VOX
Traveler's
SPANISH
and
ENGLISH
Dictionary

English-Spanish / Spanish-English

Dictionary Compiled by
the Editors of Biblograf, S. A.

North American Edition Prepared by
the Editors of National Textbook Company

National Textbook Company
4255 West Touhy Avenue
Lincolnwood, Illinois 60646-1975 U.S.A.

In Spanish, the best, by definiti

Library of Congress Catalog Card Number 87-61693

7 8 9 RP 9 8 7 6 5 4 3 2 1

ISBN 0-8442-7987-0

CONTENTS

Contents

APPENDICES / APÉNDICES

PREFACE

The *Vox Traveler's Spanish and English Dictionary* is a junior member of the Vox family of Spanish/English dictionaries, acclaimed as the world's finest. Specially designed to meet the needs of tourists and business travelers, the compact format of this dictionary makes it convenient to carry in suitcase, pocket, or purse.

In addition to its manageable size, the *Vox Traveler's* contains 6,000 of the most commonly used words in Spanish and English. This wide selection assures that visitors to a Spanish- or English-speaking country will not be at a loss for the appropriate term. Each word listed is accompanied by a transcription in the International Phonetic Alphabet (I.P.A.), so that anyone will be able to pronounce words correctly. An asterisk before a Spanish word will alert users to Latin American usage, while the same symbol before an English word indicates a North American term.

Appendices include monetary units, weights and measures, temperature conversions, clothing sizes, as well as a listing of the most commonly used abbreviations in Spanish.

In every way, the *Vox Traveler's* is ideal for anyone who needs a comprehensive and truly portable Spanish/English dictionary.

PRÓLOGO

El *Vox Traveler's Spanish and English Dictionary* es un hijo menor de la familia de diccionarios español/inglés de Vox, aclamados por ser los mejores del mundo. Diseñado específicamente para satisfacer las exigencias de turistas y viajeros de negocios, el formato compacto de este diccionario permite llevarlo en la maleta, en el bolsillo o en el bolso.

Además de su tamaño cómodo, el *Vox Traveler's* contiene 6.000 de las palabras más usadas en español e inglés. Esta gran selección asegura que los visitantes a los países de habla española o de habla inglesa siempre encuentren la expresión adecuada. Cada palabra que aparece en el diccionario va acompañada de una transcripción del Alfabeto Fonético Internacional (AFI), para que todos puedan pronunciar las palabras correctamente. Un asterisco delante de una palabra en español le avisará al lector que tal palabra se usa en Hispanoamérica. El mismo símbolo delante de una palabra en inglés indica que ésta se usa en Norteamérica.

Los apéndices incluyen tablas de unidades monetarias, pesas y medidas, conversiones de temperaturas, tallas de ropa y también una lista de las abreviaturas más usadas en español.

De todas maneras, el *Vox Traveler's* es ideal para todos los que necesiten un diccionario español/inglés comprensivo y verdaderamente portátil.

INGLÉS–ESPAÑOL
ENGLISH–SPANISH

ABREVIATURAS USADAS EN ESTE DICCIONARIO

a.	adjetivo
adv.	adverbio
AGR.	agricultura
ANAT.	anatomía
ARQ.	arquitectura
ARQUEOL.	arqueología
art.	artículo
ASTR.	astronomía
aux.	verbo auxiliar
B. ART.	bellas artes
BIB.	Biblia
BIOL.	biología
BOT.	botánica
CINEM.	cinematografía
CIR.	cirugía
COC.	cocina
COM.	comercio
compar.	comparativo
Cond.	condicional
conj.	conjunción
CONJUG.	conjugación
def.	defectivo

DEP.	deportes
DER.	derecho
dim.	diminutivo
ECLES.	eclesiástico
ECON.	economía
E. U.	Estados Unidos
ELECT.	electricidad
ENT.	entomología
f.	femenino
FERROC.	ferrocarriles
FIL.	filosofía
FÍS.	física
FISIOL.	fisiología
GEOGR.	geografía
GEOL.	geología
GEOM.	geometría
GER.	gerundio
GRAM.	gramática
HIST.	historia
ICT.	ictiología
IMPERAT.	imperativo
impers.	verbo impersonal

IMPR.	imprenta
IND.	industria
indef.	indefinido
INDIC.	indicativo
INF.	infinitivo
ING.	ingeniería
Ingl.	Inglaterra
interj.	interjección
i.	verbo intransitivo
irreg.	irregular
JOY.	joyería
LIT.	literatura
m.	masculino
MAR.	marina
MAT.	matemáticas
MEC.	mecánica
MED.	medicina
METAL.	metalurgia
MIL.	militar
MIN.	minería
MINER.	mineralogía
MÚS.	música

ORN.	ornitología
PART. P.	participio pasado
pers.	personal
pl.	plural
pos.	posesivo
p. p.	participio pasado
prep.	preposición
Pres.	presente
Pret.	pretérito
pron.	pronombre
QUÍM.	química
RADIO.	radiotelefonía, radiotelegrafía
ref.	verbo reflexivo
REL.	religión
s.	nombre substantivo
SUBJ.	subjuntivo
superl.	superlativo
TEAT.	teatro
t.	verbo transitivo
V.	véase
ZOOL.	zoología

SIGNOS DE LA A.F.I. EMPLEADOS EN LA TRANSCRIPCIÓN FONÉTICA DE LAS PALABRAS INGLESAS

Vocales

[i]	como en español en *vida, tigre*.
[e]	como en español en *guerra, dejar,* pero aún más abierta.
[æ]	sin equivalencia en español. Sonido intermedio entre la *a* en *caso* y la *e* en *perro*.
[ɑ]	como en español en *laurel, ahora,* pero enfatizada y alargada.
[ɔ]	como en español en *roca, manojo,* pero aún más abierta.
[u]	como en español en *uno,* pero con el sonido más prolongado.
[ʌ]	sin equivalencia en español. Sonido intermedio entre la *o* y la *e*.
[ə]	sin equivalencia en español. Parecida a la [ə] francesa en *venir, petit*.

Semiconsonantes

[j]	como en español en *labio, radio*.
[w]	como en español en *luego, huevo*.

Consonantes

[p]	como en español en *puerta, capa*, pero aspirada.
[t]	como en español en *todo, tienda*, pero aspirada.
[k]	como en español en *copa, queso*, pero aspirada.
[b]	como en español en *barco, vela*, pero aspirada.
[d]	como en español en *conde, candado*, pero aspirada.
[ð]	como en español en *adivinar, adorar*.
[g]	como en español en *guerra, gato*, pero aspirada.
[f]	como en español en *fuerza, fuego*.
[θ]	como en español en *hacer, ácido*.

[s] como en español en *saber, silencio.*

[ʃ] sin equivalencia en español. Fricativa palatoalveolar sorda. Parecida a la pronunciación de *chico,* si se alarga la consonante y se redondean los labios.

[v] sin equivalencia en español. Fricativa labiodental. Al pronunciarla los incisivos superiores tocan el labio inferior y hay vibración de las cuerdas vocales. Es la pronunciación del francés en *avec.*

[z] como en español en *mismo, asno.*

[ʒ] sin equivalencia en español. Fricativa palatoalveolar sonora. Parecida a la pronunciación argentina de la *ll* pero con proyección de los labios.

[tʃ] como en español en *chico, chocolate.*

[dʒ]	sin equivalencia exacta en español. Africada palatoalveolar sonora. Sonido semejante al de la *y* española en *conyuge, yugo.*
[l]	como en español en *labio, cola.*
[m]	como en español en *madre, lima.*
[n]	como en español en *nota, notable.*
[ŋ]	como en español en *cuenca, ángulo.*
[r]	sonido fricativo parecido al de la *r* española en *pero.*
[h]	sonido parecido al de la *j* española en *jerga*, pero mucho más suave.

Otros signos

[']	indica el acento tónico primario.
[ˌ]	indica el acento tónico secundario.
[:]	indica un alargamiento de la vocal.

A

a [ei, ə] *art. indef.* un, una.

abash [əˈbæʃ] *t.* avergonzar.

abate [əˈbeit] *t.* rebajar. 2 *i.* menguar.

abduct [æbˈdʌkt] *t.* raptar, secuestrar.

abide [əˈbaid] *i.* habitar. 2 permanecer. 3 *t.* esperar. 4 sufrir, tolerar. ¶ Pret. y p. p.: *abode* [əˈboud] o *abided* [əˈbaidid].

ability [əˈbiliti] *s.* habilidad, talento.

able [ˈeibəl] *a.* capaz: *to be* ~ *to*, poder.

aboard [əˈbɔːd] *adv.* a bordo.

abode [əˈboud] V. TO ABIDE. 2 *s.* morada.

abolish [əˈbɔliʃ] *t.* abolir, suprimir.

abort [əˈbɔːt] *t.* abortar.

abound [əˈbaund] *i.* abundar.

about [əˈbaut] *prep.* cerca de, junto a, alrededor de. 2 por, en. 3 sobre, acerca de. 4 hacia, a eso de: 5 *to be* ~ *to*, estar a punto de. 6 *adv.* alrededor, en torno. 7 casi, aproximadamente.

above [əˈbʌv] *prep.* sobre. 2 más de, más que. 3 *adv.* arriba, en lo alto.

abreast [əˈbrest] *adv.* de frente.

abroad [əˈbrɔːd] *adv.* afuera, en el extranjero.

absent [ˈæbsent] *t. to* ~ *oneself*, ausentarse.

absorb [əbˈsɔːb] *t.* absorber(se.

absorption [əbˈsɔːpʃən] *s.* absorción.

abstain [əb'stein] *i.* abstenerse.

abstract ['æbstrækt] *a.* abstracto.

absurd [əb'sə:d] *s.* absurdo.

abundant [ə'bʌndənt] *a.* abundante.

abuse [ə'bju:s] *s.* abuso. 2 *t.* abusar de.

abyss [ə'bis] *s.* abismo.

accede [æk'si:d] *i.* acceder.

accent [æk'sent] *t.* acentuar.

accept [ək'sept] *t.* aceptar.

acceptation [ˌæksep'teiʃən] *s.* acepción.

access ['ækses] *s.* acceso. 2 aumento.

accessory [ək'sesəri] *a.* accesorio.

accident ['æksidənt] *s.* accidente.

accommodate [ə'kɔmədeit] *t.-i.* acomodar(se, alojar(se.

accompany [ə'kʌmpəni] *t.* acompañar.

accomplish [ə'kɔmpliʃ] *t.* efectuar, llevar a cabo.

accord [ə'kɔd] *s.* acuerdo, concierto, armonía. 2 *t.* conceder.

according [ə'kɔ:diŋ] *a.* acorde, conforme. 2 ~ *to*, según, conforme a.

accordingly [ə'kɔ:diŋli] *adv.* de conformidad [con]. 2 por consiguiente.

account [ə'kaunt] *s.* cuenta. 2 *t.* tener por, estimar.

accumulate [ə'kju:mjuleit] *t.-i.* acumular(se.

accurate ['ækjurit] *a.* exacto, correcto.

accursed [ə'kə:sid] *a.* maldito.

accuse [ə'kju:z] *t.* acusar.

accustom [ə'kʌstəm] *t.* acostumbrar.

ache [eik] *s.* dolor; achaque. 2 *i.* doler.

achieve [ə'tʃi:v] *t.* realizar.

achievement [ə'tʃi:vmənt] *s.* logro.

acid ['æsid] *a.-s.* ácido.

acidity [ə'siditi], **acidness** ['æsidnis] *s.* acidez. 2 acritud.

acknowledge [ək'nɔlidʒ] *t.* reconocer. 2 agradecer.

acorn ['eikɔ:n] *s.* bellota.

acquaint [ə'kweint] *t.* enterar, informar.

acquaintance [ə'kweintəns] *s.* conocimiento.

acquiesce [ˌækwi'es] *i.* asentir, consentir.

acquiescence [ˌækwi'əs-ɔns] s. aquiescencia, conformidad.

acquire [ə'kwaiɔʳ] t. adquirir.

acquit [ə'kwit] t. absolver.

acre ['eikɔʳ] s. acre [40.47 áreas].

across [ə'krɔs] prep. a través de; al otro lado de.

act [ækt] s. acto, hecho, acción. 2 i. obrar, actuar.

action ['ækʃɔn] s. acción.

active ['æktiv] a. activo.

actor ['æktɔʳ] s. actor.

actress ['æktris] s. actriz.

actual ['æktʃuɔl] a. real, 2 actual (muy raro).

actually ['æktʃuɔli] adv. realmente.

acuity [ə'kju:iti] s. agudeza.

acumen [ə'kju:men] s. perspicacia.

acute [ə'kju:t] a. agudo.

adapt [e'dæpt] t. pr. adaptar(se.

add [æd] t. añadir.

addition [ə'diʃɔn] s. adición, suma.

address [ə'dres] s. discurso. 2 dirección, señas. 3 t. hablar, dirigirse a.

adequate ['ædikwit] a. adecuado.

adipose ['ædipəus] a. adiposo.

adjacent [ə'dʒeisɔnt] a. adyacente.

adjoin [ə'dʒɔin] t. unir.

adjourn [ə'dʒɔ:n] t. aplazar, suspender.

adjust [ə'dʒʌst] t. ajustar.

administer [əd'ministɔʳ] t.-i. administrar.

admirable ['ædmərəbl] a. admirable.

admiral ['ædmərɔl] s. almirante.

admiration [ˌædmi'reiʃɔn] s. admiración.

admire [əd'maiɔʳ] t.-i. admirar(se.

admit [əd'mit] t. admitir.

adolescent [ˌædɔu'lesɔnt] a.-s. adolescente.

adopt [ə'dɔpt] t. adoptar.

adore [ə'dɔ:ʳ] t. adorar.

adult ['ædʌlt] a.-s. adulto.

advance [əd'vɑ:ns] s. avance. 2 t.-i. adelantar(se, avanzar(se.

advantage [əd'vɑ:ntidʒ] s. ventaja; provecho. 2 t. adelantar.

adventure [əd'ventʃɔʳ] s. aventura. 2 t. aventurar(se.

adversary ['ædvɔsɔri] s. adversario.

advertise ['ædvətaiz] *t.* anunciar.

advertisement [əd'və:tismənt] *s.* anuncio.

advice [əd'vais] *s.* consejo.

advise [əd'vaiz] *t.* aconsejar.

advocate ['ædvəkeit] *t.* abogar por; defender.

aeroplane ['ɛərəplein] *s.* aeroplano.

afar [ə'fɑ:ʳ] *adv.* lejos, a lo lejos.

affair [ə'fɛəʳ] *s.* asunto, negocio.

affect [ə'fekt] *t.* afectar.

affectionate [ə'fekʃənit] afectuoso, cariñoso.

affirm [ə'fə:m] *t.* afirmar.

afford [ə'fɔ:d] *t.* dar, permitirse [un gasto].

afraid [ə'freid] *a.* temeroso.

after ['ɑ:ftəʳ] *prep.* después de.

afternoon ['ɑ:ftə'nu:n] *s.* tarde.

afterwards ['ɑ:ftəwədz] *adv.* después, luego.

again [ə'gən, ə'gein] *prep.* de nuevo, otra vez

against [ə'gənst] *prep* contra.

age [eidʒ] *s.* edad. 2 *i.-t.* envejecer.

agent ['eidʒənt] *a. - s* agente.

agglomerate [ə'glɔməreit] *t.-i.* aglomerar(se.

ago [ə'gəu] *adv.* atrás, hace, ha.

agonize ['ægənaiz] *i.* agonizar.

agony ['ægəni] *s.* agonía.

agree [ə'gri:] *i.* asentir.

agreeable [ə'griəbl] *a.* agradable.

agreement [ə'gri:mənt] *s.* acuerdo. 2 armonía.

agriculture ['ægrikʌltʃəʳ] *s.* agricultura.

ahead [ə'hed] *adv.* delante.

aid (eid) *s.* ayuda. 2 *t.* ayudar.

aim [eim] *s.* puntería. 2 *t.* apuntar.

air [ɛəʳ] *s.* aire. 2 *t.* airear, orear.

aircraft ['ɛəkrɑ:ft] *s.* avión.

airplane ['ɛə-plein] *s.* aeroplano.

airtight ['ɛə-tait] *a.* hermético.

aisle [ail] *s.* pasillo [en un teatro]; nave lateral.

alarm [ə'lɑ:m] *s.* alarma. 2 *t.* alarmar.

alarm-clock [ə'lɑ:mklɔk] *s.* despertador.

ale [eil] *s.* cerveza.

alert (ɔ'lə:t) *a.* vigilante. 2 vivo, listo.

alien ['eiljən] *a.* ajeno, extraño.

alike [ə'laik] *a.* igual, semejante.

alive [ə'laiv] *a.* vivo, viviente

all [ɔ:l] *a.-pron.* todo, -da; todos, -das: at ~, absolutamente, del todo; not at ~, de ningún modo; no hay de qué; *for ~ that*, con todo; ~ *right!*, ¡está bien!, ¡conformes!; ~ *round*, por todas partes; ~ *the better*, tanto mejor; ~ *the same*, igualmente, a pesar de todo.

allege [ə'ledʒ] *t.* alegar. 2 sostener.

allegiance [ə'li:dʒəns] *s.* obediencia, fidelidad [a un soberano].

alley ['æli] *s.* calleja.

alliance [ə'laiəns] *s.* alianza.

allied [ə'laid] *a.* aliado.

allow [ə'lau] *t.* conceder.

ally [ə'lai] *t.-i.* aliar(se.

almost ['ɔ:lməust] *adv.* casi.

aloft [ə'lɔft] *adv.* arriba, en alto.

alone [ə'ləun] *a.* solo. 2 *adv.* sólo, solamente.

along [ə'lɔŋ] *prep.* a lo

largo de. 2 *adv.* a lo largo.

aloud [ə'laud] *adv.* en voz alta.

already [ɔ:l'redi] *adv.* ya.

also ['ɔ:lsəu] *adv.* también.

alter ['ɔ:ltə'] *t.-i.* alterar(se, modificar(se.

alternate ['ɔ:ltəneit] *t.-i.* alternar(se.

alternative [ɔ:l'tə:nətiv] *a.* alternativo; el otro. 2 GRAM. disyuntivo.

although [ɔ:l'ðəu] *conj.* aunque.

altogether [ˌɔ:ltə'ɡəðə'] *adv.* enteramente, del todo.

always ['ɔ:lweiz, -əz, -iz] *adv.* siempre.

amaze [ə'meiz] *t.* asombrar.

ambassador [æm'bæsədə'] *s.* embajador.

ambition [æm'biʃən] *s.* ambición.

ambitious [æm'biʃəs] *a.* ambicioso.

ambulance ['æmbjuləns] *s.* ambulancia.

ambush ['æmbuʃ] *s.* emboscada, acecho. 2 *t.* emboscar. 3 *i.* estar emboscado.

amend [ə'mend] *t.-i.* enmendar(se.

amiable ['eimjəbl] *a.* amable.

amid [ə'mid], **amidst** [-st] *prep.* en medio de, entre.

among (st) [ə'mʌn, -st] *prep.* entre, en medio de.

amount [ə'maunt] *s.* cantidad. 2 i. to ~ to, ascender a.

ample ['æmpl] *a.* amplio.

amuse [ə'mju:z] *t.* entretener(se, divertir(se.

an [ən] *art. indef.* un, una.

analyse, -ze ['ænəlaiz] *t.* analizar.

ancestor ['ænsistər] *s.* progenitor, antepasado.

anchor ['æŋkər] *s.* ancla, áncora. 2 *t.* sujetar con el ancla. 3 *i.* anclar.

ancient ['einʃənt] *a.* antiguo.

and [ænd, ənd] *conj.* y, e.

angel ['eindʒəl] *s.* ángel.

anger ['æŋgər] *s.* cólera, ira. 2 *t.* encolerizar.

angry ['æŋgri] *a.* colérico.

anguish ['æŋgwiʃ] *s.* angustia.

ankle ['æŋkl] *s.* tobillo.

annex ['æneks] *s.* anexo.

annex [ə'neks] *t.* añadir.

announce [ə'nauns] *t.* anunciar.

annoy [ə'nɔi] *t.* molestar.

another [ə'nʌðər] *a.-pron.* otro.

answer ['ɑ:nsər] *s.* respuesta, contestación. 2 *t.-i.* responder, contestar.

ant [ænt] *s.* hormiga.

anticipate [æn'tisipeit] *t.* anticiparse a. 2 gastar antes. 3 prever. 4 gozar de antemano.

anxiety [æŋ'zaiəti] *s.* ansiedad.

anxious ['æŋkʃəs] *a.* ansioso.

any ['eni] *a.-adv.-pron.* cualquier, todo, todos los, algún, alguno; [en frases negativas] ningún, ninguno. 2 A veces no se traduce.

anybody ['eni,bɔdi] *pron.* alguien, alguno; [en frases negativas] ninguno, nadie. 2 cualquiera.

anyhow ['enihau] *adv.* de cualquier modo.

anyone ['eniwʌn] *pron.* ANYBODY.

anything ['eniθiŋ] *pron.* algo, alguna cosa, cualquier cosa, todo cuanto; [con negación] nada.

anyway ['eniwei] *adv.* de todos modos, con todo.

anywhere ['eniwɛəʳ] *adv.* doquiera; adondequiera.

apart [ə'pɑːt] *adv.* aparte; a un lado.

apartment [ə'pɑːtmənt] *s.* aposento. 2 apartamento.

ape [eip] *s.* mono, mico. 2 *t.* imitar, remedar.

apostle [ə'pɔsl] *s.* apóstol.

appall [ə'pɔːl] *t.* espantar.

apparent [ə'pærənt] *a* evidente. 2 aparente.

appeal [ə'piːl] *s.* apelación. 2 llamamiento; súplica. 3 atractivo. 4 *i.* apelar. 5 suplicar. 6 atraer.

appear [ə'piəʳ] *i.* aparecer.

applause [ə'plɔːz] *s.* aplauso.

apple ['æpl] *s.* BOT. manzana, poma. 2 ~ *of the eye*, pupila.

application [,æpli'keiʃən] *s.* aplicación. 2 petición, solicitud.

appreciate [ə'priːʃieit] *t.* apreciar, valuar.

approach [ə'prəutʃ] *s.* aproximación. 2 entrada. 3 *t.-i.* acercar(se.

appropriate [ə'prəupriit] *a.* apropiado. 2 propio, peculiar.

approval [ə'pruːvəl] *s.* aprobación.

approve [ə'pruːv] *t.* aprobar, sancionar.

apricot ['eiprikɔt] *s.* BOT. albaricoque.

April ['eiprəl] *s.* abril.

arch [ɑːtʃ] *s.* ARQ. arco; bóveda. 2 *a.* travieso, socarrón. 3 *t.-i.* arquear(se, abovedar(se.

archbishop ['ɑːtʃ'biʃəp] *s.* arzobispo.

argue ['ɑːgjuː] *i.* argüir. 2 *t.-i.* discutir.

argument ['ɑːgjumənt] *s.* argumento. 2 discusión.

arid ['ærid] *a.* árido.

arise [ə'raiz] *i.* subir, elevarse. ¶ Pret.: *arose* [ə'rouz]; p. p.: *arisen* [ə'rizn].

arm [ɑːm] *s.* brazo. 2 rama [de árbol]. 3 armas. 4 *t.-i.* armar(se.

arm-chair ['ɑːm'tʃɛəʳ] *s.* sillón.

armour ['ɑːməʳ] *s.* armadura.

army ['ɑːmi] *s.* ejército.

around [ə'raund] *adv.* alrededor.

arouse [ə'rauz] *t.* despertar.

arrange [ə'reindʒ] *t.* arreglar.

arrival [ə'raivəl] *s.* llegada.

arrive [ə'raiv] *i.* llegar.
arrow ['ærou] *s.* flecha, saeta.
art [ɑːt] *s.* arte.
artist ['ɑːtist] *s.* artista.
artistic [ɑː'tistik] *a.* artístico.
as [æz, əz] *adv.* como. 2 (en comparativos) ~ *big* ~, tan grande como. 3 ~ *for*, ~ *to*, en cuanto a; ~ *much* ~, tanto como; ~ *well* ~, así como; ~ *yet*, hasta ahora. 4 *conj.* mientras, cuando. 5 ya que.
ascend [ə'send] *i.* ascender.
ascent [ə'sent] *s.* subida.
ascertain [ˌæsə'tein] *t.* averiguar, hallar.
ash [æʃ] *s.* ceniza.
ashamed [ə'ʃeimd] *a.* avergonzado.
ashore [ə'ʃɔː, ə'ʃɔə] *adv.* en tierra, a tierra.
aside [ə'said] *adv.* al lado, a un lado, aparte.
ask [ɑːsk] *t.* preguntar. 2 pedir, solicitar, rogar que. 3 invitar, convidar.
asleep [ə'sliːp] *a.-adv.* dormido.
asparagus [əs'pærəgəs] *s.* BOT. espárrago.
aspect ['æspekt] *s.* aspecto.

aspirate ['æspəreit] *t.* aspirar.
ass [æs, ɑːs] *s.* asno.
assail [ə'seil] *t.* asaltar.
assault [ə'sɔːlt] *s.* asalto 2 *t.* asaltar.
assay [ə'sei] *s.* ensayo. 2 *t.* ensayar.
assemble [ə'sembl] *t.* congregar, reunir.
assembly [ə'sembli] *s.* asamblea, junta.
assent [ə'sent] *s.* asentimiento. 2 *i.* asentir.
assert [ə'səːt] *t.* aseverar, afirmar.
assign [ə'sain] *t.* asignar.
associate [ə'souʃiit] *a.* asociado.
associate [ə'souʃieit] *t.-i.* asociar(se, juntar(se.
assume [ə'sjuːm] *t.* asumir. 2 suponer.
assumption [ə'sʌmpʃən] *s.* suposición.
assurance [ə'ʃuərəns] *s.* seguridad, certeza.
assure [ə'ʃuər] *t.* asegurar.
astonish [əs'tɔniʃ] *t.* asombrar.
astound [əs'taund] *t.* pasmar, sorprender.
at [æt, ət] *prep.* en, a, de, con, cerca de, delante de.
ate [et] *pret.* de TO EAT.
atom ['ætəm] *s.* átomo.

attach [ə'tætʃ] t.-i. atarse, ligarse. 2 granjearse el afecto de. 3 dar, atribuir [importancia, etc.].

attack [ə'tæk] s. ataque. 2 t. atacar.

attain [ə'tein] t. lograr.

attempt [ə'tempt] s. intento. 2 atentado. 3 t. intentar. 4 atentar contra.

attend [ə'tend] t. atender a. 2 servir, escoltar. 3 asistir, concurrir. 4 aguardar.

attentive [ə'tentiv] a. atento, cuidadoso.

attire [ə'taiər] s. traje, vestidura. 2 t. vestir.

attorney [ə'tə:ni] s. apoderado. 2 procurador, abogado.

attraction [ə'trækʃən] s. atracción. 2 atractivo.

auburn ['ɔ:bən] a. castaño.

audience ['ɔ:djəns] s. auditorio, público. 2 audiencia [entrevista].

augment [ɔ:g'ment] t.-i. aumentar(se.

August ['ɔ:gəst] s. agosto.

aunt [ɑ:nt] s. tía.

austere [ɔs'tiər] a. austero.

author ['ɔ:θər] s. autor, escritor.

authority [ɔ:'θɔriti] s. autoridad: *on good* ~, de buena tinta. 2 pl. autoridades.

authorize ['ɔ:θəraiz] t. autorizar.

autumn ['ɔ:təm] s. otoño.

avail [ə'veil] s. provecho. 2 i. servir, ser útil. 3 t. aprovechar, servir [a uno].

available [ə'veiləbl] a. disponible.

avaricious [ˌævə'riʃəs] a. avaro.

avenge [ə'vendʒ] t. vengar.

avenue ['ævənju:] s. avenida, paseo, alameda.

average ['ævəridʒ] s. promedio. 2 t. determinar el promedio de.

avoid [ə'vɔid] t. evitar, eludir. 2 anular.

avow [ə'vau] t. confesar, reconocer.

await [ə'weit] t.-i. aguardar, esperar.

awake [ə'weik] a. despierto. 2 t.-i. despertar(se. ¶ Pret.: *awoke* [ə'wəuk]; p. p.: *awaked* [ə'weikt] o *awoke*.

award [ə'wɔ:d] s. adjudicación; premio. 2 *t.* conceder, otorgar.

aware [ə'wɛəʳ] *a.* sabedor, enterado.

away [ə'wei] *adv.* lejos, fuera. 2 Indica libertad o continuidad en la acción: *they fired ~*, fueron disparando.

awful ['ɔ:ful] *a.* atroz, horrible.

awhile [ə'wail] *adv.* un rato.

awkward ['ɔ:kwəd] *a.* torpe, desgarbado.

awoke [ə'wouk] V. TO AWAKE.

ax, axe [æks] *s.* hacha.

B

baby ['beibi] s. criatura, bebé.

bachelor ['bætʃələ'] s. soltero. 2 [UNIV.] licenciado.

back [bæk] s. espalda. 2 a. - adv. posterior; de vuelta, de regreso. 3 t. apoyar, sostener.

background ['bækgraund] s. fondo.

backward ['bækwəd] a. retrógrado. 2 atrasado.

backward(s ['bækwədz] adv. hacia atrás. 2 al revés.

bacon ['beikən] s. tocino.

bad [bæd] a. malo, mal.

bade [beid] V. TO BID.

baffle ['bæfl] t. confundir. 2 burlar.

bag [bæg] s. bolsa, bolso. 2 maleta. 3 t. embolsar.

baggage ['bægidʒ] s. equipaje.

bait [beit] s. cebo, carnada. 2 t. cebar.

bake [beik] t.-i. cocer(se, asar(se.

baker ['beikə'] s. panadero.

balance ['bæləns] s. balanza. 2 equilibrio. 3 t.-i. pesar, equilibrar(se.

bald [bɔːld] a. calvo.

ball [bɔːl] s. bola. 2 pelota.

balloon [bəˈluːn] s. globo.

ballot ['bælət] s. balota. 2 votación. 3 i.-t. votar.

ban [bæn] s. proscripción. 2 t. proscribir.

banana [bəˈnɑːnə] s. plátano.

band [bænd] s. faja, tira. 2 MÚS. banda. 3 pandilla. 4 t. atar, fajar.

bandage ['bændidʒ] s. venda. 2 t. vendar.

bang [bæŋ] s. golpe, porrazo. 2 t. golpear [con ruido].

banish ['bænɪʃ] t. desterrar.

bank [bæŋk] s. ribazo, talud. 2 com. banco. 3 t. amontonar. 4 depositar en un banco.

banker ['bæŋkər] s. banquero.

bankrupt ['bæŋkrʌpt] a. quebrado, insolvente.

bankruptcy ['bæŋkrəptsi] s. quiebra, bancarrota.

banner ['bænər] s. bandera.

banter ['bæntər] s. burla. 2 t. burlarse de.

baptize [bæp'taiz] t. bautizar.

bar [baːʳ] s. barra. 2 obstáculo. 3 bar; mostrador de bar. 4 t. atrancar [una puerta]. 5 obstruir.

barbarian [baːˈbɛəriən] a.-s. bárbaro.

barber ['baːbər] s. barbero.

bard [baːd] s. bardo. 2 barda.

bare [bɛəʳ] a. desnudo. 2 t. desnudar, despojar.

barefoot(ed ['bɛəfut, 'bɛəˈfutid] a. descalzo.

barely ['bɛəli] adv. apenas.

bargain ['baːgin] s. trato. 2 ganga, buen negocio. 3 i. regatear.

bark [baːk] s. corteza. 2 ladrido. 3 barca. 4 t. descortezar. 5 i. ladrar.

barley ['baːli] s. BOT. cebada.

barn [baːn] s. granero, pajar.

barn-yard ['baːn-'jad] s. patio.

baron ['bærən] s. barón.

barracks ['bærəks] s. pl. cuartel.

barrel ['bærəl] s. barril. 2 cañón [de un arma]. 3 t. embarrilar, entonelar.

barren ['bærən] a. estéril.

barrier ['bæriəʳ] s. barrera.

barrow ['bærəu] s. carretilla.

barter ['baːtəʳ] s. trueque, cambio. 2 t.-i. trocar, cambiar.

base [beis] a. bajo, vil. 2 s. base. 3 t.-i. basar(se, fundar(se.

baseball ['beisbɔːl] s. béisbol.

basement ['beismənt] s. sótano.

bashful ['bæʃful] a. vergonzoso, tímido.

basic ['beisik] *a.* básico.

basin ['beisn] *s.* jofaina.

basis ['beisis] *s.* fundamento.

bask [ba:sk] *i.* calentarse, tostarse.

basket ['ba:skit] *s.* cesto, canasta.

basket-ball ['ba:skitbɔ:l] *s.* baloncesto.

bastard ['bæstəd] *a.-s.* bastardo.

bat [bæt] *s.* ZOOL. murciélago. 2 DEPORT. bate. 3 *t.* golpear.

batch [bætʃ] *s.* hornada.

bath [ba:θ] *s.* baño. 2 bañera.

bathe [beið] *t.-i.* bañar(se.

bath-room ['ba:θrum] *s.* cuarto de baño.

battalion [bə'tæljən] *s.* batallón.

batter ['bætə'] *s.* COC. batido. 2 *t.* batir. 3 demoler.

battery ['bætəri] *s.* batería. 2 pila eléctrica.

battle ['bætl] *s.* batalla, combate. 2 *i.* combatir.

bay [bei] *a.-s.* bayo [caballo]. 2 *s.* bahía. 3 ladrido. 4 laurel. 5 *i.* ladrar.

bayonet ['beiənit] *s.* bayoneta.

baza(a)r [bə'za:'] *s.* bazar.

be (bi:) *i.* ser; estar. 2 hallarse. 3 existir. ¶ CONJUG.: INDIC. PRES.: *I am* [æm, əm, m], *you are* [a:', ə', ɔ'] *[art]*, *he is* [iz, z, s], *we are*, etc. | Pret.: *I, he was* [wə:', wɔ']. || SUBJ. PRES.: *be.* | Pret.: *were.* || PART. PAS.: *been* [bi:n, bin]. || GER.: *being* ['bi:in].

beach [bi:tʃ] *s.* playa. 2 *i.-t.* varar.

beak [bi:k] *s.* pico [de ave, etc.].

beam [bi:m] *s.* viga. 2 rayo [de luz, calor, etc.]. 3 *t.* emitir [luz, etc.].

bean [bi:n] *s.* judía.

bear [bɛə'] *s.* ZOOL. oso, osa. 2 *t.* llevar, cargar. 3 soportar. 4 dar a luz: *he was born in London*, nació en Londres. 5 [wɔz, wəz], *you, we,* Pret. *bore* [bɔ:']; p. p.: *borne* o *born* [bɔ:n].

beard [biəd] *s.* barba. 2 *t.* desafiar.

beast [bi:st] *s.* bestia, animal.

beastly ['bi:stli] *a.* bestial.

beat [bi:t] *s.* golpe; latido. 2 *t.* pegar; golpear.

¶ Pret.: **beat** [bi:t]; p. p.: *beaten* ['bi:tn].

beautiful ['bju:tiful] *a.* hermoso, bello. 2 lindo.

beauty ['bju:ti] *s.* belleza, hermosura.

became [bi'keim] V. TO BECOME.

because [bi'kɔz] *conj.* porque. 2 ~ *of*, a causa de.

beckon ['bekən] *t.* llamar por señas. 2 *i.* hacer señas.

become [bi'kʌm] *t.* convenir, sentar, caer o ir bien. 2 *i.* volverse, hacerse, convertirse en; ponerse. ¶ Pret.: *became* [bi'keim]; p. p.: *become* [bi'kʌm].

bed [bed] *s.* cama, lecho. 2 *t.-i.* acostar(se.

bedroom ['bedrum] *s.* dormitorio.

bee [bi:] *s.* abeja.

beef [bi:f] *s.* carne de vaca.

been [bi:n, bin] V. TO BE.

beer [biəʳ] *s.* cerveza.

beet [bi:t] *s.* remolacha.

beetle ['bi:tl] *s.* ENT. escarabajo.

before [bi'fɔ:ʳ, -fɔəʳ] *adv.* antes. 2 delante. 3 *prep.* antes de o que.

beforehand [bi'fɔ:hænd] *adv.* de antemano.

beg [beg] *t.* pedir, solicitar.

began [bi'gæn] V. TO BEGIN.

beggar ['begəʳ] *s.* mendigo, -ga. 2 *t.* empobrecer, arruinar.

begin [bi'gin] *t.-i.* empezar. ¶ Pret.: *began* [bi'gæn]; p. p.: *begun* (bi'gʌn]; ger.: *beginning*.

beginning [bi'giniŋ] *s.* principio.

beguile [bi'gail] *t.* engañar.

behalf [bi'hɑ:f] *s.* cuenta, interés; *on* ~ *of*, en nombre de.

behave [bi'heiv] *i.-pr.* proceder; comportarse.

behavio(u)r [bi'heivjəʳ] *s.* conducta, comportamiento.

behead [bi'hed] *t.* decapitar.

beheld [bi'held] TO BEHOLD.

behind [bi'haind] *adv.* detrás. 2 *prep.* detrás de; después de.

behold [bi'hɔuld] *t.* contemplar. ¶ Pret. y p. p.: *beheld* [bi'held].

being ['bi:iŋ] *ger.* de TO BE. 2 *s.* ser, existencia. 3 persona.

belief [bi'li:f] *s.* creencia.

believe [bi'li:v] *t.* - *i.* creer.

believer [bi'li:vəᵣ] *s.* creyente.

bell [bel] *s.* campana.

bellow ['belou] *s.* bramido, mugido. 2 *i.* bramar, mugir.

belly ['beli] *s.* vientre, panza. 2 *t.* combar, abultar.

belong [bi'lɔŋ] *i.* pertenecer.

belongings [bi'lɔŋiŋz] *s. pl.* bienes.

beloved [bi'lʌvd] *a.* querido, amado.

below [bi'lou] *adv.* abajo, debajo. 2 *prep.* bajo, debajo de.

belt [belt] *s.* cinturón, faja.

bench [bentʃ] *s.* banco. 2 tribunal.

bend [bend] *s.* inclinación. 2 *t.-i.* inclinar(se. ¶ Pret. y p. p.: *bent* [bent].

beneath [bi'ni:θ] *adv.* abajo, debajo. 2 *prep.* bajo, debajo de.

benefit ['benifit] *s.* beneficio, favor. 2 beneficio, bien. 2 *t.-i.* beneficiar(se.

bent [bent] *pret.* y *p. p.* de TO BEND. 2 *a.* torcido, doblado. 3 *s.* curvatura. 4 inclinación.

bequeath [bi'kwi:ð] *t.* legar.

bequest [bi'kwest] *s.* legado.

berry ['beri] *s.* baya; grano.

berth [bə:θ] *s.* MAR. amarradero. 2 *t.* MAR. amarrar. 3 *i.* fondear.

baseech [bi'si:tʃ] *t.* implorar; suplicar. ¶ Pret. y p. p.: *besought* [bi'sɔ:t].

beset [bi'set] *t.* asediar. ¶ Pret. y p. p: *beset; besetting.*

beside [bi'said] *adv.* cerca, al lado. 2 *prep.* al lado de, cerca de.

besides [bi'saidz] *adv.* además. 2 *prep.* además de.

besiege [bi'si:dʒ] *t.* sitiar.

besought [bi'sɔ:t] V. TO BESEECH.

best [best] *a. superl.* de GOOD: mejor, óptimo, superior. 2 *adv. superl.* de WELL: mejor; mucho; más.

bestow [bi'stou] *t.* otorgar.

bet [bet] *s.* apuesta 2 *t.-i.* apostar.

betray [bi'trei] *t.* traicionar.

betroth [bi'trouð] *t.-i.* desposar, prometer.

better ['betə^r] *a.-adv.* mejor. 2 *s.* lo mejor: so *much the* ~, tanto mejor. 3 *pl.* superiores. 4 *t.-i.* mejorar(se.

between [bi'twi:n] *adv.* en medio. 2 *prep.* entre [dos].

beverage ['bevəridʒ] *s.* bebida.

beware [bi'wɛə^r] *i.* guardarse de, precaverse.

bewilder [bi'wildə^r] *t.* desconcertar.

bewitch [bi'witʃ] *t.* embrujar.

beyond [bi'jɔnd] *adv.* más allá de.

bias ['baiəs] *s.* sesgo, oblicuidad. 2 parcialidad, prejuicio. 3 *t.* predisponer.

bib [bib] *s.* babero.

Bible ['baibl] *s.* Biblia.

bicycle ['baisikl] *s.* bicicleta.

bid [bid] *t.* decir. 2 ofrecer [un precio], pujar. 3 ordenar. 4 invitar. ¶ Pret.: *bade* [beid]; p. p.: *bidden* ['bidn].

big [big] *a.* grande, importante.

bigot ['bigət] *s.* fanático.

bigotry ['bigətri] *s.* fanatismo, intolerancia.

bill [bil] *s.* pico [de ave]. 2 pica, alabarda. 3 cuenta, nota, factura, lista: ~ *of fare*, minuta, lista de platos. 4 letra, pagaré. 5 patente, certificado. 6 cartel, programa [de teatro], prospecto. 7 proyecto de ley; ley. 8 *t.* cargar en cuenta. 9 anunciar por carteles.

billion ['biljən] *s.* [ingl.] billón. 2 (E. U.) mil millones.

billow ['bilou] *s.* oleada. 2 ola. 3 *i.* ondular.

bin [bin] *s.* caja, cubo.

bind [bin] *s.* lazo, ligadura. 2 *t.* ligar, atar, unir. 3 vendar. 4 ribetear. 5 encuadernar. 6 obligar, compeler. ¶ Pret. y p. p.: *bound* [baund].

birch [bə:tʃ] *s.* [vara de] abedul. 2 *t.* azotar.

bird [bə:d] *s.* pájaro.

birth [bə:θ] *s.* nacimiento. 2 cuna, origen. 3 linaje.

birthday ['bə:θdei] *s.* cumpleaños.

biscuit ['biskit] *s.* galleta, bizcocho.

bishop ['biʃəp] *s.* ECLES. obispo. 2 AJED. alfil.

bit [bit] *s.* trozo.

bite [bait] s. mordedura. 2 bocado, tentempié. 3 t.-i. morder. ¶ Pret.: *bit* (bit); p. p.: *bit* o *bitten* ['bitn].

biting ['baitiŋ] a. mordaz; picante.

bitten ['bitn] V. TO BITE.

bitter ['bitə'] a. amargo.

black [blæk] a. negro. 2 t.-i. ennegrecerse.

blackberry ['blækbəri] s. BOT. zarza. 2 zarzamora.

blackboard ['blækbɔ:d] s. pizarra.

blackish ['blækiʃ] a. negruzco.

blackmail ['blækmeil] s. chantaje. 2 t. hacer un chantaje a.

blackness ['blæknis] s. negrura.

blacksmith ['blæksmiθ] s. herrero.

blade [bleid] s. hoja, cuchilla. 2 pala [de remo, etc.]. 3 hoja [de hierba].

blame [bleim] s. censura, culpa. 2 t. censurar.

blank [blæŋk] a. en blanco. 2 vacío; sin interés. 3 desconcertado, confuso. 4 s. blanco, espacio, laguna. 5 diana [de un blanco].

blanket ['blæŋkit] s. manta.

blast [bla:st] s. ráfaga.

2 soplo; chorro. 3 sonido. 4 explosión, voladura. 5 ~ *furnace*, alto horno. 6 t. agostar, marchitar. 7 maldecir.

blaze [bleiz] s. llama. 2 hoguera. 3 i. arder, llamear. 4 brillar, resplandecer. 5 t. encender, inflamar.

bleak [bli:k] a. desierto, frío.

bleed [bli:d] t.-i. sangrar. ¶ Pret. y p. p.: *bled* [bled].

blemish ['blemiʃ] s. tacha, defecto. 2 t. manchar, afear.

blend [blend] s. mezcla, combinación. 2 t.-i. mezclar(se, combinar(se. 3 t. matizar, armonizar. ¶ *blended* ['blendid] o *blent* [blent].

blew [blu:] V. TO BLOW.

blind [blaind] a. ciego. 2 oscuro. 3 ~ *alley*, callejón sin salida. 4 s. pantalla, mampara, persiana. 5 engaño, disfraz, pretexto. 6 t. cegar.

blindness ['blaindnis] s. ceguera.

blink [bliŋk] s. pestañeo, guiño. 2 i. parpadear.

bliss [blis] s. bienaventuranza.

blissful ['blisful] *a*. bienaventurado, dichoso.

blister ['blistə'] *t.-i*. ampollar(se. 2 *s*. vejiga.

blithe [blaið], **blithesome** [-səm] *a*. alegre, gozoso, jovial.

block [blɔk] *s*. bloque. 2 manzana [de casas]. 3 bloc [de papel]. 4 obstáculo. 5 *t*. obstruir, bloquear.

blockade [blɔ'keid] *s*. MIL. bloqueo. 2 *t*. MIL. bloquear.

blood [blʌd] *s*. sangre.

bloodshed ['blʌdʃɔd] *s*. matanza.

bloody ['blʌdi] *a*. sangriento. 2 (*vul*.) maldito; muy.

bloom [blu:m] *s*. flor. 2 floración. 3 frescor, lozanía. 4 *i*. florecer.

blossom ['blɔsəm] *s*. flor. 2 *i*. florecer.

blouse [blauz] *s*. blusa.

blow [blou] *s*. golpe. 2 desgracia. 3 soplo [de aire]. 4 *t*. soplar. 5 *to* ~ *out*, apagar. 6 *impers*. hacer viento. ¶ Pret.: *blew* [blu:]; p. p.: *blown* [bloun].

blue [blu:] *a*. azul.

bluff [blʌf] *a*. escarpado. 2 *s*. escarpa, risco. 3 farol, envite falso. 4 *i*. hacer un farol; fanfarronear.

bluish ['blu(:)iʃ] *a*. azulado.

blunder ['blʌndə'] *s*. disparate, yerro, plancha. 2 *i*. equivocarse.

blunt [blʌnt] *a*. embotado. 2 *t.-i*. embotar(se.

blur [blə'] *s*. borrón. 2 *t*. manchar.

blush [blʌʃ] *s*. rubor, sonrojo. 2 *i*. ruborizarse, sonrojarse.

bluster ['blʌstə'] *i*. enfurecerse. 2 fanfarronear.

boar [bɔ:'] *s*. jabalí.

board [bɔ:d] *s*. tabla, tablero [de madera]. 2 *t*. entarimar, enmaderar. 3 abordar.

boast [boust] *s*. jactancia. 2 *i*. jactarse.

boastful ['boustful] *a*. jactancioso.

boat [bout] *s*. bote, barca.

bodily ['bɔdili] *a*. corporal. 2 *adv*. en persona.

body ['bɔdi] *s*. cuerpo. 2 persona, individuo.

bog [bɔg] *s*. pantano, cenagal.

boil [bɔil] *s*. ebullición. 2 *i*. hervir. 3 *t*. cocer.

boiler ['bɔilə'] *s*. olla, caldero.

boisterous ['bɔistərəs] a. estrepitoso, ruidoso, bullicioso.

bold [bould] a. atrevido.

bolster ['boulstər] s. cabezal, travesaño [de cama]. 2 t. apoyar.

bolt [boult] s. saeta, virote. 2 rayo, centella. 3 salto; fuga. 4 cerrojo, pestillo. 5 t. echar el cerrojo a. 6 engullir. 7 i. salir, entrar, etc., de repente; huir.

bomb [bɔm] s. bomba. 2 t.-i. bombardear.

bombardment [bɔm'baːdmənt] s. bombardeo.

bond [bɔnd] s. atadura. 2 lazo, vínculo. 3 trabazón. 4 pacto, compromiso. 5 fiador [pers.]. 6 COM. bono, obligación. 7 pl. cadenas, cautiverio.

bondage ['bɔndidʒ] s. esclavitud.

bone [boun] s. hueso. 2 espina [de pescado]. 3 t. deshuesar.

bonfire ['bɔn,faiər] s. fogata.

bonnet ['bɔnit] s. gorro; gorra. 2 AUTO. capó.

bonus ['bounəs] s. prima, gratificación.

bony ['bouni] a. huesudo.

book [buk] s. libro. 2 cuaderno. 3 t. anotar, inscribir.

bookcase ['bukkeis] s. estante para libros, librería.

booklet ['buklit] s. folleto.

bookshop ['bukʃɔp], **bookstore** [-tɔ:ʳ] s. librería [tienda].

boom [bu:m] s. estampido. 2 fig. auge repentino. 3 i. retumbar. 4 prosperar.

boor [buəʳ] s. patán. 2 grosero.

boot [bu:t] s. bota.

border ['bɔ:dəʳ] s. borde, orilla. 2 frontera.

bore [bɔ:ʳ] s. taladro, barreno, orificio. 2 t. horadar, taladrar. 3 V. TO BEAR.

born, borne [bɔ:n] V. TO BEAR.

borough ['bʌrə] s. villa; burgo, municipio.

borrow ['bɔrou] t. tomar o pedir prestado.

bosom ['buzəm] s. pecho, seno.

boss [bɔs] s. protuberancia, giba. 2 amo, capataz. 2 t.-i. mandar.

bossy ['bɔsi] a. mandón.

both [bouθ] a.-pron. ambos, entrambos, los dos.

bother ['bɔðər] s. preocupación. 2 t.-i. preocupar(se, molestar(se.

bottle ['bɔtl] s. botella, frasco. 2 t. embotellar.

bottom ['bɔtəm] s. fondo. 2 base, fundamento. 3 a. fundamental. 4 del fondo, más bajo. 5 t. poner asiento a. 6 t.-i. basar(se.

bough [bau] s. rama [de árbol].

bought [bɔ:t] V. TO BUY.

boulder ['bouldər] s. canto rodado.

bounce [bauns] s. salto, bote. 2 fanfarronada. 3 t. hacer botar. 4 i. lanzarse, saltar. 5 fanfarronear.

bound [baund] V. TO BIND. 2 a. obligado. 3 encuadernado. 4 destinado a. 5 s. límite, confín. 6 salto, brinco. 7 t. limitar. 8 i. lindar. 9 saltar, brincar.

boundary ['baundəri] s. límite.

bounty ['baunti] s. liberalidad, generosidad. 2 subvención.

bow [bau] s. inclinación, saludo. 2 t. saludar.

bow [bou] s. arco [arma, violín]. 2 t.-i. arquear(se.

bower ['bauər] s. glorieta.

bowl [boul] s. cuenco, escudilla. 2 t. hacer rodar. 3 i. jugar a bochas o a los bolos.

bowman ['boumən] s. arquero.

box [bɔks] s. caja, arca, baúl. 2 TEAT. palco. 3 bofetón, puñetazo. 4 t. encajonar. 5 abofetear. 6 i. boxear.

boxer ['bɔksər] s. boxeador.

boxing ['bɔksiŋ] s. boxeo.

boxwood ['bɔkswud] s. boj.

boy [bɔi] s. chico, muchacho.

brace [breis] s. abrazadera; *pl.* tirantes.

bracelet ['breislit] s. brazalete.

bracket ['brækit] s. ménsula, repisa. 2 anaquel, rinconera. 3 IMPR. corchete; paréntesis.

brain [brein] s. ANAT. cerebro, seso. 2 *pl.* inteligencia.

brake [breik] s. freno [de vehículo, etc.]. 2 helecho. 3 matorral. 4 t. frenar.

bramble ['bræmbl] s. zarza.

bran [bræn] s. salvado.

branch [bra:ntʃ] s. rama; ramo; ramal. 2 i. echar ramas. 3 bifurcarse.

brand [brænd] s. tizón, tea, 2 marca. 3 t. marcar [con hierro].

brandish ['brændiʃ] t. blandir.

brandy ['brændi] s. coñac, brandy.

brass [bra:s] s. latón, metal. 2 descaro.

brave [breiv] a. bravo, valiente. 2 t. desafiar.

brawl [bro:l] s. reyerta, riña. 2 i. alborotar.

bray [brei] s. rebuzno. 2 i. rebuznar.

brazen ['breizn] a. de latón. 2 descarado.

breach [bri:tʃ] s. brecha. 2 fractura. 3 hernia. 4 t. hacer brecha en.

bread [bred] s. pan.

breadth [bredθ] s. anchura.

break [breik] ·s. break [coche]. 2 rotura, ruptura. 3 comienzo. 4 interrupción, pausa. 5 t. romper, quebrar. 6 interrumpir. 7 to ~ down, demoler. 8 to ~ ground, comenzar una empresa. 9 to ~ up, desmenuzar, romper. 10 i. aparecer, salir, nacer, brotar; apuntar [el alba]. 11 to ~ away, soltarse; escapar. 12 to ~ down, parar por averia. 13 to ~ out, estallar, desatarse. ¶ Pret.: broke [brouk]; p. p.: broken ['broukən].

breakfast ['brekfəst] s. desayuno. 2 i. desayunarse, almorzar.

breast [brest] s. pecho, seno.

breath [breθ] s. aliento, respiración. 2 soplo.

breathe [bri:ð] i. respirar. 2 exhalar. 3 soplar.

bred [bred] V. TO BREED.

breeches ['bri:ʃiz] s. pl. pantalones.

breed [bri:d] s. casta, raza. 2 t. engendrar. ¶ Pret. p. p.: bred [bred].

breeding ['bri:diŋ] s. cria, producción. 2 crianza, educación.

breeze [bri:z] s. brisa, airecillo.

brew [bru:] s. infusión [bebida]. 2 t. hacer [cerveza]. 3 preparar [el té, un ponche, etc.].

bribe [braib] s. soborno. 2 t. sobornar.

brick [brik] s. ladrillo. 2 i. enladrillar.

bridal ['braidl] a. nupcial. 2 s. boda.

bride ['braid] *s.* novia, desposada.

bridge [bridʒ] *s.* puente. 2 *t.* tender un puente.

brief [bri:f] *a.* breve, conciso. 2 *s.* resumen.

brier ['braiəʳ] *s.* zarza; brezo.

brigantine ['brigəntain] *s.* bergantín goleta.

bright [brait] *a.* brillante. 2 *t.* abrillantar.

brightness ['braitnis] *s.* brillo.

brilliant ['briljənt] *a.* brillante 2 *s.* brillante [piedra].

brim [brim] *s.* borde [de un vaso, etc.]. 2 ala [de sombrero]. 3 *t.* llenar hasta el borde. 4 *i.* rebosar.

bring [briŋ] *t.* traer, llevar. 2 acarrear, causar. 3 inducir [persuadir]. 4 aportar, aducir. 5 poner [en un estado, condición, etc.]. ¶ Pret. y p. p.: **brought** [brɔːt].

brink [briŋk] *s.* borde, orilla.

brisk [brisk] *a.* vivo, activo.

bristle ['brisl] *s.* cerda, porcipelo. 2 *t.-i.* erizar(se.

brittle ['britl] *a.* quebradizo.

broad [brɔːd] *a.* ancho. 2 amplio.

broadcast ['brɔːdkɑːst] *s.* emisión de radio. 2 *t.* radiar.

broaden ['brɔːdn] *t.-i.* ensanchar(se.

broil [brɔil] *s.* asado a la parrilla. 2 riña, tumulto. 3 *t.* asar a la parrilla. 4 *t.-i.* asar(se, achicharrar(se.

broken ['brəukən] V. to BREAK.

broker ['brəukəʳ] *s.* COM. corredor, agente. 2 bolsista.

bronze [brɔnz] *s.* bronce. 2 *t.-i.* broncear(se.

brooch [brəutʃ] *s.* broche.

brood [bruːd] *s.* cria, pollada, nidada. 2 progenie. 3 casta. 4 *t.* empollar, incubar.

brook [bruk] *s.* arroyo, riachuelo. 2 *t.* sufrir, aguantar.

broom [bru(ː)m] *s.* escoba.

brother ['brʌðəʳ] *s.* hermano.

brother-in-law ['brʌðərinlɔː] *s.* cuñado, hermano político.

brotherly ['brʌðəli] *a.* fraternal.

brought [brɔːt] V. to BRING.

brow [brau] s. ANAT. ceja. 2 frente, entrecejo. 3 cresta, cumbre.

brown [braun] a. pardo, moreno. 2 t. tostar.

browse [brauz] t. rozar.

bruise [bru:z] s. magulladura. 2 t. magullar.

brush [brʌʃ] s. cepillo. 2 t. cepillar.

bubble [ˈbʌbl] s. burbuja. 2 i. burbujear.

buck [bʌk] s. gamo. 2 macho.

bucket [ˈbʌkit] s. cubo, balde.

buckle [ˈbʌkl] s. hebilla. 2 t. abrochar.

bud [bʌd] s. yema, capullo. 2 i. brotar, florecer.

budget [ˈbʌdʒit] s. presupuesto. 2 t.-i. presupuestar.

buff [bʌf] a. de ante 2 s. ante.

buffet [ˈbʌfit] s. bofetada. 2 t. abofetear. 3 [ˈbufei] bar [de estación]. 4 aparador [mueble].

bug [bʌg] s. insecto; chinche.

build [bild] s. estructura. 2 forma, figura, talle. 3 t. construir, edificar. 4 fundar, cimentar. ¶ Pret. y p. p.: *built* [bilt].

building [ˈbildiŋ] s. construcción, edificación. 2 edificio, casa.

built [bilt] V. TO BUILD.

bulb [bʌlb] s. BOT., ZOOL. bulbo. 2 ELECT. bombilla.

bulk [bʌlk] s. bulto. volumen, tamaño. 2 mole. 3 la mayor parte. 4 i. abultar.

bull [bul] s. ZOOL. toro: ~ ring, plaza de toros. 2 bula [pontificia].

bullfight [ˈbulfait] s. corrida de toros.

bullfighter [ˈbulfaitəʳ] s. torero.

bully [ˈbuli] s. matón, valentón. 2 t. intimidar con amenazas; maltratar.

bulwark [ˈbulwək] s. baluarte.

bump [bʌmp] s. choque, porrazo. 2 t.-i. golpear.

bun [bʌn] s. bollo [panecillo]. 2 moño, castaña.

bunch [bʌntʃ] s. manojo. 2 racimo. 3 t.-i. juntar(se, arracimar(se.

bundle [ˈbʌndl] s. atado, manojo. 2 t. liar, atar.

bungalow [ˈbʌngələu] s. casita.

buoy [bɔi] s. boya, baliza. 2 t. mantener a flote.

burden ['bə:dn] *s.* carga, peso. 2 *t.* cargar, agobiar.

burglar ['bə:glə'] *s.* ladrón.

burial ['beriəl] *s.* entierro.

burn [bə:n] *s.* quemadura. 2 *t.* quemar, abrasar. 3 *i.* arder, quemarse. ¶ Pret. y p. p.: *burned* [bə:nd] o *burnt* [bə:nt].

burner ['bə:nə'] *s.* mechero.

burnt [bə:nt] V. TO BURN.

burrow ['bʌrəu] *s.* madriguera. 2 *t.-i.* minar.

burst [bə:st] *s.* explosión. 2 *t.-i.* reventar. ¶ Pret. y p. p.: *burst.*

bury ['beri] *t.* enterrar.

bus [bʌs] *s.* autobús.

bush [buʃ] *s.* arbusto.

business ['biznis] *s.* oficio, ocupación, trabajo, asunto. 2 negocio, comercio, tráfico. 3 negocio, empresa, casa, establecimiento.

bust [bʌst] *s.* busto.

bustle ['bʌsl] *s.* movimiento, agitación. 2 *t.-i.* bullir, menearse.

busy ['bizi] *a.* ocupado, atareado. 2 *t.-ref.* ocupar(se.

but [bʌt, bət] *conj.* mas, pero; sino; [con *cannot, could not* + inf.] no puedo [evitar] menos de, sino. 2 *adv.* sólo. 3 *prep., conj.* excepto, salvo; menos.

butcher ['butʃə'] *s.* carnicero. 2 *t.* matar.

butler ['bʌtlə'] *s.* mayordomo.

butter ['bʌtə'] *s.* mantequilla. 2 *t.* untar con mantequilla.

butterfly ['bʌtəflai] *s.* ENT. mariposa.

button ['bʌtn] *s.* botón. 2 *t.-i.* abrochar(se.

buy [bai] *t.-i.* comprar. ¶ Pret. y p. p.: *bought* [bɔ:t].

buzz [bʌz] *s.* zumbido. 2 *i.* susurrar, zumbar.

by [bai] *prep.* junto a, cerca de, al lado de, cabe. 2 a, con, de, en, por, etc. 3 ~ *the way*, de paso, a propósito. 4 *a.* lateral, apartado. 5 *adv.* cerca, al lado, por el lado. 6 aparte.

C

cab [kæb] s. cabriolé. 2 taxi. 3 cabina.

cabbage ['kæbidʒ] s. col.

cabin ['kæbin] s. cabaña, choza. 2 MAR. camarote. 3 cabina.

cabinet ['kæbinit] s. gabinete; escritorio. 2 vitrina.

cable ['keibl] s. cable. 2 t. cablegrafiar.

cackle ['kækl] s. cacareo. 2 i. cacarear.

café ['kæfei] s. café [lo cal].

cage [keidʒ] s. jaula. 2 t. enjaular.

cajole [kə'dʒəul] t. engatusar, lisonjear.

cake [keik] s. pastel, bollo. 2 pastilla [de jabón, etc.].

calculate ['kælkjuleit] t.-i. calcular; hacer cálculos.

calendar ['kælindər] s. calendario, almanaque.

calf [kɑːf] s. ternero, -ra. 2 pantorrilla.

call [kɔːl] s. grito, llamada. 2 toque de señal. 3 reclamo [de caza]. 4 exigencia. 5 derecho, motivo. 6 visita corta.

call [kɔːl] t. llamar. 2 citar. 3 invocar. 4 considerar. 5 pregonar. 6 to ~ at, detenerse en; to ~ attention to, llamar la atención sobre; to ~ back, hacer volver; to ~ for, ir a buscar; pedir; to ~ forth, ser la causa de; to ~ names, insultar; to ~ off, cancelar; to ~ on, visitar; exhortar; to ~ the roll, pasar lista; to ~ up, llamar por teléfono; poner a debate. 7 i. gritar. 8

hacer una visita a. 9 [de un barco] hacer escala; [del tren] parar.

caller ['kɔ:lər] s. visitante.

calm [ka:m] s. calma, sosiego. 2 a. sosegado, tranquilo. 3 t. sosegar. 4 i. to ~ down, calmarse.

came [keim] V. TO COME.

camera ['kæmərə] s. cámara. 2 máquina fotográfica.

camp [kæmp] s. campamento. 2 t.-i. acampar.

campaign [kæm'pein] s. campaña.

camping ['kæmpiŋ] s. campamento.

can [kæn] s. lata. 2 t. enlatar. 3 [kæn, kən] aux. poder, saber. ¶ Pret. y cond: could [kud].

canal [kə'næl] s. canal.

cancel ['kænsəl] t. cancelar. 2 tachar.

cancer ['kænsər] s. cáncer.

candidate ['kændidit] s. candidato. 2 aspirante.

candle ['kændl] s. vela.

candy [kændi] s. confite.

cane [kein] s. caña.

canker ['kæŋkər] s. úlcera, cáncer. 2 t.-i. gangrenar(se.

cannot ['kænɔt], **can't** [ka:nt, kænt] de can y not.

canoe [kə'nu:] s. canoa.

canopy ['kænəpi] s. dosel.

canvas ['kænvəs] s. lona.

canyon ['kænjən] s. desfiladero, cañón.

cap [kæp] s. gorra. 2 cima. 3 t. cubrir [la cabeza]. 4 coronar.

capable ['keipəbl] a. capaz.

capacity [kə'pæsiti] s. capacidad.

cape [keip] s. cabo. 2 capa.

caper ['keipər] s. cabriola. 2 i. cabriolar.

capital ['kæpitl] a. capital. 2 a.-s. mayúscula. 3 s. capital [población].

capitalist ['kæpitəlist] a.-s. capitalista.

captain ['kæptin] s. capitán.

captivity [kæp'tiviti] s. cautividad, cautiverio.

capture ['kæptʃər] s. captura. 2 t. capturar, apresar.

car [ka:r] s. coche. automóvil.

caravan ['kærəvæn] s. caravana.

card [ka:d] s. naipe. 2

tarjeta, cédula, ficha. 3 *t*. cardar.

cardboard ['kɑ:dbɔ:d] *s*. cartón.

care [kɛɔʳ] *s*. cuidado. 2 *i*. preocuparse; cuidar [de].

career [kɔ'riɔʳ] *s*. carrera. 2 *i*. galopar.

careful ['kɛɔful] *a*. cuidadoso.

careless ['kɛɔlis] *a*. descuidado, negligente.

caress [kɔ'res] *s*. caricia, halago. 2 *t*. acariciar.

cargo ['kɑ:gou] *s*. MAR. carga, cargamento.

carol ['kærɔl] *s*. villancico.

carpenter ['kɑ:pintɔʳ] *s*. carpintero.

carpet ['kɑ:pit] *s*. alfombra. 2 *t*. alfombrar.

carrier ['kæriɔʳ] *s*. portador. 2 portaaviones. 3 transportista.

carrot ['kærɔt] *s*. zanahoria.

carry ['kæri] *t*. llevar, transportar; acarrear. 2 *to* ~ *away*, llevarse; *to* ~ *forward*, sumar y seguir; *to* ~ *off*, llevarse, lograr; *to* ~ *on*, seguir; *to* ~ *out*, llevar a cabo; *to* ~ *through*, completar.

cart [kɑ:t] *s*. carro, carreta. 2 *t*. acarrear.

cartoon [kɑ:'tu:n] *s*. caricatura. 2 dibujos animados.

cartridge ['kɑ:tridʒ] *s*. cartucho.

case [keis] *s*. caso. 2 pleito. 3 caja. 4 maleta. 5 *t*. encajonar.

cash [kæʃ] *s*. dinero en efectivo. 2 *t*. pagar al contado.

cashier [kæ'ʃiɔʳ] *s*. cajero. 2 [kɔ'ʃiɔ] *t*. destituir. 3 degradar.

cask [kɑ:sk] *s*. barril.

cast [kɑ:st] *s*. tiro, lanzamiento. 2 fundición. 3 molde. 4 tendencia. 5 matiz. 6 TEAT. reparto; actores. 7 ~ *iron*, hierro colado. 8 *t*. arrojar. 9 derramar. 10 desechar. 11 proyectar [sombra]. 12 formar. 13 fundir. 14 TEAT. repartir [los papeles]. 15 *to* ~ *away*, desechar. 16 *to* ~ *lots*, echar suertes. ¶ Pret. y p. p.: *cast*.

caste [kɑ:st] *s*. casta.

castle ['kɑ:sl] *s*. castillo. 2 AJED. torre.

casual ['kæʒjuel] *a*. casual. 2 distraído. 3 **-ly** *adv*. casualmente, etc.

casualty ['kæʒjuelti] *s*.

accidente. 2 MIL. baja.
3 víctima.

cat [kæt] s. gato.

catalogue [ˈkætəlɔg] s. catálogo. 2 t. catalogar.

catapult [ˈkætəpʌlt] s. catapulta.

catch [kætʃ] s. redada. 2 trampa. 3 cierre, pestillo. 2 t. coger, agarrar. 3 contraer. 4 sorprender. 5 i. engancharse. ¶ Pret. y. p. p.: *caught* [kɔ:t].

category [ˈkætigəri] s. categoría.

cater [ˈkeitər] i. abastecer.

cathedral [kəˈθi:drəl] s. catedral.

catholicism [kəˈθɔlisizəm] s. catolicismo.

cattle [ˈkætl] s. ganado.

caught [kɔ:t] V. TO CATCH.

cause [kɔ:z] s. causa, razón. 2 t. causar.

caution [ˈkɔ:ʃən] s. cautela, precaución. 2 t. advertir, avisar.

cautious [ˈkɔ:ʃəs] a. cabalgata.

cavalry [ˈkævəlri] s. caballería.

cave [keiv] s. cueva. 2 i. to ~ in, hundirse.

cavity [ˈkæviti] s. hoyo.

cease [si:s] t.-i. cesar, dejar de.

cede [si:d] t. ceder.

ceiling [ˈsi:liŋ] s. techo.

celebrate [ˈselibreit] t.-i. celebrar.

celebrity [siˈlebriti] s. fama.

celibacy [ˈselibəsi] s. celibato.

cell [sel] s. celda. 2 célula.

cellar [ˈselər] s. sótano.

cement [siˈment] s. cemento. 2 t. unir con cemento.

cemetery [ˈsemitri] s. cementerio.

censure [ˈsenʃər] s. censura. 2 t. censurar.

census [ˈsensəs] s. censo.

cent [sent] s. centavo.

centre [ˈsentər] s. centro. 2 t. centrar. 3 concentrar.

century [ˈsentʃəri] s. siglo.

cereal [ˈsiəriəl] a.-s. cereal.

ceremony [ˈseriməni] s. ceremonia.

certain [ˈsə:tn, -tin] a. cierto. 2 fijo.

certificate [səˈtifikit] s. certificado. 2 [səˈtifikeit] t. certificar.

chafe [tʃeif] t. frotar. 2 t.-i. rozar(se. 3 irritar(se.

chain [tʃein] s. cadena. 2 t. encadenar.

chair [tʃɛəʳ] s. silla.

chairman ['tʃɛəmən] s. presidente.

chalk [tʃɔ:k] s. yeso. 2 t. enyesar.

challenge ['tʃælindʒ] s. reto, desafío. 2 t. retar.

champion ['tʃæmpjən] s. campeón; paladín. 3 t. defender.

chance [tʃɑ:ns] s. casualidad; ocasión, oportunidad; riesgo. 2 i. suceder, encontrarse con.

chancellor ['tʃɑ:nsələʳ] s. canciller.

change [tʃeindʒ] s. cambio. 2 t. cambiar, variar, mudar.

channel ['tʃænl] s. canal. 2 t. acanalar.

chaos ['keiɔs] s. caos.

chapel ['tʃæpəl] s. capilla.

chapter ['tʃæptəʳ] s. capítulo [de un libro].

character ['kæriktəʳ] s. carácter. 2 personaje. 3 tipo.

charge [tʃɑ:dʒ] s. carga. 2 obligación, cometido. 3 cargo, acusación. 4 ataque. 5 t. cargar. 6 encargar. 7 **mandar.** 8 adeudar. 9 to ~ with, acusar. 10 t.-i. atacar.

charm [tʃɑ:m] s. encanto, hechizo. 2 amuleto. 3 t. encantar, cautivar.

chart [tʃɑ:t] s. mapa. 2 t. trazar [un mapa, etc.].

charter ['tʃɑ:təʳ] s. fuero, privilegio. 2 t. fletar. 3 alquilar.

chase [tʃeis] s. caza. 2 t. dar caza a.

chat [tʃæt] s. charla. 2 i. charlar.

chatter ['tʃætəʳ] s. charla: ~ box, parlanchín. 2 i. charlar.

cheap [tʃi:p] a.-adv. barato.

cheat [tʃi:t] s. estafa. 2 t. estafar. 3 i. hacer trampas.

check [tʃek] s. represión, obstáculo. 2 comprobación. 3 COM. cheque. 4 AJED. jaque. 5 t. detener. 6 comprobar.

cheek [tʃi:k] s. mejilla. 2 fig. descaro.

cheer [tʃiəʳ] s. alegría, ánimo. 2 viva, vítor. 3 t.-i. animar(se. 4 t. vitorear.

cheese [tʃi:z] s. queso.

chemistry ['kemistri] s. química.

cherish ['tʃeriʃ] t. acariciar. 2 apreciar.

chest [tʃest] s. pecho. 2 cofre, arca.

chew [tʃuː] *t.* mascar. 2 *t.-i.* rumiar.

chick [tʃik], **chicken** ['tʃikin] *s.* pollo, polluelo.

chide [tʃaid] *t.* regañar. ¶ Pret.: *chid* [tʃid]; p. p.: *chidden* ['tʃidn].

chief [tʃiːf] *a.* principal. 2 *s.* jefe, cabeza, caudillo.

child [tʃaild], *pl.* **children** ['tʃildrən] *s.* niño, criatura. 2 hijo: ~ *hood*, niñez.

childish ['tʃaildiʃ] *a.* infantil.

chill [tʃil] *s.* frío [sensación]. 2 escalofrío. 3 frialdad. 4 *t.* enfriar. 5 desalentar.

chimney ['tʃimni] *s.* chimenea.

chin [tʃin] *s.* barbilla.

chirp [tʃəːp] *s.* chirrido. 2 *i.* chirriar, gorjear.

choice [tʃɔis] *s.* preferencia. 2 opción. 3 *a.* escogido.

choir ['kwaiə] *s.* coro.

choke [tʃouk] *t.-i.* ahogar(se, sofocar(se. 2 *t.* ~ *up*, obstruir.

choose [tʃuːz] *t.-i.* escoger. ¶ Pret.: *chose* [tʃouz]; p. p.: *chosen* ['tʃouzn].

chop [tʃɔp] *s.* chuleta. 2 *t.* tajar; picar [carne].

chosen ['tʃouzn] V. TO CHOOSE.

Christian ['kristjən] *a.-s.* cristiano: ~ *name*, nombre de pila.

Christmas ['krisməs] *s.* Navidad.

chronicle ['krɔnikl] *s.* crónica. 2 *t.* narrar.

chuck [tʃʌk] *t.* dar un golpecito [debajo de la barba]. 2 echar, tirar, arrojar.

church [tʃəːtʃ] *s.* iglesia.

churchyard ['tʃəːtʃjɑːd] *s.* cementerio.

churn [tʃəːn] *s.* mantequera. 2 *t.* batir.

cigar [si'gɑːʳ] *s.* cigarro puro [tabaco].

cigarette [sigə'ret] *s.* cigarrillo, pitillo.

cinema ['sinəmə] *s.* cine.

cipher ['saifəʳ] *s.* cifra. 2 *t.* cifrar, calcular.

circle ['səːkl] *s.* círculo. 2 *t.* rodear. 3 *i.* girar.

circumference [sə'kʌmfərəns] *s.* circunferencia.

circus ['səːkəs] *s.* circo.

cite [sait] *t.* citar.

citizen ['sitizn] *s.* ciudadano, vecino.

citizenship ['sitiznʃip] *s.* ciudadanía.

civic ['sivik] *a.* cívico.

civil ['sivl] *a.* civil: ~

servant, funcionario público.

claim [kleim] *s.* demanda, reclamación. 2 *t.* reclamar.

clamber ['klæmbə'] *i.* trepar.

clamp [klæmp] *s.* tornillo de sujeción. 2 *t.* sujetar.

clang [klæŋ], **clank** [klæŋk] *i.* resonar. 2 *t.* hacer sonar.

clap [klæp] *s.* golpe seco; trueno. 2 aplauso. 3 *t.* golpear, aplaudir.

clash [klæʃ] *s.* fragor. 2 choque. 3 conflicto. 4 *i.* chocar. 5 oponerse.

clasp [klɑːsp] *s.* broche, cterre. 2 abrazo. 3 *t.* abrochar, cerrar. 2 asir.

class [klɑːs] *s.* clase. 2 *t.* clasificar.

clatter ['klætə'] *s.* estrépito. 2 alboroto. 3 *i.* hacer ruido, meter bulla.

claw [[klɔː] *s.* garra. 2 *t.-i.* desgarrar.

clay [klei] *s.* arcilla.

clean [kliːn] *a.* limpio. 2 *t.* limpiar. 3 purificar.

cleanly ['klenli] *a.* aseado. 2 [kliːnli] *adv.* limpiamente.

cleanse [klenz] *t.* aclarar.

clear [kliə'] *a.* claro. 2 limpio. 3 claro, espacio. 4 *t.* aclarar. 5 limpiar. 6 *i.* ~ *up*, despejarse, aclarar. 7 ~ *off, out*, largarse.

clearing ['kliəriŋ] *s.* claro [en un bosque]: ~ *house*, cámara de compensación.

1) **cleave** [kliːv] *t.-i.* pegarse, adherirse. ¶ Pret. y p. p.: *cleaved* [kliːvd].

2) **cleave** [kliːv] *t.-i.* hender(se, rajar(se, partir(se. ¶ Pret.: *cleft* [kleft], *cleaved* [kliːvd] o *clove* [klɔuv]; p. p.: *cleft, cleaved* o *cloven* [klɔuvn].

clench [klentʃ] *t.* apretar. 2 agarrar.

clerk [klɑːk] *s.* empleado, dependiente.

clever ['klevə'] *a.* listo.

click [klik] *s.* golpecito seco. 2 *i.* sonar.

cliff [klif] *s.* risco.

climate ['klaimit] *s.* clima.

climb [klaim] *s.* subida. 2 *t.* subir, escalar.

clinch [klintʃ] *s.* remache. 2 agarro. 3 *i.* agarrarse. 4 *t.* apretar.

cling [kliŋ] *i.* asirse. 2 persistir. ¶ Pret. y p. p.: *clung* [klʌŋ].

clinic ['klinik] *s.* clínica.

clip [klip] *s.* grapa. 2 corte. 3 *t.* sujetar. 4 cortar.

cloak [kləuk] s. capa. 2 t. encubrir.

clock [klɔk] s. reloj [de pared].

cloister ['klɔistər] s. claustro.

1) **close** [kləus] s. recinto. 2 a. cerrado. 3 apretado. 4 secreto. 5 espeso. 6 riguroso. 7 íntimo. 8 adv. cerca; ~ by, muy cerca.

2) **close** [kləuz] t. cerrar. 2 tapar, obstruir. 3 apretar, tupir. 4 cercar, rodear. 5 concluir, ultimar. 6 clausurar. 7 i. cerrarse. 8 acercarse. 9 luchar, agarrarse. 10 terminarse. 11 s. conclusión.

closet ['klɔzit] s. armario. 2 retrete.

cloth [klɔθ] s. tela.

clothe [kləuð] t. vestir. ¶ Pret. y p. p.: clothed [kləuðd] o clad [klæd].

clothes [kləuðz] s. pl. prendas de vestir, ropa.

cloud [klaud] s. nube. 2 t.-i. nublar(se.

cloudy ['klaudi] a. nublado. 2 oscuro.

clown [klaun] s. payaso.

club [klʌb] s. clava, porra. 2 DEP. bate; palo [de golf]. 3 trébol o bastos

[de la baraja]. 4 club, círculo, sociedad.

clue [klu:] s. pista.

clump [klʌmp] s. grupo [de árboles]. 2 masa. 3 t.-i. agrupar(se.

clumsy ['klʌmzi] a. torpe.

cluster ['klʌstər] s. ramo. 2 grupo; racimo. 3 i. agruparse. 4 t. apiñar.

clutch [klʌtʃ] s. agarro. 2 MEC. embrague. 3 t.-i. asir, agarrar.

coach [kəutʃ] s. coche, diligencia. 2 instructor. 3 t.-i. adiestrar.

coal [kəul] s. carbón. 2 t.-i. proveer de carbón.

coarse [kɔ:s] a. tosco.

coast [kəust] s. costa. 2 t. navegar costeando.

coat [kəut] s. abrigo; chaqueta. 2 cubierta. 3 t. cubrir.

coax [kəuks] t. engatusar.

cobweb ['kɔbweb] s. telaraña.

cock [kɔk] s. gallo. 2 espita. 3 i. gallear. 4 t. amartillar [un arma]. 5 levantar.

cocoa ['kəukəu] s. cacao.

coconut ['kəukənat] s. coco.

cod [kɔd] s. bacalao.

code [kəud] s. código.

coffee ['kɔfi] s. café [bebida].

coffin ['kɔfin] s. ataúd.

coil [kɔil] s. rollo, rosca. 2 t. enrollar. 3 i. enroscarse.

coin [kɔin] s. moneda. 2 t. acuñar. 3 forjar.

coincidence [kəu'insidəns] s. coincidencia.

coke [kəuk] s. cok, coque.

cold [kəuld] a.-s. frío. 2 resfriado.

collapse [kə'læps] s. fracaso. 2 MED. colapso. 3 i. derrumbarse. 4 sufrir colapso.

collar ['kɔlə'] s. cuello [de una prenda]. 2 collar.

colleague ['kɔli:g] s. colega.

collect [kə'lekt] t. recoger, coleccionar. 2 cobrar. 3 reponerse. 4 i. congregarse.

college ['kɔlidʒ] s. colegio.

collide [kə'laid] t. chocar.

collision [kə'liʒən] s. colisión. 2 oposición.

colony ['kɔləni] s. colonia.

colour ['kʌlə'] s. color. 2 pl. bandera. 3 t. pintar. 4 colorear. 5 enrojecer.

colourless ['kʌləlis] a. descolorido.

column ['kɔləm] s. columna.

comb [kəum] s. peine. 2 t. peinar. 3 rastrillar.

come [kʌm] i. venir. 2 provenir. 3 aparecer. 4 suceder. 5 to ~ about, ocurrir. 6 to ~ back, retroceder. 7 to ~ forward, avanzar. 8 to ~ in, entrar. 9 to ~ off, despegarse. 10 to ~ on, entrar. 11 to ~ out, salir. ¶ Pret.: came [keim]; p. p.: come [kʌm].

comely ['kʌmli] a. gentil.

comfort ['kʌmfət] s. comodidad. 2 t. consolar.

comfortable ['kʌmfətəbl] a. confortable, cómodo.

coming ['kʌmiŋ] a. próximo. 2 s. llegada.

command [kə'mɑ:nd] s. mandato. 2 mando. 3 t.-i. mandar, ordenar.

commander [kə'mɑ:ndə'] s. comandante, jefe.

commend [kə'mend] t. encomendar. 2 recomendar.

comment ['kɔment] s. comentario. 2 i. comentar.

commit [kə'mit] t. cometer. 2 encargar. 3 comprometerse.

committee [kə'miti] *s.* comisión, comité.

common ['komən] *a.* común. 2 vulgar.

commonwealth ['komənwelθ] *s.* comunidad de naciones.

communist ['komjunist] *a.-s.* comunista.

compact ['kompækt] *s.* pacto. 2 polvera. 3 [kəm'pækt] *a.* denso. 4 conciso. 5 *t.* condensar.

companion [kəm'pænjən] *s.* compañero; camarada.

company ['kʌmpəni] *s.* compañía.

comparison [kəm'pærisn] *s.* comparación.

compartment [kəm'pɑːtmənt] *s.* departamento.

compass ['kʌmpəs] *s.* ámbito. 2 brújula. 3 *pl.* compás. 4 *t.* planear. 5 conseguir. 6 rodear.

compassionate [kəm'pæʃənit] *a.* compasivo.

compel [kəm'pel] *t.* obligar, forzar.

compensate ['kompenseit] *t.* compensar.

competent ['kompitənt] *a.* competente, capaz.

competition [,kompi'tiʃən] *s.* competición. 2 certamen. 3 oposición(es.

competitive [kəm'petitiv] *a.* competitivo.

compile [kəm'pail] *t.* recopilar.

complain [kəm'plein] *i.* quejarse.

complaint [kəm'pleint] *s.* queja. 2 demanda.

complement ['komplimənt] *s.* complemento.

complete [kəm'pliːt] *a.* completo. 2 *t.* completar. 3 llenar.

complexion [kəm'plekʃən] *s.* cutis. 2 aspecto.

compose [kəm'pəuz] *t.* componer. 2 calmar.

compound ['kompaund] *s.* mezcla. 2 [kəm'paund] *t.* componer. 3 *i.* avenirse.

comprehend [,kompri'hend] *t.* comprender.

comprehensive [,kompri'hensiv] *a.* extenso.

compress [kəm'pres] *t.* comprimir. 2 apretar.

comprise [kəm'praiz] *t.* comprender, incluir.

compulsory [kəm'pʌlsəri] *a.* obligatorio.

conceal [kən'siːl] *t.* ocultar, encubrir.

concede [kən'siːd] *t.* conceder.

conceit [kən'siːt] *s.* vanidad. 2 concepto.

conceited [kən'siːtid] *a.* engreído, presuntuoso.

conceive [kən'siːv] *t.-i.*

concebir. 2 *t.* comprender.

concentrate ['konsentreit] *t.-i.* concentrar(se.

concept ['konsept] *s.* concepto.

concern [kən'sə:n] *s.* interés. 2 preocupación. 3 asunto. 4 *t.* concernir. 5 importar. 6 preocupar.

concert ['kɔnsə(:)t] *s.* acuerdo. 2 ['kɔnsət] concierto.

concert [kən'sə:t] *t.* concertar, planear. 2 *i.* concertarse.

concord ['kɔnkɔ:d] *s.* acuerdo.

concrete ['kɔnkri:t] *a.* concreto. 2 *s.* hormigón.

condemn [kən'dem] *t.* condenar.

condense [kən'dens] *t.-i.* condensar(se.

condescend [ˌkɔndi'send] *i.* condescender.

conduct ['kɔndʌkt] *s.* conducta.

conduct [kən'dʌkt] *t.* conducir. 2 dirigir, mandar.

conductor [kən'dʌtə'] *s.* conductor: *lightning* ~, pararrayos. 2 MÚS. director. 3 cobrador [de autobús; (E. U.) revisor de tren.

confer [ken'fə:'] *t.* conferir. 2 *i.* conferenciar.

conference ['kɔnfərəns] *s.* conferencia, entrevista.

confess [kən'fes] *t.* confesar. 2 reconocer.

confide [kən'faid] *t.-i.* confiar.

confident ['kɔnfidənt] *a.* seguro.

confine [kən'fain] *i.* confinar. 2 *t.* limitar.

confirm [kən'fə:m] *t.* confirmar, corroborar.

conflict ['kɔnflikt] *s.* conflicto.

conflict [kən'flikt] *i.* chocar, estar en conflicto.

confront [kən'frʌnt] *t.* confrontar. 2 comparar.

congenial [kən'dʒi:njəl] *a.* simpático, agradable.

congenital [kən'dʒenitl] *a.* congénito.

congest [kən'dʒest] *t.-i.* congestionar(se. 2 aglomerar(se.

congratulate [kən'grætjuleit] *t.* felicitar.

conjecture [kən'dʒektʃə'] *s.* conjetura. 2 *t.* conjeturar, presumir.

conjure [kən'dʒuə'] *t.* implorar. 2 ['kʌndʒə'] *to* ~ *up*, evocar. 3 *i.* hacer juegos de manos.

connect [kə'nekt] *t.-i.* unir(se, enlazar(se, relacionar(se. 2 *t.* conectar.

connection, connexion [kə'nekʃən] s. conexión, enlace. 2 relación.

conquer ['kɔŋkər] t. conquistar. 2 vencer, dominar.

conscience ['kɔnʃəns] s. conciencia.

conscientious [ˌkɔnʃi'enʃəs] a. concienzudo. 2 de conciencia.

conscious ['kɔnʃəs] a. consciente.

consciousness [ˌkɔnʃəsnis] s. FIL., PSIC. conciencia. 2 sentido.

consent [kən'sent] s. consenso.

conservative [kən'sə:vətiv] a. conservativo. 2 a.-s. POL. conservador.

conserve [kən'sə:v] s. conserva. 2 t. conservar, mantener.

consider [kən'sidər] t. considerar, pensar.

considering [kən'sidəriŋ] prep. considerando [que].

consign [kən'sain] t. consignar, confiar, depositar.

consist [kən'sist] i. consistir.

consistent [kən'sistənt] a. consistente, sólido. 2 compatible. 3 consecuente.

consolation [ˌkɔnsə'leiʃən] s. consolación, consuelo, alivio.

consolidate [kən'sɔlideit] t.-i. consolidar(se.

consort ['kɔnsɔ:t] s. consorte. 2 [kən'sɔ:t] i. juntarse, acompañarse.

conspiracy [kən'spirəsi] s. conspiración.

conspire [kəns'paiər] i. conspirar, conjurarse. 2 t. tramar.

constable ['kʌnstəbl] s. condestable. 2 policía [uniformado].

constipate ['kɔnstipeit] t. to be ~d, estar estreñido.

constipation [ˌkɔnsti'peiʃən] s. estreñimiento.

constituency [kən'stitjuənsi] s. distrito electoral. 2 electores.

constituent [kən'stitjuənt] a. constitutivo. 2 POL. constituyente. 3 s. componente. 4 elector.

constrain [kəns'trein] t. constreñir, obligar.

consume [kən'sju:m] t.-i. consumir(se.

consummate [kən'sʌmit] a. consumado. 2 perfecto. 3 ['kɔnsəmeit] t. consumar.

consumption [kən'sʌmpʃən] s. consumo. 2 MED. tisis.

contact ['kɔntækt] s. contacto. 2 [kən'tækt] t. ponerse o estar en contacto con.

contain [kən'tein] t. contener; tener cabida para.

contemplate ['kɔntəmpleit] t. contemplar. 2 proponerse. 3 i. meditar.

contemporaneous [kən-ˌtempə'reinjəs] a., **contemporary** [kən'tempərəri] a.-s. contemporáneo.

contempt [kən'tempt] s. desprecio, menosprecio, desdén.

contemptible [kən'temptəbl] a. despreciable. 2 desdeñable.

contend [kən'tend] i. contender. 2 competir, oponerse.

content [kən'tent] a. contento. 2 t. contentar, satisfacer.

contention [kən'tenʃən] s. contienda, disputa. 2 afirmación.

contentment [kən'tentmənt] s. satisfacción, contento.

contest ['kɔntest] s. contienda, lucha, lid. 2 disputa. 3 [kən'test] t. disputar, luchar por.

continual [kən'tinjual] a. continuo, incesante.

contour ['kɔntuə'] s. contorno.

contract [kən'trækt] t.-i. escoger(se. 2 t. contratar, pactar. 3 contraer [matrimonio]. 4 ['kɔn-trækt] s. contrato.

contradict [ˌkɔntrə'dikt] t. contradecir. 2 desmentir, negar.

contrary ['kɔntrəri] a. contrario. 2 adverso. 3 discolo, terco.

contrivance [k ə n't r a i-vəns] s. inventiva. 2 traza, invención.

contrive [kən'traiv] t. idear, inventar. 2 tramar.

control [kən'troul] s. mando, autoridad. 2 gobierno, dirección. 3 sujeción, freno. 4 inspección. 5 comprobación. 6 MEC. mando, control, regulación. 7 t. sujetar, reprimir. 8 gobernar, dirigir. 9 controlar.

convent ['kɔnvənt] s. convento.

convention [kən'venʃən] s. convocación. 2 asamblea, convención. 3 convenio.

converse ['kɔnvə:s] a.

opuesto. 2 [kən'vəːs] *i.* conversar.

convert ['kɔnvəːt] *s.* converso. 2 [kən'vəːt] *t.-i.* convertir(se.

convey [kən'vei] *t.* llevar, transportar. 2 trasmitir.

conveyance [kən'veiəns] *s.* transporte. 2 trasmisión.

convict ['kɔnvikt] *s.* presidiario. 2 [kən'vikt]. DER. declarar culpable. 3 condenar.

convince [kən'vins] *t.* convencer.

convoy ['kɔnvɔi] *s.* convoy. 2 *t.* convoyar, escoltar.

coo [kuː] *s.* arrullo. 2 *i.* arrullar(se.

cook [kuk] *s.* cocinero, -ra. 2 *t.-i.* cocer, guisar, cocinar.

cookery ['kukəri] *s.* cocina [arte].

cool [kuːl] *a.* fresco. 2 frío, tibio. 3 sereno, osado. 4 *t.-i.* refrescar(se, enfriar(se.

copper ['kɔpər] *s.* cobre. 2 penique; calderilla. 3 caldera.

copy ['kɔpi] *s.* copia, reproducción, imitación. 2 ejemplar [de un libro]; número [de un periódi-

co]. 3 IMPR. original. 4 *rough* ~, borrador. 5 *t.* copiar. 6 imitar, remedar.

copyright ['kɔpirait] *s.* [derechos de] propiedad literaria.

coral ['kɔrəl] *s.* coral.

cord [kɔːd] *s.* cordel; cuerda.

core [kɔːr] *s.* corazón, centro. 2 *t.* despepitar.

cork [kɔːk] *s.* corcho. 2 tapón de corcho. 3 ~-*oak*, alcornoque. 4 *t.* tapar [con corcho], encorchar.

corn [kɔːn] *s.* grano, trigo. 2 (E. U.) maíz. 3 mies. 4 callo. 5 *t.* salar, curar.

corner ['kɔːnər] *s.* ángulo, esquina, recodo; rincón. 3 *t.* arrinconar, poner en un aprieto.

corps [kɔːr, *pl.* kɔːz] *s.* cuerpo de ejército.

corpse [kɔːps] *s.* cadáver.

correct [kə'rekt] *a.* correcto. 2 *t.* corregir.

correspond [ˌkɔris'pɔnd] *i.* corresponder, corresponderse [en analogía]. 2 escribirse.

corridor ['kɔridɔːr] *s.* corredor, pasillo.

corrugate ['kɔrugeit] *t.*

arrugar. 2 plegar, ondular.

corsair ['kɔ:sɛəʳ] s. corsario.

cosmonaut ['kɔzmənɔːt] s. cosmonauta.

cost [kɔst] s. coste, precio. 2 i. costar, valer. ¶ Pret. y p. p.: *cost* [kɔst].

costly ['kɔstli] a. costoso, caro.

costume ['kɔstjuːm] s. traje, vestido. 2 pl. TEAT. vestuario.

cot [kɔt] s. choza. 2 camita.

cottage ['kɔtidʒ] s. casita de campo.

cotton ['kɔtn] s. algodón.

couch [kautʃ] s. cama, lecho. 2 t.-i. acostar(se, tender(st.

cough [kɔf] s. tos. 2 i. toser.

could [kud, kəd] V. CAN.

council ['kaunsil] s. concilio. 2 consejo, junta. 3 ayuntamiento.

counsel ['kaunsəl] s. consejo, parecer; deliberación, consulta. 2 asesor; abogado. 3 t. aconsejar, asesorar.

count [kaunt] s. cuenta, cálculo. 2 conde. 3 t. contar, computar. 4 considerar, tener por.

countenance ['kautinəns] s. rostro, semblante. 2 t. favorecer, apoyar, aprobar.

counter ['kauntəʳ] s. ficha, tanto. 2 computador. 3 mostrador [mesa]. 4 t. oponerse a.

counteract [,kauntəˈrækt] t. contrarrestar.

counterfeit ['kauntəfit] a. falso. 2 fingido. 3 s. falsificación. 4 t. falsificar, contrahacer. 5 fingir.

countess ['kauntis] s. condesa.

country ['kʌntri] s. país, nación, región. 2 tierra, patria. 3 campo, campiña.

county ['kaunti] s. condado. 2 distrito.

couple ['kʌpl] s. par, pareja. 2 t.-i. aparear(se, emparejar(se.

courage ['kʌridʒ] s. valor.

courageous [kəˈreidʒəs] a. valeroso, valiente.

course [kɔ:s] s. curso, marcha. 2 camino, trayecto. 3 rumbo. 4 transcurso [del tiempo]. 5 línea [de conducta]. 6 carrera [en la vida]. 7 curso [de estudios], asig-

natura. *8* plato, servicio
[de una comida]. *9*
ALBAÑ. hilada. *10* adv. *of
~*, naturalmente, desde
luego, por supuesto. *11*
t. perseguir. *12* *i.* correr.

court [kɔ:t] *s.* patio;
atrio; plazuela cerrada.
2 pista [de tenis]. *3* corte. *4* tribunal. *5* *t.* cortejar.

courteous ['kə:tjəs] *a.*
cortés.

courtesy ['kə:tisi] *s.* cortesía.

courtier ['kə:tjəʳ] *s.* cor-
tesano.

courtship ['kə:t-ʃip] *s.*
cortejo, galanteo. *2* noviazgo.

courtyard ['kə:tjɑ:d] *s.*
patio.

cousin ['kʌzn] *s.* primo,
-ma.

covenant ['kʌvinənt] *s.*
pacto. *2* *t.-i.* pactar.

cover ['kʌvəʳ] *s.* tapa,
tapadera. *2* cubierta. *3*
abrigo, cubierto, techa-
do. *4* *t.* cubrir. *5* proteger.

coverlet ['kʌvəlit] *s.* colcha.

covet ['kʌvit] *t.* codiciar.

cow [kau] *s.* vaca. *2* *t.*
acobardar.

coward ['kauəd] *a.-s.* cobarde.

cowardice ['kauədis] *s.*
cobardía.

cowardly ['kauədli] *a.*
cobarde.

cowboy ['kaubɔi] *s.* vaquero.

crab [kræb] *s.* cangrejo.

crack [kræk] *s.* crujido.
2 hendidura. *3* *a.* fam.
de primera. *4* *i.* crujir. *5*
reventar.

cracker ['krækəʳ] *s.* pe-
tardo. *2* galleta. *3* *pl.*
chiflado.

crackle ['krækl] *s.* crujido. *2* *i.* crujir.

cradle ['kreidl] *s.* cuna. *2*
t. acunar.

craft [krɑ:ft] *s.* arte,
destreza. *2* oficio; gremio.

craftsman ['krɑ:ftsmən]
s. artesano.

crafty ['krɑ:fti] *a.* astuto, artero.

crag [kræg] *s.* risco, des-
peñadero.

cram [kræm] *t.* henchir,
atestar.

cramp [kræmp] *s.* calam-
bre. *2* *t.* dar calambres.

crane [krein] *s.* ORN. gru-
lla. *2* *t.* MEC. grúa. *3* *t.*
levantar con grúa.

crash [kræʃ] *s.* estallido.
2 choque, accidente. *3* *t.-*
i. romper(se, estallar.

crater ['kreitər] s. cráter.

crave [kreiv] t.-i. pedir.

craving ['kreivin] s. deseo, anhelo, ansia.

crawl [krɔ:l] s. reptación, arrastramiento. 2 NAT. crol. 3 i. reptar, arrastrarse; gatear.

crazy ['kreizi] a. loco, insensato.

creak [kri:k] i. crujir.

cream [kri:m] s. crema, nata.

crease [kri:s] s. pliegue, doblez. 2 t. plegar, doblar, arrugar.

credit ['kredit] s. crédito. 2 honor, honra. 3 t. dar crédito a.

creditor ['kreditər] s. acreedor.

creed [kri:d] s. credo; creencia.

creek [kri:k] s. abra, cala.

creep [kri:p] i. arrastrarse, gatear. 2 correr [los insectos]; trepar [las plantas]. ¶ Pret. y p. p.: crept [krept].

crept [krept] V. TO CREEP.

crescent ['kresnt] a. creciente. 2 s. media luna.

crest [krest] s. cresta. 2 penacho.

crevice ['krevis] s. raja.

crew [kru:] s. MAR., AVIA.

tripulación, equipaje. 2 equipo, cuadrilla. 3 pret. anticuado de TO CROW.

cricket ['krikit] s. ENT. grillo. 2 DEP. criquet.

crime [kraim] s. delito. 2 crimen.

crimson ['krimzn] a.-s. carmesí.

cringe [krindʒ] s. adulación servil. 2 i. encogerse [ante un peligro, etc.]. 3 arrastrarse [servilmente].

cripple [kripl] s. cojo, lisiado. 2 t. encojar, lisiar. 3 i. cojear.

crisp [krisp] a. crespo, rizado. 2 crujiente. 3 t. encrespar, rizar. 4 tostar bien.

croak [krouk] s. graznido. 2 i. croar. 3 t. graznar. 4 gruñir.

crocodile ['krokədail] s. cocodrilo.

crook [kruk] s. curva, curvatura. 2 gancho, garfio. 3 cayado. 4 trampa. 5 fam. estafador. 6 t.-i. torcer(se, encorvar(se.

crop [krɔp] s. cosecha. 2 cabello corto. 3 buche [de ave]. 4 pl. campos, mieses. 5 t. cosechar, recolectar.

cross [krɔs] s. cruz. 2 signo de la cruz. 3 cruce [de caminos, etc.]. 4 t. atravesar. 5 cruzar [cheque; razas]. 6 to ~ one-self, santiguarse.

crouch [krautʃ] i. agacharse, agazaparse. 2 arrastrarse [servilmente].

crow [krəu] s. ORN. cuervo. 2 i. cantar [el gallo]. 3 jactarse, bravear.

crowd [kraud] s. multitud, gentío. 2 t.-i. agolpar(se, apiñar(se.

crown [kraun] s. corona. 2 cima, cumbre. 3 t. coronar.

cruise [kru:z] s. crucero, viaje. 2 t. MAR., AVIA. cruzar, navegar.

cruiser ['kru:zər] s. crucero.

crumb [krʌm] s. miga. 2 t. migar.

crumble ['krʌmbl] t. desmenuzar, deshacer.

crumple ['krʌmpl] t.-i. arrugar(se, ajar(se.

crusade [kru:'seid] s. cruzada.

crush [krʌʃ] s. aplastamiento, machacamiento. 2 t. aplastar, machacar.

crust [krʌst] s. corteza. 2 mendrugo.

crutch [krʌtʃ] s. muleta.

cry [krai] s. grito. 2 lamento. 3 i.-t. gritar. 4 llorar, lamentarse. 5 to ~ down, rebajar, desacreditar.

cub [kʌb] s. cachorro.

cube [kju:b] s. GEOM., MAT. cubo. 2 t. cubicar.

cuckoo ['kuku:] s. ORN. cuclillo.

cucumber ['kju:kʌmbər] s. BOT. cohombro; pepino.

cuddle ['kʌdl] t. abrazar, acariciar.

cudgel ['kʌdʒəl] s. garrote. 2 t. apalear, aporrear.

cue [kju:] s. señal, indicación.

cuff [kʌf] s. puño [de camisa o vestido]: ~ links, gemelos. 2 t. abofetear.

cull [kʌl] t. escoger, elegir. 2 coger [frutos, etc.].

culminate ['kʌlmineit] t. culminar.

culprit ['kʌlprit] s. culpable, reo.

cult [kʌlt]. s. culto.

cunning ['kʌniŋ] a. hábil, ingenioso. 2 s. habilidad, ingenio.

cup [kʌp] s. taza, copa.

cupboard ['kʌbəd] s. aparador.

curb [kə:b] s. barbada.
2 freno. 3 bordillo. 4 brocal. 5 t. refrenar.

curd [kə:d] s. cuajada.

curdle ['kə:dl] t.-i. cuajar(se.

cure [kjuəʳ] s. cura, curación. 2 t.-i. curar(se.

curfew ['kə:fju:] s. toque de queda.

curing ['kjuəriŋ] s. curación.

curio ['kjuəriəu] s. curiosidad, antigüedad [objeto].

curl [kə:l] s. rizo, bucle. 2 t.-i. rizar(se, ensortijar(se.

currant ['kʌrənt] s. pasa de Corinto. 2 grosella.

currency ['kʌrənsi] s. curso, circulación. 2 moneda corriente.

curse [kə:s] s. maldición. 2 t. maldecir.

curtail [kə:'teil] t. acortar.

curtain ['kə:tn] s. cortina.

curtsy ['kə:tsi] s. reverencia. 2 i. hacer una reverencia.

curve [kə:v] s. curva. 2 t.-i. encorvar(se, torcer(se.

cushion ['kuʃən] s. cojín.

custard ['kʌstəd] s. natillas.

custom ['kʌstəm] s. costumbre. 2 parroquia, clientela. 3 pl. aduana; derechos de aduana.

customary ['kʌstəməri] a. acostumbrado, habitual, usual.

customer ['kʌstəməʳ] s. parroquiano, cliente.

cut [kʌt] s. corte, incisión. 2 tajo, tallado. 3 trozo [de carne], tajada. 4 hechura, corte [de un vestido. 5 p. p. de TO CUT. 6 t. cortar, partir. 7 labrar, tallar. 8 herir. 9 to ~ down, cortar, rebajar, reducir. 10 to ~ out, cortar, quitar; desconectar. 11 to ~ short, interrumpir. 12 i. cortar. 13 salir [los dientes]. 14 to ~ in, meter baza. ¶ Pret. y p. p.: cut [kʌt].

cute [kju:t] a. listo, astuto; mono, bonito.

cycle ['saikl] i. ir en bicicleta.

cylinder ['silindəʳ] s. GEOM., MEC. cilindro.

D

dad [dæd], **daddie, daddy**
['dædi] s. fam. papá,
papaíto.
daily ['deili] a. diario,
cotidiano. 2 s. periódico
diario. 3 sirvienta. 4 adv.
diariamente.
dainty ['deinti] a. delicado, exquisito. 2 elegante. 3 s. golosina.
dairy ['dɛəri] s. lechería.
daisy ['deizi] s. вот. margarita.
dale [deil] s. cañada, va-
llecito.
dam [dæm] s. dique, presa. 2 t. embalsar.
damage ['dæmidჳ] s. daño, perjuicio. 2 t. dañar,
perjudicar.
damn [dæm] s. maldi-
ción. 2 a. maldito. 3 t.
condenar. 4 maldecir.
damp [dæmp] a. húmedo,

mojado. 2 s. humedad.
3 t. humedecer, mojar. 4
apagar, amortiguar. 5
desalentar.
dance [da:ns] s. danza,
baile. 2 i.-t. danzar, bailar.
danger ['deindჳəʳ] s. peligro.
dangerous ['deindჳrəs] a.
peligroso.
dare [dɛəʳ] s. reto, desafío. 2 t. atreverse a, osar.
¶ Pret.: *dared* [dɛəd] o
durst [də:st]; p. p.: *dared.*
dark [da:k] a. oscuro. 2
s. oscuridad, tinieblas.
darken ['da:kən] t.-i.
oscurecer(se; nublar(se.
darkness ['da:knis] s. oscuridad.
darling ['da:liŋ] a. amado.

darn [dɑ:n] *s.* zurcido. 2 *t.* zurcir.

dart [dɑ:t] *s.* dardo, flecha. 2 *t.-i.* lanzar(se, arrojar(se.

dash [dæʃ] *s.* arremetida. 2 guión. 3 *t.-i.* lanzar(se, arrojar(se.

date [deit] *s.* fecha. 2 cita. 3 dátil. 4 *t.* fechar, datar. 5 *i.* anticuarse.

daughter ['dɔ:tər] *s.* hija.

daughter-in-law ['dɔ:tərinlɔ:] *s.* nuera, hija política.

daunt [dɔ:nt] *t.* intimidar.

dawn [dɔ:n] *s.* alba, aurora. 2 *i.* amanecer, alborear.

day [dei] *s.* día.

day-break ['dei-breik] *s.* amanecer.

daylight ['deilait] *s.* luz del día.

daze [deiz] *s.* deslumbramiento. 2 *t.* deslumbrar, aturdir.

dazzle ['dæzl] *s.* deslumbramiento. 2 *t.* deslumbrar.

deacon ['di:kən] *s.* diácono.

dead [ded] *a.* muerto. 2 difunto.

deadly ['dedli] *a.* mortal.

2 *adv.* mortalmente; sumamente.

deaf [def] *a.* sordo.

deafen ['defn] *t.* ensordecer.

deal [di:l] *s.* porción, cantidad. 2 *t.* dar. 3 tratar. 4 comerciar. ¶ Pret. y p. p.: *dealt* [delt].

dealer ['di:lər] *s.* comerciante, tratante.

dear [diər] *a.* caro, querido.

death [deθ] *s.* muerte.

debate [di'beit] *s.* debate, discusión. 2 *t.-i.* debatir, discutir.

debris ['debri:] *s.* ruinas, escombros; desecho.

debt [det] *s.* deuda, débito.

debtor ['detər] *s.* deudor.

decade ['dekeid] *s.* década.

decay [di'kei] *s.* decaimiento. 2 *i.* decaer.

decease [di'si:s] *s.* defunción. 2 *i.* morir.

deceit [di'si:t] *s.* engaño.

deceitful [di'si:tful] *s.* engañoso.

deceive [di'si:v] *t.* engañar.

December [di'sembər] *s.* diciembre.

decide [di'said] *t.-i.* decidir.

decisive [di'saisiv] *a.* de-

cisivo. 2 decidido, firme.
deck [dek] s. MAR. cubierta. 2 t. adornar.

declaration [ˌdeklə'reiʃən] s. declaración. 2 manifiesto.

declare [di'klɛəʳ] t.-i. declarar.

decline [di'klain] s. declinación, decadencia. 2 t.-i. inclinar(se, bajar. 3 t. rehusar.

declivity [di'kliviti] s. declive.

decompose [ˌdiːkəm'pəuz] t.-i. descomponer(se.

decorate ['dekəreit] t. decorar, adornar. 2 condecorar.

decoy ['di'kɔi] s. señuelo, reclamo. 2 [di'kɔi] t. atraer con señuelo. 3 seducir.

decrease ['diːkriːs] s. decrecimiento, disminución. 2 [diː'kriːs] i. decrecer. 3 t.-i. menguar.

decree [di'kriː] s. decreto, orden. 2 t. decretar.

decry [di'krai] t. desacreditar, rebajar.

deed [diːd] s. hecho; acción.

deem [diːm] t.-i. juzgar, creer, estimar.

deep [diːp] a. hondo, profundo.

deepen ['diːpən] t.-i. ahondar(se, intensificar-(se.

deer [diəʳ] s. ciervo, venado.

defame [di'feim] t. difamar, infamar.

default [di'fɔːlt] s. falta, carencia. 2 t.-i. faltar.

defeat [di'fiːt] s. derrota. 2 t. derrotar, vencer.

defective [di'fektiv] a. defectivo, defectuoso.

defence [di'fens] s. defensa.

defend [di'fend] t. defender.

defendant [di'fendənt] s. DER. demandado; acusado.

defer [di'fəːʳ] t. diferir, aplazar, retardar.

defiance [di'faiəns] s. desafío.

defiant [di'faiənt] a. desafiador.

defile ['diːfail] s. desfiladero.

defile [di'fail] t. ensuciar. 2 manchar, profanar.

define [di'fain] t. definir.

definition [ˌdefi'niʃən] s. definición.

deflate [di'fleit] t.-i. desinflar(se, deshinchar(se.

defy [di'fai] *t.* desafiar.
degenerate [di'dʒenərit] *a.-s.* degenerado.
degrade [di'greid] *t.-i.* degradar(se. 2 *t.* minorar, rebajar.
degree [di'gri:] *s.* grado.
deign [dein] *i.* dignarse.
deject [di'dʒekt] *t.* abatir, desanimar.
delay [di'lei] *s.* dilación, retraso. 2 *t.* diferir, aplazar.
delegate ['deligit] *a.-s.* delegado.
delegate ['deligeit] *t.* delegar, comisionar.
deliberate [di'libəreit] *t.* reflexionar, considerar. 2 *i.* deliberar, consultar.
delicacy ['delikəsi] *s.* delicadeza.
delicious [di'liʃəs] *a.* delicioso.
delight [di'lait] *s.* deleite, delicia. 2 *t.-i.* deleitar(se, encantar(se.
delightful [di'laitful] *a.* deleitable, delicioso.
delirious [di'liriəs] *a.* delirante.
deliver [di'livə'] *t.* libertar. 2 librar, salvar. 3 entregar.
deliverance [di'livərəns] *s.* liberación, rescate.
delivery [di'livəri] *s.* liberación, rescate. 2 entrega.
deluge ['delju:dʒ] *s.* diluvio. 2 *t.* inundar.
delusion [di'lu:ʒən] *s.* engaño.
demand [di'ma:nd] *s.* demanda. 2 *t.* demandar, pedir.
demeanou(u)r [di'mi:nə'] *s.* comportamiento.
demolish [di'mɔliʃ] *t.* demoler. 2 arrasar.
demon ['di:mən] *s.* demonio.
demonstrate ['demənstreit] *t.* demostrar. 2 *i.* manifestarse.
demoralize [di'mɔrəlaiz] *t.* desmoralizar.
demur (di'mə:'] *s.* irresolución. 2 objeción. 3 *i.* objetar, poner dificultades.
den [den] *s.* caverna. 2 guarida.
denial [di'naiəl] *s.* negación.
denote [di'nout] *t.* denotar.
denounce [di'nauns] *t.* denunciar. 2 anunciar.
dense [dens] *a.* denso.
density ['densiti] *s.* densidad.
dental ['dentl] *a.* dental.
deny [di'nai] *t.* negar.

depart [[di'pɑ:t] *i.* partir.

department [di'pɑ:tmənt] *s.* departamento.

departure [di'pɑ:tʃər] *s.* partida, marcha, salida.

depend [di'pend] *i.* depender.

dependence [di'pəndəns] *s.* dependencia. 2 confianza.

depict [di'pikt] *t.* pintar, representar.

deport [di'pɔ:t] *t.* deportar, desterrar.

deportment [di'pɔ:tmənt] *s.* conducta, proceder.

depose [di'pəuz] *t.* deponer, destituir.

deposit [di'pɔzit] *s.* depósito, sedimento. 2 *t.-i.* depositar(se, sedimentar-(se. ·

depot ['depəu] *s.* depósito, almacén.

depreciate [di'pri:ʃieit] *t.* depreciar. 2 despreciar.

depress [di'pres] *t.* deprimir.

depression [di'preʃən] *s.* depresión. 2 abatimiento, desánimo.

deprive [di'praiv] *t.* privar.

depth [depθ] *s.* profundidad, hondura.

deputy [de'pjuti] *s.* diputado.

deride [di'raid] *t.* burlarse.

derive [di'raiv] *t.* derivar.

descend [di'send] *i.-t.* descender.

descent [di'sent] *s.* descenso. 2 linaje, descendencia.

descry [dis'krai] *t.* descubrir, divisar.

desert ['dezət] *a.* desierto. 2 *s.* desierto, yermo.

desert [di'zə:t] *t.* abandonar. 2 *t.-i.* desertar.

deserts [di'zə:ts] *s. pl.* lo merecido.

deserve [di'zə:v] *t.-i.* merecer.

design [di'zain] *s.* plan. 2 intención. 3 dibujo. 4 *t.* destinar. 5 proyectar. 6 trazar, diseñar.

designer [di'zainər] *s.* dibujante. 2 inventor.

desirable [di'zaiərəbl] *a.* deseable, apetecible.

desire [di'zaiər] *s.* deseo. 2 *t.* desear.

desirous [di'zaiərəs] *a.* deseoso.

desk [desk] *s.* pupitre.

desolate ['desəleit] *t.* desolar, devastar.

despair [dis'pɛər] *s.* desesperación; desesperanza. *2 i.* desesperar; desesperanzarse.

despatch = DISPATCH.

desperate ['despərit] *a.* desesperado. *2* arriesgado.

desperation [,despə'reiʃən] *s.* desesperación; furor.

despise [dis'paiz] *t.* despreciar, menospreciar.

despite [dis'pait] *prep.* ~ *of, in* ~ *of,* a pesar de.

despot ['despɔt] *s.* déspota.

dessert [di'zə:t] *s.* postres.

destination [,desti'neiʃən] *s.* destinación, destino.

destitute ['destitju:t] *a.* indigente, desamparado.

destroy [dis'trɔi] *t.* destruir. *2* demoler.

detach [di'tætʃ] *t.* separar, desprender.

detail ['di:teil] *s.* detalle, pormenor. *2 t.* detallar, especificar.

detain [di'tein] *t.* retener, detener.

detect [di'tekt] *t.* descubrir, averiguar.

deter [di'tə:'] *t.* detener, disuadir.

detest [di'test] *t.* detestar.

develop [di'veləp] *t.* fomentar. *2 t.-i.* desenvolver(se, desarrollar(se.

device [di'vais] *s.* artificio, invención.

devil ['devl] *s.* demonio, diablo.

devilish ['devliʃ] *a.* diabólico. *2* endiablado.

devise [di'vaiz] *t.* inventar.

devoid [di'vɔid] *a.* falto, exento.

devote [di'vout] *t.* consagrar, dedicar.

devout [di'vaut] *a.* devoto, piadoso.

dew [dju:] *s.* rocío; relente. *2 t.-i.* rociar, refrescar.

dexterity [deks'teriti] *s.* destreza.

dial ['daiəl] *s.* reloj de sol. *2* esfera [de reloj]. *3* disco [de teléfono, etc.]. *4 t.* TELEF. marcar.

diameter [dai'æmitə'] *s.* diámetro.

diamond ['daiəmənd] *s.* diamante. *2* GEOM. rombo.

diary ['daiəri] *s.* diario, dietario.

dice [dais] *s.* dados.

dictate ['dikteit] *s.* mandato.

dictate [dik'teit] *t.* dictar. *2* mandar.

dictionary ['dikʃənəri] *s.* diccionario, léxico.

did [did] *pret.* de TO DO.

die [dai], *pl.* **dice** [-s] *s.* dado [para jugar]. 2 cubito.

die [dai] *i.* morir, fallecer. ¶ Pret. y p. p.: *died* [daid]; ger.: *dying* ['daiiŋ].

differ ['difə'] *i.* diferir.

difficult ['difikəlt] *a.* difícil.

diffidence ['difidəns] *s.* timidez.

diffuse [di'fju:s] *a.* difuso.

diffuse [di'fju:z] *t.-i.* difundir(se.

dig [dig] *s.* empujón, codazo. 2 *t.* cavar, ahondar. ¶ Pret. y p. p.: *dug* [dʌg].

digest ['daidʒest] *s.* compendio.

digest [di'dʒest] *t.-i.* digerir(se. 2 *t.* resumir.

digress [dai'gres] *i.* divagar.

dike [daik] *s.* dique, malecón.

diligence ['dilidʒəns] *s.* diligencia, aplicación.

dilute [dai'lju:t] *t.-i.* diluir(se.

dim [dim] *a.* oscuro, opaco. 2 *t.* oscurecer.

dime [daim] *s.* (E. U.) diez centavos.

dimension [[di'menʃən] *s.* dimensión.

diminish [di'miniʃ] *t.* disminuir.

din [din] *s.* fragor, estrépito. 2 *t.* golpear con ruido.

dine [dain] *i.* comer, cenar.

diner ['dainə'] *s.* comensal. 2 vagón restaurante.

dingy ['dindʒi] *a.* oscuro, sucio.

dining-room ['daininrum] *s.* comedor [pieza].

dinner ['dinə'] *s.* cena: *to have* ~, cenar.

dip [dip] *s.* zambullida. 2 *t.* sumergir, bañar.

dire ['daiə'] *a.* horrendo.

direct [di-, dai'rekt] *a.* directo. 2 *t.* dirigir.

dirge [də:dʒ] *s.* canto fúnebre.

dirt [də:t] *s.* suciedad.

dirty ['də:ti] *a.* manchado, sucio. 2 cochino, indecente. 3 *t.-i.* ensuciar(se.

disable [dis'eibl] *t.* inutilizar.

disadvantage [ˌdisəd'vɑːntidʒ] *s.* desventaja.

disagree [ˌdisə'gri:] *i.* discordar, discrepar.

disagreeable [,disə'griəbl]
a. desagradable, ingrato.

disagreement [,disə'gri:-
mənt] *s.* discordancia,
discrepancia.

disappear [,disə'piə'] *i.*
desaparecer.

disappoint [,disə'pɔint]
t. defraudar, decepcio-
nar.

disapproval [,disə'pru:v-
əl] *s.* desaprobación.

disapprove ['disə'pru:v]
t. desaprobar.

disarm [dis'ɑ:m] *t.-i.* de-
sarmar(se. 2 calmar.

disc [disk] *s.* disco.

discard [di'kɑ:d] *t.-i.*
descartarse [de]. 2 *t.*
descartar.

discern [di'sə:n] *t.* discernir, distinguir.

discharge [dis'tʃɑ:dʒ] *s.*
descarga. 2 *t.* descargar.

disclose [dis'klouz] *t.*
descubrir.

discomfort [dis'kʌmfət]
s. incomodidad, molestia.

disconcert [,diskən'sə:t]
t. desconcertar.

discontent ['diskən'tent]
s. descontento, disgusto.
2 *a.* descontento. 3 *t.*
descontentar, disgustar.

discontinuous ['diskən-
'tinjues] *a.* discontinuo.

discord ['diskɔ:d] *s.* discordia.

discord [dis'kɔ:d] *i.* des-
convenir, discordar.

discount ['diskaunt] *s.*
descuento; rebaja 2 *t.*
descontar, rebajar.

discourage [dis'kʌridʒ] *t.*
desalentar. 2 disuadir.

discourse [di'kɔ:s] *s.* discurso. 2 *i.* discurrir, di-
sertar.

discover [dis'kʌvə'] *t.*
descubrir, hallar.

discovery [dis'kʌvəri] *s.*
descubrimiento, hallazgo.

discredit [dis'kredit] *s.*
descrédito; deshonra. 2
t. desacreditar, despres-
tigiar.

discreet [dis'kri:t] *a.*
discreto.

discretion [dis'kreʃən] *s.*
discreción.

discuss [dis'kʌs] *t.-i.* discutir.

disdain [dis'dein] *s.* desdén, menosprecio. 2 *t.*
desdeñar.

disease [di'zi:z] *s.* enfermedad.

disfigure [dis'figə'] *t.*
desfigurar, afear.

disgrace [dis'greis] *s.*
desgracia, disfavor.

disgrace [dis'greis] *t.* deshonrar.

disgraceful [dis'greisful]
a. deshonroso, vergonzoso.

disguise [dis'gaiz] s. disfraz. 2 t. disfrazar.

disgust [dis'gʌst] s. aversión. 2 t. hastiar, repugnar.

dish [diʃ] s. plato, fuente. 2 t. servir. 3 burlar, frustrar.

dishearten [dis'hɑːtn] t. descorazonar, desanimar.

dishevel [di'ʃevəl] t. desgreñar, despeinar.

dishonest [dis'ɔnist] a. tramposo, falso. 2 poco honrado.

dishono(u)r [dis'ɔnəʳ] s. deshonor, deshonra. 2 t. deshonrar.

disillusion [ˌdisi'luːʒən] s. desilusión. 2 t. desilusionar.

disinterested [dis'intristid] a. desinteresado. 2 imparcial.

disjoint [dis'dʒɔint] t. desarticular, descoyuntar.

disk [disk] s. disco.

dislike [dis'laik] s. aversión. 2 t. tener antipatía a, detestar.

dismal ['dizməl] a. triste, sombrío.

dismay [dis'mei] s. desmayo. 2 t. desanimar, espantar.

dismiss [dis'mis] t. despedir. 2 disolver.

dismount ['dis'maunt] t. desmontar. 2 i. bajar, apearse.

disobey ['disə'bei] t.-i. desobedecer.

disorder [dis'ɔːdəʳ] s. trastorno. 2 t. desordenar.

dispatch [dis'pætʃ] s. despacho. 2 t. despachar.

dispel [dis'pel] t.-i. dispersar(se, disipar(se.

dispense [dis'pens] t. dispensar, distribuir.

disperse [dis'pəːs] t.-i. dispersar(se.

displace [dis'pleis] t. cambiar de sitio, remover.

display [dis'plei] s. despliegue, exhibición, manifestación. 2 t. desplegar, abrir, extender.

displease [dis'pliːz] t. desagradar, disgustar.

displeasure [dis'pleʒəʳ] s. desagrado, descontento.

disposal [dis'pəuzəl] s. disposición, arreglo.

dipose [dis'pəuz] t. disponer [arreglar, ordenar; establecer; disponer el ánimo de].

dispute [dis'pjuːt] s. disputa, discusión. 2 t.-i. disputar, discutir. 3 controvertir.

disqualify [dis'kwɔlifai] t. inhabilitar.

disquiet [dis'kwaiət] s. inquietud. 2 t. inquietar.

disregard ['disri'gɑ:d] s. desatención, descuido. 2 t. desatender, descuidar.

disreputable [dis'repjutəbl] a. desacreditado. 2 deshonroso.

disrespect ['disris'pekt] s. falta de respeto, desacato.

disrespectful [,disris'pekful] a. irrespetuoso.

dissatisfaction ['dis,sætis-'fækʃən] s. descontento.

dissatisfy ['dis'sætisfai] t. descontentar.

dissect [di'sekt] t. disecar.

dissension [di'senʃən] s. disensión, discordia.

dissent [di'sent] s. disentimiento. 2 i. disentir, diferir. 3 disidir.

dissipate ['disipeit] t. dispersar. 2 disipar.

dissolute ['disəlu:t] a. disoluto.

dissolve [di'zɔlv] t.-i. disolver(se.

dissuade [di'sweid] t. disuadir.

distance ['distəns] s. distancia. 2 t. distanciar.

distasteful [dis'teistful] a. desagradable, repugnante.

distemper [dis'tempər] s. mal humor. 2 enfermedad. 3 t. perturbar, enfermar.

distil(l [dis'til] t. destilar.

distinct [dis'tiŋkt] a. distinto.

distort [dis'tɔ:t] t. torcer.

distract [dis'trækt] t. distraer, apartar.

distress [dis'tres] s. pena. 2 t. afligir.

distrust [dis'trʌst] s. desconfianza. 2 t. desconfiar.

disturb [dis'tə:b] t. turbar.

disturbance [dis'tə:bəns] s. perturbación, alteración.

ditch [ditʃ] s. zanja, foso.

dive [daiv] s. zambullida, inmersión. 2 buceo. 3 i. zambullirse, sumergirse.

diver ['daivər] s. buzo.

divert [dai'və:t] t. desviar, apartar. 2 divertir.

divine [di'vain] a. divino: sublime. 2 s. sacerdote; teólogo. 3 t.-i. adivinar. 4 conjeturar.

diviner [di'vainər] s. adivino.

diving ['daiviŋ] s. buceo.

divinity [di'viniti] s. divinidad. 2 teología.

divorce [di'vɔ:s] s. divorcio. 3 t.i-. divorciarse de.

dizziness ['dizinis] s. vértigo, mareo, vahído.

dizzy ['dizi] a. vertiginoso, que marea.

do [du:] t. [en sentido general] hacer [justicia; un favor, etc.]. 2 concluir, despachar. 3 cumplir con [un deber, etc.]. 4 producir, preparar. arreglar. 5 cocer, guisar. 6 i. obrar, portarse; estar: how ~ you ~?, ¿cómo está usted? 7 servir, bastar: that will ~, esto basta. ¶ INDIC. Pres., 3.ª pers.: does [dʌz, dɔz]. | Pret.: did [did]. | Part. p.: done [dʌn].

dock [dɔk] s. dique; dársena. 2 t. cortar, cercenar.

doctor ['dɔktər] m. doctor. 2 t. doctorar.

doctrine ['dɔktrin] s. doctrina.

dodge [dɔdʒ] s. regate. 2 argucia, artificio. 3 i. regatear; evitar, burlar.

doe [dou] s. ZOOL. gama.

doer ['du(:)ər] s. autor, agente.

does [dʌz, dɔz] V. TO DO.

dog [dɔg] s. perro, perra, can. 2 t. perseguir, seguir.

doing ['du(:)iŋ] ger. de TO DO. 2 s. pl. hechos, acciones.

doll [dɔl] s. muñeca, muñeco.

dollar ['dɔlər] s. dólar.

dolly ['dɔli] s. muñequita.

dolphin ['dɔlfin] s. ZOOL. delfín.

domain [də'mein] s. finca.

dome [doum] s. ARQ. cúpula.

dominion [də'minjən] s. dominación, señorío.

don [dɔn] t. vestirse.

done [dʌn] p. p. de TO DO.

donkey ['dɔŋki] s. asno, burro.

doom [du:m] s. sentencia, condena. 2 destino. 3 t. condenar.

door [dɔ:r, dɔər] s. puerta.

door-keeper ['dɔ:ˌki:pər] s. portero.

doorway ['dɔ:wei] s. puerta, entrada, portal.

dope [doup] s. droga, narcótico. 2 t. drogar, narcotizar.

dose [dous] s. dosis, toma. 2 t. medicinar. 3 dosificar.

dot [dɔt] s. punto, señal.
2 t. puntear, salpicar.

double ['dʌbl] a. doble,
duplo. 2 doble [de dos
partes; insincero, ambi-
guo]. 3 t. doblar, dupli-
car.

doubt [daut] s. duda. 2
t.-i. dudar.

doubtful ['dautful] a. dudoso.

doubtless ['dautlis] a. in-
dudable.

dough [dəu] s. masa [del
pan].

dove [dʌv] s. palomo, pa-
loma.

down [daun] s. plumón.
2 bozo, vello. 3 pelusa. 4
duna. 5 loma. 6 ups and
downs, altibajos. 7 adv.-
prep. abajo, hacia abajo,
por. 8 t. derribar.

downright ['daunrait] a.
a. claro, categórico.

downstars ['daun'stɛəz]
adv. abajo [en el piso
inferior].

downward ['daunwəd] a.
descendente. 2 a d v .
DOWNWARDS.

downwards ['daunwədz]
adv. hacia abajo.

downy ['dauni] a. vello-
so.

dowry ['dauəri] s. dote.

doze [dəuz] s. sueño li-
gero. 2 i. dormitar.

dozen ['dʌzn] s. docena.

drab [dræb] s. pardusco.

draft, draught [dra:ft]
s. acción de sacar. 2 co-
rriente [de aire]. 3 tiro
[de chimenea]. 4 inhala-
ción, trago; bebida. 5
atracción, tracción, tiro.
6 redada. 7 trazado; bo-
ceto, dibujo. ¶ En las
acepciones 4 y 6 úsase de
preferencia draught.

draft, draught [dra:ft] t.
hacer el borrador de, re-
dactar.

drag [dræg] s. rastra,
grada. 2 t. arrastrar.

drain [drein] s. drenaje.
2 t. desaguar, drenar.

drainage ['dreinidʒ] s.
desagüe.

drake [dreik] s. pato
[macho].

drank [dræŋk] V. TO
DRINK.

drape [dreip] s. colgadu-
ra. 2 t. entapizar.

drapery ['dreipəri] s. pa-
ñería.

draught [dra:ft] s. DRAFT.

draw [drɔ:] s. arrastre,
tracción. 2 t. arrastrar.
2 dibujar. ¶ Pret.: drew
[dru:]; p. p.: drawn
[drɔ:n].

drawback ['drɔ:bæk] s.
inconveniente, desventa-
ja.

drawer [drɔ:ˁ, drɔəˁ] *s.* cajón.

drawl [drɔ:l] *s.* enunciación lenta. 2 *t.-i.* arrastrar las palabras.

drawn [drɔ:n] *p. p.* de TO DRAW. 2 *a.* de aspecto fatigado.

dread [dred] *s.* miedo, temor. 2 *a.* temible, terrible. 3 *t.-i.* temer [a].

dreadful ['dredful] *a.* terrible, espantoso.

dream [dri:m] *s.* sueño. 2 *t.-i.* soñar. ¶ Pret. y p. p.: *dreamed* o *dreamt* [dremt].

dreamt [dremt] V. TO DREAM.

dreary ['driəri] *a.* triste.

drench [drentʃ] *t.* mojar.

dress [dres] *s.* vestido, indumentaria. 2 *t.-i.* vestir(se, ataviar(se. 3 peinar, arreglar [el cabello].

dresser ['dresəˁ] *s.* cómoda con espejo.

dressmaker ['dres,meikəˁ] *s.* modista, costurera.

drew [dru:] V. TO DRAW.

dried [draid] V. TO DRY.

drift [drift] *s.* lo arrastrado por el mar, el viento, etc. 2 rumbo, dirección, giro. 3 *t.* impeler, llevar, amontonar. 4 *i.* flotar, ir a la deriva.

drill [dril] *s.* taladro. 2 ejercicio. 3 *t.* taladrar.

drink [driŋk] *s.* bebida. 2 trago. 3 *t.* beber. 4 *i.* emborracharse. ¶ Pret.: *drank* [dræŋk]; p. p.: *drunk* [drʌŋk].

drinking ['driŋkiŋ] *s.* bebida.

drip [drip] *s.* goteo. 2 gotera. 3 *i.* gotear, chorrear.

drive [draiv] *s.* paseo en coche. 2 *t.* impeler, impulsar, mover, llevar. 3 guiar, conducir. ¶ Pret.: *drove* [drouv]; p. p.: *driven* ['drivn].

driver ['draivəˁ] *s.* conductor.

driving ['draiviŋ] *s.* conducción. 2 impulso.

drone [droun] *s.* ENT. y fig. zángano. 2 zumbido. 3 *t.* zumbar.

droop [dru:p] *s.* inclinación, caída. 2 *t.-i.* inclinar(se, bajar(se.

drop [drɔp] *s.* gota [de líquido]. 2 JOY. pendiente. 3 *t.* dejar caer, soltar, echar, verter. 4 *i.* gotear, chorrear.

drought [draut] *s.* sequía.

drove [drouv] V. TO DRIVE. 2 *s.* manada, rebaño.

drown [draun] *t.-i.* ahogar(se, anegar(se. 2 *t.* inundar.

drowsy ['drauzi] *a.* soñoliento.

drudgery ['drʌdʒəri] *s.* trabajo penoso.

drug [drʌg] *s.* droga; medicamento. 2 *t.* narcotizar; medicinar.

druggist ['drʌgist] *s.* (Ingl.) droguero, farmacéutico; (E. U.) dueño de un DRUG-STORE.

drug-store ['drʌgstoː'] *s.* (E. U.) tienda a la vez farmacia, perfumería, colmado, comedor, etcétera.

drum [drʌm] *s.* tambor. 2 *i.* tocar el tambor.

drunk [drʌŋk] *p. p.* de TO DRINK. 2 *a.* borracho, embriagado.

drunkard ['drʌŋkəd] *s.* borrachín.

drunken ['drʌŋkən] *a.* borracho.

dry [drai] *a.* seco; árido. 2 *t.-i.* secar(se, enjugar(se.

duchess ['dʌtʃis] *s.* duquesa.

duchy ['dʌtʃi] *s.* ducado [territorio].

duck [dʌk] *s.* ORN. ánade, pato. 2 *t.-i.* zambu-

llir(se. 3 agachar(se rápidamente.

due [dju:] *a.* debido: ~ to, debido a.

duel ['dju(ː)əl] *s.* duelo, desafío.

dug [dʌg] V. TO DIG. 2 *s.* teta, ubre.

duke [dju:k] *s.* duque.

dull [dʌl] *a.* embotado, obtuso. 2 torpe, lerdo. 3 *t.* embotar.

dullness ['dʌlnis] *s.* embotamiento. 2 torpeza, estupidez.

duly ['dju:li] *adv.* debidamente.

dumb [dʌm] *a.* mudo, callado.

dump [dʌmp] *s.* vertedero; depósito 2 *t.* descargar, verter.

dunce [dʌns] *s.* zote, ignorante.

dung [dʌŋ] *s.* estiércol. 2 *t.* estercolar.

dungeon ['dʌndʒən] *s.* calabozo.

duplicate ['dju:plikeit] *t.* duplicar.

durable ['djuərəbl] *a.* durable, duradero.

during ['djuəriŋ] *prep.* durante.

dusk [dʌsk] *s.* crepúsculo. 2 sombra.

dusky ['dʌski] *a.* oscuro. 2 sombrío.

dust [dʌst] *s.* polvo. 2 restos mortales. 3 basura. 4 *t.* desempolvar.

dusty ['dʌsti] *a.* polvoriento.

duty ['dju:ti] *s.* deber, obligación. 2 obediencia, respeto.

dwarf [dwɔ:f] *a.-s.* enano, -na. 2 *t.* impedir el crecimiento de. 3 empequeñecer; achicar.

dwell [dwel] *i.* habitar, residir, vivir. 2 permanecer. ¶ Pret. y p. p.: *dwelt* [dwelt].

dweller ['dwelǝʳ] *s.* habitante, inquilino.

dwindle ['dwindl] *i.* menguar, disminuirse.

dye [dai] *s.* tintura, tinte, color. 2 *t.-i.* teñir(se.

E

each [i:tʃ] *a.-pr.* cada, todo; cada uno: ~ *other*, uno a otro, los unos a los otros.

eager ['i:gəʳ] *a.* ávido, ansioso.

eagerness ['i:gənis] *s.* avidez, ansia, afán, ardor.

eagle ['i:gl] *s.* águila.

ear [iəʳ] *s.* oreja. 2 oído, oídos. 3 BOT. espiga, mazorca [de cereal].

earl [ə:l] *s.* conde [título].

early ['ə:li] *a.* primitivo, antiguo, remoto. 2 *adv.* temprano, pronto.

earn [e:n] *t.* ganar, merecer, lograr.

earnest ['ə:nist] *a.* serio. 2 sincero.

earnestness ['ə:nistnis]

s. seriedad, buena fe. 2 ahínco, ardor.

earnings ['ə:ninz] *s. pl.* ganancias; sueldo, salario.

ear·ring ['iərin] *s.* pendiente.

earshot ['iə-ʃɔt] *s.* alcance del oído.

earth [ə:θ] *s.* tierra, barro. 2 tierra [mundo; país; suelo]. 3 madriguera.

earthen ['ə:θən] *a.* de barro.

earthenware ['ə:θənwɛəʳ] *s.* ollería, vasijas de barro.

earthly ['ə:θli] *a.* terrestre. 2 terrenal. 3 mundano, carnal.

earthquake ['ə:θkweik] *s.* terremoto.

earthworm [ˈəːθ-wəːm] s. lombriz de tierra.

ease [iːz] s. alivio, descanso. 2 t. aliviar, moderar.

easily [ˈiːzili] adv. fácilmente.

east [iːst] s. este, oriente, levante. 2 a. oriental, del este.

Easter [ˈiːstəʳ] s. Pascua de Resurrección.

eastern [ˈiːstən] a. oriental.

easy [ˈiːzi] a. fácil. 2 sencillo. 3 cómodo.

eat [iːt] t.-i. comer. ¶ Pret.: ate [et, eit]; p. p.: eaten [ˈiːtn].

eaves [iːvz] s. pl. alero.

ebb [eb] s. MAR. menguante, reflujo. 2 i. menguar [la marea]. 3 decaer.

ebony [ˈebəni] s. BOT. ébano.

ecclesiastic [ikliːziˈæstik] a.-s. eclesiástico.

echo [ˈekou] s. eco. 2 t. hacer eco. 3 i. repercutir, resonar.

economics [ˌiːkəˈnɔmiks] s. economía [ciencia].

ecstasy [ˈekstəsi] s. éxtasis.

eddy [ˈedi] s. remolino. 2 i. arremolinarse.

edge [edʒ] s. filo, corte.

2 canto, borde, esquina. 3 t. afilar, aguzar. 4 ribetear.

edict [ˈiːdikt] s. edicto, decreto.

edifice [ˈedifis] s. edificio.

edit [ˈedit] t. revisar, preparar para la publicación. 2 redactar, dirigir [un periódico].

edition [iˈdiʃən] s. edición.

editor [ˈeditəʳ] s. director, redactor [de una publicación].

editorial [ˌediˈtɔːriəl] a. de dirección o redacción: ~ staff, redacción [de un periódico]. 2 s. editorial, artículo de fondo.

educate [ˈedjukeit] t. educar.

education [ˌedjuˈkeiʃən] s. educación. 2 enseñanza.

eel [iːl] s. ICT. anguila.

effect [iˈfekt] s. efecto. 2 t. efectuar, realizar.

effective [iˈfektiv] a. efectivo.

effort [ˈefət] s. esfuerzo. 2 obra, trabajo.

egg [eg] s. huevo. 2 t. cubrir con huevo. 3 to ~ on, incitar, instigar.

egress [ˈiːgres] s. salida.

eight [eit] *a.-s.* ocho; **-h** [eitθ] octavo; **-een** ['ei-ti:n] dieciocho; **-eenth** [-θ] decimoctavo; **-y** ['eiti] ochenta; **-ieth** ['eitiiθ] octogésimo.

either ['aiðər, 'i:ðər] *a.-pr.* [el] uno o [el] otro; [el] uno y [el] otro. 2 *adv.* también; [con negación] tampoco. 3 *conj.* ~ ... *or*, o ... o.

elaborate [i'læbəreit] *t.* elaborar. 2 *i.* extenderse.

elbow ['elbəu] *s.* codo. 2 recodo. 3 brazo [de sillón].

elder ['eldər] *a.* mayor [en edad]. 2 *s.* persona mayor. 3 saúco.

elderly ['eldəli] *a.* mayor, anciano.

eldest ['eldist] *a. superl.* mayor [en edad]. 2 primogénito.

elect [i'lekt] *a.* elegido, escogido. 2 electo. 3 *t.* elegir.

election [i'lekʃən] *s.* elección.

electricity [ilek'trisiti] *s.* electricidad.

elegant ['eligənt] *a.* elegante.

element ['elimənt] *s.* elemento. 2 *pl.* elementos [rudimentos; fuerzas naturales].

elementary [,eli'mentəri] *a.* elemental.

elephant ['elifənt] *s.* ZOOL. elefante.

elevate ['eliveit] *t.* elevar, levantar, alzar.

elevation [,eli'veiʃən] *s.* elevación. 2 exaltación. 3 altura. 4 GEOGR. altitud.

elevator ['eliveitər] *s.* elevador. 2 montacargas. 3 (E. U.) GEOGR. ascensor. (Ingl.) escalera mecánica. 5 almacén de granos.

eleven [i'levn] *a.-s.* once; **~th** [θ] *a.* undécimo.

elf [elf] *s.* duende. 2 diablillo.

elicit [i'lisit] *t.* sacar, arrancar, sonsacar.

elm [elm] *s.* BOT. olmo.

eloquent ['eləkwənt] *a.* elocuente.

else [els] *a.* más, otro: *nobody* ~, nadie más. 2 *adv.* de otro modo. 3 *conj.* si no.

elsewhere ['els'wɛər] *adv.* en [cualquier] otra parte.

elucidate [i'lu:sideit] *t.* elucidar, dilucidar.

elude [i'lu:d] *t.* eludir.

elusive [i'lu:siv] *a.* huidizo, esquivo.

embankment [im'bæŋk-mənt] *s.* terraplén, dique, presa.

embark [im'ba:k] *t.-i.* embarcar(se.

embarrass [im'bærəs] *t.* turbar, desconcertar. 2 embarazar, estorbar. 3 poner en apuros.

embassy ['embəsi] *s.* embajada.

embitter [im'bitə'] *t.* amargar. 2 enconar.

emblem ['embləm] *s.* emblema.

embody [im'bɔdi] *t.* encarnar, personificar. 2 incorporar.

embrace [im'breis] *s.* abrazo. 2 *t.-i.* abrazar(se. 3 *t.* abarcar.

embroider [im'brɔidə'] *t.* bordar, recamar. 2 adornar.

embroidery [im'brɔidəri] *s.* bordado, bordadura.

embroil [im'brɔil] *t.* embrollar, enredar.

emerald ['emərəld] *s.* esmeralda.

emerge [i'mə:dʒ] *i.* emerger.

emergence [i'mə:dʒəns] *s.* emergencia; salida, aparición.

emergency [i'mə:dʒənsi] *s.* emergencia, apuro.

emigrant ['emigrənt] *s.* emigrante, emigrado.

emigrate ['emigreit] *i.* emigrar.

emit [i'mit] *t.* emitir.

emotional [i'məuʃənl] *a.* emotivo.

emperor ['empərə'] *s.* emperador.

emphasis ['emfəsis] *s.* énfasis

emphasize ['emfəsaiz] *t.* dar énfasis a. 2 recalcar, acentuar.

emphatic(al [im'fætik, -əl] *a.* enfático. 2 enérgico, fuerte.

empire ['empaiə'] *s.* imperio.

employ [im'plɔi] *s.* empleo, servicio. 2 *t.* emplear. 3 ocupar.

employee [,emplɔi'i:] *s.* empleado, dependiente.

employer [im'plɔiə'] *s.* patrón, amo, jefe.

employment [im'plɔimənt] *s.* empleo. 2 trabajo, colocación.

empower [im'pauə'] *t.* autorizar, facultar.

empty ['empti] *a.* vacío. 2 vacante. 3 *t.-i.* vaciar(se.

enable [i'neibl] *t.* habilitar, facultar. 2 facilitar.

enact [i'nækt] t. aprobar y sancionar [una
ley]. 2 TEAT. representar
[una escena]; desempe-
ñar [un papel].

enactment [i'næktmənt]
estatuto. 2 ejecución.

enchant [in'tʃɑ:nt] t.
encantar, hechizar. 2 de-
leitar.

enchantment [in'tʃɑ:nt-
mənt] s. encantamien-
to, hechicería. 2 encan-
to, hechizo, embeleso.

enclose [in'klauz] t. cercar, rodear. 2 incluir.

enclosure [in'klauʒəʳ] s.
cercamiento. 2 cerca, va-
llado.

encounter [in'kauntəʳ] s.
encuentro 2 choque,
combate. 3 t. encontrar,
tropezar con. 4 comba-
tir, luchar con. 5 i. en-
contrarse, entrevistarse.

encourage [in'kʌridʒ] t.
alentar, animar.

end [end] s. fin, cabo,
extremo: on ~, dere-
cho; de punta, erizado;
seguido, consecutivo. 2
colilla. 3 conclusión,
muerte. 4 fin, objeto. 5
resultado. 6 FÚTBOL ex-
tremo. 7 t. acabar, ter-
minar.

endear [in'diəʳ] t. hacer
amar, hacer querido o
amado.

endearment [in'diəmənt]
s. expresión cariñosa,
terneza.

endeavo(u)r [in'devəʳ] s.
esfuerzo, empeño, tenta-
tiva. 2 i. esforzarse, empeñarse.

ending ['endiŋ] s. fin, final, conclusión. 2 GRAM
terminación.

endorsement [in'dɔsmənt]
s. endoso.

endow [in'dau] t. dotar
[una fundación; de cua-
lidades].

endure [in'djuəʳ] t. soportar, sufrir, resistir. 2
i. durar.

enemy ['enimi] s. enemigo.

energy ['enədʒi] s. energía.

enforce [in'fɔ:s] t. hacer cumplir. 2 imponer.

engage [in'geidʒ] t.-i.
comprometer(se, empe-
ñarse. 2 tomar, contra-
tar. 3 ocupar(se, absor-
ber(se. 4 trabar.

engagement [in'geidʒ-
mənt] s. compromiso,
cita. 2 palabra de casa-
miento; noviazgo. 3 ajus-
te, contrato. 4 MIL. en-
cuentro, combate.

engine ['endʒin] *s.* máquina, motor; locomotora.

engineer [ˌendʒi'niə'] *s.* ingeniero. 2 (E. U.) maquinista. 3 *t.* proyectar. 4 arreglar.

enhance [in'hɑ:ns] *t.* acrecentar, realzar.

enjoy [ind'dʒɔi] *t.* gozar o disfrutar de.

enlarge [in'lɑ:dʒ] *t.-i.* agrandar(se; aumentar. 2 ampliar(se.

enlighten [in'laitn] *t.* iluminar, alumbrar. 2 ilustrar.

enlist [in'list] *t.-i.* alistar(se.

enmity ['enmiti] *s.* enemistad.

ennoble [i'nəubl] *t.* ennoblecer.

enormous [i'nɔ:məs] *a.* enorme.

enough [i'nʌf] *a.* bastante, suficiente. 2 *adv.* bastante.

enquire ≡ TO INQUIRE.

enrage [in'reidʒ] *t.* enfurecer, encolerizar.

enrich [in'ritʃ] *t.* enriquer. 2 AGR. fertilizar.

enrol(l [in'rəul] *t.* alistar, matricular. 2 *i.* alistarse.

ensing ['ensain. *in the navy* 'ensn] *s.* bandera, pabellón, enseña. 2 insignia. 3 (E. U.) alférez [de marina]. 4 *ensign- -bearer*, abanderado.

ensue [in'sju:] *i.* seguirse; suceder. 2 resultar.

entail [in'teil] *s.* vinculación. 2 *t.* vincular [bienes]. 3 ocasionar.

entangle [in'tæŋgl] *t.* enredar, enmarañar.

enter ['entə'] *i.* entrar.

enterprise ['entəpraiz] *s.* empresa. 2 energía. resolución.

entertain [ˌentə'tein] *t.* entretener, divertir. 2 hospedar, agasajar. 3 tomar en consideración. 4 tener, abrigar [ideas, sentimientos]. 5 *i.* recibir huéspedes, dar comidas o fiestas.

entertainment [ˌentə'teinmənt] *s.* acogida, hospitalidad; fiesta. 2 entretenimiento, diversión; función, espectáculo.

enthusiasm [in'θju:ziæzəm] *s.* entusiasmo.

entice [in'tais] *t.* atraer, tentar, incitar, seducir.

entire [in'taiə'] *a.* entero, completo, íntegro.

entitle [in'taitl] *t.* titular. 2 dar derecho **a**, autorizar.

entrance ['entrəns] *s.* entrada, acceso, ingreso: *no* ~, se prohibe la entrada.

entreat [in'tri:t] *t.-i.* suplicar, rogar, implorar.

entrust [in'trʌst] *t.* confiar.

entry ['entri] *s.* entrada, ingreso. 2 puerta, vestíbulo, zaguán. 3 asiento, anotación.

enunciate [i'nʌnsieit] *t.* enunciar. 2 pronunciar.

envelop [in'veləp] *t.* envolver, cubrir, forrar.

envelope ['envələup] *s.* sobre [de carta]. 2 envoltura, cubierta.

enviable ['enviəbl] *a.* envidiable.

envious ['enviəs] *a.* envidioso.

environment [in'vaiərənmənt] *s.* ambiente, medio ambiente. 2 alrededores.

envoy ['envɔi] *s.* mensajero.

envy ['envi] *s.* envidia. 2 *t.* envidiar.

epic ['epik] *a.* épico. 2 *s.* epopeya; poema épico.

epidemic [,epi'demik] *a.* epidémico. 2 *s.* epidemia.

episcopal [i'piskəpəl] *a.* episcopal.

episode ['episəud] *s.* episodio.

epitaph ['epitɑf] *s.* epitafio.

epoch ['i:pɔk] *s.* época, edad.

equal ['i:kwəl] *a.* igual. 2 justo, imparcial. 3 *t.* igualar.

equality [i:'kwɔliti] *s.* igualdad.

equation [i'kweiʒən] *s.* ecuación.

equator [i'kweitəʳ] *s.* ecuador.

equilibrium [,i:kwi'libriəm] *s.* equilibrio.

equip [i'kwip] *t.* equipar.

equipage ['ekwipidʒ] *s.* equipo.

equipment [i'kwipmənt] *s.* equipo, equipaje. 2 pertrechos.

equivalence [i'kwivələns] *s.* equivalencia.

era ['iərə] *s.* era [de tiempo].

erase [i'reiz] *t.* borrar. 2 tachar, rayar, raspar.

erode [i'roud] *t.* corroer.

err [əːʳ] *i.* errar, equivocarse, pecar. 2 vagar.

errand ['erənd] *s.* encargo, recado, mandado.

erroneous [i'rəunjəs] *a.* erróneo.

error ['erəʳ] *s.* error.

eructate [i'rʌkteit] *i.* eructar.

escalade [ˌeskə'leid] *s.* MIL. escalada. 2 *t.* escalar [una pared, etc.].

escalator ['eskəleitəʳ] *s.* escalera mecánica.

escape [is'keip] *s.* escape, fuga. 2 *t.* escapar(se; huir. 3 *t.* evitar, rehuir.

escort [is'kɔ:t] *t.* escoltar, convoyar, acompañar.

especial [is'peʃəl] *a.* especial. 2 **-ly** *adv.* especialmente.

espy [is'pai] *t.* divisar, columbrar.

esquire [is'kwaiəʳ] *s.* título pospuesto al apellido en cartas [Esq.]. Equivale a Señor Don.

essay ['esei] *s.* tentativa, esfuerzo. 2 ensayo [literario].

essence ['esns] *s.* esencia.

essential [i'senʃəl] *a.* esencial. 2 vital, indispensable.

establishment [is'tæbliʃmənt] *s.* establecimiento. 2 fundación.

estate [is'teit] *s.* estado [orden, clase de pers.]. 2 bienes. 3 heredad, finca. 4 herencia [bienes].

esteem [is'ti:m] *t.* apreciar.

estimate ['estimeit] *t.* estimar, evaluar, juzgar.

eternity [i'tə:niti] *s.* eternidad.

etiquette ['etiket] *s.* etiqueta.

evade [i'veid] *t.* evadir.

eve [i:v] *s.* víspera, vigilia.

even ['i:vən] *a.* llano. 2 uniforme. 3 ecuánime. 4 equilibrado. 5 igual. 6 par [número]. 7 en paz, desquitado. 8 *adv.* aun, hasta, también, incluso; ~ if, aunque, aun cuando; ~ so, aun así. 9 siquiera: not ~, ni siquiera. 10 *t.* igualar, allanar, nivelar.

evening ['i:vniŋ] *s.* tarde [después de la merienda].

event [i'vent] *s.* caso, suceso.

eventual [i'ventʃuəl] *a.* final, definitivo. 2 **-ly** *adv.* finalmente.

ever ['evəʳ] *adv.* siempre. 2 alguna vez.

evergreen ['evəgri:n] *s.* siemprepreviva.

evermore [ˌevə'mɔ:ʳ] *adv.* eternamente, siempre.

every ['evri] *a.* cada, todo, todos.

everybody ['evribɔdi]
pron. todos, todo el mundo; cada uno.

everyday [i'vridei] a. diario, cotidiano, ordinario.

everyone ['evriwʌn] pron. EVERYBODY.

everything ['evriθiŋ]
pron. todo, cada cosa.

everywhere ['evriwɛəʳ]
adv. por todas partes;
a todas partes.

evidence ['evidəns] s.
evidencia. 2 prueba.

evil ['iːvl] a. malo. 2
maligno. 3 s. mal; desastre. 4 adv. mal, malignamente.

evince [i'vins] t. mostrar.

ewe [juː] s. oveja.

exact [ig'zækt] a. exacto. 2 t. exigir, imponer.

exacting [ig'zæktiŋ] a.
exigente.

examination [ig,zæmi'neiʃən] s. examen. 2 DER.
interrogatorio.

examine [ig'zæmin] t.
examinar. 2 DER. interrogar.

example [ig'zaːmpl] s.
ejemplo.

excavate ['ekskəveit] t.
excavar. 2 extraer cavando.

exceed [ik'siːd] t. exceder.

exceeding [ik'siːdiŋ] a.
a. grande, extremo.

excel [ik'sel] t. aventajar, superar. 2 i. distinguirse.

excellence ['eksələns] s.
excelencia.

except [ik'sept] prep. excepto, salvo, a excepción
de. 2 conj. a menos que.

except [ik'sept] t. exceptuar.

excerpt ['eksəːpt] s. cita,
pasaje, fragmento.

exchange [iks'tʃeindʒ] s.
cambio. 2 t. cambiar,
canjear.

exchequer [iks'tʃekəʳ] s.
(Ingl.) hacienda pública:
Chancellor of the ~, Ministro de Hacienda. 2
bolsa, fondos.

excite [ik'sait] t. excitar.

exciting [ik'saitiŋ] a. excitante. 2 emocionante.

exclaim [iks'kleim] t.-i.
exclamar.

exclude [iks'kluːd] t. excluir.

excursion [iks'kəːʃən] s.
excursión.

excuse [iks'kjuːs] s. excusa. 2 [-z] t. excusar.
3 perdonar, dispensar.

execrable ['eksikrəbl] a.
execrable, abominable.

execute ['eksikju:t] *t.* ejecutar, cumplir. 2 TEAT. desempeñar. 3 ejecutar, ajusticiar.

executive [ig'zekjutiv] *a.* ejecutivo. 2 *s.* poder ejecutivo. 3 director, gerente.

exempt [ig'zempt] *a.* exento. 2 *t.* eximir, exceptuar.

exercise ['eksəsaiz] *s.* ejercicio. 2 *t.* ejercer, practicar. 3 *t.-i* ejercitar(se.

exert [ig'zə:t] *t.* ejercer, poner en acción. 2 *t. pr.* esforzar(se.

exertion [ig'zə:ʃən] *s.* esfuerzo.

exhale [eks'heil] *t.-i.* exhalar(se.

exhaust [ig'zɔ:st] *s.* MEC. escape, descarga [de gases, vapor, etc.]. 2 tubo de escape. 3 *t.* agotar. 4 MEC. dar salida o escape a

exhaustion [ig'zɔ:stʃən] *s.* agotamiento. 2 MEC. vaciamiento.

exhibit [ig'zibit] *s.* objeto expuesto. 2 *t.* exhibir. 3 exponer [a la vista].

exhibition [,eksi'biʃən] *s.* exhibición. 2 exposición

[de productos, cuadros, etcétera].

exile ['eksail] *s.* destierro, exilio. 2 desterrado, exilado. 3 *t.* desterrar.

exist [ig'zist] *i.* existir.

exit ['eksit] *s.* salida.

expand [iks'pænd] *t.-i.* extender(se; dilatar(se. 2 abrir(se; desplegar(se. 3 desarrollar(se. 4 *i.* expansionarse.

expanse [iks'pæns] *s.* extensión.

expansion [iks'pænʃən] *s.* expansión. 2 dilatación.

expect [iks'pekt] *t.* esperar. 2 suponer.

expectant [iks'pektənt] *a.* encinta.

expectation [,ekspek'teiʃən] *s.* espera, expectación. 2 perspectiva.

expel [iks'pel] *t.* expeler.

expenditure [iks'penditʃə'] *s.* gasto, desembolso.

expense [iks'pens] *s.* gasto, desembolso.

expensive [iks'pensiv] *a.* costoso, caro.

experience [iks'piəriəns] *s.* experiencia. 2 experimento. 3 *t.* experimentar.

experiment [iks'perimənt] s. experimento, prueba. 2 [-ment] t.-i. experimentar, probar.

expert ['ekspə:t] a.-s. experto.

expire [iks'paiər] i. expirar, morir. 2 expirar [un plazo].

explain [iks'plein] t. explicar, exponer, aclarar.

explanation [,eksplə'neiʃən] s. explicación.

exploit ['eksplɔit] s. hazaña.

exploit [iks'plɔit] t. explotar.

export ['ekspɔ:t] s. exportación. 2 [eks'pɔ:t] t. exportar.

expose [iks'pəuz] t. poner a la vista, a un riesgo]; poner en peligro, comprometer.

exposition [,ekspə'ziʃən] s. exposición. 2 explicación.

exposure [iks'pəuʒər] s. exposición [a la intemperie, al peligro, etc.]; falta de protección.

express [iks'pres] a. expreso, claro, explícito. 2 t. expresar(se. 3 t. prensar.

exquisite ['ekskwizit] a. exquisito. 2 primoroso.

extend [iks'tend] t.-i. extender(se, prolongar(se. 2 t. dar, ofrecer.

extension [iks'tenʃən] s. extensión. 2 prolongación.

extensive [iks'tensiv] a. extensivo. 2 extenso, ancho.

extent [iks'tent] s. extensión; amplitud, magnitud.

exterior [eks'tiəriər] a. exterior.

external [elks'tə:nl] a. externo.

extinct (iks'tiŋkt] a. extinto.

extinguish [iks'tiŋgwiʃ] t. extinguir. 2 apagar.

extol [iks'təul] t. exaltar.

extract ['ekstrækt] s. quím. extracto. 2 cita.

extract [iks'trækt] t. extraer.

extreme [iks'tri:m] a. extremo. 2 extremado, riguroso. 3 s. extremo, extremidad.

extricate ['ekstrikeit] t. desembarazar, desenredar.

exultation [,egzʌl'teiʃən] s. alborozo, alegría.

eye [ai] s. ojo [órgano de la visión; atención, vigilancia], vista, mirada: *to catch the* ~ *of,* llamar la atención; *to see* ~ *to* ~, estar completamente de acuerdo.

2 ojo [de una aguja, del pan, del queso]. 3 COST. corcheta, presilla. 4 *t.* mirar, clavar la mirada en.

F

fable ['feibl] *s.* fábula; ficción.

fabric ['fæbrik] *s.* tejido, tela. 3 fábrica, edificio.

fabulous ['fæbjuləs] *a.* fabuloso.

face (feis) *s.* cara, rostro, semblante; *in the ~ of*, ante, en presencia de. *2* osadía, descaro. *3* mueca, gesto. *4* aspecto, apariencia: *on the ~ of it*, según las apariencias. *5* superficie; frente, fachada. *6* esfera [de reloj]. *7 t.* volverse o mirar hacia. *8* enfrentarse con; afrontar. *9* dar a, estar encarado a. *10* cubrir, revestir.

fact [fækt] *s.* hecho; verdad, realidad.

factious ['fækʃəs] *a.* faccioso.

factory ['fæktəri] *s.* fábrica.

fade [feid] *t.-i.* marchitar(se.

fail [feil] *s.* suspenso: *without ~*, sin falta. *2 i.* faltar. *3* decaer. *4* fallar, inutilizarse. *5* fracasar. *6* errar, equivocarse. *7 to ~ to*, dejar de.

failure ['feiljər] *s.* fracaso, fiasco.

faint [feint] *a.* débil. *2* desfallecido. *3 s.* desmayo. *4 i.* desmayarse.

fair [fɛər] *a.* hermoso, bello. *2* blanca [tez]; rubio [cabello]. *3 adv.* favorablemente. *4 s.* feria, mercado.

fairness ['fɛənis] *s.* limpieza, pureza. *2* hermosura.

fairy ['fɛəri] s. hada, duende.

faith [feiθ] s. fe.

faithful ['feiθful] a. fiel. 2 leal.

fall [fɔ:l] s. caida. 2 decadencia, ruina. 3 (E. U.) otoño. 4 i. caer. 5 disminuir. 6 decaer. 7 ponerse. 8 tocar, corresponder [a uno una cosa]. 9 to ~ away, enflaquecer; desvanecerse; rebelarse; apostatar. 10 to ~ in love, enamorarse. 11 to ~ in with, estar de acuerdo con; coincidir; armonizar con. 12 to ~ out, reñir, desavenirse; acontecer. 13 to ~ through, fracasar. 14 to ~ upon, atacar, embestir. ¶ Pret.: *fell* (fel); p. p.: *fallen* ['fɔːlən].

fallen ['fɔːlən] p. p. de TO FALL.

false [fɔːls] a. falso.

fame [feim] s. fama.

familiarity [fəˌmiliˈæriti] s. familiaridad. 2 intimidad.

family ['fæmili] s. familia. 2 sangre, linaje. 3 a. familiar, de familia: ~ *name*, apellido.

famine ['fæmin] s. hambre.

famous ['feiməs] a. famoso.

fan [fæn] s. abanico. 2 ventilador. 3 hincha, aficionado. 4 t. abanicar. 5 aventar.

fancy ['fænsi] s. fantasia, imaginación. 2 capricho, antojo 3 t. imaginar, figurarse. 4 encapricharse por.

far [fɑːr] adv. lejos, a lo lejos: ~ *and wide*, por todas partes; hasta: en cuanto; *as* ~ *as I know*, que yo sepa; *in so* ~ *as*, en cuanto, en lo que; *so* ~, hasta ahora; ~*-fetched*, rebuscado. 2 muy, mucho: ~*-away*, muy lejos; ~ *off*, lejano; a lo lejos. 3 a. lejano, distante: *Far East*, Extremo Oriente.

fare [fɛər] s. pasajero; pasaje. 2 billete; precio. 3 comida. 4 i. pasarlo [bien o mal]. 5 pasar, ocurrir.

farewell ['fɛəˈwel] interj. ¡adiós! 2 s. despedida.

farm [fɑːm] s. granja, cortijo. 2 t. cultivar, labrar.

farmer ['fɑːmər] s. granjero, labrador.

farmhouse ['fɑːmhaus] s. granja.

farmyard ['fɑ:m-jɑ:d] *s.* corral.

farther [['fɑ:ðəʳ] *adv.* más lejos. 2 además.

farthest ['fɑ:ðist] *a. superl.* [el más lejano]. 2 *adv.* más lejos.

fashion ['fæʃən] *s.* forma. 2 modo, manera. 3 moda, costumbre, uso. 4 elegancia, buen tono. 5 *t.* formar, hacer, labrar. 6 amoldar.

fashionable ['fæʃnəbl] *a.* a la moda. 2 elegante.

fast [fɑ:st] *a.* firme, seguro. 2 atado, fijo; íntimo. 3 rápido, veloz. 4 adelantado [reloj]. 5 *adv.* firmemente. 6 aprisa. 7 *s.* ayuno, abstinencia. 8 amarra, cable.

fasten ['fɑ:sn] *t.-i.* fijar(se, atar(se.

fat [fæt] *a.* gordo, obeso. 2 fértil. 3 *s.* gordura; grasa.

fate [feit] *s.* hado. 2 sino.

father ['fɑ:ðəʳ] *s.* padre. 2 Dios Padre. 3 *t.* engendrar.

father-in-law ['fɑ:ðərinlɔ:] *s.* padre político, suegro.

fathom ['fæðəm] *s.* braza [medida]. 2 *t.* MAR. sondar.

fatigue [fə'ti:g] *s.* fatiga. 2 *t.* fatigar, cansar.

fatten ['fætn] *t.* engordar. 2 fertilizar.

fault [fɔ:lt] *s.* falta, defecto, error, culpa.

faultless ['fɔ:ltlis] *a.* impecable.

favo(u)r ['feivəʳ] *s.* favor. 2 *t.* favorecer.

favo(u)rable ['feivərəbl] *a.* favorable, propicio.

fawn [fɔ:n] *s.* ZOOL. cervato. 2 *i.* *to* ~ *on* o *upon*, adular, halagar.

fear [fiəʳ] *s.* miedo, temor. 2 *t.-i.* temer.

feasible ['fi:zəbl] *a.* posible.

feast [fi:st] *s.* fiesta. 2 *t.* festejar.

feat [fi:t] *s.* proeza, hazaña.

feather ['feðəʳ] *s.* pluma [de ave]. 2 *t.* emplumar.

feature ['fi:tʃəʳ] *s.* rasgo, facción [del rostro]

febrile ['fi:brail] *a.* febril.

February ['februəri] *s* febrero.

fed [fed] *pret.* y *p. p.* de TO FEED.

federal ['fedərəl] *a.* federal.

fee [fi:] *s.* honorarios, derechos. 2 *t.* retribuir, pagar.

feeble ['fi:bl] *a.* débil. 2 flaco.

feed [fi:d] *s.* alimento, comida [esp. de los animales]. 2 *t.-i.* alimentar(se. ¶ Pret. y p. p.: *fed* (fed).

feel [fi:l] *s.* tacto. 2 sensación. 2 *t.* tocar, tentar. 3 sentir, experimentar. 4 *i.* sentirse, tener: *to ~ cold*, tener frío. *to ~ like*, tener ganas de. ¶ Pret. y p. p.: *felt* [felt].

feeling ['fi:liŋ] *s.* tacto [sentido]. 2 sensación, percepción.

feet [fi:t] *s. pl.* de FOOT. pies.

feign [fein] *t.* fingir.

fell [fel] *pret.* de TO FALL. 2 *a.* cruel. 3 *s.* tala [de árboles]. 4 *t.* derribar, tumbar.

fellow ['feləu] *s.* compañero.

felt [felt] V. TO FEEL. 2 *s.* fieltro.

female ['fi:meil] *s.* hembra. 2 *a.* femenino.

feminine ['feminin] *a.* femenino.

fence [fens] *s.* valla. 2 esgrima. 3 *t.* vallar. 4 *i.* esgrimir. 5 proteger.

ferment [fə(:)'ment] *i.-t.* fermentar.

fern [fə:n] *s.* BOT. helecho.

ferocious [fə'rəuʃəs] *a.* fiero, terrible.

ferry ['feri] *s.* barca, balsa. 2 *~-boat*, barca de pasaje. 3 *t.-i.* cruzar [un río] en barca.

fertilize ['fə:tilaiz] *t.* fertilizar. 2 fecundar.

fertilizer ['fə:tilaizər] *s.* fertilizante, abono.

fervour ['fə:vər] *s.* fervor, ardor.

festoon [fes'tu:n] *s.* festón.

fetch [fetʃ] *t.* ir por, ir a buscar. 2 venderse a o por.

fetter ['fetər] *s.* grillete, prisión. 2 *t.* encadenar.

feud [fju:d] *s.* rencilla.

fever ['fi:vər] *s.* MED. fiebre.

feverish ['fi:vəriʃ] *a.* febril.

few [fju:] *a.-pron.* pocos: *a ~*, unos cuantos, algunos.

fiancé [fi'ɑ̃:nsei] *s.* novio, prometido.

fiancée [fi'ɑ̃:nsei] *s.* novia, prometida.

fiber, fibre ['faibər] *s.* fibra.

fickle ['fikl] *a.* inconstante.

fiddle ['fidl] *s.* MÚS. fam. violín.

fidget ['fidʒit] *i.* estar inquieto, agitarse.

field [fi:ld] *s.* campo.

fiend [fi:nd] *s.* demonio, diablo.

fierce [fiəs] *a.* fiero, feroz.

fiery ['faiəri] *a.* ardiente, encendido.

fife [faif] *s.* pífano.

fifth [fifθ] *a.-s.* quinto.

fifteen ['fif'ti:n] quinto; **-th** [-θ] decimoquinto; **fifty** ['fifti] cincuenta; **fiftieth** [-iiθ] quincuagésimo.

fight [fait] *s.* lucha. 2 *i.* luchar. 3 lidiar. ¶ Pret. y p. p.: **fought** [fɔ:t].

figure ['figər] *s.* figura. 2 tipo, cuerpo, talle. 3 ARIT. cifra, número. 4 *t.* adornar con [dibujos, etc.]. 5 figurarse, imaginar.

file [fail] *s.* lima. 2 carpeta. 3 expediente. 4 fila. 5 *t.* limar. 6 archivar, registrar. 7 *i.* desfilar.

fill [fil] *s.* hartazgo. 2 colmo. 3 *t.-i.* llenar(se. 4 *t.* llevar a cabo.

film [film] *s.* película, filme. 2 *t.* filmar.

filter ['filtər] *s.* filtro. 2 *t.-i.* filtrar(se.

filth [filθ] *s.* suciedad.

filthy ['filθi] *a.* sucio.

final ['fainl] *a.* final.

finance [fai'næns, fi-] *s.* ciencia financiera. 2 *pl.* hacienda. 3 *t.* financiar.

find [faind] *t.* encontrar: *to ~ fault with*, hallar defectos; *to ~ out*, averiguar. ¶ Pret. y p. p.: **found** [faund].

fine [fain] *s.* multa. 2 *a.* fino. 3 hermoso, bello. 4 bueno, excelente. 5 guapo, elegante. 6 *t.* multar.

finger ['fingər] *s.* dedos. 2 *t.* tocar, manosear. 3 hurtar, escamotear.

finish ['finiʃ] *s.* fin, final. 2 *t.* acabar, terminar, concluir.

fir [fə:r] *s.* BOT. abeto.

fire ['faiər] *s.* fuego, lumbre. 2 fuego, incendio. 3 fuego [disparos]. 4 ardor, pasión. 5 *t.-i.* encender(se. 6 *t.* disparar.

fireman ['faiəmən] *s.* bombero.

fire-place ['faiə-pleis] *s.* hogar, chimenea.

firm [fə:m] *a.* firme. 2 *s.* firma, casa, razón social.

first [fə:st] *a.* primero.

first-rate ['fə:st'reit] *a.* excelente, de primera.

fish [fiʃ] *s.* ICT. pez. 2 pescado. 3 *t.-i.* pescar.

fisherman ['fiʃəmən] *s.* pescador.

fishmonger ['fiʃˌmʌŋgə'] *s.* pescador.

fist [fist] *s.* puño.

fit [fit] *s.* ataque, acceso. 2 capricho, antojo. 3 ajuste, encaje. 4 *a.* apto, capaz. 5 *t.-i.* adaptarse, ajustarse [a]. 6 *t.* ajustar, encajar.

fitting ['fitiŋ] *a.* propio, adecuado, conveniente. 2 *s.* ajuste.

five [faiv] *a.-s.* cinco.

fix [fiks] *s.* apuro, aprieto. 2 *t.-i.* fijar(se. 3 *t.* reparar, arreglar.

fixture ['fikstʃə'] *s.* cosa, mueble. 2 *pl.* instalación [de gas, etc.].

flabby ['flæbi] *a.* fláccido, flojo; soso.

flag [flæg] *s.* bandera. 2 *i.* desanimarse.

flake [fleik] *s.* copo [de nieve].

flame [fleim] *s.* llama; fuego. 2 *i.* llamear, flamear.

flank [flæŋk] *s.* ijada. 2 costado, lado. 3 *t.* flanquear.

flannel ['flænl] *s.* TEJ. franela.

flap [flæp] *s.* golpe, aletazo. 2 *t.* batir, agitar.

flare [flɛə'] *s.* llamarada. 2 *i.* llamear, fulgurar.

flash [flæʃ] *s.* ráfaga de luz. 2 *t.* encender. 3 *i.* relampaguear.

flask [flɑ:sk] *s.* frasco, redoma.

flat [flæt] *a.* plano, llano. 2 *s.* llanura. 3 piso, apartamento.

flatter ['flætə'] *t.* adular.

flattery ['flætəri] *s.* adulación.

flavo(u)r ['fleivə'] *s.* sabor. 2 *t.* sazonar, condimentar.

flaw [flɔ:] *s.* grieta, raja. 2 defecto.

flax [flæks] *s.* lino.

flea [fli:] *s.* pulga.

fled [fled] V. TO FLEE.

flee [fli:] *i.* huir. 2 *t.* huir de, evitar. ¶ Pret. y p. p.: *fled* [fled].

fleece [fli:s] *s.* vellón, lana. 2 *t.* esquilar.

fleet [fli:t] *s.* armada. 2 flota. 3 *a.* veloz, ligero.

flesh [fleʃ] *s.* carne: *to put on* ~, engordar.

flew [flu:] V. TO FLY.

flexible ['fleksəbl] *a.* flexible.

flick [flik] *s.* golpecito.

flicker ['flikə^r] *s.* luz trémula. 2 *i.* vacilar.

flight [flait] *s.* vuelo. 2 bandada; escuadrilla. 3 fuga. 4 tramo de escaleras.

flinch [flintʃ] *i.* vacilar.

fling [fliŋ] *s.* tiro. 2 prueba. 3 *t.-i.* echar(se, lanzar(se. ¶ Pret. y p. p.: *flung* [flʌŋ].

flint [flint] *s.* pedernal.

flip [flip] *t.* arrojar, lanzar [con el pulgar y otro dedo].

flirt [flə:t] *s.* galanteador. 2 coqueta. 3 *i.* flirtear, coquetear.

flit [flit] *i.* revolotear.

float [flout] *s.* corcho. 2 boya. 3 balsa. 4 *i.* flotar. 5 *t.* hacer flotar.

flock [flɔk] *s.* rebaño; manada. 2 *i.* reunirse, congregarse.

flog [flɔg] *t.* azotar.

flood [flʌd] *s.* riada, crecida. 2 *t.* inundar.

floor [flɔ:^r, 'floə^r] *s.* suelo, piso.

flounder ['flaundə^r] *s.* esfuerzo torpe. 2 *i.* esforzarse torpemente. 3 vacilar.

flour ['flauə^r] *s.* harina.

flourish ['flʌriʃ] *s.* rasgo caprichoso. 2 toque de trompetas. 3 prosperidad. 4 *i.* prosperar. 5 rasguear. 6 *t.* blandir.

flow [flou] *s.* flujo, corriente. 2 *i.* fluir, manar.

flower ['flauə^r] *s.* BOT. flor. 2 *i.* florecer.

flown [floun] *p. p.* de TO FLY.

flu [flu:] *s.* MED. fam. gripe.

flung [flʌŋ] V. TO FLING.

flurry ['flʌri] *s.* agitación, excitación. 2 *t.* agitar.

flush [flʌʃ] *a.* lleno, rico. 2 *s.* flujo rápido. 3 rubor, sonrojo. 4 *i.* afluir [la sangre]. 5 ruborizarse.

flutter ['flʌtə^r] *s.* vibración. 2 *i.* temblar, aletear.

fly [flai] *s.* ENT. mosca. 2 *pl.* TEAT. bambalinas. 3 *i.* volar. ¶ Pret.: *flew* [flu:]; p. p.: *flown* [floun].

foam [foum] *s.* espuma. 2 *i.* echar espuma.

focus ['foukəs] *s.* foco; enfoque. 2 *t.* enfocar.

fodder ['fodər] *s.* forraje, pienso.

foe [fou] *s.* enemigo.

fog [fog] *s.* niebla, bruma.

foggy ['fogi] *a.* neblinoso.

foist [foist] *t.* endosar.

fold [fould] *s.* pliegue, doblez. 2 *t.-i.* doblar(se, plegarse.

folk [fouk] *s.* gente, pueblo.

folk-lore ['fouk-lɔːʳ] *s.* folklore.

follow ['folou] *t.* seguir.

follower ['folouəʳ] *s.* seguidor.

following ['folouiŋ] *a.* siguiente.

folly ['foli] *s.* tontería.

fond [fond] *a.* cariñoso. 2 to be ~ of, ser aficionado a.

fondle ['fondl] *t.* mimar.

food [fuːd] *s.* alimento, comida.

fool [fuːl] *s.* tonto, bobo. 2 *t.* engañar.

foolish ['fuːliʃ] *a.* tonto, necio.

foolishness ['fuːliʃnis] *s.* tontería, simpleza.

foot [fut], *pl.* feet [fiːt] *s.* pie: on ~, a pie.

football ['futbɔːl] *s.* DEP. fútbol.

for [fɔːʳ, fəʳ] *prep.* para; por; a causa de. 2 durante. 3 as ~ me, por mi parte. 4 *conj.* [fɔːʳ] ya que, pues.

forage ['forid͡ʒ] *s.* forraje. 2 *t.* forrajear.

foray ['forei] *s.* correría.

forbade [fəˈbæd] V. TO FORBID.

forbear [fɔːˈbɛəʳ] *s.* antepasado. 2 [fɔːˈbɛəʳ] *t.* dejar de, abstener de. ¶ forbore [fɔːˈbɔːʳ]; forborne [fɔːˈbɔːn].

forbid [fəˈbid] *t.* prohibir. ¶ Pret.: forbade [fəˈbæd]; p. p.: forbidden [fəˈbidn].

force [fɔːs] *s.* fuerza. 2 *t.* forzar.

forcible ['fɔːsəbl] *a.* fuerte.

ford [fɔːd] *s.* vado. 2 *t.* vadear.

fore [fɔː, fɔəʳ] *a.* delantero. 2 *s.* parte delantera; proa. 3 *adv.* a proa.

forecast ['fɔːkɑːst] *s.* pronóstico. 2 *t.* pronosticar, predecir. ¶ Pret. y p. p.: forecast o -ted [-tid].

forefather ['fɔːˌfɑːðəʳ] s. antepasado.

forefinger ['fɔːˌfɪŋgəʳ] s. dedo índice.

foregoing [fɔːˈgouiŋ] s. anterior.

forehead ['fɔrid] s. ANAT. frente.

foreign ['fɔrin] a. extranjero, exterior.

foreigner ['fɔrinəʳ] s. extranjero [pers.].

foresee [fɔːˈsiː] t. prever. ¶ Pret.: *foresaw* [fɔːˈsɔː]; p. p.: *foreseen* [fɔːˈsiːn].

foresight ['fɔːsait] s. previsión, perspicacia.

forest ['fɔrist] s. bosque. selva.

forestall [fɔːˈstɔːl] t. anticiparse a; prevenir.

foretell [fɔːˈtel] t. predecir. ¶ Pret. y p. p.: *foretold* [fɔːˈtould].

forever [fɔˈrevəʳ] adv. siempre.

forfeit ['fɔːfit] s. pena, multa. 2 prenda [en los juegos]. 3 t. perder [algo] como pena o castigo.

forge [fɔːdʒ] s. fragua; herrería. 2 t. forjar, fraguar; falsificar.

forgery ['fɔːdʒəri] s. falsificación.

forget [fɔˈget] t.-i. olvi-

dar. ¶ Pret.: *forgot* [fɔˈgɔt]; p. p. *forgotten* [fɔˈgɔtn].

forgetful [fɔˈgetful] a. olvidadizo.

forgive [feˈgiv] t. perdonar. ¶ Pret.: *forgave* [fɔˈgeiv]; p. p.: *forgiven* [fɔˈgivn].

fork [fɔːk] s. tenedor. 2 horca. 3 i. bifurcarse.

forlorn [fɔˈlɔːn] a. abandonado.

former ['fɔːməʳ] a. anterior; antiguo. 2 pron. the —, the latter, aquél éste.

formerly ['fɔːmɔli] adv. antes.

forsake [fɔˈseik] t. abandonar, desamparar. ¶ Pret.: *forsook* [fɔˈsuk]; p. p.: *forsaken* [fɔˈseikɔn].

forswear [fɔːˈswɛəʳ] t. abjurar, renunciar. ¶ Pret.: *forswore* [fɔːˈswɔː]; p. p.: *forsworn* [fɔːˈswɔːn].

forth [fɔːθ] adv. delante, adelante. 2 en adelante.

forthcoming [fɔːθˈkʌmiŋ] a. venidero, próximo.

fortnight ['fɔːtnait] s. quincena.

fortress ['fɔ:tris] s. fortaleza.

fortune ['fɔ:tʃən] s. fortuna.

forty ['fɔ:ti] a.-s. cuarenta. 2 -ieth [-iiθ] cuadragésimo.

forward ['fɔ:wəd] a. delantero. 2 precoz, adelantado. 3 t. enviar, remitir. 4 promover.

forward(s ['fɔ:wəd(z] adv. [hacia] adelante; más allá.

foster ['fɔstər] a. de leche; adoptivo. 2 t. criar, nutrir.

fought [fɔ:t] V. TO FIGHT.

foul [faul] a. sucio, asqueroso. 2 t.-i. ensuciar(se.

found [faund] TO FIND. 2 t. fundar.

founder ['faundər] s. fundador. 2 t.-i. irse a pique.

foundry ['faundri] s. fundición.

fountain ['fauntin] s. fuente. 2 ⁓-pen, pluma estilográfica.

four [fɔ:r, fɔər] a.-s. cuatro; -fold ['fɔ:-fəuld] cuádruplo; -teen [-'ti:n] catorce; [-'ti:nθ] decimocuarto; -th [-θ] cuarto; forty ['fɔ:ti] cuarenta; for-

tieth ['fɔ:tüθ] cuadragésimo.

fowl [faul] s. ave de corral.

fox [fɔks] s. zorro, -ra.

frail [freil] a. frágil. 2 débil.

frame [freim] s. armazón, marco. 2 t. formar, construir.

framework ['freimwə:k] s. armazón, esqueleto.

franchise ['fræntʃaiz] s. privilegio. 2 derecho político.

frank [fræŋk] a. franco [sincero, claro]. 2 s. franquicia postal.

frankfurter ['fræŋk,fɔ:tər] s. salchicha de Francfort.

frankness ['fræŋknis] a. franqueza.

frantic ['fræntik] a. frenético, furioso.

fraud [frɔ:d] s. fraude.

freak [fri:k] s. capricho, antojo. 2 monstruosidad.

freckle ['frekl] s. peca.

free [fri:] a. libre. 2 t. librar.

freedom ['fri:dəm] s. libertad.

freeze [fri:z] s. helada. 2 t.-i. helar(se. ¶ Pret.: froze [frəuz]; p. p.: frozen ['frəunzn].

freight [freit] *s.* carga, flete.

French [frentʃ] *a.* - *s.* francés.

frenzy ['frenzi] *s.* frenesi.

frequency ['fri:kwənsi] *s.* frecuencia.

frequent ['fri:kwənt] *a.* frecuentar.

fresh [freʃ] *a.* fresco, nuevo. 2 ~ *water*, agua dulce.

freshness ['freʃnis] *s.* frescor.

fret [fret] *s.* roce. 2 *t.-i.* rozar(se.

fretful ['fretful] *a.* irritable.

friction ['frikʃən] *s.* fricción.

Friday ['fraidi] *s.* viernes.

friend [frend] *s.* amigo, amiga; *boy* ~, novio; *girl* ~, novia.

friendly ['frendli] *a.* amistoso.

friendship ['frendʃip] *s.* amistad.

fright [frait] *s.* miedo, terror.

frighten ['fraitn] *t.* asustar.

frightful ['fraitful] *a.* espantoso.

fringe [frindʒ] *s.* franja, fleco. 2 *t.* orlar, adornar con flecos.

frisk [frisk] *i.* retozar.

frisky ['friski] *a.* juguetón.

fro [frou] *adv. to and* ~. de un lado a otro.

frock [frok] *s.* hábito [monacal]. 2 vestido [de mujer]. 3 ~ *coat*, levita.

frog [frog] *s.* rana. 2 *t.* alarmar.

frolic ['frolik] *s.* juego, retozo. 2 *i.* juguetear, retozar.

from [from, frəm] *prep.* de, desde. 2 a partir de. 3 de parte de. 4 según. 5 por, a causa de.

front [frʌnt] *s.* frente, fachada. 2 *in* ~ *of*, delante de, frente a. 3 *t.* hacer frente a.

frontier ['frʌntiəᵊ] *s.* frontera. 2 *a.* fronterizo.

frost [frost] *s.* escarcha, helada.

froth [froθ] *s.* espuma.

frothy ['froθi] *a.* espumoso.

frown [fraun] *s.* ceño, entrecejo. 2 *i.* fruncir el entrecejo.

fruit [fru:t] *s.* fruto. 2 *i.* fructificar.

FRUITFUL 82

fruitful ['fru:tful] *a.* fructífero.

fry [frai] *t.-i.* freír(se).

fuel [fjuəl] *s.* combustible, carburante.

fulfil(l [ful'fil] *t.* cumplir, realizar, verificar, efectuar.

fulfilment [ful'filmənt] *s.* ejecución, realización. 2 colmo.

full [ful] *a.* lleno, repleto.

fullness ['fulnis] *s.* llenura, plenitud, colmo. 2 abundancia.

fully ['fuli] *adv.* plenamente.

fumble ['fʌmbl] *i.* buscar a tientas, revolver.

fume [fju:m] *s.* humo. 2 *t.* ahumar.

fun [fʌn] *s.* broma, diversión: *to be* ~, ser divertido.

function ['fʌŋkʃən] *s.* función. 2 *i.* funcionar.

fund [fʌnd] *s.* fondo, capital.

funeral ['fju:nərəl] *s.* entierro. 2 *a.* fúnebre.

fungus ['fʌŋgəs] *f.* BOT. hongo.

funnel ['fʌnl] *s.* embudo; chimenea de vapor.

funny ['fʌni] *a.* cómico, gracioso, divertido.

fur [fə:ʳ] *s.* piel.

furious ['fjuəriəs] *a.* furioso.

furnace ['fə:nis] *s.* horno.

furnish ['fə:niʃ] *t.* surtir, proveer. 2 equipar, amueblar.

furniture ['fə:nitʃəʳ] *s.* mobiliario, muebles: *piece of* ~, mueble.

furrow ['fʌrou] *s.* surco. 2 arruga. 3 *t.* surcar.

further ['fə:ðəʳ] *a.* adicional, ulterior. 2 más lejano. 3 *adv.* más allá. 4 además, aún. 5 *t.* adelantar, fomentar.

furthermore ['fə:ðə'mɔːʳ] *adv.* además.

fury ['fjuəri] *s.* furia. 2 entusiasmo, frenesí.

fuse [fju:z] *s.* espoleta, cebo. 2 ELECT. fusible. 3 *t.-i.* fundir(se.

fuss [fʌs] *s.* alboroto, alharaca. 2 *i.* bullir, ajetrearse.

fussy ['fʌsi] *a.* bullidor, inquieto. 2 minucioso, exigente.

futile ['fju:tail] *a.* fútil. 2 frívolo. 3 vano, inútil.

future ['fju:tʃəʳ] *a.* futuro.

G

gabble ['gæbl] s. charla. 2 t. charlar.

gad [gæd] i. callejear.

gag [gæg] s. mordaza. 2 TEAT. morcilla. 3 t. amordazar. 4 TEAT. meter morcilla.

gaiety ('geiəti] s. alegría.

gain [gein) s. ganancia. 2 ventaja. 3 t. ganar.

gainful ['geinful] a. provechoso.

gait [geit] s. paso, marcha.

gale [geil) s. vendaval.

gall [gɔːl] s. bilis, hiel. 2 descaro. 3 t. mortificar.

gallant ['gælənt] a. gallardo, valiente. 2 [gə-'lænt] galante, cortés.

gallon ['gælən] s. galón [medida].

gallop ['gæləp] s. galope. 2 i. galopar.

gallows ['gæləuz] s. horca, patíbulo: ~-ɒtɾd, reo de muerte.

gamble ['gæmbl] s. juego [por dinero]. 2 i. jugar [dinero].

game [geim] s. juego, diversión. 2 partida [de juego]. 3 DEP. partido. 4 caza [animales]. 5 a. valiente, dispuesto.

gander ['gændəʳ] s. ZOOL. ganso.

gang [gæŋ] s. cuadrilla.

gangster ['gæŋstəʳ] s. gángster.

gaol! [dʒeil] s. cárcel.

gap [gæp] s. boquete, brecha.

gape [geip] s. bostezo. 2 i. bostezar.

garage ['gærɑːʒ, -ridʒ] s. garaje.

garbage ['gɑːbidʒ] s. basura.

garden ['gɑːdn] s. jardín.

gardener ['gɑːdnər] s. jardinero.

gardening ['gɑːdniŋ] s. jardinería, horticultura.

garland ['gɑːlənd] s. guirnalda.

garlic ['gɑːlik] s. BOT. ajo.

garment ['gɑːmənt] s. vestido.

garner ['gɑːnər] s. granero.

garnish ['gɑːniʃ] s. adorno. 2 t. adornar.

garret ['gærət] s. desván.

garrison ['gærisn] s. guarnición. 2 t. MIL. guarnecer.

gas [gæs] s. gas: ~ range, cocina de gas. 2 (E. U.) gasolina.

gaslight ['gæslait] s. luz de gas.

gasp [gɑːsp] s. boqueada. 2 i. boquear. 3 t. decir de manera entrecortada.

gate [geit] s. puerta [de ciudad, muro, etc.]; verja; barrera.

gateway ['geit-wei] s. puerta; pórtico.

gather ['gæðər] t. recoger, juntar. 2 cosechar. 3 deducir, inferir. 4 i. reunirse.

gaudy ['gɔːdi] a. ostentoso.

gauge [geidʒ] s. medida, calibre. 2 t. medir.

gaunt [gɔːnt] a. flaco, desvaído.

gauze [gɔːz] s. gasa, cendal.

gave [geiv] pret. de TO GIVE.

gay [gei] a. alegre. 2 vistoso.

gaze [geiz] s. mirada fija. 2 i. mirar fijamente.

gear [giər] s. vestidos, atavíos. 2 t. herramientas. 3 engranaje. 4 t. ataviar.

geese [giːs] s. pl. de GOOSE.

gem [dʒem] s. gema.

gender ['dʒendər] a. género.

general ['dʒenərəl] a. general. 2 m. MIL. general.

generate ['dʒenəreit] t. producir.

generous ['dʒenərəs] a. generoso. 2 noble. 3 amplio.

genius ['dʒiːnjəs], pl. **geniuses** ['dʒiːniəsiz] genio [fuerza creadora]. 2 carácter particular [de una nación, época, etc.].

genteel [dʒen'tiːl] a. [hoy, irónico] cursi; [antes] carácter corté, bien criado.

gentle ['dʒentl] a. de buena posición social. 2 dócil. 3 afable.

gentleman ['dʒentlmən] s. caballero.

gentleness ['dʒentlnis] s. mansedumbre. 2 afabilidad.

gently ['dʒentli] adv. suavemente; despacio.

gentry ['dʒentri] s. alta burguesía. 2 irón. gente bien.

genuine ['dʒenjuin] a. genuino; legítimo; sincero.

geographer [dʒi'ɔgrəfər] s. geógrafo.

geranium [dʒi'reinjəm] s. BOT. geranio.

germ [dʒəːm] s. germen.

germinate ['dʒəːmineit] i. germinar. 2 t. hacer germinar.

gesture ['dʒestʃər] s. ademán, gesto, señal.

get [get] t. obtener, conseguir. 2 hallar. 3 coger, atrapar. 4 vencer. 5 mandar; hacer que. 6 poner [en un estado, etc.]. 7 procurar, proporcionar. 8 comprender. 9 i. ganar dinero. 10 estar, hallarse. 11 ir, llegar, meterse, introducirse, pasar. 12 hacerse,

volverse, ponerse. ¶ Pret. y p. p.: **got** [gɔt].

ghastly ['gɑːstli] a. horrible.

ghost [gəust] s. espíritu, alma. 2 espectro, fantasma.

giant ['dʒaiənt] a.-s. gigante.

giddy ['gidi] a. vertiginoso; mareado.

gift [gift] s. donación. 2 regalo.

gifted ['giftid] a. dotado.

giggle ['gigl] s. risita nerviosa. 2 i. reír nerviosa y tontamente.

gild [gild] t. dorar.

gill [gil] s. agalla.

gingerly ['dʒindʒəli] adv. cautelosamente, con precaución.

gipsy ['dʒipsi] s. GYPSY.

gird [gəːd] t. ceñir, cercar. ¶ Pret. y p. p.: **girded** ['gəːdid] o **girt** [gəːt].

girl [gəːl] f. niña, muchacha.

give [giv] t. dar; regalar. 2 ofrecer. 3 to ~ back, devolver; to ~ up, renunciar a. 4 i. dar de sí, ceder. ¶ Pret.: **gave** [geiv]; p. p.: **given** ['givn].

glad [glæd] a. alegre, contento.

gladness ['glædnis] s. alegría.

glamo(u)r ['glæmər] s. encanto.

glance [glɑːns] s. mirada. 2 i.-t. dar una mirada.

gland [glænd] s. glándula.

glare [glɛər] s. fulgor, resplandor. 2 i. brillar, deslumbrar.

glass ['glɑːs] s. vidrio, cristal. 2 vaso, copa. 3 espejo. 4 ópt. lente; anteojo.

glaze [gleiz] s. vidriado. 2 t. vidriar, barnizar. 3 velar [los ojos]. 4 poner cristales a.

gleam [gliːm] s. destello. 2 i. destellar.

glean [gliːn] t. espigar.

glee [gliː] s. alegría, gozo.

glen [glen] s. cañada.

glide [glaid] s. deslizamiento. 2 i. deslizarse, resbalar.

glimmmer ['glimər] s. vislumbre. 2 i. brillar; v slumbrarse.

glimpse [glimps] s. resplandor fugaz. 2 i. echar una ojeada. 3 t. vislumbrar.

glisten ['glisn] i. brillar.

glitter ['glitər] s. resplandor. 2 i. brillar.

globe [gloub] s. globo.

gloom [gluːm] s. oscuridad.

gloomy ['gluːmi] a. oscuro.

glorify ['glɔːrifai] t. glorificar. 2 ensalzar.

glorious ['glɔːriəs] a. glorioso.

gloss [glɔs] s. lustre, brillo. 2 t. lustrar, pulir.

glossy ['glɔsi] a. brillante.

glove [glʌv] s. guante.

glow [glou] s. luz, resplandor. 2 i. dar luz o calor vivos, brillar.

glue [gluː] s. cola [para pegar]. 2 t. encolar, pegar.

gluey ['gluːi] a. pegajoso.

gnarl [nɑːl] s. nudo [en madera].

gnash [næʃ] i. hacer rechinar los dientes.

gnat [næt] s. ENT. mosquito.

gnaw [nɔː] t. roer.

go [gou] s. ida. 2 marcha. 3 empuje. 4 tentativa. 5 moda: *it is all the* ~, hace furor.

go [gou] i. ir. 2 irse, marchar, partir. 3 an-

dar, funcionar. *4* [el
traje] caer bien. *5* morir; decaer. *6* tener éxito. *7* resultar. ¶ Pres.
3.ª pers.: *goes* [gouz];
pret.: *went* [went]; p.p.:
gone [gɔn].
goad [goud] *s.* pincho,
aguijón. 2 *t.* aguijar,
aguijonear.
goal [goul] *s.* DEP. meta,
portería; gol: *to score*
a ~, marcar un tanto.
2 fin, objeto.
goat [gout] *s.* cabra; cabrón.
gobble ['gɔbl] *t.* engullir.
God [gɔd] *n. pr.* Dios. 2
m. dios.
goddess ['gɔdis] *s.* diosa,
diva.
godly ['gɔdli] *a.* piadoso,
devoto.
gold [gould] *s.* oro.
golden ['gouldən] *a.* de
oro, áureo, dorado.
goldsmith ['gouldsmiθ] *s.*
orfebre.
golf [gɔlf] *s.* DEP. golf.
gone [gɔn] *p. p.* de TO GO.
good [gud] *a.* bueno. 2 *s.*
bien; provecho; *for* ~,
para siempre.
good-by, good-bye [gud-
'bai] *s.* adiós: *to say* ~
to. despedirse de. 2
['gu(d)'bai] *intej.* ¡adiós!

goodness ['gudnis] *s.*
bondad.
goods [gudz] *s. pl.* géneros, mercancías.
goose [gu:s], *pl.* **geese**
[gi:s] *s.* ORN. ganso,
oca.
gore [gɔ:ʳ] *s.* sangre.
gorgeous ['gɔ:dʒəs] *a.*
brillante, suntuoso.
gospel ['gɔspəl] *s.* evangelio.
gossip ['gɔsip] *s.* chismorreo; chismoso. 2 *i.* cotillear.
got [gɔt] V. TO GET.
govern ['gʌvən] *t.* gobernar.
governess ['gʌvənis] *s.*
aya; institutriz.
government ['gʌvnmənt,
'gʌvə-] *s.* gobierno, dirección.
governor ['gʌvənəʳ] *s.*
gobernador. 2 director.
gown [gaun] *s.* vestido de
mujer. 2 bata; toga.
grab [græb] *t.* agarrar.
grace [greis] *s.* gracia
[física; espiritual]. 2 *t.*
adornar.
gracious ['greiʃəs] *a.* gracioso, amable.
grade [greid] *s.* grado. 2
clase. *3 t.* graduar.
graduate [græd3uət] *a.*
graduado. 2 ['grædjueit]
t.-i. graduar(se.

grain [grein] s. grano. 2 cereales. 3 átomo, pizca.

grammar ['græməʳ] s. gramática. 2 ~-school, instituto de segunda enseñanza; (E. U.) escuela primaria.

grand [grænd] a. magnífico; sublime; distinguido.

grandfather ['grænd͵faːðəʳ] s. abuelo.

grandmother ['græn͵mʌðəʳ] s. abuela.

grandson ['grænsʌn] s. nieto.

granny, -nie ['græni] s. abuela.

grant [graːnt] s. concesión. 2 beca. 3 t. conceder, otorgar.

grape [greip] s. BOT. uva.

grasp [graːsp] s. asimiento. 2 apretón de manos. 3 comprensión. 4 t. asir, empuñar. 5 comprender.

grass [graːs] s. hierba, césped.

grate [greit] s. reja, verja. 2 t. rallar. 3 raspar.

grateful ['greitful] a. agradecido.

gratify ['grætifai] t. satisfacer, contentar.

grave [greiv] a. grave, serio. 2 s. tumba, sepulcro.

gravel ['grævəl] s. arena gruesa, grava.

gravity ['græviti] s. gravedad, peso. 2 seriedad.

gravy ['greivi] s. coc. salsa, jugo.

graze [greiz] s. roce. 2 i. pacer. 3 t. raspar.

grease [griːs] s. grasa. 2 [griːz]. t. engrasar.

great [greit] a. grande, gran.

greatness ['greitnis] s. grandeza.

green [griːn] a. verde.

greengrocer ['griːn͵grəusəʳ] s. verdulero.

greenhouse ['griːnhaus] s. invernáculo.

greet [griːt] t. saludar.

greeting ['griːtiŋ] s. saludo.

grew [gruː] pret. de TO GROW.

grey [grei] a. gris, pardo.

greyhound ['greihaund] s. galgo.

grief [griːf] s. dolor, pena.

grieve [griːv] t.-i. afligir(se.

grim [grim] a. torvo, ceñudo.

grime [graim] s. mugre. 2 t. ensuciar.

grimy ['graimi] a. sucio.

grin [grin] *s.* mueca de dolor o cólera. 2 sonrisa bonachona. 3 *i.* hacer muecas. 4 sonreírse.

grind [graind] *t.* moler. ¶ Pret. y p. p.: *ground* [graund].

grip [grip] *s.* presa. 2 poder. 3 puño, mango. 4 maletín. 5 *t.-i.* agarrar(se.

groan [groun] *s.* gemido. 2 *i.* gemir.

grocer ['grousər] *s.* tendero [de comestibles].

grocery ['grousəri] *s.* tienda de comestibles. 2 *pl.* comestibles.

groom [grum] *s.* mozo de cuadra. 2 lacayo. 3 novio. 4 *t.* cuidar [caballos].

groove [gru:v] *s.* ranura, surco. 2 *t.* acanalar.

grope [group] *t.-i.* tentar, ir a tientas.

gross [grous] *a.* grueso.

ground [graund] *s.* tierra, suelo, piso. 2 terreno. 3 *pret.* y *p. p.* de TO GRIND. 4 *t.* fundamentar, apoyar. 5 *i.* basarse.

group [gru:p] *s.* grupo, conjunto. 2 *t.-i.* agrupar(se.

grove [grouv] *s.* bosquecillo.

grow [grou] *i.* Crecer, desarrollarse. 2 nacer. 3 plantar. 4 ponerse, volverse. ¶ Pret.: *grew* [gru:]; p. p.: *grown* [groun].

grown-up ['grounʌp] *a.-s.* adulto.

grudge [grʌdʒ] *s.* resentimiento. 2 *t.* regatear, escatimar.

gruesome ['gru:səm] *a.* horrible.

grumble ['grʌmbl] *s.* refunfuño, queja. 2 *i.* refunfuñar.

grunt [grʌnt] *s.* gruñido. 2 *i.* gruñir.

guarantee [ˌgærən'ti:] *s.* garantía. 2 *t.* garantizar.

guard [gɑ:d] *s.* guardia. 2 *t.-i.* guardar(se.

guess [ges] *s.* conjetura. 2 *t.* conjeturar, suponer.

guest [gest] *s.* huésped.

guidance ['gaidəns] *s.* guía, dirección.

guide [gaid] *s.* guía [persona, libro]. 2 *t.* guiar.

guild [gild] *s.* gremio, cofradía.

guile [gail] *s.* astucia, dolo.

guilt [gilt] *s.* culpa, delito.

guilty ['gilti] *a.* culpable.

guise [gaiz] *s.* guisa, modo.

guitar [gi'tɑ:ʳ] *s.* MÚS. guitarra.

gulf [gʌlf] *s.* GEOGR. golfo.

gull [gʌl] *s.* ORN. gaviota. 2 *t.* estafar, engañar.

gullet ['gʌlit] *s.* gaznate.

gulp [gʌlp] *s.* trago, engullida. 2 *t.* tragar, engullir.

gum [gʌm] *s.* encía. 2 goma. 3 *t.* engomar.

gun [gʌn] *s.* ARTILL. cañón. 2 fusil, escopeta. 3 (E. U.) pistola, revólver.

gunner ['gʌnəʳ] *s.* artillero.

gunpowder ['gʌn,paudəʳ] *s.* pólvora.

gush [gʌʃ] *s.* chorro, borbotón. 2 *i.* brotar, manar a borbotones.

gust [gʌst] *s.* ráfaga, racha.

gutter ['gʌtəʳ] *s.* arroyo. 2 *i.* correrse [una vela].

gypsy ['dʒipsi] *a.-s.* gitano.

H

hack [hæk] *s.* rocín. 2 corte, hachazo. 3 *t.* tajar, cortar.

had [hæd, həd, d] V. TO HAVE.

haggard ['hægəd] *a.* macilento.

hail [heil] *s.* granizo, pedrisco. 2 saludo, llamada. 3 *interj.* ¡ave!, ¡salud! 4 *i.-t.* granizar, pedriscar. 5 saludar, llamar.

hair [hɛəʳ] *s.* cabello, pelo.

hairdresser ['hɛə͵dresəʳ] *s.* peluquero, -ra. 2 peluquería.

half [hɑ:f], *pl.* **halves** [hɑ:vz] *s.* mitad. 2 *a.-adv.* medio; semi, casi.

hallow ['hælou] *t.* santificar; reverenciar.

halt [hɔ:lt] *s.* alto, parada. 2 cojera. 3 *a.* cojo.

4 *i.* detenerse. 5 cojear. 6 vacilar.

halter ['hɔ:ltəʳ] *s.* cabestro.

ham [hæm] *s.* pernil, jamón.

hammer ['hæmə] *s.* martillo. 2 *t.* martillar, golpear.

hammock ['hæmək] *s.* hamaca.

hamper ['hæmpəʳ] *s.* cesta. 2 estorbo. 3 *t.* estorbar.

hand [hænd] *s.* mano. 2 operario; mano de obra. 3 manecilla [del reloj]. 4 letra. 5 mano [en las cartas]. 6 *t.* dar; entregar, pasar. 7 conducir, guiar.

handicap ['hændikæp] *s.* obstáculo, desventaja. 2 *t.* DEP. poner obstáculos.

handicraft ['hændikra:ft] s. trabajo manual.

handkerchief ['hæŋkə-ʃif] s. pañuelo.

handle ['hændl] s. asa, asidero. 2 t. tocar, manejar. 3 tratar.

handsome ['hænsəm] a. hermoso. 2 guapo.

hang [hæŋ] s. caída [de un vestido, etc.]. 2 sentido, intención. 3 t. colgar, suspender. ¶ Pret. y p. p.: *hung* [hʌŋ].

happen ['hæpən] i. acontecer, ocurrir. 2 acertar a [ser, estar, etc.]. 3 to ~ on, encontrar, dar con.

happening ['hæpəniŋ] s. acontecimiento, suceso.

happiness ['hæpinis] s. felicidad.

happy ['hæpi] a. feliz.

harass ['hærəs] t. atormentar. 2 acosar, hostigar.

harbo(u)r ['ha:bər] s. puerto. 2 refugio, asilo. 3 t.-i resguardar(se, amparar(se.

hard [ha:d] a. duro. 2 adv. duramente. 3 difícilmente. 4 s. suelo o piso duro.

hardness [ha:dnis] s. dureza. 2 penalidad.

hardware ['ha:d-wɛər] s. quincalla, ferretería.

hardship ['ha:dʃip] s. penalidad. 2 privación.

hardy ['ha:di] a. fuerte, robusto.

hare [hɛər] s. liebre.

harehound ['hɛəˈhaund] s. lebrel.

harm [ha:m] s. mal, daño. 2 t. dañar, perjudicar.

harmful ['ha:mful] a. dañoso.

harmless ['ha:mlis] a. inofensivo.

harmonious [ha:ˈməu-njəs] a. armonioso.

harness ['ha:nis] s. arneses. 2 t. enjaezar.

harp [ha:p] s. MÚS. arpa. 2 i. tocar el arpa.

harrow ['hærəu] s. AGR. grada. 2 t. desgarrar, atormentar.

harsh [ha:ʃ] a. áspero.

hart [ha:t] s. ciervo, venado.

harvest ['ha:vist] s. cosecha. 2 t.-i. cosechar; segar.

has [hæz, həz] 3.ª pers. pres. ind. de TO HAVE.

haste [heist] s. prisa; presteza. 2 i. TO HASTEN.

hasten ['heisn] t. apresurar. 3 i. darse prisa.

hat [hæt] *s.* sombrero.
hatchet ['hætʃit] *s.* hacha.
hate [heit] *s.* odio, aversión. 2 *t.* odiar, aborrecer.
hateful ['heitful] *a.* odioso.
hatred ['heitrid] *s.* odio.
haughty ['hɔːti] *a.* altivo, orgulloso.
haunt [hɔːnt] *s.* guarida. 2 morada. 3 *t.* rondar, frecuentar.
have [hæv o həv] *aux.* haber. 2 *I had rather*, más quisiera; *we had rather*, vale más que. 3 *t.* haber, tener, poseer. 4 saber: *he has no latin*, no sabe latín. 5 tomar, comer, beber. 6 *to ~ to* + *infinit.* tener que, haber que. ¶ 3.ª pers. pres. ind.: *has* [hæz, həz]; pret. y p. p.: *had* [hæd, həd].
haven ['heivn] *s.* puerto. 2 asilo.
havoc ['hævək] *s.* estrago, destrucción.
hay [hei] *s.* heno, forraje.
hazard ['hæzəd] *s.* azar, acaso. 2 *t.-i.* arriesgar(se.
haze [heiz] *s.* niebla, calina.

hazy ['heizi] *a.* brumoso.
he [hiː, hi] *pron. pers.* él. 2 *pron. indef.* el, aquel: *~ who*, el o aquel que, quien. 3 *a.* macho, varón: *~-bear*, oso [macho].
head [hed] *s.* cabeza. 2 cabecera. 3 cima. 4 puño [de bastón]. 5 título. 6 espuma [de un líquido]. 7 MAR. proa. 8 jefe, principal. 9 *t.* encabezar.
headache ['hedeik] *s.* dolor de cabeza.
headland ['hedlənd] *s.* GEOGR. cabo.
headline ['hedlain] *s.* titulares [de periódico]. 2 título.
headmaster ['hed'maːstə²], **headmistress** [-'mistris] *s.* director, -ra [de un colegio].
headquarters ['hed'kwɔː-təz] *s.* MIL. cuartel general.
heal [hiːl] *t.-i.* curar(se, sanar(se. 2 *t.* remediar.
health [helθ] *s.* salud, sanidad.
healthful ['helθful], **healthy** ['helθi] *a.* sano, saludable.
heap [hiːp] *s.* montón, pila. 2 *t.* amontonar.

hear [hiəʳ] *t.-i.* oir. 2 escuchar. ¶ Pret. y p. p.: *heard* [həːd].

heart [haːt] *s.* corazón; *to take to* ~, tomar en serio; *by* ~, de memoria.

heartache ['haːt-eik] *s.* aflicción.

hearty ['haːti] *a.* cordial, sincero.

heat [hiːt] *s.* calor. 2 *t.* calentar.

heating ['hiːtiŋ] *s.* calefacción.

heave [hiːv] *s.* esfuerzo para levantar o levantarse. 2 jadeo. 3 *t.* levantar; mover con esfuerzo. 4 *i.* jadear. ¶ Pret. y p. p.: *heaved* [hiːvd] o *hove* [həuv].

heaven ['hevn] *s.* cielo.

heavily ['hevili] *adv.* pesadamente. 2 fuertemente.

heavy ['hevi] *a.* pesado. 2 *adv.* pesadamente.

hedge [hedʒ] *s.* seto vivo; cerca. 2 *t.* cercar, vallar.

heed [hiːd] *s.* atención; caso. 2 *t.* prestar atención a.

heel [hiːl] *s.* talón; tacón.

height [hait] *s.* altura, altitud.

heighten ['haitn] *t.* levantar.

heir [ɛəʳ] *s.* heredero.

held [held] V. TO HOLD.

he'll [hiːl] contract. de HE SHALL y de HE WILL.

hell [hel] *s.* infierno.

hello ['he'ləu] *interj.* ¡hola! 2 ¡diga!, ¡oiga! [en el teléfono].

helm [helm] *s.* timón.

helmet ['helmit] *s.* yelmo, casco.

help [help] *s.* ayuda, auxilio. 2 *t.* ayudar.

helpful ['helpful] *a.* útil.

helpless ['helplis] *a.* desvalido.

hem [hem] *s.* COST. dobladillo, bastilla. 2 *t.* dobladillar. 3 cercar, rodear.

hen [hen] *f.* ORN. gallina.

hence [hens] *adv.* desde aquí o ahora. 2 de aquí a, dentro de.

her [haːʳ, əːʳ, həʳ əʳ] *pron. f.* (ac. o dat.) la, le. 2 [con prep.] ella. 3 *a. pos. f.* su, sus [de ella].

herald ['herəld] *s.* heraldo. 2 *t.* anunciar.

herb [həːb] *s.* hierba.

herd [həːd] *s.* rebaño. 2 *t.-i.* juntar o juntarse en rebaño.

here [hiəⁱ] *adv.* aquí, acá.

herebouts ['hiərəˌbauts] *adv.* por aquí cerca.

hereafter [hiəⁱ'ɑːftəⁱ] *adv.* en lo futuro.

heritage ['heritidʒ] *s.* herencia.

hermit ['həːmit] *s.* ermitaño.

hero ['hiərəu] *s.* héroe.

herring ['heriŋ] *s.* ICT. arenque.

hers [həːz] *pron. f.* [el] suyo, [la] suya [los] suyos, [las] suyas [de ella].

herself [həː'self] *pron. pers. f.* ella misma, se, sí misma.

he's [hiːz, hiz] contrac. de HE IS y de HE HAS.

hesitate ['heziteit] *i.* vacilar.

hew [hjuː] *t.* cortar, labrar. ‖ Pret.: *hewed* [hjuːd]; p. p.: *hewn* [hjuːn].

hidden ['hidn] V. TO HIDE.

hide [haid] *s.* piel, cuero. 2 *t.-i.* esconder(se, ocultar(se. ‖ Pret.: *hid* [hid]; p. p.: *hidden* ['hidn] o *hid*.

hideous ['hidiəs] *a.* horrible.

high [hai] *a.* alto.

highland ['hailənd] *s.* región montañosa.

highway ['haiwei] *s.* carretera.

hiker ['haikəⁱ] *s.* excursionista.

hill [hil] *s.* colina, collado.

hilt [hilt] *s.* puño, empuñadura.

him [him, im] *pron. m.* [ac. o dat.] lo, le. 2 [con prep.] él: *to ~*, a él.

himself [him'self] *pron. pers. m.* él, él mismo, se, sí, sí mismo.

hind [haind] *a.* trasero, posterior. 2 *s.* cierva.

hinder ['hindəⁱ] *t.-i.* impedir, estorbar.

hinge [hindʒ] *s.* gozne, bisagra. 2 *t.* engoznar.

hint [hint] *s.* indicación. 2 *t.-i.* indicar.

hip [hip] *s.* cadera.

hire ['haiəⁱ] *s.* alquiler. 2 *t.* alquilar.

his [hiz, iz] *a.-pron. m.* [el] suyo, [la] suya; [los] suyos, [las] suyas [de él].

historic(al [his'tɔrik, -əl] *a.* histórico.

hit [hit] *s.* golpe. 2 éxito. 3 *t.* golpear, dar con. ‖ Pret. y p. p.: *hit* [hit].

hitch [hitʃ] *s.* tropiezo. 2 *t.* mover [a tirones].

hither ['hiðə'] *adv.* acá, hacia acá.

hitherto ['hiðə'tu:] *adv.* hasta aquí, hasta ahora.

hoard [hɔ:d] *s.* depósito. 2 *t.* acumular, atesorar.

hoarse [hɔ:s] *a.* ronco, áspero.

hoary ['hɔ:ri] *a.* cano, canoso.

hobble ['hɔbl] *s.* cojera. 2 *i.* cojear.

hobby ['hɔbi] *s.* afición.

hog [hɔg] *s.* cerdo, cochino.

hold [hould] *s.* presa. 2 asidero. 3 fortaleza. 4 receptáculo. 5 MAR. bodega. 6 dominio, poder. 7 *t.* tener, poseer. 8 sujetar, aguantar, sostener. 10 considerar, tener por. 11 *i.* agarrarse, asirse. ¶ Pret. y p. p.: *held* [held].

holder ['houldə'] *s.* tenedor, poseedor. 2 mango, agarrador.

hole [houl] *s.* agujero, boquete. 2 *t.* agujerear, horadar.

holiday ['hɔlədi, -lid-, -dei] *s.* fiesta, festividad. 2 *pl.* vacaciones. 3 *a.* festivo.

hollow ['hɔlou] *a.* hueco, 2 falso. 3 *s.* hueco.

holy ['houli] *a.* santo; sagrado.

homage ['hɔmidʒ] *s.* homenaje.

home [houm] *s.* hogar, casa.

homeless ['houmlis] *a.* sin casa.

homely ['houmli] *a.* llano, sencillo, casero. 2 feo, vulgar.

homicide ['hɔmisaid] *s.* homicidio. 2 homicida.

honest ['ɔnist] *a.* honrado.

honesty ['ɔnisti] *s.* honradez.

honey ['hʌni] *s.* miel.

hood [hud] *s.* capucha, caperuza.

hoof [hu:f] *s.* casco, pezuña.

hook [huk] *s.* gancho, garfio. 2 *t.* encorvar.

hoop [hu:p] *s.* aro, cerco.

hoot [hu:t] *s.* grito. 2 *i.-t.* gritar.

hooter ['hu:tə'] *s.* sirena.

hop [hɔp] *s.* salto, brinco. 2 *i.* brincar, saltar.

hope [houp] *s.* esperanza. 2 *t.-i.* esperar, confiar.

hopeful ['houpful] *a.* esperanzado.

hopeless ['həuplis] *a.* desesperado.

horizon [hə'raizn] *s.* horizonte.

horn [hɔ:n] *s.* asta, cuerno.

horrid ['hɔrid] *a.* horroroso.

horse [hɔ:s] *s.* ZOOL. caballo.

horseman ['hɔ:smən] *s.* jinete.

hose [həuz] *s.* calza(s, media(s. 2 manguera.

hospitable ['hɔspitəbl] *a.* hospitalario, acogedor.

hospital ['hɔspitl] *s.* hospital.

host [həust] *s.* hospedero, mesonero. 2 huésped, anfitrión.

hostage ['hɔstidʒ] *s.* rehén.

hostess ['həustis] *s.* mesonera. 2 anfitriona. 3 AVIA. azafata.

hot [hɔt] *a.* caliente.

hound [haund] *s.* perro de caza.

hour ['auər] *s.* hora.

house [haus, *pl.* 'hauziz] *s.* casa. 2 TEAT. sala, público.

household ['haushəuld] *s.* casa, familia.

housekeeper ['haus,ki:-pər] *s.* ama de llaves.

housewife ['haus-waif] *s.* ama de casa.

hove [həuv] V. TO HEAVE.

how [hau] *adv.* cómo, de qué manera; por qué. 2 qué, cuán [admirativos].

however [hau'evər] *adv.* como quiera que, por muy ... que. 2 *conj.* sin embargo, no obstante.

howl [haul] *s.* aullido. 2 grito. 3 *i.* aullar.

huddle ['hʌdl] *s.* montón, tropel. 2 *t.-i.* amontonar(se.

hue [hju:] *s.* color, matiz.

hug [hʌg] *s.* abrazo. 2 *t.* abrazar.

huge [hju:dʒ] *a.* enorme.

hulk [hʌlk] *s.* buque viejo.

hull [hʌl] *s.* cáscara, corteza. 2 *t.* mondar.

hum [hʌm] *s.* zumbido. 2 *i.* zumbar.

humble ['hʌmbl] *a.* humilde. 2 *t.-ref.* humillar(se.

humiliate [hju(:)'milieit] *t.* humillar.

humility [hju(:)'militi] *s.* humildad, sumisión.

humour ['hju:mər] *s.* humorismo. 2 humor, genio. 2 *t.* complacer.

humo(u)rous ['hju:mərəs] *a.* humorístico, gracioso.

hump [hʌmp] *s.* jiba, joroba.

hunch [hʌntʃ] *s.* joroba, jiba. 2 *t.-i.* encorvar [la espalda].

hundred ['hʌndrəd] *a.* cien. 2 **-th** [-θ] centésimo.

hung [hʌŋ] V. TO HANG.

hunger ['hʌŋgəʳ] *s.* hambre. 2 *i.* tener hambre.

hungry [hʌŋgri] *a.* hambriento.

hunk [hʌŋk] *s.* fam. trozo.

hunt [hʌnt] *s.* caza. 2 *t.-i* cazar.

hunter ['hʌntəʳ] *s.* cazador.

hurl [hə:l] *s.* tiro, lanzamiento. 2 *t.* lanzar, tirar.

hurricane ['hʌrikən] *s.* huracán.

hurry ['hʌri] *s.* prisa, premura. 2 *t.-i.* dar(se prisa, apresurar(se.

hurt [hə:t] *s.* herida, lesión. 2 *a.* herido, lastimado. 3 *t.* herir, lastimar. ¶ Pret. y p. p.: *hurt* [hə:t].

husband ['hʌzbənd] *s.* marido. 2 *t.* economizar.

husbandman ['hʌzbəndmən] *s.* agricultor.

husbandry ['hʌzbəndri] *s.* agricultura. 2 economía.

hush [hʌʃ] *s.* quietud, silencio. 2 *t.-i.* callar.

hustle ['hʌsl] *s.* actividad. 2 *t.-i.* apresurar(se.

hut [hʌt] *s.* choza, cabaña.

hydraulic [hai'drɔ:lik] *a.* hidráulico.

hypocrisy [hi'pɔkrəsi] *s.* hipocresía.

hypocrite ['hipəkrit] *s.* hipócrita.

hypothesis [hai'pɔθisis]

hysterical [his'tərikəl] *a.* histérico.

I

I [ai] pron. pers. yo.
ice [ais] s. hielo. 2 t. helar.
icy ['aisi] a. helado, frío.
idea [ai'diə] s. idea.
identify [ai'dentifai] t. identificar.
idiom ['idiəm] s. modismo.
idiot ['idiət] s. idiota.
idle ['aidl] a. ocioso. 2 t. estar ocioso.
if [if] conj. si.
ignoble [ig'noubl] a. innoble.
ignorance ['ignərəns] s. ignorancia.
I'll [ail] contr. de I SHALL y I WILL.
ill [il] a. enfermo. 2 s. mal, desgracia. 3 adv. mal.
illicit [i'lisit] a. ilícito.
illiterate [i'litərit] a. iletrado, analfabeto.

illness ['ilnis] s. enfermedad.
I'm [aim] contr. de I AM.
image ['imidʒ] s. imagen.
immigrant ['imigrənt] a.-s. inmigrante.
immigration [ˌimi'greiʃən] s. inmigración.
imminent ['iminənt] a. inminente.
immortal [i'mɔːtl] a.-s. inmortal.
immovable [i'muːvəbl] a. inamovible, inmóvil.
immunize ['imju(ː)naiz] t. inmunizar.
impact ['impækt] s. golpe, choque, impacto.
impair [im'pɛəʳ] t. dañar.
impartial [im'pɑːʃəl] a. imparcial.
impatient [im'peiʃənt] a.

impede [im'pi:d] *t.* impedir, estorbar.

impediment [im'pediment] *s.* impedimento, estorbo.

impel [im'pel] *t.* impulsar.

impeding [im'pendiŋ] *a.* inminente, amenazador.

imperious [im'piəriəs] *a.* imperioso.

impious ['impiəs] *a.* impío.

implement ['implimənt] *s.* instrumento. 2 *pl.* enseres.

implicate ['implikeit] *t.* implicar. 2 entrelazar.

implore [im'plɔ:r] *t.* implorar.

imply [im'plai] *t.* implicar.

import [im'pɔ:t] *s.* importancia. 2 importación. 3 [im'pɔ:t] *t.-i.* importar. 4 *t.* significar.

importance [im'pɔ:təns] *s.* importancia. 2 cuantía.

impose [im'pəuz] *t.* imponer.

impoverish [im'pɔvəriʃ] *t.* empobrecer.

impress ['impres] *s.* impresión. 2 [im'pres] *t.* imprimir.

impressive [im'presiv] *a.* impresionante, emocionante.

imprint ['imprint] *s.* impresión, huella. 2 [im'print] *t.* imprimir, estampar. 2 grabar.

imprison [im'prizn] *t.* encarcelar.

improbable [im'prɔbəbl] *s.* improbable. 2 inverosímil.

improper [im'prɔpər] *a.* impropio. 2 indecoroso.

improve [im'pru:v] *t.* mejorar, desarrollar.

impute [im'pju:t] *t.* imputar, atribuir.

in [in] *prep.* en, con, de, dentro de, durante, entre, por.

inability [,inə'biliti] *s.* incapacidad, impotencia.

inaccessible [,inæk'sesəbl] *a.* inaccesible.

inadequate [in'ædikwit] *a.* inadecuado. 2 insuficiente.

inasmuch as [inəz'mʌtʃ æz, -əz] *conj.* considerando que; ya que.

inaugurate [i'nɔ:gjureit] *t.* inaugurar.

incapable [in'keipəbl] *a.* incapaz.

incessant [in'sesnt] *a.* incesante.

inch [intʃ] *s.* pulgada [2'54 cm].

income ['inkəm] s. ingresos.

incomprehensible [in͵kɔmpri'hensəbl] a. incomprensible.

inconceivable [͵inkən'si:vəbl] a. inconcebible. 2 increíble.

inconsistent [͵inkən'sistənt] a. incompatible, contradictorio.

inconvenience [͵inkən'vi:njəns] s. inconveniencia. 2 t. incomodar.

increase ['inkri:s] s. aumento. 2 [in'kri:s] t. aumentar. 3 agrandar. 4 i. aumentarse.

incumbent [in'kʌmbənt] a. to be ~ on, incumbir a.

incur [in'kə:ʳ] t. incurrir en; contraer; hacer.

incurable [in'kjuərəbl] a. incurable.

indebted [in'detid] a. endeudado.

indeed [in'di:d] adv. realmente, ¡claro que sí!

indefatigable [͵indi'fætigəbl] a. infatigable.

indemnity [in'demniti] s. indemnidad.

indent [in'dent] t. mellar, dentar.

independence [͵indi'pendəns] s. independencia.

indescribable [͵indis'kraibəbl] a. indescriptible.

index ['indeks] s. índice.

Indian ['indjən] a.-s. indio.

indict [in'dait] t.-s. acusar.

indignant [in'dignənt] a. indignado.

indite [in'dait] t. redactar.

individual [͵indi'vidjuəl] a. individual. 2 s. individuo.

indomitable [in'dɔmitəbl] a. indomable.

indoors ['in'dɔ:z] adv. dentro de casa; en local cerrado.

indorse, indorsee, etc., V. ENDORSE (TO), ENDORSEE, etcétera.

induce [in'dju:s] t. inducir.

inducement [in'dju:smənt] s. móvil, aliciente.

indulge [in'dʌldʒ] t. satisfacer [pasiones, etc.]. 2 consentir.

industrial [in'dʌstriəl] a. industrial.

industrious [in'dʌstriəs] a. industrioso, laborioso.

industry ['indəstri] s. industria. 2 diligencia, laboriosidad.

ineffectual [,ini'fektʃual] a. ineficaz. 2 inútil, vano.

inept [i'nept] a. inepto.

inequality [,ini(:)'kwɔliti] s. desigualdad. 2 desproporción.

inexpensive [,iniks'pensiv] a. barato, poco costoso.

inexperience [,iniks'piəriəns] s. inexperiencia, impericia.

infamous ['infəməs] a. infame.

infantry ['infəntri] s. MIL. infantería.

infect [in'fekt] t. infectar.

infer [in'fə:ʳ] t. inferir.

infest [in'fest] t. infestar.

infirmity [in'fə:miti] s. enfermedad.

inflate [in'fleit] t. inflar.

inflict [in'flikt] t. infligir.

informant [in'fɔ:mənt] s. informador.

infuriate [in'fjuərieit] t. enfurecer.

ingenious [in'dʒi:njəs] a. ingenioso, hábil, sutil.

inhabit [in'hæbit] t. habitar, morar en.

inhabitant [in'hæbitənt] s. habitante.

inhale [in'heil] i. inhalar.

inherit [in'herit] t. heredar.

inheritance [in'heritəns] s. herencia.

inject [in'dʒekt] t. inyectar.

injunction [in'dʒʌŋkʃən] s. orden, mandato.

injure ['indʒəʳ] t. dañar, perjudicar.

injury ['indʒəri] s. daño.

ink [iŋk] s. tinta.

inkling ['iŋkliŋ] s. insinuación, indicio.

inland ['inlænd] a.-n.-adv. de tierra adentro.

inlay [in'lei] t. incrustar. ' Pret. p. p.: inlaid ['inleid].

inlet ['inlet] s. caleta; ría.

inmate ['inmeit] s. asilado, preso; residente.

inn [in] s. posada, fonda.

inner ['inəʳ] a. interior, íntimo.

inordinate [i'nɔ:dinit] a. inmoderado, excesivo.

inquest ['inkwest] s. información judicial.

inquire [in'kwaiəʳ] t. averiguar, investigar.

inquiry [in'kwaiəri] s. indagación, investigación, pregunta.

inroad ['inrəud] *s.* incursión.

insane [in'sein] *a.* loco, demente.

insect ['insekt] *s.* ZOOL. insecto.

insert [in'sə:t] *t.* insertar.

inside ['in'said] *s.* interior.

insight ['insait] *s.* perspicacia, intuición.

insist [in'sist] *i.* insistir.

install [ins'tɔ:l] *t.* instalar.

instance ['instəns] *s.* ejemplo.

instant ['instənt] *s.* instante, momento. 2 *a.* instante, insistente. 3 corriente, actual: *the 10th* ~, el diez del corriente.

instead [ins'ted] *adv.* en cambio. 2 ~ *of,* en lugar de.

instinct ['instiŋkt] *s.* instinto.

insulate ['insjuleit] *t.* aislar.

insult ['insʌlt] *s.* insulto; [in'sʌlt] *t.* insultar.

insurance [in'ʃuərəns] *s.* COM. seguro.

insure [in'ʃuər] *t.* COM. asegurar. 2 garantizar.

insurgent [in'sə:dʒənt]

a.-s. insurgente, insurrecto.

insurmountable [,insə(:)'mauntəbl] *a.* insuperable.

insurrection [,insə'rekʃən] *s.* insurrección.

intemperate [in'tempərit] *a.* excesivo, extremado. 2 intemperante. 3 bebedor.

intend [in'tend] *t.* proponerse. 2 querer decir.

intensify [in'tensifai] *f.* intensificar.

intent [in'tent] *a.* atento. 2 *s.* intento, propósito.

inter [in'tə:r] *t.* enterrar.

interchange ['intə'tʃeindʒ] *s.* intercambio. 2 comercio; [,intə'tʃeindʒ] *t.* cambiar, trocar.

intercourse ['intəkɔ:s] *s.* trato, comunicación. 2 comercio.

interest ['intrist] *s.* interés. 2 *t.* interesar.

interesting ['intristiŋ] *a.* interesante.

interfere [,intə'fiər] *i.* interponerse, entrometerse.

intervene [,intə'vi:n] *i.* intervenir.

interview ['intəvju:] *s.*

entrevista. 2 *t.* entrevistar.

interweave [ˌintə'wiːv] *t.* entretejer.

intestine [in'testin] *a.* intestino.

intimate ['intimit] *a.* íntimo. 2 ['intimeit] *t.* notificar, intimar.

into ['intu] *prep.* en, dentro [indicando movimiento, transformación, penetración, inclusión].

intoxicate [in'tɔksikeit] *t.* embriagar. 2 MED. intoxicar.

intrigue [in'triːg] *s.* intriga. 2 *t.-i.* intrigar.

introduce [ˌintrə'djuːs] *t.* introducir.

intrude [in'truːd] *t.* imponer. 2 *i.* estorbar.

invade [in'veid] *t.* invadir.

invaluable [in'væljuəbl] *a.* inestimable, precioso.

invasion [in'veiʒən] *s.* invasión.

invent [in'vent] *t.* inventar.

invert [in'vəːt] *t.* invertir.

invest [in'vest] *t.* invertir [dinero]. 2 MIL. sitiar, cercar.

investigate [in'vestigeit]

t. investigar. 2 indagar.

investment [in'vestmənt] *s.* investidura. 2 inversión. 3 MIL. cerco, sitio.

invite [in'vait] *t.* invitar.

invoke [in'vəuk] *t.* invocar.

involve [in'vɔlv] *t.* envolver.

inward ['inwəd] *a.* interior.

inwards ['inwədz] *adv.* hacia dentro.

Irish ['aiəriʃ] *a.* irlandés.

iron ['aiən] *s.* hierro. 2 plancha. 3 *t.* planchar.

irony ['aiərəni] *s.* ironía.

irrigate ['irigeit] *t.* regar.

irritable ['iritəbl] *a.* irritable.

island ['ailənd] *s.* isla, ínsula.

isle [ail] *s.* isla. 2 isleta.

isolate ['aisəleit] *t.* aislar.

issue ['iʃuː, 'isjuː] *s.* salida. 2 principio. 3 edición. 4 *t.* verter. 5 expedir. 6 publicar. 7 *i.* nacer.

it [it] *pr. neutro* él, ella, ello, eso, lo, la, le.

italic [i'tælik] *a.* itálico. 2 *s. pl.* IMPR. bastardilla, cursiva.

itch [itʃ] s. MED. sarna.
2 picazón, comezón. 3 i.
sentir picazón.

item ['aitəm] adv. item.
2 s. partida [de una
cuenta]. 3 punto, deta-
lle. 4 artículo. 5 noticia.

its [its] a.-pron. neutro
su, sus, suyo, suyos [de
él, ella, etc.].

itself [it'self] pron. neutro él mismo, ella mis-
ma, ello mismo, si, si
mismo.

ivory ['aivəri] s. marfil.

ivy ['aivi] s. hiedra.

J

jab [dʒæb] *s.* pinchazo; golpe. 2 *t.* pinchar; golpear.

jack [dʒæk] *s.* hombre, mozo. 2 gato [del coche].

jacket ['dʒækit] *s.* chaqueta, americana.

jade [dʒeid] *s.* rocín, jamelgo.

jail [dʒeil] *s.* cárcel. 2 *t.* encarcelar.

jam [dʒæm] *s.* confitura. 2 atasco. 3 *t.* obstruir.

January ['dʒænjuəri] *s.* enero.

Japanese [ˌdʒæpə'ni:z] *a.-s.* japonés.

jar [dʒɑ:ʳ] *s.* jarra, tarro. 2 sonido áspero. 3 *t.-i.* [hacer] sonar, vibrar con sonido áspero.

jaunty ['dʒɔ:nti] *a.* vivo, garboso, airoso.

jaw [dʒɔ:] *s.* ZOOL. mandíbula.

jazz [dʒæz] *s.* jazz.

jealous ['dʒeləs] *a.* celoso.

jean [dʒein, dʒi:n] *s.* TEJ. dril. 2 [dʒi:nz] *pl.* pantalones tejanos.

jeer [dʒiəʳ] *s.* burla, mofa. 2 *t.-i.* burlarse, mofarse [de].

jelly ['dʒeli] *s.* jalea. 2 gelatina.

jeopardize ['dʒepədaiz] *t.* arriesgar, exponer.

jerk [dʒɔ:k] *s.* tirón, sacudida. 2 *t.* sacudir, traquetear.

jest [dʒest] *s.* broma, burla. 2 *i.* bromear, chancearse.

jet [dʒet] *s.* MINER. azabache. 2 surtidor, chorro. *3* reactor [avión]. *4 i.* salir, brotar en chorro.

Jew [dʒuː] *a.-s.* judío, israelita.

jewel ['dʒuːəl] *s.* joya, alhaja.

jewellery, jewelry ['dʒuːəlri] *s.* joyas, pedrería.

Jewish ['dʒuːiʃ] *a.* judío.

jib [dʒib] *s.* MAR. foque.

jingle ['dʒiŋgl] *s.* tintineo. *2 i.* hacer sonar.

job [dʒɔb] *s.* trabajo, tarea. *2* empleo, ocupación.

jocund ['dʒɔkənd] *s.* jocundo.

jog [dʒɔg] *s.* empujoncito.

join [dʒɔin] *t.* unir, juntar.

joining ['dʒɔiniŋ] *s.* unión, juntura.

joke [dʒouk] *s.* chiste; chanza. *2 i.* bromear.

jolly ['dʒɔli] *a.* alegre, divertido. *2 adv.* muy.

jolt [dʒoult] *s.* traqueteo. *2 i.* dar tumbos.

jostle ['dʒɔsl] *t.* empujar.

journal ['dʒəːnl] *s.* diario, periódico.

journey ['dʒəːni] *s.* viaje. *2 i.* viajar.

joust [dʒaust] *s.* justa. *2 i.* justar.

jovial ['dʒouvjəl] *a.* jovial.

joy [dʒɔi] *s.* gozo, júbilo.

joyful ['dʒɔiful] *a.* jubiloso, alegre, gozoso.

judge [dʒʌdʒ] *s.* juez, magistrado. *2 t.-i.* juzgar. *3* creer, suponer.

judg(e)ment ['dʒʌdʒmənt] *s.* decisión. *2* juicio.

juice [dʒuːs] *s.* zumo; jugo.

juicy ['dʒuːsi] *a.* jugoso.

July [dʒu(ː)'lai] *s.* julio [mes].

jump [dʒʌmp] *s.* salto, brinco. *2 i.* saltar, brincar.

jumpy ['dʒʌmpi] *a.* saltón.

junction ['dʒʌŋkʃən] *s.* unión.

June [dʒuːn] *s.* junio [mes].

jungle ['dʒʌŋgl] *s.* selva virgen.

junior ['dʒuːnjər] *a.* menor, más joven, hijo.

jurisdiction [,dʒuəris'dikʃən] *s.* jurisdicción.

jury ['dʒuəri] *s.* DER. jurado.

just [dʒʌst] *a.* justo, recto. 2 merecido. 3 fiel, exacto. 4 *adv.* justamente, precisamente. 5 hace poco: ~ *now*, ahora mismo.

justice ['dʒʌstis] *s.* justicia.

jut [dʒʌt] *i.* salir, sobresalir.

jute [dʒuːt] *s.* yute.

K

keel [ki:l] *s.* quilla.
keen [ki:n] *a.* agudo, afilado. 2 aficionado a.
keep [ki:p] *s.* mantenimiento, subsistencia. 2 *t.* guardar. 3 tener, mantener. 4 cuidar, custodiar, guardar. 5 detener, impedir. 6 retener. 7 callar, ocultar. 8 celebrar, tener [reunión, sesión, sesión, etc.]. 9 *i.* mantenerse, conservarse. ¶ Pret. p. p.: *kept* [kept].
keeper [ˈki:pəʳ] *s.* guardián. 2 custodio, velador, defensor.
keg [keg] *s.* cuñete, barril.
kennel [ˈkenl] *s.* perrera.
kept [kept] V. TO KEEP.
kerb [kə:b] *s.* encintado, bordillo [de la acera].
kerchief [ˈkə:tʃif] *s.* pañuelo.

kernel [ˈkə:nl] *s.* grano, almendra, núcleo del fruto.
kettle [ˈketl] *s.* caldero, olla.
key [ki:] *s.* llave. 2 clave.
kick [kik] *s.* puntapié, patada. 2 *t.* dar puntapiés a.
kid [kid] *s.* cabrito. 2 chaval.
kidnap [ˈkidnæp] *t.* secuestrar, raptar.
kill [kil] *t.* matar.
kin [kin] *s.* parientes, parentela.
kind [kaind] *a.* bueno, bondadoso, benévolo. 2 *s.* género, especies, clase.
kindle [ˈkindl] *t.-i.* encender(se. 2 inflamar(se.
kindly [ˈkaindli] *a.* amable. 2 *adv.* amablemente.

king [kiŋ] *s.* rey, monarca.

kingdom ['kiŋdəm] *s.* reino.

kiss [kis] *s.* beso. 2 *t.-i.* besar(se.

kitchen ['kitʃin] *s.* cocina.

kite [kait] *s.* cometa [juguete].

kitty [kiti] *s.* gatito, minino.

knave [neiv] *s.* bribón, pícaro.

knead [ni:d] *t.* amasar.

knee [ni:) *s.* ANAT. rodilla.

kneel [ni:l] *i.* arrodillarse. ¶ Pret. y p. p.: *knelt* [nelt] o *kneeled* ['ni:ld].

knew [nju:] *pret.* de TO KNOW.

knife, *pl.* **knives** [naif, naivz] *s.* cuchillo; cuchilla; navaja.

knight [nait] *s.* caballero [de una orden]. 2 *t.* armar caballero.

knit [nit] *t.* tejer [a punto de aguja o malla]. ¶ Pret. y p. p.: *knit* [nit] o *knited* ['nitid].

knob [nɔb] *s.* bulto, protuberancia. 2 botón, tirador [de puerta, etc.].

knock [nɔk] *s.* golpe, porrazo. 2 *t.-i.* golpear.

knoll [nəul] *s.* loma, otero.

knot [nɔt] *s.* nudo, lazo. 2 *t.* anudar.

know [nəu] *t.* conocer. 2 saber. 3 ver, comprender. ¶ Pret.: *knew* [nju:] p. p.: *known* [nəun].

knowing ['nəuin] *a.* inteligente; astuto; entendido; enterado.

knowledge ['nɔlidʒ] *s.* conocimiento.

known [nəun] *p.* p. de TO KNOW.

knuckle ['nʌkl] *s.* ANAT. nudillo. 2 *t.* golpear o apretar con los nudillos.

L

label ['leibl] s. rótulo, etiqueta. 2 t. rotular.

laboratory [lə'bɔrətri] s. laboratorio.

labo(u)r ['leibər] s. trabajo, labor. 2 Partido Laborista. 3 i. trabajar, esforzarse, forcejear. 4 t. trabajar; arar, cultivar.

labo(u)rer ['leibərər] s. trabajador, obrero.

lace [leis] s. cordón, cinta. 2 t. atar.

lack [læk] s. falta, carencia. 2 i.-t. carecer de, necesitar.

lad [læd] s. muchacho, mozo.

ladder ['lædər] s. escalera [de mano].

lade [leid] t. cargar. ¶ P. p.: *laded* ['leidid] o *laden* ['leidn].

lady ['leidi] s. señora, dama.

lag [læg] s. retardo, retraso. 2 i. rezagarse.

laid [leid] V. TO LAY.

lain [lein] p. p. de TO LIE.

lake [leik] s. lago, laguna. 2 laca, carmín [color].

lamb [læm] s. cordero.

lame [leim] a. cojo, lisiado. 2 t. encojar, lisiar.

lamp [læmp] s. lámpara.

land [lænd] s. tierra. 2 t. desembarcar. 3 coger, sacar [un pez]. 4 conseguir. 5 aterrizar.

landlady ['læn‚leidi] s. propietaria; casera. 2 mesonera.

landlord ['lænlɔ:d] s. propietario [de tierras]; casero; mesonero.

landowner ['lænd‚ounər]

s. hacendado, terrateniente.

landscape ['lænskeip] s. paisaje.

lane [lein] s. senda, vereda.

language ['læŋgwidʒ] s. lenguaje.

languish ['læŋgwiʃ] i. languidecer. 2 consumirse.

lap [læp] s. falda, regazo. 2 t. sobreponer, encaballar.

lapse [læps] s. lapso, error. 2 i. pasar, transcurrir.

lard [lɑ:d] s. tocino gordo. 2 manteca de cerdo.

large [lɑ:dʒ] a. grande, grueso. 2 amplio. 3 extenso, lato.

lass [læs] f. chica, moza.

last [lɑ:st] a. último, final: ~ *but one*, penúltimo. 2 s. fin, final. 3 i. durar, permanecer.

late [leit] a. retrasado, tardío. 2 adv. tarde.

lately ['leitli] adv. últimamente, recientemente.

later ['leitər] a.-adv. comp. de LATE: ~ *on*, más adelante.

lather ['lɑ:ðər] s. espuma. 2 t. enjabonar. 3 i. hacer espuma.

latter ['lætər] a. más reciente, último: *the former* ... *the* ~, aquél ... éste.

laugh [lɑ:f] s. risa. 2 i. reir, reirse.

laughter ['lɑ:ftər] s. risa.

launch [lɔ:ntʃ] s. MAR. botadura. 2 MAR. lancha. 3 t.-i. lanzar(se. 4 MAR. botar.

laundry ['lɔ:ndri] s. lavadero. 2 lavandería. 3 ropa lavada.

lavender ['lævindər] s. espliego.

lavish ['læviʃ] a. pródigo. 2 t. prodigar.

law [lɔ:] s. ley, regla, precepto. 2 derecho, jurisprudencia.

lawful ['lɔ:ful] a. legal.

lawless ['lɔ:lis] a. sin ley. 2 ilegal, ilícito.

lawn [lɔ:n] s. césped, prado.

lawsuit ['lɔ:sju:t] s. pleito, litigio. 2 proceso.

lawyer ['lɔ:jər] s. letrado, abogado.

lax [læks] a. laxo.. 2 impreciso.

1) **lay** (lei) pret. de TO LIE.

2) **lay** [lei] a. seglar. 2 lego. 3 s. situación. 4 LIT. lay, balada.

3) **lay** [lei] *t.* tumbar, acostar, tender. 2' poner, dejar; colocar. 3 extender, aplicar. 4 exponer. 5 apostar. ¶ Pret. y p. p.: *laid* [leid].

lazy ['leizi] *a.* perezoso, holgazán.

1) **lead** [led] *s.* plomo. 2 *t.* emplomar.

2) **lead** [li:d] *s.* primacía, primer lugar. 2 dirección, mando, guía. 3 *t.* conducir, guiar; dirigir; impulsar. ¶ Pret. y p. p.: *led* [led]

leader ['li:dər] *s.* conductor, guía. 2 jefe, líder.

leadership ['li:dəʃip] *s.* dirección, jefatura.

leaf [li:f], *pl.* **leaves** [li:vz] hoja [de planta, libro, etc.].

league [li:g] *s.* liga, unión. 2 *t.-i.* unir(se, aliar(se.

leak [li:k] *s.* escape [de un fluido]. 2 *i.* tener escasez o pérdidas [un recipiente].

lean [li:n] *a.* delgado, flaco. 2 *t.-i.* unir(se. ¶ Pret. y p. p.: *leant* [lent] o *leaned* [li:nd].

leap [li:p] *s.* salto, brinco. 2 *i.* saltar, brincar. ¶ Pret. y p. p.: *leapt* [lept] o *leaped* [li:pt].

learn [lə:n] *t.-i.* aprender. ¶ Pret. y p. p.: *learned* [lə:nd] o *learnt* [lə:nt].

learned ['lə:nid] *a.* ilustrado, sabio, versado en.

learning ['lə:niŋ] *s.* instrucción.

learnt [lə:nt] V. TO LEARN.

lease [li:s] *t.* arrendar.

least [li:st] *a. superl.* de LITTLE. mínimo, menor.

leather ['leðər] *s.* cuero.

leave [li:v] *s.* permiso, licencia. 2 *t.* dejar. 3 *i.* partir. ¶ Pret. y p. p.: *left* [left].

lecture ['lektʃər] *s.* conferencia. 2 *i.* dar una conferencia.

lecturer ['lektʃərər] *s.* conferenciante; lector [Universidad].

led [led] V. TO LEAD.

ledge [ledʒ] *s.* repisa.

lees [li:z] *s. pl.* heces, poso.

left [left] V. TO LEAVE. 2 *a.* izquierdo. 3 *s.* izquierda.

leg [leg] *s.* pierna.

legal ['li:gəl] *s.* legal.

legend ['ledʒənd] *s.* leyenda.

legislation [ˌledʒisˈleiʃən] *s.* legislación.

legitimate [li'dʒitimit] *a.* legítimo. 2 [li'dʒitimeit] *t.* legitimar.

leisure ['leʒəʳ] *s.* ocio, tiempo libre.

leisurely ['leʒəli] *a.* lento. 2 *adv.* despacio.

lemon ['lemən] *s.* limón.

lemonade [,lemə'neid] *s.* limonada.

lend [lend] *t.* prestar. ¶ Pret. y p. p.: *lent* [lent].

length [leŋθ] *s.* longitud; extensión; duración.

lengthen ['leŋθən] *t.-i.* alargar(se; prolongar(se.

lent [lent] V. TO LEND.

less [les] *a.-adv.-prep.* menos.

lessen ['lesn] *t.-i.* disminuir.

lesser ['lesəʳ] *comp. de* LES menor.

lesson ['lesn] *s.* lección.

lest [lest] *conj.* no sea que, para que no.

let [let] *s.* estorbo, obstáculo. 2 *t.* arrendar, alquilar. 3 dejar, permitir. 4 AUX. ~ *us run,* corramos; ~ *him come,* que venga. ¶ Pret. y p. p.: *let* [let].

letter ['letəʳ] *s.* letra [del alfabeto, signo]. 2 letra [sentido literal]. 3 carta; documento.

lettuce ['letis] *s.* BOT. lechuga.

level ['levl] *a.* liso, llano, horizontal. 2 igual. 3 equilibrado. 4 juicioso. 5 *s.* nivel. 6 llano, llanura. 7 *t.* nivelar.

lever ['li:vəʳ] *s.* palanca.

levy ['levi] *s.* leva, recluta. 2 *t.* reclutar.

lewd [lu:d] *a.* lujurioso.

liability [,laiə'biliti] *s.* riesgo. 2 responsabilidad.

liable ['laiəbl] *a.* expuesto, sujeto, propenso.

liar ['laiəʳ] *s.* embustero.

liberal ['libərəl] *a.* liberal. 2 abundante.

liberate ['libəreit] *t.* libertar.

librarian [lai'brɛəriən] *s.* bibliotecario, -ria.

library ['laibrəri] *s.* biblioteca.

license, licence ['laisəns] *s.* licencia, libertinaje. 2 licencia [poética]. 3 licencia, permiso. 4 *t.* autorizar, dar permiso.

lick [lik] *s.* lamedura. 2 *t.* lamer.

lid [lid] *s.* tapa. 2 párpado.

1) **lie** [lai] *s.* mentira. 2 *i.* mentir. ¶ Pret. y p. p.:

lied [laid] ger.: *lying*
['laiiŋ].
2) lie [lai] *i.* tenderse;
apoyarse. 2 estar. 3 constituir. ¶ Pret.: *lay* [lei];
p. p.: *lain* [lein]; ger.:
lying ['laiiŋ].

lieutenant [lef'tenənt] *s.*
lugarteniente.

life [laif], *pl.* lives [laivz]
s. vida. 2 animación.

lift [lift] *s.* elevación, alzamiento. 2 (Ingl.) ascensor. 3 *t.-i.* alzar(se,
levantar(se.

light [lait] *s.* luz. 2 fuego, cerilla. 3 aspecto,
punto de vista. 4 *a.* de
luz. 5 blondo, rubio;
blanca [tez]. 6 leve. 7
adv. ligeramente; fácilmente. 8 *t.-i.* encender(se. 4 *a.* de
lighted ['laitid] o *lit*
[lit].

lighten ['laitn] *t.-i.* iluminar(se. 2 aclarar(se.
3 *i.* relampaguear. 4 *t.-i.*
aligerar(se. 5 alegrar(se.

lighter ['laitər] *s.* encendedor.

lighthouse ['laithaus] *s.*
MAR. faro, farola.

lighting ['laitiŋ] *s.* iluminación; alumbrado.

lightning ['laitniŋ] *s.* relámpago.

like [laik] *a.* igual, semejante, como. 2 *t.* querer,
gustarle a uno: *I like
him*, me gusta.

likely ['laikli] *a.* probable.

liken ['laikən] *t.* asemejar.

liking ['laikiŋ] *s.* inclinación. 2 preferencia.

limb [lim] *s.* miembro
[de hombre o animal].

lime [laim] *s.* cal.

limestone ['laimstəun] *s.*
piedra caliza.

limp [limp] *s.* cojera. 2 *i.*
cojear.

linden ['lindən] *s.* BOT.
tilo.

line [lain] *s.* cuerda, cabo, cordel. 2 línea. 3
conducción, tubería. 4
verso [línea]. 5 arruga
[en la cara]. 6 TEAT. papel. 7 *t.* linear, rayar. 8
arrugar [el rostro]. 9
alinearse.

lineage ['liniidʒ] *s.* linaje.

linen ['linin] *s.* lienzo,
lino.

liner ['lainər] *s.* vapor o
avión de línea.

linger ['liŋgər] *i.* demorar.

lining ['lainiŋ] *s.* forro.

link [liŋk] *s.* eslabón. 2 vínculo, enlace. 3 *t.-i.* eslabonar(se.

linoleum [li'nəuljəm] *s.* linóleo.

lion ['laiən] *s.* león.

lioness ['laiənis] *s.* leona.

lip [lip] *s.* labio. 2 pico.

lip-stick ['lip-stik] *s.* lápiz para labios.

liquid ['likwid] *a.-s.* líquido. 2 *a.* claro, cristalino.

lisp [lisp] *i.* cecear.

list [list] *s.* lista, catálogo. 2 *t.* poner en lista.

listen ['lisn] *i.* escuchar, oír, atender. | Gralte. con *to*.

listener ['lisnə'] *s.* oyente.

lit [lit] *pret.* y *p. p.* de TO LIGHT.

lithe [laið], **lithesome** [-səm] *a.* flexible, cimbreño, ágil.

litter ['litə'] *s.* litera. 2 camilla. 3 basura. 4 *t.* poner o dejar en desorden.

little ['litl] *a.* pequeño, chico, menudo. 2 *a.-adv.-s.* poco; un poco de; algo.

live [laiv] *a.* vivo. 2 [liv] *i.-t.* vivir.

lively [laivli] *a.* vivo, vivaz, vivaracho. 2 animado. 3 *adv.* vivamente.

liver ['livə'] *s.* hígado.

livery ['livəri] *s.* librea.

livestock ['laivstɔk] *s.* ganado, ganadería.

lizard ['lizəd] *s.* ZOOL. lagarto.

load [ləud] *s.* carga. 2 peso. 3 *t.* cargar.

loaf [ləuf] *s.* pan, hogaza. 2 *i.* holgazanear.

loan [ləun] *s.* préstamo. 2 *t.-i.* prestar.

loath [ləuθ] *a.* poco dispuesto.

loathe [ləuð] *t.* aborrecer, detestar.

lothsome ['ləuðsəm] *a.* aborrecible, odioso.

lobster ['lɔbstə'] *s.* ZOOL. langosta; bogavante.

lock [lɔk] *s.* rizo, bucle. 2 cerradura. 3 *t.* cerrar [con llave].

lockout ['lɔkaut] *s.* lockout [cierre de fábrica por los patronos].

locomotive ['ləukə,məutiv] *a.-s.* locomotora.

lodge [lɔdʒ] *s.* casita, pabellón. 2 *t.* alojar, hospedar.

lodging ['lɔdʒiŋ] *s.* alojamiento.

loft [lɔft] *s.* desván.

lofty ['lɔti] *a*. alto, elevado. 2 altanero.

log [lɔg] *s*. leño, tronco.

logic ['lɔdʒik] *s*. lógica.

logical ['lɔdʒikəl] *a*. lógico.

loiter ['lɔitər] *i*. holgazanear.

lone [loun] *a*. solo.

loneliness ['ləunlinis] *s*. soledad.

lonely ['ləunli] *a*. solo, solitario.

long [lɔŋ] *a*. largo. 2 *s*. longitud, largo. 3 *i*. [con *for, after* o *to*] ansiar, anhelar.

longing ['lɔŋiŋ] *s*. ansia. 2 *a*. ansioso.

look [luk] *s*. mirada. 2 semblante. 3 aspecto. 4 *i*. mirar; considerar. 5 *i*. parecer. 6 ~ *at*, mirar. 7 ~ *after*, cuidar de, 8 ~ *for*, buscar.

looking-glass ['lukiŋglɑːs] *s*. espejo.

lookout ['luk'aut] *s*. vigía. 2 atalaya, miradero. 3 *pl*. perspectivas.

loom [luːm] *s*. TEJ. telar. 2 *t.-i*. vislumbrarse, amenazar.

loop [luːp] *s*. curva. 2 lazo. 3 rizo. 4 *t*. doblar.

loose [luːs] *a*. suelto, flojo. 2 *t*. soltar, desatar, aflojar.

loosen ['luːsn] *t*. soltar, desatar.

lord [lɔːd] *s*. señor, dueño, amo. 2 lord [título].

lordship ['lɔːdʃip] *s*. señoría.

lorry ['lɔri] *s*. camión.

lose [luːz] *t*. perder. 2 *i*. perderse; extraviarse. ¶ Pret. y p. p.: *lost* [lɔst].

loss [lɔs] *s*. pérdida.

lost [lɔst] V. TO LOSE.

lot [lɔt] *s*. lote, parte. 2 solar. 3 suerte. 4 colección. 5 *a* ~ *of*, lots of, mucho(s.

loud [laud] *a*. fuerte [sonido]. 2 alta [voz]

loud-speaker ['laud'spiːkər] *s*. RADIO altavoz.

lounge [laundʒ] *s*. salón de descanso o tertulia. 2 *i*. pasear, pasar el rato.

louse [laus], *pl*. **lice** [lais] *s*. ENT. piojo.

love [lʌv] *s*. amor, cariño, afecto, afición. 2 *t*. amar, querer. 3 gustar de, tener afición a.

lovely ['lʌvli] *a*. amable, adorable, encantador.

lover ['lʌvər] *s*. enamorado; amante.

low [ləu] *a*. bajo. 2 pobre. 3 escaso, insuficiente. 4 débil, enfermo. 5 *adv*. bajo.

lower ['louǝ^r] *t.* bajar. 2 arriar. 3 *comp.* de LOW. 4 ['lauǝ^r] *i.* mirar ceñudo. 5 encapotarse [el cielo].

loyal ['lɔiǝl] *a.* leal, fiel.

luck [lʌk] *s.* suerte, fortuna.

luckless ['lɔklis] *a.* desafortunado.

lucky ['lʌki] *a.* afortunado.

luggage ['lʌgidʒ] *s.* equipaje [de viajero].

lull [lʌl] *s.* momento de calma. 2 *t.-i.* calmar(se.

lumber ['lʌmbǝ^r] *s.* madera.

lump [lʌmp] *s.* pedazo, terrón.

lunch [lʌntʃ], **luncheon** [-ǝn] *s.* almuerzo. 2 *i.* almorzar.

lung [lʌŋ] *s.* pulmón.

lure [ljuǝ^r] *s.* señuelo, reclamo. 2 *t.* atraer.

lurk [lǝ:k] *i.* acechar.

lush [lʌʃ] *a.* lujuriante.

lust [lʌst] *s.* avidez. 2 lujuria. 3 *t.* codiciar [con lujuria].

lustre ['lʌstǝ^r] *s.* lustre, brillo.

lustrous ['lʌstrɔs] *a.* lustroso.

lusty ['lʌsti] *a.* lozano, fuerte.

luxuriant [lʌg'zjuǝriǝnt] *a.* lujuriante, exuberante.

luxury ['lʌkʃǝri] *s.* lujo, fausto.

lying ['laiiŋ] *ger.* de TO LIE. 2 *a.* mentiroso. 3 tendido, echado. 4 situado.

M

machine [mə'ʃi:n] s. máquina. 2 bicicleta, automóvil, etc.

machinery [mə'ʃi:nəri] s. maquinaria.

mad [mæd] a. loco.

madam ['mædəm, mæ-'dɑ:m] s. señora [tratamiento de respeto].

madden ['mædn] t.-i. enloquecer.

made [meid] V. TO MAKE.

magazine [ˌmægə'zi:n] s. almacén, depósito. 2 revista [periódico].

magic ['mædʒik] s. magia. 2 a. mágico.

magistrate ['mædʒistreit] s. magistrado.

maid [meid] s. doncella, criada, camarera.

maiden ['meidn] s. doncella, joven soltera.

mail [meil] s. malla. 2

correo, correspondencia. 3 t. echar al correo, enviar por correo.

main [mein] a. primero; principal. 2 s. cañería principal.

maintain [me(i)n'tein] t. mantener, sostener.

maize [meiz] s. BOT. maíz.

majestic [mə'dʒestik] a. majestuoso.

majesty ['mædʒisti] s. majestad.

major ['meidʒəʳ] a. mayor, principal. 2 s. DER. mayor de edad.

majority [mə'dʒɔriti] s. mayoría. 2 mayor edad.

make [meik] s. hechura, forma. 2 obra, fabricación. 3 t. hacer [crear, elaborar, fabricar; formar; causar, producir; preparar; efectuar, etc.].

¶ Pret. y p. p.: *made* [meid].

male [meil] *a.* macho. 2 masculino. 3 *s.* varón.

malice ['mælis] *s.* malicia.

man [mæn), *pl.* **men** [men] *s.* hombre.

manacles ['mænəklz] *s. pl.* manillas, esposas.

manage ['mænidʒ] *t.* manejar. 2 dirigir, regir.

management ['mænidʒmənt] *s.* manejo, gobierno, administración; cuidado.

manager ['mænidʒəʳ] *s.* director.

mane [mein] *s.* crin, melena.

manger ['meindʒəʳ] *s.* pesebre.

mangle ['mæŋgl] *s.* máquina para exprimir ropa. 2 *t.* destrozar, mutilar.

manhood ['mænhud] *s.* virilidad, valor. 2 los hombres.

manifest ['mænifest] *a.* manifiesto, patente. 2 *t.-i.* manifestar(se.

mankind [mæn'kaind] *s.* género humano. 2 los hombres.

manly ['mænli] *a.* varonil, viril.

manner ['mænəʳ] *s.* manera, modo.

manufacture [ˌmænju'fæktʃəʳ] *s.* manufactura. 2 *t.* manufacturar.

manufacturer [ˌmænju'fæktʃərəʳ] *s.* fabricante.

many ['meni] *a.-pron.* muchos, -chas.

map [mæp] *s.* mapa, carta.

mar [maːʳ] *t.* estropear.

marble ['maːbl] *s.* mármol.

March [maːtʃ] *s.* marzo [mes].

march [maːtʃ] *s.* marcha. 2 *i.* marchar, andar.

margin ['maːdʒin] *s.* margen.

mariner ['mærinəʳ] *s.* marinero.

mark [maːk] *s.* marca, señal. 2 mancha. 3 huella. 4 signo, indicio. 5 rótulo. 6 importancia, distinción. 7 punto, nota, calificación. 8 blanco, hito, fin, propósito. 9 marco [moneda]. 10 *t.* marcar, señalar. 11 indicar. 12 delimitar. 13 notar, observar, advertir. 14 puntuar, calificar.

market ['maːkit] *s.* mercado, bolsa.

marquis, -quess ['mɑ:k-wis] s. marqués.
marriage ['mæridʒ] s. matrimonio.
married ['mærid] a. casado.
marry ['mæri] t. casar, desposar. 2 i. casarse con.
marshy ['mɑ:ʃi] a. pantanoso.
marvel ['mɑ:vəl] s. maravilla. 2 i. maravillarse.
marvellous ['mɑ:vələs] a. maravilloso, prodigioso.
mask [mɑ:sk] s. máscara. 2 i. ponerse careta. 3 disfrazarse.
mason ['meisn] s. albañil. 2 masón.
mass [mæs] s. masa, bulto, mole. 2 misa.
massive ['mæsiv] a. macizo, masivo.
mast [mɑ:st] s. MAR. mástil, palo. 2 asta.
master ['mɑ:stər] s. amo, patrón, dueño. 2 señor, señorito [dicho por un criado]. 3 t. dominar, vencer, subyugar.
masterful ['mɑ:stəful] a. dominante, autoritario. 2 hábil.
masterly ['mɑ:stəli] a. magistral.
masterpiece ['mɑ:təpi:s] s. obra maestra.

mastery ['mɑ:stəri] s. dominio, autoridad.
match [mætʃ] s. fósforo, cerilla. 2 pareja, igual. 3 contrincante temible. 4 juego [de dos cosas]. 5 DEP. lucha, partida, partido. 6 casamiento, partido. 7 t. casar, hermanar. 8 oponer, equiparar. 9 igualar a.
mate [meit] s. compañero, -ra. 2 consorte, cónyuge. 3 t. casar, desposar.
material [mə'tiəriəl] a. material. 2 físico, corpóreo. 3 importante, esencial. 4 s. material, materia. 5 tela, género.
mathematics [ˌmæθi'mætiks] s. matemáticas.
matter ['mætər] s. materia. 2 cosa. 3 importancia. 4 *what is the ~?*, ¿qué ocurre? 5 i. importar.
mattress ['mætris] s. colchón.
mature [mə'tjuər] a. maduro. 2 t.-i. madurar.
May [mei] s. mayo [mes].
may [mei] v. aux. poder [tener facultad, libertad, oportunidad o permiso ser posible o contingente]. ¶ Pret.: *might*

[mait]. | Sólo tiene pres. y pret.

maybe ['meibi:] *adv.* acaso.

mayor [mɛɔʳ] *s.* alcalde.

me [mi:, mi] *pron. pers.* me, mi: *with me*, conmigo.

meadow ['medəu] *s.* prado.

meal [mi:l] *s.* comida. 2 harina [de maíz, etc.].

mean [mi:n] *s.* bajo, humilde. 2 ruin, bajo, vil. 3 mezquino, tacaño. 4 (E. U.) avergonzado. 5 medio, mediano, intermedio. 6 *s.* medio [término medio]. 7 *pl.* medio, medios. 8 *t.* significar, querer decir. 9 decir en serio. 10 pretender. 11 destinar. ¶ Pret. y p. p.: *meant* [ment].

meaning ['mi:niŋ] *s.* significación, sentido, acepción. 2 intención.

meantime ['mi:n'taim], **meanwhile** [-'wail] *adv.* entretanto.

measure ['meʒəʳ] *s.* medida. 2 cantidad, grado, extensión. 3 ritmo. 4 *t.-i.* medir.

meat [mi:t] *s.* carne [como alimento]. 2 vianda, comida.

mechanics [mi'kæniks] *s.* mecánica [ciencia].

mechanism ['mekənizəm] *s.* mecanismo. 2 mecanicismo.

medal ['medl] *s.* medalla.

meddle ['medl] *i.* entrometerse, meterse [en].

medicine ['medsin] *s.* medicina [medicamento]; ciencia].

meet [mi:t] *t.* encontrar, hallar, topar con; enfrentarse con. 2 conocer, ser presentado a. 3 reunirse, entrevistarse con. 4 hacer frente a [gastos, etc.]. ¶ Pret. y p. p.: *met* [met].

meeting ['mi:tiŋ] *s.* reunión, junta, sesión. 2 asamblea, mitin.

mellow ['melou] *a.* maduro, sazonado [fruto]. 2 tierno, blando. 3 suave [vino]. 4 lleno, puro, suave [voz, sonido, color, luz]. 5 *t.-i.* madurar.

melody ['melədi] *s.* melodía, aire.

melt [melt] *t.-i.* fundir(se, derretir(se.

member ['membəʳ] *s.* miembro.

memorial [mi'mɔ:riəl] *a.* conmemorativo. 2 *s.* monumento conmemorativo. 3 memorial, petición. 4 nota, apunte.

men [men] *s. pl.* de MAN.

menace ['menəs] *s.* amenaza. 2 *t.-i.* amenazar.

mend [mend] *t.* componer, reparar. 2 *i.* corregirse, enmendarse.

merchandise ['mə:tʃəndaiz] *s.* mercancía, géneros.

mercy ['mə:si] *s.* misericordia, clemencia, compasión. 2 merced, gracia.

mere [miər] *a.* mero, solo.

merge [mə:dʒ] *t.-i.* unirse, combinar(se, fusionar(se.

merit ['merit] *s.* mérito. 2 *t.* merecer.

merriment ['merimənt] *s.* alegría.

merry ['meri] *a.* alegre

mesh [meʃ] *s.* malla [de red].

mess [mes] *s.* enredo, lío; asco, suciedad. 2 *t.* enredar, ensuciar.

message ['mesidʒ] *s.* mensaje.

messenger ['mesindʒər] *s.* mensajero.

met [met] V. TO MEET.

method ['meθəd] *s.* método.

metre (E.U.) **meter** ['mi:-tər] *s.* metro.

mice V. MOUSE.

mid [mid] *a.* medio.

middle ['midl] *a.* medio, de en medio, mediano, intermedio. 2 *s.* medio, mediados, mitad, centro.

midnight ['midnait] *s.* medianoche.

midst [midst] *s.* centro, medio.

midsummer ['mid͵sʌmər] *s.* canícula.

might [mait] *pret.* de MAY. 2 *s.* poderío, fuerza.

mighty ['maiti] *a.* poderoso. 2 vigoroso, potente. 3 importante.

mild [maild] *a.* apacible, blando. 2 manso, dócil. 3 leve, moderado, templado. 4 dúctil.

mile [mail] *s.* milla.

milk [milk] *s.* leche. 2 *t.* ordeñar.

mill [mil] *s.* molino. 2 fábrica. 2 *t.* moler, triturar.

mind [maind] *s.* mente, espíritu, entendimiento, juicio; ánimo. 2 mentalidad. 3 intención, propósito, deseo. 4 pensamiento, mientes, memoria, recuerdo. 5 opinión, parecer. 6 *t.* tener en cuenta; hacer caso de. 7

tener inconveniente en; molestarle una [una cosa]. *8* cuidar de, atender, ocuparse de. *9* tener cuidado con. *10* recordar, acordarse de. *11* i. *never* ~, no importa, no se preocupe.

mine [main] *pron. pos.* mío, -a; míos, -as. *2 s.* MIN., FORT., MIL. mina. *3 t.* minar. *4* extraer [mineral].

miner ['mainə'] *s.* minero.

mineral ['minərəl] *a.-s.* mineral.

mingle ['mingl] *t.-i.* mezclar(se, juntar(se.

minister ['ministə'] *s.* ministro. *2 t.* dar, suministrar. *3 i.* oficiar. *4* asistir, auxiliar.

ministry ['ministri] *s.* ministerio. *2* clero.

minor ['mainə'] *a.-s.* menor.

mint [mint] *s.* casa de moneda. *2* BOT. menta. *3 t.* acuñar.

minute [mai'nju:t] *a.* diminuto. *2* minucioso. *3* ['minit] *s.* minuto. *4* minuta.

miracle ['mirəkl] *s.* milagro.

miraculous [mi'rækjuləs]

a. milagroso. *2* maravilloso.

mirror ['mirə'] *s.* espejo. *2 t.-i.* reflejar(se.

mirth [mə:θ] *s.* alegría.

mischief ['mis-tʃif] *s.* mal, daño.

mischievous ['mis-tʃivəs] *a.* malo, dañino.

miser ['maizə'] *a.-s.* misero.

miserable ['mizərəbl] *a.* desdichado; abatido.

miserly ['maizəli] *a.* avaro, tacaño.

misery ['mizəri] *s.* miseria. *2* desdicha, infelicidad.

misfortune [mis'fɔ:tʃən] *s.* infortunio, desdicha.

Miss [mis] *s.* señorita [antepuesto al nombre].

miss [mis] *s.* errada; fracaso. *2 t.* errar. *3* perder [un tren, la ocasión, etc.]. *4* echar de menos.

missing ['misiŋ] *a.* extraviado, perdido.

mission ['miʃən] *s.* misión.

mist [mist] *s.* niebla, vapor.

mistake [mis'teik] *s.* equivocacón, error, confusión. *2 t.* equivocar; confundir. ¶ Pret.: *mistook;* p. p.: ~ *taken.*

mistaken [mis'teikən] _p._
_p._ de TO MISTAKE.
mistress ['mistris] _s._
ama, dueña, señora. 2
maestra. 3 amante.
misty ['misti] _a._ brumoso.
misunderstand ['misʌndə-
'stænd] _t._ entender mal.
mitten ['mitn] _s._ mitón.
mix [miks] _s._ mezcla. 2
_t.-i._ mezclar(se.
mixture ['mikstʃəʳ] _s._
mezcla.
moan [moun] _s._ gemido,
quejido. 2 _i._ gemir, quejarse.
mob [mɔb] _s._ populacho.
2 _t._ atacar en tumulto.
mock [mɔk] _a._ ficticio. 2
burlesco. 3 _s._ burla 4 _t._
mofarse de.
model ['mɔdl] _s._ modelo.
2 _t._ modelar, moldear.
moderate ['mɔdərit] _a._
moderado; templado. 2
['mɔdəreit] _t.-i._ mode-
rar(se, templar(se.
modern ['mɔdən] _a._ moderno.
modest ['mɔdist] _a._ modesto.
modify ['mɔdifai] _t._ modificar. 2 moderar.
moist [mɔist] _a._ húmedo.
moisten ['mɔisn] _t.-i._ hu-
medecer(se, mojar(se.

mole [moul] _s._ lunar. 2
rompeolas; muelle.
moment ['moumənt] _s._
momento, instante. 2
importancia.
momentum [mou'men-
təm] _s._ ímpetu, impulso.
monarch ['mɔnək] _s._ monarca.
Monday ['mʌndi, -dei] _s._
lunes.
money ['mʌni] _s._ moneda, dinero.
mongrel ['mʌŋgrəl] _a.-s._
mestizo, cruzado.
monk [mʌŋk] _s._ monje,
fraile.
monkey ['mʌŋki] _s._ ZOOL.
mono.
monkish ['mʌŋkiʃ] _a._
monacal.
monotony [mə'nɔtəni] _s._
monotonía.
monster ['mɔnstəʳ] _s._
monstruo.
month [mʌnθ] _s._ mes.
monument ['mɔnjumənt]
_s._ monumento.
mood [mu:d] _s._ genio,
talante. 2 humor, dispo-
sición.
moody ['mu:di] _a._ mal-
humorado, triste, cavilo-
so.
moon [mu:n] _s._ ASTR. luna.
Moor [muəʳ] _s._ moro, sa-
rraceno.

mop [mɔp] *s.* bayeta. 2 greña. 3 *t.* limpiar al suelo, fregar.

moral ['mɔrəl] *a.* moral. 2 *s.* moraleja. 3 *pl.* moral, ética.

more [mɔːʳ, mɔəʳ] *a.- adv.* más: *the ~ the merrier*, cuantos más mejor.

moreover [mɔ:'rəuvəʳ] *adv.* además, por otra parte.

morning ['mɔ:niŋ] *s.* [la] mañana. 2 *a.* matinal, matutino.

morrow ['mɔrəu] *s.* mañana, día siguiente.

morsel ['mɔ:səl] *s.* bocado.

mortar ['mɔ:təʳ] *s.* mortero.

mortgage ['mɔ:gidʒ] *s.* hipoteca. 2 *t.* hipotecar.

moss [mɔs] *s.* BOT. musgo; moho.

most [məust] *adj. superl.* de MORE, MUCH y MANY. 2 muchos, los más, la mayoría de. 3 *adv.* sumamente, muy; más. 4 *s.* lo más, lo sumo.

moth [mɔθ] *s.* ENT. polilla.

mother ['mʌðəʳ] *s.* madre.

motion ['məuʃən] *s.* movimiento. 2 seña. 3 *pl.* cine. 4 *i.-t.* hacer seña o ademán [a uno].

motionless ['məuʃenlis] *a.* inmóvil.

motive ['məutiv] *s.* motivo. 2 *a.* motor, motriz.

motor ['məutəʳ] *s.* motor. 2 *a.* motor, motriz.

mound [maund] *s.* montículo. 2 montón.

mount [maunt] *s.* monte. 2 montura, cabalgadura. 3 *t.-i.* subir. 4 montar(se en o sobre.

mountain ['mauntin] *s.* montaña.

mountaineer [‚maunti-'niəʳ] *s.* montañés. 2 alpinista.

mountainous ['mauntinəs] *a.* montañoso, montuoso.

mourn [mɔ:n] *t.-i.* lamentar(se, llorar.

mouse [maus], *pl.* **mice** [mais] *s.* ZOOL. ratón.

mouth [mauθ, *pl.* mauðz] *s.* boca.

move [mu:v] *s.* movimiento. 2 jugada. 3 *t.* mover. 4 conmover, enternecer. 5 jugar. 6 *i.* moverse, andar. 7 irse.

movie [mu:vi] *s.* película [de cine]. 2 *pl. the movies*, el cine.

much [mʌtʃ] *a.* mucho, -cha. 2 *adv.* muy, mucho.

mud [mʌd] *s.* barro, lodo.

muddy ['mʌdi] *a.* barroso, fangoso.

muffle ['mʌfl] *t.* envolver. 2 amortiguar.

mule [mjuːl] *s.* ZOOL. mulo.

multiply ['mʌltiplai] *t.-i.* multiplicar(se.

multitude ['mʌltitjuːd] *s.* multitud, muchedumbre.

munch [mʌntʃ] *t.* mascar.

murder ['məːdər] *s.* asesinato. 2 *t.* asesinar, matar.

murderer ['məːdərər] *s.* asesino.

murderous ['məːdərəs] *a.* asesino, homicida. 2 cruel.

murmur ['məːmər] *s.* murmullo.

murmur ['məːmər] *i.-t.* murmurar. 2 *i.* quejarse.

muscle ['mʌsl] *s.* ANAT. músculo.

muse [mjuːz] *i.* meditar. 2ª *s.* musa.

museum [mjuː(ː)'ziəm] *s.* museo.

mushroom ['mʌʃrum] *s.* BOT. seta, champiñón.

music ['mjuːzik] *s.* música.

musician [mjuː(ː)'ziʃən] *s.* músico.

must [mʌst, məst] *aux. defect.* [usado sólo en el presente] deber, haber de, tener que. 2 deber de. 3 ser necesario.

mutiny ['mjuːtini] *s.* motín. 2 *i.* amotinarse.

mutter ['mʌtər] *s.* murmullo. 2 *t.-i.* murmurar, refunfuñar.

mutton ['mʌtn] *s.* carnero, carne de carnero.

mutual ['mjuːtʃuəl] *a.* mutuo.

my [may] *a. pos.* mi, mis. 2 *interj.* oh, my!, ¡carampa!

myself [mai'self] *pron.* yo, yo mismo; a mí, a mí mismo, me.

N

nail [neil] *s.* ANAT., ZOOL. uña. 2 clavo. 3 *t.* clavar; fijar.

naked ['neikid] *a.* desnudo.

name [neim] *s.* nombre. 2 *t.* llamar. 3 nombrar.

nameless ['neimlis] *a.* anónimo. 2 innominado. 3 humilde.

namely ['neimli] *adv.* a saber.

nap [næp] *s.* siesta, sueñecito. 2 *i.* dormitar.

napkin ['næpkin] *s.* servilleta.

narrative ['nærətiv] *a.* narrativo. 2 *s.* narración, relato.

narrow ['nærəu] *a.* estrecho. 2 escaso. 3 mezquino. 4 *t.-i.* estrechar(se, angostar(se.

nation ['neiʃən] *s.* nación.

native ['neitiv] *a.* nativo [metal]. 2 natal.

nature ['neitʃə] *s.* naturaleza. 2 carácter. 3 natural, índole, genio.

naught [nɔ:t] *s.* cero. 2 nada.

naughty ['nɔ:ti] *a.* travieso.

naval ['neivəl] *a.* naval.

navigation [,nævi'geiʃən] *s.* navegación.

navy ['neivi] *s.* armada, flota.

near [niə'] *a.* cercano, próximo. 2 *adv.* cerca. 3 *t.-i.* acercar(se.

nearby ['niəbai] *a.* cercano. 2 *adv.* cerca.

nearly ['niəli] *adv.* cerca. 2 casi.

neat [ni:t] *a.* pulcro, ordenado.

necessary ['nesisəri] *a.* necesario.

necessity [ni'sesiti] *s.* necesidad.

neck [nek] *s.* cuello, garganta.

necklace ['neklis] *s.* collar.

need [ni:d] *s.* necesidad. 2 *t.* necesitar.

needful ['ni:dful] *a.* necesario.

needless ['ni:dlis] *a.* innecesario.

neglect [ni'glekt] *s.* abandono. 2 *t.* abandonar, descuidar.

negro ['ni:grəu] *a.-s.* negro [pers.].

neighbo(u)r ['neibə'] *s.* vecino.

neighbo(u)rhood ['neibəhud] *s.* vecindad 2 cercanías.

neighbo(u)ring ['neibəriŋ] *a.* vecino, adyacente.

neither ['naiðə', 'ni:ðə'] *a.* ninguno [de los dos], ningún, -na. 2 *conj.* ni. 3 *adv.* tampoco, ni siquiera. 4 *pron.* ninguno, ni el uno ni el otro.

nephew ['nevju(:)] *s.* sobrino.

nerve [nə:v] *s.* ANAT., BOT. nervio. 2 valor. 3 descaro.

nervous ['nə:vəs] *a.* nervioso. 2 vigoroso. 3 timido.

nest [nest] *s.* nido. 2 *i.* anidar. 3 buscar nidos.

net [net] *s.* red. 2 malla. 3 *a.* COM. neto.

never ['nevə'] *adv.* nunca, jamás.

nevertheless [,nevəðə'les] *adv. conj.* no obstante, sin embargo.

news [nju:z] *s.* noticia, noticias. 2 prensa, periódicos.

newspaper ['nju:s,peipə'] *s.* diario, periódico.

next [nekst] *a.* próximo, inmediato, contiguo. 2 *adv.* luego, después, a continuación. 3 *prep.* al lado de. 4 después de.

nice [nais] *s.* bueno, agradable. 2 lindo. 3 elegante. 4 exacto, preciso.

nickel ['nikl] *s.* QUÍM. niquel. 2 fam. (E. U.) moneda de cinco centavos.

nickname ['nikneim] *s.* apodo.

niece [ni:s] *s. f.* sobrina.

night [nait] *s.* noche. 2 *a.* nocturno.

nightingale ['naitiŋgeil] *s.* ORN. ruiseñor.

nine [nain] *a.-s.* nueve.

nineteen ['nain'ti:n] *a.-s.* diecinueve. 2 **-th** [-θ] decimonono.

ninetieth ['naintiiθ] *a.-s.* nonagésimo.

ninety ['nainti] *a.-s.* noventa.

ninth [nainθ] *a.* nono, noveno.

nit [nit] *s.* liendre.

no [nəu] *adv.* no. 2 *a.* ningún, ninguno: ~ *one*, ninguno, nadie.

nobility [nəu'biliti] *s.* nobleza.

noble ['nəubl] *a.-s.* noble.

nobody ['nəubədi] *pron.* nadie, ninguno.

nod [nɔd] *s.* inclinación de cabeza. 2 cabezada. 3 *i.-t.* inclinar la cabeza [para asentir o saludar]. 4 dormitar.

noise [nɔiz] *s.* ruido, sonido. 2 *t.* divulgar, rumorear.

noisome ['nɔisəm] *a.* nocivo, asqueroso.

noisy ['nɔizi] *a.* ruidoso.

nominate ['nɔmineit] *t.* nombrar. 2 proponer.

none [nʌn] *pron.* ninguno nada. 2 nadie. 3 *adv.* no, en ningún modo: ~

the less, no obstante, sin embargo.

nonsense ['nɔnsəns] *s.* disparate, tonterías.

noon [nu:n] *s.* mediodía.

nor [nɔ:'] *conj.* ni. 2 tampoco.

north [nɔ:θ] *s.* norte. 2 *a.* del norte, septentrional.

northern ['nɔ:ðən] *a.* del norte, septentrional.

nose [nəuz] *s.* ANAT., ZOOL. nariz. 2 *t.* oler, olfatear.

nostril ['nɔstril] *s.* ventana de la nariz. 2 ollar.

not [nɔt] *adv.* no.

notable ['nəutəbl] *a.* notable.

notch [nɔtʃ] *s.* muesca. 2 *t.* hacer muescas en. 3 mellar, dentar.

note [nəut] *s.* nota, señal. 2 *t.* notar, observar.

nothing ['nʌθiŋ] *s.* nada. 2 ARIT. cero.

notice ['nəutis] *s.* informe, aviso, advertencia. 2 despido. 3 *t.* notar, observar.

noticeable ['nəutisəbl] *a.* notable.

notion ['nəuʃən] *s.* noción. 2 idea, concepto. 3 *pl.* (E. U.) mercería.

notorious [nəu'tɔ:riəs]

a. notorio, conocido, famoso. | Ús. gralte. en sentido peyorativo.

notwithstanding [ˌnɔtwiθ-ˈstændiŋ] *adv.* no obstante. *2 prep.* a pesar de *3 conj.* aunque, por más que.

nought [nɔ:t] *s.* NAUGHT.

noun [naun] *s.* GRAM. nombre.

nourish [ˈnʌriʃ] *t.* nutrir, alimentar, sustentar.

novelty [ˈnɔvəlti] *s.* novedad.

November [nəuˈvembəʳ] *s.* noviembre.

now [nau] *adv.* ahora; hoy día; actualmente.: ~ *and then*, de vez en cuando.

nowadays [ˈnauədeiz] *adv.* hoy día, hoy en día.

nowhere [ˈnəu(h)wɛəʳ] *adv.* en ninguna parte.

nucleus [ˈnju:kliəs] *s.* núcleo.

nuisance [ˈnju:sns] *s.* fastidio. *2 pers.* o cosa molesta, fastidiosa.

number [ˈnʌmbəʳ] *s.* número. *2 t.* numerar. *3* contar.

numerous [ˈnju:mərəs] *a.* numeroso. *2* muchos.

nurse [nə:s] *s.* ama, niñera. *2* enfermera. *3 t.* criar. *4* cuidar.

nursery [ˈnə:sri] *s.* cuarto de los niños: ~ *rhymes*, cuentos en verso. *2* criadero, vivero.

nut [nʌt] *s.* BOT. nuez.

nymph [nimf] *s.* ninfa.

O

oak [əuk] s. roble.

oar [ɔ:ʳ, əəʳ] s. remo.

oat [əut] s. BOT. avena.

oath [əuθ] s. juramento, jura. 2 blasfemia.

obedience [ə'bi:djəns] s. obediencia.

obey [ə'bei] t.-i. obedecer.

object ['ɔbdʒikt] s. objeto. 2 [əb'dʒekt] t. objetar.

objection [əb'dʒekʃən] s. objeción, reparo, inconveniente.

obligation [ˌɔbli'geiʃən] s. obligación, deber.

oblige [ə'blaidʒ] t. obligar. 2 complacer.

obscure [əbs'kjuəʳ] a. oscuro. 2 t. oscurecer. 3 ocultar.

observation [ˌɔbzə(:)-'veiʃən] s. observación.

observe [əb'zə:v] t. observar. 2 guardar [una fiesta].

obsolete ['ɔbsəli:t] a. anticuado.

obtain [əb'tein] t. obtener.

obvious ['ɔbviəs] a. obvio, evidente, palmario.

occasion [ə'keiʒən] s. ocasión, oportunidad, caso, circunstancia. 2 t. ocasionar, causar.

occasional [ə'keiʒənl] a. ocasional, casual.

occupy ['ɔkjupai] t. ocupar, habitar. 2 emplear, invertir.

occur [ə'kə:ʳ] i. hallarse. 2 ocurrir, suceder.

ocean ['əuʃən] s. océano.

October [ɔk'təubəʳ] s. octubre.

odd [ɔd] *a.* impar, non. 2 ocasional. 3 y tantos; y pico. *4* raro, extraño.

odo(u)r [ˈoudəʳ] *s.* olor.

of [ɔv, əv] *prep.* En muchos casos se traduce por *de*; en otros, por *a, en, con, por,* etc.

off [ɔːf, ɔf] *adv.* lejos, fuera; enteramente, del todo; indica alejamiento, ausencia, separación, disminución, privación, cesación. 2 *prep.* lejos de 3 *a.* alejado, ausente. *4* FÚTBOL ~ *side,* fuera de juego.

offence [əˈfens] *s.* ofensa, agravio.

offer [ˈɔfəʳ] *s.* oferta. 2 *t.-i.* ofrecer(se.

office [ˈɔfis] *s.* oficio, función. 2 cargo. 3 oficina, despacho.

officer [ˈɔfisəʳ] *s.* MIL., MAR. oficial. 2 funcionario.

official [əˈfiʃəl] *a.* oficial. 2 *s.* funcionario.

oft [ɔ(ː)ft], **often** [ˈɔ(ː)fn] *adv.* a menudo, frecuentemente.

oil [ɔil] *s.* aceite; óleo. 2 petróleo.

old [əuld] *a.* viejo; anciano.

old-fashioned [ˈəuldˈfæ-**

ʃənd] *a.* anticuado; pasado de moda.

olive [ˈɔliv] *s.* BOT. olivo. 2 aceituna, oliva.

omelet, omelette [ˈɔmlit] *s.* tortilla de huevos.

omit [əˈmit] *t.* omitir.

on [ɔn, ɔn] *prep.* en, sobre; a; de; con; por; bajo; ~ *foot,* a pie; ~ *arriving,* al llegar; ~ *duty,* de servicio. 2 adelante, continuando. 3 *a.* abierto, encendido.

once [wʌns] *adv.-s.* vez, una vez: *at* ~, a la vez; en seguida; ~ *upon a time there was,* érase una vez.

one [wʌn] *a.* uno, una. 2 *pron.* uno, una: ~ *another,* el uno al otro.

onion [ˈʌnjən] *s.* BOT. cebolla.

only [ˈəunli] *s.* solo, único. 2 *adv.* solo, solamente. 3 *if* ~, ojalá, si, si al menos. *4 conj.* sólo que, pero.

onto [ˈɔntu, -te] *prep.* hacia, sobre.

onward(s [ˈɔnwəd(z] *adv.* hacia adelante.

open [ˈəupən] *a.* abierto: *in the open air,* al aire libre. 2 *t.* abrir. 3 iniciar, empezar.

opening ['əupəniŋ] *s.* apertura. 2 abertura, entrada. 3 TEAT. estreno.

operate ['opəreit] *t.* hacer funcionar, mover. 2 *i.* obrar, producir efecto.

opinion [ə'pinjən] *s.* opinión, buen concepto.

oppose [ə'pəuz] *t.* oponer.

opposite ['opəzit] *a.* opuesto. 2 *prep.* enfrente de. 3 *adv.* enfrente.

oppress [ə'pres] *t.* oprimir.

oppression [ə'preʃən] *s.* opresión.

optimistic [,opti'mistik] *a.* optimista.

or [ɔ:ʳ] *conj.* o, u.

oral ['ɔ:rəl] *a.* oral.

orange ['orindʒ] *s.* BOT. naranja: ~ **blossom**, azahar.

orb [ɔ:b] *s.* orbe, esfera.

orbit ['ɔ:bit] *s.* ASTR. órbita.

orchard ['ɔ:tʃəd] *s.* huerto.

orchestra ['ɔ:kistrə] *s.* orquesta. 2 TEAT. platea.

ordain [ɔ:'dein] *t.* ordenar.

order ['ɔ:dəʳ] *s.* orden: *in ~ to*, para, a fin de. 2 COM. pedido. 3 *t.* orde-

nar. 4 COM. hacer un pedido.

orderly ['ɔ:dəli] *a.* ordenado.

ordinary ['ɔ:din(ə)ri] *a.-s.* ordinario, corriente.

ore [ɔ:ʳ, ɔəʳ] *s.* MIN. mineral, ganga, mena.

organ ['ɔ:gən] *s.* órgano.

organization [,ɔ:gənai'zeiʃən] *s.* organización.

organize ['ɔ:gənaiz] *t.-i.* organizar(se.

origin ['oridʒin] *s.* origen.

original [ə'ridʒənl] *a.* original.

ornament ['ɔ:nəmənt] *s.* ornamento. 2 [-ment] *t.* ornamentar.

orphan [,ɔ:fən] *a.-s.* huérfano.

other ['ʌðəʳ] *a.-pron.* otro, otra, otras, otras: *every ~ day*, días alternos.

otherwise ['ʌðə-waiz] *adv.* de otra manera.

otter ['ɔtəʳ] *s.* ZOOL. nutria.

2) **ought** [ɔ:t] *def.* y *aux.* [seguido de infinitivo con *to*] deber [en presente o mejor condicional].

ounce [auns] *s.* onza [28.35 gr.].

our ['auə^r] *a.* nuestro, -a, -os, -as.

ours ['auəz] *pron. pos.* [el, lo] nuestro, [la] nuestra, [los] nuestros, [las] nuestras.

ourselves [,auə'selvz] *pron.* nosotros mismos. 2 nos, a nosotros mismos.

out [aut] *adv.* fuera, afuera, hacia fuera. 2 claro, sin rodeos. 3 *a.* ausente, fuera de casa.

outbreak ['autbreik] *s.* erupción.

outdoor ['aut'dɔ:] *a.* al aire libre. 2 **-s** [-z] *adv.* fuera de casa, al aire libre.

outer ['autə^r] *a.* exterior.

outfit ['autfit] *s.* equipo. 2 *t.* equipar.

outlet ['aut-let] *s.* salida.

outline ['aut-lain] *s.* contorno, perfil. 2 bosquejo, esbozo.

output ['autput] *s.* producción; rendimiento.

outrage ['aut-reidʒ] *s.* ultraje. 2 *t.* ultrajar, atropellar.

outrageous [aut'reidʒəs] *a.* ultrajante. 3 violento.

outside ['aut'said] *s.-adj.*

exterior. 2 *adv.* fuera, afuera, por fuera. 3 *prep.* fuera de, más allá; excepto.

outstanding [aut'stændiŋ] *a.* saledizo, saliente. 2 destacado.

outstretch [aut'stretʃ] *t.* extender, alargar.

outward ['autwed] *a.* exterior. 2 **-s** [-z] *adv.* hacia fuera.

oval ['əuvəl] *a.* oval, ovalado.

oven ['ʌvn] *s.* horno, hornillo.

over ['əuvə^r] *adv.* arriba, por encima. 2 al otro lado. 3 completamente. 4 más o de más. 5 *prep.* sobre, encima de. 6 al lado o a la vuelta de. 7 más de. 8 durante. 9 *a.* superior, más alto. 10 acabado.

overcoat ['əuvəkəut] *s.* sobretodo, gabán, abrigo.

overcome [,əuvə'kʌm] *t.* vencer, triunfar.

overflow ['əuvə-fləu] *s.* inundación. 2 [,əuvə-'fləu] *t.-i.* inundar(se.

overhead ['əuvə'hed] *a.-adv.* [situado] arriba, en lo alto.

overlook [,əuvə'luk] *t.*

mirar desde lo alto. 2 pasar por alto, disimular.

overrun [ˌəuvəˈrʌn] *t.* cubrir enteramente, invadir.

oversea [ˈəuvəˈsiː] *a.* de ultramar. 2 -s (-z) *adv.* ultramar.

overtake [ˌəuvəˈteik] *t.* alcanzar, atrapar.

overthrow [ˌəuvəˈθrəu] *t.* volcar, tumbar, derribar.

overwhelm [ˌəuvəˈwelm] *t.* aplastar. 2 abrumar.

owe [əu] *t.* deber, adeudar.

owl [aul] *s.* ORN. búho.

own [əun] *a.* propio, mismo, de uno. 2 *s. one's* ~, lo suyo, lo de uno. 3 *t.* poseer, tener. 4 reconocer, confesar.

owner [ˈəunəʳ] *s.* dueño.

ox [ɔks], *pl.* **oxen** [ˈɔksən] *s.* buey.

oxygen [ˈɔksidʒən] *s.* oxígeno.

oyster [ˈɔistəʳ] *s.* ostra.

P

pace [peis] *s.* paso. *2 i.* andar, pasear.

pacific [pə'sifik] *a.* pacífico.

pack [pæk] *s.* lío, fardo, bala. *2 t.-i.* empacar, empaquetar.

package ['pækidʒ] *s.* fardo.

pad [pæd] *s.* cojincillo, almohadilla. *2 t.* rellenar, acolchar.

page [peidʒ] *s.* paje. *2* botones. *3* página.

pageant ['pædʒənt] *s.* cabalgata.

paid [peid] V. TO PAY.

pail [peil] *s.* balde, cubo.

pain [pein] *s.* dolor, pena. *2 t.* doler. *3* causar dolor.

painful ['peinful] *a.* doloroso, penoso.

paint [peint] *s.* pintura, color. *2 t.-i.* pintar.

painter ['peintər] *s.* pintor.

painting ['peintiŋ] *s.* pintura. *2* pintura, cuadro.

pair [pɛər] *s.* par, pareja. *2 t.-i.* aparear(se, acoplar(se.

palace ['pælis] *s.* palacio.

pale [peil] *a.* pálido. *2 s.* estaca, palizada. *3 i.* palidecer.

palm [pɑːm] *s.* BOT. palma. *2* palma [de la mano]. *3 t.* manosear.

pan [pæn] *s.* cacerola, cazuela.

pane [pein] *s.* cristal, vidrio. *2* cara, faceta.

pang [pæŋ] *s.* punzada.

panic ['pænik] *a.-s.* pánico.

pant [pænt] *s.* jadeo, resuello. 2 *i.* jadear, resollar.

pantry ['pæntri] *s.* despensa.

papa [pə'pɑ:] *s.* fam. papá.

paper ['peipə'] *s.* papel. 2 papel, periódico, diario. 3 *t.* empapelar.

parade [pə'reid] *s.* ostentación; alarde; desfile. 3 *t.* desfilar por; hacer alarde de. 4 *i.* pasar revista.

paradise ['pærədais] *s.* paraíso.

paragraph ['pærəgrɑ:f] *s.* párrafo. 2 suelto, artículo corto.

parallel ['pærəlel] *a.* paralelo. 2 *s.* paralelismo, semejanza. 3 *t.* igualar, parangonar.

paralise ['pærəlaiz] *t.* paralizar.

parcel [pɑ:sl] *s.* paquete, bulto. 2 parcela. 3 *t.* parcelar. 4 empaquetar.

pardon ['pɑ:dn] *s.* perdón. 3 *t.* perdonar.

parent ['pɛərənt] *s.* padre o madre. 2 *pl.* padres.

parish ['pæriʃ] *s.* parroquia.

park [pɑ:k] *s.* parque. 2 *t.-i.* aparcar.

parliament ['pɑ:ləmənt] *s.* parlamento, cortes.

parlo(u)r ['pɑ:lə'] *s.* sala de estar o recibimiento. 2 (E. U.) salón [de belleza]; sala [de billares]. 3 locutorio.

parson ['pɑ:sn] *s.* párroco, cura, clérigo.

part [pɑ:t] *s.* parte. 2 cuidado, deber. 3 TEAT. papel. 4 (E. U.) raya [del cabello]. 5 *t.* dividir, partir. 6 irse, despedirse.

particle ['pɑ:tikl] *s.* partícula.

particular [pə'tikjulə'] *a.* particular. 2 minucioso. 3 *s.* pormenor, detalle.

partition [pɑ:'tiʃən] *s.* partición. 2 división.

partner ['pɑ:tnə'] *s.* socio. 2 compañero. 3 pareja [de baile]. 4 cónyuge.

partridge ['pɑ:tridʒ] *s.* perdiz.

party ['pɑ:ti] *s.* partido. 2 reunión, fiesta. 3 parte [en un contrato, una contienda, etc.]. 4 individuo.

pass [pɑ:s] *s.* paso, pasaje. 2 pase. 3 aprobación. 4 *t.-i.* pasar. 5

aprobar. ¶ Part. p.:
passed o *past*.

passage ['pæsidʒ] *s.* paso,
pasaje, tránsito.

passenger ['pæsindʒəʳ]
s. viajero.

passionate ['pæʃənit] *a.*
apasionado.

past [pɑːst] *a.-s.* pasado, pretérito. 2 *prep.* pasado, después de.

paste [peist] *s.* pasta,
masa.

pastor ['pɑːstəʳ] *s.* pastor [esp. espiritual].

pastry ['peistri] *s.* paste-
lería.

pasture ['pɑːstʃəʳ] *s.*
pasto. 2 *t.-i.* pacer, apa-
centarse.

pat [pæt] *a.* exacto, oportuno. 2 *adv.* oportuna-
mente. 3 *s.* golpecito,
palmadita. 4 *t.* dar pal-
maditas o golpecitos.

path [pɑːθ] *s.* camino,
senda.

patience ['peiʃəns] *s.* pa-
ciencia.

patient ['peiʃənt] *a.* paciente.

patron ['peitrən] *a.* patrón. 2 patrono.

pattern ['pætən] *s.* modelo. 2 patrón, plantilla.

pause [pɔːz] *s.* pausa. 2
i. pausar.

pave [peiv] *t.* pavimen-
tar.

pavement ['peivmənt] *s.*
pavimiento. 2 acera; an-
dén.

pawn [pɔːn] *s.* peón [de
ajedrez]. 2 empeño, ga-
rantía. 3 *t.* empeñar
[un objeto].

pay [pei] *s.* paga, sueldo. 2 *t.-i.* pagar. 3 *t.*
costear, sufragar. 4 ren-
dir [homenaje]; prestar
[atención]. 5 *i.* compensar, ser provechoso. ¶
Pret. y p. p.: *paid* [peid].

payment ['peimənt] *s.*
pago.

pea [piː] *s.* guisante.

peace [piːs] *s.* paz.

peaceful ['piːsful] *a.* pacífico.

peach [piːtʃ] *s.* melocotón.

peacock ['piːkɔk] *s.* pavo real.

peak [piːk] *s.* pico, cumbre.

pear [pɛəʳ] *s.* BOT. pera.

pearl [pɑːl] *s.* perla,
margarita. 2 *t.* perlar.

peasant ['pezənt] *s.* labriego.

pebble ['pebl] *s.* guija,
guijarro.

peck [pek] *s.* picotazo. 2
t. picar.

peculiar [pi'kju:liə^r] *a.* peculiar.

peel [pi:l] *s.* piel, corteza. 2 *t.* pelar, mondar.

peep [pi:p] *s.* atisbo, ojeada. 2 pío [de ave]. 3 *i.* atisbar, fisgar. 4 piar.

peer [piə^r] *s.* par, igual. 2 *i.* mirar [atentamente]. 3 asomar.

peg [peg] *s.* clavija, estaquilla. 2 percha, colgador.

pelt [pelt] *s.* pellejo, cuero. 2 *t.* tirar, arrojar. 3 *i.* caer con fuerza [la lluvia].

pen [pen] *s.* pluma. 2 *t.* escribir. ¶ Pret. y p. p.: *penned* o *pent.*

penalty ['penəlti] *s.* castigo.

pencil ['pensl] *s.* lápiz, lapicero.

penetrate ['penitreit] *t.-i.* penetrar. 2 *t.* atravesar.

penny ['peni], *pl.* **pennies** ['peniz] o [en comp.] **pence** [pens] *s.* penique.

pension ['penʃən] *s.* pensión, jubilación. 2 ['pɑ:ŋsiɔ:ŋ] pensión, casa de huéspedes.

pension ['penʃən] *t.* pensionar, retirar, jubilar.

people ['pi:pl] *s.* pueblo, nación. 2 gente, personas. 3 *t.* poblar.

pepper ['pepə^r] *s.* pimienta. 2 *t.* sazonar con pimienta.

perceive [pə'si:v] *t.* percibir, ver.

percentage [pə'sentidʒ] *s.* porcentaje.

perception [pə'sepʃən] *s.* percepción.

perch [pə:tʃ] *s.* percha. 2 pértiga, palo. 3 *t.-i.* encaramar(se.

perfect ['pə:fikt] *a.* perfecto. 2 [pə'fekt] *t.* perfeccionar.

perfection [pə'fekʃən] *s.* perfección.

perform [pə'fɔ:m] *t.* hacer, realizar. 2 *i.* actuar. 3 desempeñar un papel, tocar un instrumento, etcétera.

performance [pə'fɔ:məns] *s.* cumplimiento, desempeño. 2 acción. 3 función, representación, concierto; actuación de un artista, etc.

perfume ['pə:fju:m] *s.* perfume.

perfume [pə'fju:m] *t.* perfumar, embalsamar.

perhaps [pə'hæps, præps] *adv.* quizá, tal vez.

peril ['peril] *s.* peligro, riesgo.

perilous ['perilǝs] *a.* peligroso.

period ['piǝriǝd] *s.* período.

perish ['periʃ] *i.* perecer.

perjury ['pǝ:dʒǝri] *s.* perjurio.

permanent ['pǝ:mǝnǝnt] *a.* permanente, estable, duradero.

permission [pǝ'miʃǝn] *s.* permiso, licencia, venia.

permit ['pǝ:mit] *i.* permiso. 2 [pǝ'mit] *t.* permitir.

pernicious [pǝ:'niʃǝs] *a.* pernicioso. 2 malvado.

perpetual [pǝ'petjuǝl, -tʃuǝl] *a.* perpetuo. 2 continuo.

perplex [pǝ'pleks] *t.* dejar perplejo; confundir.

persevere [,pǝ:si'viǝ'] *i.* perseverar.

persist [pǝ'sist] *i.* persistir.

person ['pǝ:sn] *s.* persona.

personable ['pǝ:sǝnǝbl] *a.* bien parecido.

personal ['pǝ:sǝnl] *a.* personal.

personality [,pǝ:sǝ'næliti] *s.* personalidad.

personnel [,pǝ:sǝ'nel] *s.* personal, dependencia.

persuade [pǝ'sweid] *t.* persuadir, inducir.

pertain [pǝ:'tein] *i.* pertenecer; corresponder.

pertinent ['pǝ:tinǝnt] *a.* pertinente, oportuno, atinado.

perturb [pǝ'tǝ:b] *t.* perturbar, agitar.

pet [pet] *a.* querido, mimado. 2 *s.* animal doméstico. 3 *t.-i.* acariciar(se.

petition [pi'tiʃǝn] *s.* petición. 2 *t.* solicitar.

petty ['peti] *a.* pequeño, insignificante, mezquino.

phase [feiz] *s.* fase.

philosopher [fi'lɔsǝfǝ'] *s.* filósofo.

philosophy [fi'lɔsǝfi] *s.* filosofía.

phone [fǝun] *s.* fam. teléfono. 2 *t.-i.* telefonear.

photograph ['fǝutǝgrɑ:f] *s.* fotografía. 2 *t.-i.* fotografiar.

phrase [freiz] *s.* frase, locución.

physical ['fizikǝl] *a.* físico.

physician [fi'ziʃǝn] *s.* médico.

piano ['pjænǝu, 'pjɑ:nǝu) *s.* piano.

pick [pik] s. pico [herramienta]. 2 cosecha. 3 selección. 4 t. picar, agujerear. 5 coger [flores, frutos, etc.]. 6 escoger.

picket ['pikit] s. piquete.

pickle ['pikl] s. salmuera, escabeche. 2 t. escabechar.

picnic ['piknik] s. comida al aire libre. 2 i. comer en el campo.

picture ['piktʃər] s. pintura, cuadro. 2 imagen, retrato. 3 escena, cuadro. 4 descripción. 5 *the pictures*, el cine. 6 t. pintar, retratar.

pie [pai] s. pastel, empanada.

piece [pi:s] s. pieza, trozo, pedazo: ~ *of furniture*, mueble. 2 t. apedazar.

pier [piər] s. pilar, estribo. 2 embarcadero.

pierce [piəs] t. atravesar.

pile [pail] s. pelo, lana. 2 pila, montón. 3 ELECT. pila, batería. 4 pira. 5 estaca. 6 t. amontonar. 7 sostener con pilotes. 8 i. acumularse.

pilgrim ['pilgrim] s. peregrino, romero.

pillar ['pilər] s. pilar, columna.

pillow ['pilou] s. almohada.

pilot [['pailət] m. piloto. 2 t. pilotar.

pin [pin] s. alfiler. 2 broche. 3 clavija, chaveta. 4 bolo [para jugar]. 5 t. prender; clavar, sujetar.

pinch [pintʃ] s. apuro. 2 punzada. 3 pellizco. 4 t. pellizcar. 5 coger, prender. 6 i. economizar.

pine [pain] s. BOT. pino: ~ *cone*, piña; ~ *nut*, piñón. 2 i. desfallecer.

pineapple ['pain,æpl] s. BOT. ananás, piña de América.

pink [pink] s. BOT. clavel. 2 color de rosa. 3 estado perfecto. 4 a. rosado.

pint [paint] s. pinta.

pioneer [,paiə'niər] s. pionero.

pious ['paiəs] a. pío, piadoso.

pipe [paip] s. tubo, cañería. 2 flauta, caramillo. 3 pitido, silbido. 4 pipa [para fumar]. 5 MÚS. gaita. 6 t.-i. tocar [en] el caramillo. 7 chillar, pitar.

piper ['paipər] s. gaitero.

pique [piːk] s. pique, resentimiento. 2 t. picar, irritar.

pirate ['paiərit] s. pirata. 2 t.-i. piratear.

pistol ['pistl] s. pistola.

pit [pit] s. hoyo; foso, pozo. 2 boca [del estómago]. 3 hueso [de fruta].

pitch [pitʃ] s. pez, brea. 2 echada, tiro [en ciertos juegos]. 3 inclinación, pendiente. 4 MÚS., FONÉT. tono. 5 DEP. campo. 6 t. empecinar, embrear. 7 tirar, arrojar. 8 clavar; poner, colocar.

pitcher ['pitʃər] s. jarro, cántaro. 2 DEP. lanzador.

pitiful ['pitiful] a. PITIABLE. 2 compasivo.

pity ['piti] s. piedad. 2 what a ~!, ¡qué lástima! 3 t. compadecer, apiadarse de.

pivot ['pivət] s. eje, pivote.

place [pleis] s. lugar, sitio. 2 puesto; rango, dignidad. 3 plazuela; calle corta. 4 t. colocar, poner.

plague [pleig] s. plaga. 2 peste. 3 t. plagar, infestar.

plain [plein] a. llano. 2 evidente. 3 franco. 4 simple. 5 feo. 6 s. llanura.

plan [plæn] s. plano, diseño. 2 plan, proyecto. 3 t. planear, proyectar.

plane [plein] a. plano. 2 s. plano [superficie]. 3 nivel. 4 aeroplano, avión. 5 cepillo, garlopa. 6 BOT. ~ tree, plátano [árbol]. 7 i. AVIA. volar; planear.

planet ['plænit] s. ASTR. planeta.

plank [plæŋk] s. tablón, tabla. 2 t. entarimar.

plant [plɑːnt] s. BOT. planta. 2 equipo, instalación. 3 fábrica, taller. 4 t. plantar, sembrar. 5 implantar.

plantation [plæn'teiʃən] s. plantación. 2 plantío.

plaster ['plɑːstər] s. yeso. 2 FARM. parche. 3 t. enyesar. 4 emplastar.

plate [pleit] s. placa. 2 grabado, lámina. 3 plato, fuente. 4 vajilla [de plata, etc.]. 5 t. planchar. 6 dorar, platear, niquelar, chapear.

platform ['plætfɔːm] s. plataforma. 2 FERROC. andén.

play [plei] *s.* juego, broma. 2 TEAT. representación. 3 comedia, drama, etc. 4 *t.* jugar. 5 TEAT. representar [una obra]; hacer [un papel]. 6 MÚS. tocar, tañer.

player ['pleiə*r*] *s.* jugador. 2 TEAT. actor. 3 ejecutante.

playground ['plei-graund] *s.* patio de recreo. 2 campo de juego.

plea [pli:] *s.* pretexto; disculpa. 2 súplica; defensa.

plead [pli:d] *t.* alegar. 2 *i.* pleitear, abogar.

pleasant ['pleznt] *a.* agradable.

please [pli:z] *t.-i.* agradar, gustar; complacer.

pleasing ['pli:ziŋ] *a.* agradable.

pleasure ['pleʒə*r*] *s.* placer, deleite, goce, gusto.

pleat [pli:t] *s.* pliegue, doblez.

pledge [pledʒ] *s.* prenda [garantía], rehén, fianza. 2 brindis. 3 *t.* dar en prenda, empeñar. 4 brindar por.

plentiful ['plentiful] *a.* abundante, copioso.

plenty ['plenti] *s.* abundancia; ~ of, mucho.

plight [plait] *s.* condición, estado. 2 apuro, aprieto.

plod [plɔd] *i.* afanarse.

plot [plɔt] *s.* solar, parcela. 2 conspiración, complot. 3 LIT. trama, argumento. 4 *t.* tramar, urdir.

plough, (E. U.) **plow** [plau] *s.* arado. 2 *t.-i.* arar, labrar.

ploughman, (E. U.) **plowman** ['plaumən] *s.* arador, labrador.

pluck [plʌk] *s.* valor, resolución. 2 tirón, estirón. 3 *t.* coger, arrancar. 4 desplumar. 5 MÚS. puntear.

plug [plʌg] *s.* tapón, espita. 2 clavija, enchufe. 3 *t.* tapar. 4 enchufar.

plum [plʌm] *s.* ciruela.

plume [plu:m] *s.* pluma. 2 plumaje.

plump [plʌmp] *a.* regordete. 2 *t.-i.* engordar(se.

plunder ['plʌndə*r*] *s.* pillaje. 2 *t.* pillar, saquear.

plunge [plʌndʒ] *s.* zambullida. 2 *t.-i.* zambullir(se.

plus [plʌs] *prep.* más.

ply [plai] *s.* pliegue, doblez. 2 *t.* usar, manejar. 3 trabajar con ahínco en.

pocket ['pɔkit] s. bolsillo. 2 t. embolsar(se.

pocket-book ['pɔkitbuk] s. libro de bolsillo. 2 billetero, cartera.

poem ['pouim] s. poema.

poet ['pouit] s. poeta, vate.

poetry ['pou(u)itri] s. poesía.

point [pɔint] s. punta. 2 punzón, buril, puñal, etc. 3 punto. 4 t. aguzar, sacar punta a. 5 apuntar, asestar, encarar. 6 señalar, indicar, hacer notar.

poise [pɔiz] s. equilibrio. 2 t. equilibrar.

poison ['pɔizn] s. veneno. 2 t. envenenar.

poke [pouk] s. empujón, codazo. 2 t. picar, atizar.

pole [poul] s. polo. 2 (con may.) polaco, ca.

police [pə'li:s] s. policía.

policeman [pə'li:smən] s. policía; guardia de seguridad, urbano.

policy ['pɔlisi] s. política, línea de conducta; maña. 2 póliza [de seguro].

polish ['pɔliʃ] s. pulimento; betún; cera. 2 lustre, brillo. 3 t. pulir, bruñir, lustrar.

polite [pə'lait] a. cortés.

political [pə'litikəl] a. político [de la política].

politician [ˌpɔli'tiʃən] s. político.

politics ['pɔlitiks] s. pl. política.

poll [poul] s. cabeza [pers.]. 2 votación. 3 lista electoral. 4 pl. colegio electoral. 5 urnas electorales. 6 t. recibir y escrutar [los votos]. 7 dar [voto].

pollution [pə'lu:ʃən, -'lju:-] s. contaminación.

pomp [pɔmp] s. pompa, fausto.

pond [pɔnd] s. estanque, charca.

ponder ['pɔndər] t. ponderar, pesar.

pony ['pouni] s. jaquita.

pool [pu:l] s. charco, balsa; piscina.

poop [pu:p] s. MAR. popa.

poor [puər] a. pobre. 2 malo, de mala calidad. 3 débil; enfermo.

pop [pɔp] s. estallido, taponazo. 2 t. hacer estallar.

Pope [poup] s. papa, pontífice.

popular ['pɔpjulər] a. popular.

popularity [ˌpɔpjuˈlæriti] s. popularidad.

population [ˌpɔpjuˈleiʃən] s. población [habitantes].

porch [pɔːtʃ] s. porche, atrio.

pork [pɔːk] s. cerdo.

port [pɔːt] s. puerto.

portable [ˈpɔːtəbl] a. portátil.

porter [ˈpɔːtəʳ] s. portero. 2 mozo de cuerda o estación.

portion [ˈpɔːʃən] s. porción, parte. 2 herencia, dote. 3 sino, suerte. 4 t. distribuir.

portrait [ˈpɔːtrit] s. retrato.

pose [pəuz] s. actitud. 2 afectación. 3 t. plantear [un problema, etc.]. 4 t. B. ART. posar por.

position [pəˈziʃən] s. posición.

positive [ˈpɔzitiv] a. positivo. 2 seguro.

possess [pəˈzəs] t. poseer.

possibility [ˌpɔsiˈbiliti] s. posibilidad.

possible [ˈpɔsibl] a. posible.

possibly [ˈpɔsibli] adv. posiblemente, tal vez.

post [pəust] s. poste, pilar. 2 puesto, empleo. 3 correo, estafeta; correos. 4 t. anunciar [con carteles]. 5 apostar, situar. 6 enviar por correo.

postage [ˈpəustidʒ] s. franqueo; ~ stamp, sello de correos.

postal [ˈpəustəl] a. postal: ~ order, giro postal.

pot [pɔt] s. olla, puchero. 2 maceta, tiesto.

potato [pəˈteitəu] s. BOT. patata: sweet ~, batata, boniato.

poultry [ˈpəultri] s. pollería.

pound [paund] s. libra. 2 t. moler, majar, machacar.

pour [pɔːʳ, pɔəʳ] t. verter. 2 i. fluir, correr.

poverty [ˈpɔvəti] s. pobreza.

powder [ˈpaudəʳ] s. polvo. 2 polvos [de tocador]. 3 pólvora. 4 t. polvorear. 5 t.-i. pulverizar(se.

power [ˈpauəʳ] s. poder, facultad. 2 potencia.

powerful [ˈpauəful] a. poderoso.

practical [ˈpræktikəl] a. práctico. 2 ~ joke, broma, chasco.

practically [ˈprætikəli] adv. prácticamente.

practice ['præktis] *s.* práctica.

practise ['præktis] *t.-i.* practicar.

prairie ['prɛəri] *s.* pradera.

praise [preiz] *s.* alabanza. 2 *t.* alabar, ensalzar.

pray [prei] *t.-i.* rogar.

prayer [prɛəʳ] *s.* ruego, súplica, rezo, oración.

preach [pri:tʃ] *t.-i.* predicar, sermonear.

preacher ['pri:tʃəʳ] *s.* predicador.

precarious [pri'kɛəriəs] *a.* precario. 2 incierto, inseguro.

precaution [pri'kɔ:ʃən] *s.* precaución.

precede [pri(:)'si:d] *t.-i.* preceder.

precious ['preʃəs] *a.* precioso.

precipitate [pri'sipitit] *a.* precipitado, súbito. 2 quím. precipitado.

predict [pri'dikt] *t.* predecir, vaticinar.

predominate [pri'dɔmineit] *i.* predominar, prevalecer.

preface ['prefis] *s.* prefacio.

prefer [pri'fə:ʳ] *t.* preferir, anteponer.

preference ['prefərəns] *s.* preferencia. 2 predilección.

preferential [,prefə'renʃəl] *a.* preferente.

pregnant ['pregnənt] *a.* preñada. 2 importante.

prejudice ['predʒudis] *s.* prejuicio. 2 perjuicio. 3 *t.* perjudicar. 4 perjudicar.

preliminary [pri'liminəri] *a.-s.* preliminar.

premier ['premjəʳ] *a.* primero. 2 *s.* primer ministro.

premise ['premis] *s.* premisa. 2 *pl.* casa, finca. 3 [pri'maiz] *t.* suponer, dar por sentado.

preparation [,prepə'reiʃən] *s.* preparación. 2 preparativo.

preparative [pri'pærətiv], **preparatory** [pri'pærətəri] *a.* preparatorio.

prepare [pri'pɛəʳ] *t.* preparar. 2 prevenir, disponer.

prescribe [pris'kraib] *t.* prescribir [ordenar; recetar].

presence ['prezns] *s.* presencia.

present ['preznt] *a.* presente. 2 *s.* presente, regalo. 3 [pri'zent] *t.* presentar.

presentation [,prezen'teiʃən] s. presentación. 2 regalo, obsequio.

preserve [pri'zə:v] s. conserva, confitura. 2 t. preservar, conservar.

preside [pri'zaid] t.-i. presidir; dirigir.

president ['prezidənt] s. presidente.

press [pres] s. muchedumbre. 2 empuje, presión. 3 prisa, apremio. 4 prensa [máquina; periódicos]. 5 imprenta. 6 t. apretar. 7 prensar. 8 urgir, apremiar.

pressure ['preʃər] s. presión. 2 impulso, empuje. 3 urgencia, apremio.

prestige [pres'ti:ʒ] s. prestigio.

presume [pri'zju:m] t. presumir, suponer. 2 i. atreverse.

pretence [pri'tens] s. pretensión. 2 pretexto.

pretend [pri'tend] t. aparentar, fingir. 2 t.-i. pretender.

pretext ['pri:tekst] s. pretexto.

pretty ['priti] a. lindo, bonito. 2 adv. muy, casi.

prevail [pri'veil] i. prevalecer. 2 predominar.

prevalent ['prevələnt] a. reinante, corriente, general.

prevent [pri'vent] t. prevenir, evitar, impedir.

previous ['pri:vjəs] a. previo.

prey [prei] s. presa, rapiña. 2 i. to ~ on, upon o at, hacer presa; pillar.

price [prais] s. precio. 2 t. apreciar, estimar.

prick [prik] s. pinchazo, picadura, resquemor. 2 aguijón. 3 t. pinchar, punzar, picar.

pride [praid] s. orgullo.

pride [praid] t. to ~ oneself on, enorgullecerse de.

priest [pri:st] m. sacerdote.

primary ['praiməri] a. primario.

prime [praim] a. primemero, principal. 2 albor, amanecer. 3 lo mejor. 4 t. cebar [un arma, etc.].

primitive ['primitiv] a. primitivo. 2 prístino.

prince [prins] s. príncipe.

princess [prin'ses] f. princesa.

principle ['prinsəpl] s. principio.

print [print] s. impresión. 2 t.-i. imprimir, estampar.

printing ['printiŋ] *s.* impresión, estampado. 2 imprenta. 3 impreso.

prior ['praiəʳ] *a.* anterior, previo. 2 *s.* prior.

prison ['prizn] *s.* prisión, cárcel.

prisoner ['priznəʳ] *s.* preso.

private ['praivit] *a.* privado, personal, particular.

privilege ['privilidʒ] *s.* privilegio.

privy ['privi] *a.* privado, oculto.

prize [praiz] *s.* premio. 2 presa, captura. 3 *t.* apreciar, estimar.

probability [,probə'biliti] *s.* probabilidad. 2 verosimilitud.

probable ['probəbl] *a.* probable, verosímil.

procedure [prə'si:dʒəʳ] *s.* proceder. 2 procedimiento.

proceed [prə'si:d] *i.* proseguir, seguir adelante. 2 proceder, provenir.

proceeding [prə'si:diŋ, prəu-] *s.* proceder, procedimiento.

process ['prəuses] *s.* proceso, marcha. 2 procedimiento.

proclaim [prə'kleim] *t.* proclamar. 2 promulgar.

proclamation [,proklə'meiʃən] *s.* proclamación. 2 edicto.

procure [prə'kjuəʳ] *t.* lograr, obtener, procurar.

produce ['prodju:s] *s.* producto. 2 [prə'dju:s] *t.* presentar. 3 producir.

producer [prə'dju:səʳ] *s.* productor. 2 TEAT. director.

production [prə'dʌkʃən] *s.* producción. 2 TEAT. dirección escénica, representación.

productive [prə'dʌktiv] *a.* productivo. 2 producente.

profess [prə'fes] *t.* profesar. 2 declarar, confesar.

professor [prə'fesəʳ] *s.* profesor, catedrático.

profit ['profit] *s.* provecho. 2 *t.* aprovechar, ser útil a.

profitable ['profitəbl] *a.* provechoso, beneficioso.

profound [prə'faund] *a.* profundo. 2 hondo. 3 abstruso.

program(me ['prəugræm] *s.* programa. 2 plan.

progress ['prəugres] *s.*

progreso. 2 [prə'gres] *i.* progresar.

progressive [prə'gresiv] *a.* progresivo.

prohibit [prə'hibit] *t.* prohibir. 2 impedir.

prohibition [ˌprəui'biʃən] *s.* prohibición.

project ['prɔdʒekt] *s.* proyecto. 2 [prə'dʒekt] *t.* proyectar.

prolong [prə'lɔŋ] *t.* prolongar.

prominent ['prɔminənt] *a.* prominente, saliente. 2 notable.

promise ['prɔmis] *s.* promesa. 2 *t.-i.* prometer.

promontory ['prɔmentri] *s.* promontorio.

promote [prə'mout] *t.* promover, ascender.

promotion [prə'mouʃən] *s.* promoción.

prompt [prɔmpt] *a.* pronto, presto, puntual. 2 *t.* incitar.

prong [prɔŋ] *s.* gajo, púa.

pronounce [prə'nauns] *t.-i.* pronunciar(r.

proof [pru:f] *s.* prueba, demostración. 2 ensayo.

proper ['prɔpər] *a.* propio, característico. 2 propio, apropiado. 3 correcto [en su uso, etc.].

property ['prɔpəti] *s.* propiedad.

prophecy ['prɔfisi] *s.* profecía.

prophet ['prɔfit] *s.* profeta.

proportion [prə'pɔ:ʃən] *s.* proporción; armonía, correlación. 2 *t.* proporcionar.

proportional [prə'pɔ:-ʃənl], **proportionate** [prə'pɔ:ʃənit] *a.* proporcional.

proposal [prə'pəuzəl] *s.* propuesta, proposición.

propose [prə'pəuz] *t.* proponer. 2 brindar por.

proposition [ˌprɔpə'ziʃən] *s.* proposición. 2 (E. U.) cosa, asunto, negocio.

proprietor [prə'praiətər] *s.* propietario, dueño.

propriety [prə'praiəti] *s.* propiedad, cualidad de apropiado. 2 corrección, decencia. 3 *pl.* urbanidad, reglas de conducta.

prose [prəuz] *s.* prosa.

prosecute ['prɔsikju:t] *t.* proseguir, continuar. 2 procesar, enjuiciar.

prospect ['prɔspekt] *s.* perspectiva, paisaje, panorama. 2 [prəs'pekt] *t.-i.* explorar.

prospective [prəs'pektiv]

prosper [ˈprɔspər] *t.-i.*
prosperar.

prosperity [prɔsˈperiti] *s.*
prosperidad.

prosperous [ˈprɔspərəs]
a. próspero. 2 favorable.

protect [prəˈtekt] *t.* proteger.

protection [prəˈtekʃən]
s. protección.

protective [prəˈtektiv] *a.*
protector. 2 proteccionista.

protest [ˈproutest] *s.* protesta. 2 [prəˈtest] *t.-i.*
protestar.

Protestant [ˈprɔtistənt]
a.-s. protestante.

proud [praud] *a.* orgulloso, sobebio, altanero.

prove [pruːv] *t.* probar;
comprobar. 2 resultar.

provide [prəˈvaid] *t.* proveer.

provided [prəˈvaidid]
conj. ~ *that*, con tal que,
siempre que.

providence [ˈprɔvidəns]
s. providencia, previsión.

province [ˈprɔvins] *s.*
provincia. 2 región, distrito.

provision [prəˈviʒən] *s.*
provisión.

provocative [prəˈvɔkətiv]
a. provocativo. 2 irritante

provoke [prəˈvouk] *t.*
provocar. 2 irritar.

prowess [ˈprauis] *s.* valor. 2 proeza; destreza.

prudent [ˈpruːdənt] *a.*
prudente; previsor.

prune [pruːn] *t.* podar.

pry [prai] *i.* espiar, acechar.

psalm [sɑːm] *s.* salmo.

psychologic(al [ˌsaikəˈlɔdʒik(əl] *a.* psicológico.

psychology [saiˈkɔledʒi]
s. psicología.

pub [pʌb] *s.* pop. (Ingl.)
cervecería, taberna.

public [ˈpʌblik] *a.* público. 2 *s.* público.

publication [ˌpʌbliˈkeiʃən] *s.* publicación. 2
edición.

publicity [pʌbˈlisiti] *s.*
publicidad. 2 notoriedad.

publish [ˈpʌbliʃ] *t.* publicar.

publisher [ˈpʌbliʃər] *s.*
editor.

pucker [ˈpʌkər] *s.* arruga. 2 *t.* arrugar.

pudding [ˈpudiŋ] *s.* budín, pudín.

Puerto Rican [ˈpweːtəuˈriːkən] *a.-s.* portorriqueño.

puff [pʌf] s. soplo, bufido. 2 bocanada. 3 coc. bollo. 4 i. soplar, jadear; echar bocanadas.

pugilist ['pju:dʒilist] s. púgil.

pull [pul] s. tirón, sacudida. 2 tirador. 3 esfuerzo prolongado. 4 atracción. 5 trago. 6 chupada [a un cigarro]. 7 ventaja, superioridad. 8 t. tirar de. 9 beber, chupar.

pulse [pʌls] s. pulso, pulsación. 2 i. pulsar, latir.

pump [pʌmp] s. MEC. bomba. 2 t. impeler.

pumpkin ['pʌmpkin] s. BOT. calabaza.

punch [pʌntʃ] s. ponche. 2 puñetazo. 3 empuje, vigor. 4 punzón. 5 (mayúsc.) Polichinela. 6 t. picar; perforar.

punctual ['pʌŋktjuəl] a. puntual, exacto.

punish ['pʌniʃ] t. castigar.

punishment ['pʌniʃmənt] s. castigo. 2 vapuleo.

pupil ['pju:pl, -pil] s. discípulo. 2 ANAT. pupila.

puppet ['pʌpit] s. títere, marioneta.

purchase ['pə:tʃəs] s. compra. 2 t. comprar, adquirir.

pure ['pjuər] a. puro.

Puritan ['pjuəritən] a.-s. puritano.

purple ['pə:pl] a. purpúreo. 2 s. púrpura.

purport ['pə:pət] s. significado. 2 t. significar, quere decir.

purpose ['pə:pəs] s. propósito, intención. 2 t.-i. proponerse, intentar.

purse [pə:s] s. bolsa, bolsillo. 2 t. arrugar, fruncir.

pursue [pə'sju:] t. seguir, perseguir. 2 i. proseguir, continuar.

pursuit [pə'sju:t] s. seguimiento, caza, busca.

purveyor [pə:'veiər] s. proveedor.

push [puʃ] s. empujón. 2 impulso. 3 t. empujar, impeler. 4 apretar.

put [put] s. acción de to PUT. 2 golpe, lanzamiento. 3 t. poner, colocar. 4 hacer [una pregunta]. 5 to ~ on, ponerse [una prenda]. 6 to ~ over, aplazar. 7 to ~ up, levantar, erigir. ¶ Pret. y p. p.: put [put]; ger.: putting ['putiŋ].

puzzle ['pʌzl] s. embarazo, perplejidad. 2 enredo, embrollo. 3 acertijo, rompecabezas. 4 t. confundir. 5 embrollar.

Q

quaint [kweint] *a.* curioso, original, pintoresco.

qualification [ˌkwɔlifiˈkeiʃən] *s.* calificación. 2 condición, requisito. 3 capacidad, idoneidad.

qualify [ˈkwɔlifai] *t.* calificar, capacitar.

quality [ˈkwɔliti] *s.* calidad, cualidad.

quantity [ˈkwɔntiti] *s.* cantidad.

quarrel [ˈkwɔrəl] *s.* riña. 2 *i.* reñir.

quarry [ˈkwɔri] *s.* cantera.

quart [kwɔːt] *s.* cuarto de galón.

quarter [ˈkwɔːtər] *s.* cuarto, cuarta parte. 2 cuarto [de hora; de la luna]. 3 (E. U.) veinticinco centavos. 4 trimestre. 5 parte, dirección. 6 barrio, vecindad, 7 *pl.* cuartel, oficina; vivienda, alojamiento. 8 *t.* alojar.

queen [kwiːn] *s.* reina.

queer [kwiər] *a.* raro, extraño.

quench [kwentʃ] *t.* apagar.

quest [kwest] *s.* busca. 2 *t.* buscar.

question [ˈkwestʃən] *s.* pregunta. 2 objeción, duda. 3 cuestión, problema, asunto. 4 *t.* preguntar, interrogar.

queue [kjuː] *s.* cola, hilera. 2 *i.* hacer cola.

quick [kwik] *a.* vivo, rápido. 2 **-ly** *adv.* vivamente, prontamente, aprisa.

quicken ['kwikən] *t.* vivificar, resucitar.

quiet ['kwaiət] *a.* quieto, inmóvil. 2 callado, silencioso. 3 *s.* quietud, silencio. 4 *t.* aquietar.

quit [kwit] *a.* absuelto, descargado. 2 libre, exento. 3 *t.* abandonar. 4 *i.* irse. 5 dimitir.

quite [kwait] *adv.* completamente, del todo;

realmente, verdaderamente.

quiver ['kwivər] *s.* aljaba, carcaj. 2 vibración, temblor. 3 *t.* vibrar, temblar.

quotation [kwəu'teiʃən] *s.* cita [texto citado].

quote [kwəut] *t.* citar [un texto, un autor].

quoth [kwəuθ] ~ *I*, dije; ~ *he*, dijo.

R

rabbit [ˈræbit] s. ZOOL. conejo.

race [reis] s. raza; casta. 2 carrera, regata. 3 i. correr [en una carrera, etcétera].

rack [ræk] s. estante. 2 aparato de tortura. 3 t. torturar.

racket [ˈrækit] s. raqueta. 2 alboroto. 3 diversión. 4 i. armar jaleo.

radiant [ˈreidjənt] a. radiante.

radical [ˈrædikəl] a.-s. radical. 2 a. esencial, fundamental.

radio [ˈreidiəu] s. ELECT. radio: ~ set, aparato de radio.

rag [ræg] s. trapo, harapo.

rage [reidʒ] s. rabia, ira. 2 i. rabiar, encolerizarse.

ragged [ˈrægid] a. andrajoso, harapiento.

raid [reid] s. incursión, ataque. 2 t. hacer una incursión en.

rail [reil] s. barra; pasamano. 2 raíl; ferrocarril. 3 t. cercar, poner barandilla a.

railroad [ˈreilrəud] (E. U.), **railway** [-wei] (Ingl.) s. ferrocarril, vía férrea.

rain [rein] s. lluvia: ~ bow, arco iris; ~ drops, gota de agua; ~ fall, chaparrón. 2 i.-impers.- t. llover.

rainy [ˈreini] a. lluvioso.

raise [reiz] s. aumento. 2 t. levantar, alzar, elevar. 3 cultivar [plantas], criar [animales]. 4 (E. U.) criar, educar.

raisin ['reizn] *s.* pasa.

rake [reik] *s.* libertino. 2 AGR. rastro, rastrillo. 3 *t.* AGR. rastrillar. 4 atizar, hurgar [el fuego].

rally ['ræli] *s.* reunión. 2 *t.-i.* reunir(se, concentrar(se.

ran [ræn] *pret.* de TO RUN.

ranch [ra:ntʃ] *s.* rancho.

random ['rændəm] *s.* azar, acaso. 2 *a.* ocasional, fortuito.

rang [ræŋ] *pret.* de TO RING.

range [reindʒ] *s.* fila, hilera. 2 esfera [de una actividad]. 3 escala, gama, serie. 4 extensión [de la voz]. 5 alcance [de un arma, etc.]. 6 *t.* alinear, arreglar, ordenar. 7 *i.* alinearse. 8 extenderse, variar.

rank [ræŋk] *a.* lozano, lujuriante, vicioso. 2 rancio. 3 grosero. 4 *s.* línea, hilera, fila. 5 rango, grado. 6 *t.* alinear. 7 ordenar, arreglar.

ransom ['rænsəm] *s.* rescate. 2 *t.* rescatar, redimir.

rap [ræp] *s.* golpe seco. 2 *t.-i.* golpear.

rapacious [rə'peiʃəs] *a.* rapaz.

rapid ['ræpid] *a.* rápido.

rapture ['ræptʃəʳ] *s.* rapto, arrobamiento, éxtasis.

rare [rɛəʳ] *a.* raro.

rascal ['ra:skəl] *s.* bribón, pillo.

rat [ræt] *s.* ZOOL. rata.

rate [reit] *s.* razón, proporción, velocidad. 2 precio, valor. 3 clase, orden. 4 *at any* ~, al menos, de todos modos. 5 *t.* valuar, tasar. 6 estimar, juzgar. 7 reñir, regañar.

rather ['ra:ðəʳ] *adv.* bastante. 2 mejor, más: *I would* ~, me gustaría más.

rattle ['rætl] *s.* tableteo. 2 estertor. 3 cascabel [de serpiente]. 4 sonajero. 5 matraca. 6 *t.* hacer sonar. 7 aturdir. 8 *i.* tabletear, matraquear.

raw [rɔ:] *a.* crudo, en bruto, en rama. 2 crudo, húmedo, frío [viento, tiempo]. 3 novato.

ray [rei] *s.* rayo [de luz, etc.]. 2 GEOM. radio. 3 ICT. raya.

reach [ri:tʃ] *s.* alcance, poder. 2 *t.* alargar, extender, tender. 3 llegar.

reactor [ri(:)'æktəʳ] *s.* reactor.

read [ri:d] *t.* leer. ¶
Pret. y p. p.: *read* [red].
reader ['ri:dəʳ] *s.* lector.
2 libro de lectura.
readily ['redili] *adv.*
prontamente. 2 de buena
gana.
reading ['ri:diŋ] *s.* lectura.
ready ['redi] *a.* prepara-
do, pronto, listo, dis-
puesto.
real [riəl] *a.* real, verdadero.
reality [ri(:)'æliti] *s.* realidad.
realize ['riəlaiz] *t.* comprender, darse cuenta de.
2 realizar, efectuar.
realm [relm] *s.* reino. 2
campo, dominio, región.
reap [ri:p] *t.* segar, gua-
dañar. 2 recoger, cose-
char.
reaper ['ri:pəʳ] *s.* sega-
dor.
reappear ['ri:ə'piəʳ] *i.*
reaparecer.
rear [riəʳ] *a.* trasero, último, posterior. 2 *s.* tra-
sera, parte de atrás. 3 *t.*
levantar, alzar; erigir. 4
criar, cultivar.
reason ['ri:zn] *s.* razón.
2 *t.-i.* razonar. 3 *i.* persuadir o disuadir con ra-
zones.

reasonable ['ri:zənəbl] *a.*
racional [ser]. 2 razona-
ble.
reasoning ['ri:z(ə)niŋ] *s.*
razonamiento.
reassure [,ri:ə'ʃuəʳ] *t.*
tranquilizar; alentar.
rebel ['rebl] *a.-s.* rebelde. 2 [ri'bel] *i.* rebelarse, sublevarse.
rebellion [ri'beljən] *s.* re-
belión.
rebuke [ri'bju:k] *s.* reproche. 2 *t.* increpar, reprender.
recall [ri'kɔ:l] *s.* llamada [para hacer volver].
2 anulación, revocación.
3 *t.* llamar, hacer volver.
4 anular, revocar.
receipt [ri'si:t] *s.* recepción. 2 cobranza. 3 reci-
bo. 4 receta. 5 ingresos.
receive [ri'si:v] *t.* recibir; tomar, aceptar.
receiver [ri'si:vəʳ] *s.* receptor. 2 cobrador, te-
sorero.
recent ['ri:snt] *a.* reciente.
reception [ri'sepʃən] *s.*
recepción. 2 admisión,
aceptación.
recess [ri'ses] *s.* hueco,
entrada. 2 suspensión,
descanso.

recipe ['resipi] *s.* récipe, receta.

recite [ri'sait] *t.-i.* recitar. 2 *t.* narrar.

reckon ['rekən] *t.-i.* contar, calcular.

reclaim [ri'kleim] *t.* poner en cultivo; hacer utilizable. 2 DER. reclamar.

recognize ['rekəgnaiz] *t.* reconocer.

recollection [,rekə'lekʃən] *s.* recuerdo, memoria.

recommend [,rekə'mend] *t.* recomendar. 2 alabar.

recommendation [,rekəmen'deiʃən] *s.* recomendación.

reconcile ['rekənsail] *t.* reconciliar.

reconstruct ['ri:-kəns-'trΛkt] *t.* reconstruir.

record ['rekɔ:d] *s.* inscripción. 2 acta, historia. 3 DER. expediente. 4 disco; grabación [en disco]. 5 DEP. récord, marca. 6 [ri'kɔ:d] *t.* inscribir, registrar. 7 fijar en la memoria. 8 grabar en disco o en cinta magnetofónica.

recover [ri'kΛvər] *t.* recobrar, recuperar.

recovery [ri'kΛvəri] *s.* recobro, recuperación.

recreation [,rekri'eiʃən] *s.* recreación, recreo.

recruit [ri'kru:t] *s.* recluta. 2 *t.* reclutar, alistar.

rector ['rektər] *s.* rector.

recur [ri'kə:'] *t.* volver [a un tema]. 3 volver a ocurrir, repetirse.

red [red] *a.* encarnado, rojo.

redeem [ri'di:m] *t.* redimir.

redress [ri'dres] *s.* reparación. 2 *t.* corregir, reparar.

reduce [ri'dju:s] *t.* reducir. 2 rebajar, diluir.

reduction [ri'dΛkʃən] *s.* reducción.

reed [ri:d] *s.* BOT. caña.

reel [ri:l] *s.* carrete; rollo. 2 *t.* devanar.

re-enlist ['ri:in'list] *t.-i.* reenganchar(se.

refer [ri'fə:'] *t.* referir.

reference ['refrəns] *s.* referencia, relación.

refine [ri'fain] *t.* refinar.

refinement [ri'fainmənt] *s.* refinamiento. 2 sutileza.

reflect [ri'flekt] *t.* reflejar.

reflection [ri'flekʃən] *s.* reflexión, reverberación.

reform [ri'fɔ:m] *s.* reforma. 2 *t.* reformar, mejorar.

refrain [ri'frein] *s.* estribillo. 2 *t.* refrenar, contener.

refresh [ri'freʃ] *t.* refrescar. 2 renovar, restaurar.

refreshment [ri'freʃmənt] *s.* refrescadura. 2 refresco.

refrigerator [ri'fridʒəreitər] *s.* refrigerador. 2 nevera, frigorífico.

refuge ['refju:dʒ] *s.* refugio.

refugee [ˌrefju(:)'dʒi:] *s.* refugiado. 2 asilado.

refusal [ri'fju:zəl] *s.* rechazamiento. 2 negativa, denegación.

refuse ['refju:s] *s.* desecho, basura. 2 [ri'fju:z] *t.* rehusar, rechazar.

regain [ri'gein] *t.* recobrar.

regal ['ri:gəl] *a.* real, regio.

regard [ri'gɑ:d] *s.* miramiento. 2 afecto, respeto. 3 relación, respecto. 4 *pl.* recuerdos. 5 *t.* mirar, contemplar. 6 tocar a, concernir, referirse a: *as regards*, en cuanto a.

regarding [ri'gɑ:diŋ] *prep.* tocante a, respecto de.

region ['ri:dʒən] *s.* región.

register ['redʒistər] *s.* registro; archivo, protocolo. 2 *t.-i.* registrar(se, inscribir(se.

regret [ri'gret] *s.* pesar, sentimiento. 2 remordimiento. 3 *i.* sentir, lamentar. 4 arrepentirse.

regretful [ri'gretful] *a.* arrepentido, pesaroso.

regular ['regjulə] *a.* normal, corriente.

regulate ['regjuleit] *t.* regular, arreglar, reglamentar.

regulation [ˌregju'leiʃən] *s.* regulación. 2 reglamentación.

reign [rein] *s.* reino, soberanía. 2 reinado. 3 *i.* reinar.

rein [rein] *s.* rienda.

reject [ri'dʒekt] *t.* rechazar, rehusar.

rejoice [ri'dʒɔis] *t.-i.* alegrar(se, regocijar(se.

rejoicing [ri'dʒɔisiŋ] *s.* alegria.

relate [ri'leit] *t.* relatar, referir. 2 relacionar.

relation [ri'leiʃən] *s.* relación, relato. 2 parentesco, afinidad. 4 pariente, deudo.

relationship [ri'leiʃənʃip] s. relación [entre cosas o pers.]. 2 parentesco.

relative ['relətiv] a. relativo. 2 s. pariente, deudo, allegado.

relax [ri'læks] t.-i. relajar(se, descansar. 2 s. descanso; diversión.

release [ri'li:s] s. libertad. 2 estreno. 3 t. libertar 4 estrenar; publicar.

reliable [ri'laiəbl] a. confiable, digno de confianza.

relic ['relik] s. reliquia. 2 pl. restos, ruinas.

relief [ri'li:f] s. ayuda, auxilio. 2 alivio. 3 relieve, realce. 4 MIL. relevo.

relieve [ri'li:v] t. remediar, auxiliar, socorrer. 2 realzar, hacer resaltar. 3 MIL. relevar.

religion [ri'lidʒən] s. religión.

religious [ri'lidʒəs] a. religioso.

relish ['reliʃ] s. buen sabor. 2 t. saborear. 3 i. gustar, agradar.

rely [ri'lai] i. [con *on* o *upon*] confiar o fiar en.

remain [ri'mein] i. quedar. 2 permanecer, continuar. 3 s. pl. restos; sobras.

remainder [ri'meindər] s. resto.

remark [ri'ma:k] s. observación. 2 t. observar, advertir, notar.

remarkable [ri'ma:kəbl] a. observable. 2 notable.

remedy ['remidi] s. remedio. 2 t. remediar.

remember [ri'membər] t. recordar, acordarse de.

remind [ri'maind] t. to ~ *of*, recordar.

remnant ['remnənt] s. remanente, resto, residuo. 2 vestigio.

remote [ri'məut] a. remoto.

removal [ri'mu:vəl] s. remoción, levantamiento. 2 mudanza.

remove [ri'mu:v] t.-i. trasladar(se, mudar(se.

render ['rendər] t. dar, entregar. 2 devolver. 3 volver, hacer, poner.

renew [ri'nju:] t.-i. renovar(se 2 reanudar(se.

renown [ri'naun] s. renombre.

rent [rent] s. renta, arriendo. 2 grieta. 3 cisma. 4 p. p. de TO REND. 5 t.-i. arrendar(se.

repair [ri'pɛər] s. reparación. 2 t. reparar.

repay [ri:'pei] t. pagar, corresponder a.

repeal [ri'pi:l] *s.* abrogación. 2 *t.* abrogar.

repeat [ri'pi:t] *t.-i.* repetir(se.

repent [ri'pent] *i.* arrepentirse. 2 *t.* arrepentirse de.

repetition [,repi'tiʃən] *s.* repetición. 2 repaso.

replace [ri'pleis] *t.* reponer.

reply [ri'plai] *s.* respuesta. 2 *t.* responder.

report [ri'pɔ:t] *s.* voz, rumor. 2 noticia. 3 relato. 4 *t.* relatar. 5 informar.

reporter [ri'pɔ:tər] *s.* reportero.

repose [ri'pəuz] *s.* reposo. 2 *t.* descansar, reclinar.

represent [,repri'zent] *t.* representar, significar.

representation [,reprizen-'teiʃən] *s.* representación.

representative [,repri'zentətiv] *a.* representativo. 2 (E. U.) diputado.

reproach [ri'prəutʃ] *s.* reproche. 2 *t.* reprochar.

reproduce [,ri:prə'dju:s] *t.-i.* reproducir(se.

republic [ri'pʌblik] *s.* república.

repulse [ri'pʌls] *s.* repulsa. 2 *t.* rechazar, repeler.

reputation [,repju(:)'teiʃən] *s.* reputación, fama.

request [ri'kwest] *s.* ruego. 2 *t.* rogar, solicitar.

require [ri'kwaiər] *t.-i.* requerir, pedir, demandar.

requirement [ri'kwaiəmənt] *s.* requisito, condición.

requisite ['rekwizit] *a.* requerido. 2 *s.* requisito, cosa esencial.

rescue ['reskju:] *s.* rescate. 2 *t.* libertar, rescatar, salvar.

research [ri'sə:tʃ] *s.* búsqueda, investigación. 2 *t.* buscar, investigar.

resemblance [ri'zembləns] *s.* parecido, semejanza.

resemble [ri'zembl] *t.* parecerse, asemejarse a.

resent [ri'zent] *t.* resentirse.

resentment [ri'zentmənt] *s.* resentimiento, enojo.

reservation [,rezə'veiʃən] *s.* reserva. 2 terreno reservado.

reserve [ri'zə:v] *s.* reserva, repuesto. 2 reserva [discreción]. 3 *t.* reservar.

reside [ri'zaid] *i.* residir.

residence ['rezidəns] *s.* residencia, morada, mansión.

resident ['rezidənt] *a.* residente.

resign [ri'zain] *t.* dimitir.

resignation [,rezig'neiʃən] *s.* dimisión. 2 resignación.

resin ['rezin] *s.* resina.

resist [ri'zist] *t.-i.* resistir.

resistance [ri'zistəns] *s.* resistencia.

resistant [ri'zistənt] *a.* resistente.

resolution [,rezə'luːʃən] *s.* resolución. 2 propósito.

resolve [ri'zɔlv] *s.* resolución. 2 *t.* resolver.

resonance ['rezənəns] *s.* resonancia.

resort [ri'zɔːt] *s.* recurso, medio. 2 refugio. 3 balneario. 4 *i.* acudir; recurrir.

resource [ri'sɔːs] *s.* recurso.

respect [ris'pekt] *s.* respeto. 2 *t.* respetar. 3 respectar; atañer.

respectable [ris'pektəbl] *a.* respetable.

respond [ris'pɔnd] *i.* responder, contestar.

response [ris'pɔns] *s.* respuesta.

responsibility [ris,pɔnsi-'biliti] *s.* responsabilidad. 2 cometido.

responsible [ris'pɔnsəbl] *a.* responsable.

rest [rest] *s.* descanso, reposo. 2 apoyo, soporte. 3 resto, restante. 4 *i.* descansar. 5 apoyarse, basarse [en]. 6 quedar, permanecer.

restaurant ['restərɔːŋ] *s.* restaurante.

restless ['restlis] *a.* inquieto.

restoration [,restə'reiʃən] *s.* restauración. 2 restitución.

restore [ris'tɔːʳ] *t.* restaurar. 2 restablecer.

restrain [ris'trein] *t.* refrenar, contener, reprimir.

restraint [ris'treint] *s.* refrenamiento, cohibición.

restriction [ris'trikʃən] *s.* restricción, limitación.

result [ri'zʌlt] *s.* resultado. 2 *i.* to ~ from, resultar. 3 to ~ in, dar por resultado.

resume [ri'zjuːm] *t.* reasumir, volver a tomar.

resumption [ri'zʌmpʃən] *s.* reasunción. 2 recobro.

retain [ri'tein] *t*. retener.

retire [ri'taiər] *t.-i.* retirar(se.

retort [ri'tɔ:t] *s.* réplica mordaz. 2 *t.-i.* replicar, redargüir.

retreat [ri'tri:t] *s.* retirada. 2 *i.* retirarse, retroceder.

return [ri'tə:n] *s.* vuelta, regreso, retorno. 2 *i.* volver, regresar. 3 *t.* volver, devolver.

reveal [ri'vi:l] *t.* revelar.

revelation [,revi'leiʃən] *s.* revelación. 2 Apocalipsis.

revenge [ri'vendʒ] *s.* venganza. 2 *t.* vengar, vindicar.

revenue ['revinju:] *s.* renta.

reverence ['revərəns] *s.* reverencia, respeto. 2 *t.* reverenciar.

reverend ['revərənd] *a.* reverendo, venerable.

reverse [ri'və:s] *a.* inverso. 3 *t.* invertir.

review [ri'vju:] *s.* revista. 2 revisión. 3 reseña. 4 *t.* rever. 5 revisar.

revive [ri'vaiv] *t.* reanimar, restablecer.

revolt [ri'vəult] *s.* revuelta. 2 *i.* sublevarse, amotinarse.

revolution [,revə'lu:ʃən] *s.* revolución.

reward [ri'wɔ:d] *s.* premio, recompensa. 2 *t.* recompensar.

rhyme [raim] *s.* LIT. rima. 2 *t.-i.* rimar. 3 *t.* consonar.

rib [rib] *s.* ANAT., BOT., MAR. costilla. 2 ENT. nervio [de ala]. 3 varilla [de paraguas o abanico].

ribbon ['ribən] *s.* cinta, galón.

rice [rais] *s.* arroz.

rich [ritʃ] *a.* rico.

riches ['ritʃiz] *s. pl.* riqueza.

rid [rid] *t.* librar, desembarazar; *to get ~ of*, librarse de. ¶ Pret. y p. p.: *rid* [rid] o *ridded* ['ridid].

ridden ['ridn] v. TO RIDE.

riddle ['ridl] *s.* enigma. 2 *t.* resolver, descifrar.

ride [raid] *s.* paseo o viaje a caballo, en bicicleta, en coche. 2 *i.* ir a caballo, en bicicleta, en coche, etc. ¶ Pret.: *rode* [rəud]; p. p.: *ridden* ['ridn].

ridge [ridʒ] *s.* cerro, cresta.

ridiculous [ri'dikjuləs] *a.* ridículo.

rifle ['raifl] s. rifle. fusil. 2 t. pillar, saquear.

right [rait] a. recto, derecho. 2 justo, honrado. 3 derecho, diestro, de la derecha. 4 adv. exactamente. 5 bien; justamente. 6 a la derecha. 7 interj. all ~!, ¡está bien!, ¡conformes! 8 s. derecho, justicia, razón. 9 t. hacer justicia a.

rigid ['ridʒid] a. rígido.

rim [rim] s. borde, margen.

ring [riŋ] s. anillo, sortija. 2 BOX. ring, cuadrilátero. 3 corro, círculo. 4 pista, arena.

1) **ring** [riŋ] t. cercar, circundar. 2 poner anillos a. ¶ Pret. y p. p.: ringed [riŋd].

2) **ring** [riŋ] i. hacer sonar; tocar, tañer, repicar: to ~ up, llamar por teléfono. ¶ Pret.: rang [ræŋ]; p. p.: rung [rʌŋ].

riot ['raiət] s. tumulto, alboroto. 2 i. armar alboroto.

rip [rip] s. rasgadura. 2 t. rasgar, abrir.

ripe [raip] a. maduro.

ripen ['raipən] t.-i. madurar.

ripple ['ripl] s. onda, rizo. 2 i. rizarse, ondear.

rise [raiz] s. levantamiento, subida. 2 elevación. 3 salida [de un astro]. 4 causa, origen. 5 i. subir, ascender, elevarse, alzarse, remontarse. 6 salir [un astro]. 7 nacer, salir, originarse. ¶ Pret.: rose [rəuz]; p.p.: risen ['rizn].

risen [rizn] p. p. de TO RISE.

risk [risk] s. riesgo, peligro. 2 t. arriesgar, aventurar.

rite [rait] s. rito.

rival ['raivəl] a. competidor. 2 s. rival. 3 t. competir.

river ['rivə'] s. río, cuenca.

road [rəud] s. carretera. camino.

roam [rəum] i. rodar, vagar, errar. 2 t. vagar por.

roar [rɔːʳ, rɔəʳ] s. rugido. 2 i. rugir.

roast [rəust] s. asado. 2 t.-i. asar(se. 3 tostar(se.

rob [rɔb] t. robar, hurtar.

robber ['rɔbəʳ] s. ladrón.

robe [rəub] s. ropaje, vestidura. 2 bata. 3 vestido de mujer. 4 t.-i. vestirse.

robust [rə'bʌst] *a.* robusto.

rock [rɔk] *s.* roca, peña. 2 *t.* acunar. 3 *t.-i.* mecer(se, balancear(se.

rocket ['rɔkit] *s.* cohete.

rocky ['rɔki] *a.* rocoso, pedregoso.

rod [rɔd] *s.* vara, varilla. 2 caña [de pescar].

rode [rəud] *pret.* de TO RIDE.

rogue [rəug] *s.* pícaro, bribón.

role, rôle [rəul] *s.* papel [que se hace o representa].

roll [rəul] *s.* rollo. 2 lista, nómina. 3 bollo, panecillo. 4 ARQ. voluta. 5 retumbo [del trueno]; redoble [del tambor]. 6 balanceo. 7 oleaje; rodadura. 8 *t.* hacer rodar. 9 *i.* rodar, girar. 10 retumbar, tronar.

roller ['rəulə'] *s.* MEC. rodillo. 2 rueda.

Roman ['rəumən] *a.-s.* romano. 2 *a.* latina [lengua]. 3 *s.* latín. 4 IMPR. redondo [tipo].

romance [rə'mæns] *s.* romance; novela. 2 idilio amoroso. 3 ficción, invención.

romantic [rəu'mæntik, -rə-] *a.* romántico.

roof [ru:f] *s.* techo. 2 *t.* cubrir, techar.

room [rum, ru:m] *s.* cuarto, pieza, habitación, sala.

roost [ru:st] *s.* percha; gallinero. 2 *i.* dormir [las aves en la percha].

root [ru:t] *s.* raíz. 2 *i.-t.* hozar. 3 *t.* arraigar, implantar.

rope [rəup] *s.* cuerda, soga.

rose [rəuz] *s.* BOT. rosal. 2 rosa [flor, color]: ~ bud, capullo de rosa. 3 *pret.* de TO RISE.

rosy ['rəuzil] *a.* rosado.

rot [rɔt] *s.* putrefacción. 2 *t.-i.* pudrir(se, corromper(se.

rotary ['rəutəri] *a.* rotatorio.

rotate [rəu'teit] *i.* rodar, girar.

rotten ['rɔtn] *a.* podrido.

rouge [ru:ʒ] *s.* colorete, arrebol.

rough [rʌf] *a.* áspero, tosco. 2 *t.* hacer o labrar toscamente.

round [raund] *a.* redondo. 2 rollizo. 3 circular. 4 claro, categórico. 5 fuerte, sonoro. 6 cabal, completo. 7 *s.* círculo, esfera; corro. 8 redondez.

9 recorrido, ronda. 10 ronda [de bebidas, etc.]. 11 serie [de sucesos, etc.], rutina. 12 salva [de aplausos]. 13 descarga, salva, disparo. 14 BOX. asalto. 15 adv. alrededor; por todos lados. 16 t. redondear. 17 rodear, cercar.

roundabout ['raundəbaut] a. indirecto, hecho con rodeos. 2 s. circunloquio. 3 tiovivo.

rouse [rauz] t.-i. despertar.

route [ru:t] s. ruta, camino.

routine [ru:'ti:n] s. rutina.

rove [rəuv] i. vagar, errar.

rover ['rəuvəʳ] s. vagabundo, andariego.

1) **row** [rau] s. riña, pendencia

2) **row** [rəu] s. fila, hilera. 2 paseo en bote.

1) **row** [rau] t. fam. pelearse con. 2 i. pelearse.

2) **row** [rəu] i. remar, bogar. 2 t. mover al remo.

royal ['rɔiəl] a. real, regio.

royalty ['rɔiəlti] s. realeza. 2 derechos de autor.

rub [rab] s. friega, frote. 2 t. estregar, restregar.

rubber ['rabəʳ] s. goma; caucho.

rubbish ['rabiʃ] s. basura, escombros; tonterías.

ruby ['ru:bi] s. MINER. rubí.

rudder ['radəʳ] s. timón.

ruddy ['radi] a. colorado.

rude [ru:d] a. rudo.

ruffle ['rafl] s. volante fruncido. 2 t. rizar, alechugar, fruncir.

rug [rag] s. alfombra.

rugged ['ragid] a. rugoso, escabroso, accidentado.

ruin [ruin] s. ruina. 2 t. arruinar.

rule [ru:l] s. regla, precepto. 2 t.-i. gobernar, regir.

ruler ['ru:ləʳ] s. gobernante. 2 regla [instrumento].

rumble ['rambl] s. rumor. 2 i. retumbar.

rumo(u)r ['ru:məʳ] s. rumor. 2 t. rumorear, propalar.

run [ran] s. corrida, carrera. 2 curso, marcha, dirección. 3 viaje, paseo. 4 t.-i. correr. 5 dirigir [un negocio]. 6 extenderse; llegar, alcanzar [hasta]. ¶ Pret.: *ran* [ræn]; p. p.: *run* [ran]; ger; *running*.

runner ['rʌnəʳ] s. corredor. 2 contrabandista.

running ['rʌniŋ] s. carrera, corrida, curso. 2 marcha, funcionamiento. 3 dirección, manejo. 4 a. corredor. 5 corriente.

rural ['ruərəl] a. rural, rústico.

rush [rʌʃ] s. movimiento o avance impetuoso. 2 prisa, precipitación. 3 i. arrojarse, abalanzarse, precipitarse. 4 t. empujar.

Russian ['rʌʃən] a.-s. ruso.

rust [rʌst] s. moho, orín. 2 t. enmohecer(se.

rustic ['rʌstik] a.-s. rústico. 2 campesino. 3 a. campestre.

rustle ['rʌsl] s. susurro, crujido. 2 i. susurrar, crujir.

rusty ['rʌsti] a. mohoso.

rye [rai] s. BOT. centeno. 2 BOT. ~ grass, ballico, césped inglés.

S

sack [sæk] *s.* saco. 2 saqueo. 3 despido. 4 *t.* saquear. 4 ensacar. 5 despedir.

sacred ['seikrid] *a.* sagrado.

sacrifice ['sækrifais] *s.* sacrificio.

sacrifice ['sækrifais] *t.* sacrificar; inmolar.

sacrilege ['sækrilidʒ] *s.* sacrilegio.

sad [sæd] *a.* triste.

saddle ['sædl] *s.* silla de montar. 2 *t.* ensillar.

sadness [s'ædnis] *s.* tristeza.

safe [seif] *a.* salvo, ileso. 2 *s.* arca, caja de caudales.

safeguard ['seifgɑ:d] *s.* salvaguardia, resguardo.

safety ['seifti] *s.* seguridad.

sage [seidʒ] *s.* BOT. salvia. 2 *a.-s.* sabio, filósofo, hombre prudente.

said]sed] V. TO SAY.

sail [seil] *s.* MAR. vela. 2 aspa [de molino]. 3 *i.* navegar.

sailor ['seilər] *s.* marinero.

saint [sent, sən(t)] *s.* san, santo, -ta.

sake [seik] *s.* causa, amor: for God's —, por el amor de Dios.

salad ['sæləd] *s.* ensalada.

salary ['sæləri] *s.* salario.

sale [seil] *s.* venta.

salesman ['seilzmən] *s.* vendedor. 2 viajante de comercio.

salmon ['sæmən] *s.* ICT. salmón.

saloon [sə'luːn] *s.* salón. [gran sala]. 2 (E. U.) taberna, bar.

salt [sɔːlt] *s.* QUÍM. sal. 2 sal común. 3 *a.* salado, salino. 4 *t.* salar.

salute [sə'luːt] *s.* saludo. 2 *t.-i.* saludar.

same [seim] *a.-pron.* mismo, misma, etc.

sample ['saːmpl] *s.* COM. muestra. 2 muestra, cala. 3 *t.* sacar muestra de; probar, catar.

sanction ['sæŋkʃən] *s.* sanción. 2 *t.* sancionar.

sanctuary ['sæŋktjuəri] *s.* santuario.

sand [sænd] *s.* arena.

sandwich ['sænwidʒ] *s.* emparedado, bocadillo.

sane [sein] *a.* sano. 2 cuerdo.

sang [sæŋ] V. TO SING.

sap [sæp] *s.* savia. 2 vigor. 3 *t.* zapar, minar.

sash [sæʃ] *s.* faja, ceñidor; ~ window, ventana de guillotina.

satin ['sætin] *s.* TEJ. raso.

satiric [sə'tirik] *a.* satírico.

satisfaction [ˌsætis'fækʃən] *s.* satisfacción.

satisfactory [ˌsætis'fæktəri] *a.* satisfactorio. 2 suficiente.

satisfy ['sætisfai] *t.* satisfacer. 2 contentar. 3 convencer.

sausage ['sɔsidʒ] *s.* salsicha.

savage ['sævidʒ] *a.* salvaje.

save [seiv] *prep.* salvo, excepto. 2 *t.* salvar, librar.

saving ['seiviŋ] *s.* economía, ahorro. 2 *pl.* ahorros. 3 *prep.* salvo, excepto.

saw [sɔː] *s.* sierra [herramienta]. 2 dicho, refrán. 3 *pret.* de TO SEE. 4 *t.-i.* serrar, aserrar. ¶ Pret.: *sawed* [sɔːd]; p. p.: *sawn* [sɔːn].

say [sei] *s.* dicho, aserto. 2 turno para hablar. 3 *t.* decir. ¶ Pres.: *says* [sez]; pret. y p. p.: *said* [sed].

saying ['seiiŋ] *s.* dicho, sentencia.

scale [skeil] *s.* platillo. 2 balanza, báscula. 3 escala. 4 *t.* pesar.

scalp [skælp] *s.* cuero cabelludo. 3 *t.* arrancar la cabellera.

scandal ['skændl] *s.* escándalo. 2 ignominia. 3 difamación.

scandalous ['skændələs]

a. escandaloso, vergonzoso.

scanty ['skænti] *a.* escaso, insuficiente, exiguo.

scar [ska:^r] *s.* cicatriz.

scarce [skɛəs] *a.* escaso, raro.

scare [skɛə^r] *s.* susto, alarma. 2 *t.* asustar, alarmar.

scarf [ska:f] *s.* echarpe.

scarlet ['ska:lit] *a.* rojo, de color escarlata.

scatter ['skætə^r] *t.* dispersar. 2 disipar, desvanecer.

scene [si:n] *s.* escena. 2 escenario. 3 TEAT. decorado.

scenery ['si:nəri] *s.* paisaje. 2 THEAT. decorado.

scent [sent] *s.* olfato. 2 olor. 3 *t.* oler, husmear.

schedule ['ʃedju:l], (E. U.) 'skedju:l] *s.* lista, inventario; horario.

scheme [ski:m] *s.* esquema. 2 *t.* proyectar, idear.

schism ['sizəm] *s.* cisma.

scholar ['skɔlə^r] *s.* colegial, -a. 2 becario. 3 sabio, erudito.

scholarship ['skɔləʃip] *s.* saber, erudición. 2 beca [para estudiar].

school [sku:l] *s.* escuela. 2 *t.* enseñar, instruir.

schoolmaster ['sku:lˌma:stə^r] *s.* profesor de instituto.

science ['saiens] *s.* ciencia. 2 ciencas naturales.

scientist ['saiəntist] *s.* hombre de ciencia.

scold [skəuld] *t.* reñir, regañar.

scope [skəup] *s.* alcance [de un arma]. 2 campo o radio [de acción]. 3 mira, designio.

score [skɔ:^r, skɔə^r] *s.* muesca, entalladura. 2 cuenta [de lo que se debe]. 3 tantos, tanteo. 4 razón, motivo. 5 veintena. 6 MÚS. partitura. 7 *t.* esclopear. 8 marcar, ganar [puntos, tantos]. 9 rayar. 10 MÚS. orquestar.

scorn [skɔ:n] *s.* desdén, desprecio. 2 *t.* desdeñar, despreciar.

Scot [skɔt], *s.*, **Scotch** [skɔtʃ] *a.-s.* escocés.

scourge [ska:dʒ] *s.* látigo. 2 *t.* azotar, flagelar.

scout [skaut] *s.* MIL. explorador, escucha. 2 *t.-i.* explorar.

scowl [skaul] *s.* ceño, sobrecejo. 2 *i.* mirar con ceño.

scramble ['skræmbl] s. lucha, arrebatiña. 2 gateamiento. 3 i. trepar, gatear. 4 andar a la arrebatiña.

scrap [skræp] s. trozo, pedazo.

scrape [skreip] s. raspadura, rasguño. 3 t. raspar, rascar.

scratch [skrætʃ] s. arañazo. 2 t. arañar, rayar.

scream [skri:m] s. chillido, grito. 2 t.-i. chillar, gritar.

screen [skri:n] s. pantalla. 2 t. ocultar, tapar.

screw [skru:] s. tornillo, rosca. 2 t. atornillar.

script [skript] s. escritura. 2 manuscrito; guión [cine].

Scripture ['skriptʃəʳ] s. Sagrada Escritura.

scrub [skrʌb] a. desmirriado. 2 s. fregado, fregoteo. 3 t. fregar, estregar.

sculptor ['skʌlptəʳ] s. escultor.

sculpture ['skʌlptʃəʳ] s. escultura.

sea [si:] s. mar, océano.

seal [si:l] s. ZOOL. foca. 2 sello, sigilo. 3 t. sellar, precintar.

seam [si:m] s. costura. 2 t. coser.

seaman ['si:mən] s. marinero.

search [sə:tʃ] s. busca, búsqueda. 2 t.-i. buscar.

season ['si:zn] s. estación [del año]. 2 tiempo, temporada. 3 t. sazonar. 4 habituar, aclimatar.

seat [si:t] s. asiento. 2 sitio, sede, residencia. 3 t. sentar. 4 establecer, instalar.

secede [si'si:d] i. separarse.

second ['sekənd] a. segundo. 2 secundario, subordinado. 3 inferior. 4 s. segundo [división del minuto]. 5 t. secundar, apoyar.

secondary ['sekəndəri] a. secundar.

secret ['si:krit] a. secreto. 2 callado, reservado. 3 s. secreto.

secretary ['sekrətri] s. secretario.

section ['sekʃən] s. sección.

secular ['sekjuləʳ] a. secular. 2 seglar, lego.

secure [si'kjuəʳ] a. seguro. 2 t. asegurar; afianzar.

security [si'kjuəriti] s. seguridad. 2 protección.

see (si:) s. ECLES. sede, silla. 2 t.-i. ver. 3 mirar, observar. 4 considerar, juzgar. 5 to ~ after, cuidar. ¶ Pret.: saw (sɔ:); p. p.: seen [si:n].

seed [si:d] s. BOT. semilla. 2 t.-i. sembrar.

seek [si:k] t. buscar. ¶ Pret. y p. p.: sought [sɔ:t].

seem [si:m] i. parecer.

seen [si:n] V. TO SEE.

seize [si:z] t. asir, agarrar.

seldom ['seldəm] adv. raramente, rara vez.

select [si'lekt] a. selecto. 2 t. escoger, elegir.

selection [si'lekʃən] s. selección.

self [self], pl. selves [selvz] a. mismo; idéntico. 2 self-, [en compuestos] auto-, por sí mismo; ~ conscious, tímido; ~ sufficient, presuntuoso.

selfish ['selfiʃ] a. interesado, egoísta. 2 -ly adv. interesadamente, egoístamente.

sell [sel] s. fam. engaño, estafa. 2 t.-i. vender[se. ¶ Pret. y p. p.: sold [sould].

seller ['selər] s. vendedor.

senate ['senit] s. senado.

send [send] t. enviar, mandar. 2 lanzar. ¶ Pret. y p. p.: sent [sent].

senior ['si:njər] a. mayor, de más edad; más antiguo; decano. 2 (E. U.) del último curso de una facultad. 3 s. anciano.

sense [sens] s. sentido [corporal; del humor, etc.]. 2 cordura, buen sentido. 3 inteligencia. 4 significado, acepción. 5 sensación, impresión, conciencia. 6 t. sentir, percibir, darse cuenta.

sensible ['sensibl] a. juicioso, prudente, sensato, cuerdo.

sensitive ['sensitiv] a. sensitivo. 2 sensible, impresionable.

sent [sent] V. TO SEND.

sentence ['sentəns] s. sentencia; fallo; condena. 2 sentencia, máxima. 3 GRAM. oración, período.

sentiment ['sentimənt] s. sentimiento. 2 sensibilidad. 3 parecer, opinión. 4 concepto, frase.

separate ['seprit] a. separado. 2 ['sepəreit] t. separar. 3 despegar.

separation [,sepə'reiʃən] s. separación. 2 porción.

September [səp'tembər] *s.* septiembre.

serene [si'ri:n] *a.* sereno, claro.

sergeant ['sɑːdʒənt] *s.* MIL. sargento.

series ['siəriːz] *s.* serie.

serious ['siəriəs] *a.* serio.

sermon ['sɔːmən] *s.* sermón.

serpent ['sɔːpənt] *s.* serpiente.

servant ['sɔːvənt] *s.* sirviente, criado.

serve [sɔːv] *t.-i.* servir. 2 surtir, abastecer.

service ['sɔːvis] *s.* servicio.

servile ['sɔːvail] *a.* servil.

session ['seʃən] *s.* sesión.

set [set] *s.* juego, servicio, colección; grupo. 2 aparato [de radio, etc.]. 3 *a.* resuelto, determinado. 4 fijo, inmóvil. 5 *t.* poner, colocar. 6 destinar, fijar. 7 *to* ~ *about*, poner a. 8 *to* ~ *aside*, dejar a un lado. 9 *to* ~ *fire to*, pegar fuego a. 10 *to* ~ *free*, libertar. 11 *to* ~ *going*, poner en marcha. ¶ Pret y p. p.: *set* [set]; ger.: *setting* ['setiŋ]

settle ['setl] *t.* escaño, banco. 2 *t.* colocar, establecer. 3 fijar, asegurar.

4 colonizar, poblar. 5 *i.* establecerse, instalarse.

settler ['setlər] *s.* poblador, colono.

seven ['sevn] *a.-s.* siete. 2 **-teen** [-'tiːn] diecisiete. 3 **-teenth** [-'tiːnθ] decimoséptimo. 4 **-th** [-θ] séptimo. 5 **-tieth** [-tiəθ, -tiiθ] septuagésimo. 6 **-ty** [-ti] setenta.

several ['sevrəl] *a.* varios.

severe [si'viər] *a.* severo.

sew [sou] *t.-i.* coser. ¶ Pret.: *sewed* [soud]; p. p.: *sewn* [soun] o *sewed*.

sewing ['souiŋ] *s.* costura: ~ *machine*, máquina de coser.

sex [seks] *s.* sexo.

shabby ['ʃæbi] *a.* raído.

shade [ʃeid] *s.* sombra. 2 matiz, tinte. 3 pantalla [de lámpara]. 4 visillo, cortina. 5 *t.* hacer o dar sombra. 6 proteger, esconder.

shadow ['ʃædou] *s.* sombra. 2 *t.* sombrear; oscurecer.

shaft [ʃɑːft] *s.* astil. 2 asta. 3 saeta.

shake [ʃeik] *s.* meneo, sacudida. 2 apretón [de manos]. 3 *t.* sacudir, agitar, blandir. ¶ Pret.:

shook [ʃuk]; p. p.: *shaken* [ˈʃeikən].

shall [ʃæl, ʃəl] *v. def. aux.* del futuro. En 1.ª personas denota simple acción futura; en 2.ª y 3.ª, voluntad, intención, mandato: *I shall go*, iré; *he shall go*, tiene que ir. 2 **SHOUL** [ʃud, ʃəd] pret. de *shall*. En 1.ª personas, forma potencial; en 2.ª y 3.ª, voluntad, intención, mandato: *I should come*, vendría; *you should come*, deberías venir.

shallow [ˈʃæləu] *a.* bajo, poco profundo. 2 superficial, frívolo.

shame [ʃeim] *s.* vergüenza. 2 *t.* avergonzar.

shameful [ˈʃeimful] *a.* vergonzoso.

shape [ʃeip] *s.* forma, figura. 2 *t.* formar, dar forma a; modelar.

share [ʃɛəʳ] *s.* parte, porción. 2 participación. 3 *t.* distribuir, repartir.

sharp [ʃɑːp] *a.* agudo, aguzado, afilado, cortante, punzante.

sharpen [ˈʃɑːpən] *t.* afilar.

shatter [ˈʃætəʳ] *t.* romper, hacer estallar.

shave [ʃeiv] *t.-i.* afeitar(se.

shaving [ˈʃeiviŋ] *s.* afeitado.

shawl [ʃɔːl] *s.* chal, mantón.

she [ʃiː, ʃi] *pron. pers.* ella. 2 hembra: *she-ass*, borrica.

shear [ʃiəʳ] *s.* esquileo. 2 lana esquilada. 3 *t.* esquilar, trasquilar. ¶ P. p.: *shorn* [ʃɔːn].

shed [ʃed] *s.* cobertizo, alpende. 2 *t.* verter, derramar. 3 *i.* mudar [la piel, etc.]. ¶ Pret. y p. p.: *shed*.

sheep [ʃiːp] *s. sing.* y *pl.* carnero(s, oveja(s.

sheer [ʃiəʳ] *a.* puro, mero. 2 *t.-i.* desviar(se.

sheet [ʃiːt] *s.* lámina, plancha. 2 sábana.

shelf [ʃelf], *pl.* **shelves** [ʃelvz] *s.* anaquel; *pl.* estantería.

shell [ʃel] *s.* ZOOL. concha, caparazón. 2 cáscara [de huevo, nuez, etc.]. 3 bala [de cañón], bomba, granada. 4 *t.* descascarar, mondar. 5 bombardear.

shelter [ˈʃeltəʳ] *s.* abrigo, refugio. 2 *t.-i.* guarecer(se, abrigar(se.

shelves [ʃelvz] s. pl. de SHELF.

shepherd ['ʃepəd] s. pastor.

sheriff ['ʃerif] s. alguacil mayor, sheriff.

shield [ʃi:ld] s. escudo. 2 t. proteger, escudar.

shift [ʃift] s. recurso, maña. 2 tanda, turno [de obreros; de trabajo]. 3 cambio, desviación. 4 t.-i. cambiar, mudar [de posición, etc.]. 5 usar subterfugios.

shilling ['ʃiliŋ] s. chelin.

shine [ʃain] s. brillo. 2 i. brillar. ¶ Pret. y p. p.: *shone* [ʃɔn].

ship [ʃip] s. buque, barco. 2 t. embarcar(se. 3 t. transportar.

shipping ['ʃipiŋ] s. embarque.

shirk [ʃə:k] t. eludir.

shirt [ʃə:t] s. camisa.

shiver ['ʃivə'] s. temblor. 2 i.-t. temblar, tiritar.

shoal [ʃoul] s. bajo, banco [de arena o de peces].

shock [ʃɔk] s. golpe, choque. 2 conmoción. 3 t. chocar; ofender. 4 conmover.

shoe [ʃu:] s. zapato: ~

black, limpiabotas; ~ polish, betún; ~ calzador. 2 t. calzar; herrar [a un caballo]. ¶ Pret. y p. p.: *shod* [ʃɔd].

shoemaker ['ʃu:,meikə'] s. zapatero.

shone [ʃɔn] TO SHINE.

shook [ʃuk] V. TO SHAKE.

shoot [ʃu:t] s. BOT. vástago, retoño. 2 cacería. 3 t. fusilar. 4 disparar. 5 DEP. chutar. 6 i. ir de caza. 7 to ~ up, brotar [las plantas, etc.]. ¶ Pret. y p. p.: *shot* [ʃɔt].

shop [ʃɔp] s. tienda, comercio. 2 i. comprar: to go shopping, ir de compras.

shore [ʃɔ:'] s. orilla, costa, playa.

shorn [ʃɔ:n] V. TO SHEAR.

short [ʃɔ:t] a. corto; breve, escaso, poco. 2 bajo [de estatura]. 3 seco, brusco. 4 ~ hand, taquígrafo, taquigrafía; ~ sighted, corto de vista. 5 adv. brevemente, cortamente; ~ of, excepto, si no. 6 s. CINEM. película corta. 7 pl. pantalones cortos [para deporte].

shot [ʃɔt] a. tornasolado, matizado. 2 s. tiro,

disparo. 3 bala. 4 tirada
[en ciertos juegos]. 6 V.
TO SHOOT.

should [ʃud, ʃed] V.
SHALL.

shoulder ['ʃəuldəʳ] s.
hombro. 2 t. echar o lle-
var al hombro; cargar
con.

shout [ʃaut] s. grito, gri-
terío. 2 t.-i. gritar, vo-
cear.

shove [ʃʌv] s. empujón,
empuje. 2 t.-i. empujar,
dar empujones.

shovel ['ʃʌvl] s. pala. 2
palada.

show [ʃou] s. presentación. 2 exposición. 3 es-
pectáculo; función [de
teatro, cine]. 4 ostenta-
ción. 5 t. mostrar, ense-
ñar, exhibir. 6 hacer ver,
demostrar. 7 to ~ how
to, enseñar a [hacer al-
go]. 8 to ~ up, destacar.
9 TEAT. actuar. ¶ Pret.:
showed [ʃoud]; p. p.:
shown [ʃəun] o showed.

shower ['ʃauəʳ] s. chu-
basco, chaparrón. 2 abun-
dancia. 3 ~ bath, ducha.

shown [ʃəun] V. TO SHOW.

shrewd [ʃru:d] a. sagaz,
listo.

shriek [ʃri:k] s. chillido,
alarido. 2 i. chillar, gritar.

shrill [ʃril] a. agudo, chi-
llón. 2 t.-i. chillar.

shrine [ʃrain] s. urna,
relicario.

shrink [ʃriŋk] t.-i. enco-
ger(se, contraerse; dis-
minuir. ¶ Pret.: shrank
[ʃræŋk] o shrunk
[ʃrʌŋk]; p. p.: shrunk
o shrunken ['ʃrʌŋkən].

shrub [ʃrʌb] s. arbusto.

shrug [ʃrʌg] t.-i. enco-
ger(se [de hombros].

shrunk [ʃrʌŋk] V. TO
SHRINK.

shudder ['ʃʌdəʳ] s. temblor. 2 i. estremecerse.

shun [ʃʌn] t. rehuir.

shut [ʃʌt] t. cerrar [una
puerta, etc.]. 2 tapar,
obstruir. 3 to ~ down,
cerrar una fábrica; to ~
up, tapar; callarse. ¶
Pret. y p. p.: shut [ʃʌt];
ger.: shutting.

shutter ['ʃʌtəʳ] s. posti-
go.

shy [ʃai] a. tímido, asus-
tadizo. 2 i. esquivar;
asustarse.

sick [sik] a.-s. enfermo.
2 mareado. 3 to be ~ of,
estar harto de.

sickness ['siknis] s. enfermedad.

side [said] s. lado, costado. 2 orilla, margen. 3

falda [de montaña]. *4* partido, bando. *5 a.* lateral; secundario. *6 t.* ponerse o estar al lado de.

sidewalk ['said-wɔːk] *s.* (E. U.) acera.

siege [siːdʒ] *s.* sitio, asedio, cerco.

sift [sift] *t.* cerner, tamizar, cribar.

sigh [sai] *s.* suspiro. *2 i.* suspirar.

sight [sait] *s.* vista, visión: *at* ~, *on* ~, a primera vista. 2 escena, espectáculo. 3 monumentos. *4* **-ly** *a.* vistoso, hermoso.

sight [sait] *t.-i.* ver, mirar.

sign [sain] *s.* signo, señal. 2 *t.-i.* firmar, rubricar.

signal ['signəl] *s.* señal, seña. 2 *a.* señalado, notable. 3 *t.-i.* hacer señales.

signature ['signətʃər] *s.* firma.

signify ['signifai] *t.* significar. 2 *i.* importar.

silence ['sailəns] *s.* silencio. 2 *t.* imponer silencio.

silent ['sailənt] *a.* silencioso.

silhouette [ˌsiluˈet] *s.* silueta.

silk [silk] *s.* seda [materia, hilo, tejido]: ~ *hat*, sombrero de copa.

silken ['silkən] *a.* de seda.

silliness ['silinis] *s.* tontería.

silly ['sili] *a.* tonto, necio.

silver ['silvər] *s.* plata. 2 *a.* de plata.

similar ['similər] *a.* similar.

simple ['simpl] *a.* simple. 2 tonto, bobo.

simplicity [simˈplisiti] *s.* simplicidad. 2 sencillez.

simply ['simpli] *adv.* simplemente; meramente.

sin [sin] *s.* pecado. 2 *i.* pecar.

since [sins] *adv.* desde. 2 *prep.* desde, después de 3 *conj.* desde que, después que. *4* ya que, puesto que.

sincere [sinˈsiər] *a.* sincero.

sing [siŋ] *t.-i.* cantar. ¶ Pret.: *sang* [sæŋ]; p. p.: *sung* [sʌŋ].

singer ['siŋər] *s.* cantante.

single ['siŋgl] *a.* único. 2 célibe: ~ *man*, soltero.

3 sencillo, simple. 4 individual. 5 t. to ~ out, singularizar.

singular ['siŋgjulər] a. singular. 2 raro, estrafalario.

sink [siŋk] s. sumidero. 2 fregadero. 3 t.-i. hundir(se, sumergir(se. 4 to ~ down, derrumbarse. 5 ponerse [el sol]. ¶ Pret.: *sank* [sæŋk] o *sunk* [sʌŋk]; p. p.: *sunk* o *sunken* ['sʌŋkən].

sinner ['sinə'] s. pecador.

sinuosity ['sinju'ɔsiti] s. sinuosidad, tortuosidad.

sinuous ['sinjuəs] a. sinuoso.

sir [sə:', sə'] s. señor. 2 [Ingl.] tratamiento que se antepone al nombre de un caballero o baronet: *Sir Winston Churchill.*

sire ['saiə'] s. señor [tratamiento del soberano]. 2 progenitor.

sister ['sistə'] s. hermana. 2 sor, monja. 3 enfermera. 4 *sister-in-law,* cuñada.

sit [sit] t.-i. sentar(se; posarse [un pájaro]; estar sentado. 2 empollar [las gallinas]. 3 celebrar sesión. 4 sentar bien [un

traje]. 5 to ~ down, sentarse; establecerse. 6 to ~ for, representar [un distrito]; servir de modelo. 7 to ~ on o upon, deliberar sobre. 8 to ~ up, incorporarse [en la cama]. ¶ Pret. y p. p.: *sat* [sæt].

site [sait] s. sitio, escenario. 2 asiento, situación.

situation [,sitju'eiʃən] s. situación. 2 empleo.

six [siks] a.-s. seis. 2 **-teen** [-'ti:n] dieciséis. 3 **-teenth** [-'ti:nθ] decimosexto. 4 **-th** [-θ] sexto. 5 **-tieth** [-tiəθ] sexagésimo. 6 **-ty** [-ti] sesenta.

size [saiz] s. medida, tamaño. 2 t. clasificar según tamaño.

skate [skeit] s. patín. 2 i. patinar.

skeleton ['skelitn] s. esqueleto. 2 armazón. 3 esbozo, esquema. 4 ~ *key,* llave maestra.

sketch [sketʃ] s. boceto. 2 t. esbozar.

skilful ['skilful] a. diestro.

skill [skil] s. habilidad.

skilled [skild] a. práctico.

skim [skim] t. espumar.

skin [skin] s. piel, cutis. 2 odre. 3 cáscara, hollejo. 4 *skin-deep*, superficial. 5 t. desollar, despellejar.

skip [skip] s. salto. 2 omitir, pasar por alto.

skirt [skə:t] s. falda. 2 orilla. 3 *t.-i.* bordear, rodear.

skull [skʌl] s. cráneo, calavera.

sky [skai] s. cielo, firmamento.

slain [slein] V. TO SLAY.

slam [slæm] s. golpe, portazo. 2 t. cerrar de golpe.

slander ['slɑ:ndə'] s. calumnia. 2 t. calumniar, difamar.

slap [slæp] s. palmada; bofetón. 2 insulto. 3 t. pegar, abofetear.

slate [sleit] s. pizarra.

slaughter ['slɔ:tə'] s. matanza. 2 t. matar. 3 sacrificar [reses].

slave [sleiv] s. esclavo.

slavery ['sleivəri] s. esclavitud.

slay [slei] t. matar. ¶ Pret.: *slew* [slu:]; p. p.: *slain* [slein].

sled [sled], **sledge** [sledʒ] s. trineo, rastra.

sleep [sli:p] s. sueño. 2 i. dormir. ¶ Pret. y p. p.: *slept* [slept].

sleeping ['sli:piŋ] a. dormido.

sleepy ['sli:pi] a. soñoliento.

sleeve [sli:v] s. manga.

slender ['slendə'] a. delgado.

slept [slept] V. TO SLEEP.

slew [slu:] V. TO SLAY.

slice [slais] s. rebanada, lonja. 2 t. rebanar. 3 tajar.

slid [slid] V. TO SLIDE.

slide [slaid] s. corrimiento de tierra; falla. 2 *i.-t.* resbalar. ¶ Pret. y p. p.: *slid* [slid].

slight [slait] a. ligero. 2 pequeño, insignificante. 3 delgado. 4 s. desaire. 5 t. despreciar.

slim [slim] a. delgado, esbelto.

slip [slip] s. resbalón. 2 huida, esquinazo. 3 tira [trozo estrecho]. 4 combinación [de mujer]. 5 *t.-i.* resbalar(se.

slipper ['slipə'] s. zapatilla.

slippery ['slipəri] a. resbaladizo.

slope [sləup] s. cuesta. 2 ladera. 3 i. inclinarse.

slow [slou] *a.* lento, tardo. 2 torpe. 3 atrasado. 4 *adv.* lentamente, despacio. 5 *t.-i.* retardar.

slumber ['slʌmbər] *s.* sueño. 2 *i.* dormitar. 3 dormirse.

sly [slai] *a.* astuto, socarrón. 2 *on the* ~, a hurtadillas. 3 **-ly** *adv.* astutamente.

small [smɔ:l] *a.* pequeño, insignificante: ~ *change*, dinero suelto. 2 bajo [estatura].

smart [sma:t] *a.* elegante: *the* ~ *set*, la gente distinguida. 2 listo, astuto. 3 fuerte, violento. 4 *s.* dolor. 5 *i.* escocer doler.

smash [smæʃ] *s.* rotura, destrozo. 2 choque [de vehículos, etc.]. 3 fracaso, bancarrota. 4 *t.-i.* romper(se, destrozar(se. 5 quebrar. 6 chocar.

smell [smel] *s.* olfato [sentido]. 2 olor. 3 *t.* oler. 4 olfatear, husmear. ¶ Pret. y p. p.: *smelt* [smelt].

smile [smail] *s.* sonrisa. 2 *i.* sonreír(se.

smite [smait] *t.* golpear. 2 asolar. 3 remorder [la conciencia]. ¶ Pret.:

smote [smout] p. p.: *smiten* ['smitn].

smoke [smouk] *s.* humo. 2 *t.-i.* fumar. 3 ahumar.

smooth [smu:ð] *a.* liso. 2 cepillar, pulir. 3 facilitar [las cosas]. 4 suavizar. 5 calmar. 6 *a.* liso, llano. 7 afable.

smote [smout] V. TO SMITE.

smother ['smʌðər] *t.-i.* ahogar(se. 2 sofocar(se.

snake [sneik] *s.* culebra, serpiente. 2 *i.* serpentear.

snap [snæp] *s.* chasquido. 2 mordisco. 3 energía, vigor. 4 ~ *shot*, foto instantánea. 5 *t.-i.* chasquear. 6 tirar un bocado a. 4 hacer una instantánea.

snare [snɛər] *s.* lazo. 2 celada. 3 *t.* atrapar.

snarl [sna:l] *s.* gruñido. 2 *i.* regañar; gruñir.

snatch [snætʃ] *s.* acción de arrebatar. 2 trozo, pedacito. 3 rato. 4 *t.* coger, arrebatar, quitar.

sneak [sni:k] *s.* persona ruin. 2 *t.-i.* andar u obrar furtivamente. 3 hurtar, ratear.

sneer [sniə^r] s. burla, mofa. 2 i. reirse con burla o desprecio; burlarse.

sniff [snif] s. olfato, husmeo. 2 t. olfatear, husmear.

snob [snɔb] s. esnob [persona con pretensiones sociales.]

snow [snou] s. nieve. 2 i. nevar.

snuffle ['snʌfl] i. respirar con la nariz obstruida.

so [sou] adv. asi; eso, lo mismo: I hope ~, asi lo espero. 2 ~ that, para que. 3 tan, tanto: ~ good, tan bueno. 4 y asi, por tanto. 5 conj. con tal que; para que. 6 and ~ forth, etcétera; ~ far as, hasta; ~ long, hasta la vista; ~ much, tanto; ~ many, tantos; so-so, regular; so-and-so, fulano [de tal]; ~ far hasta ahora, hasta aqui; ~ to say, o to speak, por decirlo asi.

soak [souk] s. remojo, remojón. 2 borrachin. 3 t.-i. remojar(se, empapar-(se.

soap [soup] s. jabón. 2 t. jabonar.

soar [sɔː^r, souə^r] i. elevarse.

sob [sɔb] s. sollozo. 3 i. sollozar.

sober ['soubə^r] a. sobrio.

so-called ['sou'kɔːld] a. llamado.

social ['souʃəl] a. social.

society [sə'saiəti] s. sociedad.

sock [sɔk] s. calcetin. 2 golpe.

sod [sɔd] s. césped.

soft [sɔft] a. blando, maleable.

soften ['sɔfn] t.-i. ablandar(se, suavizar(se.

soil [sɔil] s. tierra, terreno. 2 t. ensuciar, manchar.

sold [sould] V. TO SELL.

soldier ['souldʒə^r] s. soldado.

sole [soul] s. planta [del pie]; palma [del casco del caballo]. 2 suela [del zapato]. 3 suelo, base. 4 ICT. lenguado. 5 a. solo, único: ~ right, exclusiva.

solemn ['sɔləm] a. solemne.

solid ['sɔlid] a. sólido.

solitude ['sɔlitjuːd] s. soledad.

solution [sə'luːʃən] s. solución.

solve [sɔlv] *t.* resolver.

some [sʌm, səm] *a.-pron.* algún, algunos. 2 un poco de.

somebody ['sʌmbədi] *pron.* alguien, alguno.

somehow ['sʌmhau] *adv.* de algún modo.

someone ['sʌmwʌn] *pron.* SOMEBODY.

something ['sʌmθiŋ] *s.* algo, alguna cosa.

sometimes ['sʌmtaimz] *adv.* algunas veces, a veces.

somewhat ['sʌmwɔt] *s.* algo, un poco. 2 *adv.* algo, algún tanto; en cierto modo.

somewhere ['sʌmwɛɔʳ] *adv.* en alguna parte.

son [sʌn] *s.* hijo. 2 *son-in-law,* yerno.

song [sɔŋ] *s.* canto. 2 MÚS., LIT. canción. canto, copla, cantar.

soon [su:n] *adv.* pronto, luego: *I had (would) sooner not do it,* preferiría no hacerlo.

soothe [su:ð] *t.* aliviar.

sophisticated [sɔ'fistikeitid] *a.* sofisticada. 2 artificial.

sore [sɔ:ʳ, soəʳ] *a.* dolorido. 2 *s.* herida, llaga.

sorrow ['sɔrou] *s.* dolor, pesar. 2 *i.* afligirse.

sorry ['sɔri] *a.* afligido, pesaroso, triste: *I am* ∼, lo siento.

sort [sɔ:t] *s.* clase, especie. 2 modo, manera: *in a* ∼, en cierto modo. 3 *t.* ordenar, clasificar.

sought [sɔ:t] V. TO SEEK.

soul [soul] *s.* alma.

sound [saund] *a.* sano. 2 *s.* son, sonido. 3 *i.* sonar. 4 *t.* tocar, tañer.

soup [su:p] *s.* sopa.

sour ['sauɔʳ] *a.* ácido, agrio. 2 *i.-t.* agriarse. 3 enranciarse.

source [sɔ:s] *s.* fuente, manantial.

south [sauθ] *s.* sur, mediodía.

southern ['sʌðən] *a.* del sur.

sovereign ['sɔvrin] *a.* soberano. 2 *s.* soberano [monarca; moneda].

soviet ['souviet] *s.* soviet. 2 *a.* soviético.

1) **sow** [sau] *s.* cerda, marrana.

2) **sow** [sou] *t.* sembrar. ¶ Pret.: *sowed* [soud]; p. p.: *sown* [soun] o *sowed.*

space [speis] *s.* espacio. 2 oportunidad. 3 *t.* espaciar.

spacious ['speiʃəs] *a.* espacioso.

spade [speid] s. laya, pala.

span [spæn] s. palmo. 2 ojo [de puente]. 3 extensión. 4 V. TO SPIN.

Spaniard ['spænjəd] s. español.

Spanish ['spæniʃ] a. español. 2 s. lengua española o castellana.

spare [spɛəʳ] a. de repuesto. 2 flaco, enjuto. 3 sobrio, frugal. 4 t. ahorrar, economizar. 5 prescindir de, pasar sin.

spark [spɑ:k] s. chispa; centella. 2 i. chispear, echar chispas.

sparkle ['spɑ:kl] s. chispa. 2 i. chispear.

sparrow ['spærəu] s. gorrión.

speak [spi:k] i. hablar: to ~ out, hablar claro. 2 t. hablar, decir, expresar. 3 hablar [una lengua]. ¶ Pret.: spoke [spəuk]; p. p.: spoken ['spəukən].

speaker ['spi:kəʳ] s. el que habla. 2 orador. 3 presidente [de una asamblea]. 4 RADIO locutor.

spear [spiəʳ] s. lanza, venablo. 2 arpón [para pescar]. 3 t. alancear. 4 atravesar con arpón.

special ['speʃəl] a. especial. 2 particular, peculiar. 3 s. tren, autobús, etc., especial.

species ['spi:ʃi:z] s. especie [imagen: apariencia]. 2 clase, suerte. 3 género humano.

specific(al [spə'sifik, -əl] a. específico. 2 preciso. 3 característico. 4 s. FARM. específico.

specimen ['spesimin] s. espécimen.

speck [spek] s. manchita. 2 t. manchar.

spectacle ['spektəkl] s. espectáculo. 2 pl. gafas, anteojos.

spectator [spek'teitəʳ] s. espectador.

speech [spi:tʃ] s. palabra, lenguaje. 2 idioma. 3 discurso. 4 TEAT. parlamento. 5 conversación.

speed [spi:d] s. rapidez, prisa. 2 t. acelerar, dar prisa a. ¶ Pret. y p. p.: sped [sped] o speeded ['spi:did].

spell [spel] s. hechizo, encanto. 2 turno, tanda. 3 t.-i. deletrear. ¶ Pret. y p. p.: spelled [speld] o spelt [spelt].

spend [spen] t. gastar. 2

pasar [el tiempo]. ¶
Pret. y p. p.: *spent*
sphere [sfiəʳ] *s.* esfera. 2
globo.

spice [spais] *s.* especia. 2
t. condimentar con especias.

spider ['spaidəʳ] *s.* araña.

spill [spil] *t.-i.* derramar-
(se. ¶ Pret. y p. p.:
spilled [spild] o *spilt*
[spilt].

spin [spin] *s.* giro, vuelta. 2 *t.-i.* hilar. 3 hacer
girar. ¶ Pret.: *spun*
[spʌn] o *span* [spæn];
p. p.: *spun* [spʌn].

spine [spain] *s.* espinazo.

spire ['spaiəʳ] *s.* cima,
aguja de campanario.

spirit ['spirit] *s.* espiritu.
2 *pl.* alcohol, bebida es-
pirituosa. 3 *t.* alentar,
animar.

spiritual [['spiritjuəl] *a.*
espiritual. 2 *s.* espiritual
[canto religioso de los
negros].

spit [spit] *s.* asador. 2
esputo. 3 *i.* escupir, es-
putar. 4 lloviznar. ¶
Pret. y p. p.: *spat*
[spæt].

spite [spait] *s.* despecho,
rencor. 2 *in* ~ *of*, a pesar de. 3 *t.* molestar.

splash [splæʃ] *s.* salpica-
dura. 2 *t.* salpicar, rociar.

splendid ['splendid] *a.*
espléndido. 2 ilustre, glorioso.

splendo(u)r ['splendəʳ] *s.*
brillo. 2 magnificencia.

splinter ['splintəʳ] *s.* astilla. 2 *t.-i.* astillar(se.

split [split] *s.* grieta. 2
división. 3 *t.-i.* hender-
(se, partir(se. ¶ Pret. y
p. p.: *split* [split].

spoil [spɔil] *s.* despojo,
botín. 2 *t.* saquear, robar. 3 estropear. 4 mi-
mar, malcriar. ¶ Pret.
y p. p.: *spoiled* [spɔild]
o *spoilt* [spɔilt].

spoke [spɔuk] *pret.* de TO
SPEAK. 2 *s.* rayo [de rue-
da].

spoken ['spɔukən] V. TO
SPEAK.

sponge [spʌndʒ] *s.* esponja. 2 *t.* lavar con esponja, borrar.

spoon [spuːn] *s.* cuchara.

sport [spɔːt] *s.* deporte.
2 *t.* ostentar. 3 *i.* jugar.

spot [spɔt] *s.* mancha,
borrón. 2 sitio, lugar. 3
a. disponible [dinero]. 4
t. manchar. 5 localizar.

sprang [spræŋ] V. TO
SPRING.

spray [sprei] *s.* líquido pulverizado; rocío [del mar, etc.]. 2 *t.* pulverizar.

spread [spred] *s.* despliegue, desarrollo, extensión [de terreno, etc.]. 2 *t.-i.* extender(se, desplegar(se. 3 *t.* ofrecer a la vista. ¶ Pret. y p. p.: *spread* [spred].

sprig [sprig] *s.* ramita.

spring [spriŋ] *s.* primavera. 2 fuente. 3 origen. 4 salto. 5 muelle. 6 elasticidad. 7 vigor. 8 *i.* saltar. 9 nacer, brotar. 10 provenir, seguirse. 11 *t.* hacer saltar o estallar [una mina]. ¶ Pret.: *sprang* [spræŋ]; p. p.: *sprung* [spraŋ].

sprinkle ['spriŋkl] *s.* rocío. 2 *t.* rociar.

sprint [sprint] *s.* esprint. 2 *i.* esprintar.

spruce [spru:s] *a.* pulcro. 2 *t.-i.* asear(se.

sprung [spraŋ] V. TO SPRING.

spun [spʌn] V. TO SPIN.

spur [spəːʳ] *s.* espuela. 2 estímulo. 3 *t.* espolear. 4 estimular.

spy [spai] *s.* espía. 2 *t.* espiar.

squadron ['skwɔdrən] *s.* escuadra; escuadrilla.

square [skwɛəʳ] *s.* GEOM. cuadro, cuadrado. 2 MAT. cuadrado. 3 casilla [ajedrez, etc.]. 4 plaza [de ciudad]. 5 escuadra, cartabón. 6 *a.* fornido. 7 exacto, justo. 8 recto, honrado. 9 saldado en paz; empatado. 10 rotundo, categórico. 11 abundante [comida]. 12 *t.* GEOM., MAT. cuadrar. 13 elevar al cuadrado. 14 saldar [cuentas].

squeak [ski:k] *s.* chillido. 2 *i.* chillar, chirriar.

squeeze [skwi:z] *s.* apretón. 2 *t.* apretar.

squire ['skwaiəʳ] *s.* escudero. 2 (Ingl.) hacendado; caballero.

squirrel ['skwirəl] *s.* ardilla.

stable ['steibl] *a.* estable. 2 *s.* establo, cuadra. 3 *t.-i.* poner, tener o estar en un establo.

stack [stæk] *s.* almiar. 2 pila, montón. 3 pabellón [de fusiles]. 4 cañón [de chimenea]. 5 *t.* apilar, amontonar.

staff [stɑːf] *s.* palo, bastón. 2 personal. 3 *t.* proveer de personal técnico o directivo.

stage [steidʒ] *s.* escenario. 2 campo [de actividades]. 3 parada; jornada. 4 grado, fase. 5 t. poner en escena.

stagger ['stægəᵊ] i. vacilar.

stain [stein] s. mancha. 2 t.-i. manchar(se.

stair [stɛəᵊ] s. escalón, peldaño.

stake [steik] s. estaca; poste. 2 t. estacar. 3 apostar.

stale [steil] a. pasado, rancio, no fresco.

stalk [stɔːk] s. BOT. tallo, caña. 2 t. andar majestuosamente. 3 espiar, acechar.

stall [stɔːl] s. establo. 2 puesto de venta. 3 t.-i. poner en establo. 4 i. pararse.

stalwart ['stɔːlwət] a.-s. fornido. 2 valiente; leal.

stammer ['stæməᵊ] s. tartamudeo. 2 i. tartamudear.

stamp [stæmp] s. estampa, huella. 2 sello. 3 género, suerte. 4 t. estampar, imprimir. 5 caracterizar. 6 poner sello a.

stand [stænd] s. posición, puesto. 2 alto, parada. 3 resistencia. 4 tablado, tribuna. 5 puesto [en el mercado]; quiosco [de

venta]. 6 velador, pie, soporte. 7 i. estar, tenerse o ponerse en pie; levantarse: ~ up, ponte en pie. 8 detenerse. 9 mantenerse firme, resistir. 10 aguantar. 11 to ~ aside, apartarse. 12 to ~ by, apoyar; estar alerta. 13 to ~ for, representar. 14 to ~ off, apartarse. 15 to ~ out, sobresalir. ¶ Pret. y p. p.: *stood* [stud].

standard ['stændəd] s. norma; nivel. 2 modelo. 3 estandarte. 4 a. normal, corriente.

standing ['stændiŋ] a. derecho, de pie. 2 parado. 3 fijo. 4 vigente [ley]. 5 s. posición.

star [stɑːʳ] s. ASTR. estrella, astro. 2 t. tachonar de estrellas.

starch [stɑːtʃ] s. almidón. 2 t. almidonar.

stare [stɛəʳ] s. mirada fija. 2 t.-i. mirar fijamente.

start [stɑːt] s. sobresalto. 2 marcha, partida. 3 ventaja. 4 by starts, a ratos; a empujones. 5 i. sobresaltarse. 6 salir; arrancar [el motor, etc.]. 7 t. empezar.

startle ['stɑ:tl] *t.-i.* asustar(se; sobresaltar(se.

starve [stɑ:v] *i.* morir o padecer hambre. 2 *t.* matar de hambre.

state [steit] *s.* estado, situación. 2 *t.* exponer, declarar.

stately ['steitli] *a.* majestuoso.

statement ['steitmənt] *s.* declaración, afirmación.

statesman ['steitsmən] *s.* estadista, hombre de estado.

station ['steiʃən] *s.* estación. 2 parada, apeadero. 3 puesto. 4 *t.* estacionar, situar.

statistics [stə'tistiks] *s.* estadística.

stay [stei] *s.* MAR. estay, tirante. 2 sostén, apoyo. 3 parada, estancia. 4 aplazamiento. 5 varilla [de corsé]. 6 *pl.* corsé. 7 *t.* sostener, apoyar. 8 resistir. 9 detener, frenar. 10 aplazar. 11 *i.* estar de pie o quieto; pararse. 12 estar o quedarse en casa; to ~ up, velar.

steady ['stedi] *a.* firme. 2 *t.-i.* afianzar(se, dar firmeza.

steak [steik] *s.* tajada, bistec.

steal [sti:l] *s.* hurto, robo. 2 *t.-i.* hurtar, robar. 3 to ~ away, escabullirse, escapar. ¶ Pret.: **stole** [stɔul]; p. p.: **stolen** ['stɔulən].

stealthy ['stelθi] *a.* furtivo.

steam [sti:m] *s.* vapor: *t.* cocer o preparar al vapor. 3 *i.* emitir vaho.

steamboat ['sti:mbəut], **steamer** ['sti:mər], **steamship** ['sti:mʃip] *s.* vapor [buque].

steed [sti:d] *s.* corcel.

steel [sti:l] *s.* acero. 2 *t.* acerar.

steep [sti:p] *a.* empinado. 2 excesivo. 3 *s.* cuesta. 4 *t.* empapar.

steer [stiə] *t.* gobernar [una embarcación]; conducir, guiar [un vehículo].

stem [stem] *s.* BOT. tallo, tronco. 2 tronco [de una familia]. 3 raíz [de una palabra]. 4 *t.* estancar, represar. 5 navegar contra [la corriente].

step [step] *s.* paso. 2 estribo. 3 huella, pisada. 4 *i.* andar, caminar; to ~ aside, apartarse; to ~

back, retroceder 5 t. sentar [el pie].

stern [stə:n] a. duro, riguroso. 2 s. popa.

stew [stju:] s. estofado, guisado. 2 t. estofar, guisar.

steward ['stjuəd] s. mayordomo.

stick [stik] s. palo, garrote. 2 t. clavar, hincar. 3 levantar [con up]. ¶ Pret. y p. p.: stuck [stʌk].

stiff [stif] a. tieso. 2 duro, difícil. 3 terco, obstinado. 4 ~ neck, torticolis; obstinación; stiffnecked, obstinado.

stifle ['staifl] t.-i. ahogar(se; sofocar(se.

still [stil] a. quieto, inmóvil. 2 suave [voz, ruido]. 3 adv. aún, todavía. 4 conj. no obstante, a pesar de eso. 5 s. silencio, quietud. 6 i. acallar. 7 detener(se; calmar(se.

stillness ['stilnis] s. quietud.

stimulate ['stimjuleit] t.-i. estimular.

sting [stiŋ] s. picadura, punzada. 2 t.-i. picar, punzar. ¶ Pret. y p. p.: stung [stʌŋ].

stir [stə:ˈ] s. movimien-

to. 2 t.-i. mover(se, menear(se.

stitch [stitʃ] s. puntada [de costura]. 2 t. pespuntar.

stock [stɔk] s. tronco. 2 zoquete. 3 pilar. 4 provisión, existencia. 5 TEAT. repertorio. 6 inventario. 7 ganado. 8 capital de un negocio. 9 COM. título; acción. 10 mang:les. 11 mango [de caña de pescar, etc.]; caja [de fusil, etc.]. 12 valores públicos. 13 pl. cepo [castigo]. 14 a. común, usual. 15 t. tener en existencia. 16 abastecer, proveer.

stocking ['stɔkiŋ] s. media, calceta.

stole [stəul], stolen ['stəulən] V. TO STEAL.

stolid ['stɔlid] a. estólido.

stomach ['stʌmək] s. estómago.

stone [stəun] s. piedra. 2 hueso [de fruta]. 3 (Ingl.) peso de 14 libras. 4 t. apedrear.

stony ['stəuni] a. pedregoso.

stood [stud] V. TO STAND.

stool [stu:l] s. taburete, escabel. 2 excremento.

stoop [stu:ɒ] s. inclinación. 2 *i.* agacharse, doblar el cuerpo.

stop [stɔp] *s.* alto, parada. 2 *t.-i.* detener(se, parar(se.

storage ['stɔːridʒ] *s.* almacenamiento. 2 almacenaje.

store [stɔr, stɔər] *s.* abundancia; provisión. 2 tesoro. 3 ~*-house*, almacén. 4 [E. U.] tienda, comercio. 5 *pl.* reservas. 6 *t.* proveer, abastecer.

storey ['stɔːri] *s.* piso, planta.

storm [stɔːm] *s.* tempestad. 2 *t.* tomar al asalto. 3 *i.* haber tempestad.

stormy ['stɔːmi] *a.* tempestuoso.

story ['stɔːri] *s.* historieta, leyenda, cuento. 2 *fam.* chisme. 3 ARQ. piso [de edificio].

stout [staut] *a.* fuerte, recio.

stove [stəuv] *s.* estufa; hornillo. 2 V. TO STAVE.

stow [stəu] *t.* apretar.

straight [streit] *a.* recto, derecho. 2 erguido. 3 sincero; honrado. 4 puro, sin mezcla. 5 *adv.* seguido: *for two hours* ~, dos horas seguidas; ~ *away*, en seguida; ~ *ahead*,

enfrente. 6 *s.* recta, plano. 7 escalera [en póker].

straighten ['streitn] *t.-i.* enderezar(se. 2 arreglar.

straightway ['streit-wei] *adv.* inmediatamente, en seguida.

strain [strein] *s.* tensión o esfuerzo excesivo. 2 esguince. 3 estirpe. 4 tono, acento. 5 aire, melodía. 6 *t.* estirar demasiado. 7 torcer, violentar.

strait [streit] *a.* estrecho. 2 difícil. 3 *s.* GEOGR. estrecho. 4 *pl.* apuros.

strand [strænd] *s.* playa, ribera. 2 *t.-i.* embarrancar.

strange [streindʒ] *a.* extraño. 2 ajeno. 3 raro.

stranger ['streindʒər] *s.* extraño.

strap [stræp] *s.* correa, tira. 2 *t.* atar con correas.

straw [strɔː] *s.* paja.

strawberry ['strɔːbəri] *s.* fresa.

stray [strei] *a.* descarriado. 2 *i.* desviarse. 3 descarriarse.

streak [striːk] *s.* raya, línea. 2 *t.* rayar, listar.

stream [striːm] *s.* corriente. 2 *i.* fluir, manar.

street [stri:t] *s.* calle: *streetcar*, (E. U.) tranvia.

strength [strenθ] *s.* fuerza.

strengthen ['strenθən] *t.-i.* fortalecer(se, reforzar(se.

stress [stres] *s.* esfuerzo; tensión. 2 acento. 3 *t.* acentuar; recalcar.

stretch [stretʃ] *s.* extensión. 2 *t.-i.* extender(se, alargar(se.

stricken ['strikən] *p. p.* de TO STRIKE.

strict [strikt] *a.* estricto.

stridden ['stridn] V. TO STRIDE.

stride [straid] *s.* zancada. 2 *i.* andar a pasos largos. ¶ Pret.: *strode* [stroud]; p. p.: *stridden* ['stridn].

strife [straif] *s.* disputa.

strike [straik] *s.* golpe. 2 huelga: *to go on* ~, declararse en huelga; ~ *breaker*, esquirol. 3 *t.* golpear. 4 encender [una cerilla]. 5 producir un efecto súbito. 6 acuñar [moneda]. 7 MÚS. tocar. 8 *how does she* ~ *you?*, ¿qué opina de ella? 9 *i.* marchar, partir. 10 declararse en huelga. 11

[del reloj] dar la hora. ¶ Pret.: *struck* [strʌk]; p. p.: *struck* o *stricken* ['strikən].

string [striŋ] *s.* cordón, cordel. 2 *t.* atar. ¶ Pret. y p. p.: *strung* [strʌŋ].

strip [strip] *s.* tira, lista. 2 *t.-i.* despojar(se, desnudarse. ¶ Pret. y p. p.: *stripped* [stript].

stripe [straip] *s.* raya, lista. 2 *t.* rayar, listar: *striped*, rayado, listado.

strive [straiv] *i.* esforzarse. ¶ Pret.: *strove* [strouv]; p. p.: *striven* ['strivn].

strode [stroud] *pret.* le TO STRIDE.

stroke [strouk] *s.* golpe. 2 brazada [del que nada]. 3 MED. ataque [de apoplejía, etc.]. 4 trazo, rasgo, pincelada. 5 caricia. 6 *t.* acariciar.

stroll [stroul] *s.* paseo. 2 *i.* pasear.

strong [stroŋ] *a.* fuerte. 2 *strong-minded*, de creencias arraigadas.

strove [strouv] V. TO STRIVE.

struck [strʌk] V. TO STRIKE.

structure ['strʌktʃər] *s.* estructura. 2 construcción, edificio.

struggle ['strʌgl] s. esfuerzo. 2 i. luchar.

stubborn ['stʌbən] a. obstinado.

stuck [stʌk] V. TO STICK.

student ['stju:dənt] s. estudiante.

study ['stʌdi] s. estudio. 2 t.-i. estudiar.

stuff [stʌf] s. material, materia prima. 2 tonterías. 3 t. llenar. 4 disecar [un animal].

stumble ['stʌmbl] s. tropiezo. 2 i. tropezar. 3 vacilar.

stump [stʌmp] s. tocón, cepa. 2 muñón [de miembro cortado]; raigón [de muela, etc.]. 3 colilla [de cigarro]. 4 (E. U.) *to be up a ~*, estar en un brete. 5 t. cortar en el tronco de un árbol]. 6 tropezar. 7 (E. U.) recorrer haciendo discursos electorales.

stung [stʌŋ] V. TO STING.

stunk [stʌŋk] V. TO STINK.

stupid ['stju:pid] a.-s. estúpido.

sturdy ['stə:di] a. robusto.

style [stail] s. estilo.

subdue [səb'dju:] t. sojuzgar.

subject ['sʌbdʒikt] a. sometido. 2 a.-s. súbdito. 3 s. sujeto, asunto, tema; asignatura. 4 [səb-'dʒekt] t. sujetar, someter.

sublime [sə'blaim] a. sublime.

submarine [,sʌbmə'ri:n] a.-s. submarino.

submerge [səb'mə:dʒ] t.-i. sumergir(se. 2 t. inundar.

submit [səb'mit] t.-i. someter(se. 2 presentar.

subsequent ['sʌbsikwənt] a. subsiguiente.

substance ['sʌbstəns] s. substancia.

substantial [səb'stænʃəl] a. substancial. 2 esencial.

substitute ['sʌbstitju:t] s. substituto, suplente. 2 t. substituir.

subtle ['sʌtl] a. sutil.

suburb ['sʌbə:b] s. suburbio.

subway ['sʌbwei] s. paso subterráneo. 2 (E. U.) ferrocarril subterráneo.

succeed [sək'si:d] i. suceder [a una pers.]. 2 tener buen éxito; salir bien.

success [sək'ses] s. éxito.

succesful [sək'sesful] a. afortunado.

succession [sək'sefən] s. sucesión.

successive [sək'sesiv] a. sucesivo.

successor [sək'sesər] s. sucesor.

such [sʌtʃ] a.-pron. tal(es, semejante(s. 2 pron. éste, -ta, etc.; as ~, como a tal. 3 ~ as, el, la, los, las que; tal(es como. 4 adv. tan, así, tal: ~ a good man, un hombre tan bueno.

suck [sʌk] t.-i. chupar.

sudden ['sʌdn] a. súbito.

suffering ['sʌfəriŋ] s. sufrimiento, padecimiento. 2 a. doliente, enfermo. 3 sufrido.

suffice [sə'fais] i. bastar, ser suficiente.

sufficient [sə'fiʃənt] a. suficiente, bastante.

suffrage ['sʌfridʒ] s. sufragio, voto.

sugar ['ʃugər] s. azúcar. 2 t. azucarar.

suggest [sə'dʒest] t. sugerir.

suggestion [sə'dʒestʃən] s. sugestión. 2 indicación. 3 señal.

suicide ['sjuisaid] s. suicidio. 2 suicida.

suit [sjuːt] s. petición. 2 cortejo, galanteo. 3 DER.

demanda; pleito. 4 traje. 5 colección. 6 palo de la baraja. 7 t. vestir. 8 t.-i. convenir, ir o venir bien.

suitable ['sjuːtəbl] a. propio, conveniente, apropiado.

sullen ['sʌlən] a. hosco, huraño.

sulphur ['sʌlfər] s. azufre.

sultry ['sʌltri] a. bochornoso; sofocante.

sum [sʌm] s. MAT. suma. 2 total. 3 t.-i. sumar.

summer ['sʌmər] s. verano. 2 i. veranear.

summit ['sʌmit] s. cúspide, cumbre, cima.

summon ['sʌmən] t. llamar. 2 citar, emplazar.

sun [sʌn] s. sol. 2 t. asolear. 3 i. tomar el sol.

sunbeam ['sʌnbiːm] s. rayo de sol.

Sunday ['sʌndi, -dei] s. domingo.

sunder ['sʌndər] s. separación. 2 t.-i. separar(se, dividir(se.

sung [sʌŋ] V. TO SING.

sunk [sʌŋk] V. TO SINK.

sunlight ['sʌnlait] s. sol, luz de sol.

sunny ['sʌni] a. soleado.

sunrise ['sʌnraiz] s. salida del sol, amanecer.

sunset ['sʌnset] *s.* ocaso.

sunshine ['sʌnʃain] *s.* luz del sol.

sup [sʌp] *t.-i.* cenar. 2 *t.* beber, tomar a sorbos.

superb [su:'pə:b] *a.* soberbio.

superintendent [ˌsjuːpərin'tendənt] *s.* superintendente, inspector.

superior [sju(:)'piəriəʳ] *a.-s.* superior.

supervision [ˌsjuːpə'viʒən] *s.* ispección, vigilancia.

supper ['sʌpəʳ] *s.* cena.

supply [sə'plai] *s.* provisión. 2 *t.* suministrar.

support [sə'pɔːt] *s.* apoyo, ayuda. 2 sustento. 3 *t.* apoyar, sostener. 4 mantener.

suppose [sə'pauz] *t.* suponer. 2 creer.

supposed [sə'pauzd] *a.* supuesto, presunto. 2 **-ly** *adv.* supuestamente.

suppress [sə'pres] *t.* suprimir. 2 contener.

supreme [su'pri:m] *a.* supremo; sumo.

sure [ʃuəʳ] *a.* seguro, firme; *to make ~* asegurar(se de. 2 **-ly** seguramente.

surface ['sə:fis] *s.* superficie.

surge [sə:dʒ] *s.* oleaje. 2 *i.* hinchar(se, agitar(se.

surgeon ['sə:dʒən] *s.* cirujano.

surpass [sə:'pɑːs] *t.* sobrepujar, aventajar.

surprise [sə'praiz] *s.* sorpresa. 2 *t.* sorprender.

surrender [sə'rendəʳ] *s.* rendición. 2 entrega, renuncia. 3 *t.-i.* rendir(se, entregar(se.

surround [sə'raund] *t.* rodear, cercar.

surrounding [sə'raundiŋ] *a.* circundante, vecino. 2 *s. pl.* alrededores.

survey ['sə:vei] *s.* medición; plano [de un terreno]. 2 inspección, examen. 3 perspectiva, bosquejo [de historia, etc.]. 4 [sə:'vei] *t.* medir, deslindar [tierras]. 5 levantar el plano de. 6 inspeccionar, examinar. 7 dar una ojeada general a.

surveyor [sə(:)'veiəʳ] *s.* agrimensor; topógrafo. 2 inspector. 3 vista [de aduanas]

survive [sə:'vaiv] *t.-i.* sobrevivir.

suspect ['sʌspekt] *a.-s.* sospechoso. 2 [səs'pekt] *t.* sospechar.

suspend [səs'pend] *t.* suspender, colgar. 2 aplazar.

suspicion [səs'piʃən] *s.* sospecha.

suspicious [səs'piʃəs] *a.* sospechoso. 2 suspicaz.

sustain [səs'tein] *t.* sostener. 2 mantener, sustentar.

swallow ['swɔləu] *s.* ORN. golondrina. 2 gaznate. 3 trago. 4 ~-*tail*, frac. 5 *t.-i.* tragar, engullir.

swam [swæm] V. TO SWIM.

swamp ['swɔmp] *s.* pantano. 2 *t.-i.* sumergir(se, hundir(se.

swan [swɔn] *s.* cisne.

swarm [swɔːm] *s.* enjambre, multitud. 2 *i.* pulular, hormiguear.

sway [swei] *s.* oscilación. 2 poder, dominio. 3 *i.* oscilar. 4 *t.-i.* dominar, influir en.

swear [swɛəˈr] *t.-i.* jurar. ¶ Pret.: *swore* [swɔː]; p. p.: *sworn* [swɔːn].

sweat [swet] *s.* sudor; trasudor. 2 *t.-i.* sudar; trasudar. 3 *t.* hacer sudar; explotar [al que trabaja].

sweep [swiːp] *s.* barrido. 2 redada. 3 extensión. 4 deshollinador. 5 *t.* ba-

rrer. 6 deshollinar. ¶ Pret. y p. p.: *swept* [swept].

sweet [swiːt] *a.* dulce, azucarado. 2 amable. 3 *s. pl.* dulces, caramelos.

sweetheart ['swiːthɑːt] *s.* novio,-a; amor.

swell [swel] *s.* hinchazón. 2 *t.-i.* hinchar(se, inflar(se. ¶ Pret.: *swelled* [sweld]; p. p.: *swollen* ['swəulən] y *swelled*.

swept [swept] V. TO SWEEP.

swift [swift] *a.* rápido, veloz.

swim [swim] *s.* acción o rato de nadar. 2 *swimming-pool*, piscina. 3 *i.* nadar. ¶ Pret.: *swam* [swæm]; p. p.: *swum* [swʌm].

swing [swiŋ] *s.* oscilación, giro; ritmo. 2 columpio. 3 *t.-i.* balancear(se, columpiar(se. 4 *t.* hacer oscilar o girar. 5 suspender, colgar. ¶ Pret. y p. p.: *swung* [swʌŋ].

swirl [swəːl] *s.* remolino. 2 *t.-i.* girar.

Swiss [swis] *a.-s.* suizo, -za.

switch [switʃ] *s.* vara flexible; látigo. 2 latigazo. 3 ELECT. interruptor, conmutador. 4 cambio.

5 *t.* azotar, fustigar. *6* cambiar, desviar. 7 ELECT. *to* ~ *on,* conectar [dar la luz]; *to* ~ *off,* desconectar.

sword [sɔːd] *s.* espada [arma].

swore [swɔːˈ], **sworn** [swɔːn] V. TO SWEAR.

swum [swʌm] V. TO SWIM.

swung [swʌŋ] V. TO SWING.

syllable [ˈsiləbl] *s.* sílaba.

symbol [ˈsimbl] *s.* símbolo.

symmetric(al [siˈmetrik, -əl] *a.* simétrico.

sympathetic(al [ˌsimpəˈθetik, -əl] *a.* compasivo; comprensivo.

sympathy [ˈsimpəθi] *s.* solidaridad. 2 comprensión.

symptom [ˈsimptəm] *s.* síntoma.

system [ˈsistəm] *s.* sistema.

T

table ['teibl] s. mesa: ~ cloth, mantel; ~ ware, vajilla, servicio de mesa. 2 tabla [de materias, etc.]; lista, catálogo. 3 t. poner sobre la mesa. 4 poner en forma de índice.

tablet ['tæblit] s. tablilla. 2 lápida, placa. 3 FARM. tableta. 4 bloc de papel.

tackle ['tækl] s. equipo, aparejos. 2 t. agarrar. 3 abordar [un problema, etcétera].

tactless ['tæktlis] a. falto de tacto.

tail [teil] s. cola, rabo. 2 SAST. faldón: ~ coat, frac.

tailor ['teilə'] s. sastre.

take [teik] s. toma, tomadura. 2 redada. 3 recaudación [de dinero]. 4

take-off, remedo, parodia; despegue [del avión]. 5 t. tomar, coger; agarrar; apoderarse de. 6 asumir. 7 deleitar, cautivar. 8 llevar, conducir. 9 dar [un golpe, un paseo, un salto, etc.]. 10 hacer [ejercicio, etc.]. 11 arraigar [una planta]. 12 prender [el fuego; la vacuna]. 13 tener éxito. 14 to ~ a chance, correr el riesgo. 15 to ~ after, parecerse a. 16 to ~ amiss, interpretar mal. 17 to ~ care of, cuidar de. 18 to ~ cold, resfriarse. 19 to ~ down, descolgar. 20 to ~ in, meter en; abarcar. 21 I ~ it that, supongo que... 22 to ~ leave, despedirse. 23 to ~ off, descontar, rebajar; despegar [el avión]; remedar. 24 to ~ place, ocurrir, tener lugar. ¶ Pret.: took [tuk]; p. p.: taken ['teikən].

tale [teil] s. cuento, fábula.

talent ['tælənt] s. talento.

talk [tɔːk] s. conversación. 2 i. hablar; conversar. 3 to ~ into, persuadir a. 4 to ~ out of, disuadir de. 5 to ~ over, examinar. 6 to ~ up, alabar; hablar claro.

tall [tɔːl] a. alto [pers., árbol]. 2 excesivo, exorbitante.

tame [teim] a. manso, 2 t. domar, domesticar.

tan [tæn] s. color tostado. 2 a. tostado, de color de canela. 2 t. curtir [las pieles]. 2 tostar, atezar.

tangle ['tæŋgl] s. enredo. 2 t.-i. enredar(se, enmarañar(se.

tank [tæŋk] s. tanque, cisterna.

tap [tæp] s. grifo, espita. 2 golpecito, palmadita. 3 t. poner espita a. 4 t.-i. dar golpecitos o palmadas [a o en].

taper ['teipər] s. candela. 2 t.-i. adelgazar(se.

tariff ['tærif] s. tarifa.

tarnish ['taːniʃ] t.-i. deslustrar(se. empañar(se.

task [taːsk] s. tarea, labor.

taste [teist] s. gusto [sentido]. 2 sabor. 3 afición. 4 gusto [por lo bello, etc.]. 5 sorbo, bocadito. 6 muestra, prueba. 7 t. gustar, saborear. 8 probar, catar 9 i. to ~ of, saber a.

tavern ['tævən] s. taberna.

taxation [tæk'seiʃən] s. impuestos.

taxi ['tæksi], taxicab ['tæksikæb] s. taxi [coche].

tea [tiː] s. té: ~ party, té [reunión]; ~ set, juego de té.

teach [tiːtʃ] t.-i. enseñar, instruir. ¶ Pret. y p. p.: taught [tɔːt]

teacher ['tiːtʃər] s. maestro, -tra.

team [tiːm] s. tiro [de nimales]. 2 grupo, cuadrilla. 3 DEP. equipo. 4 t. enganchar, uncir.

1) tear [tiər] s. lágrima.
2) tear [tɛər] s. rotura,

desgarro. 2 *t.* romper, rasgar. ¶ Pret.: *tore* [tɔːʳ, tɔəʳ]; p. p.: *torn* [tɔːn].

tease [tiːz] *t.* fastidiar.

teaspoonful ['tiːspu(ː)n,ful] *s.* cucharadita.

technical ['teknikəl] *a.* técnico.

tedious ['tiːdjəs] *a.* tedioso.

teeth [tiːθ] *s. pl.* de TOOTH.

telegram ['teligræm] *s.* telegrama.

telegraph ['teligrɑːf, -græf] *s.* telégrafo. 2 telegrama. 3 *t.-i.* telegrafiar.

telephone ['telifəun] *s.* teléfono. 2 *t.-i.* telefonear.

telescope ['teliskəup] *s.* telescopio.

tell [tel] *t.* contar, numerar. 2 narrar, relatar, decir. 3 mandar, ordenar. 4 distinguir, conocer; adivinar. 5 *there is no telling*, no es posible decir o prever. 6 *it tells*, tiene su efecto. ¶ Pret. y p. p.: *told* [təuld].

temper ['tempəʳ] *s.* temple [del metal]. 2 genio; humor. 3 cólera, mal genio. 4 *t.* templar, moderar. 5 templar [el metal].

temperament ['tempərəmənt] *s.* temperamento [de una pers.].

temperate ['tempərit] *a.* templado, sobrio, moderado.

temperature ['tempritʃəʳ] *s.* temperatura: *to have a ~*, tener fiebre.

tempest ['tempist] *s.* tempestad.

temple ['templ] *s.* templo. 2 ANAT. sien.

temporary ['tempərəri] *a.* temporal, provisional, interino.

tempt [tempt] *t.* tentar.

temptation [temp'teiʃən] *s.* tentación. 2 incent. vo.

ten [ten] *a.-s.* diez. 2 **-th** [-θ] décimo.

tenant ['tenənt] *s.* inquilino.

tend [tend] *t.* cuidar, atender. 2 *i.* tender [a un fin].

tendency ['tendənsi] *s.* tendencia; propensión.

tender ['tendəʳ] *a.* tierno. 2 delicado [escrupuloso]. 3 *s.* cuidador, guardián. 4 oferta, propuesta. 5 *t.* ofrecer, presentar. 6 *t.-i.* ablandar(se.

tendernes ['tendənis] *s.* ternura, suavidad. 2 debilidad.

tennis ['tenis] *s.* tenis.

tent [tent] *s.* tienda de campaña. 2 *i.* acampar.

term [tə:m] *s.* plazo, período. 2 trimestre. 3 *pl.* condiciones; acuerdo. 4 *t.* nombrar.

terrace ['terəs] *s.* terraza.

terrible ['teribl] *a.* terrible.

terrific [te'rifik] *a.* terrorífico.

terrify ['terifai] *t.* aterrar.

territory ['teritəri] *s.* territorio.

terror ['terər] *s.* terror, espanto.

test [test] *s.* copela. 2 prueba, ensayo. 3 PSIC. test. 4 *t.* examinar, probar, ensayar.

testify ['testifai] *t.* testificar, testimoniar.

testimony ['testiməni] *s.* testimonio, declaración.

text [tekst] *s.* texto.

than [ðæn, ðən] *conj.* que [después de comparativo]. 2 de: *more ~ once,* más de una vez.

thank [θæŋk] *t.* dar gracias. 2 *s. pl. thanks,* gracias.

thankful ['θæŋkful] *a.* agradecido.

thanksgiving ['θæŋks¡giviŋ] *s.* acción de gracias.

that [ðæt] *a.* ese, esa, aquel, aquella. 2 *pron.* ése, ésa, eso, aquél, aquélla, aquello. 3 *pron. rel.* [ðət, ðæt] que. 4 *conj.* [ðət, ðæt] que: *so ~,* para que. 5 *adv.* así, tan: *~ far,* tan lejos; *~ long,* de este tamaño.

thaw [θɔ:] *s.* deshielo. 2 *t.-i.* deshelar(se.

the [ðə: ante vocal, ði] el, la, lo; los, las. 2 *adv.* *~ more he has, ~ more he wants,* cuanto más tiene [tanto] más quiere.

theater, theatre ['θiətər] *s.* teatro.

their [ðɛər, ðər] *a. pos.* su, sus [de ellos o de ellas].

theirs [ðɛəz] *prons. pos.* [el] suyo [la] suya, [los] suyos, [las] suyas [de ellos o de ellas].

them [ðem, ðəm] *pron. pers.* [sin prep.] los, las, les. 2 [con prep.] ellos, ellas.

theme [θi:m] *s.* tema, materia.

themselves [ðəm'selvz] *pron. pers.* ellos mismos, ellas mismas. 2 se [reflx.],, a sí mismos.

then [ðen] *adv.* entonces. 2 luego, después; además. 3 *conj.* por consiguiente. 4 *now* ~, ahora bien; ~ *and there*, allí mismo; *now and* ~, de vez en cuando.

thence [ðens] *adv.* desde allí, desde entonces: ~ *forth*, desde entonces. 2 por lo tanto, desde.

theory ['θiəri] *s.* teoría.

there [ðɛəʳ, ðəʳ] *adv.* allí, allá ahí: ~ *is*, ~ *are*, hay; ~ *was*, ~ *were*, había; ~ *he is*, helo ahí. 2 *interj.* ¡eh!, ¡vaya!, ¡ea! 3 *thereabuts*, por allí, aproximadamente. 4 *thereafter*, después de ello; por lo tanto. 5 *thereby*, en relación con esto. 6 *therefore*, por lo tanto. 7 *therein*, en eso; allí dentro. 8 *thereof*, de eso, de ellos. 9 *thereon*, encima de ello, en seguida. 10 *thereupon*, por tanto; inmediatamente.

thermometer [θə'mɔmitəʳ] *s.* termómetro.

these [ðiːz] *a.* estos, estas. 2 *pron.* éstos, éstas.

they [ðei] *pron. pers.* ellos, ellas.

thick [θik] *a.* espeso, grueso. 2 espeso, poblado [barba], tupido. 3 *s.* grueso, espesor.

thicket ['θikit] *s.* espesura, matorral.

thickness ['θiknis] *s.* espesor.

thief [θi:f] *s.* ladrón, ratero.

thigh [θai] *s.* ANAT. muslo.

thin [θin] *s.* delgado, fino. 2 ligero, transparente. 3 *t.-i.* adelgazar(se. 4 aclarar(se.

thine [ðain] *pron. pos.* [el] tuyo [la] tuya, [los] tuyos, [las] tuyas. 2 *a.* tu, tus. | Úsase sólo en poesía y en la Biblia.

thing [θiŋ] *s.* cosa: *poor* ~!, ¡pobrecito!

think [θiŋk] *t.-i.* pensar, juzgar, creer. ¶ Pret. y p. p.: *though* [θɔːt].

third [θəːd] *a.* tercero. 2 *s.* tercio [tercera parte].

thirst [θəːst] *s.* sed. 2 anhelo. 3 *i.* tener sed. 4 anhelar, ansiar.

thirsty ['θəːsti] *a.* sediento.

thirteen ['θəː'tiːn] a.-s.
trece. 2 -th [-θ] decimo-
tercero.

thirty ['θəːti] a.-s. treinta.

this [ðis] a. este, esta. 2
pron. éste, ésta, esto.

thither ['ðiðəʳ] adv. allá,
hacia allá.

thorn [θɔːn] s. espina.

thorough ['θʌrə] a. com-
pleto, total, acabado. 2
perfecto.

those [ðəuz] a. esos, esas;
aquellos, aquellas. 2 pron.
ésos,   ésas;   aquéllos,
aquéllas.

thou [ðau] pron. tú. |
Usase sólo en poesía y
en la Biblia.

though [ðəu] conj. aun-
que, si bien; sin em-
bargo. 2 as ~, como si.

thought [θɔːt] V. TO
THINK. 2 s. pensamien-
to, idea, intención.

thoughtful ['θɔːtful] a.
pensativo, meditabundo.
2 atento.

thoughtfulness ['θɔːtful-
nis] s. consideración,
atención.

thoughtless ['θɔːtlis] a.
irreflexivo, atolondrado,
incauto.

thoughtlessness ['θɔːtlis-

nis] s. irreflexión, lige-
reza.

thousand ['θauzənd] a.
mil. 2 -th ['θauzənθ]
milésimo.

thrash [θræʃ] t.-i. tri-
llar.

thrashing ['θræʃiŋ] s.
THRESHING. 2 zurra, pa-
liza.

thread [θred] s. hilo. 2
fibra. 3 t. enhebrar, en-
sartar.

threat [θret] s. amenaza.

threaten ['θretn] t.-i.
amenazar.

three [θriː] a.-s. tres:
~ fold, triple; tres ve-
ces más.

thresh [θreʃ] t.-i. trillar,

threshing ['θreʃiŋ] s. tri-
lla.

theshold ['θreʃ(h)əuld]
s. umbral.

threw [θruː] pret. de TO
THROW.

thrill [θril] s. emoción. 2
t. hacer estremecer. 3 i.
temblar.

thrive [θraiv] i. crecer.
2 prosperar, medrar. ¶
Pret.: throve [θrəuv] o
thrived [θraivd]; p.
p.: thrived o thriven
['θrivn].

throat [θrəut] s. gargan-
ta.

throe [θrəu] *s.* angustia.

throne [θrəun] *s.* trono.

throng [θrɔŋ] *s.* muchedumbre. 2 *i.* apiñarse.

throttle ['θrɔtl] *s.* garganta. 2 *t.-i.* ahogar(se.

through [θru:] *prep.* por, a través de. 2 por medio de, a causa de. 3 *adv.* de un lado a otro, de parte a parte, hasta el fin; completamente, enteramente. 4 *a.* directo: ~ *train,* tren directo. 5 de paso. 6 *to be* ~ *with,* haber acabado con.

throughout [θru:'aut] *prep.* por todo, durante todo, a lo largo de. 2 *adv.* por o en todas partes, desde el principio hasta el fin.

throw [θrəu] *s.* lanzamiento, tiro. 2 *t.* tirar, arrojar, lanzar. 3 derribar. 4 *to* ~ *away,* desperdiciar. 5 *to* ~ *back,* devolver; replicar. 6 *to* ~ *off,* librarse de; improvisar [versos]. 7 *to* ~ *out,* echar fuera, proferir. 8 *to* ~ *over,* abandonar. ¶ Pret.: *threw* [θru:]; p. p.: *thrown* [θrəun].

thrust [θrʌst] *s.* estocada, lanzada. 2 *t.* meter, clavar, hincar. 3 empujar.

4 *i.* meterse, abrirse paso. ¶ Pret. y p. p.: *thrust* [θrʌst].

thumb [θʌm] *s.* pulgar.

thump [θʌmp] *s.* golpe, porrazo. 2 *t.-i.* golpear, aporrear.

thunder ['θʌndər] *s.* trueno. 2 *i.* tronar.

Thursday [θə:zdi, -dei] *s.* jueves.

thus [ðʌs] *adv.* así, de este modo. 2 hasta este punto: ~ *far,* hasta aquí; hasta ahora.

thyself [ðai'self] *pron.* tú mismo, ti mismo. | Úsase sólo en poesía y en la Biblia.

ticket ['tikit] *s.* billete, boleto, entrada: *return* ~, billete de ida y vuelta. 2 lista de candidatos. 3 etiqueta.

tide [taid] *s.* marea; corriente. 2 época.

tidings ['taidiŋz] *s.* noticias.

tie [tai] *s.* cinta, cordón. 2 lazo, nudo. 3 corbata. 4 empate. 5 *t.* atar. 6 *t.-i.* empatar.

tiger ['taigər] *s.* tigre.

tight [tait] *a.* bien cerrado, hermético. 2 tieso, tirante. 3 duro, severo. 4 tacaño.

tighten ['taitn] *t.-i.* apretar(se, estrechar(se.

tile [tail] *s.* teja. 2 *t.* tejar.

till [til] *prep.* hasta. 2 *conj.* hasta que. 3 *t.-i.* labrar.

tilt [tilt] *s.* inclinación, ladeo. 2 lanza, torneo. 3 lanzada, golpe. 4 disputa. 5 *t.-i.* inclinar(se. 6 volcar(se. 7 *t.* dar lanzadas, acometer.

timber ['timbə'] *s.* madera, viga. 2 bosque.

time [taim] *s.* tiempo. 1 No tiene el sentido de estado atmosférico. 2 hora; vez; plazo: *behind* ~, retrasado [el tren]; *behind the times,* anticuado; *on* ~, puntual; *to have a good* ~, divertirse, pasar un buen rato; *what's the* ~?, *what* ~ *is it?,* ¿qué hora es? 3 *t.* escoger el momento. 4 regular, poner en hora [el reloj]. 5 cronometrar.

timid ['timid] *a.* tímido.

tin [tin] *s.* QUÍM. estaño. 2 lata, hojalata. 3 lata, bote. 4 *t.* estañar. 5 enlatar: *tinned goods,* conservas.

tinge [tindʒ] *s.* tinte,

matiz. 2 *t.* teñir, matizar.

tingle ['tingl] *s.* hormigueo. 2 *i.* hormiguear.

tinkle ['tiŋkl] *s.* tintineo. 2 *i.* retiñir, tintinear.

tint [tint] *s.* tinte, matiz. 2 *t.* teñir, matizar.

tiny ['taini] *a.* pequeñito.

tip [tip] *s.* extremo, punta. 2 propina. 3 soplo, aviso confidencial. 4 *t.-i.* inclinar(se, volcar(se. 5 *t.* dar propina a. 6 dar un soplo o aviso confidencial a.

tiptoe ['tiptəu] *s.* punta de pie. 2 *i.* andar de puntillas.

tirade [tai'reid] *s.* andanada, invectiva.

tire ['taiə'] *s.* AUT. neumático. 2 *t.-i.* cansar(se.

tireless ['taiəlis] *a.* incansable.

tiresome ['taiəsəm] *a.* cansado.

tissue ['tisju:, 'tiʃju:] *s.* tisú, gasa.

tit [tit] *s.* ~ *for tat,* golpe por golpe.

title ['taitl] *s.* título.

to [tu:, tu, tə] *prep.* a, hacia, para; hasta: *a quarter* ~ *five,* las cinco menos cuarto; *I have* ~ *go,* tengo que ir. 2 *to* ante verbo es signo de infinitivo y no se traduce. 3 adv. to come ~, volver en sí; ~ and fro, de acá para allá.

toad [toud] s. sapo.

toast [toust] s. tostada. 2 brindis. 3 t. -i. tostar(se.

tobacco [tə'bækəu] s. tabaco.

today, **to-day** [te'dei] adv. hoy, hoy en día. 2 s. el día de hoy.

toe [tou] s. dedo del pie.

together [tə'geðər] adv. junto; juntos, reunidos, juntamente; de acuerdo; to call ~, convocar. 2 al mismo tiempo. 3 sin interrupción.

toil [toil] s. trabajo, esfuerzo. 2 i. afanarse, esforzarse.

toilet ['toilit] s. tocador; cuarto de baño; retrete. 2 tocado; peinado; aseo personal.

token ['toukən] s. señal, indicio. 2 moneda, ficha.

told [tould] V. TO TELL.

tomato [tə'ma:təu; (E. U.) tə'meitəu] s. tomate.

tomb [tu:m] s. tumba.

tomorrow [tə'mərəu] adv. mañana.

ton [tʌn] s. tonelada.

tone [toun] s. tono. 2 t. dar tono a.

tongue [tʌŋ] s. lengua. 2 idioma.

tonight [tə'nait] s. esta noche.

too [tu:] adv. demasiado. 2 a. ~ much, demasiado; ~ many, demasiados. 2 3 también, además.

took [tuk] V. TO TAKE.

tool [tu:l] s. instrumento, herramienta.

tooth [tu:θ], pl. **teeth** [ti:θ] s. diente; muela: ~ hache, dolor de muelas; ~ pick, mondadientes; ~ paste, pasta dentífrica.

top [tɔp] s. parte superior, cima, cumbre. 2 a. superior. 3 t. desmochar. 4 coronar. 5 sobresalir.

topic ['tɔpik] s. asunto, tema. 2 pl. tópicos, lugares comunes.

torch [tɔ:tʃ] s. hacha, antorcha; linterna.

tore [tɔ:r] V. TO TEAR.

torment ['tɔ:ment] s. tormento, tortura. 2 [tɔ:'ment] t. atormentar.

torn [tɔ:n] V. TO TEAR. 2 a. roto.

torrent ['tɔrənt] s. torrente.

torrid ['tɔrid] a. tórrido.

torture ['tɔːtʃəʳ] s. tortura. 2 t. torturar.

toss [tɔs] s. sacudida. 2 tiro. 3 t. sacudir. 4 arrojar. 5 i. agitarse.

total ['toutl] a. entero. 2 s. total.

totter ['totəʳ] i. vacilar.

touch [tʌtʃ] s. toque. 2 tacto; contacto. 3 t. tocar, tantear. 4 conmover. 5 alcanzar, llegar a.

tough [tʌf] a. duro, correoso. 2 fuerte. 3 (E. U.) pendenciero. 4 terco, tenaz. 5 penoso.

tour [tuəʳ] s. viaje, excursión. 2 i. viajar por, hacer turismo.

tourist ['tuərist] s. turista.

tournament ['tuənəmənt] s. torneo, justa. 2 certamen.

toward [təˈwɔːd], **towards** [-z] prep. hacia. 2 cerca de. 3 para. 4 con, para con.

towel ['tauəl] s. toalla.

tower ['tauəʳ] s. torre, torreón. 2 i. descollar, sobresalir.

town [taun] s. población, ciudad, pueblo; municipio: ~ council, ayuntamiento; ~ hall, casa del ayuntamiento

toy [tɔi] s. juguete. 2 i. jugar.

trace [treis] s. huella, pisada. 2 t. trazar, esbozar. 3 rastrear.

track [træk] s. rastro, pista. 2 vía [de tren, tranvía, etc.]. 3 t. rastrear.

tract [trækt] s. área, región.

tractor ['træktəʳ] s. tractor.

trade [treid] s. profesión, ocupación; oficio, arte mecánica; ~ union, sindicato obrero. 2 comercio, tráfico; ~ mark, marca registrada. 3 parroquia, clientela. 4 i. comerciar, negociar, tratar.

trader ['treidəʳ] s. comerciante.

tradition [trəˈdiʃən] s. tradición.

traduce [trəˈdjuːs] t. difamar, calumniar.

traffic ['træfik] s. tráfico. 2 tránsito: ~ lights, semáforo.

tragedy ['trædʒidi] s. tragedia.

trail [treil] s. cola [de vestido, cometa, etc.]. 2 rastro, huella. 3 t.-i.

arrastrar(se. *4* seguir la pista.

train [trein] s. tren. *2* fila, recua. *3* cola [de cometa, vestido, etc.]. *4* t.-i. ejercitar(se. *5* DEP. entrenar. *6* apuntar [un cañón, etc.].

trainer ['treinər] s. amaestrador. *2* DEP. preparador.

training ['treiniŋ] s. adiestramiento. *2* DEP. entrenamiento.

traitor ['treitər] a.-s. traidor.

tramp [træmp] s. vagabundo. *2 i.* viajar a pie, vagabundear. *3 t.* pisar; apisonar.

transfer ['trænsfə:ʳ] s. transferencia, traslado. *2* [træns'fə:ʳ] *t.* transferir, trasladar.

transform [træns'fɔ:m] *t.-i.* transformar(se.

translate [træns'leit] *t.* traducir. *2* trasladar.

translation [træns'leiʃən] s. traducción. *2* trasladar.

transparent [træns'pɛərənt] *a.* transparente. *2* franco, ingenuo.

transport ['trænspɔ:t] s. transporte, acarreo. *2* rapto, éxtasis. *3* [træns'pɔ:t] *t.* transportar,

acarrear. *4* transportar, enajenar.

transportation [,trænspɔ:'teiʃən] s. transporte, sistemas de transporte. *2* (E. U.) coste del transporte; billete, pasaje.

trap [træp] s. trampa, lazo. *2 t.* atrapar.

travel ['trævl] s. viaje. *2 i.* viajar.

travel(l)er ['trævlər] s. viajero.

traverse ['trævə(:)s] s. travesaño. *2 t.* cruzar, atravesar.

tray [trei] s. bandeja.

treacherous ['tretʃərəs] *a.* traidor, falso, engañoso.

treachery ['tretʃəri] s. traición.

tread [tred] s. paso. *2* huella. *3 t.* pisar, hollar. ¶ Pret.: *trod* [trɔd]; p. p.: *trodden* ['trɔdn] o *trod.*

treason ['tri:zn] s. traición.

treasure ['treʒəʳ] s. tesoro. *2 t.* atesorar.

treasurer ['treʒərəʳ] s. tesorero.

treasury ['treʒəri] s. tesorería.

treat [tri:t] s. agasajo,

convite. 2 *t.-i.* tratar. 3 *t.* convidar.

treatment ['tri:tmənt] *s.* trato.

treaty ['tri:ti] *s.* tratado.

tree [tri:] *s.* árbol: *apple ~,* manzano.

tremble ['trembl] *v.* temblor. 2 *i.* temblar.

tremendous [tri'mendəs] *a.* tremendo.

trench [trentʃ] *s.* foso, zanja. 2 *t.* abrir fosos o zanjas en.

trial ['traiəl] *s.* prueba, ensayo. 2 aflicción. 3 juicio, proceso.

tribe [traib] *s.* tribu.

tributary ['tribjutəri] *a.-s.* tributario; afluente [río].

tribute ['tribju:t] *s.* tributo.

trick [trik] *s.* treta, ardid. 2 *t.-i.* engañar, estafar.

trickle ['trikl] *i.* gotear.

tried [traid] V. TO TRY. 2 *a.* probado, fiel.

trifle ['traifl] *s.* frusleria. 2 *i.* bromear, chancear(se.

trim [trim] *a.* bien arreglado. 2 elegante; pulcro, acicalado. 3 *s.* adorno, aderezo. 4 buen es-

tado. 5 *t.* arreglar, disponer. 6 cortar [el pelo, etc.]; podar.

trip [trip] *s.* viaje, excursión. 2 *i.* saltar, brincar. 3 tropezar.

triumph ['traiəmf] *s.* triunfo. 2 *i.* triunfar.

troop [tru:p] *s.* tropa, cuadrilla.

tropical ['trɔpikəl] *a.* tropical.

trot [trɔt] *s.* trote. 2 *i.* trotar.

trouble ['trʌbl] *s.* perturbación, molestia. 2 apuro. 3 avería. 4 *t.* turbar, perturbar.

trousers ['trauzəz] *s. pl.* pantalon(es.

trout [traut] *s.* trucha.

truant ['tru(:)ənt] *s.* tunante, holgazán. 2 *a.* ocioso; perezoso.

truck [trʌk] *s.* (Ingl.) vagón de plataforma. 2 (E. U.) camión. 3 carretilla de mano. 4 cambio, trueque. 5 *garden ~,* hortalizas frescas.

truculence ['trʌkjuləns] *s.* truculencia, crueldad.

truculent ['trʌkjulənt] *a.* truculento.

true [tru:] *a.* verdadero, cierto.

truism ['tru(:)izəm] *s.*

verdad manifiesta; perogrullada.

truly ['tru:li] *adv.* verdaderamente. 2 sinceramente: *yours (very) truly,* su afectísimo.

trumpet ['trʌmpit] *s.* trompeta.

trunk [trʌŋk] *s.* tronco [de árbol; del cuerpo, etc.]. 2 cofre, baúl. 3 trompa [de elefante]. 4 *pl.* pantalones cortos [para deporte]. 5 ~ *call,* conferencia interurbana.

trust [trʌst] *s.* confianza, fe. 2 depósito, cargo, custodia. 3 com. crédito. 4 trust, asociación de empresas. 5 *t.* confiar en.

truth [tru:θ] *s.* verdad.

try [trai] *s.* prueba, ensayo. 2 *t.* probar, intentar: ~ *on,* probarse [un traje].

trying ['traiiŋ] *a.* molesto; cansado; difícil.

tub [tʌb] *s.* tina, baño.

tuberculosis [tju,bə:kju-'ləusis] *s.* tuberculosis.

tuck [tʌk] *t.* hacer alforzas o pliegues.

Tuesday ['tju:zdi, -dei] *s.* martes.

tug [tʌg] *s.* tirón, estirón. 2 *t.* arrastrar. 3 remolcar.

tumble ['tʌmbl] *s.* tumbo, voltereta. 2 desorden. 3 *i.* dar volteretas, voltear. 4 *t.* derribar.

tumult ['tju:mʌlt] *s.* tumulto.

tune [tju:n] *s.* melodía; tonada. 2 *i.* templar, afinar. 3 *i.* armonizar.

tunnel ['tʌnl] *s.* túnel.

Turk [tə:k] *s.* turco.

turkey ['tə:ki] *s.* pavo.

turn [tə:n] *s.* vuelta, giro. 2 turno. 3 *t.-i.* volver(se; voltear(se. 4 girar, dar vueltas. 5 trastornar. 6 volverse. 7 *to* ~ *away,* despedir; echar; desviar. 8 *to* ~ *back,* volver atrás, devolver. 9 *to* ~ *down,* rechazar [una oferta]. 10 *to* ~ *inside out,* volver al revés. 11 *to* ~ *off,* cortar [el agua, etc.], apagar [la luz]; ~ *on,* dar [la luz, el agua, etc.].

turnip ['tə:nip] *s.* nabo.

turtle ['tə:tl] *s.* zool. tortuga.

tutor ['tju:tər] *s.* preceptor. 2 *t.* enseñar, instruir.

twelfth [twelfθ] *a.-s.* duodécimo: ~ *night,* noche de reyes, epifanía.

twelve [twelv] *a.-s.* doce.

twentieth ['twentiiθ] *a.-s.* vigésimo.

twenty ['twenti] *a.-s.* veinte.

twice [twais] *adv.* dos veces.

twig [twig] *s.* ramita.

twilight ['twailait] *s.* crepúsculo.

twin [twin] *s.* gemelo, mellizo.

twine [twain] *s.* cordel. *2 t.* torcer; tejer.

twinkle ['twiŋkl] *s.* destello. *2* parpadeo. *3 i.* destellar. *4* parpadear; guiñar.

twist [twist] *s.* torsión, torcedura. *2 t.-i.* torcer(se, retorcer(se.

two [tu:] *a.-s.* dos. *2 twofold,* doble.

type [taip] *s.* tipo, modelo, ejemplar: ⁓ *writing,* mecanografía; *typist,* mecanógrafa.

typewriter ['taip,raitər] *s.* máquina de escribir.

typical ['tipikl] *a.* típico.

tyranny ['tirəni] *s.* tiranía.

tyrant ['taiərənt] *s.* tirano.

tyre ['taiər] *s.* neumático.

U

ugly ['ʌgli] *a.* feo. 2 horroroso. 3 (E. U.) de mal genio.

ultimate ['ʌltimit] *a.* último. 2 fundamental, esencial.

umbrella [ʌm'brelə] *s.* paraguas.

umpire ['ʌmpaiə'] *s.* árbitro.

unable ['ʌn'eibl] *a.* incapaz.

uncle ['ʌŋkl] *s.* tío.

under ['ʌndə'] *prep.* bajo, debajo de. 2 menos de; dentro. 3 en tiempo de. 4 conforme a, según. 5 4. inferior.

underbrush ['ʌndəbrʌʃ] *s.* maleza [de un bosque].

undergo [ˌʌndə'gou] *t.* sufrir, padecer, aguan-

tar. ¶ Pret.: *underwent* [ˌʌndə'went]; p. p.: *undergone* [ˌʌndə'gɔn].

underground [ˌʌndə-graund] *a.* subterráneo. 2 secreto, clandestino. 3 *s.* subterráneo. 4 metro, ferrocarril subterráneo. 5 [ˌʌndə'graund] *adv.* bajo tierra. 6 en secreto.

underlying [ˌʌndə'laiiŋ] *a.* subyacente. 2 fundamental.

underneath [ˌʌndə'niːθ] *adv.* debajo. 2 *prep.* debajo de.

understand [ˌʌndə'stænd] *t.* entender, comprender. ¶ Pret. y p. p.: *understood* [ˌʌndə'stud].

understanding [ˌʌndə-'stændiŋ] *s.* inteligencia, comprensión. 2 *a.*

inteligente; comprensivo.

understood [ˌʌndəˈstud] V. TO UNDERSTAND.

undertake [ˌʌndəˈteik] t. emprender, acometer. 2 comprometerse a. ¶ Pret.: *undertook* [ˌʌndəˈtuk]; p. p.: *undertaken* [ˌʌndəˈteikən].

undertaking [ˌʌndəˈteikiŋ] s. empresa. 2 promesa. 3 [ˈʌndəˌteikiŋ] funeraria.

underwear [ˈʌndəwɛəʳ] s. ropa interior.

uneasy [ʌnˈiːzi] a. intranquilo, incómodo.

unfit [ˈʌnˈfit] a. incapaz, inepto. 2 inadecuado, impropio.

unfold [ˈʌnˈfəuld] t.-i. desplegar(se, extender(se.

unhappy [ʌnˈhæpi] a. infeliz, desgraciado. 2 triste.

union [ˈjuːnjən] s. unión: *the Union*, los Estados Unidos. 2 asociación o sindicato obrero: *Trade Union*, sindicato obrero.

unique [juːˈniːk] a. único; singular, raro.

unit [ˈjuːnit] s. unidad.

unite [juːˈnait] t.-i. unir(se.

unity [ˈjuːniti] s. unidad.

universal [ˌjuːniˈvəːsəl] a. universal.

universe [ˈjuːnivəːs] s. universo.

university [ˌjuːniˈvəːsiti] s. universidad. 2 a. universitario.

unknown [ˈʌnˈnəun] a. desconocido, ignorado, ignoto.

unless [ənˈles] conj. a menos que, a no ser que. 2 salvo, excepto.

unlike [ˈʌnˈlaik] a. desemejante, diferente. 2 adv. de diferente modo que. 3 prep. a diferencia de.

unpleasant [ʌnˈpleznt] a. desagradable, molesto. 2 -ly adv. desagradablemente.

until [ənˈtil] prep. hasta [con sentido temporal]. 2 conj. hasta que.

unto [ˈʌntu] prep. (poét. y ant.) hacia, a, hasta, contra, en.

unwilling [ˈʌnˈwiliŋ] a. reacio.

up [ʌp] adv. hacia arriba. 2 en alto. 3 a la altura de: *well ~ in*, bien enterado. 4 enteramente, completamente. *tu burn ~*, quemar del todo. 5 en contacto o proximidad: *close ~ to*, tocando a. 6

en reserva: *to lay* ~, acumular. 7 hasta: ~ *to date*, hasta la fecha. 8 *prep.* subido a, en lo alto de: ~ *a tree*, subido a un árbol. 9 hacia arriba: ~ *the river*, río arriba. 10 *a.* ascendente: ~ *train*, tren ascendente. 11 derecho; levantado [no acostado]. 12 que está en curso: *what is* ~?, ¿qué ocurre? 13 entendido, enterado. 14 capaz, dispuesto. 15 acabado: *the time is* ~, expiró el plazo. 16 s. *ups and downs*, altibajos. 17 *interj.* ¡arriba!, ¡aúpa! 18 ~ *there!*, ¡alto ahí!

plift ['ʌplift] s. levantamiento.

upon [ə'pɔn] *prep.* sobre, encima. 2 *nothing to live* ~, nada con qué vivir; ~ *pain of*, bajo pena de; ~ *seeing this*, viedo esto.

upper ['ʌpəʳ] *a. comp.* de **up**: superior, alto, más elevado: ~ *classes*, la clase alta ~ *House*, cámara alta; *to have the* ~ *hand of*, ejercer el mando. 2 s. pala y caña del zapato. 3 litera alta.

upright ['ʌp'rait] *a.* de-

recho, vertical. 2 ['ʌprait] recto, honrado.

uproar ['ʌp.rɔ:] s. gritería, alboroto, tumulto.

upset ['ʌpset] *a.* volcado, tumbado. 2 trastornado, desarreglado. 3 [ʌp'set] s. vuelco. 4 trastorno. 5 [ʌp'set] *t.* volcar. 6 trastornar, desarreglar. ¶ Pret. y p. p.: *upset*.

upstairs ['ʌp'stɛəz] *adv.* arriba, al o en el piso de arriba. 2 *a.* de arriba.

urge [ə:dʒ] s. impulso. 2 ganas. 3 *t.* insistir en. 4 recomendar. 5 instar.

us [ʌs, əs, s] *pron. pers.* [caso objetivo] nos. 2 [con prep.] nosotros.

use [ju:s] s. uso, empleo. 2 utilidad, servicio, provecho. 3 práctica, costumbre. 4 [ju:z] *t.* usar, emplear. 5 practicar, hacer. 6 tratar [bien, mal].

useful ['ju:sful] *a.* útil.

useless ['ju:slis] *a.* inútil.

usual ['ju:ʒuəl] *a.* usual, habitual: *as* ~, como de costumbre.

usury ['ju:ʒuri] s. usura.

utility [ju:'tiliti] *s.* utilidad, provecho. 2 empre-
sa de servicio público.

utilize ['ju:tilaiz] *t.* utilizar, emplear, explotar.

utmost ['ʌtməust, -məst]
a. sumo, extremo. 2 *s.*
lo más posible.

utter ['ʌtər] *a.* absoluto,
total. 2 *t.* pronunciar,
articular. 3 decir, expresar.

V

vacation [vəˈkeiʃən] s. vacación.

vague [veig] a. vago, indefinido.

vain [vein] a. vano, fútil.

vale [veil] s. valle, cañada.

valentine [ˈvæləntain] s. tarjeta o regalo el día de san Valentín. 2 novio, novia.

valiant [ˈvæljənt] a. valiente.

valley [ˈvæli] s. valle, cuenca.

valo(u)r [ˈvælər] s. valor.

valuable [ˈvæljuəbl] a. valioso, costoso. 2 s. pl. objetos de valor.

value [ˈvælju:] s. valor [de una cosa]; precio, mérito. 2 t. valorar. 3 apreciar, estimar.

van [væn] s. furgón; camioneta. 2 vanguardia.

vanish [ˈvæniʃ] i. desaparecer, desvanecerse.

vanity [ˈvæniti] s. vanidad.

vapo(u)r [ˈveipər] s. vapor, vaho. 2 niebla ligera.

variety [vəˈraiəti] s. variedad.

various [ˈvɛəriəs] a. vario [diverso; variable]. 2 varios.

vary [ˈvɛəri] t.-i. variar. 2 i. diferenciarse.

vase [vɑ:z] s. jarrón; florero.

vassal [ˈvæsəl] s. vasallo.

vast [vɑ:st] a. vasto. 2 inmenso.

vat [væt] s. tina, tanque.

vault [vɔ:lt] s. ARQ. bóveda. 2 sótano; cripta tumba o panteón subte-

rráneo. 3 salto [con pér- | vaso. 2 nave, embarca-
tiga, etc.]. 4 *t.* above- | ción.
dar. 2 *t.-i.* saltar [por | **vest** [vest] *s.* chaleco. 2
encima], saltar con pér- | *t. to — in,* dar, atribuir,
tiga. | conferir a.

vaunt [vɔːnt] *i.* jactarse. | **vex** [veks] *t.* vejar, mo-

veal [viːl] *s.* ternera | lestar. 2 disgustar, desa-
[carne]. | zonar.

vegetable ['vedʒitəbl] *a.* | **vibrate** [vaiˈbreit] *t.-i.*
vegetal. 2 *s.* vegetal. 3 | vibrar, hacer vibrar.
legumbre, hortaliza. | **vice** [vais] *s.* vicio. 2 tor-

veil [veil] *s.* velo. 2 *t.* | no de banco. 3 fam. sus-
velar. | tituto, suplente.

vein [vein] *s.* ANAT. vena. | **vicinity** [viˈsiniti] *s.* ve-
2 humor, disposición. | cindad.

velvet ['velvit] *s.* tercio- | **victim** ['viktim] *s.* vícti-
pelo. | ma.

vengeance ['ven(d)ʒəns] | **victor** ['viktəʳ] *m.* ven-
s. venganza. | cedor.

verdict ['vəːdikt] *s.* ve- | **view** [vjuː] *s.* vista, vi-
redicto. | sión, consideración; mi-

verse [vəːs] *s.* LIT. verso. | rada. 2 opinión, punto

version ['vəːʃən] *s.* ver- | de vista. 3 aspecto. 4
sión. | propósito. 5 *t.* ver, mi-

vertical ['vəːtikəl] *a.* | rar. 6 examinar, inspec-
vertical. | cionar. 7 considerar.

very ['veri] *a.* mismo, | **vigorous** ['vigərəs] *a.*
idéntico: *at that — mo-* | vigoroso.
ment, en aquel mismo | **vigo(u)r** ['vigəʳ] *s.* vi-
instante. 2 verdadero, | gor.
puro, solo: *the — truth,* | **vile** [vail] *a.* vil, ruin.
la pura verdad. 3 *adv.* | **village** ['vilidʒ] *s.* aldea,
muy, sumamente: — | lugar.
much, mucho, muchísi- | **villain** ['vilən] *s.* bribón,
mo. | canalla.

vessel ['vesl] *s.* vasija, | **vine** [vain] *s.* BOT. vid,
 | parra.

vinegar ['vinigə'] *s.* vinagre.

violate ['vaiəleit] *t.* violar.

violence ['vaiələns] *s.* violencia.

violet ['vəiəlit] *s.* violeta. 2 color de violeta.

violin [,vaiə'lin] *s.* violín.

virgin ['və:dʒin] *s.* virgen, doncella. 2 *a.* virgen; virginal.

virtue ['və:tju:] *s.* virtud.

visible ['vizibl] *a.* visible.

vision ['viʒən] *s.* vista [sentido]. 2 visión.

visit ['vizit] *s.* visita. 2 *t.* visitar. 3 afligir, castigar.

visitor ['vizitə'] *s.* visita, visitante. 2 visitador.

vivid ['vivid] *a.* vívido. 2 vivo, animado.

voice [vois] *s.* voz. 2 habla, palabra. 3 opinión,

voto. 2 *t.* expresar, decir.

void [void] *s.* vacío; vacante.

volcano [vol'keinou] *s.* volcán.

volume ['voljum] *s.* volumen, tomo, libro.

volunteer [,volən'tiə'] *s.* voluntario. 2 *t.-i.* ofrecer(se voluntariamente.

vote [vout] *s.* voto, votación. 2 *t.-i.* votar [dar su voto].

voter ['voutə'] *s.* votante.

vow [vau] *s.* voto, promesa solemne. 2 voto, deseo; súplica. 3 *t.* hacer voto de; prometer solemnemente.

voyage ['voiidʒ] *s.* viaje por mar o por el aire, travesía. 2 *i.* viajar, navegar.

vulgar ['vʌlgə'] *a.* vulgar. 2 común, ordinario. de mal gusto.

W

wade [weid] *i.* andar sobre terreno cubierto de agua, lodo, etc. 2 *t.* vadear.

wag [wæg] *s.* meneo. 2 bromista, guasón, 3 *t.-i.* menear(se.

wage [weidʒ] *s.* paga, jornal. 2 *t.* hacer; librar; proseguir.

wag(g)on [ˈwægən] *s.* carromato, furgón.

waif [weif] *s.* cosa o animal sin dueño. 2 niño abandonado; golfillo.

wail [weil] *s.* lamento, gemido. 2 *t.-i.* lamentar(se, deplorar.

waist [weist] *s.* cintura, talle.

wait [weit] *s.* espera. 2 detención, demora. 3 *i.-t.* esperar, aguardar [con *for*]. 4 *i.* servir: *to ~ at*

table, servir a la mesa.

waiter [ˈweitər] *s.* mozo, camarero.

waiting [ˈweitiŋ] *s.* espera. 2 servicio.

wake [weik] *s.* estela, aguaje. 2 vela, velatorio. 3 [a veces con *up*] *t.-i.* despertar(se, despabilarse. ¶ Pret. *waked* [weikt] o *woke* [wouk]; p. p.: *waked* o *woken* [ˈwoukən].

waken [ˈweikən] *t.-i.* despertar.

walk [wɔːk] *s.* paseo, vuelta. 2 paseo, alameda, senda. 3 paso [del caballo, etc.]. 4 *i.* andar, caminar: *to ~ away,* irse; *to ~ out, to ~ out with,* salir con, ser novio de; *to ~ up to,* acercarse a; *to ~ the hospi-*

tals, estudiar medicina. *5 t.* sacar a paseo. *6* recorrer.

walking ['wɔ:kiŋ] *s.* marcha, paseo.

wall [wɔ:l] *s.* pared, muro.

walnut ['wɔ:lnʌt] *s.* BOT. nuez.

wand [wɔnd] *s.* vara.

wander ['wɔndər] *t.-i.* errar, vagar.

want [wɔnt] *s.* falta, necesidad, carencia, escasez. *2 t.* necesitar. *3* querer, desear.

wanting ['wɔntiŋ] *a.* falto, defectuoso. *2* necesitado.

war [wɔ:] *s.* guerra. *2 i.* guerrear, estar en guerra.

ward [wɔ:d] *s.* guarda, custodia. *2 t.* guardar, proteger.

wardrobe ['wɔ:droub] *s.* armario, guardarropa.

ware [wɛər] *s. sing.* o *pl.* géneros, mercancías.

warehouse ['wɛəhaus] *s.* almacén.

warfare ['wɔ:fɛər] *s.* guerra.

warm [wɔ:m] *a.* caliente, cálido, caluroso; *I am* ~, tengo calor; *it is* ~, hace calor. *2 t.-i.* calentar(se.

warmth [wɔ:mθ] *s.* calor moderado. *2* afecto, cordialidad.

warn [wɔ:n] *t.* avisar, advertir, prevenir. *2* amonestar.

warning ['wɔ:niŋ] *s.* aviso, advertencia. *2* amonestación.

warp [wɔ:p] *s.* TEJ. urdimbre. *2 t.* urdir.

warrant ['wɔrənt] *s.* autorización, poder. *2 t.* autorizar.

warrior ['wɔriər] *s.* guerrero.

wash [wɔʃ] *s.* lavado, ablución. *2* baño, capa. *3* loción. *4 t.* lavar. *5* bañar, regar; *to* ~ *up,* lavar los platos.

washing ['wɔʃiŋ] *s.* acción de TO WASH. *2* colada. *3 a.* de lavar: ~*-machine,* lavadora.

wasp [wɔsp] *s.* avispa.

waste [weist] *a.* yermo, inculto. *2 s.* extensión, inmensidad. *3 t.* devastar, destruir. *4* gastar, mermar.

watch [wɔtʃ] *s.* reloj de bolsillo. *2* vela, vigilia: ~ *night,* noche vieja. *3* vigilancia, observación. *4* centinela, vigilante. *5 i.* velar [estar despierto]. 6 vigilar, estar alerta.

watchful ['wɔtʃful] a. desvelado. 2 vigilante, en guardia.

water ['wɔ:tə'] s. agua: *in deep ~*, o *waters*, en apuros. 2 agua, de agua, acuático. 3 t. regar, rociar, mojar. 4 i. chorrear agua o humedad; llorar.

waterfall [['wɔ:tɔfɔ:l] s. cascada, catarata.

wave [weiv] s. ola. 2 onda. 3 i. flotar, ondear.

waver ['weivə'] s. oscilación. 2 i. ondear, oscilar.

wax [wæks] s. cera. 2 t. encerar. 3 i. crecer, aumentar.

way [wei] s. vía, camino, calle, canal, conducto. 2 viaje, rumbo, curso, dirección, sentido: *the other ~ round*, al revés; *this ~*, por aquí. 3 paso. 4 espacio, distancia, trecho. 5 marcha, progreso. 6 modo, manera: *anyway*, de todos modos. 7 lado, aspecto. 8 medio. 9 sistema de vida, costumbre. 10 estado, condición. 11 pl. maneras [de una persona]. 12 by *~ of*, pasando por, por vía de. 13 by the *~*, a

propósito. 14 a. de camino, de tránsito: *~ train*, tren, tranvía.

we [wi:, wi) pron. nosotros.

weak [wi:k] a. débil, flojo.

weaken ['wi:kən] t.-i. debilitar(se.

weakness ['wi:knis] s. debilidad.

wealth [welθ] s. riqueza.

wealthy ['welθi] a. rico.

weapon ['wepən] s. arma.

wear [wɛə'] s. uso [de ropa, calzado, etc.]. 2 ropa, vestidos. 3 t. traer puesto, usar, llevar. 4 t.-i. gastar(se, deteriorar(se. 5 to *~ away*, gastar(se, consumir(se. ¶ Pret.: *wore* [wɔ:', wɔə']; p. p.: *worn* [wɔ:n]

weariness ['wiərinis] s. cansancio, fatiga. 2 aburrimiento.

weary ['wiəri] a. fatigado. 2 t.-i. cansar(se, fatigar(se.

weather ['weðə'] s. tiempo [estado de la atmósfera]. 2 t.-i. curar(se, secar(se a la intemperie.

weave [wi:v] s. tejido, textura. 2 t. tejer. 3 urdir, tramar. ¶ Pret.: *wore* [wɔuv]; p. p.:

woven ['wouvən] o *wove*.

web [web] *s.* tejido, tela; telaraña.

we'd [wi:d] *contrac.* de WE HAD, WE SHOLD o WE WOULD.

wedding ['wediŋ] *s.* boda.

wedge [wedʒ] *s.* cuña, calce. 2 *t.* acuñar, meter cuñas.

Wednesday ['wenzdi, -dei] *s.* miércoles.

weed [wi:d] *s.* yerbajo. 2 *t.* desyerbar.

week [wi:k] *s.* semana: *a ~ from today,* de hoy en ocho días.

weep [wi:p] *t.-i.* llorar. ¶ Pret. y p. p.: *wept* [wept].

welcome ['welkəm] *a.* bien venido. 2 grato, agradable. 3 *you are ~,* no hay de qué. 4 *s.* bienvenida, buena acogida. 5 *t.* dar la bienvenida, acoger.

welfare ['welfɛəʳ] *s.* bienestar.

we'll [wi:l] *contrac.* de WE SHALL y WE WILL.

1) **well** [wel] *a.* bien hecho, satisfactorio, bueno, apto. 2 *s. well-being,* bienestar. 3 pozo. 4 *adv.*

bien, felizmente. 5 *as ~,* además; también.

2) **well** [wel] *t.-i.* manar.

went [went] *pret.* de TO GO.

wept [wept] V. TO WEEP.

we're [wiəʳ] *contrac.* de WE ARE.

were [wəːʳ, wəʳ] V. TO BE.

west [west] *s.* oeste, occidente. 2 *a.* occidental, del oeste.

wet [wet] *a.* mojado. 2 húmedo. 3 *s.* humedad. 4 *t.* mojar. ¶ Pret. y p. p.: *wet* o *wetted*.

wetness ['wetnis] *s.* humedad.

wharf [(h)wɔ:f] *s.* muelle.

what [(h)wɔt] *a.* y *pron. interr.* qué; cuál: *~ for?,* ¿para qué? 2 *pron. rel.* lo que. 3 *a. rel.* que: *~ a man!,* ¡qué hombre! 4 *interj.* ¡eh!, ¡qué!

whatever [wɔt'evəʳ] *pron.* cualquier cosa que, todo lo que. 2 *a.* cualquiera que.

whatsoever [ˌwɔtsəu'evəʳ] *pron.* y *a.* WHATEVER.

wheat [(h)wi:t] *s.* trigo.

wheel [(h)wi:l] *s.* rueda. 2 torno. 3 AUTO. volante.

when [(h)wen] *adv.-conj.* cuando.

whence [(h)wens] *adv.* de
donde; por lo cual.
whenever [(h)wen'evər]
adv. cuando quiera que,
siempre que.
where [wɛər] *adv.-conj.*
donde, en donde, adon-
de, por donde.
whereas [wɛər'æz] *conj.*
considerando que. 2
mientras que.
wherever [wɛər'evər] *adv.*
dondequiera que, adon-
dequiera que, por donde-
quiera que.
whether ['weðər] *conj.* si.
2 sea, ya sea que, tanto
si... (como).
which [(h)witʃ] *a.* y *pron.*
interrogativo [selectivo]
¿qué?, ¿cuál?, ¿cuáles?
2 *pron. rel.* lo que, lo
cual. 3 *a. rel.* que [cuan-
do el antecedente es co-
sa].
whichever [(h)witʃ'evər]
pron. y *a.* cual(es)quiera
[que].
while [(h)wail] *s.* rato,
tiempo: *be worth* ~, va-
ler la pena. 2 *conj.* mientras [que]. 3 *t.* pasar [el
rato, etc.].
whine [(h)wain] *s.* gemido. 2 *i.* gemir, quejar-
se.
whip [(h)wip] *s.* látigo,

azote. 2 *t.* fustigar, azotar.
whir [(h)wə:r] *s.* zumbido. 2 *i.* zumbar.
whirl [(h)wə:l] *s.* remolino. 2 *i.* girar rápidamente. 3 *t.* hacer girar.
whisper ['(h)wispər] *s.*
susurro. 2 *i.-t.* susurrar,
murmurar.
whistle ['(h)wisl] *s.* silba-
to, pito. 2 *i.-t.* silbar,
pitar.
whit [(h)wit] *s.* pizca.
white [(h)wait] *a.* blanco:
~-*hot*, candente. 2 *s.*
clara [de huevo].
whither ['(h)wiðər] *adv.*
adonde.
who [hu:, hu] *pron. rel.*
quien, quienes, que, el
que, la que, los que, las
que. 2 *pron. interr.*
¿quién?, ¿quiénes?
whoever [hu(:)'evər]
pron. rel. quienquiera
que, cualquiera que.
whole [haul] *a.* todo, entero. 2 *s.* total, conjunto.
wholesale ['haul-seil] *a.-
adv.* al por mayor. 2 *s.*
venta al por mayor.
wholesome ['haulsəm] *a.*
sano.
whom [hu:m, hum] *pron.*
caso oblicuo de WHO) a

quien, a quienes; que, al que, etc.

whose [hu:z] *pron.* (genitivo de WHO y WHICH) cuyo -s, cuyos -as, del que, de quien(es.

why [(h)wai] *adv. conj.* ¿por qué?, ¿cómo? 2 *interj.* ¡cómo!, ¡toma! 3 *s.* porqué, causa.

wicked ['wikid] *a.* malo, perverso.

wide [waid] *a.* ancho. 2 amplio, extenso. 3 *adv.* ampliamente. 4 lejos, a distancia.

widen ['waidn] *t.-i.* ensanchar(se, extender(se.

widow ['widəu] *s.* viuda.

width [widθ] *s.* anchura, ancho.

wife [waif], *pl.* **wives** [waivz] *s.* esposa.

wild [waild] *a.* salvaje, montaraz, silvestre.

wilderness ['wildənis] *s.* tierra inculta, desierto.

will [wil] *s.* voluntad.

1) **will** [wil] *t.* querer, ordenar. ╒ Pret. y p. p.: *willed.*

2) **will** (sin **to**) [wil] *t.* querer, desear. ╒ Pret.: *would* [wud]. | No se usa otro tiempo.

3) **will** (sin **to**) [wil] *v. defect* y *aux.* pret. y

condicional: *would* [wud, wəd]. Se usa *will* para formar el fut. y *would* en condicional en 2.ª y 3.ª pers.

willing ['wiliŋ] *a.* deseoso, dispuesto. 2 gustoso.

willow ['wiləu] *s.* sauce.

wilt [wilt] *t.-i.* marchitar(se.

win [win] *t.* ganar. 2 *i.* vencer, triunfar. ╒ Pret. y p. p.: *won* [wʌn].

wind [wind] *s.* viento, aire. 2 rumbo, punto cardinal. 3 aliento, respiración.

1) **wind** [wind] *t.-i.* husmear, olfatear. 2 *t.* airear. ╒ Pret. y p. p.: *winded* ['windid].

2) **wind** [waind] *t.* devanar. 2 dar cuerda a [un reloj]. 3 izar, elevar. ╒ Pret. y p. p.: *wound* [waund].

3) **wind** [waind] *t.* soplar. ╒ Pret. y p. p.: *winded* ['waindid] o *wound* [waund].

window ['windəu] *s.* ventana.

wine [wain] *s.* vino.

wing [wiŋ] *s.* ala. 2 vuelo. 3 TEAT. bastidor.

wink [wiŋk] *s.* parpadeo. 2 guiño. 3 destello. 4 *i.*

pestañear. 5 hacer gui-
ños. 6 centellear.

winner ['winər] s. ganador.

winning ['winiŋ] a.
triunfante, ganador. 2
atractivo. 3 -s s. pl. ganancias [en el juego].

winter ['wintər] s. invierno.

wipe [waip] t. limpiar.

wire ['waiər] s. alambre.
2 telegrama; telégrafo.
3 t. poner un telegrama.

wireless ['waiəlis] s. radio.

wisdom ['wizdəm] s. sa-
biduria.

wise [waiz] a. cuerdo,
prudente. 2 s. manera:
in no ~, de ningún mo-
do.

wish [wiʃ] s. deseo, anhelo. 2 t. desear, anhe-
lar, ansiar.

wit [wit] s. agudeza, ingenio.

witch [witʃ] s. bruja, he-
chicera.

with [wið] prep. con;
para con; a, de, en, en-
tre: charged ~, acusado
de.

withdraw [wið'drɔ:] t.-i.
retirar(se. 2 apartar(se,
separar(se.   ¶ Pret.:

withdrew [wið'dru:]; p.
p.: withdrawn [wið-
'drɔ:n].

wither ['wiðər] t. mar-
chitar(se, secar(se, ajar-
(se.

withhold [wið'houl] t.
detener, contener. 2 sus-
pender [un pago]. 3 ne-
gar. ¶ Pret. y p.
p.: withheld [wið'held].

within [wi'ðin] prep.
dentro de [los límites
de], en. 2 al alcance de.
3 adv. dentro, en o al
interior, en la casa.

without [wi'ðaut] prep.
sin. 2 falto de. 3 fuera
de. 4 adv. fuera. 5 conj.
si no, a menos de.

witness ['witnis] s. testigo. 2 t. dar testimonio
de, atestiguar.

witty ['witi] a. ingenioso,
agudo.

wives [waivz] s. pl. de
WIFE.

woe [wou] s. pena, aflicción.

woke [wouk] V. TO WAKE.

wolf [wulf] pl. wolves
[wulvz] s. lobo: ~ cub,
lobezno.

woman ['wumən] pl.
women ['wimin] s. mu-
jer.

won [wʌn] V. TO WIN.

wonder ['wʌndər] s. admiración, asombro: *no ~*, no es de extrañar. 2 incertidumbre. 3 t. desear saber, preguntarse.

wonderful ['wʌndəful] a. admirable, maravilloso.

wondrous ['wʌndrəs] a. sorprendente, asombroso.

wont [wount] a. acostumbrado: *to be ~ to*, soler, acostumbrar. 2 s. costumbre, hábito.

won't [wount] contr. de WILL NOT.

woo [wu:] t.-i. cortejar.

wood [wud] s. bosque, selva. 2 madera, leña.

wool [wul] s. lana.

word [wo:d] s. palabra, vocablo. 2 palabra, promesa. 3 aviso, recado. 4 pl. palabras, disputa: *to have words*, disputar. 5 t. expresar [con palabras].

wore [wo:ʳ, woəʳ] V. to WEAR.

work [wo:k] s. trabajo, labor; ocupación, empleo; operación, funcionamiento. 2 obra. 3 pl. fábrica, taller. 4 maquinaria [de un artefacto]. 5 i. trabajar; laborar. 6 surtir efecto, dar resultado. 7 *to ~ out*, resultar [bien o mal]; DEP.

entrenarse. 8 t. fabricar, producir. 9 *to ~ off*, deshacerse de. 10 *to ~ up*, inflamar.

worker ['wo:kəʳ] s. obrero.

workman ['wo:kmən] s. obrero.

world [wo:ld] s. mundo.

worm [wo:m] s. gusano. 2 *i.-ref.* introducirse, insinuarse.

worn [wo:n] p. p. de to WEAR. 2 *~ out*, usado, gastado.

worried ['wʌrid] a. angustiado, preocupado.

worry ['wʌri] s. preocupación. 2 *t.-i.* inquietar(se, preocupar(se. 3 *to ~ out*, hallar solución.

worse [wo:s] a. - adv. comp. de *bad*, peor.

worship ['wo:ʃip] s. culto, adoración. 2 t. adorar.

worst [wo:st] s. superl. peor [en sentido absoluto]: *the ~*, el peor. 2 adv. superl. peor, pésimamente. 3 t. vencer, derrotar.

worth [wo:θ] s. valor, precio. 2 a. digno, merecedor de.

worthless ['wo:θlis] a. sin valor.

worthy ['wo:ði] a. estimable, excelente. 2 digno, merecedor.

would [wud, wəd] *pret.* de WILL 2; *pret. y condicional* de WILL 3.

would-be ['wudbi:] *a.* supuesto, seudo. 2 aspirante.

wouldn't ['wudənt] *contracción* de WOULD NOT.

wound [wu:nd] *s.* herida. 2 *t.* herir, lastimar.

wove [wəuv], **woven** ['wəuven] V. TO WEAVE.

wrap [ræp] *s.* envoltura. 2 manta, abrigo. 3 *t.-i.* cubrir(se, envolver(se.

wrath [rɔθ] *s.* cólera, ira.

wreak [ri:k] *t.* infligir.

wreath [ri:θ] *s.* corona, guirnalda.

wreck [rek] *s.* naufragio; ruina, destrucción. 2 *t.* hacer naufragar, echar a pique. 3 *t.-i.* arruinar(se, destruir(se.

wrench [rentʃ] *s.* tirón. 2 *t.* tirar de.

wrestle ['resl] *i.* luchar a brazo partido.

wretch [retʃ] *s.* miserable, infeliz.

wretched ['retʃid] *a.* infeliz. 2 malo, ruin.

wrinkle ['riŋkl] *s.* arruga, surco.

wrist [rist] *s.* ANAT. muñeca.

write [rait] *t.-i.* escribir; *to ~ back,* contestar por carta; *to ~ down,* anotar; *to ~ out,* redactar; *to ~ up,* poner al día. ¶ Pret.: *wrote* [rəut]; p. p.: *written* ['ritn].

writer ['raitə'] *s.* escritor, autor.

writing ['raitiŋ] *s.* escritura, escrito.

wrong [rɔŋ] *a.* malo, injusto. 2 erróneo, equivocado. 2 *the ~ side,* el revés (de una tela). 3 *adv.* mal, al revés. 4 *s.* agravio, injusticia. 5 *t.* agraviar, ofender.

wrought [rɔ:t] *pret. y p. p. irreg.* de TO WORK. 2 *a.* trabajado, labrado, forjado.

wrung [rʌŋ] V. TO WRING.

X

Xmas ['krisməs] *s. abrev.* de CHRISTMAS.

X-rays ['eks'reiz] *s. pl.* rayos X.

Y

yard [jɑːd] *s.* yarda [medida inglesa de longitud = 0'914 m]. 2 patio, corral.

yarn [jɑːn] *s.* hebra, hilo. 2 cuento increíble.

yawn [jɔːn] *s.* bostezo. 2 *i.* bostezar.

year [jeːʳ] *s.* año.

yearly ['jeːli] *a.* anual.

yearn [jeːn] *i.* [con *for* o *after*], anhelar, suspirar por.

yell [jel] *s.* grito, alarido. 2 *i.* gritar, dar alaridos.

yellow ['jelou] *a.* amarillo.

yeoman ['joumən] *s.* hacendado. 2 ~ *of the guard*, guardián de la Torre de Londres.

yes [jes] *adv.-s.* sí [respuesta afirmativa].

yesterday ['jestədi, -dei] *s.* y *adv.* ayer.

yet [jet] *adv.* todavía, aún. 2 *conj.* aún así, no obstante.

yield [jiːld] *s.* producto, rendimiento. 2 *t.* producir, rendir. 3 entregar, ceder. 4 rendirse.

yoke [jouk] *s.* yugo; esclavitud. 2 *t.* uncir, acoyundar.

yon [jɔn], **yonder** ['jɔndəʳ] *a.* aquel, aquella, etc., aquellos, aquellas, etc. 2 *adv.* allá; más allá.

you [juː, ju] *pron.* de 2.ª pers. *sing.* y *pl.* tú, usted, vosotros, ustedes. 2 a ti, te; le, a usted; os, a vosotros; les, a ustedes.

young [jʌŋ] *a.* joven.

youngster ['jʌŋstər] s.
muchacho, joven.
your [juər, jɔ:'] a. tu,
tus, vuestro, -a, -os,
-as; su, de usted, de
ustedes.
yours [juəz, jɔ:z] pron.
pos. [e] tuyo, -a, -os,
-as, [el] vuestro, -a, -os,
-as; [el] suyo, -a, -os,
-as [de usted o uste-
des].

yourself [juə'self, jɔ:-]
pron. pers. tú, ti, usted
mismo; te, se [reflexi-
vos].
yourselves [juə'selvz,
jɔ:-] pron. pl. de YOUR-
SELF.
youth [ju:θ] s. juventud.
youthful ['ju:θful] a. joven, juvenil. 2 fresco,
vigoroso.

Z

zeal [zi:l] s. celo, fervor.
zealous ['zeləs] a. celoso,
entusiasta.
zero ['ziərəu] s. cero.
zest [zest] s. sabor, gusto. 2 entusiasmo; ali-
ciente.

zigzag ['zigzæg] s. zigzag.
2 i. zigzaguear.
zinc [ziŋk] s. cinc, zinc.
zone [zəun] s. zona.
zoological [ˌzəuə'lɔdʒikl]
a. zoológico.

SPANISH–ENGLISH
ESPAÑOL–INGLÉS

ABBREVIATIONS USED IN THIS DICTIONARY

a.	adjective
adv.	adverb
AER.	aeronautics
AGR.	agriculture
Am.	Spanish America
ANAT.	anatomy
ARCH.	architecture
art.	article
ARTILL.	artillery
ARTS	fine arts
AUTO.	automobile
aux.	auxiliary verb
BIB.	Bible; Biblical
BIOL.	biology
BOOKKEEP.	bookkeeping
BOT.	botany
BOX.	boxing
BULLF.	bullfighting
CARDS	playing cards; card games
CARP.	carpentry
CHEM.	chemistry
CINEM.	cinema; movies

COM.	commerce
comp.	comparative
COND.	conditional
conj.	conjunction
CONJUG.	conjugation
COOK.	cooking
def.	defective; definite
dem.	demonstrative
dim.	diminutive
ECCL.	ecclesiastical
ECON.	economics
EDUC.	education
ELEC.	electricity
ELECT.	electricity
ENTOM.	entomology
exclam.	exclamatory; exclamation
F. ARTS.	fine arts
FUT.	future
GEOG.	geography
GEOL.	geology
GEOM.	geometry
GER.	gerund

GOLF	golf
GRAM.	grammar
HIST.	history
HUNT.	hunting
i.	intransitive
ICHTH.	ichthyology
IMPER.	imperative
Imperf.	imperfect
impers.	impersonal verb
IND.	industry
indef.	indefinite
INDIC.	indicative
Instit.	secondary school; high school
interrog.	interrogative
interr. pron.	interrogative pronoun
LAW	law
LIT.	literature
LOG.	logic
m.	masculine; masculine noun
MACH.	machinery
MATH.	mathematics

MEC.	mechanics
MECH.	mechanics
MED.	medicine
MIL.	military
MIN.	mining
MUS.	music
n.	neuter
NAUT.	nautical
ORN.	ornithology
p.	pronominal (reflexive) verb
PAINT.	painting
PAST P.	past participle
pers.	personal
PHIL.	philosophy
PHYS.	physics
PHYSIOL.	physiology
pl.	plural
POL.	politics
poss.	possessive
p.p.	past participle
prep.	preposition
Pres.	present

Pret.	preterite
PRINT.	printing
pron.	pronoun
prn.	pronoun
RADIO	radio; broadcasting
ref. prn.	reflexive pronoun
rel.	relative
RLY.	railway; railroad
sing.	singular
SPORT.	sports
SUBJ.	subjunctive
superl.	superlative
SURG.	surgery
TELEPH.	telephone
TELEV.	television
THEAT.	theater
Univers.	University
ZOOL.	zoology

KEY TO SPANISH PRONUNCIATION ACCORDING TO THE INTERNATIONAL PHONETIC ALPHABET (I. P. A.)

SPANISH VOWELS

Spanish vowels always have the same value. The pronunciation of Spanish vowels, compared with vowels in English, is much more tense.

Spanish vowels	phonetic symbols	explanation of the sounds
i	[i]	The Spanish /i/ is not as closed as in the English *seat*, but not as open as in *sit*. It resembles the French i in *fille*: i*sla* [ízla], *avisar* [aβisár].
e	[e]	The Spanish /e/ is more closed than the English e in *men*. It is similar to the French e in *chanté*: *queso* [késo], *noche* [nótʃe].
a	[a]	The Spanish /a/ is not like the English a in *father* or in *hat*. It is similar to the English o in *son*, but more open and frontal. It is similar to the French a in *chat*: *arte* [árte], *amor* [amór].

Spanish vowels	phonetic symbols	explanation of the sounds
o	[o]	It is similar to the English **ou** in *bou*ght, but not so long. It resembles the French **eau** in *b*eau: *o*la [óla], *ric*o [rríko].
u	[u]	It is more closed than the English **u** in *fu*ll. It is similar to the English **oo** in *foo*l [fu:l], but not so long and tense. It resembles the French **ou** in *pou*le: *l*una [lúna], *r*utina [rrutína]. NOTE. It is silent after **q** and in **gue, gui,** unless marked by a diaeresis: *vergü*enza [berɣwénθa], *argü*ir [arɣwir].

SPANISH SEMIVOWELS

Spanish semi-vowels	phonetic symbols	explanation of the sounds
i, y	[i]	When it is the second element in Spanish falling diphthongs (see below), it resembles the **i** in the English *voi*ce. In Spanish it is louder and much more

prominent than in English: *aire* [áire], *rey* [rréi].

u   [u̯]   When it is the second element in Spanish falling diphthongs, it is like the **u** in the English *house* [haus]. In Spanish it is louder and much more prominent than in English: *causa* [káusa].

SPANISH SEMICONSONANTS

Spanish semicon-sonants	phonetic symbols	explanation of the sounds
i, y	[j]	When it is the first element in Spanish rising diphthongs (see below), this sound is similar to the English **y** in *yes* or *yet*: *siete* [sjéte], *hacia* [áθja].
u	[w]	This sound is similar to the English **w** in *wait*: *cuatro* [kwátro], *bueno* [bwéno].

SPANISH DIPHTHONGS

There are two kinds of diphthongs in Spanish: falling and rising diphthongs.

Falling diphthongs: /ai/, c**ai**go [káiɣo]. h**ay** [ái]; /ei/, r**ei**na [rréina], l**ey** [léi]; /oi/, o**ig**a [óiɣa]; h**oy** [ói]; /au/, c**au**to [káuto]; /eu/, d**eu**da [déuða]; /ou/, b**ou** [bóu].

In falling diphthongs, the first elements **e, o** are more closed than in English. The second elements **i, u,** called semivowels, are louder and much more prominent in Spanish than in English.

Rising diphthongs: /ja/, hac**ia** [áθja], /je/, t**ie**mpo [tjémpo]; /jo/, lab**io** [láβjo]; /ju/, v**iu**da [bjúða]; /w/, c**ua**tro [kwátro]; /we/ b**ue**no [bwéno]; /wi/, f**ui** [fwi]; /wo/, ard**uo** [árðwo].

SPANISH TRIPHTHONGS

The strong vowels **a, e** in the middle of two weak vowels (**i, u**) take the stress. The final vowel **i** is much more prominent in Spanish than in English.

/jai/, estud**iái**s [estuðjáis]; /jei/, limp**iéi**s [limpjéis]; /wai/, averig**uái**s [aβeriɣwáis], Parag**uay** [paraɣwái]; /wei/, santig**üéi**s [santiɣwéis], b**uey** [bwéi].

SPANISH CONSONANTS

Spanish consonants	phonetic symbols	explanation of the sounds
p (pe)	[p]	Like the English /p/, but without any aspiration, as in *spin:* **p**adre [páðre], ca**p**a [kápa].

NOTE: a) Omitted in sé(p)-
tiembre, suscri(p)tor, sé(p)-
timo.

b) It can be dropped, except in affected speech, in the initial
groups *ps-*: (p)sicología.—

c) **p** in end syllable position followed by a consonant becomes
[β]: *apto* [áβto].

b (be)   The Spanish letters **b** and **v** have
v (uve)   the same sound. There are two
pronunciations: [b] and [β] ac-
cording to position:

[b]   Like the English /b/ in the initial
position and after **m** or **n (mb,
n b, nv**): *bueno* [bwéno]; *venir*
[beníɾ]; *hombre* [ómbre];
un buen día [um bwén día];
envidia [embídja]; *un vals* [um
bals].

[β]   In any other position not mentioned above. Try to pro-
nounce it with your lips slight-
ly open, as if blowing out a
candle and making the vocal
cords vibrate: *lobo* [lóβo]; *la
vaca* [la βáka]; *ábside*
[áβsiðe].

t (te)   [t]   The Spanish /t/ is pronounced as in English, but

a) with the tip of the tongue behind the upper teeth (not between the teeth);

b) without any aspiration or puff of air.

It is similar to the English /t/ in the group *st-*: **st**one [stəun]. Examples: **t**ener [tenér], **t**inta [tínta].

NOTE: /t/ at the end of a syllable followed by a consonant becomes /ð/: *atlas* [áðlas].

d (de)   This Spanish letter has two different pronunciations /d/ and /ð/ according to position.

         [d]   In the initial position and after **i** or **n**, the Spanish /d/ is similar to the English /d/, but with the tip of the tongue behind the upper teeth (not between the teeth): **d**inero [dinéro], *fa***ld**a [fálda], *co***nd**e [kóde], *un_di*ente [un djénte].

         [ð]   In any other position not mentioned above, the sound of the Spanish letter **d** is similar to

the English **th** in th*is*: *tu* d*inero*
[tu ðinéro], *cada* [káða],
ciudad [θjuðáð].

NOTE a) The final **-d** of some
words tends to disappear altogether: **virtu***(d),* **verda***(d),*
juventu*(d),* **uste***(d),* **Madri***(d).*

b) In words ending in **-ado**, the
pronunciation of [ð] is even
softer and in popular speech
tends to disappear.

c) The Spanish letter **z** in end syllable position followed by a
voiced consonant (b, v, d, g, l,
m, n, r) is pronounced [ð]:
juzgar [xuðɣár].

c (ce) [k] This Spanish sound is similar to
en ca, co, the English /k/, but without
cu, que, any aspiration, like in *scar*
qui, k [ska:].

This [k] sound is represented in
Spanish by

1.° **c** followed by **a, o, u, l** or **r**: *caro*
[káro], *saco* [sáko], *cubo*
[kuβo], *claro* [kláro], *cristal*
[kristál].

2.° **qu** followed by **e, i**: The **u** is silent: *quedar* [keðár], *quinto*
[kinto].

3.° **k** in a few words of foreign origin: **k**i*lómetro* [kilómetro].

NOTE: **c** at the end of a syllable followed by a consonant becomes [ɣ]: *acto* [áɣto].

g (ge)　　　　The Spanish letter **g** has three different sounds: /g/, /ɣ/, /x/.

en **ga, go,**　　[g]　　This Spanish sound is similar to
gu, gue,　　　　　　the English /g/ in good [gud]. It
gui　　　　　　　　is represented in Spanish by **g**
　　　　　　　　　　followed by **a, o, u** at the beginning of a breath group or after
　　　　　　　　　　n: **ga***nar* [ganár], **go***ta* [góta],
　　　　　　　　　　gu*sano* [gusáno], *ten***g***o*
　　　　　　　　　　[téngo].

The **u** is silent in **gu***e,* **gu***i,* unless marked with a diaeresis: **gu***erra* [gérra], **gu***itarra* [gitárra]. But, *ver***gü***enza* [berɣwénθa], *ar***gü***ir* [arɣwir].

　　　　　　　　[ɣ]　　In any other position not mentioned above, the Spanish /g/ has no equivalent in English. The contact of the back of the tongue with the soft palate is not complete and the air passing through the narrow pas-

		sage produces a slight friction: el **g**allo [el ɣáʎo], ha**g**o [áɣo], di**g**no [díɣno].
	[x]	For the third pronunciation of /g/ see the phonetic symbol [x].
m (eme)	[m]	Like the English /m/ in **my**: **m**adre [máðre], a**m**or [amór].
		NOTE a) Final **m** is pronounced as **n**: hare**m** [arén], álbu**m** [álβun].
		b) **n** before **p, b, β, v, f,** and **m** is pronounced like English /m/: co**n** pa**n** blando [kom pam βlándo], e**n**vidia [embíðja], e**n**fado [emfáðo], co**n**migo [kommiɣo].
n (ene)	[n]	The Spanish **n** is pronounced like the English **n** in ni**n**e [nain]: **n**adar [naðár].
		NOTE: **n** before **p, b, β, v, f** and **m** is pronounced like the English /m/ (see phonetic symbol [m]).
ng, nca,	[ŋ]	The Spanish letter **n** before **g, j, c** (in **ca, co, cu**) and **qu** (in **que, qui**) is pronounced like the English **n** in si**ng** or i**nk**. Its phonetic symbol is /ŋ/: te**ng**o
nco, ncu,		
nque,		
nqui,		
nj		

		[téngo], *b*anco [bánko], *m*on*j*a [mónxa].
ñ (eñe)	[ɲ]	This sound has no equivalent in English. The closest sound in English is *ni* in o*ni*on; a*ñ*o [áɲo], *ri*ñ*ón* [rriɲón].
l (ele)	[l]	Like the English l in *l*et: *l*ado [láðo], *ci*e*l*o [θjélo].
ll (elle)	[ʎ]	This sound, as it exists in Castilian Spanish, has no equivalent in English. The closest sound in English is *li* in mi*lli*on pronounced rapidly: *ll*ave [ʎáβe], *ca*lle [káʎe].
		In some parts of Spain and in most Spanish-speaking countries of Latin America, ll is pronounced like the English y in y*et* (yeísmo) or like s in *mea*sure [¹meʒoʳ]: *ca*lle [káje or káʒe].
f (efe)	[f]	Like the English f in *f*oot [fut]: *f*iloso*f*ía [filosofía].
ce, ci	[θ]	In Castilian Spanish this sound is like the English th in *th*in [θin].
za, zo		It is represented by ce, ci, za, zo
zu		and zu: *ce*ro [θéro], *ci*ento [θjénto], *za*pato [θapáto].

		In Andalusia and in Spanish-speaking American countries this sound is pronounced like the s in s*oul.*
s (ese)	[s]	It is similar to the English s in s*oul,* except in the instances mentioned in [z] (below): s*illa* [síʎa], *casa*s [kásas].
s + $\begin{cases} \text{b, v,} \\ \text{d, g,} \\ \text{l, m,} \\ \text{n} \end{cases}$	[z]	The Spanish s when followed by a voiced consonant (**b, v, d, g, l, m, n**) is pronounced like the English s in *rose* [rəuz]: i*s*la [izla], mi*s*mo [mizmo], e*s*belto [ezβélto], de*s*de [dézðe].
ya, ye, yo, yu, hi-	[j]	This sound has no equivalent in English. The Spanish groups **ya, ye, yo, yu** and **hi-,** when not at the beginning of a breath group and not preceded by **n** or **l,** have a sound similar to the English y in y*es,* but more closed and tense: *la* **hi***erba* [la jérβa], *mayo* [májo], *mi* **ye***rno* [mi jérno].
ya, ye, yo, yu, hi-	[dʒ]	The groups **ya, ye, yo, yu, hi-** at the beginning of a syllable and preceded by **n** or **l** have a sound similar to the English j

		in *jump* [dʒʌmp], though not as strong: *cónyuge* [kóndʒuxe], *inyección* [indʒekθjón], *el yugo* [el dʒüyo].
che (che)	[tʃ]	This symbol represents one sound. It is similar to the English *ch* in **ch**urch [tʃɔ:tʃ]: *muchacho* [mutʃátʃo].
j (jota) ge, gi	[x]	This sound has no equivalent in English. It is similar to the composer's name, **Bach**. The back of the tongue is brought close to the soft palate and friction is produced by the air passing through them. It is represented in Spanish by a) the letter **j**: *jabón* [xaβón]. b) **ge, gi**: *co***ger** [koxér], **gi***tano* [xitáno]. The letter **j** is silent in *reloj* [rreló].
r (ere)	[r]	The pronunciation of the Spanish [r] has no equivalent in English. It is pronounced with a single trill of the tongue against the teeth. NOTE: A single *r* is pronounced like the double *rr*: 1) at the be-

		ginning of a word: **r**io [rrío]. 2) when preceded by **n**, **l** or **s**: ho**nr**a [ónrra], a**lr**ededor [alrreðeðór], **Isr**ael [i(s)rraél].
r (erre)	[rr]	The pronunciation of the Spanish [rr] has no equivalent in English.
		It is pronounced with several trills (two or three) of the tip of the tongue against the teeth: to**rr**e [tórre].
		Remember (see the NOTE on the preceding sound) that a single /r/ is pronounced as double /rr/ 1) at the beginning of a word: **r**io [rrío]. 2) when preceded by **n**, **l** or **s**: ho**nr**a [ónrra], a**lr**ededor [alrreðeðór], **isr**aelita [i(s)rraelíta].
		NOTE: It is very important to notice the opposition between /r/ one trill, and /rr/ two or three trills: *caro/carro, cero/cerro, coral/corral.*
h (hache)		Always silent in Spanish: **h**umo [úmo].
w (uve doble)		This is not a letter of the Spanish alphabet. It is only used in re-

cent loanwords. It has two
pronunciations:

1) as /b/ or /β/ in assimilated
English or German words:
w*atio* [b-, βátjo], w*ater* [b-,
βáter]; w*alkiria* [b-, βalkirja],
W*agner* [b-, βáɣner].

2) as the English /w/ in non-
assimilated English words:
w*eek-end* [wikén]; w*hisky*
[wíski or ɣwíski].

x (equis)   This letter is pronounced [ɣs],
never [gz]: *examen* [eɣsámen].
In ordinary speech it is pronounced like the English **s** in
soul: *exponer* [e(ɣ)sponér],
excelente [e(ɣ)sθelénte].

A

a [a] *prep.* to, at, by, in.

abad [aβáð] *m.* abbot.

abadia [aβaðía] *f.* abbey.

abajo [aβáxo] *adv.* down. 2 below, under. 3 downstairs.

abandonar [aβandonár] *t.* to abandon, leave. 2 to give up. 3 *p.* to neglect oneself.

abandono [aβandóno] *m.* ease, indolence.

abanicar [aβanikár] *t.* to fan. 2 *p.* to fan oneself.

abanico [aβaníko] *m.* fan.

abarcar [aβarkár] *t.* to clasp, grasp, include.

abarrotar [aβarrotár] *t.* to cram, overstock.

abastecer [aβasteθér] *t.* to purvey, supply. ¶ Conjug. like *agradecer*.

abatimiento [aβatimjénto] *m.* low spirits.

abatir [aβatír] *t.-p.* to bring down, throw down; dishearten; to be disheartened.

abeja [aβéxa] *f.* bee: ～ *reina*, queen-bee.

abertura [aβertúra] *f.* opening, aperture, gap.

abeto [aβéto] *m.* fir, silver fir; spruce.

abierto [aβjérto] *p. p.* opened. 2 open. 3 sincere, frank.

abismo [aβísmo] *m.* abyss, gulf.

abnegación [aβneɣaθjón] *f.* abnegation, selfdenial.

abogado [aβoɣáðo] *m.* lawyer, barrister.

abonar [aβonár] *t.* to approve. 2 to guarantee. 3

to improve. 4 to manure. 5 COM. to credit; to discount. 6 *t.-p.* to subscribe [for].

abono [aβóno] *m.* payment. 2 fertilizer. 3 subscription.

aborrecer [aβorreθér] *t.* to abhor, hate. ¶ CONJUG. like *agradecer*.

abrasar [aβrasár] *t.* to burn, sear, scorch. 2 *p.* to feel very hot; to burn with [love, etc.].

abrazar [aβraθár] *t.* to embrace, hug, clasp. 2 to include. 3 *p.* to embrace each other.

abrazo [aβráθo] *m.* embrace, hug.

abrigar [aβriɣár] *t.* to cover, wrap. 2 to shelter. 3 to entertain [hopes, etc.]. 4 *p.* to take shelter.

abrigo [aβríɣo] *m.* protection. 2 shelter. 3 overcoat.

abril [aβríl] *m.* April.

abrir [aβrír] *t.* to open. 2 to unfold; to split. 3 to lead [a procession]. 4 ~ *paso*, to make way. 5 *p.* to blossom. ¶ Past. p.: *abierto*.

absoluto [aβsolúto] *a.* absolute. 2 *en* ~, not at all, certainly not.

absurdo [aβsúrðo] *a.* absurd. 2 *m.* nonsense.

abuela [aβwéla] *f.* grandmother.

abuelo [aβwélo] *m.* grandfather. 2 *pl.* grandparents.

abundancia [aβundánθja] *f.* abundance, plenty.

abundante [aβundánte] *a.* abundant, copious.

aburrido [aβurríðo] *a.* bored, weary. 2 boring, tedious.

aburrir [aβurrír] *t.* to annoy, bore. 2 *p.* to get bored.

abusar [aβusár] *i.* to abuse; to take undue advantage of.

abuso [aβúso] *m.* abuse, misuse.

acá [aká] *adv.* here, hither; ~ *y acullá*, here and there.

acabar [akaβár] *t.-i.* to finish, end: ~ *con*, to destroy; ~ *en*, to end in; ~ *por*, to end by. 2 to kill. 3 *i.* to die. 4 *p.* to end, be over. 5 *acaba de llegar*, he has just arrived.

academia [akaðémja] *f.* academy.

académico [akaðémiko] *a.* academic. 2 *m.* academician.

acariciar [akariθjár] *t.* to caress, fondle. 2 to cherish (hopes, etc.).

acaso [akáso] *m.* chance, hazard. 2 *adv.* by chance; perhaps.

acceder [ayθeðér] *i.* to accede, agree, consent.

accidente [ayθiðénte] *m.* accident.

acción [ayθjón] *f.* action, act. 2 COM. share, *stock. 3 THEAT. plot.

aceite [aθéite] *m.* olive oil.

aceituna [aθeitúna] *f.* olive.

acento [aθénto] *m.* accent. 2 stress.

acentuar [aθentuár] *t.* to accent. 2 to stress. 3 to emphasize.

aceptar [aθeβtár] *t.* to accept.

acera [aθéra] *f.* pavement, *sidewalk.

acerca de [aθérka ðe] *adv.* about, concerning, with regard to.

acercamiento [aθerka- mjénto] *m.* approach, approximation.

acercar [aθerkár] *t.* to bring or place near. 2 *p.* to come near.

acero [aθéro] *m.* steel.

acertar [aθertár] *t.* to hit [the mark]. 2 to guess.

3 to do well, right; to succeed [in]. 4 *i.* to happen, chance. ¶ CON- JUG. INDIC. Pres.: *acier- to, aciertas, acierta; aciertan.* | SUBJ. Pres.: *acierte, aciertes, acierte; acierten.* | IMPER.: *acier- ta, acierte; acierten.*

ácido [áθiðo] *a.* acid, sour, tart. 2 *a.-m.* acid.

acierto [aθjérto] *m.* good aim, hit. 2 good guess. 3 wisdom. 4 knack; suc- cess.

aclamar [aklamár] *t.* to acclaim, cheer, hail, applaud.

aclarar [aklarár] *t.* to clear, clarify. 2 to rinse. 3 to explain. 4 *i.* to clear up. 5 to dawn. 6 *p.* to become clear.

acoger [akoxér] *t.* to re- ceive, admit. 2 to shel- ter. 3 *p.* to take refuge [in].

acomodar [akomoðár] *t.* to accommodate.

acompañar [akompaɲár] *t.* to accompany, go with. 2 to enclose.

acongojar [akoŋgoxár] *t.* to grieve. 2 *p.* to feel anguish.

aconsejar [akonsexár] *t.* to advise. 2 *p.* to take advice.

acontecer [akonteθér] impers. to happen, occur. ¶ CONJUG. like *agradecer.*

acontecimiento [akonteθimjénto] *m.* event, happening.

acordar [akorðár] *t.* to decide. 2 MUS. to attune. 3 *i.* to agree. 4 *p.* to come to an agreement. 5 *acordarse de,* to remember. ¶ CONJUG. like *contar.*

acorde [akórðe] *a.* agreeing. 2 *m.* chord.

acostar [akostár] *t.* to put to bed; to lay down. 2 *p.* to go to bed. ¶ CONJUG. like *contar.*

acostumbrar [akostumbrár] *t.* to accustom. 2 *i.* to be used [to]. 3 *p.* to get used [to].

acreditado [akreðitáðo] *a.* reputable, well-known.

acreditar [akreðitár] *t.* to accredit. 2 to prove to be. 3 to bring credit to. 4 *p.* to win credit.

actitud [aγtitúð] *f.* attitude.

actividad [aγtiβiðáð] *f.* activity.

activo [aγtiβo] *a.* active. 2 *m.* assets.

acto [áγto] *m.* act, action, deed: *en el* ~, at

once. 2 meeting, public function. 3 act [of a play].

actor [aγtór] *m.* actor.

actriz [aγtriθ] *f.* actress.

actuación [aγtwaθjón] *f.* action, performance. 2 *pl.* law proceedings.

actual [aγtwál] *a.* present, current.

actualidad [aγtwaliðáð] *f.* present time. 2 current events. 3 *pl.* CINEM. news-reel.

acuático [akwátiko] *a.* aquatic.

acudir [akuðír] *i.* to go or come [to]. 2 to frequent.

acueducto [akweðúγto] aqueduct.

acuerdo [akwérðo] *m.* agreement, understanding: *estar de* ~, to agree; *de común* ~, by mutual agreement. 2 solution.

acusación [akusaθjón] *f.* accusation, charge.

acusado [akusáðo] *a. m.-f.* accused, defendant.

acusar [akusár] *t.* to accuse, charge. 2 to acknowledge.

adaptar [aðaβtár] *t.-p.* to adapt, fit, suit.

adecuado [aðekwáðo] *a.* adequate, fit, suitable.

adelantar [aðelantár] *t.* to advance. 2 to get ahead of. 3 *i.* to be fast. 4 to overtake. 5 to improve.

adelante [aðelánte] *adv.* forward, ahead, onward: en ~, henceforth. 2 *interj.* come in!

adelanto [aðelánto] *m.* progress. 2 advance.

ademán [aðemán] *m.* gesture; attitude. 2 *pl.* manners.

además [aðemás] *adv.* moreover, besides. 2 ~ de, besides.

adentro [aðéntro] *adv.* within, inside, indoors.

adiós [aðjós] *interj.* good-bye!

adivinanza [aðiβinánθa] *f.* prediction; riddle.

adivinar [aðiβinár] *t.* to guess, foresee. 2 to solve.

adjetivo [aðxetíβo] *a.-n.* adjective.

administración [aðministraθjón] *f.* administration, management.

administrador [aðministraðór] *m.* administrator, manager, trustee.

administrar [aðministrár] *t.* to administer, manage.

admirable [aðmiráβle] *a.*

admirable. 2 **-mente** *adv.* admirably.

admiración [aðmiraθjón] *f.* admiration. 2 wonder. 3 exclamation mark (!).

admirar [aðmirár] *t.* to admire. 2 *p.* to be astonished.

admitir [aðmitír] *t.* to admit. 2 to accept.

adonde [aðónde] *adv.* where.

adoptar [aðoptár] *t.* to adopt.

adoración [aðoraθjón] *f.* worship.

adornar [aðornár] *t.* to adorn, embellish, garnish.

adorno [aðórno] *m.* adornment, ornament.

adquirir [aðkirir] *t.* to acquire. 2 to buy. ¶ CONJUG. INDIC. Pres.: *adquiero, adquieres, adquiere; adquieren.* ‖ SUBJ. Pres.: *adquiera, adquieras, adquiera; adquieran.* ‖ IMPER.: *adquiere, adquiera; adquieran.*

aduana [aðwána] *f.* customs, customs-house.

adulto [aðúlto] *a.-n.* adult, grown-up.

adverbio [aðβérβjo] *m.* adverb.

adversario [aðβersárjo] *m.* adversary, opponent.

advertir [aðβertír] *t.* to notice, realize. 2 to advise, warn. ¶ CONJUG. like *discernir*.

aéreo [aéreo] *a.* aerial. 2 *correo* ~, air-mail.

aeroplano [aeropláno] *m.* aeroplane, airplane.

aeropuerto [aeropwérto] *m.* airport.

afable [afáβle] *a.* kind.

afán [afán] *m.* anxiety, eagerness, desire.

afanarse [afanárse] *p.* to strive to, toil.

afectar [afeɣtár] *t.* to affect. 2 *p.* to be affected.

afecto [aféɣto] *a.* fond. 2 *m.* affection, love.

afición [afiθjón] *f.* fondness, liking. 2 hobby.

aficionado [afiθjonáðo] *m.* amateur. 2 fan, devote, keen on, fond of.

aficionarse [afiθjonárse] *p.* to grow fond of, take a liking to.

afilar [afilár] *t.* to sharpen, whet, point; to taper

afirmar [afirmár] *t.* to make firm. 2 to affirm, say. 3 *p.* to steady oneself.

aflicción [afliɣθjón] *f.* grief, sorrow, distress.

afligir [aflixír] *t.* to afflict. 2 *t.-p.* to grieve.

afortunadamente [afortunáðaménte] *adv.* luckily, fortunately.

afortunado [afortunáðo] *a.* lucky, happy.

afrontar [afrontár] *t.* to confront, face.

afuera [afwéra] *adv.* out, outside. 2 *f. pl.* outskirts, environs.

agachar [aɣatʃár] *t.* to lower. 2 *p.* to stoop; to crouch, squat.

agarrar [aɣarrár] *t.* to seize, catch; grasp. 2 *p.* to take hold of.

agencia [axénθja] *f.* agency.

agente [axénte] *m.* agent. 2 ~ *de cambio y bolsa*, stockbroker; ~ *de policía*, policeman.

ágil [áxil] *a.* agile, nimble.

agitación [axitaθjón] *f.* agitation, excitement.

agitar [axitár] *t.* to agitate; to flurry, excite. 2 to shake, stir. 3 *p.* to be agitated.

agosto [aɣósto] *m.* August.

agotar [aɣotár] *t.* to exhaust, work out, sell out. 2 *p.* to run out; to be sold out.

agradable [aɣraðáβle] *a.* agreeable, pleasant, enjoyable.

agradar [aɣraðár] *t.* to please; to like.

agradecer [aɣraðeθér] *t.* to thank for, be grateful for. ¶ CONJUG. INDIC. Pres.: *agradezco, agradeces,* etc. ‖ SUBJ. Pres.: *agradezca, agradezcas,* etc. ‖ IMPER.: *agradezca, agradezcamos, agradezcan.*

agradecimiento [aɣraðeθimjénto] *m.* gratitude, thankfulness.

agrado [aɣráðo] *m.* affability. 2 pleasure, liking.

agregar [aɣreɣár] *t.* to add, join.

agricultor [aɣrikultór] *m.* farmer.

agricultura [aɣrikultúra] *f.* agriculture, farming.

agrio [áɣrjo] *a.* sour. 2 bitter. 3 rough, tart.

agrupar [aɣrupár] *t.* to group, gather.

agua [áɣwa] *f.* water: ~ *dulce,* fresh water; ~ *salada,* salt water.

aguantar [aɣwantár] *t.* to bear, endure, suffer. 2 *p.* to restrain oneself.

aguardar [aɣwarðár] *t.* to wait [for]; to expect, await.

agudo [aɣúðo] *a.* acute [sharp; keen]. 2 witty. 3 oxytone [word].

águila [áɣila] *f.* eagle.

aguinaldo [aɣináldo] *m.* Christmas box.

aguja [aɣúxa] *f.* needle. 2 hand [of clock]. 3 steeple. 4 *pl.* RLY. switch.

agujero [aɣuxéro] *m.* hole.

ahí [ai] *adv.* there.

ahogar [aoɣár] *t.* to choke, smother, suffocate; to strangle; to quench. 2 to drown. 3 *p.* to be drowned.

ahora [aóra] *adv* now; at present.

ahorcar [aorkár] *t.* to hang.

ahorrar [aorrár] *t.* to save, spare.

ahorro [aórro] *m.* saving. 2 *pl.* savings.

aire [áire] *m.* air: *al* ~ *libre,* in the open air.

aislar [aizlár] *t.* to isolate. 2 *p.* to seclude oneself.

¡ajá! [axá] *interj.* good!

ajeno [axéno] *a.* another's, strange, alien. 2 foreing [to].

ají [axi] *m.* red pepper, chili.

ajuar [axwár] *m.* household furniture. 2 trousseau.

ajustar [axustár] *t.* to adjust, fit. 2 to make [an agreement]. 3 to settle. 4 *i.* to fit tight. 5 *p.* to conform [to].

al [al] *contr.* of A & EL.

ala [ála] *f.* wing. 2 brim [of a hat]. 3 flap [of a table].

alabanza [alaβánθa] *f.* praise.

alabar [alaβár] *t.* to praise. 2 *p.* to boast.

alacena [alaθéna] *f.* cupboard, closet.

alacrán [alakrán] *m.* scorpion.

alambre [alámbre] *m.* wire.

alameda [alaméða] *f.* poplar grove. 2 avenue.

alargar [alарγár] *t.* to lengthen, extend. 3 to stretch out.

alarma [alárma] *f.* alarm.

alarmar [alarmár] *t.* to alarm. 2 *p.* to be alarmed.

alba [álβa] *f.* dawn.

albañil [alβaɲíl] *m.* mason, bricklayer.

albergar [alβerγár] *t.* to shelter, lodge. 2 *p.* to take shelter, lodge.

albergue [alβérγe] *m.* shelter, lodging, harbour, refuge.

alborotar [alβorotár] *t.* to disturb. 2 *p.* to get excited. 3 to riot.

alboroto [alβoróto] *m.* uproar, noise. 2 riot.

álbum [álβun] *m.* album.

alcalde [alkálde] *m.* mayor.

alcaldía [alkaldía] *f.* town-hall.

alcance [alkánθe] *m.* overtaking. 2 reach: *al ~ de uno*, within one's reach. 3 range, consequence. 4 understanding.

alcanzar [alkanθár] *t.* to overtake. 2 to reach. 3 to get, obtain. 4 to understand. 5 *i.* to reach [to]. 6 to be sufficient.

alcoba [alkóβa] *f.* bedroom.

alcohol [alkoól] *m.* alcohol.

aldaba [aldáβa] *f.* knocker.

aldea [aldéa] *f.* village.

aldeano [aldeáno] *m.* villager, countryman.

alegar [aleγár] *t.* to allege, plead.

alegrar [aleγrár] *t.* to cheer. 2 to enliven. 3 *p.* to be glad. 4 to rejoice, cheer.

alegre [aléɣre] *a.* glad, joyful. 2 cheerful, merry, gay, bright.

alegría [aleɣría] *f.* joy, pleasure. 2 merriment.

alejar [alexár] *t.* to remove to a distance, to move away. 2 to separate. 3 *p.* to go or move away.

aleluya [alelúja] *f.* hallelujah. 2 *f. pl.* doggerel.

alemán [alemán] *a.-n.* German.

alentar [alentár] *i.* to breathe. 2 *t.* to encourage, cheer. ¶ CONJUG. like *acertar*.

alerta [alérta] *adv.* on the watch. 2 *interj.* look out! 3 *m.* sentinel's call.

alfabeto [alfaβéto] *m.* alphabet.

alfiler [alfilér] *m.* pin.

alfombra [alfómbra] *f.* floor carpet, rug.

algo [álɣo] *pron.* something. 2 *adv.* somewhat.

algodón [alɣoðón] *m.* cotton.

alguien [álɣjen] *pron.* somebody, someone.

algún -o [alɣún -o] *a.* some, any: ~ vez, sometimes. 2 *pron.* someone, anyone, somebody, anybody.

aliado [aliáðo] *m.* ally. 2 *a.* allied.

alianza [aljánθa] *f.* alliance, league.

aliar [aliár] *t.-p.* to ally.

aliento [aljénto] *m.* breath. 2 courage.

alimentación [alimentaθjón] *f.* food, feeding, nourishment.

alimentar [alimentár] *t.* to feed, nourish.

alimenticio [alimentíθjo] *a.* nutritious, nourishing.

alimento [aliménto] *m.* food, nourishment.

aliviar [aliβjár] *t.* to lighten. 2 to alleviate, allay. 3 *p.* to get better.

alivio [alíβjo] *m.* alleviation, allay; relief.

alma [álma] *f.* soul. 2 bore. 3 core, heart.

almacén [almaθén] *m.* store, warehouse, shop. 2 depot; magazine.

almacenar [almaθenár] *t.* to store. 2 to hoard.

almanaque [almanáke] *m.* almanac.

almendra [alméndra] *f.* almond.

almidón [almiðón] *m.* starch.

almirante [almiránte] *m.* admiral.

almohada [almoáða] *f.* pillow; cushion.

almorzar [almorθár] *i.* to lunch, have lunch.

almuerzo [almwérθo] *m.* lunch, luncheon.

alojar [aloxár] *t.* to lodge, billet. 2 *p.* to put up.

alondra [alóndra] *f.* lark.

alquilar [alkilár] *t.* to let, rent; to hire.

alrededor [alrreðeðór] *adv.* around, about.

alrededores [alrreðeðóres] *m. pl.* outskirts, surroundings.

altanero [altanéro] *a.* haughty.

alterar [alterár] *t.* to alter, change. 2 to excite. 3 to disturb. 4 *p.* to become altered.

altercar [alterkár] *t.* to dispute, argue.

alternar [alternár] *t.-i.* to alternate. 2 *i.* to mix.

altivo [altíβo] *a.* haughty.

alto [álto] *a.* high. 2 tall. 3 upper. 4 excellent. 5 loud. 6 *m.* height. 7 halt. 8 *interj.* stop!

altura [altúra] *f.* height. 2 tallness. 3 top.

aludir [aluðir] *i.* to allude, mention.

alumbrado [alumbráðo] *m.* lights; ~ *público,* public lighting.

alumbrar [alumbrár] *t.* to light. 2 *i.* to give birth.

alumno [alúmno] *m.* pupil.

alzar [alθár] *t.* to raise, lift, hoist. 2 to build. 3 *p.* to rise; to get up, stand up. 4 to rebel.

allá [aʎá] *adv.* there; yonder: *más* ~, farther.

allí [aʎí] *adv.* there.

amable [amáβle] *a.* kind, nice, friendly.

amado [amáðo] *m.* loved.

1) **amanecer** [amaneθér] *i.* to dawn. ¶ CONJUG. like *agradecer.*

2) **amanecer** [amaneθér] *m.* dawn, daybreak.

amante [amánte] *m.-f.* lover; paramour; *f.* mistress.

amapola [amapóla] *f.* corn poppy.

amar [amár] *t.* to love 2 to like, be fond of.

amargo [amáryo] *a.* bitter. 2 sour [temper].

amargura [amaryúra] *f* bitterness. 2 grief.

amarillento [amariʎénto] *a.* yellowish. 2 pale.

amarillo [amariʎo] *a.-m.* yellow.

amarrar [amarrár] *t.* to tie, fasten, rope.

ambición [ambiθjón] *f.* ambition.

ambicioso [ambiθjóso] *a.* covetous, eager.

ambiente [ambjénte] *m.* atmosphere, setting.

ambos [ámbos] *a.-pron.* both.

ambulancia [ambulánθeja] *f.*

amenaza [amenáθa] *f.* threat, menace.

amenazar [amenaθár] *t.* to threaten, menace

americano [amerikáno] *a.-n.* American.

ametralladora [ametraʎaðóra] *f.* machine-gun.

amigo [amiɣo] *m.* friend.

amistad [amistáð] *f.* friendship.

amistoso [amistóso] *a.* friendly, amicable.

amo [ámo] *m.* master, lanlord, owner. 2 boss.

amontonar [amontonár] *t.* to heap, pile. 2 *p.* to crowd, throng.

amor [amór] *m.* love, affection; ~ propio, conceit, self-esteem.

amoroso [amoróso] *a.* loving, affectionate.

amparar [amparár] *t.* to protect, shelter.

amparo [ampáro] *m.* protection, shelter.

amplio [ámpljo] *a.* ample, 2 wide. 3 large.

amueblar [amweβlár] *t.* to furnish.

análisis [análisis] *m.* analysis. 2 GRAM. parsing.

anaranjado [anaraŋxáðo] *a.-n.* orange-(coloured).

anarquía [anarkía] *f.* anarchy.

anciano [anθjáno] *a.* old, aged. 2 *m.-f.* old man or woman; elder.

ancla [áŋkla] *f.* anchor.

ancho [ántʃo] *a.* broad, wide. 2 lax.

anchura [antʃúra] *f.* breadth, width.

andaluz [andalúθ] *a.-n.* Andalusian.

andante [andánte] *a.* walking. 2 [knight-]errant.

andar [andár] *i.* to walk, go, move; [of a machine] to run, work. ¶ CONJUG. INDIC. Pret.: *anduve, anduviste,* etc. ‖ SUBJ. Imperf.: *anduviera, anduvieras,* etc., or *anduviese, anduvieses,* etc. ‖ Fut.: *anduviere, anduvieres,* etc.

andrajoso [andraxóso] *a.* ragged, in tatters.

anécdota [anéɣðota] *f.* anecdote, story.

angosto [aŋgósto] *a.* narrow.

ángulo [ángulo] *m.* angle.

angustia [angústja] *f.* anguish, distress.

angustiar [angustjár] *t.* to afflict, distress, worry.

anhelar [anelár] *i.* to pant. 2 *t.* to long for.

anhelo [anélo] *m.* longing, yearning, desire.

anidar [aniðár] *i.* to nest.

anillo [aníʎo] *m.* ring, finger ring.

ánima [ánima] *f.* soul.

animado [animáðo] *a.* animate. 2 lively. 3 full of people.

animal [animál] *m.* animal. 2 blockhead.

animar [animár] *t.* to animate. 2 to cheer up 3 to encourage. 4 to enliven. 5 *p.* to take heart.

ánimo [ánimo] *m.* mind. 2 courage. 3 intention. 4 *interj.* cheer up!

anis [anís] *m.* anise. 2 anissette.

aniversario [aniβersárjo] *m.* anniversary.

anoche [anótʃe] *adv.* last night.

1) **anochecer** [anotʃeθér] *i.* to grow dark. ¶ Conjug. like *agradecer*.

2) **anochecer** [anotʃeθér] *m.* nightfall, evening.

anotación [anotaθjón] *f.* annotation. 2 entry.

anotar [anotár] *t.* to write, note down.

ansia [ánsja] *f.* anguish. 2 eagerness, longing.

ansiedad [ansjeðáð] *f.* anxiety, uneasiness.

ansioso [ansjóso] *a.* anxious, eager, greedy.

1) **ante** [ánte] *m.* elk, moose. 2 muff, buckskin.

2) **ante** [ánte] *prep.* before. 2 ~ *todo*, above all.

anteayer [anteaʝér] *adv.* the day before yesterday.

antemano (de) [antemáno] *adv.* beforehand.

anteojo [anteóxo] *m.* spyglass. 2 *pl.* binocular. 3 spectacles.

antepasado [antepasáðo] *m.* ancestor, forefather.

anterior [anterjór] *a.* anterior, former, previous.

anteriormente [anterjórménte] *adv.* previously, before.

antes [ántes] *adv.* before. 3 *conj.* ~ *bien*, rather.

anticipar [antiθipár] *t.* to bring forward, advance. 2 *p.* to forestall.

antigüedad [antiɣweðáð] *f.* seniority 2 *pl.* antiques.

antiguo [antiɣwo] a. ancient, old; antique.

antipático [antipátiko] a. disagreeable; unpleasant.

antojarse [antoxárse] p. to take a fancy to; to long.

antorcha [antórtʃa] f. torch, flambeau.

anual [anwál] a. yearly. 2 **-mente** adv. annually, yearly.

anunciar [anunθiár] t. to announce. 2 to advertise.

anuncio [anúnθjo] m. announcement. 2 advertisement.

anzuelo [anθwélo] m. fish-hook.

añadir [aɲaðír] t. to add.

año [áɲo] m. year: ~ bisiesto, leap-year. 2 tengo 20 años, I'm 20 years old.

apacible [apaθíβle] a. gentle, mild, calm.

apadrinar [apaðrinár] t. to act as godfather to; to support; to sponsor.

apagar [apaɣár] t. to put out, turn out. 2 to quench. 3 to soften.

aparato [aparáto] m. apparatus, device, set. 2 machine, airplane. 3 display, show.

aparcar [aparkár] t. to park [cars, etc.].

aparecer [apareθér] i.-p. to appear, turn up. ¶ CONJUG. like agradecer.

aparejar [aparexár] t. to prepare, get ready. 2 to saddle. 3 to rig out.

aparición [apariθjón] f. apparition, appearance. 2 ghost.

apariencia [aparjénθja] f. appearance, aspect. 2 guardar las apariencias, to keep up appearances.

apartado [apartáðo] a. retired, distant. 2 m. post-office box. 3 section [of a law, etc.].

apartamento [apartaménto] m. retirement. 2 flat, apartment.

apartar [apartár] t. to separate, set apart. 2 to turn aside; to remove, move away. 3 p. to move away.

aparte [apárte] a. separate, other. 2 adv. apart, aside. 3 m. THEAT. aside. 4 punto y ~, paragraph.

apasionar [apasjonár] t. to excite strongly. 2 p. to become impassioned. 3 to become passionately fond [of].

apear [apeár] t.-p. to dismount, alight.

apelación [apelaθjón] f. appeal.

apelar [apelár] *i.* to appeal, have recourse to.

apellido [apeʎíðo] *m.* surname.

apenado [apenáðo] *a.* sorry, troubled.

apenas [apénas] *adv.* scarcely, hardly. 2 no sooner than.

apetito [apetíto] *m.* hunger, appetite.

ápice [ápiθe] *m.* summit.

aplastar [aplastár] *t.* to flatten. 2 to crush. 3 *p.* to become flat.

aplaudir [aplauðír] *t.-i.* to applaud, clap.

aplicación [aplikaθjón] *f.* application, studiousness.

aplicado [aplikáðo] *a.* applied. 2 diligent.

aplicar [aplikár] *t.* to apply. 2 *p.* to devote oneself to.

apoderar [apoðerár] *t.* to empower. 2 *p.* to seize.

aportar [aportár] *t.* to contribute, bring.

aposento [aposénto] *m.* room, apartment.

apóstol [apóstol] *m.* apostle.

apoyar [apojár] *t.* to rest, lean. 2 to support; to found. 3 to prove. 4 to prop. 5 *i.-p.* to rest, lean [on]; to be sup-

ported [on or by]. 6 *p.* to base oneself.

apoyo [apójo] *m.* support. 2 protection, help.

apreciar [apreθjár] *t.* to estimate, value. 2 to esteem, like, appreciate.

aprender [aprendér] *t.* to learn.

apresurar [apresurár] *t.* to hasten. 2 *p.* to hurry up.

apretar [apretár] *t.* to press down. 2 to tighten. 3 [of garments] to fit pinch. 4 to urge. 5 ~ *el paso,* to quicken the pace. 6 *i.* ~ *a correr,* to start running. 7 *p.* to crowd. ¶ CONJUG. like *acertar.*

aprisa [aprísa] *adv.* quickly, hurriedly.

aprobación [aproβaθjón] *f.* approbation, approval; applause.

aprobado [aproβáðo] *m.* pass mark, pass.

aprobar [aproβár] *t.* to approve. 2 to pass. ¶ CONJUG. like *contar.*

apropiado [apropjáðo] *a.* fit, appropriate, suitable.

aprovechar [aproβetʃár] *t.* to make use of, profit by. 2 to use up. 3 *i.* to be useful. 4 *p.* to avail oneself of, take advantage of.

aproximadamente [aproɣsimáðaménte] *adv.* approximately.

aproximar [aproɣsimár] *t.* to bring near. 2 *p.* to approach, come near.

aptitud [aβtitúθ] *f.* aptitude, fitness, talent.

apuesta [apwésta] *f.* bet, wager.

apuntar [apuntár] *t.* to aim. 2 to point out. 3 to note, write down. 4 to stitch, pin lightly. 5 THEAT. to prompt. 6 *i.* to dawn.

apuñalar [apuɲalár] *t.* to stab, knife.

apurar [apurár] *t.* to use up, exhaust. 2 to hurry, press. 3 to worry. 4 *p.* to be worried.

aquel [akél] *m.*, **aquella** [akéʎa] *f. dem. a. sing.* that. **aquellos** [akéʎos] *m.*, **aquellas** [akéʎas] *f. pl.* those.

aquél [akél] *m.*, **aquélla** [akéʎa] *f. dem. pron. sing.* that one; the former. **aquello** [akéʎo] *neut.* that, that thing. **aquéllos** [akéʎos] *m.*, **aquéllas** [akéʎas] *f. pl.* those [ones]; the former.

aquí [akí] *adv.* here. 2 *de ~ en adelante*, from now on.

arado [aráðo] *m.* plough.

araña [aráɲa] *f.* spider. 2 chandelier, lustre.

arañar [araɲár] *t.* to scratch; to scrape up.

arar [arár] *t.* to plough.

árbitro [árβitro] *m.* arbiter. 2 umpire. 3 referee.

árbol [árβol] *m.* tree. 2 shaft. 3 mast.

arboleda [arβoléða] *f.* grove, woodland.

arbusto [arβústo] *m.* shrub, bush.

arca [árka] *f.* coffer, chest. 2 safe. 3 ark.

arcángel [arkáɲxel] *m.* archangel.

arcilla [arθíʎa] *f.* clay.

arco [árko] *m.* arc. 2 bow: *~ iris*, rainbow.

arder [arðér] *t.* to burn.

ardid [arðíθ] *m.* stratagem, trick.

ardiente [arðjénte] *a.* burning, hot. 2 passionate.

ardor [arðór] *m.* ardour, heat. 2 courage.

área [área] *f.* area.

arena [aréna] *f.* sand.

arenque [aréŋke] *m.* herring.

argentino [arxentíno] *m.* Argentine, Argentinean.

argumentación [aryumentaθjón] *f.* argumentation.

argumento [aryuménto] *m.* argument. 2 plot [of a play].

árido [árioo] *a.* dry, arid.

aritmética [ariometíka] *f.* arithmetic.

arma [árma] *f.* weapon, arm.

armada [armáoa] *f.* navy. 2 fleet. 3 armada.

armadura [armaoúra] *f.* armo(u)r. 2 framework.

armar [armár] *t.* to arm. 2 to fit out [a ship]. 3 to set up, mount. 4 *p.* to arm oneself.

armario [armárjo] *m.* cupboard, wardrobe.

armonía [armonía] *f.* harmony.

armonioso [armonjóso] *a.* harmonious.

aro [áro] *m.* hoop, ring.

aroma [aróma] *f.* aroma, scent, fragance.

arpa [árpa] *f.* harp.

arquitectura [arkiteytúra] *f.* architecture.

arrabal [arraβál] *m.* suburb. 2 *pl.* outskirts.

arrancar [arraŋkár] *t.* to uproot, pull out. 2 to pluck [feathers]. 3 *i.* to start.

arrastrar [arrastrár] *t.* to drag, trail. 2 to carry away. 3 *p.* to crawl.

arrebatar [arreβatár] *t.* to snatch. 2 to carry away. 3 *p.* to be led away [by emotion].

arreglar [arreγlár] *t.-p.* to arrange. 2 to put in order. 3 to smarten up. 4 to mend, fix up.

arreglo [arréγlo] *m.* arrangement. 2 settlement. 3 mending. 4 *con* ~ *a,* according to.

arrepentimiento [arrepentimjénto] *m.* repentance; regret.

arrepentirse [arrepentírse] *p.* to repent, regret. ¶ CONJUG. like *hervir.*

arrestar [arrestár] *t.* to arrest, imprision.

arriba [arríβa] *adv.* up, upwards; upstairs; above, at top: *cuesta* ~, up the hill; *de* ~ *abajo,* from top to bottom.

arribar [arríβár] *i.* to arrive. 2 to put into port.

arriesgar [arrjezγár] *t.* to risk, hazard, venture. 2 *p.* to expose oneself to danger. 3 to dare.

arrimar [arrimár] t. to bring close [to]. 2 p. to go near; to lean against.

arrodillarse [arroðiʎárse] p. to kneel [down].

arrojado [arroxáðo] a. bold, dashing, rash.

arrojar [arroxár] t. to throw, fling. 2 to vomit. 3 to show [a balance]. 4 p. to throw oneself.

arrollar [arroʎár] t. to roll up. 2 to run over.

arroyo [arróʝo] m. brook, stream. 2 gutter.

arroz [arróθ] m. rice.

arruga [arrúʝa] f. wrinkle, crease, line.

arrugar [arruʝár] t. to wrinkle; to crease. 2 to fold. 3 ~ la frente, to frown.

arruinar [arrwinár] t. to ruin. 2 p. to go to ruin.

arrullo [arrúʎo] m. lullaby. 2 cooing.

arte [árte] m.-f. art: bellas artes, fine arts. 2 craft, skill.

artificial [artifiθjál] a. artificial.

artificio [artifíθjo] m. skill. 2 trick. 3 device.

artista [artísta] m.-f. artist; actor, actress.

artístico [artístiko] a. artistic.

as [as] m. ace; champion.

asaltar [asaltár] t. to assail, assault.

asalto [asálto] m. assault. 2 BOX. round.

asamblea [asambléa] f. assembly, meeting.

asar [asár] t.-p. to roast.

ascender [asθendér] i. to ascend, climb. 2 to accede. 3 to amount [to]. 4 to be promoted. ¶ CONJUG. like entender.

aseado [aseáðo] a. clean, tidy.

asegurar [aseʝurár] t. to secure. 2 to fasten. 3 to ensure. 4 to assure. 5 to assert. 6 COM. to insure. 7 p. to make sure.

asentar [asentár] t. to seat. 2 to place, stablish. 3 to affirm. 4 to enter. 5 p. to sit down. ¶ CONJUG. like acertar.

aseo [aséo] m. tidiness. 2 cleaning: cuarto de ~, toilet-room.

asesinar [asesinár] t. to murder, assassinate.

asesinato [asesináto] m. murder, assassination.

asesino [asesíno] m. murderer.

así [así] adv. so, thus.

asiento [asjénto] *m.* seat, chair; situation.

asignación [asiɣnaθjón] *f.* assignation. 2 allowance.

asignar [asiɣnár] *t.* to assign, appoint.

asignatura [asiɣnatúra] *f.* subject of study.

asilo [asílo] *m.* asylum, shelter.

asimismo [asímízmo] *adv.* likewise, also.

asistencia [asisténθja] *f.* audience. 2 help.

asistir [asistír] *i.* to attend, be present. 3 *t.* to help.

asno [ázno] *m.* ass, donkey, jackass.

asociación [asoθjaθjón] *f.* association.

asociar [asoθjár] *t.* to associate.

asolar [asolár] *t.* to raze. ¶ CONJUG. like *contar.*

asomar [asomár] *i.* to begin to appear. 2 *t.* to put out. 3 *p.* to look out.

asombrar [asombrár] *t.* to frigten. 2 to astonish. 3 *p.* to be astonished.

asombro [asómbro] *m.* amazement, astonishment. 2 fright.

aspecto [aspéɣto] *m.* aspect, look, appearance.

áspero [áspero] *a.* rough. 2 harsh. 3 rude.

aspirar [aspirár] *t.* to breathe in. 2 to draw in. 3 *i.* to aspire to.

astilla [astíʎa] *f.* chip, splinter.

astro [ástro] *m.* star.

astucia [astúθja] *f.* cunning. 2 trick.

asueto [aswéto] *m.* day off, school holiday.

asumir [asumír] *t.* to assume, take upon oneself.

asunto [asúnto] *m.* matter, subject. 2 affair.

asustar [asustár] *t.* to frighten. 2 *p.* to be frightened.

atacar [atakár] *t.* to attack, impugn.

ataque [atáke] *m.* attack. 2 fit, stroke.

atar [atár] *t.* to tie, bind.

1) **atardecer** [ataɾðeθéɾ] *impers.* to grow dark.

2) **atardecer** [ataɾðeθéɾ] *m.* evening, nightfall.

atención [atenθjón] *f.* attention. 2 kindness.

atender [atendér] *i.-t.* to attend, pay attention. 2 to heed. 3 to take care [of]. 4 *t.* to listen to. ¶ CONJUG. like *entender.*

atentado [atentáðo] *m.* crime. 2 attempted murder.

atentamente [aténtaménte] *adv.* attentively. 2 politely.

atento [aténto] *a.* attentive. 2 polite.

aterrizar [aterriθár] *t.* to land, alight.

atleta [aδléta] *m.* athlete.

atlético [aδlétiko] *a.* athletic.

atmósfera [aδmósfera] *f.* atmosphere.

atómico [atómiko] *a.* atomic.

atormentar [atormentár] *t.* to torment. 2 torture. 3 *p.* to worry.

atracción [atraɣθjón] *f.* attraction, appeal.

atractivo [atraɣtíβo] *a.* attractive. 2 *m.* charm.

atraer [atraér] *t.* to attract, draw. 2 to lure. 3 to charm. ¶ CONJUG. like *traer.*

atrás [atrás] *adv.* back, backward(s, behind.

atrasado [atrasáδo] *a.* behind [time]. 2 backward. 3 slow.

atravesar [atraβesár] *t.* to cross. 2 to pierce; to pass through. ¶ CONJUG. like *acertar.*

atreverse [atreβérse] *p.* to dare, venture, risk.

atrevido [atreβíδo] *a.* daring, bold.

atribuir [atriβuír] *t.* to attribute, ascribe. 2 *p.* to assume. ¶ CONJUG. like *huir.*

atrio [átrjo] *m.* courtyard; portico.

atropellar [atropeλár] *t.* to run over, trample. 2 to knock down. 3 to outrage. 4 *p.* to be hasty.

aturdir [aturδír] *t.* to deafen. 2 to make giddy. 3 to bewilder. 4 to amaze.

audaz [aŭδáθ] *a.* audacious, bold, daring.

audición [aŭδiθjón] *f.* hearing. 2 concert.

audiencia [aŭδjénθja] *f.* audience. 2 Spanish provincial high court.

auditor [aŭδitór] *m.* judge-advocate.

aula [áŭla] *f.* class-room.

aumentar [aŭmentár] *t.-i.-p.* to increase. 2 *i.-p.* to grow larger.

aumento [aŭménto] *m.* enlargement, increase.

aun [áun] *adv.* even, still; ~ *cuando,* although.

aún [aún] *adv.* yet, as yet, still.

aunque [áuŋke] *conj.* though, although.

ausencia [aŭsénθja] *f.* absence; lack.

ausentarse [aŭsentárse] *p.* to be absent; to leave.

auto [áŭto] *m.* judicial decree, writ, warrant. 2 car. 3 religious play. 4 *pl.* LAW proceedings.

autobús [aŭtoβús] *m.* bus.

automático [aŭtomátiko] *a.* automatic(al.

automóvil [aŭtomóβil] *m.* automobile, motorcar.

autor [aŭtór] *m.-f.* author, authoress [writer]. 2 perpetrator.

autoridad [aŭtoriðáð] *f.* authority.

autorizar [aŭtoriθár] *t.* to authorize, empower, permit, legalize, approve.

autostop [aŭtostóp] *m.* hitch-hiking: hacer ~, to hitch-hike.

1) **auxiliar** [aŭsiljár] *t.* to help, assist.

2) **auxiliar** [aŭsiljár] *a.* auxiliary. 2 *m.* assistant.

auxilio [aŭsíljo] *m.* help, aid, assistance.

avance [aβánθe] *m.* advance payment. 2 trailer.

avanzar [aβanθár] *i.* to improve, progress.

avariento [aβarjénto], **avaro** [aβáro] *a.* miserly, niggard. 2 *m.-f.* miser.

ave [áβe] *f.* bird; fowl: ~ de rapiña, bird of prey.

avemaría [aβemaría] *f.* Hail Mary.

avena [aβéna] *f.* oats.

avenida [aβeníða] *f.* flood, freshet. 2 avenue.

aventura [aβentúra] *f.* adventure. 2 chance, risk, hazard.

avergonzar [aβerɣonθár] *t.* to shame. 2 *p.* to be ashamed. 3 to blush. ¶ CONJUG. like *contar.*

averiguar [aβeriɣwár] *t.* to inquire, find out.

aviación [aβjaθjón] *f.* aviation; air force.

aviador [aβjaðór] *m.* aviator, airman, air pilot.

avión [aβjón] *m.* airplane, aircraft.

avisar [aβisár] *t.* to inform. 2 to warn; to advise.

aviso [aβíso] *m.* notice, advice; warning.

avispa [aβíspa] *f.* wasp.

bastón [bastón] *m.* cane, walking stick.

basura [basúra] *f.* rubbish, garbage, sweepings, refuse.

bata [báta] *f.* dressing-gown. 2 white coat.

batalla [batáʎa] *f.* battle, fight, struggle.

batería [batería] *f.* battery: ~ *de cacina*, pots and pans.

batir [batír] *t.* to beat, strike. 2 to flop [wings]. 3 to beat, defeat. 4 to clap [hands]. 5 MIL. to reconnoitre the ground. 6 *p.* to fight.

baúl [baúl] *m.* luggage trunk, portmanteau.

bautismo [baŭtizmo] *m.* baptism; christening.

bautizar [baŭtiθár] *t.* to baptize, christen. 2 to name. 3 to water [wine].

beber [beβér] *t.-p.* to drink.

bebida [beβíða] *f.* drink.

becerro [beθérro] *m.* calf, young bull. 2 calf-skin. 3 ~ *marino*, seal.

bejuco [bexúko] *m.* liana; rattan.

belleza [beʎéθa] *f.* beauty.

bello [béʎo] *a.* beautiful, fine, lovely, handsome.

bellota [beʎóta] *f.* acorn.

bendecir [bendeθír] *t.* to bless.

bendición [bendiθjón] *f.* benediction, blessing. 2 *pl.* wedding ceremony.

bendito [bendíto] *a.* holy, blessed. 2 happy. 3 *m.* simple-minded soul.

beneficiar [benefiθjár] *t.* to benefit. 2 to improve [land]. 3 *p.* to profit.

beneficio [benefíθjo] *m.* benefit, advantage, profit.

beneficioso [benefiθjóso] *a.* profitable, advantageous, useful.

berenjena [berenxéna] *f.* egg-plant.

besar [besár] *t.* to kiss.

beso [béso] *m.* kiss.

bestia [béstja] *f.* beast. 2 idiot.

Biblia [bíβlja] *f.* Bible.

bíblico [bíβliko] *a.* Biblical.

biblioteca [biβljotéka] *f.* library.

bicicleta [biθikléta] *f.* bicycle, bike, cycle.

1) bien [bjén] *adv.* well, properly, right 2 ~ ... ~, either ... or. 3 *ahora* ~, now then. 4 *má* ~, rather. 5 *si* ~, although.

2) bien [bjén] *m.* good. 2 welfare, benefit: *ha*

¡**ay!** [áĭ] *interj.* alas!

ayer [ajér] *adv. - m.* yesterday, in the past.

ayuda [ajúða] *f.* help, aid, assistance.

ayudante [ajuðánte] *m.* aid, assistant.

ayudar [ajuðár] *t.* to help, aid, assist.

ayuntamiento [ajunta-mjénto] *m.* town council. 2 town hall.

azada [aθáða] *f.* hoe.

azar [aθár] *m.* hazard, chance: *al* ~, at random.

azotar [aθotár] *t.* to whip, flog. 2 to spank. 3 [of sea, etc.] to beat.

azote [aθóte] *m.* scourge, whip, birch, thong.

azotea [aθotéa] *f.* flat roof, terrace roof.

azúcar [aθúkar] *m.-f.* sugar.

azucarar [aθukarár] *t.* to sugar, sweeten.

azucena [aθuθéna] *f.* white lily.

azul [aθúl] *a.-m.* blue: ~ *celeste*, sky blue; ~ *marino*, navy blue.

B

bacalao [bakaláo] *m.* cod-fish.

bacteria [baktérja] *f.* bacterium, *pl.* -a; germ.

bachillerato [batʃiʎeráto] *m.* the Spanish certificate of secondary education.

bahia [baia] *f.* bay.

bailar [baïlár] *i.* to dance. 2 [of a top] to spin.

bailarín [baïlarín] *a.* dancing. 2 *m.-f.* dancer.

baile [báïle] *m.* dance; ball.

bajar [baxár] *i.* to come down, go down. 2 to fall. 3 *t.-i.* to get down. 4 *t.* to lower [prices, etc.].

1) **bajo** [báxo] *adv.* in a low voice. 2 *prep.* beneath, under.

2) **bajo** [báxo] *a.* low. 2 short. 3 lower: *la clase baja*, the lower classes. 4 *piso ~, planta baja*, ground floor. 5 *m.* hollow, deep. 6 shoal. 7 bass.

bala [bála] *f.* bullet, shot. 2 bale [of goods].

balancear [balanθeár] *i.-p.* to rock, swing, roll. 2 *t.* to balance.

balanza [balánθa] *f.* [pair of] scales, balance.

balar [balár] *i.* to bleat.

balcón [balkón] *m.* balcony.

balón [balón] *m.* ball; football. 2 bag. 3 CHEM. balloon.

baloncesto [balonθésto] *m.* basket-ball.

balsa [bálsa] *f.* pool. 2 NAUT. raft.

ballena [baʎéna] *f.* whale; whalebone.

bambú [bambú] *m.* bamboo.

banca [báŋka] *f.* COM. banking. 2 bank. 3 bench.

banco [báŋko] *m.* bench. 2 COM. bank.

banda [bánda] *f.* sash. 2 band, gang. 3 side [of ship]. 4 MUS. band.

bandada [bandáða] *f.* flock [of birds].

bandeja [bandéxa] *f.* tray, salver.

bandera [bandéra] *f.* flag, banner, standard.

bandido [bandíðo] *m.* outlaw. 2 bandit, highwayman.

banquete [baŋkéte] *m.* banquet, feast.

bañar [baɲár] *t.-p.* to bathe, take a bath.

baño [báɲo] *m.* bath; bathing. 2 bathtub.

bar [bar] *m.* bar.

baraja [baráxa] *f.* pack [of cards].

barato [baráto] *a.* cheap.

barba [bárβa] *f.* chin. 2 beard.

bárbaro [bárβaro] *a.* barbarous. 2 *m.-f.* barbarian.

barberia [barβería] *f.* barber's shop.

barbero [barβéro] *m.* barber.

barbudo [barβúðo] *a.* bearded.

barca [bárka] *f.* boat, ferry-boat.

barco [bárko] *m.* ship.

barómetro [barómetro] *m.* barometer.

barra [bárra] *f.* bar. 2 MECH. lever. 2 ~ *de labios*, lipstick.

barraca [barráka] *f.* cabin, hut. 2 farmhouse.

barrer [barrér] *t.* to sweep. 2 NAUT. to rake.

barriada [barriáða] *f.* quarter, district; slum quarter.

barriga [barríγa] *f.* belly.

barril [barríl] *m.* barrel. keg.

barrio [bárrjo] *m.* town ward, quarter: *barrios bajos*, slums.

barro [bárro] *m.* mud.

basar [basár] *t.* to base, found. 2 *p.* to be based upon.

base [báse] *f.* basis, base.

bastante [bastánte] *a.* sufficient, enough. 2 *adv.* enough, rather.

bastar [bastár] *i.* to suffice, be enough.

cer ~, to do good. 3 pl.
property, estate, goods:
bienes inmuebles, real
estate; bienes muebles,
movables.

bienaventurado [bjena-
βenturáðo] a. blessed,
happy. 2 simple.

bienestar [bjenestár] m.
well-being, comfort.

bienhechor [bjenetʃór]
m. benefactor.

bigote [biɣóte] m.
m(o)ustache. 2 whis-
kers [of a cat].

billar [biʎár] m. billiards
[-table, -room, -hall].

billete [biʎéte] m. short
letter. 2 love-letter. 3
ticket. 4 ~ de banco,
bank-note.

bisabuelo, la [bisaβwélo,
la] m.-f. great-grand-
father; great-grand-
mother. 2 m. pl. great-
grandparents.

bistec [bisté] m. beef-
steak.

bizco [biθko] a. squint-
-eyed, cross-eyed.

bizcocho [biθkótʃo] m.
biscuit. 2 sponge cake.

blanco [blánko] a. white.
2 fair [complexion]. 3
m.-f. white person. 4 m.
white colour. 5 target,
mark. 6 aim, goal. 7
interval. 8 blank.

blancura [blankúra] f.
whiteness. 2 fairness.

blando [blándo] a. soft.
2 gentle, mild.

blanquear [blaŋkeár] t.
to whiten. 2 to white-
wash.

bloque [blóke] m. block.

blusa [blúsa] f. blouse.

bobo [bóβo] a. silly,
foolish. 2 m.-f. fool.

boca [bóka] f. mouth. 2
entrance, opening.

bocado [bokáðo] m.
mouthful. 2 bit.

bocina [boθína] f. horn.

boda [bóða] f. marriage,
wedding.

bodega [boðéɣa] f. wine-
cellar. 2 wine shop. 3
NAUT hold.

bola [bóla] f. ball.

boletín [boletín] m.
bulletin, journal.

boleto [boléto] m. (Am.)
ticket.

bolígrafo [boliɣrafo] m.
ball-point pen, biro.

bolo [bólo] m. skittle,
ninepin.

bolsa [bólsa] f. bag. 2
purse. 3 stock exchange.

bolsillo [bolsíʎo] m.
pocket; purse.

bomba [bómba] f. pump.
2 bomb; shell.

bombero [bombéro] m.
fireman; pl. fire brigade.

bombilla [bombíʎa] *f.* light bulb.

bondad [bondáð] *f.* goodness. 2 kindness.

bondadoso [bondaðóso] *a.* kind, good.

bonito [bonito] *a.* pretty, nice. 2 *m.* ICHTH. bonito, striped tunny.

bono [bóno] *m.* COM. bond, certificate; ~ *del tesoro,* exchequer bill.

bordado [borðáðo] *m.* embroidering; embroidery.

bordar [borðár] *t.* to embroider.

borde [bórðe] *m.* border, edge. 2 hem.

borracho [borrátʃo] *a.* drunk. 2 *m.-f.* drunkard.

borrador [borraðór] *m.* draft. 2 duster, eraser.

borrar [borrár] *t.* to cross, rub out, blot out; to erase.

borrico [borríko] *m.* ass, donkey.

bosque [bóske] *m.* forest, wood, grove, thicket.

bosquejar [boskexár] *t.* to sketch, outline.

bosquejo [boskéxo] *m.* sketch, outline.

bota [bóta] *f.* leather wine bag. 2 cask. 3 boot.

botar [botár] *t.* to throw, fling out. 2 to launch. 3 *i.* to bound. 4 to jump.

bote [bóte] *m.* small boat: ~ *salvadidas,* life-boat. 2 bound, bounce. 3 pot. 4 *de* ~ *en* ~, crowded.

botella [botéʎa] *f.* bottle, flask, jar.

botica [botíka] *f.* chemist's shop, drugstore.

botiquín [botikín] *m.* medicine case; first-aid kit.

botón [botón] *m.* button.

boxeador [boɣseaðór] *m.* boxer.

boxear [boɣseár] *i.* to box.

boxeo [boɣséo] *m.* boxing.

bravo [bráβo] *a.* brave, courageous. 2 excellent. 3 ferocious [animal].

brazalete [braθaléte] *m.* bracelet, armlet.

brazo [bráθo] *m.* arm. 2 power. 3 branch [of river]. 4 forelegs.

brea [bréa] *f.* tar, pitch.

breve [bréβe] *a.* short, brief. 2 *f.* MUS. breve. 3 *adv. en* ~, soon, shortly. 4 **-mente** *adv.* briefly.

brillante [briʎánte] *a.* brilliant, shining, bright.

2 *m.* brilliant [diamond].
3 **-mente** *adv.* brilliantly.
brillar [briʎár] *i.* to
shine. 2 to glitter. 3 to
be outstanding.
brillo [bríʎo] *m.* brilliance, brightness, shine.
brincar [briŋkár] *i.* to
spring, leap, jump, hop.
brinco [bríŋko] *m.*
spring, leap, jump, hop.
brindar [brindár] *i.* to
toast. 2 *t.* to offer,
afford. 3 *p.* to offer to
[do something].
brío [brío] *m.* strength,
spirit. 2 liveliness;
courage.
brioso [brióso] *a.* vigorous, spirited, lively.
brisa [brísa] *f.* breeze.
británico [britániko] *a.*
British.
broma [bróma] *f.* fun,
merriment; joke: *gastar una ~ a*, to play
a joke on; *en ~*, in
fun; *~ pesada*, practical joke.
bronce [brónθe] *m.*
bronze.
brotar [brotár] *i.* to
sprout; to bud, shoot.
2 to spring. 3 *t.* to put
forth [plants, etc.].
bruja [brúxa] *f.* witch,
sorceress.

brújula [brúxula] *f.* compass; magnetic needle.
brusco [brúsko] *a.* rude.
2 sudden. 3 sharp
[curve].
bruto [brúto] *a.* brute,
brutish. 2 stupid, ignorant. 3 rough.
bueno [bwéno] *a.* good.
2 kind. 3 suitable. 4
well. 5 *por las buenas*,
willingly; *buenos días*,
good morning.
buey [bwéi] *m.* ox: *carne de ~*, beef.
buhardilla [bwardíʎa] *f.*
garret, attic. 2 (Am.)
skylight.
bujía [buxía] *f.* wax
candle. 2 candlestick. 3
spark-plug.
bulto [búlto] *m.* volume,
size, bulk. 2 form,
body. 3 swelling. 4
bundle.
buque [búke] *m.* ship,
vessel: *~ de guerra*,
warship; *~ de vela*,
sailboat; *~ cisterna*,
tanker; *~ mercante*,
merchant ship.
burla [búrla] *f.* mockery,
scoff: *hacer ~ de*, to
mock, make fun of. 2
joke, jest: *de burlas*,
in fun. 3 trick.
burlar [burlár] *t.* to

mock. 2 to deceive, se-
duce. 3 to frustrate. 4
i.-p. *burlarse de*, to
make fun of, laugh at.
burro [búrro] *m*. donkey,
ass.

buscar [buskár] *t*. to
look for, search for,
seek.
butaca [butáka] *f*. arm-
-chair. 2 orchestra
stall.

C

caballería [kaβaʎería] *f.* riding animal. 2 cavalry. 3 knighthood: ~ andante, knight-errantry.

caballero [kaβaʎéro] *m.* rider, horseman. 2 ~ andante, knight-errant. 3 gentleman. 4 sir.

caballo [kaβáʎo] *f.* horse. 2 knight [in chess]. 3 CARDS queen. 4 horsepower. 5 a ~, on horseback.

cabaña [kaβáɲa] *f.* cabin, hut. 2 large number of cattle.

of honour. 3 headboard. 4 bedside.

cabellera [kaβeʎéra] *f.* hair. 2 scalp.

cabello [kaβéʎo] *m.* hair, head of hair.

caber [kaβér] *i.* to fit into, go in; to hold; to have enough room for. ¶ CONJUG. INDIC. Pres.: quepo, cabes, cabe, etc. | Pret.: cupe, cupiste, etc. ‖ COND.: cabría, cabrías, etc. ‖ SUBJ. Pres.: quepa, quepas, etc.. | Imperf.: cupiera, cupieras, etc., or cupiese, cupieses, etc. | Fut.: cupiere, cupieres, etc. ‖ IMPER.: cabe, quepa; quepamos, cabed, quepan.

cabeza [kaβwθa] *f.* head. 2 mind, understanding. 3 source [of a river].

cable [káβle] *m.* cable.

cabo [káβo] *m.* end, extremity: de ~ a rabo, from head to tail. 2 llevar a ~, to carry out. *3* strand. *4* GEOG. cape. *5* MIL. corporal.

cabra [káβra] *f.* goat.

cabrito [kaβríto] *m.* kid.

cacao [kakáo] *m.* cacao [tree]; cocoa [drink].

cacarear [kakareár] *i.* to cackle, crow. 2 to boast.

cacería [kaθería] *f.* hunt, hunting, shoot, shooting.

cacerola [kaθeróla] *f.* casserole, saucepan, pan.

cacique [kaθíke] *m.* Indian chief. 2 political boss.

cacharro [katʃárro] *m.* piece of crockery. 2 rickety machine.

cachete [katʃéte] *m.* slap, punch in the face.

cachorro [katʃórro] *m.-f.* puppy, cub.

cada [káða] *a.* each, every; ~ *cual*, ~ *uno*, every one.

cadáver [kaðáβer] *m* corpse, dead body.

cadena [kaðéna] *f.* chain: ~ *perpetua*, life imprisonment.

caer [kaér] *t.-p.* to fall, drop, fall down, come down; to fall off, fall out. 2 ~ *en la cuenta de*, to realize. 3 to lie, be located. 4 ~ *bien* or *mal*, to suit, fit, or not to suit, fit. ¶ CONJUG.

INDIC. Pres.: *caigo*, caes, etc. | Pret.: caí, caíste, *cayó*; caímos, caísteis, *cayeron*. ‖ SUBJ. Pres.: *caiga*, *caigas*, etc. | Imperf.: *cayera*, *cayeras*; etc., or *cayese*, *cayeses*, etc. ‖ IMPER.: cae, *caiga*; *caigamos*, caed, *caigan*. ‖ GER.: *cayendo*.

café [kafé] *m.* coffee. 2 café [tea-shop].

cafetal [kafetál] *m.* coffee plantation.

cafetera [kafetéra] *f.* coffee-pot.

caída [kaíða] *f.* fall, drop; downfall: *a la* ~ *del sol*, at sunset.

caja [káxa] *f.* box, chest, case. 2 cashbox; cashier's office. 3 ~ *de ahorros*, savings-bank.

cal [kal] *f.* lime.

calamidad [kalamiðáð] *f.* disaster, misfortune.

calavera [kalaβéra] *f.* skull. 2 *m.* madcap.

calcio [kálθjo] *m.* calcium.

calcular [kalkulár] *t.-i.* to calculate. 2 *t.* to conjecture, guess.

cálculo [kálkulo] *m.* calculation, estimate.

caldero [kaldéro] *m.*

small kettle or cauldron.

caldo [káldo] *m.* broth. 2 *pl.* vegetal juices.

calendario [kalendárjo] *m.* calendar, almanac.

calentar [kalentár] *t.* to warm, heat. 2 to spank. 3 *p.* to become heated, excited or angry.

calentura [kalentúra] *f.* fever, temperature.

calidad [kaliðáð] *f.* quality. 2 nature. 3 rank.

cálido [káliðo] *a.* warm, hot.

caliente [kaljénte] *a.* warm, hot.

calificar [kalifikár] *t.* to qualify, rate, class as. 2 to award marks to [in examination].

calma [kálma] *f.* calm. 2 composure. 3 slowness.

calmar [kalmár] *t.* to calm, quiet. 2 to soothe. 3 to calm oneself.

calor [kalór] *m.* heat, warmth: *hace* ~, it is hot: *tengo* ~, I feel warm, hot. 2 enthusiasm, ardour.

calumnia [kalúmnja] *f.* calumny, slander.

caluroso [kaluróso] *a.* hot [weather]. 2 warm, hearty.

calvario [kalβárjo] *m.* calvary, suffering.

calzado [kalθáðo] *a.* shod. 2 *m.* footwear; boots, shoes.

calzar [kalθár] *t.-p.* to put on [one's shoes, gloves].

callar [kaʎár] *i.-p.* to be, keep or become silent; to shut up, be quiet; to stop [talking].

calle [káʎe] *f.* street, road: ~ *mayor*, high street.

cama [káma] *f.* bed, couch; bedstead.

cámara [kámara] *f.* chamber, room, hall. 2 granary. 3 ~ *alta*, upper house; ~ *baja*, lower house. 4 inner tube [of tire].

camarada [kamaráða] *m.* comrade, companion, pal, friend.

cambiar [kambjár] *t.-i.* to change, shift. 2 *t.* to convert: ~ *por*, to exchange for.

cambio [kámbjo] *m.* change; shifting. 2 exchange. 3 RLY. switch. 4 *libre* ~, free trade; *a* ~ *de*, in exchange for; *en* ~, on the other hand; in exchange; ~

de marchas, AUTO. gear-shift.

camello [kaméʎo] *m.* camel.

caminante [kaminánte] *m.-f.* traveller, walker.

caminar [kaminár] *i.* to travel, journey. 2 to walk, march, go.

camino [kamíno] *m.* path, road, way, track, course, journey, travel.

camión [kamjón] *m.* lorry, *truck.

camisa [kamísa] *f.* shirt; chemise.

camiseta [kamiséta] *f.* vest, undershirt.

campamento [kampaménto] *m.* camp, encampment.

campana [kampána] *f.* bell.

campaña [kampáɲa] *f.* countryside, level country. 2 campaign.

campeón [kampeón] *m.* champion; defender.

campeonato [kampeonáto] *m.* championship.

campesino [kampesíno] *a.* rural. 2 *s.* peasant, countryman.

campiña [kampíɲa] *f.* arable land; fields, countryside.

campo [kámpo] *m.* fields, country, countryside. 2 cultivated land. 3 ground. 4 GOLF. links.

canal [kanál] *m.* canal [artificial channel]. 2 GEOG. channel, strait. 3 *m.-f.* gutter.

canario [kanárjo] *a.-n.* Canarian. 2 *m.* ORN. canary.

canasta [kanásta] *f.* basket, hamper.

cancelar [kanθelár] *t.* to cancel, annul.

cáncer [kánθer] *m.* cancer.

canción [kanθjón] *f.* song.

cancionero [kanθjonéro] *m.* collection of lyrics. 2 song-book.

cancha [kántʃa] *f.* sports ground; court; cockpit.

candado [kandáðo] *m.* padlock.

candela [kandéla] *f.* candle, taper. 2 candlestick. 3 fire.

candidato [kandiðáto] *m.-f.* candidate.

canela [kanéla] *f.* cinnamon.

canoa [kanóa] *f.* canoe.

canoso [kanóso] *a.* gray-haired, hoary.

cansado [kansáðo] *a.* tired. 2 worn-out.

cansancio [kansánθjo] *m.* weariness, fatigue.

cansar [kansár] *t.-i.* to tire. 2 *t.* to weary, bore. 3 *t.* to exhaust. *4 p.* to get tired. 5 *i.* to be tiring.

cantante [kantánte] *a.* singing. 2 *m.-f.* singer.

1) **cantar** [kantár] *m.* song: ~ *de gesta*, epic poem.

2) **cantar** [kantár] *t.-i.* to sing. 2 *i.* coll. to confess. 3 [of cocks] to crow.

cántaro [kántaro] *m.* pitcher, jug.

cantera [kantéra] *f.* quarry, stone pit.

cántico [kántiko] *m.* canticle, religious song.

cantidad [kantiðáð] *f.* quantity, amount.

cantina [kantína] *f.* canteen, refreshment room.

canto [kánto] *m.* singing, chant, song. 2 crow [of cock]: chirp [of insects]. 3 corner. 4 edge: *siempre de ~*, this side upside. 5 stone: ~ *rodado*, boulder.

cantor [kantór] *m.-f.* singer.

caña [kápa] *f.* cane; reed: ~ *de azúcar*, sugar--cane. 2 ~ *de pescar*, fishing-rod.

cañería [kapería] *f.* pipe.

caño [kápo] *m.* short tube or pipe.

cañón [kapón] *m.* tube, pipe. 2 barrel [of gun]. 3 flue [of chimney]. 4 ARTILL. cannon, gun. 5 canyon, ravine. 6 quill.

caoba [kaóβa] *f.* mahogany.

capa [kápa] *f.* cloak, mantle, cape. 2 coat [of paint, etc.]. 3 stratum.

capacidad [kapaθiðáð] *f.* capacity, content. 2 ability.

capataz [kapatáθ] *m.* foreman, overseer.

capaz [kapáθ] *a.* roomy. 2 capable. 3 able, competent.

capilla [kapíʎa] *f.* hood, cowl. 2 chapel: oratory.

capital [kapitál] *a.* capital [main, great]: *pena ~*, capital punishment. 2 *m.* property, fotune. 3 ECON. capital. 4 *f.* capital, chief town.

capitán [kapitán] *m.* captain.

capítulo [kapítulo] *m.* chapter.

capricho [kaprítʃo] *m.* caprice, whim, fancy. 2 longing.

capturar [kaβturár] *t.* to capture, arrest.

capullo [kapúʎo] *m.* cocoon. 2 flower bud.

cara [kára] *f.* face, visage, countenance: *echar en ~*, to reproach; *de ~ a*, opposite, facing; *~ a ~*, face to face. 2 look, aspect, front, façade. 2 head [of a coin]: *~ y cruz*, heads or tails.

carabela [karaβéla] *f.* caravel.

caracol [karakól] *m.* snail. 2 *escalera de ~*, spiral staircase.

carácter [karáyter], *pl.* **caracteres** [karaytéres] *m.* character [type, letter; distinctive qualities]. 2 nature.

caracterizar [karayteriθár] *t.* to characterize. 2 to give distinction, etc. 3 *p.* THEAT. to dress up, make up.

¡caramba! [karámba] *interj.* good gracious!

caramelo [karamélo] *m.* caramel, sweetmeat, sweet.

carbón [karβón] *m.* coal; charcoal. 2 ELEC. carbon, crayon.

cárcel [kárθel] *f.* jail, gaol, prison.

cardenal [karðenál] *m.* cardinal. 2 bruise.

carecer de [kareθér] *i.* to lack, be in need of. ¶ CONJUG. like *agradecer.*

careta [karéta] *f.* mask.

carga [kárɣa] *f.* loading; charging. 2 burden. 3 cargo, freight.

cargar [karɣár] *t.* to load. 2 to burden. 3 to charge. 4 to assume responsibilities. 5 to impute. 6 to annoy. 7 *i.* to load up: *~ con*, to shoulder, take the weigh of. 8 *p.* to lean [the body towards].

cargo [kárɣo] *m.* loading. 2 burden, weight. 3 employment, post. 4 charge, responsibility. 5 accusation. 6 *hacerse ~ de*, to take charge of; to understand.

caricia [kariθja] *f.* caress.

caridad [kariðáð] *f.* charity.

cariño [kariɲo] *m.* love, affection, fondness.

cariñoso [kariɲóso] *a.* loving, affectionate.

caritativo [karitatíβo] *a.* charitable.

carne [kárne] *f.* flesh. 2 meat [as a food].

carnero [karnéro] *m.* sheep; mutton; ram.

carnicería [karniθería] *f.* butcher's [shop]. 2 massacre.

carnicero [karniθéro] *m.* butcher. 2 carnivorous.

caro [káro] *a.* dear, costly; expensive.

carpeta [karpéta] *f.* table cover. 2 portfolio.

carpintería [karpintería] *f.* carpentry. 2 carpenter's shop.

carpintero [karpintéro] *m.* carpenter: *pájaro* ~, woodpecker.

carrera [karréra] *f.* running. 2 road, highway. 3 race. 4 ladder [in a stocking]. 5 career. 6 profession. 7 *pl.* horse-racing.

carreta [karréta] *f.* long, narrow cart.

carretera [karretéra] *f.* highway, main road.

carro [kárro] *m.* cart. 2 (Am.) car. 3 chariot.

carroza [karróθa] *f.* coach, carriage.

carruaje [karruáxe] *m.* carriage; vehicle.

carta [kárta] *f.* letter, epistle; note: ~ *certificada*, registered letter. 2 chart, map. 3 playing-card.

cartel [kartél] *m.* poster, placard, bill.

cartera [kartéra] *f.* wallet. 2 portfolio; brief-case. 3 satchel.

cartero [kartéro] *m.* postman; mailman.

cartón [kartón] *m.* cardboard, pasteboard.

casa [kása] *f.* house, building: ~ *consistorial*, town hall: ~ *de socorro*, first-aid hospital; ~ *solariega*, manor. 2 home, family: *en* ~, at home. 3 firm.

casamiento [kasamjénto] *m.* marriage, wedding.

casar [kasár] *i.* to marry; to match [colours]; to blend. 2 *p.* to get married, marry.

cáscara [káskara] *f.* rind, peel [of orange, etc.]; shell [of egg, etc.]. 2 crust, hull.

casco [kásko] *m.* helmet. 2 skull. 3 cask [for liquids]. 4 hull [of ship]. 5 hoof [of horse, etc.]. 6 *pl.* brains.

casero [kaséro] *a.* homely; informal. 2 home-made. 3 home-loving. 4 *m.-f.* landlord, landlady. 5 renter, tenant.

casi [kási] *adv.* almost, nearly.

caso [káso] GRAM., MED. case. 2 event: *venir al* ~, to be relevant; *vamos al* ~, let's come to the point; *en* ~ *de que*, in case; *en todo* ~, anyhow, at any rate. 3 notice; *hacer* ~ *omiso*, to take no notice.

casta [kásta] *f.* caste. 2 race, stock. 3 lineage. 4 kind.

castaña [kastáɲa] *f.* chestnut.

castellano [kasteʎáno] *a.-n.* Castilian.

castigar [kastiɣár] *t.* to punish, chastise. 2 to mortify.

castigo [kastiɣo] *m.* punishment; penance, penalty.

castillo [kastíʎo] *m.* castle.

casualidad [kaswaliðáð] *f.* chance, accident; event: *por* ~, by chance.

catálogo [katáloɣo] *m.* catalogue.

catarata [kataráta] *f.* waterfall.

catarro [katárro] *m.* catarrh; cold.

cátedra [káteðra] *f.* chair [professorship].

catedral [kateðrál] *a.-f.* cathedral.

catedrátrico [kateðrátiko]

m. (Univers.) professor; (Instit.) grammar-school teacher.

categoria [kateɣoría] *f.* category, rank, quality. 2 class, kind.

católico [katóliko] *a.-n.* catholic.

catorce [katórθe] *a.-n.* fourteen.

catre [kátre] *m.* cot, light bed.

cauce [káuθe] *m.* river-bed. 2 channel, ditch.

caudal [kauðál] *m.* fortune; abundance. 3 volume [of water].

caudaloso [kauðalóso] *a.* full-flowing. 2 rich.

caudillo [kauðíʎo] *m.* chief, leader.

causa [káusa] *f.* cause, origin, reason, motive.

causar [kausár] *t.* to cause, give rise to, bring about.

cautivo [kautíβo] *a.-n.* captive, prisoner.

cavar [kaβár] *t.-i.* to dig, excavate.

caverna [kaβérna] *f.* cavern, cave.

caza [káθa] *f.* hunting, chase; shooting. 2 game. 3 *m.* AER. fighter.

cazador [kaθaðór] *m.* hunter. 3 *f.* huntress. 4 hunting jacket.

cazar [kaθár] *t.-i.* to hunt, chase, shoot.

cazuela [kaθwéla] *f.* earthen pan; large casserole.

cebada [θeβáða] *f.* barley.

cebolla [θeβóʎa] *f.* onion.

ceder [θeðér] *t.* to cede. 2 *i.* to yield, give in, give way.

cedro [θéðro] *m.* cedar.

ceja [θéxa] *f.* brow, eyebrow.

celda [θélda] *f.* cell.

celebración [θeleβraθjón] *f.* celebration. 2 holding. 3 applause.

celebrar [θeleβrár] *t.* to celebrate; to make [a festival]; to hold [a meeting]. 2 to praise. 3 to be glad of. 4 to say Mass. 5 *p.* to take place.

célebre [θéleβre] *a.* famous, remarkable.

celeste [θeléste] *a.* heavenly.

celestial [θelestjál] *a.* heavenly.

celo [θélo] *m.* zeal. 2 heat, rut. 3 *pl.* jealousy.

celoso [θelóso] *a.* zealous. 2 jealous.

célula [θélula] *f.* cell.

cementerio [θementérjo] *m.* cemetery, graveyard.

cemento [θeménto] *m.* cement; concrete.

cena [θéna] *f.* supper; dinner.

cenar [θenár] *i.* to have supper, have dinner.

ceniza [θeniθa] *f.* ash. 2 *pl.* cinders.

censura [θensúra] *f.* censure. 2 censorship.

centenar [θentenár] *m.* hundred.

centeno [θenténo] *m.* rye.

centímetro [θentímetro] *m.* centimetre.

céntimo [θéntimo] *m.* centime, cent.

centinela [θentinéla] *m.-f.* sentinel, sentry.

central [θentrál] *a.* central. 2 *f.* main office. 3 TELEPH. exchange, *central. 4 ELEC. power-station.

centro [θéntro] *m.* centre, middle. 2 club. 3 main office.

ceñir [θeɲír] *t.* to gird; to girdle. 2 to fit tight. 3 ~ *espada*, to wear a sword. 4 *p.* to be concise. ¶ CONJUG. like *reir*.

cepillo [θepíʎo] *m.* brush; ~ *de dientes*, tooth-brush. 2 CARP. plane. 3 alms box.

cera [θéra] *f*. wax.

1) cerca [θérca] *f*. hedge, fence.

2) cerca *adv*. near, close, nigh. 2 ~ *de*, nearly, about.

cercado [θerkáðo] *a*. fenced-in, walled-in. 2 *m*. enclosure.

cercano [θerkáno] *a*. near. 2 neighbouring.

cercar [θerkár] *t*. to fence in. 2 to surround. 3 MIL. to lay siege to.

cerco [θérko] *m*. circle; edge. 2 rim. 3 MIL. siege, blockade.

cerdo [θérðo] *m*. swine, hog, pig. 2 pork [meat].

cereal [θereál] *a.-m*. cereal.

cerebro [θeréβro] *m*. head, brains.

ceremonia [θeremónja] *f*. ceremony. 2 formality.

cereza [θeréθa] *f*. cherry.

cerilla [θeriʎa] *f*. match.

cero [θéro] *m*. zero, nought; nothing; nil.

cerrado [θerráðo] *a*. closed, shut; locked.

cerradura [θerraðúra] *f*. lock.

cerrar [θerrár] *t*. to close, shut. 2 to fasten, bolt, lock. 3 to clench [the fist]. 4 to block up, bar. 5 to wall. 6

to seal [a letter]. 7 to turn off [the water, etc.]. 8 *i*. [of a shop, etc.] to shut.

cerro [θérro] *m*. neck. 2 back, backbone. 3 hill.

certeza [θertéθa] *f*. certainty.

certificado [θertifikáðo] *a*. registered. 2 *m*. registered letter. 3 certificate.

cerveza [θerβéθa] *f*. beer, ale.

césped [θéspeð] *m*. lawn, grass.

cesta [θésta] *f*. basket, hamper.

ciclón [θiclón] *m*. cyclone, hurricane.

ciegamente [θjéɣaménte] *adv*. blindly.

ciego [θjéɣo] *a*. blind. 2 blocked. 3 *m.-f*. blind man.

cielo [θjélo] *m*. sky. 2 heaven. 3 ~ *raso*, ceiling.

cien [θjén] *a*. [a, one] hundred.

ciencia [θjénθja] *f*. science; learning, knowledge.

científico [θjentifiko] *a*. scientific. 2 *m.-f*. scientist.

cierto [θjérto] *a*. certain, sure: *por ~ que*, by the way.

cifra [θífra] *f.* cipher, figure, number. 2 amount.

cigarillo [θiɣarríʎo] *m.* cigarette.

cigarro [θiɣárro] *m.* cigar.

cigüeña [θiɣwéɲa] *m.* stork. 2 MACH. crank, winch.

cilindro [θilíndro] *m.* cylinder. 2 roller.

cima [θíma] *f.* summit, top, peak. 2 *dar ~*, to carry out, complete.

cinco [θíŋko] *a.* five.

cincuenta [θiŋkwénta] *a.-m.* fifty.

cine [θíne] *m.* cinema, movies, pictures.

cinta [θínta] *f.* ribbon, tape. 2 film.

cintura [θintúra] *f.* waist.

cinturón [θinturón] *m.* belt, girdle.

circo [θírko] *m.* circus.

circulación [θirkulaθjón] *f.* circulation. 2 currency. 3 traffic.

1) **circular** [θirkulár] *a.* circular. 2 *f.* circular letter.

2) **circular** *i.* to pass along, cross.

círculo [θírkulo] *m.* circle. 2 club.

circunstancia [θirkunstánθja] *f.* circumstance.

ciruela [θirwéla] *f.* plum: *~ pasa*, prune.

cirugía [θiruxía] *f.* surgery.

cirujano [θiruxáno] *m.* surgeon.

cisne [θízne] *m.* swan.

cita [θíta] *f.* appointment, date. 2 quotation.

citar [θitár] *t.* to make an appointment. 2 to cite, quote. 3 LAW to summon.

ciudad [θjuðáð] *f.* city, town.

ciudadano [θjuðaðáno] *m.-f.* citizen.

cívico [θíβiko] *a.* civic.

civil [θiβíl] *a.* civil. 2 *a.-n.* civilian.

civilización [θiβiliθaθjón] *f.* civilization.

clamar [klamár] *t.-i.* to clamour for, cry out for.

claramente [kláraménte] *adv.* clearly. 2 frankly, openly.

claro [kláro] *a.* bright. 2 clear. 3 obvious. 4 light [colour]. 5 outspoken. 6 *adv.* clearly. 7 *interj.* of course! 8 *m.* space, interval. 9 clearing [in woods]. 10

poner en ~, to make plain, to clear up.

clase [kláse] *f.* class: ~ alta, media, baja, upper, middle, lower classes; ~ obrera, working class. 2 kind, sort: toda ~ de, all kind of. 3 RLY., EDUC. class. 4 classroom.

clásico [klásiko] *a.* classic(al. 2 *m.* classic [author].

clasificar [klasifikár] *t.* to classify. 2 to sort, file.

claustro [kláŭstro] *m.* cloister.

clavar [klaβár] *t.* to drive, stick, stab with. 2 to nail. 3 to fix [eyes, etc.].

clave [kláβe] *f.* key. 2 code. 3 MUS. clef.

clavel [klaβél] *m.* pink, carnation.

clavo [kláβo] *m.* nail.

cliente [kliénte] *m.-f.* client. 2 customer.

clima [klíma] *m.* climate.

clínica [klínika] *f.* clinic.

club [kluβ] *m.* club, society.

cobarde [koβárðe] *a.* cowardly. 2 *m.-f.* coward.

cobijar [koβixár] *t.* to cover, shelter. 2 *p.* to take shelter.

cobrar [koβrár] *t.* to collect, receive; to cash: ~ ánimo, to take courage; ~ fuerzas, to gather strength. 4 HUNT. to retrieve.

cobre [kóβre] *m.* copper.

cocer [koθér] *t.* to cook. 2 to boil. 3 to bake [bread, etc.].

cocido [koθíðo] *a.* cooked, boiled, baked. 2 *m.* Spanish stew.

cocina [koθína] *f.* kitchen: ~ económica, cooking range.

cocinar [koθinár] *t.* to cook. 2 *i.* to do the cooking.

cocinero [koθinéro] *m.* cook.

cocodrilo [kokoðrílo] *m.* crocodile.

coche [kótʃe] *m.* coach, carriage, car: ~ de alquiler, cab, taxi. 2 AUTO. car. 3 RLY. car, carriage: ~ cama, sleeping-car; ~ restaurante, dining-car.

cochino [kotʃíno] *a.* filthy, dirty. 2 *m.* ZOOL. pig, hog. 3 *m.-f.* dirty person.

código [kóðiyo] *m.* code.

codo [kóðo] *m.* elbow.

2 bend [in tube, etc.].

coger [koxér] *t.* to take, seize, grasp; to take hold of. 2 to pick, gather. 3 to catch.

cohete [koéte] *m.* rocket.

cojín [koxín] *m.* cushion.

cojo [kóxo] *a.* lame, crippled.

col [kol] *f.* cabbage.

cola [kóla] *f.* tail; end. 2 train [of gown]. 3 queue: *hacer* ~, to queue up. 4 glue.

colaboración [kolaβoraθjón] *f.* collaboration.

colar [kolár] *t.* to strain, filter; to bleach with lye. 3 *p.* to sneak in. ¶ CONJUG. like *contar*.

colcha [kóltʃa] *f.* quilt.

colchón [koltʃón] *m.* mattress.

colchoneta [koltʃonéta] *f.* thin mattress.

colección [koleyθjón] *f.* collection.

colectivo [koleytíβo] *a.* collective.

colegial, la [kolexjál, la] *m.* schoolboy. 2 schoolgirl.

colegio [koléxjo] *m.* school. 2 college. 3 ~ *electoral,* polling station.

cólera [kólera] *f.* anger, rage. 2 *m.* cholera.

colgar [kolγár] *t.* to hang, suspend. 2 to impute. 3 *i.* to hang [be suspended], dangle.

colina [kolína] *f.* hill, hillock.

colmado [kolmáðo] *a.* full, abundant. 2 *m.* grocer's, *foodstore.

colmena [kolména] *f.* beehive.

colocación [kolokaθjón] *f.* location. 2 placement. 3 employment; job. 4 investment [of capital].

colocar [kolokár] *t.* to place, put; to set, lay. 3 *p.* to get a job.

colonia [kolónja] *f.* colony. 2 eau-de-Cologne.

colonial [kolonjál] *f.* colonial.

colono [kolóno] *m.* colonist, settler. 2 farmer.

color [kolór] *m.* colo(u)r; colo(u)ring.

colorado [koloráðo] *a.* colo(u)red. 2 red: *ponerse* ~, to blush.

columna [kolúmna] *f.* column.

columpio [kolúmpjo] *m.* swing; seesaw.

collar [koʎár] *m.* necklace. 2 collar.

coma [kóma] *f.* GRAM. comma. 2 *m.* MED. coma.

comadre [komáðre] *f.*
midwife; godmother.

comandante [komandán-
te] *m.* MIL. commander.
2 major.

comarca [komárka] *f.*
region, district, country.

combate [kombáte] *m.*
combat, fight, battle. 2
BOX. fight.

combatir [kombatír] *t.-i.*
to combat, fight.

combinación [kombina-
θjón] *f.* combination.

combustible [kombusti-
βle] *a.* combustible. 2
m. fuel.

comedia [koméðja] *f.* co-
medy, play. 2 farce.

comedor [komeðór] *m.*
dining-room.

comentar [komentár] *t.*
to comment on.

comentario [komentárjo]
m. LIT. commentary. 2
comment.

comenzar [komenθár] *t.-
i.* to start, begin.

comer [komér] *t.-p.* to
eat [up]. 2 *i.* to eat,
feed. 3 to dine; to have
a meal.

comercial [komerθjál] *a.*
commercial.

comerciante [komerθján-
te] *m.* merchant, trad-
er, tradesman.

comercio [komérθjo] *m.*
commerce, trade. 2 shop,
store.

comestible [komestíβle]
a. eatable. 2 *m. pl.*
food, groceries; vict-
uals, provisions: *tienda
de comestibles,* grocer's
[shop], grocery.

cometer [kometér] *t.* to
entrust, commit. 2 to
do, perpetrate.

cómico [kómiko] *a.* com-
ic, amusing. 2 comical,
funny. 3 *m.* actor. 4
f. actress.

comida [komíða] *f.* food;
meal. 2 dinner.

comienzo [komjénθo] *m.*
m. commencement, be-
ginning.

comisión [komisjón] *f.*
commission. 2 commit-
tee.

como [kómo] *adv.* as,
like: *tanto* ~, as much
as. 2 *conj. asi* ~, as
soon as. 3 if. 4 because,
as. 5 ~ *quiera que,*
since, as, inasmuch. 6
adv. interrg. how: *¿cómo está usted?,* how
do you do? 7 why;
what. 8 *interj.* why!,
how now!

comodidad [komoðiðáð]
f. comfort, convenience,
ease, leisure.

cómodo [kómoðo] a. comfortable. 2 handy, cosy.

compadecer [kompaðeθér] t. to pity, feel sorry for. 2 p. to have pity on.

compañero [kompaɲéro] m. companion, fellow, mate, partner.

compañía [kompaɲía] f. society. 2 THEAT. company.

comparación [komparaθjón] f. comparison.

comparar [komparár] t. to compare. 2 to confront.

comparecer [kompareθér] i. to appear [before a judge, etc.].

compartir [kompartír] t. to share.

compás [kompás] m. [a pair of] compasses. 2 MUS. time, measure.

compasión [kompasjón] f. compassion, pity.

compatriota [kompatrjóta] m.-f. fellow-countryman, compatriot.

compendio [kompéndjo] m. summary, digest.

competencia [kompeténθja] f. ability. 2 rivalry.

competente [kompeténte] a. competent, suitable. 2 qualified

competir [kompetír] i. to compete. ¶ CONJUG. like servir.

complacer [komplaθér] t. to please. 2 p. to be pleased. ¶ CONJUG. like agradecer.

complemento [kompleménto] m. complement. 2 GRAM. object.

completar [kompletár] t. to complete, finish.

completo [kompléto] a. complete. 2 full up.

complicado [komplikáðo] complicate(d, complex.

componer [komponér] t. to compose; compound. 2 to fix. 3 to adorn. 4 to settle [a dispute]. 5 p. to dress up, make up. 6 componerse de, to consist of. 7 to manage.

comportamiento [komportamjénto] m. behavio(u)r, conduct.

composición [komposiθjón] f. composition. 2 agreement.

compositor [kompositór] m. composer.

comprar [komprár] t. to purchase, buy.

comprender [komprendér] t. to comprehend. 2 to understand.

comprensión [komprensjón] *f.* comprehension. 2 understanding.

comprobar [komproβár] *t.* to verify, check. 2 to prove.

comprometer [komprometér] *t.* to risk, jeopardize. 2 *p.* to become engaged.

compromiso [kompromíso] *m.* engagement, obligation. 3 trouble.

comulgar [komulɣár] *i.* to take, receive Communion.

común [komún] *a.* common. 2 ordinary. 3 *por lo* ~, generally.

comunicación [komunikaθjón] *f.* communication.

comunicar [komunikár] *t.* to communicate, report. 3 *i.* [of the telephone] to be engaged.

comunidad [komuniðáð] *f.* community.

comunión [komunjón] *f.* communion.

comunismo [komunízmo] *m.* communism.

comunista [komunísta] *a.-s.* communist.

con [kon] *prep.* with.

concebir konθeβír] *t.-i.* to conceive. ¶ Conjug. like *servir*.

conceder [konθeðér] *t.* to grant, award. 2 to admit.

concentrar [konθentrár] *t.-p.* to concentrate.

concepto [konθépto] *m.* concept, idea. 2 opinion.

concertar [konθertár] *t.* to arrange; to conclude; to agree upon. 2 *i.-p.* to agree. ¶ Conjug. like *acertar.*.

concesión [konθesjón] *f.* concession. 2 grant.

conciencia [konθjénθja] *f.* conscience. 2 consciousness.

concierto [konθjérto] *m.* agreement. 2 mus. concert.

concluir [konkluír] *t.-i.p.* to finish, end. 2 to conclude.

conclusión [konklusjón] *f.* end, conclusion.

concretar [konkretár] *i.* to summarize; to fix details. 2 *p.* to keep close to the point.

concreto [konkréto] *a.* concrete; definite.

concurrencia [konkurrénθja] *f.* concurrence; audience.

concurso [konkúrso] *m.* competition.

concha [kóntʃa] *f.* shell.

conde [kónde] _m._ earl, count.

condenar [kondenár] _t._ condemn, sentence. 2 _p._ to be damned.

condición [kondiθjón] _f._ condition: _a ~ de que,_ provided that. 2 _pl._ terms.

conducir [konduθír] _t._ to lead. 2 to manage. 3 to drive [a vehicle]. 4 _p._ to behave. ¶ CONJUG. INDIC. Pres.: _conduzco,_ conduces, etc. | Pret.: _conduje, condujiste,_ etc. ‖ SUBJ. Pres.: _conduzca, conduzcas,_ etc. | Imperf.: _condujera,_ etc., or _condujese,_ etc. | Fut.: _condujere,_ etc. ‖ IMPERAT.: conduce, _conduzca; conduzcamos,_ conducid, _conduzcan._

conducta [kondùkta] _f._ conduct, behavio(u)r. 2 management.

conductor [konduktór] _m._ guide, leader. 2 driver [of a vehicle]. 4 PHYS., RLY. conductor.

conectar [koneктár] _t._ to connect; to switch on, turn on.

conejo [konéxo] _m._ rabbit: _conejillo de Indias,_ guinea-pig.

conferencia [komferénθja] _f._ lecture. 2 conference. 3 TELEPH. trunk call.

confesar [komfesár] _t.-i._ to confess. 2 to acknowledge.

confesión [komfesjón] _f._ confession.

confiado [komfjáðo] _a._ _a._ unsuspecting. 2 self-confident.

confianza [komfjánθa] _f._ confidence, reliance, trust. 4 familarity.

confiar [komfjár] _i._ to confide, trust, rely on. 2 to entrust.

confirmación [komfirmaθjón] _f._ confirmation.

confirmar [komfirmár] _t._ to confirm.

conflicto [komflikto] _m._ conflict, struggle. 2 difficulty.

conformar [komformár] to adjust. 2 to agree. 3 _p._ to yield.

conforme [komfórme] _a._ alike; in agreement; resigned; ready to. 2 _adv._ according to.

confundir [komfundir] _t._ to mix up. 2 to confound. 3 _p._ to get mixed up. 4 to get mistaken; to make a mistake.

confusión [komfusjón] *f.* confusion. 2 disorder. 3 shame.

confuso [komfúso] *a.* confused. 2 troubled. 3 obscure.

congregación [kongreɣaθjón] *f.* congregation.

congresista [kongresísta] *m.* congress-man.

congreso [kongréso] *m.* congress, assembly.

conjugación [konxuɣaθjón] *f.* conjugation.

conjunto [konxúnto] *a.* conjunt, united. 2 *m.* total: *en ~*, altogether.

conmemoración [kommemoraθjón] *f.* commemoration.

conmemorar [kommemorár] *t.* to commemorate

conmigo [kommíɣo] *pron.* with me, with myself.

conmover [kommoβér] *t.* to move, touch, excite. 2 *p.* to be touched.

conocedor [konoθeðór] *m.-f.* connoisseur, judge.

conocer [konoθér] *t.* to know. 2 to be acquainted with, meet [a person]. 3 *p.* to be acquainted with each other.

conocimiento [konoθimjénto] *m.* knowledge;

information. 2 intelligence.

conque [kónke] *conj.* so, so then, well then.

conquista [konkísta] *f.* conquest.

conquistador [konkistaðór] *m.* conqueror. 2 *m.* lady-killer.

conquistar [konkistár] *t.* to conquer; to win, gain.

consagración [konsaɣraθjón] *f.* consecration.

consagrar [konsaɣrár] *t.* to consecrate, hallow.

consecuencia [konsekwénθja] *f.* consequence.

consecutivo [konsekutíβo] *a.* consecutive.

conseguir [konseɣír] *t.* to obtain, attain, get. 2 to succeed in, manage to.

consejo [konséxo] *m.* advice; piece of advice. 2 council, board.

consentir [konsentír] *t.* to allow, permit. ¶ CONJUG. like *hervir*.

conserje [konsérxe] *m.* door-keeper, porter.

conservación [konserβaθjón] *f.* conservation.

conservador [konserβaðór] *m.* curator. 2 *a.-n.* POL. conservative.

conservar [konserβár] *t.* to keep, maintain.

considerable [konsiðerá-βle] a. considerable.

consideración [konsiðera-θjón] f. consideration.

considerar [konsiðerár] t. to consider, think over.

consigo [konsíγo] *pron.* with him [her, it, one]; with them, with you.

consiguiente [konsiγjén-te] a.-n. consequent. 2 *por ~*, therefore.

consistente [konsisténte] a. consistent, firm, solid.

consistir [konsistír] i. to consist [of, in, with]; to be based on.

consolador [konsolaðór] a. consoling, comforting.

consolar [konsolár] t. to console, comfort, cheer. ¶ Conjug. like *contar*.

constante [konstánte] a. constant, steady. 2 **-mente** adv. constantly.

constar [konstár] i. to be on record. 2 to consist of. 3 to be clear from.

constitución [konstitu-θjón] f. constitution.

constituir [konstituír] t. to constitute; to establish. ¶ Conjug. like *huir*.

construcción [konstruy-θjón] f. construction, building; structure.

construir [konstrwír] t. to construct, build.

consuelo [konswélo] m. consolation, comfort. 2 relief.

consulta [konsúlta] f. consultation. 2 reference.

consultar [konsultár] t.-i. to consult, take advice.

consumidor [konsumiðór] m. consumer.

consumir [konsumír] t. to consume. 2 to waste away, spend. 3 p. to burn out.

consumo [konsúmo] m. consumption.

contabilidad [kontaβili-ðáð] f. accounting, book-keeping.

contacto [kontáγto] m. contact. 2 touch.

contado [kontáðo] a. counted. 2 rare. 3 m. *al ~*, cash down.

contador [kontaðór] m. computer. 2 counter. 3 meter. 4 book-keeper.

contagioso [kontaxjóso] a. contagious, infectious.

contar [kontár] t. to count. 2 to tell, narrate: *~ con*, to rely on.

contemplar [kontemplár] t. to contemplate, look at. 2 to pamper.

contener [kontenér] t to contain, check. 2 to restrain, refrain. 3 to hold back.

contenido [konteníðo] a. moderate. 2 m. contents.

contento [konténto] a. pleased, glad. 2 m. joy.

contestación [kontestaθjón] f. answer, reply. 2 debate.

contestar [kontestár] t. answer, write back.

contigo [kontíγo] pron. with you.

contiguo [kontíγwo] a. next, neighbouring.

continente [kontinénte] m. continent.

continuación [kontinwaθjón] f. continuation.

continuamente [kontinwaménte] adv. incessantly.

continuar [kontinuár] t. to continue. 2 i. to go on.

continuo [kontínwo] a. continuous; steady.

contra [kóntra] prep. against. 2 m. con: el pro y el ~, the pros and cons.

contraer [kontraér] t.-p. to contract, shrink. 2 to get, catch. ¶ CONJUG. like traer.

contrariedad [kontrarjeðáð] f. contrariety. 2 set-back, disappointment.

contrario [kontrárjo] a. contrary. 2 harmful. 3 m.-f. opponent, adversary. 4 al ~, on the contrary.

contraste [kontráste] m. opposition. 2 contrast.

contratar [kontratár] t. to contract for. 2 to engage, hire.

contrato [kontráto] m. contract.

contribución [kontriβuθjón] f. contribution. 2 tax.

contribuir [kontriβuir] i. to contribute to.

contrincante [kontriŋkánte] m. competitor, rival.

control [kontról] m. control, check.

convencer [kombenθér] t. to convince.

conveniencia [kombenjénθja] f. utility, advantage. 2 pl. income, property.

conveniente [kombenjénte] a. convenient, advantegeous. 3 **-mente** *adv.* conveniently.

convenio [kombénjo] *m.* agreement, pact.

convenir [kombenír] *i.* to agree. 2 to come together. 3 to be convenient. advantageous.

convento [kombénto] *m.* convent.

conversación [kombersaθjón] *f.* conversation, talk.

conversar [kombersár] *i.* to converse, talk.

convertir [kombertír] *t.* to convert, transform 2 *p.* to be or become converted.

convicción [kombiɣθjón] *f.* conviction, belief

convidar [kombiðár] *t.* to invite.

convocar [kombokár] *t.* to convoke, call together.

coñac [koɲá] *m.* cognac, brandy.

cooperación [kooperaθjón] *f.* co-operation.

cooperar [kooperár] *t.* to co-operate.

cooperativa [kooperatíβa] *f.* co-operative.

copa [kópa] *f.* wineglass. 2 *tomar una* ~, to have a drink. 3 cup. 4 top.

copia [kópja] *f.* copy. 2 imitation.

copiar [kopjár] *t.* to copy. 2 to take down.

copla [kópla] *f.* folksong, ballad.

coqueta [kokéta] *f.* coquette, flirt. 2 *a.* coquettish.

coraje [koráxe] *m.* courage. 2 anger.

coral [korál] *m.* coral.

corazón [koraθón] *m.* heart. 2 вот. core.

corbata [korβáta] *f.* tie.

corcel [korθél] *m.* steed, charger.

corcho [kórtʃo] *m.* cork.

cordel [korðél] *m.* string.

cordero [korðéro] *m.* lamb.

cordial [korðjál] *a.* friendly, hearty. 2 **-mente** *adv.* heartily.

cordillera [korðiʎéra] *f.* mountain range.

cordón [korðón] *m.* braid; yarn, cord, string 2 lace. 3 cordon.

coro [kóro] *m.* choir. 2 chorus.

corona [koróna] *f.* crown; wreath.

coronel [koronél] *m.* colonel.

corporación [korporaθjón] *f.* corporation.

corpulento [korpulénto] a. bulky, stout.

corral [korrál] m. yard, farm yard.

correa [korréa] f. leather strap, leash.

correcto [korréyto] a. correct, proper, right.

corredor [korreðór] a. running. 2 m. SPORT. runner. 3 COM. broker 4 corridor.

corregir [korrexír] t. to correct. 2 to reprimand. ¶ CONJUG. like *servir*.

correo [korréo] m. postman; courier. 2 post-office. 3 mail, post.

correr [korrér] i. to run. 2 to blow. 3 to spread. 4 to pass. 5 to hurry. 6 t. to run [a horse; a risk]. 7 to fight. 8 to draw. 9 ~ prisa, to be urgent, pressing. 10 p. to slide, slip. 11 to be ashamed.

correspondencia [korrespondénθja] f. correspondence, letter-writing.

corresponder [korrespondér] i. to correspond, answer. 2 to pertain. 4 p. to love each other.

correspondiente [korrespondjénte] a. suitable, appropriate.

corrida [korríða] f. course, race. 2 ~ de toros, bullfight.

corriente [korrjénte] a. flowing, running. 2 current. 3 usual. 4 f. stream. 5 ELEC. current.

cortar [kortár] t. to cut, slash; to cut away, off, out or up; to sever. 2 to carve, chop. 3 to cross. 4 to hew. 5 to cut short. 6 to stop, bar. 7 p. [of milk] to sour, curdle.

1) **corte** [kórte] m. cutting edge. 2 cut. 3 art of cutting clothes. 4 length. 5 felling [of trees]. 6 ELECT. break.

2) **corte** [kórte] f. court. 2 city. 3 (Am.) court [of justice]. 4 courtship: *hacer la ~ a*, to pay court to.

cortés [kortés] a. courteous, polite.

cortesía [kortesía] f. politeness.

corteza [kortéθa] f. bark [of tree]; crust [of bread, etc.]; rind [of cheese, etc.]; peel [of orange, etc.].

cortina [kortína] f. curtain; screen, flap.

corto [kórto] a. short, brief. 2 wanting. 3 shy. 4 dull, 5 ELEC. ~ circuito, short circuit. 6 ~ de vista, short-sighted.

cosa [kósa] f. thing, matter: como si tal ~, as if nothing had happened.

cosecha [kosétʃa] f. harvest, crop; vintage. 2 reaping. 3 harvest time.

cosechar [kosetʃár] t.-i. to harvest, crop, reap.

coser [kosér] t. to sew; to seam. 2 to stab.

costa [kósta] f. coast, shore. 2 cost: a toda ~, at all costs; a ~ de, at the expense of.

costar [kostár] i. to cost. ¶ CONJUG. like contar.

coste [kóste] m. cost, price: ~ de vida, cost of living.

costilla [kostíʎa] f. rib. 2 chop, cutlet [to eat].

costo [kósto] m. cost, price.

costoso [kostóso] a. costly, expensive. 2 difficult.

costumbre [kostúmbre] f. custom; habit.

costura [kostúra] f. sewing, needlework. 2 seam.

cotorra [kotórra] f. parrot. 2 chatterbox.

cráneo [kráneo] m. skull.

creación [kreaθjón] f. creation.

creador [kreaðór] m. creator. 2 maker.

crear [kreár] t. to create. 2 to make.

crecer [krθér] t. to grow, increase. 2 to swell.

crecimiento [kreθimjénto] m. growth, increase.

crédito [kréðito] m. credit, credence: dar ~ a, to believe. 2 good reputation: a ~, on credit.

creencia [kreénθja] f. belief, creed.

creer [kreér] t.-i.-p. to believe. 2 to think, suppose.

crema [kréma] f. cream.

crepúsculo [krepúskulo] m. twilight; dawn.

cresta [krésta] f. crest, comb [of a bird]; cock's comb. 2 crest of mountain. 3 tuft.

creyente [krejénte] m.-f. believer, faithful.

cría [kría] f. suckling 2 breeding. 3 brood, young [animals].

criado [kriáðo] a. bred.

2 *m.* manservant. 3 *f.* maid, maidservant.

crianza [kriánθa] *f.* nursing. 2 bringing up, 3 manners.

criar [kriár] *t.* to nurse, suckle. 2 to rear, breed, grow. 3 to bring up, educate.

criatura [kriatúra] *f.* creature. 2 baby, child.

crimen [krímen] *m.* crime, felony.

criminal [kriminál] *a.-n.* criminal.

crisis [krísis] *f.* crisis. 2 COM. depression; shortage.

cristal [kristál] *m.* crystal. 2 window-pane.

cristalino [kristalíno] *a.* crystalline. 2 *m.* crystalline lens.

cristiano [kristjáno] *a.-n.* Christian.

Cristo [krísto] *m. pr. n.* Christ. 2 *m.* crucifix.

criterio [kritérjo] *m.* criterion. 2 judgement.

crítica [krítika] *f.* criticism. 2 faultfinding, gossip. 3 the critics.

crítico [krítiko] *a.* critical. 2 *m.* critic.

crucificar [kruθifikár] *t.* to crucify. 2 to torture.

crudo [krúðo] *a.* raw,

underdone [food]. 2 bitter [weather]. 3 harsh, rough.

cruel [krwél] *a.* cruel, ruthless, harsh.

cruz [kruθ] *m.* cross: ~ *Roja,* Red Cross. 2 tails [of coin]: *cara o* ~, heads or tails.

cruzar [kruθár] *t.* to cross, lie across. 2 *p.* to pass each other.

cuaderno [kwaðérno] *m.* exercise-book.

cuadra [kwáðra] *f.* stable.

cuadrado [kwaðráðo] *a.-m.* square.

cuadrar [kwaðrár] *t.* to square. 2 *i.* to fit, suit. 3 *p.* MIL. to stand at attention.

cuadro [kwáðro] *m.* square: *a cuadros,* checkered. 2 picture, painting. 3 frame [of door, etc.]. 4 LIT. picture, description. 5 scene. 6 flower-bed. 7 table, synopsis.

cual, cuales [kwál, kwáles] *rel. pron.* who, which, that. 2 as, such as. 3 *adv.* like.

cuál, cuáles [kwál, kwáles] *interr. pron.* who, which [one, ones], what. 2 *adv.* how.

cualidad [kwaliðáð] *f.*
quality.
cualquiera [kwalkjéra],
pl. **cualesquiera** [kwa-
leskjéra] *pron.* anyone,
anybody. 2 ~ *que*, wha-
tever, whichever.
cuan [kwán] *adv. tan…
cuan*, as… as.
cuán [kwán] *interrog.-
exclam.* how.
cuando [kuándo] *adv.*
when: *aun* ~, even
though; *de* ~ *en* ~,
now and then.
1) **cuanto** [kwánṭo] *adv.*
en ~ *a*, with regard
to, as for. 2 ~ *antes*,
as soon as possible. 3
~ *más … tanto más*,
the more … the more.
4 **cuánto** *adv.* how;
how much, how long,
how far.
2) **cuanto** [kwánto] *a.*
all the, every, as much
[sing.], as many [pl.].
2 *pron.* all [that], as
much as [sing.], as
many as [pl.], all who.
3 *a.-pron. unos cuantos*,
some, a few.
3) **cuánto** [kwánto], **cuán-
tos** [kwántos] (with in-
terrog. or exclam.) *a.-
pron.* how much [sing.],
how many [pl.], what.

cuarenta [kwarénta] *a.-
n.* forty.
cuartel [kwartél] *m.*
ward [of a town]. 2
MIL. barracks. 3 MIL.
quarters.
cuartilla [kwartíʎa] *f.*
sheet of paper.
cuarto [kwárto] *a.*
fourth. 2 *m.* quarter. 3
room: ~ *de baño*, bath-
-room; ~ *de estar*,
living-room.
cuatro [kwátro] *a.* four.
2 roof(ing. 3 outer tyre.
4 NAUT. deck.
cubo [kúβo] *m.* bucket,
pail. 2 GEOM. cube. 3
hub [of a wheel].
cubrir [kuβrír] *t.* to
cover [up]. 2 to hide.
3 to roof [a building].
cucaracha [kukarátʃa] *f.*
cockroach.
cuchara [kutʃára] *f.*
spoon. 2 dipper.
cucharada [kutʃaráða] *f.*
spoonful.
cuchilla [kutʃíʎa] *f.* large
knife, cleaver. 2 blade.
cuchillo [kutʃíʎo] *m.*
knife.
cuello [kwéʎo] *m.* neck,
throat. 2 collar [of a
garment].
cuenta [kwénta] *f.* account; count; bill, note·

hacer cuentas, to cast accounts. 2 com. account: ~ *corriente*, current account; *por* ~ *de*, for account of. 3 report, information: *dar* ~ *de*, to inform of. 4 *caer en la* ~, *darse* ~, to realize. 5 *tener en* ~, to take into account.

cuento [kwénto] *m.* tale, story: ~ *de hadas*, fairy tale. 2 gossip; 3 count: *sin* ~, numberless.

cuerda [kwérða] *f.* rope, cord, string: *dar* ~ *a un reloj*, to wind up a watch.

cuerdo [kwérðo] *a.* sane, wise, prudent.

cuerno [kwérno] *m.* horn.

cuero [kwéro] *m.* hide, raw hide. 2 leather. 3 *en cueros*, stark naked.

cuerpo [kwérpo] *m.* body; trunk: *luchar* ~ *a* ~, to fight hand to hand. 3 corpse. 4 ~ *de ejército*, army corps.

cuervo [kwérβo] *m.* raven, crow.

cuesta [kwésta] *f.* slope, hill.

cuestión [kwestjón] *f.* question; affair, business. 2 quarrel.

cueva [kwéβa] *f.* cave.

cuidado [kwiðáðo] *m.* care, charge: *al* ~ *de*, in care of; *tener* ~, to be careful: *¡—!*, look out!

cuidadosamente [kwiðaðósaménte] *adv.* carefully.

cuidadoso [kwiðaðóso] *a.* careful.

cuidar [kwiðár] *t.-i.* to take care of, keep, look after, mind. 3 *p.* to take care of oneself.

culebra [kuléβra] *f.* snake.

culpa [kúlpa] *f.* guilt, fault, blame.

culpable [kulpáβle] *a.* guilty.

cultivar [kultiβár] *t.* to cultivate, labour, farm [land, soil].

cultivo [kultíβo] *m.* cultivation, farming.

1) **culto** [kúlto] *m.* cult, worship.

2) **culto** [kúlto] *a.* educated. 2 learned.

cultura [kultúra] *f.* culture.

cumbre [kúmbre] *f.* summit, top, peak. 2 height.

cumpleaños [kumpleáɲos] *m.* birthday.

cumplimiento [kumplimjénto] *m.* fulfilment. 2 observance [of law]. 3 compliment, politeness.

cumplir [kumplír] *t.* to accomplish, perform, fulfil. 2 to keep [a promise]. 3 to do [one's duty]; to observe [a law]. 4 to finish [a term in prison]. 5 reach [of age]. 6 *i.-p.* [of time] to expire. 7 *p.* to be fulfilled.

cuna [kúna] *f.* cradle. 2 lineage.

cuneta [kunéta] *f.* ditch, gutter.

cuñada [kuɲáða] *f.* sister-in-law.

cuñado [kuɲáðo] *m.* brother-in-law.

cuota [kwóta] *f.* membership fee. 2 quota.

cura [kúra] *m.* parish priest. 2 cure: *primera* ~, first aid.

curar [kurár] *i.-p.* to cure, heal, recover, get well. 2 to take care of; to mind. 3 MED. to treat.

curiosidad [kurjosiðáð] *f.* curiosity.

curioso [kurjóso] *a.* curious. 2 clean, tidy.

cursar [kursár] *t.* to frequent. 2 to study [law]. 3 to make [a petition].

curso [kúrso] *m.* course, direction. 2 EDUC. course; school year.

cutis [kútis] *m.* skin; complexion.

cuyo [kújo] *poss. pron.* whose, of which, of whom.

CH

chancleta [tʃaŋkléta] *f.* slipper.

chaqueta [tʃakéta] *f.* jacket, sack coat.

charca [tʃárka] *f.* pool, pond.

charco [tʃárko] *m.* puddle, pond.

charla [tʃárla] *f.* chatter. 2 chat. 3 talk.

charlar [tʃarlár] *i.* to chatter. 2 to chat, talk.

charlatán [tʃarlatán] *m.-f.* chatterbox.

cheque [tʃéke] *m.* cheque, check: ~ *de viajero*, traveller's check.

chicle [tʃiklé] *m.* chewing-gum.

chico [tʃíko] *a.* small, little. 2 *m.* boy, lad. 3 *f.* girl, lass.

chicharrón [tʃitʃarrón] *m.* fried piece of fat.

chillar [tʃiʎár] *i.* to shriek, scream. 2 to shout.

chimenea [tʃimenéa] *f.* chimney. 2 fireplace. 3 funnel.

china [tʃína] *f.* pebble. 2 China silk.

chino [tʃíno] *a.-n.* Chinese.

chiquillo [tʃikíʎo] *a.* small. 2 *m.-f.* little boy or girl.

chispa [tʃíspa] *f.* spark, sparkle.

chiste [tʃíste] *m.* joke.

chistoso [tʃistóso] *a.* witty, funny, amusing.

chocar [tʃokár] *i.* to collide; to clash, bump together. 3 to surprise.

chocolate [tʃokoláte] *m.* chocolate.

chófer [tʃófer] *m*. driver.

choque [tʃóke] *m*. collision, clash; shock. 2 MIL. encounter. 3 quarrel.

chorizo [tʃoríθo] *m*. pork sausage.

chorro [tʃórro] *m*. jet, spout, flow, stream.

choza [tʃóθa] *f*. hut, cabin.

chuleta [tʃuléta] *f*. chop, cutlet.

chupar [tʃupár] *t*. to suck, draw.

D

dado [dáðo] *m.* die [*pl.* dice].

dama [dáma] *f.* lady, dame. 2 king [in draughts]. 3 queen [in chess].

danza [dánθa] *f.* dance.

danzar [danθár] *i.* to dance.

dañar [danár] *t.* to harm, damage, injure, hurt. 2 to spoil. 3 *p.* to get hurt.

dañino [danino] *a.* harmful.

daño [dáno] *m.* harm, damage, loss, injury.

dar [dar] *t.* to give, hand, deliver, grant. 2 to bear, yield. 3 ~ comienzo, to begin; ~ un paseo, to take a walk. 4 dar como or por, to consider. 5 ~ a conocer, to make known; ~ a luz, to give birth to; to publish; ~ que pensar, to arouse suspicions. 6 *i.* ~ con, to meet, find. 7 ~ de sí, to yield, stretch. 8 *p.* to give oneself. 9 to yield, surrender. 10 darse a la bebida, to take to drink. 11 darse la mano, to shake hands. ¶ Conjug. Indic. Pres.: doy, das, da; damos, dais, dan. | Imperf.: daba, dabas, etc. | Pret.: di, diste, dio; dimos, disteis, dieron. | Fut.: daré, darás, etc. ‖ Con.: daría, darías, etc. ‖ Subj. Pres.: dé, des, etc. | Imperf.: diera, dieras, etc., or diese, dieses, etc.

| Fut.: *diere, dieres*, etc. || IMPER.: *da, dé; demos, dad, den.* || PAST. P.: *dado.* || GER.: *dando*

dato [dáto] *m.* datum, fact, piece of information.

de [de] *prep.* of; from, by, with: ~ *dia*, by day; ~ *noche*, at night.

debajo [deβáxo] *adv.* underneath, below: ~ *de*, under, beneath.

debate [deβáte] *m.* debate, discussion.

1) **deber** [deβér] *m.* duty, obligation 2 homework.

2) **deber** [deβér] *t.* to owe. 2 *aux.* [with an inf.] must, have to; ought to, should.

débil [déβil] *a.* weak, feeble. 2 slight, sickly.

decano [dekáno] *m.* dean.

decena [deθéna] *f.* ten.

decente [deθénte] *a.* decent, proper.

decidir [deθiðir] *t.* to decide, determine. 2 *p.* to make up one's mind.

décima [déθima] *f.* a stanza of ten octosyllabic lines.

decir [deθir] *t.* to say, talk, tell, speak: ~ *para si*, to say to oneself;

querer ~, to mean; *es* ~, that is to say. ¶ CONJUG. INDIC. Pres.: *digo, dices, dice;* decimos, *decís, dicen.* | Imperf.: *decia, decias*, etc. | Pret.: *dije, dijiste, dijo; dijimos, dijísteis, dijeron.* | Fut.: *diré, dirás,* etc. || COND.: *diria, dirias,* etc. || SUBJ. Pres.: *diga, digas,* etc. | Imperf.: *dijera, dijeras,* etc., or *dijese, dijeses,* etc. || Fut.: *dijere, dijeres,* etc. | IMPER.: *di, diga; digamos, decid, digan.* || P. P.: *dicho.* | GER.: *diciendo.*

decisión [deθisjón] *f.* decision.

decisivo [deθisiβo] *a.* decisive.

declaración [deklaraθjón] *f.* statement.

declarar [deklarár] *t.* to declare. 2 to state. 3 LAW to find (guilty).

decorar [dekorár] *t.* to decorate.

dedal [deðál] *m.* thimble.

dedicación [deðikaθjón] *f.* dedication.

dedicar [deðikár] *t.* to dedicate. 2 to devote. 3 *p.* to devote oneself to.

dedo [déðo] m. ~ de la mano, finger; ~ del pie, toe.

defecto [deféγto] m. defect, fault, blemish.

defender [defendér] t.-p. to defend. ¶ CONJUG. like *entender*.

defensor [defensór] m.-f. defender. 2 supporter.

deficiencia [defiθjénθja] f. deficiency.

definición [definiθjón] f. definition.

definido [definíðo] a. definite.

definir [definír] t. to define.

definitivo [definitíβo] a. definitive.

defraudar [defrauðár] t. to defraud, cheat. 2 to frustrate, disappoint. 3 to deceive.

degollar [deγoʎár] t. to behead; to slash the throat. ¶ CONJUG. like *contar*.

dejar [dexár] t. to leave: ~ en paz, to let alone. 2 to let go. 3 to quit. 4 to allow, let.

del [del] contraction of DE and EL: of the.

delantal [delantál] m. apron; pinafore.

delante [delánte] adv. before, in front of; ahead.

delantero [delantéro] m. SPORT. forward.

delegación [deleγaθjón] f. delegation. 2 COM. branch.

delicia [delíθja] f. delight; pleasure, joy.

delicioso [deliθjóso] a. delicious, delightful.

delincuente [delinkwénte] a.-n. delinquent.

delito [delíto] m. offence, crime, guilt, misdemeano(u)r.

demanda [demánda] f. petition, request. 2 COM. demand. 3 LAW claim, lawsuit.

demandar [demandár] t. to demand, ask for, beg. 2 LAW to sue.

demás [demás] a. the rest of the. 2 pron. other, others; por lo ~, for the rest.

demasiado [demasjáðo] adv. too, excessively; 2 a.-pron. too much, too many.

demente [deménte] a. mad, insane. 2 m.-f. lunatic, maniac.

democracia [demokráθja] f. democracy.

democrático [demokrátiko] a. democratic.

demonio [demónjo] *m.* demon, devil, fiend.

demostración [demostr-θjón] *f.* demonstration; show; proof.

demostrar [demostrár] *t.* to demonstrate, show; to prove.

denominador [denomina-ðór] *m.* MATH. denominator.

denominar [denominár] *t.* to denominate, name, call.

denso [dénso] *a.* dense, compact, thick.

dentista [dentísta] *m.* dentist.

dentro [déntro] *adv.* in, inside, within: ~ *de poco*, shortly.

denunciar [denunθjár] *t.* *t.* to denounce. 2 to accuse. 3 to report. 4 to claim. 5 to charge with.

departamento [departa-ménto] *m.* department. 2 compartment.

depender [depender] *i.* ~ *de*, to depend on, rely upon.

dependiente [dependjénte] *a.* depending, subordinate. 2 *m.* clerk, assistant.

deporte [depórte] *m.* sport.

deportista [deportísta] *m.* sportsman.

deportivo [deportiβo] *a.* sports, sporting, sportive.

depositar [depositár] *t.* to deposit. 2 to place, put.

depósito [depósito] *m.* trust. 2 sediment. 3 storehouse. 4 tank, reservoir.

derecha [derétʃa] *f.* right. 2 right hand. 3 POL. right wing. 4 *a la* ~, to the right.

derecho [derétʃo] *a.* right side, right-hand. 2 straight. 3 standing, upright. 4 *adv.* straight on. 5 *m.* right; justice. 6 law.

derivar [deriβár] *i.-p.* to derive, come from.

derramar [derramár] *t.* to pour out, spill. 2 to shed. 3 *p.* to overflow, run over.

derredor [derreðór] *m.* circuit; contour: *al* ~, *en* ~, around.

derretir [derretír] *t.-p.* to melt, thaw.

derribar [derriβár] *t.* to pull down. 2 to overthrow, knock down.

derrota [derróta] *f.* defeat, rout, disaster.

derrotar [derrotár] *t.* to defeat, rout, beat.

desacato [desakáto] *m.* disrespect. 2 disobedience.

desafío [desafío] *m.* challenge.

desagradable [desaɣraðáβle] *a.* disagreeable, unpleasant.

desaliento [desaljénto] *m.* discouragement, dejection.

desamparar [desamparár] *t.* to forsake, leave helpless.

desagradable [desaɣraðáβle] *a.* unpleasant, disagreeable.

desaparecer [desapareθér] *i.-p.* to disappear.

desarrollar [desaroʎár] *t.* to develop.

desarrollo [desaróʎo] *m.* development.

desastre [desástre] *m.* disaster, calamity.

desatar [desatár] *t.* to untie, loose, loosen, unfasten. 2 [of a storm] to break out.

desayunar(se [desajunár-(se] *i.-p.* to breakfast, have breakfast.

desayuno [desajúno] *m.* breakfast.

desbaratar [dezβaratár] *t.* to destroy, ruin. 2 to frustrate.

desbordar [dezβorðár] *i.-p.* to overflow.

descabellado [deskaβeʎáðo] *a.* preposterous, absurd.

descalzo [deskálθo] *a.* barefooted.

descansar [deskansár] *i.* to rest; to lie in sleep. 2 to rely on.

descanso [deskánso] *m.* rest, relaxation. 2 break [half-time].

descarga [deskárɣa] *f.* unloading. 2 discharge. 3 volley.

descargar [deskarɣár] *t.* to unload, unburden. 2 to strike [a blow]. 3 to vent [one's fury, etc.]. 4 to fire, discharge.

descartar [deskartár] *t.* to put aside, lay aside.

descendencia [desθendénθja] *f.* descent. 2 lineage.

descender [desθendér] *i.* to go down. 2 to drop. ¶ CONJUG. like *entender.*

descendiente [desθendjénte] *m.-f.* descendant.

descomponer [deskompo-nér] *t.* to put out of order, disarrange, upset. 2 fig. to set at odds. 3 *p.* to decompose; to become putrid. 4 to get out of order. 5 to be altered. 6 to lose one's temper.

desconocer [deskonoθér] *t.* not to know. 2 to fail to recognize. ¶ CONJUG. like *agradecer*.

desconocido [deskonoθíðo] *a.* unknown. 2 unfamiliar. 3 *m.-f.* stranger.

descontar [deskontár] *t.* to discount, deduct.

descontento [deskonténto] *a.* displeased. 2 *m.* displeasure.

descortés [deskortés] *a.* impolite.

describir [deskriβír] *t.* to describe.

descripción [deskripθjón] *f.* description.

descubrimiento [desku-βrimjénto] *m.* discovery, invention. 2 disclosure.

descubrir [deskuβrír] *t.* to discover, reveal. 2 to make known. 3 to find out. 4 *p.* to take off one's hat.

descuidado [deskwiðáðo]

a. careless. 2 slovenly.

descuidar [deskwiðár] *t.-i.-p.* to neglect, be careless.

descuido [deskwíðo] *m.* negligence, carelessness. 2 oversight.

desde [dézðe] *prep.* from, since.

desdén [dezdén] *m.* disdain.

desdeñoso [dezðeɲóso] *a.* disdainful, contemptuous.

desdicha [dezðítʃa] *f.* misfortune, unhappiness.

desdichado [dezðitʃáðo] *a.* unfortunate, unhappy.

desear [deseár] *t.* to desire, wish, want.

desechar [desetʃár] *t.* to cast aside, refuse.

desembarcar [desembar-kár] *t.* to disembark, land, go ashore.

desembocar [desembokár] *i.* to flow. 2 to end [at], lead into.

desempeñar [desempe-ɲár] *t.* to discharge [a duty]. 2 to act, play.

desengaño [desengáɲo] *m.* disappointment.

desenvolver [desembol-βér] *t.* to unfold. 2 to develop.

deseo [deséo] *m.* desire; wish, longing.

deseoso [deseóso] *a.* desirous, eager.

desesperación [desesperaθjón] *f.* despair, desperation.

desesperar [desesperár] *t.* to drive mad. 2 *i.-p.* to despair; to be exasperated.

desfilar [desfilár] *t.* to march past. 2 to file out.

desfile [desfíle] *m.* defiling; marching past, parade, review.

desgarrar [dezɣarrár] *t.* to tear, rend.

desgracia [dezɣráθja] *f.* misfortune. 2 bad luck, mischance.

desgraciado [dezɣraθjáðo] *a.* unfortunate, unlucky. 2 *m.-f.* wretch.

deshacer [desaθér] *t.* to undo, unmake. 2 to loosen. 3 to destroy. 4 to upset. 5 *p.* to melt, dissolve: *deshacerse de,* to get rid of.

desierto [desjérto] *a.* deserted. 2 *m.* desert, wilderness.

designar [desiɣnár] *t.* to purpose. 2 to designate, appoint.

designio [desíɣnjo] *m.* design, purpose, plan.

desinteresado [desinteresáðo] *a.* disinterested. 2 unselfish.

desistir [desistír] *i.* to desist; to stop, give up.

deslizar [dezliθár] *t.-i.-p.* to slide, glide, slip.

deslumbrar [dezlumbrár] *t.* to dazzle, daze.

desmayar [dezmajár] *t.* to discourage. 2 *p.* to faint, swoon.

desnivel [dezniβél] *m.* unevennness; slope.

desnudo [deznúðo] *a.* nake. 2 bare.

desobedecer [desoβeðeθér] *t.* to disobey. ¶ Conjug. like *agradecer.*

desobediencia [desoβeðjénθja] *f.* disobedience.

desocupado [desokupáðo] *a.* free. 2 idle. 3 unemployed.

desocupar [desokupár] *t.* to empty. 2 *p.* to disengage oneself.

desolar [desolár] *t.* to desolate. ¶ Conjug. like *contar.*

desorden [desórðen] *m.* disorder. 2 riot.

desordenado [desorðenáðo] *a.* disorderly. 2 licentious.

despacio [despáθio] *adv.* slowly.

despachar [despatʃár] *t.* to dispatch. 2 to attend to; to sell [goods]. 3 to dismiss. 4 *i.-p.* to hasten, be quick.

despacho [despátʃo] *m.* dispatch. 2 sale [of goods]. 4 office.

despedida [despeδiδa] *f.* farewell, leave. 2 dismissal.

despedir [despeδír] *t.* to throw. 2 to emit, send forth. 3 to dismiss. 4 to say good-bye to. 5 *p.* to take one's leave. 6 to leave [a post]. ¶ Conjug. like *servir*.

despegar [despeɣár] *t.* to detach. 2 *i.* AER. to take off.

despensa [despénsa] *f.* pantry, larder, store-room.

desperdicio [desperδiθio] *m.* waste. 2 leavings.

despertar [despertár] *t.* to wake, awaken. 2 to excite. 3 *i.-p.* to wake up, awake. ¶ Conjug. like *acertar*.

despierto [despjérto] *a.* awake. 2 lively.

desplegar [despleɣár] *t.* to unfold, spread. 2 to display.

desplomarse [desplomárse] *p.* to tumble down. 2 to collapse.

despojar [despoxár] *t.* to despoil, plunder. 2 *p.* to take off.

despojo [despóxo] *m.* plundering. 2 spoils. 3 *pl.* leavings, scraps.

desposado [desposáδo] *a.* newly married.

despreciar [despreθjár] *t.* to despise.

desprecio [despréθjo] *m.* contempt, disdain, scorn.

desprender [desprendér] *t.* to detach. 2 *p.* to withdraw from. 3 to fall down. 4 to follow.

desprendimiento [desprendimjénto] *m.* disinterestedness. 2 landslide.

después [despwés] *adv.* after, afterwards, later.

destacar [destakár] *t.* to detach. 2 *t.-p.* to stand out.

destapar [destapár] *t.* to uncover, uncork. 2 to take off the lid of.

destello [destéʎo] *m.* sparkle. 2 flash; beam.

desterrar [desterrár] *t.* to exile, banish. ¶ Conjug. like *acertar*.

destierro [destjérro] *m.* exile, banishment.

destilería [destilería] *f.* distillery.

destinar [destinár] *t.* to destine. 2 to assign.

destino [destíno] *m.* destiny, fate: con ~ *a*, bound for, going to. 3 employment.

destituir [destituír] *t.* to dismiss. ¶ CONJUG. like *huir*.

destreza [destréθa] *f.* skill; cleverness.

destrozar [destroθár] *t.* to break to pieces, shatter, destroy.

destrucción [destruγθjón] *f.* ruin, destruction.

destruir [destruír] *t.* to destroy. 2 to waste. ¶ CONJUG. like *huir*.

desvalido [dezβalíðo] *a.* helpless, destitute.

desvanecerse [dezβaneθérse] *p.* to vanish. 2 to faint, swoon. 3 to fade. ¶ CONJUG. like *agradecer*.

desvelar [dezβelár] *t.* to keep awake. 2 *p.* to stay awake.

desvelo [dezβélo] *m.* wakefulness. 2 care.

desventaja [dezβentáxa] *f.* disadvantage; drawback.

desventura [dezβentúra] *f.* misfortune.

desviar [dezβiár] *t.* to turn aside. 2 RLY. to switch. 3 *p.* to deviate, swerve.

desvío [dezβío] *m.* deviation. 2 RLY. side-track.

detalle [detáʎe] *m.* detail.

detective [deteγtíβe] *m.* detective.

detener [detenér] *t.* to detain, stop. 2 to arrest, capture. 3 *p.* to stop, halt. 4 to delay. ¶ CONJUG. like *tener*.

determinación [determinaθjón] *f.* determination. 2 decision.

determinar [determinár] *t.* to determine. 2 to decide.

detrás [detrás] *adv.* behind, back, in the rear.

deuda [déuða] *f.* debt.

deudor [deuðór] *m.-f.* debtor.

devoción [deβoθjón] *f.* piety, devoutness.

devolver [deβolβér] *t.* to give back.

devorar [deβorár] *t.* to devour.

devoto [deβóto] *a.* devout, pious.

dia [día] *m.* day: ~ *de fiesta,* holiday; ~ *laborable,* workday; *hoy* ~, nowadays. 2 daylight, daytime.

diablo [djáβlo] *m.* devil; wicked person.

diáfano [djáfano] *a.* transparent, clear.

diálogo [djáloγo] *m.* dialogue.

diamante [diamánte] *m.* diamond.

diámetro [djámetro] *m.* diameter.

diantre [djántre] *interj.* the deuce!

diariamente [djárjaménte] *adv.* daily, every day.

diario [djárjo] *a.* daily. 2 *m.* daily newspaper. 3 day-book.

dibujar [diβuxár] *t.* to draw, make a drawing of; to sketch, design.

dibujo [diβúxo] *m.* drawing, sketch, portrayal.

diccionario [diγθjonárjo] *m.* dictionary.

diciembre [diθjémbre] *m.* December.

dictadura [diγtaðúra] *f.* dictatorship.

dictar [diγtár] *t.* to dictate. 2 to issue. 3 to suggest.

dicha [dítʃa] *f.* happiness.

dicho [dítʃo] *a.* said. 2 *m.* saying, proverb.

dichoso [dítʃóso] *a.* happy, lucky.

diecinueve [djeθinwéβe] nineteen.

dieciocho [djeθiótʃo] *a.-m.* eighteen.

dieciséis [djeθiséĭs] *a.-m.* sixteen.

diecisiete [djeθisjéte] *a.-m.* seventeen.

diente [djénte] *m.* tooth: *hablar entre dientes,* to mutter, mumble; *hincar el* ~ *en,* to backbite. 2 clove [of garlic].

diestro [djéstro] *a.* right, right-hand. 2 skilful.

dieta [diéta] *f.* diet. 2 assembly.

diez [diéθ] *a.-m.* ten.

diferencia [diferénθja] *f.* difference.

diferenciar [diferenθjár] *t.* to differentiate.

diferente [diferénte] *a.* different.

diferir [diferír] *t.* to delay, postpone, put off. ¶ CONJUG. like *hervir.*

difícil [difíθil] *a.* difficult, hard.

dificultad [difikultáð] *f.* difficulty.

difundir [difundír] *t.-p.* to diffuse, spread out.

difunto [difúnto] *m.-f.* deceased, dead.

digerir [dixerír] *t.* to digest. ¶ CONJUG. like *hervir*.

digestión [dixestjón] *f.* digestion.

dignarse [diɣnárse] *p.* to deign, condescend.

dignidad [diɣniðáð] *f.* dignity.

digno [díɣno] *a.* worthy. 2 deserving.

dilatar [dilatár] *t.-p.* enlarge, widen.

diligencia [dilixénθja] *f.* diligence. 2 stage-coach.

diligente [dilixénte] *a.* diligent.

dimensión [dimensjón] *f.* dimensión, size.

diminuto [diminúto] *a.* little, tiny.

dimisión [dimisjón] *f.* resignation.

dimitir [dimitír] *t.* to resign, give up.

dinero [dinéro] *m.* money, currency, wealth.

Dios [djós] *pr. n.* God: *¡adiós!*, farewell, good-bye.

diosa [djósa] *f.* goddess.

diploma [diplóma] *m.* diploma. 2 licence.

diplomático [diplomátiko] *a.* tactful. 2 *m.-f.* diplomat.

diputado [diputáðo] *m.* deputy, representative.

dique [díke] *m.* mole, dike. 2 dry dock.

dirección [direɣθjón] *f.* direction: ~ *única*, one way. 2 management; postal address.

directamente [diréytaménte] *adv.* directly.

directivo [direɣtíβo] *m.* manager, executive.

directo [diréyto] *a.* direct, straight.

director [direɣtór] *m.-f.* director, manager. 2 MUS. conductor.

dirigente [dirixénte] *a.* leading. 2 *m.-f.* leader.

dirigir [dirixír] *t.* to direct. 2 to manage, govern; to lead. 3 MUS. to conduct. 4 to address [a letter, etc.]. 5 *p.* to speak to. 6 to go to. 7 to apply to.

disciplina [disθiplína] *f.* discipline. 2 teaching. 3 science. 4 *pl.* scourge.

discípulo [disθípulo] *m.-f.* disciple. 2 pupil.

disco [dísko] *m.* disk. 2 record.

discreción [diskreθjón] *f.*
discretion: *a* ~, at will.

discreto [diskréto] *a.* discreet, prudent. 2 fairly good.

discurrir [diskurrír] *i.* to go about, roam. 2 to flow. 3 to pass. 4 to reason, infer. 5 to contrive.

discurso [diskúrso] *m.* talk, speech, lecture.

discusión [diskusjón] *f.* discussion.

discutir [diskutír] *t.-i.* to discuss, debate.

disfrazar [disfraθár] *t.* to disguise, conceal, mask.

disfrutar [disfrutár] *t.* to enjoy, possess, benefit by.

disgustar [dizɣustár] *f.* to displease, annoy. 2 *p.* to be displeased or hurt.

disgusto [dizɣústo] *m.* displeasure, trouble: *a* ~, against one's will.

disipar [disipár] *t.* to dissipate, scatter, squander.

disminuir [dizminuír] *t.-i.-p.* to diminish, decrease. ¶ CONJUG. like *huir.*

disolver [disolβér] *t.-p.* to dissolve. ¶ CONJUG. like *mover.*

disparar [disparár] *t.* to discharge, fire, shoot. 2 to throw. 3 *p.* to dash off; to bolt. 4 to go off.

disparate [disparáte] *m.* nonsense. 2 blunder, mistake.

disparo [dispáro] *m.* shot, report.

dispensar [dispensár] *t.* to grant. 2 to exempt. 3 to excuse.

dispersar [dispersár] *t.* to scatter.

disponer [disponér] *t.* to dispose. 2 to prepare, get ready.

disposición [disposiθjón] *f.* disposition. 2 disposal. 3 natural aptitude. 4 order.

disputar [disputár] *t.* to dispute. 2 *i.* to argue.

distancia [distánθja] *f.* distance.

distante [distánte] *a.* distant, far.

distinción [distinθjón] *f.* privilege; rank. 2 clarity.

distinguido [distiŋgíðo] *a.* distinguished.

distinguir [distingír] *t.* to distinguish. 2 *p.* to be distinguished; to differ.

distinto [distínto] *a.* distinct. 2 different.

distraer [distraér] *t.* to amuse, entertain. 2 to distract. 3 *p.* to amuse oneself. 4 to be inattentive.

distribución [distribuθjón] *f.* distribution. 2 arrangement.

distribuir [distribuír] *t.* to distribute. ¶ CONJUG. like *huir*.

distrito [distríto] *m.* district, region.

diurno [djúrno] *a.* daily, diurnal; day.

diversión [diβersjón] *f.* amusement, entertainment.

diverso [diβérso] *a.* diverse, different. 2 *pl.* sundry.

divertido [diβertíðo] *a.* amusing, funny.

divertir [diβertír] *t.* to amuse, entertain. ¶ CONJUG. like *hervir*.

dividendo [diβiðéndo] *m.* dividend.

dividir [diβiðír] *t.* to divide, split, separate.

divino [diβíno] *a.* divine, heavenly.

divisar [diβisár] *t.* to perceive, make out.

división [diβisjón] *f.* division.

divorcio [diβórθjo] *m.* divorce, separation.

doblar [doβlár] *t.* to double. 2 to fold. 3 to bend, bow. 4 to turn [a page; a corner]. 5 *i.* to toil. 6 *p.* to stoop, give in.

doble [dóβle] *a.* double, twofold.

doce [dóθe] *a.-m.* twelve.

docena [doθéna] *f.* dozen.

docente [doθénte] *a.* teaching.

doctor [doʏtór] *m.* doctor.

doctrina [doʏtrína] *f.* doctrine. 2 catechism.

documento [documénto] *m.* document.

dólar [dólar] *m.* dollar.

doler [dolér] *i.* to ache, hurt, pain. 2 *p. dolerse de*, to repent; to feel sorry for. ¶ CONJUG. like *mover*.

dolor [dolór] *m.* pain, ache, aching; ~ *de cabeza*, headache. 2 sorrow, grief.

doloroso [dolURASO] *a.* painful, distressing.

domar [domár] *t.* to tame. 2 to break in [horses, etc.].

doméstico [doméstiko] *a.* domestic. 2 *m.-f.* house servant.

domicilio [domiθiljo] *m.* domicile, home, abode.

dominar [dominár] *t.* to dominate. 2 to domineer. 3 to rule over. 4 to control. 5 to master [a subject]. 6 to overlook.

domingo [domiŋgo] *m.* Sunday.

dominio [dominjo] *m.* dominion. 2 control. 3 mastery. 4 domain.

don [don] *m.* gift, present. 2 talent; knack. 3 Don [equiv. to Mr. before Christian name].

donar [donár] *t.* to bestow, grant.

doncella [donθéʎa] *f.* virgin, maiden, maid. 2 maidservant.

donde [dónde] *adv.* where, wherein, whither, in which.

dondequiera [dondekjéra] *adv.* anywhere, wherever.

doña [dóɲa] *f.* [equiv. to Mrs. before Christian name].

doquier, ra [dokjér, ra] *adv.* anywhere.

dorado [doráðo] *a.* gilt, golden. 2 *m.* gilding.

dorar [dorár] *t.* to gild. 2 COOK. to brown.

dormir [dormir] *i.* to sleep, rest. 2 *p.* to go to sleep, fall asleep. ¶ CONJUG. INDIC. Pres.: *duermo, duermes, duerme; dormimos, dormís, duermen.* | Pret.: *dormí, dormiste, durmió; dormimos, dormisteis, durmieron.* ‖ SUBJ. Pres.: *duerma, duermas, duerma; durmamos, durmáis, duerman.* | Imperf.: *durmiera, durmieras,* etc., or *durmiese, durmieses,* etc. | Fut.: *durmiere, durmieres,* etc. ‖ IMPER.: *duerme, duerma; durmamos, dormid, duerman.* | GER.: *durmiendo.*

dormitorio [dormitórjo] *m.* bedroom.

dos [dos] *a.-n.* two.

doscientos [dosθjéntos] *a.-m.* two hundred.

dotar [dotár] *t.* to endow, dower, bestow.

drama [dráma] *m.* drama.

dramático [dramátiko] *a.* dramatic.

ducat [coin].

ducha [dútʃa] *f.* shower-bath.

duda [dúða] *f.* doubt.

dudar [duðár] *i.-t.* to doubt.

dudoso [duðóso] *a.* doubtful.

duelo [dwélo] *m.* duel. 2 grief, sorrow. 3 mourning.

duende [dwénde] *m.* goblin, elf; ghost.

dueño [dwéɲo] *m.* owner, master, landlord.

dulce [dúlθe] *a.* sweet. 2 saltless. 3 fresh [water]. 4 *m.* sweet, candy.

dulcería [dulθería] *f.* confectionery shop.

duodécimo [dwoðéθimo] *a.-m.* twelfth.

duque [dúke] *m.* duke.

durante [duránte] *prep.* during, for.

durar [durár] *i.* to endure, last, continue.

duro [dúro] *a.* hard. 2 harsh. 3 hardy. 4 *adv.* hard. 5 *m.* five-peseta piece.

E

e [e] *conj.* and.

ébano [éβano] *m.* ebony.

ebrio [éβrjo] *a.* drunk, intoxicated.

eclesiástico [eklesjástiko] *a.* ecclesiastic(al; 2 *m.* clergyman.

eclipse [eklíβse] *m.* eclipse.

eco [éko] *m.* echo.

economía [ekonomía] *f.* economy. 2 saving, thrift.

económico [ekonómiko] economic. 2 thrifty, saving.

economizar [ekonomiθár] *t.* to economize. 2 to save, spare.

echar [etʃár] *t.* to throw, cast. 2 to put in, add. 3 to give off [sparks, etc.]. 4 to dismiss. 5

to pour [wine, etc.]. 6 ~ *un trago,* to take a drink; ~ *a perder,* to spoil; ~ *a pique,* to sink; ~ *de menos,* to miss. 7 *i.-p.* ~ *a correr,* to begin to run. 8 *p.* to lie down. 9 to throw oneself into.

edad [eðáð] *f.* age.

edición [eðiθjón] *f.* edition. 2 issue. 3 publication.

edificar [eðifikár] *t.* to build.

edificio [eðifíθjo] *m.* building.

editorial [eðitorjál] *m.* editorial, leading article. 2 *f.* publishing house.

educación [eðukaθjón] *f.* education, training. 2 manners; politeness.

educar [eðukár] *t.* to educate; to train, bring up.

efectivamente [efeɣtiβaménte] *adv.* really. 2 indeed.

efectivo [efeɣtiβo] *a.* effective, real. 2 *m.* cash: *en* ~, in cash.

efecto [eféɣto] *m.* effect, result: *en* ~, in fact, indeed. 2 impression.

efectuar [efeɣtuár] *t.* to carry out. 2 *p.* to take place.

eficaz [efikáθ] *a.* efficient; efficacious.

eficiente [efiθjénte] *a.* efficient.

egoismo [eɣoizmo] *m.* selfishness.

egoista [eɣoísta] *a.* selfish.

eje [éxe] *m.* axis. 2 axle, shaft.

ejecución [exekuθjón] *f.* execution; performance, fulfilment.

ejecutar [exekutár] *t.* to execute, fulfil, perform.

ejecutivo [exekutíβo] *a.-s.* executive.

ejemplar [exemplár] *a.* exemplary. 2 *m.* pattern. 3 copy.

ejemplo [exémplo] *m.* example: *por* ~, for instance.

ejercer [exerθér] *t.* to exercise. 2 to practise.

ejercicio [exerθíθjo] *m.* exercise, training. 2 MIL. drill.

ejercitar [exerθitár] *t.* practise. 2 *t.-p.* to exercise.

ejército [exérθito] *m.* army.

el [el] *def. art. masc. sing.* the.

él [el] *pers. pron. masc. sing.* he; him, it [after prep.].

elaborar [elaβorár] *t.* to elaborate, manufacture.

elección [eleɣθjón] *f.* election. 2 choice. 3 election.

electricidad [eleɣtriθiðáð] *f.* electricity.

electricista [eleɣtriθísta] *m.* electrician; electrical engineer.

eléctrico [eléɣtriko] *a.* electric(al.

elefante [elefánte] *m.* elephant.

elegante [eleɣánte] *a.* elegant, smart.

elegir [elexír] *t.* to choose. ¶ CONJUG. like *servir*.

elemental [elementál] *a.* elementary.

elemento [eleménto] *m.* element.

elevación [eleβaθjón] *f.* elevation. 2 height.

elevar [eleβár] *t.* to elevate, raise. 2 *p.* to rise, soar.

eliminación [eliminaθjón] *f.* elimination, removal.

eliminar [eliminár] *t.* to eliminate, remove.

elocuente [elokwénte] *a.* eloquent.

elogio [elóxjo] *m.* praise, eulogy.

ella [éʎa] *pron.* she; her, it [after prep.].

ello [éʎo] *pron.* it.

ellos, ellas [éʎos, éʎas] *pron.* they; them [after prep.].

embajador [embaxaðór] *m.* ambassador.

embarcación [embarkaθjón] *f.* boat, ship, vessel.

embarcar [embarkár] *t.-i.-p.* to embark.

embargar [embaryár] *t.* to restrain. 2 to overcome. 3 to seize.

embargo [embáryo] *m.* seizure. 2 embargo. 3 *sin ~,* nevertheless, however.

embarque [embárke] *m.* shipment.

embellecer [embeʎeθér] *t.* to embellish, beautify. ¶ CONJUG. like *agradecer.*

emblema [embléma] *m.* emblem, symbol.

emborrachar [emborratʃár] *t.* to intoxicate, make drunk. 2 *p.* to get drunk.

emboscada [emboskáða] *f.* ambuscade, ambush.

embriagado [embrjayáðo] *a.* intoxicated; drunk.

embrujar [embruxár] *t.* to bewitch, enchant.

embuste [embúste] *m.* lie, fib, trick, fraud.

embustero [embustéro] *m.-f.* liar.

emergencia [emerxénθja] *f.* emergency.

emigración [emiyraθjón] *f.* emigration.

eminente [eminénte] *a.* eminent, excellent.

emitir [emitír] *t.* to issue. 2 to broadcast.

emoción [emoθjón] *f.* emotion, excitement, thrill.

emocionante [emoθjonánte] *a.* moving, touching, thrilling, exciting.

emocionar [emoθjonár] *t.* to move, touch, thrill. 2 *p.* to be moved.

empalizada [empaliθáða] *f.* stockade, palisade.

empapar [empapár] *t.* to soak, drench.

empatar [empatár] *t.-i.-p.* to tie, draw.

empate [empáte] *m.* tie, draw.

empeñar [empeɲár] *t.* to pledge; to pawn. 2 to engage. 3 *p.* to get into debt. 4 *empeñarse en,* to insist on; to engage in.

empeño [empéɲo] *m.* pledge. 2 pawn: *casa de empeños,* pawnbroker. 3 insistence.

emperador [emperaðór] *m.* emperor.

empero [empéro] *conj.* yet, however; but.

empezar [empeθár] *t.-i.* to begin, start. ¶ CONJUG. like *acertar.*

empleado [empleáðo] *m.* employee; clerk.

emplear [empleár] *t.* to employ. 2 to spend, invest [money].

empleo [empléo] *m.* employment, job. 2 use, 3 investment [of money].

empolvarse [empolβárse] *p.* to powder one's face.

empollar [empoʎár] *t.* to brood, hatch. 2 to swot up, grind [a subject].

emprender [emprendér] *t.* to undertake; to begin, start out.

empresa [emprésa] *f.* enterprise. 2 firm. 3 management.

empresario [empresárjo] *m.* manager; impresario.

empujar [empuxár] *t.* to push, shove, drive.

empuñar [empuɲár] *t.* to handle. 2 to clutch, grasp.

en [en] *prep.* in, into.

enamorado [enamoráðo] *a.* in love. 2 *m.-f.* lover.

enamorar [enamorár] *t.* to make love to, court. 2 *p.* to fall in love.

enano [enáno] *a.-m.-f.* dwarf.

encabezamiento [eŋkaβeθamiénto] *m.* heading, headline.

encabezar [eŋkaβeθár] *t.* to head.

encajar [eŋkaxár] *t.* to fit into; to put or force in. 2 to take [a blow]. 3 to be relevant.

encaje [eŋkáxe] *m.* fitting in. 2 socket, groove. 3 lace.

encallecerse [eŋkaʎeθérse] *p.* to become hardened. ¶ CONJUG. like *agradecer.*

encaminar [eŋkaminár]

t. to direct. 2 *p.* to set out for.

encantador [eŋkantaðór] *a.* charming, delightful.

encantar [eŋkantár] *t.* to enchant, charm.

encanto [eŋkánto] *m.* enchantment. 2 charm, delight.

encaramar [eŋkaramár] *t.* to raise, hoist. 2 *p.* to climb.

encarcelar [eŋkarθelár] *t.* to put in prison. ¶ CONJUG. like *agradecer.*

encargar [eŋkaryár] *t.* to entrust. 2 to order. 3 *p.* ~ *de,* to take charge of.

encargo [eŋkáryo] *m.* charge. 2 errand. 3 order.

encarnado [eŋkarnáðo] *a.* flesh-coloured. 2 red.

encendedor [enθendeðór] *m.* cigarette-lighter.

encender [enθendér] *t.* to light, set fire to. 2 *p.* to burn. 3 [of war] to break out. ¶ CONJUG. like *entender.*

encendido [enθendíðo] *a.* red, flushed.

encerrar [enθerrár] *t.* to shut in, lock up. 2 to

enclose, contain. ¶ CONJUG. like *acertar.*

encima [enθíma] *adv.* on, upon, over, above.

encina [enθína] *f.* evergreen oak, holm oak.

encomendar [eŋkomendár] *t.* to commend. ¶ CONJUG. like *acertar.*

encontrar [eŋkontrár] *t.-p.* to find; to meet. 2 *p.* to be [in a place]. 3 to feel [ill, well, etc.]. 4 *encontrarse con,* to come across. ¶ CONJUG. like *contar.*

encorvar [eŋkorβár] *t.* to bend, curve. 2 *p.* to stoop.

encuentro [eŋkwéntro] *m.* meeting, encounter.

enderezar [endereθár] *t.* to straighten. 2 to set upright. JUG. like *agradecer.*

enemigo [enemíyo] *a.* enemy, hostile. 3 *m.-f.* enemy, foe.

energía [enerxía] *f.* energy: ~ *eléctrica,* electric power.

enérgico [enérxico] *a.* energetic, active, lively.

enero [enéro] *m.* January.

enfadar [enfaðár] *t.* to annoy, anger. 2 *p.* to get angry, be cross.

enfermar [emfermár] *i*
to fall ill.

enfermedad [emfermeðáð]
f. illness, disease, sickness.

enfermera [emferméra]
f. nurse.

enfermo [emférmo] *a.*
sick, ill. 2 *m.-f.* patient.

enfocar [emfokár] *t.* to
focus. 2 to envisage; to
approach.

enfrascar [emfraŋskár]
t. to bottle. 2 *p.* to become absorbed in.

enfrentar [emfrentár] *t.-
p.* to confront, face.

enfrente [emfrénte] *adv.*
in front, opposite.

enfriar [emfriár] *t.* to
cool. 2 *p.* to cool
down. 3 to get cold.
up.

enganchar [eŋgantʃár] *t.*
to hook. 2 to hitch. 3
RLY. to couple. 4 MIL.
to recruit.

engañar [eŋgaɲár] *t.* to
deceive, dupe, cheat. 2
p. to be mistaken.

engaño [eŋgáɲo] *m.* deceit, fraud. 2 error.

engañoso [eŋgaɲóso] *a.*
deceptive. 2 deceitful.

engarzar [eŋgarθár] *t.* to
link. 2 to set, mount.

engendrar [eŋxendrár] *t.*
to engender, beget. 2
to originate.

engordar [eŋgorðár] *t.*
to fatten. 2 *i.* to grow
fat.

engrandecer [eŋgrande-
θér] *t.* to enlarge. ¶
CONJUG. like *agradecer*.

enjambre [eŋxámbre] *m.*
swarm of bees. 2 crowd.

enjaular [eŋxaŭlár] *t.* to
cage, pen in.

enjugar [eŋxuɣár] *t.* to
dry; to wipe.

enlace [enláθe] *m.* tie,
bond. 2 link. 3 RLY.
junction; connection.

enlatar [enlatár] *t.* to
can, tin.

enlazar [enlaθár] *t.* to
lace. 2 to link. 3 *p.* to
marry. 4 to be connected.

enmarañar [emmaraɲár]
t. to entangle. 2 *p.* to
get tangled.

enmendar [emmendár]
t. to amend [law]. 2 to
repair, correct, reform.
3 *p.* to mend one's ways.
¶ CONJUG. like *acertar*.

enmienda [emmjénda] *f.*
amendment.

enojar [enoxár] *t.* to
make angry, vex, annoy.
2 *p.* to get cross.

enojo [enóxo] *m.* anger, annoyance; rage, trouble.

enorme [enórme] *a.* enormous, huge.

enredadera [enrreðaðéra] *f.* creeper. 2 bindweed.

enredar [enrreðár] *t.* to tangle. 2 to net. 3 to embroil. 4 *i.* to be mischievous. 5 *p.* to get entangled.

enriquecer [enrrikeθér] *t.* enrich. 2 *p.* to become wealthy. ¶ CONJUG. like *agradecer*.

ensalada [ensaláða] *f.* salad.

ensanchar [ensantʃár] *t.-p.* to widen, enlarge. 2 to strech, expand.

ensayar [ensajár] *t.* to assay. 2 to try out, test. 3 to rehearse.

ensayo [ensájo] *m.* assay. 2 rehearsal.

enseñanza [enseɲánθa] *f.* teaching, education.

enseñar [enseɲár] *t.* to teach. 2 to train. 3 to show.

ensuciar [ensuθjár] *t.* to dirty, soil. 2 *p.* to get dirty.

ensueño [enswéɲo] *m.* day-dream, illusion.

entender [entendér] *t.* to understand. 2 *p.* to

along well together. ¶ CONJUG. INDIC. Pres.: *entiendo, entiendes, entiende;* entendemos, entendéis, *entienden.* ‖ SUBJ. Pres.: *entienda, entiendas, entienda;* entendamos, entendáis, *entiendan.* ‖ IMPER.: *entiende, entienda;* entendamos, entended, *entiendan.*

entendimiento [entendimjénto] *m.* understanding.

enterar [enterár] *t.* to inform, acquaint. 2 *p.* to learn, be informed of; to know.

entero [entéro] *a.* entire, whole. 2 honest, upright.

enterrar [enterrár] *t.* to bury, inter. 2 *p.* to retire, bury oneself. ¶ CONJUG. like *acertar*.

entidad [entiðáð] *f.* entity, organization.

entierro [entjérro] *m.* burial, funeral.

entonar [entonár] *t.* to sing in tune, intone.

entonces [entónθes] *adv.* then: *por ~,* at that time.

entrada [entráða] *f.* entrance, gate. 2 entry; admission. 3 ticket.

entrambos [entrámbos] *a.* both.

entraña [entráɲa] *f.* the innermost part. 2 *pl.* entrails. 3 heart.

entrar [entrár] *i.* to enter, go in(to, come in(to, get in(to.

entre [éntre] *prep.* between, among, amongst. 2 ~ *tanto*, meanwhile.

entregar [entreɣár] *t.* to deliver, hand over. 2 *t.-p.* to give up, surrender. 3 *p.* to gield. 4 to devote oneself to.

entretanto [entretánto] *adv.* meanwhile.

entretener [entretenér] *t.-p.* to delay, detain. 2 to entertain, amuse.

entrevista [entreβísta] *f.* interview, meeting.

entrevistar [entreβistár] *t.* to interview. 2 *p.* to have an interview with.

entristecer [entristeθér] *t.* to sadden. 2 *p.* to become sad. ¶ CONJUG. like *agradecer*.

entusiasmar [entusjazmár] *t.* to captivate, excite. 2 *p.* to get excited about.

entusiasmo [entusjázmo] *m.* enthusiam, keenness.

entusiasta [entusjásta] *m.-f.* enthusiast, fan.

enumerar [enumerár] *t.* to enumerate.

envase [embáse] *m.* container. 2 bottling.

enviar [embjár] *t.* to send, dispatch.

envidia [embiðja] *f.* envy, jealousy.

envidiar [embiðjár] *t.* to envy, covet.

envidioso [embiðjóso] *a.-n.* envious, jealous.

envío [embio] *m.* sending, shipment; dispatch.

envolver [embolβér] *t.* to cover, envelop, wrap up. 2 to involve. ¶ CONJUG. like *mover*.

epidemia [epiðémja] *f.* epidemic.

episodio [episóðjo] *m.* episode; incident.

época [époka] *f.* epoch, time.

equilibrio [ekiliβrjo] *m.* balance, poise.

equipaje [ekipáxe] *m.* luggage, baggage. 2 outfit.

equipar [ekipár] *t.* to equip, fit out.

equipo [ekipo] *m.* equipment. 2 squad. 3 SPORT team.

equivaler [ekiβalér] *i.* to be equivalent; to be equal.

equivocación [ekiβoka-θjón] *f.* mistake, error.

equivocado [ekiβokáðo] *a.* mistaken. 2 wrong.

equivocarse [ekiβokárse] *p.* to be mistaken; to make a mistake; to be wrong.

erguir [eryír] *t.* to raise, erect, lift. 2 *p.* to sit up. ‖ CONJUG. INDIC. Pres.: *irgo* or *yergo, irgues* or *yergues, irgue* or *yergue;* erguimos, erguís, *irguen* or *yerguen.* ‖ Pret.: ergui, erguiste, irguió; erguimos, erguisteis, *irguieron.* ‖ SUBJ. Pres.: *irga* or *yerga, irgas* or *yergas,* etc. ‖ Imperf.: *irguiera* o *irguiese,* etc. ‖ Fut.: *irguiere, irguieres,* etc. ‖ IMPER.: *irgue* or *yergue, irga* or *yerga; irgamos* or *yergamos,* erguid, *irgan* or *yergan.* ‖ P. P.: erguido. ‖ GER.: *irguiendo.*

erizar [eriθár] *t.* to bristle. 2 *p.* to stand on end.

erizo [eríθo] *m.* hedgehog, porcupine. 2 sea-urchin.

ermita [ermíta] *f.* hermitage.

ermitaño [ermitáɲo] *m.* hermit.

errante [erránte] *a.* errant, wandering, strolling.

erróneo [erróneo] *a.* erroneous, wrong.

error [errór] *m.* error.

erudito [eruðíto] *m.-f.* scholar, learned.

esbelto [ezβélto] *a.* slender, slim, graceful.

escabroso [eskaβróso] *a.* rough, rugged. 2 harsh. 3 indecent, blue.

escala [eskála] *f.* ladder, step-ladder. 2 port of call.

escalar [eskalár] *t.* to scale, climb.

escalera [eskaléra] *f.* stair, staircase. 2 ladder.

escalón [eskalón] *m.* step, stair; rung.

escándalo [eskándalo] *m.* scandal. 2 noise.

escapar [eskapár] *i.-p.* to escape; to flee, run away.

escape [eskápe] *m.* escape, flight. 2 leak.

escarabajo [eskaraβáxo] *m.* beetle.

escarbar [eskarβár] *t.* to scratch.

escasear [eskaseár] *t.* to be scarce, fall short.

escasez [eskaséθ] *f.* lack, shortage.

escaso [eskáso] *a.* scarce, scant. 2 short.

escena [esθéna] *f.* stage. 2 scene. 3 scenery.

escenario [esθenárjo] *m.* stage; setting; scene.

esclavitud [esklaβitúð] *f.* slavery.

esclavo [eskláβo] *m.-f.* slave.

escoba [eskóβa] *f.* broom.

escoger [eskoxér] *t.* to choose, select, pick out.

escolar [eskolar] *m.* schoolboy, schoolgirl; student. 2 *a.* school: año ~, school year.

esconder [eskondér] *t.* to hide, conceal.

escondite [eskondite] *m.* hiding-place.

escopeta [eskopéta] *f.* shot-gun.

escribir [eskriβir] *t.-i.* to write.

escritor [eskritór] *m.-f.* writer, author.

escritorio [eskritórjo] *m.* writing-desk. 2 office.

escritura [eskritúra] *f.* writing; hand-writing. 2 LAW deed.

escuchar [eskutʃár] *t.* to listen to.

escudero [eskuðéro] *m.* squire.

escudo [eskúdo] *m.* shield, buckler. 2 coat of arms. 3 gold crown [coin].

escuela [eskwéla] *f.* school.

escultura [eskultúra] *f.* sculpture.

escupir [eskupir] *i.* to spit.

ese [ése] *dem. a.* that; *pl.* those.

ése [ése] *dem. pron.* that one; *pl.* those.

esencia [esénθja] *f.* essence. 2 perfume.

esencial [esenθjál] *a.* essential.

esfera [esféra] *f.* sphere. 2 rank. 3 dial.

esforzarse [esforθárse] *p.* to try hard, strive.

esfuerzo [esfwérθo] *m.* effort.

esfumarse [esfumárse] *p.* to disappear.

eslabón [ezlaβón] *m.* link.

esmerado [ezmeráðo] *a.* careful; neat.

esmeralda [ezmerálda] *f.* emerald.

esmero [ezméro] *m.* great care; neatness.

espacio [espáθjo] *m.* space. 2 room. 3 delay.

espacioso [espaθjóso] *a.* spacious, roomy.

espada [espáda] *f.* sword.

espalda [espálda] *f.* back; shoulders.

espantar [espantár] *t.* to frighten, scare. 2 *p.* to be afraid.

espanto [espánto] *m.* fright, dread.

espantoso [espantóso] *a.* frightful, dreadful.

español [espaɲól] *a.* Spanish. 2 *m.-f.* Spaniard.

esparcir [esparθír] *t.-p.* to scatter, spread. 2 *p.* to amuse oneself.

especia [espéθja] *f.* spice.

especial [espeθjál] *a.* especial. 2 special. 3 **-mente** *adv.* especially, specially.

especialidad [espeθjalidáð] *f.* speciality.

especialista [espeθjalista] *a.-n.* specialist.

especie [espéθje] *f.* kind, sort.

espectáculo [espeɣtákulo] *m.* spectacle; show. 2 scene.

espectador [espeɣtaðór] *m.-f.* spectator. 2 *pl.* audience.

espectro [espéɣtro] *m.* spectre, ghost. 2 spectrum.

espejo [espéxo] *m.* mirror, looking-glass.

esperanza [esperánθa] *f.* hope. 2 expectation.

esperar [esperár] *t.* to hope; to expect. 2 to look forward to. 3 *t.-i.* to await, wait [for].

espeso [espéso] *a.* thick.

espetar [espetár] *t.* to spit; to pierce. 2 to read.

espia [espia] *m.* *f.* spy.

espiga [espiɣa] *f.* spike, ear.

espina [espina] *f.* thorn.

espiritismo [espiritizmo] *m.* spiritism, spiritualism.

espiritista [espiritista] *m.-f.* spiritist, spiritualist.

espíritu [espíritu] *m.* spirit; soul. 2 ghost: *Espíritu Santo,* Holy Ghost. 3 courage.

espiritual [espirituál] *a.-m.* spiritual.

espléndido [espléndiðo] *a.* splendid.

esplendor [esplendór] *m.* splendour.

espolvorear [espolβoreár] *t.* to powder.

esponja [espóŋxa] *f.* sponge.

esposa [espósa] *f.* wife. 2 *pl.* handcuffs.

esposo [espóso] *m.* husband.

espuela [espwéla] *f.* spur.

espuma [espúma] *f.* foam, froth. 2 lather. 3 scum.

esqueleto [eskeléto] *m.* skeleton.

esquiar [eskjár] *i.* to ski.

esquimal [eskimál] *a.-n.* Eskimo.

esquina [eskina] *f.* corner.

estable [estáβle] *a.* steady; firm; regular.

establecer [estaβleθér] *t.* to establish. 2 to decree. 3 *p.* to settle down. ¶ Conjug. like *agradecer.*

establecimiento [estaβleθimjénto] *m.* settlement. 2 establishment, shop, store.

establo [estáβlo] *m.* stable.

estaca [estáka] *f.* stake. 2 stick, cudgel.

estación [estaθjón] *f.* season. 2 RLY. station.

estadio [estáðjo] *m.* stadium.

estado [estáðo] *m.* state, condition. 2 order, class. 3 POL. state, govern-

ment. 4 MIL. ~ *mayor,* staff.

estallar [estaʎár] *i.* to burst, explode. 2 to break out.

estambre [estámbre] *m.* worsted. 2 BOT. stamen.

estampa [estámpa] *f.* print, engraving.

estancar [estaŋkár] *t.* to stem, sta(u)nch, hold up or back. 2 *p.* to stagnate.

estancia [estánθja] *f.* stay. 2 living-room. 3 Am.) ranch, farm.

estanco [estáŋko] *m.* tobacconist's.

estanque [estáŋke] *m.* pond, reservoir.

estante [estánte] *m.* shelf.

estar [estár] *i.p.* to be; to stay, stand: ~ *quieto,* to stand still. ¶ Conjug. Indic. Pres.: *estoy, estás, está;* estamos, estáis, *están.* | Pret.: *estuve, estuviste, estuvo, etc.* ‖ Subj. Pres.: *esté, estés, esté;* estemos, estéis, *estén.* | Imperf.: *estuviera, estuvieras, etc., or estuviese, estuvieses, etc.* | Fut.: *estuviere, estuvieres, etc.* ‖ Imper.: *está, esté;* estemos, estad, *es-*

tén. ‖ P. p.: **estado.** ‖ GER.: **estando.**

estatua [estátwa] *f.* statue.

estatura [estatúra] *f.* stature, height.

estatuto [estatúto] *m.* statute, regulation.

1) **este** [éste] *m.* east.

2) **este** [éste] *dem. a.* this; *pl.* these.

éste [éste] *dem. pron.* this one; *pl.* these.

estera [estéra] *f.* mat.

estéril [estéril] *a.* sterile, barren.

estiércol [estjérkol] *m.* dung, manure.

estilo [estílo] *m.* style. 2 use.

estima [estíma] *f.* esteem, appreciation.

estimar [estimár] *t.* to esteem, hold in regard. 2 to think. 3 to value.

estimular [estimulár] *t.* to stimulate. 2 to incite, encourage.

estímulo [estímulo] *m.* stimulus. 2 encouragement.

estío [estío] *m.* summer.

estirar [estirár] *t.* to stretch, pull out. 2 *p.* to stretch out.

estómago [estómaɣo] *m.* stomach.

estorbar [estorβár] *t.* to hinder, obstruct. 2 to annoy.

estrechar [estretʃár] *t.* to narrow. 2 to take in. 3 to tighten. 4 ~ la mano, to shake hands with.

estrecho [estrétʃo] *a.* narrow. 2 tight. 3 close. 4 *m.* GEOG. strait(s.

estrella [estréʎa] *f.* star.

estrellar [estreʎár] *t.-p.* to smash, shatter.

estremecer [estremeθér] *t.-p.* to shake, shiver, shudder; to thrill. ‖ CONJUG. like *agradecer.*

estrenar [estrenár] *t.* to wear for the first time. to perform [a play] or to show [a film] for the first time.

estrépito [estrépito] *m.* noise, din.

estribar [estriβár] *i.* to rest on; to lie on.

estribo [estríβo] *c.* stirrup.

estricto [estríkto] *a.* strict; severe.

estrofa [estrófa] *f.* strophe, stanza.

estropear [estropeár] *t.* to spoil, ruin, damage. 2 *p.* to get spoiled, ruined.

estructura [estruɣtúra] f. structure.

estruendo [estrwéndo] m. clangour, crash. 2 uproar.

estuche [estútʃe] m. case, sheath, container.

estudiante [estuðjánte] m. student.

estudiar [estuðjár] t. to study. 2 i. to be a student.

estudio [estúðjo] m. study. 2 studio. 3 pl. learning.

estudioso [estuðjóso] a. studious.

estufa [estúfa] f. stove, heater: ~ eléctrica, electric fire.

estúpido [estúpiðo] a.-n. stupid.

etcétera [etθétera] f. etcetera, and so on.

eternamente [etérnaménte] adv. eternally.

eternidad [eterniðáð] f. eternity.

eterno [etérno] a. eternal.

etiqueta [etikéta] f. label. 2 formality.

eucalipto [eukalípto] m. eucalyptus.

europeo [európéo] a.-n. European.

evadir [eβaðir] t. to evade, elude. 2 p. to escape, break out.

evangélico [eβaŋxéliko] a. evangelical.

evangelio [eβaŋxéljo] m. gospel.

evaporar [eβaporár] t.-p. to evaporate.

evidencia [eβiðénθja] f. evidence.

evidente [eβiðénte] a. evident, obvious.

evitar [eβitár] t. to avoid, elude, shun. 2 to prevent.

exactamente [esáytaménte] adv. exactly.

exactitud [esaytitúð] f. exactness, accuracy.

exacto [esáyto] a. exact, accurate. 2 adv. right.

exaltar [eɣsaltár] t. to praise. 2 p. to become excited.

examen [eɣsámen] m. examination. 2 investigation.

examinar [eɣsaminár] t. to examine. 2 to look into. 3 p. to sit for an examination.

exceder [esθeðér] t. to exceed, surpass, outdo.

excelente [esθelénte] a. excellent.

excelso [eɣθélso] a. sublime, exalted.

excepción [esθeβθjón] *f.*
exception.

excepto [esθéβto] *adv.*
except, save.

exceptuar [esθeβtuár] *t.*
to except, leave out.

excesivo [esθesíβo] *a.*
excessive, too much.

exceso [esθéso] *m.* excess. 2 intemperance.

excitar [esθitár] *t.* to
excite. 2 *p.* to get ex-
cited.

exclamar [esklamár] *i.*
to exclaim, cry out.

excluir [eskluír] *t.* to
exclude. ¶ CONJUG. like
huir.

exclusivamente [esklusí-
βaménte] *adv.* exclus-
ively.

exclusivo [esklusíβo] *a.*
exclusive, sole.

excursión [eskursjón] *f.*
excursion, trip, tour.

excusa [eskúsa] *f.* excuse, apology.

exhibir [eγsiβír] *t.* to
exhibit, show. 2 *p.* to
show off.

exigir [eγsixír] *t.* to
require, demand.

existencia [eγsisténθja]
f. existence. 2 life. 3 *pl.*
stocks.

existir [eγsistír] *i.* to
exist, be.

éxito [éγsito] *m.* issue.
2 success.

expansión [espansjón] *f.*
expansion. 2 effusion. 3
relaxation.

expedición [espeðiθjón]
f. expedition. 2 dispatch.

experiencia [esperjénθja]
f. experience.

experimentar [esperimen-
tár] *t.* to experiment,
try, test. 2 to experience,
undergo.

experto [espérto] *a.* skilful. 2 *m.* expert.

expiación [espjaθjón] *f.*
expiation.

explicación [esplikaθjón]
f. explanation.

explicar [esplikár] *t.* to
explain, lecture on, teach.

explorador [esploraðór]
m. f. explorer; pioneer
2 boy scout.

explorar [esplorár] *t.* to
explore.

explosión [esplosjón] *f.*
explosion; outburst.

explotar [esplotár] *t.* to
exploit. 2 to explode.

exponer [esponér] *t.* to
explain, state. 2 to ex-
pose, show. 3 to exhibit.

exportación [esportaθjón]
f. exportation, export.

exportar [esportár] *t.* to
export.

exposición [esposiθjón]
f. exposition. 2 exhibition, show.

expresar [espresár] *t.-*
p. to express.

expresión [espresjón] *f.*
expression.

expresivo [espresíβo] *a.*
expressive. 2 kind.

expreso [espréso] *a.* expressed. 2 clear. 3 *m.*
RLY. express train.

expuesto [espuésto] *a.*
exposed. 2 exhibited. 3
dangerous. 4 liable.

expulsar [espulsár] *t.* to
expel, drive out.

exquisito [eskisíto] *a.*
exquisite.

extender [estendér] *t.*
to spread out. 2 to
stretch out. ¶ CONJUG.
like *entender*.

extensión [estensjón] *f.*
extension. 2 range. 3
expanse, stretch.

extenso [esténso] *a.* extensive, vast, spacious.

exterior [esterjór] *a.* exterior, outer. 2 foreign.
3 *m.* outside. 4 appear-

ance. 5 **-mente** externally.

exterminar [esterminár]
to exterminate.

extinguir [estiŋgír] *t.* to
extinguish, quench, put
out. 2 *p.* to go out.

extraer [estraér] *t.* to
extract, draw out.

extranjero [estraŋxéro]
a. foreing. 2 *m.-f.*
alien, foreigner: *al* or
en el ~, abroad.

extrañar [estrapár] *t.*
to surprise. 2 (Am.) to
miss. 3 *p.* to be suprised,
wonder.

extraño [estrápo] *a.*
foreign. 2 strange, peculiar.

extraordinario [estraorðinárjo] *a.* extraordinary,
uncommon.

extraviar [estraβjár] *t.*
to mislay. 2 *p.* to stray,
get lost.

extremidad [estremiðáð]
f. extremity, end, border. 3 *pl.* extremities.

extremo [estrémo] *a.* extreme, farthest. 2 excessive.

F

fábrica [fáβrika] *f.* factory, works, plant, mill.

fabricación [faβrikaθjón] *f.* manufacture.

fabricante [faβrikánte] *m.* manufacturer.

fabricar [faβrikár] *t.* to make, manufacture.

fábula [fáβula] *f.* fable.

fácil [fáθil] *a.* easy. 2 **-mente** *adv.* easily.

facilidad [faθiliðáð] *f.* facility; fluency.

facilitar [faθilitár] *t.* to make easy, facilitate.

factor [faγtór] *m.* cause. 2 RLY. luggage clerk. 3 MATH. factor.

factoría [faγtoría] *f.* agency. 2 trading post.

facultad [fakultáð] *f.* faculty. 2 power. 3 ability. 4 *pl.* mental powers.

faena [faéna] *f.* work, toil. 2 task, job, *chore.

faja [fáxa] *f.* scarf. 2 wrapper. 3 stripe, band.

fajar [faxár] *t.* to band, girdle, wrap up.

falda [fálda] *f.* skirt. 2 lap. 3 foothill, slope.

falso [fálso] *a.* false. 2 untrue. 3 sham. 4 treacherous. 6 counterfeit [money].

falta [fálta] *f.* lack, want, shortage: *a ~ de*, for want of. 2 fault. 3 misdeed. 4 mistake. 5 *hacer ~*, to be necessary.

faltar [faltár] *i.* to be lacking, wanting or missing. 2 to be absent. 3 to offend. 4 to break [one's word].

falto [fálto] *a.* wanting, short.

fallar [faʎár] *t.* to pass sentence. 2 to trump [at cards]. 3 *i.* to fail, miss.

fallecer [faʎeθér] *i.* to expire, decease, die. ¶ CONJUG. like *agradecer*.

fama [fáma] *f.* fame, renown. 2 rumour.

familia [famílja] *f.* family. 2 household.

familiar [familjár] *a.* informal. 2 colloquial. 3 *m.* relative.

famoso [famóso] *a.* famous, renowned.

fanático [fanátiko] *a.* fanatic(al. 2 *m.-f.* fanatic, fan, bigot.

fango [fáŋgo] *m.* mud.

fantasía [fantasía] *f.* fancy, imagination.

fantasma [fantázma] *m.* phantom. 2 ghost.

fantástico [fantástiko] *a.* fantastic, fanciful.

fariseo [fariséo] *m.* pharisee; hypocrite.

farmacéutico [farmaθéŭtiko] *m.-f.* chemist, pharmacist.

farmacia [farmáθja] *f.* pharmacy. 2 chemist's [shop], *drugstore.

faro [fáro] *m.* lighthouse. 2 headlight.

farol [faról] *m.* street lamp, lamp-post.

fase [fáse] *f.* phase, aspect, stage.

fatal [fatál] *a.* fatal. 2 bad, deadly.

fatiga [fatíɣa] *f.* fatigue, weariness. 2 *pl.* hardships.

fatigar [fatiɣár] *t.* to fatigue, weary, tire. 2 *p.* to get tired.

favor [faβór] *m.* help, aid. 2 favo(u)r: *por ~,* please.

favorable [faβoráβle] *a.* favo(u)rable. 2 advantageous. 3 **-mente** *adv.* favo(u)rably.

favorecer [faβoreθér] *t.* to help, aid, favo(u)r. ¶ CONJUG. like *agradecer.*

favorito [faβorito] *a.-n.* favo(u)rite.

faz [faθ] *f.* face, visage.

fe [fe] *f.* faith: *dar ~,* to believe. 2 ~ *de bautismo,* cerfificate of baptism.

febrero [feβréro] *m.* February.

fecundo [fekúndo] *a.* fruitful, fertile.

fecha [fétʃa] *f.* date. 2 day.

federal [feðerál] *a.* federal.

felicidad [feliθiðáð] *f.* happiness. 2 *pl.* congratulations!

felicitación [feliθitaθjón] *f.* congratulation.

felicitar [feliθitár] *t.* to congratulate.

feliz [feliθ] *a.* happy, lucky. 2 **-mente** *adv.* happily.

femenino [femeníno] *a.* femenine.

fenómeno [fenómeno] *m.* phenomenon. 2 monster, freak.

feo [féo] *a.* ugly.

feria [férja] *f.* fair: ~ de muestras, trade exhibition or show.

feroz [feróθ] *a.* ferocious. 2 wild, fierce, savage.

ferretería [ferretería] *f.* hardware. 2 ironmonger's [shop].

ferrocarril [ferrokarríl] *m.* railway, *railroad.

fértil [fértil] *a.* fertile.

fertilizar [fertiliθár] *t.* to fertilize.

ferviente [ferβjénte] *a.* FERVOROSO.

fervor [ferβór] *m.* fervour, zeal, warmth.

fervoroso [ferβoróso] *a.* fervent; devout, zealous.

festejar [festexár] *t.* to celebrate. 2 to feast.

festín [festín] *m.* feast, banquet.

festivo [festíβo] *a.* festive, gay. 2 día ~, holiday, 3 witty, humorous.

fianza [fiánθa] *f.* bail, security. 2 guarantee.

fiar [fiár] *t.* to answer for. 2 *t.-i.* to sell on credit. 3 *p.* to trust.

fibra [fíβra] *f.* fibre; staple.

fidelidad [fiðeliðáð] *f.* fidelity, faithfulness.

fideos [fiðéos] *m. pl.* vermicelli, noodles.

fiebre [fjéβre] *f.* fever. 2 excitement.

fiel [fjél] *a.* faithful. 2 *m.* faithful. 3 pointer. 4 **-mente** *adv.* faithfully.

fiera [fjéra] *f.* wild beast or animal.

fiero [fjéro] *a.* fierce, ferocious. 2 wild [beast].

fiesta [fjésta] *f.* feast, entertainment, party; public rejoicing. 2 holiday. 3 endearment.

figura [fiɣúra] *f.* figure, shape.

figurar [fiɣurár] *t.* to figure, shape. 2 *i.* to be counted [among]. 3 *p.* to fancy.

fijar [fixár] *t.* to fix, fasten. 2 to stick. 3 to

set. 4 p. to settle; to pay attention.

fijo [fíxo] a. fixed. 2 firm, steady, set. 3 fast [colour].

fila [fíla] f. row, line; file: en ~, in a row.

filosofía [filosofía] f. philosophy.

filósofo [filósofo] a. philosophic. 2 m.-f. philosopher.

filtro [fíltro] m. filter, strainer.

fin [fin] m. end: poner ~ a, to put an end to; al ~, at the end; finally; por ~, at last. 2 aim, purpose: a ~ de [que], in order to, to.

final [finál] a. final, last. 2 m. end. 3 **-mente** adv. finally.

finalizar [finaliθár] t.-i. to end, finish.

finca [fínka] f. property, land, house, real estate.

fingir [finxír] t. to feign, simulate, sham. 2 p. to pretend to be.

fino [fíno] a. fine. 2 thin. 3 polite. 4 sharp.

firma [fírma] f. signature. 2 signing. 3 firm.

firmamento [firmaménto] m. sky, firmament.

firmar [firmár] t. to sign, subscribe.

firme [fírme] a. firm, strong, steady.

fiscal [fiskál] m. public prosecutor, *district attorney.

física [física] f. physics.

físico [físiko] a. physical. 2 m. physicist. 3 looks.

flaco [fláko] a. lean, thin. 2 weak.

flauta [fláuta] f. flute.

flecha [flétʃa] f. arrow.

flexible [fleɣsíβle] a. flexible, pliant, supple.

flojo [flóxo] a. slack. 2 weak. 3 lax.

flor [flor] f. flower, blossom.

florecer [floreθér] i. to flower, blossom. ¶ Conjug. like agradecer.

florero [floréro] m. flower vase.

florido [floríðo] a. a-bloom, flowery.

flota [flóta] f. fleet.

flotar [flotár] i. to float.

fluido [flwíðo] a.-m. fluid. 2 a. fluent.

foco [fóko] m. focus, centre. 2 headlight, spotlight.

fogón [foɣón] m. hearth. 2 cooking-range.

follaje [foʎáxe] m. foliage.

fomentar [fomentár] t. to promote, encourage.

fomento [foménto] m. fostering; encouragement.

fonda [fónda] f. inn.

fondo [fóndo] m. bottom. 2 depth. 3 farthest end. 4 background. 5 nature. 6 s. pl. funds

forma [fórma] f. form, shape.

formación [formaθjón] f. formation. 2 shape.

formal [formál] a. formal. 2 serious.

formar [formár] t. to form, shape.

formidable [formiðáβle] a. formidable, fearful.

fórmula [fórmula] f. 2 recipe. 3 prescription.

formular [formulár] t. to formulate, make out.

foro [fóro] m. forum. 2 bar. 3 back-stage.

forrar [forrár] t. to line. 2 to cover [a book].

forro [fórro] m. lining; book-cover.

fortalecer [fortaleθér] t. to strengthen. 2 p. to grow strong. ¶ CONJUG. like agradecer.

fortaleza [fortaléθa] f. fortitude. 2 vigour. 3 fortress.

fortuna [fortúna] f. fortune, chance, luck. 2 wealth.

fósforo [fósforo] m. phosphorus. 2 match.

fósil [fósil] a.-m. fossil.

fotografía [fotoɣrafía] f. photography. 2 photograph.

fotógrafo [fotóɣrafo] m. photographer.

fracasar [frakasár] i. to fail, be unsuccessful.

fracaso [frakáso] m. failure, collapse.

fracción [fraɣθjón] f. fraction.

fragancia [fraɣánθja] f. fragrance.

fragante [fraɣánte] a. fragrant, scented.

frágil [fráxil] a. fragile, brittle. 2 frail.

fragmento [fraɣménto] m. fragment, piece, bit.

fraile [fráile] m. friar.

francés [franθés] a. French. 2 m. Frenchman. 3 f. Frenchwoman.

franco [fránko] a. frank, open. 2 generous. 3 free. 4 m. franc.

franja [fránxa] f. band; stripe. 2 stripe.

frasco [frásko] m. bottle, flask, vial.

frase [fráse] f. phrase, sentence.

fraternidad [fraterniðáð] *f.* brotherhood, fraternity.

fray [fraĭ] *m.* brother.

frecuencia [frekwénθja] *f.* frequency: con ~, frequently.

frecuente [frekwénte] *a.* frequent. 2 **-mente** *adv.* frequently, often.

fregadero [freɣaðéro] *m.* kitchen sink.

fregar [freɣár] *t.* to rub, scrub. 2 to mop [the floor]; to wash up [dishes]. ¶ CONJUG. like *acertar*.

freir [freír] *t.* to fry. ¶ CONJUG. like *reir*.

freno [fréno] *m.* bridle. 2 brake. 3 control, restraint.

frente [frénte] *f.* forehead; face: *hacer ~ a*, to face, meet. 2 *m.* front: ~ *a*, in front of; *en ~*, opposite.

fresa [frésa] *f.* strawberry.

fresco [frésko] *a.* cool, fresh. 2 cheeky. 3 *m.* cool air: *hacer ~*, to be cool. 4 PAINT. fresco.

frio [frío] *a.* cold. 2 cool, calm. 3 *m.* cold, coldness: *hace ~*, it is cold.

frondoso [frondóso] *a.* leafy, luxuriant.

frontera [frontéra] *f.* frontier, border.

frotar [frotár] *t.* to rub, scour, strike.

fruta [frúta] *f.* fruit.

frutal [frutál] *a.* fruit-bearing. 2 *m.* fruit tree.

frutero [frutéro] *m.-f.* fruiterer. 2 *m.* fruit-dish.

fruto [frúto] *m.* fruit.

fuego [fwéɣo] *m.* fire.

fuente [fwénte] *f.* spring; fountain. 2 dish.

fuera [fwéra] *adv.* out [of], outside, with-out.

fuerte [fwérte] *a.* strong. 2 healthy. 3 loud [voice]. 4 *m.* fortress. 5 **-mente** *adv.* strongly.

fuerza [fwérθa] *f.* strength, force, power. 2 violence. 3 vigour. 4 *sing.-pl.* MIL. force(s).

fuga [fúɣa] *f.* flight, escape. 2 leak.

fugarse [fuɣárse] *p.* to flee, escape.

fugaz [fuɣáθ] *a.* fugitive.

fulgor [fulɣór] *m.* brilliancy, glow.

fumar [fumár] *t.-i.* to smoke.

función [funθjón] *f.* function. 2 show, performance.

funcionamiento [funθjonamjénto] *m.* functioning, working, operation.

funcionar [funθjonár] *i.* to function, work.

funcionario [funθjonárjo] *m.* civil servant, official.

funda [fúnda] *f.* case, sheath, cover.

fundación [fundaθjón] *f.* foundation.

fundador [fundaðór] *m.-f.* founder.

fundamental [fundamentál] *a.* fundamental, essential. 2 **-mente** *adv.* basically.

fundamento [fundaménto] *m.* foundation. 2 ground.

fundar [fundár] *t.* to found, establish, base, ground.

fundición [fundiθjón] *f.* melting. 2 foundry.

fundir [fundír] *t.* to fuse, melt. 2 to found, cast.

furia [fúrja] *f.* fury, rage, violence. 2 speed.

furioso [furjóso] *a.* furious, angry, raging, frantic.

furor [furór] *m.* fury, rage; frenzy; passion.

fusil [fusil] *m.* rifle, gun.

fútbol [fúðβol] *m.* football.

futuro [futúro] *a.* future. 2 *m.* future [tense; time].

G

gabán [gaβán] *m.* overcoat, topcoat.

gabinete [gaβinéte] *m.* private room. 2 study. 3 cabinet.

gala [gála] *f.* best dress. 2 grace. 3 finery.

galán [galán] *a.* lover. 2 THEAT. leading man.

galardón [galarðón] *m.* reward, recompense.

galería [galería] *f.* gallery; corridor.

galés [galés] *a.* Welsh. 2 *n* Welshman.

galón [galón] *m.* braid. 2 MIL. stripe. 3 gallon.

gallardo [gaʎárðo] *a.* elegant. 2 brave.

gallego [gaʎéyo] *a.-n.* Galician.

galleta [gaʎéta] *f.* biscuit, cooky.

gallina [gaʎína] *f.* hen.

gallo [gáʎo] *m.* cock, rooster.

gana [gána] *f.* appetite, desire, will: *tener ganas de*, to wish, feel like; *de buena ~*, willingly; *de mala ~*, reluctantly.

ganadería [ganaðería] *f.* cattle raising, stockbreeding. 2 live-stock.

ganado [ganáðo] *m.* stock, livestock, cattle.

ganador [ganaðór] *m. f.* winner.

ganancia [ganánθja] *f.* gain, profit.

ganar [ganár] *t.-p.* to gain, earn, win. 2 to beat. 3 *i.* to improve.

gancho [gántʃo] *m.* hook, crook.

gandul [gandúl] *a.* idle.
2 *m.-f.* idler.

ganga [gánga] *f.* MIN.
gangue. 2 bargain.

ganso [gánso] *m.* goose,
gander.

garaje [garáxe] *m.* garage.

garantía [garantía] *f.*
guarantee, pledge, secu-
rity.

garantizar [garantiθár]
t. to guarantee. 2 to
warrant. 3 to vouch for.

garganta [garɣánta] *f.*
throat. 2 ravine.

garra [gárra] *f.* paw,
claw; talon. 2 *fig.*
clutch.

garza [gárθa] *f.* heron.

gas [gas] *m.* gas. 2 gaslight.

gasa [gása] *f.* gauze,
chiffon.

gaseoso [gaseóso] *a.* gas-
eous.

gasolina [gasolína] *f.*
gasoline, petrol, *gas.

gastar [gastár] *t.* to
spend. 2 to use, wear.
3 to waste. 4 *p.* to wear
out.

gasto [gásto] *m.* expense. 2 *pl.* expenses,
costs.

gato [gáto] *m.* cat, tom-
-cat. 2 *f.* she-cat: *a*

gatas, on all fours. 3
lifting jack.

gaveta [gaβéta] *f.* drawer, till.

gavilán [gaβilán] *m.*
sparrow hawk.

gemelo [xemélo] *a.-n.*
twin. 2 *m. pl.* cuff-
-links. 3 binoculars.

gemir [xemír] *i.* to
moan, groan. ¶ CONJUG.
like *servir*.

generación [xeneraθjón]
f. generation.

general [xenerál] *a.* general: *en ~, por lo ~*,
in general. 2 common.
3 *m.* MIL. general.

género [xénero] *m.* kind,
sort. 2 race. 3 GRAM.
gender. 4 BIOL., LOG.
genus. 5 F. ARTS., LIT.
genre. 6 COM. cloth,
goods.

generoso [xeneróso] *a.*
generous, liberal.

genio [xénjo] *m.* temper.
2 temperament. 3 genius.

gente [xénte] *f.* people,
folk; nation; men.

gentil [xentíl] *a.-n.* gen-
tile. 2 *a.* courteous,
graceful.

genuino [xenuíno] *a.*
genuine, true.

geografía [xeoɣrafía] *f.*
geography.

geográfico [xeoɣráfiko] *a.* geographic(al.

gerente [xerénte] *m.* manager.

germen [xérmen] *m.* germ. 2 origin.

gestión [xestjón] *f.* negotiation, conduct, management.

gestionar [xestjonár] *t.* to take steps to; to manage.

gesto [xésto] *m.* gesture: *hacer gestos a,* to make faces at.

gigante [xiɣánte] *m.* giant. 2 *f.* giantess.

gimnasio [ximnásjo] *m.* gymnasium, gym.

girar [xirár] *i.* to gyrate, revolve, whirl, spin. 2 *t.-i.* to draw.

girasol [xirasól] *m.* BOT. sunflower.

giro [xíro] *m.* revolution, turn. 2 course, trend. 3 COM. draft; ~ *postal,* money order. 4 COM. trade.

gitano [xitáno] *a.-n.* gypsy.

globo [glóβo] *m.* globe, sphere. 2 world. 3 balloon.

gloria [glórja] *f.* glory. 2 heaven. 3 delight.

gloriarse [glorjárse] *p.*

to boast of; to glory in.

glorificar [glorifikár] *t.* to glorify. 2 *p.* GLORIARSE.

glorioso [glorjóso] *a.* glorious.

gobernador [goβernaðór] *m.* governor, ruler, governor, ruler.

gobernar [goβernár] *t.-i.* to govern, rule. 2 *t.* to lead. 3 to steer ¶ CONJUG. like *acertar.*

gobierno [goβjérno] *m.* government, cabinet, administration. 2 control, management.

golondrina [golondrína] *f.* swallow.

golpe [gólpe] *m.* blow, strike, beat, hit, knock. coup d'état; *de* ~, suddenly.

golpear [golpeár] *t.-i.* to strike, beat, hit, knock.

goma [góma] *f.* gum, rubber. 2 eraser.

gordo [górðo] *a.* fat, stout. 2 thick.

gorra [górra] *f.* cap, bonnet.

gorrión [gorrjón] *m.* sparrow.

gorro [górro] *m.* cap.

gota [góta] *f.* drop. 2 MED. gout.

gozar [goθár] *t.-i.* to

enjoy, have. 2 p. to rejoice.

gozo [góθo] m. joy, delight, pleasure.

gozoso [goθóso] a. joyful, delighted.

grabado [graβáðo] a. engraved, stamped. 2 m. engraving, print. picture.

gracia [gráθja] f. gracefulness. 2 charm. 3 kindness. 4 elegance. 5 joke, wittiness. 6 *tener ~*, to be funny; *¡gracias!*, thank you.

gracioso [graθjóso] a. graceful, charming. 2 gracious. 3 witty. 4 funny. 5 m.-f. THEAT. fool.

grado [gráðo] m. step. 2 degree. 3 grade. 4 rank, class.

graduación [graðwaθjón] f. graduation, grading. 2 strength. 3 MIL. rank. 4 admission to a degree.

graduar [graðuár] t. to graduate. 2 to gauge, measure. 3 p. to take a degree.

gramo [grámo] m. gramme.

granada [granáða] f. BOT. pomegranate. 2 handgrenade, shell.

gran, grande [gran, gránde] a. large, big; great, grand.

grandeza [grandéθa] f. bigness. 2 greatness, grandeur.

grandioso [grandjóso] a. grand, magnificent.

granero [granéro] m. granary, barn.

granizo [graníθo] m. hail; hailstorm.

granja [gránxa] f. farm. 2 dairy.

grano [gráno] m. grain. 2 seed. 3 grape, corn. 4 pimple. 5 *ir al ~*, to come to the point.

grasa [grása] f. grease, fat, suet.

gratis [grátis] adv. gratis, free.

gratitud [gratitúð] f. gratitude gratefulness.

grato [gráto] a. pleasant. 2 grave, weighty, serious. 3 difficult.

grave [gráβe] a. heavy. 2 grave, weighty, serious. 3 difficult.

gravedad [graβeðáð] f. gravity. 2 seriousness.

griego [grjéɣo] a.-n. Greek.

grillo [gríʎo] m. cricket. 2 sprout. 3 pl. fetters.

gris [gris] a. grey.

gritar [gritár] i.-t. to shout, cry out, scream.

grito [gríto] *m.* shout; cry, hoot.

grosero [groséro] *a.* coarse. 2 rude. 3 *m.-f.* boor.

grúa [grúa] *f.* crane, derrick.

grueso [grwéso] *a.* thick. 2 fat, stout. 3 big. 4 *m.* bulk. 5 main body. 6 thickness.

grupo [grúpo] *m.* group, cluster. 2 set, assembly.

guante [gwánte] *m.* glove.

guapo [gwápo] *a.* handsome, good-looking.

guardar [gwaröár] *t.* to keep, watch over. 2 to lay up, store. 3 to observe. 4 *p.* to keep from.

guardia [gwáröja] *f.* guard: ~ *urbano*, policeman. 2 defense. 3 *estar de* ~, to be on duty.

guardián [gwaröján] *m.-f.* guardian, watchman.

guerra [gérra] *f.* war, warfare.

guerrear [gerreár] *i.* to wage war against, fight.

guerrero [gerréro] *m.-f.* warrior, soldier.

guía [gía] *m.-f.* guide, leader. 2 guide-book. 3 ~ *de teléfonos*, directory.

guiar [giár] *t.* to guide, lead. 2 to drive, steer. 3 AER. to pilot.

guirnalda [girnálda] *f.* garland, wreath.

guisante [gisánte] *m.* pea, sweet pea.

guisar [gisár] *t.* to cook.

guitarra [gitárra] *f.* guitar.

gusano [gusáno] *m.* worm; caterpillar. 2 silkworm.

gustar [gustár] *t.* to taste. 2 to please. 3 to like: *me gusta*, I like.

gusto [gústo] *m.* taste. 2 flavour. 3 pleasure: *con mucho* ~, with pleasure.

gustoso [gustóso] *a.* tasty. 2 pleasant. 3 glad.

H

haba [áβa] *f.* (broad) bean.

haber [aβér] *t. aux.* to have. 2 (with *de*) to have to, must. 3 *impers.* hay, there is, there are. 4 (with *que*) it is necessary. 5 *cinco dias ha*, five days ago. ¶ Conjug. Indic. Pres.: *he, has, ha* or *hay; hemos* or *habemos, habéis, han.* | Imperf.: *habia, habías,* etc. | Pret.: *hube, hubiste,* etc. | Fut.: *habré, habrás,* etc. | Cond.: *habria, habrias,* etc. ‖ Subj. Pres.: *haya, hayas,* etc. | Imperf.: *hubiera, hubieras,* etc., or *hubiese, hubieses,* etc. | Fut.: *hubiere, hubieres,* etc. ‖ Imper.: *he, haya; ha-*
yamos, habed, hayan. ‖ Past. p.: habido. ‖ Ger.: habiendo.

habichuela [aβitʃwéla] *f.* kidney bean, French bean.

hábil [áβil] *a.* skilful, clever. 2 **-mente** *adv.* skilfully.

habilidad [aβiliðáð] *f.* ability, skill, cleverness.

habitación [aβitaθión] *f.* room.

habitante [aβitánte] *m.-f.* inhabitant; tenant.

habitar [aβitár] *t.-i.* to inhabit; to dwell, live.

hábito [áβito] *m.* habit, custom. 2 habit [of monk].

habitual [aβituál] *a.* habitual, customary.

hablador [aβlaðór] *a.* talkative. 2 *m.-f.* chatterer.

hablar [aβlár] *i.* to speak [to], talk [to, with].

Hacedor [aθeðór] *m.* Maker.

hacer [aθér] *t.* to make [create, build]. 2 to do [perform, carry out]. 3 3 ~ *bien* o *mal*, to do it rightly, wrongly; ~ *burla de*, to mock; ~ *caso*, to pay attention; ~ *daño*, to hurt; ~ *pedazos*, to break to pieces; ~ *preguntas*, to ask questions. 4 *i.* no *hace al caso*, it is irrelevant; ~ *de*, to act as a [chairman]. 5 *p.* to become, grow: *me hice limpiar los zapatos*, I had my shoes cleaned. 6 impers. *hace frío*, it's cold; *hace tres días*, three days ago; *hace un año que no le veo*, it's a year since I saw him; *se hace tarde*, it's getting late. ‖ Conjug. Indic. Pres.: *hago*, *haces*, etc. ‖ Imperf.: *hacía*, *hacías*, etc. ‖ Pret.: *hice*, *hiciste*, etc. ‖ Fut.: *haré*, *harás*, etc. ‖ Conjug.: *haría*, *harías*, etc. ‖ Subj. Pres.: *haga*, *hagas*, etc. ‖ Imperf.: *hiciera*, *hi-* cieras, etc., or *hiciese*, *hicieses*, etc. | Fut.: *hiciere*, *hicieres*, etc. ‖ *haz*, *haga*; *hagamos*, ha-ced, *hagan*. ‖ Past. p.: *hecho*. ‖ Ger.: ha-ciendo.

hacia [áθja] *prep.* toward(s, to, for): ~ *adelante*, forwards; ~ *atrás*, backwards.

hacienda [aθjénda] *f.* farm. 2 (Am.) ranch. 3 property: ~ *pública*, Treasury, Exchequer.

hacha [átʃa] *f.* axe, hatchet. 2 torch.

hada [áða] *f.* fairy.

hallar [aʎár] *t.* to find, come across, meet with. 2 to find out, discover. 3 to think. 5 *p.* to be [present].

hamaca [amáka] *f.* hammock, swing.

hambre [ámbre] *f.* hunger, starvation, famine: *tener* ~, to be hungry.

hambriento [ambrjénto] *a.* hungry. 2 greedy.

harina [arína] *f.* flour, meal, powder.

hartar [artár] *t.* to satiate, glut. 2 to fill up. 3 to tire, sicken. 4 *p.* to become fed up [with].

harto [árto] *a.* satiated. 2 tired, sick; fed up [with].

hasta [ásta] *prep.* till, until; to, as far as; ~ *ahora*, till now; ~ *aquí*, so far; ~ *luego*, goodbye, see you later.

hazaña [aθáɲa] *f.* deed, exploit, achievement.

he [e] *adv. heme aquí*, here I am.

hebilla [eβíʎa] *f.* buckle, clasp.

hebra [éβra] *f.* thread. 2 fibre, staple. 3 filament.

hectárea [eɣtárea] *f.* hectare.

hecho [étʃo] *p. p.* made, done. 2 grown. 3 ready- -made. 4 used. 5 *m.* fact. 6 happening. 7 act, feat.

helada [eláða] *f.* frost.

helado [eláðo] *a.* frozen. 2 frost-bitten. 3 cold. 4 *m.* ice-cream.

helar [elár] *t.* to freeze. 2 to frostbite. ¶ CON-JUG. like *acertar*.

hembra [émbra] *f.* female. 2 MEC. nut.

henchir [entʃír] *t.* to fill, stuff. 2 to swell. 3 *p.* to be filled. ¶ CON-JUG. like *servir*.

hender [endér] *t.-p.* to cleave, split, slit, crack.

¶ CONJUG. like *entender*.

heredar [ereðár] *t.* to inherit.

heredero [ereðéro] *m.-f.* inheritor. 2 *m.* heir. 3 *f.* heiress.

herencia [erénθja] *f.-f.* inheritance. 2 heredity.

herida [eríða] *f.* wound, injury.

herido [eríðo] *a.* wound- ed, injured, hurt.

herir [erír] *t.* to wound, injure, hurt. 2 to of-fend. 3 to strike, hit. ¶ CONJUG. like *servir*.

hermano [ermáno] *m.* brother: ~ *político*, brother-in-law; *primo* ~, cousin german.

hermoso [ermóso] *a.* beautiful, fair, lovely. 2 handsome, good-looking.

hermosura [ermosúra] *a.* beauty, fairness.

héroe [éroe] *m.* hero.

heroico [eróiko] *a.* her-oic.

heroismo [eroizmo] *m.* heroism.

herramienta [erramjén-ta] *f.* tool, implement.

hervir [erβir] *i.* to boil. 2 to bubble. 3 to swarm. ¶ CONJUG. INDIC. Pres.: *hiervo, hierves, hierve;*

hervimos, hervís, *hierven*. | Pret.: herví, herviste, *hirvió;* hervimos, hervisteis, *hirvieron*. || Subj. Pres.: *hierva, hiervas, hierva; hirvamos, hirvais, hiervan*. | Imperf.: *hirviera, hirvieras*, etc., or *hirviese, hirvieses*, etc. | Fut.: *hirviere, hirvieres*, etc. || Imper.: *hierve, hierva; hirvamos, hervid, hiervan*. || Past. p.: hervido. || Ger.: *hirviendo*.

hielo [jélo] *m.* ice. 2 frost. 3 coldness.

hierba [jérβa] *f.* grass.

hierro [jérro] *m.* iron.

hígado [íγaðo] *m.* liver.

higiénico [ixjéniko] *a.* sanitary, hygienic.

higo [íγo] *m.* fig.

hijo [íxo] *m.-f.* child; *m.* son; *f.* daughter: *hijo político*, son-in-law; *hija política*, daughter--in-law.

hilar [ilár] *t.* to spin.

hilera [iléra] *f.* file, row.

hilo [ílo] *m.* thread. 2 yarn. 3 wire.

himno [ímno] *m.* hymn: ~ *nacional*, national anthem.

hincar [iŋkár] *t.* to drive [in], thrust [in]: ~ *el diente*, to bite. 2 *p.* ~ *de rodillas*, to kneel down.

hinchar [intʃár] *t.* to swell; to blow up, pump up.

hipnotizar [iβnotiθár] *t.* to hypnotize.

hipódromo [ipóðromo] *m.* race-track, race-course.

hipoteca [ipotéka] *f.* mortgage.

hipotético [ipotétiko] *a.* hypothetic(al.

hispánico [ispániko] *a.* Spanish.

hispanoamericano [ispanoamerikáno] *a.* Spanish-American.

historia [istórja] *f.* history.

historiador [istorjaðór] *m.-f.* historian.

histórico [istóriko] *a.* historic(al.

hocico [oθíko] *m.* snout, muzzle, nose.

hogar [oγár] *m.* fireplace, hearth. 2 home.

hoguera [oγéra] *f.* bonfire, fire, blaze.

hoja [óxa] *f.* leaf [of tree, etc.]; blade [of grass, etc.]; petal. sheet [of paper]. 3 foil, pane [of metal]; ~ *de* afeitar, razor blade. 4 shutter.

¡hola! [óla] *interj.* hello!, hullo!, hey!, I say!

holandés [olandés] *a.* Dutch. 2 *m.* Dutchman.

holgazán [olɣaθán] *a.* idle, lazy.

hombre [ómbre] *m.* man [male; human bieng; mankind]. 2 husband.

hombro [ómbro] *m.* shoulder.

homenaje [omenáxe] *m.* homage. derer.

hondamente [óndaménte] *adv.* deeply.

hondo [óndo] *a.* deep, profound. 2 *m.* depth, bottom.

honesto [onésto] *a.* chaste. 2 honest, decent.

honor [onór] *m.* honour. 2 honesty. 3 *pl.* honours (civilties).

honorable [onoráβle] *a.* honourable.

honra [ónrra] *f.* honour, dignity.

honrado [onrráðo] *a.* honest, upright, fair, just.

honrar [onrrár] *t.* to honour. 2 *p.* to be proud of.

hora [óra] *f.* hour; time: ¿qué ~ es?, what time is it?

horario [orárjo] *m.* hour-hand. 2 time-table.

horizonte [oriθónte] *m.* horizon.

hormiga [ormíɣa] *f.* ant.

horno [órno] *m.* oven; kiln; alto ~, blast-furnace.

horrible [orríβle] *a.* horrible, fearful.

horror [orrór] *m.* horror, fright. 2 grimness.

horroroso [orroróso] *a.* horrible, dreadful. 2 frightful.

hortaliza [ortalíθa] *f.* vegetables, greens.

hospital [ospitál] *m.* hospital; infirmary.

hostil [ostíl] *a.* hostile.

hotel [otél] *m.* hotel.

hoy [oĭ] *adv.* today; now.

hoyo [ójo] *m.* hole. 2 dent.

hueco [wéko] *a.-m.* hollow.

huelga [wélɣa] *f.* strike.

huelguista [welɣísta] *m.-f.* striker.

huella [wéʎa] *f.* tread. 2 print; track, footprint.

huérfano [wérfano] *a.-n.* orphan.

huerto [wérto] *m*. orchard. 2 kitchen garden.

hueso [wéso] *m*. bone.

huésped [wéspeð] *m*.-*f*. guest.

huevo [wéβo] *m*. egg.

huir [uir] *i*. to flee, fly, escape, run away [from]. 2 *t*. to avoid, shun. ‖ Conjug.: Indic.: Pres.: *huyo, huyes, huye;* huimos, huis, huyen. ‖ Pret:; hui, huiste, *huyó;* huimos, huisteis, huyeron. ‖ Subj. Pres.: *huya, huyas,* etc. | Imperf.: *huyera, huyeras,* etc., or *huyese, huyeses,* etc. | Fut.: *huyere, huyeres,* etc. ‖ Imperat.: *huye, huya; huyamos,* huid, *huyan.* ‖ Ger.: *huyendo.*

humanidad [umaniðáð] *f*. humanity. 2 mankind. 3 kindness. 4 corpulence. 5 *pl*. humanities.

humanitario [umanitárjo] *a*. humanitarian.

humano [umáno] *a*. human. 2 humane.

humedad [umeðáð] *f*. humidity, moisture, dampness.

húmedo [úmeðo] *a*. humid, moist, damp, wet.

humildad [umildáð] *f*. humility, humbleness.

humilde [umilde] *a*. humble. 2 meek. 3 **-mente** *adv*. humbly.

humillar [umiʎár] *t*. to humble. 3 to shame. 4 to lower [one's head]. 5 *p*. to humble oneself.

humo [úmo] *m*. smoke. 2 steam, vapour.

humor [umór] *m*. humour, temper, mood: *buen, mal* ~, good, bad humour. 4 wit.

hundir [undir] *t*. to sink. 2 naut. to founder. 3 *p*. to sink. 4 to collapse.

huracán [urakán] *h*. hurricane.

ida [íða] f. going, departure: billete de ~ y vuelta, return ticket.

idea [iðéa] f. idea; notion. 2 purpose. 3 opinion.

ideal [iðeál] a.-m. ideal.

idear [iðeár] t. to conceive, think. 2 to plan, design.

identificar [iðentifikár] t. to identify.

idioma [iðjóma] m. language.

idiota [iðjóta] a. silly 2 m.-f. idiot.

ídolo [íðolo] m. idol.

iglesia [iɣlésja] f. church.

ignorancia [iɣnoránθja] f. ignorance, illiteracy.

ignorante [iɣnoránte] a. ignorant. 2 m.-f. ignoramus.

ignorar [iɣnorár] t. not to know.

igual [iɣwál] a. equal [to]. 2 the same. 3 level, even. 4 sin ~, matchless. 5 adv. ~ que, as well as; me es ~, I don't mind.

igualar [iɣwalár] t. to equalize. 2 to even, level. 3 to match.

igualdad [iɣwaldáð] f. equality, sameness.

igualmente [iɣwálménte] adv. similarly. 3 likewise, also.

ilimitado [ilimitáðo] a. unlimited, limitless.

iluminar [iluminár] t. to light up. 2 to enlighten.

ilusión [ilusjón] f. illusion, day-dream.

ilustrado [ilustráðo] a. cultured, educated.

ilustrar [ilustrár] *t.* to illustrate. *2* to explain. *3 p.* to learn.

ilustre [ilústre] *a.* celebrated, illustrious.

imagen [imáxen] *f.* image.

imaginación [imaxinaθjón] *f.* imagination, fancy.

imaginar [imaxinár] *t.* to imagine, fancy. *2 t.-p.* suppose.

imán [imán] *m.* magnet. *2* loadstone.

imitar [imitár] *t.* to imitate, ape; to follow.

impaciente [impaθjénte] *a.* impatient, anxious.

imparcial [imparθjál] *a.* impartial, fair.

impedir [impeðír] *t.* to impede, hinder, prevent. ¶ CONJUG. like *servir*.

imperativo [imperatíβo] *a.-m.* imperative.

imperdible [imperðíβle] *m.* safety-pin.

imperfecto [imperféγto] *a.-m.* imperfect.

imperial [imperjál] *a.* imperial.

imperio [impérjo] *m.* empire.

ímpetu [ímpetu] *m.* impetus, impulse. *2* rush.

impío [impío] *a.* impious.

implicar [implikár] *t.* to implicate. *2* to imply.

implorar [implorár] *t.* to implore, entreat, beg.

imponente [imponénte] *a.* impressive, imposing. *2* grandiose.

imponer [imponér] *t.* to impose. *2* to inspire. *3* to deposit. *4 p.* to assert oneself. *5* to be necessary. *6* to impose one's authority on.

importancia [importánθja] *f.* importance, consequence.

importante [importánte] *a.* important, urgent, serious.

importar [importár] *i.* to be important; to matter. *2* to amount to. *3* to import.

importe [impórte] *m.* amount.

imposible [imposíβle] *a.* impossible. *2 m.* impossibility.

imprenta [imprénta] *f.* press; printing office.

imprescindible [impresθindíβle] *a.* indispensable.

impresión [impresjón] *f.* stamp, imprint. *2* footprint. *3* impression.

impresionar [impresjonár] *t.* to impress, affect. 2 to touch. 3 to record sounds. 4 p. to be moved.

imprimir [imprimír] t to print; to stamp.

impropio [imprópjo] a improper. 2 unfitting.

impuesto [impwésto] m. tax, duty, levy.

impulsar [impulsár] t. to impel. 3 to drive, force.

impulso [impúlso] m. impulse. 2 force, push.

inauguración [inauɣura-θjón] f. inauguration, opening.

inaugurar [inauɣurár] t. to inaugurate, open.

incapaz [inkapáθ] a. incapable. 2 unable, inefficient.

incendio [inθéndjo] m. fire. 2 arson.

incentivo [inθentíβo] m. incentive, encouragement.

incesante [inθesánte] a. incessant, unceasing.

incidente [inθiðénte] a. incidental. 2 m. incident.

incierto [inθjérto] a. uncertain.

inclinación [inklinaθjón] f. slope. 2 liking. 3 bow, nod.

inclinar [inklinár] t.-p. to slant, bow. 2 t. to

dispose. 3 p. lean, be disposed.

incluir [inkluír] t. to include. 2 to enclose. ¶ CONJUG. like huir.

inclusive [inklusíβe] adv. including.

incluso [inklúso] a. included. 2 adv. even, besides.

incomparable [inkompa-ráβle] a. incomparable.

inconveniente [inkombe-njénte] a. inconvenient. 2 m. drawback.

incorporar [inkorporár] t. to incorporate. 2 p. to sit up. 3 to join.

incrédulo [inkréðulo] a. incredulous; 2 m.-f. unbeliever.

increíble [inkreíβle] a. incredible, unbelievable.

incurrir [inkurrír] i. to incur. 2 to fall into.

indefenso [indefénso] a. defenceless.

independencia [independén θja] f. independence.

independiente [indepen-djénte] a. independent.

indicación [indikaθjón] f. indication. 2 hint.

indicar [indikár] t. to point out, show. 2 to hint.

índice [índiθe] m. index, forefinger. 2 sign.

indicio [indíθjo] *m.* sign, token; clue; trace.
indiferencia [indiferén-θja] *f.* indifference.
indiferente [indiferénte] *a.* indifferent.
indígena [indíxena] *a.* indigenous. 2 *m.-f.* native.
indignar [indiɣnár] *t.* to irritate, anger. 2 *p.* to become indignant.
indigno [indíɣno] *a.* unworthy.
indio [índjo] *a.-n.* Indian. 2 Hindu.
indiscutible [indiskutíβle] *a.* unquestionable.
indispensable [indispen-sáβle] *a.* indispensable.
individual [indiβiðuál] *a.* individual. 2 **-mente** *adv.* individually.
individuo [indiβiðówo] *a.-n.* individual.
índole [índole] *f.* nature. 2 class, kind.
inducir [induθír] *t.* to induce, instigate. ¶ CONJUG. like *conducir*.
industria [indústrja] *f.* industry.
industrial [industrjál] *a.* industrial. 2 *m.* manufacturer.
infame [imfáme] *a.* hateful, odious, vile.

infancia [imfánθja] *f.* infancy, childhood.
infantería [imfantería] *f.* infantry; ~ *de marina*, marines.
infantil [imfantíl] *a.* infantile. 2 childish.
infección [imfeɣθjón] *f.* infection, contagion.
infeliz [imfelíθ] *a.* unhappy, wretched.
inferior [imferjór] *a.-n.* inferior. 2 *a.* lower.
infiel [imfjél] *a.* unfaithful. 2 *a.-n.* infidel, pagan.
infierno [imfjérno] *m.* hell, inferno.
infinidad [imfiniðáð] *f.* infinity, great quantity.
infinito [imfiníto] *a.* infinite. 2 *m.* infinite space.
influencia [imfluénθja] *f.* influence.
influir [imfluír] *t.* to influence.
información [imforma-θjón] *f.* information. 2 inquiry.
informar [imformár] *t.* to inform [tell]. 2 *i.* to report. 3 *p.* to inquire, find out.
informe [imfórme] *a.* shapeless. 2 *m.* information, report. 3 *pl.* references.

ingeniero [inxenjéro] *m.* engineer.

ingenio [inxénjo] *m.* genius; mind, talent. 2 cleverness, wit. 3 machine.

inglés [inglés] *a.* English. 2 *m.* Englishman. 3 *f.* Englishwoman.

ingratitud [ingratitúð] *f.* ingratitude.

ingrato [ingráto] *a.* ungrateful.

ingresar [ingresár] *i.* to enter; to become a member of; to join. 3 *t.* to deposit [money].

ingreso [ingréso] *m.* entrance. 2 *pl.* income. pioneer.

iniciar [iniθjár] *t.* to begin, start, initiate.

iniciativa [iniθjatíβa] *f.* initiative, enterprise.

iniquidad [inikiðáð] *f.* iniquity, wickedness.

injusticia [inxustíθja] *f.* injustice.

injusto [inxústo] *a.* unjust, unfair.

inmediatamente [immeðjátaménte] *adv.* immediately.

inmediato [immeðjáto] *a.* immediate. 2 close [to], next [to].

inmensidad [immensiðáð] *f.* immensity. 2 great number.

inmenso [imménso] *a.* immense. 2 vast, huge.

inmóvil [immóβil] *a.* motionless, fixed. 2 constant.

inmundo [immúndo] *a.* dirty, filthy.

innecesario [inneθesárjo] *a.* unnecessary.

innumerable [innumeráβle] *a.* numberless.

inocente [inoθénte] *a.-s.* innocent.

inofensivo [inofensíβo] *a.* harmless, inoffensive.

inolvidable [inolβiðáβle] *a.* unforgettable.

inquieto [inkjéto] *a.* restless. 2 worried, anxious.

inquietud [inkjetúð] *f.* restlessness, anxiety.

inscribir [inskríβir] *t.* to inscribe. 2 *p.* to register.

inscripción [inskriβθjón] *f.* inscription. 2 registration.

insecto [inséγto] *m.* insect.

insensato [insensáto] *a.* stupid, foolish.

insignificante [insiγnifikánte] *a.* insignificant.

insistir [insistír] *i.* to insist [on, that].

inspección [inspeγθjón] *f.* inspection, survey.

inspector [inspeytór] *m.-f.* inspector, surveyor.

inspiración [inspiraθjón] *f.* inspiration.

inspirar [inspirár] *t.* to inspire, breathe in.

instalación [instalaθjón] *f.* installation. 2 plant.

instalar [instalár] *t.* to set up. 2 *p.* to settle.

instante [instánte] *m.* instant: al ~, immediately.

instinto [instínto] *m.* instinct; impulse, urge.

institución [instituθjón] *f.* institution.

instituir [instituír] *t.* to establish, found. 2 LAW appoint [as heir]. ¶ CONJUG. like *huir*.

instituto [institúto] *m.* institute. 2 state secondary school.

instrucción [instruyθjón] *f.* instruction, teaching, learning. 2 MIL. drill. 3 *pl.* orders.

instruir [instruír] *t.* to instruct, teach. 2 MIL. to drill. 3 *p.* to learn. ¶ CONJUG. like *huir*.

instrumento [instruménto] *m.* instrument, tool.

insultar [insultár] *t.* to insult; to call names.

insuperable [insuperáβle] *a.* unsurpassable.

integrar [inteγrár] *t.* to form, make up.

integridad [inteγriðáð] *f.* integrity. 2 honesty.

intelectual [inteleytwál] *a.-n.* intellectual.

inteligencia [intelixénθja] *f.* intelligence, understanding.

inteligente [intelixénte] intelligent.

intención [intenθjón] *f.* intention, purpose, mind.

intensidad [intensiðáð] *f.* intensity.

intenso [inténso] *a.* intense, powerful, strong.

intentar [intentár] *t.* to try, attempt. 2 to intend.

intento [inténto] *m.* intent, purpose. 2 attempt.

interés [interés] *m.* interest, concern.

interesante [interesánte] *a.* interesting.

interesar [interesár] *t.* to interest. 2 to concern. 3 MED. to affect. 4 *i.* to be interesting. 5 to be necessary. 6 *p.* to be interested.

interino [interíno] *a.* temporary.

interior [interjór] *a.* interior, inside. 2 *m.* inland.

intermedio [interméðjo] *a.* intermediate. 2 *m.* interval.

interminable [interminá-βle] *a.* endless.

internacional [interna-θjonál] *a.* international.

interpretación [interpreta-θjón] *f.* interpretation, explanation.

interpretar [interpretár] *t.* to interpret. 2 THEAT. to play.

intérprete [intérprete] *m.-f.* interpreter.

interrogar [interroɣár] *t.* to interrogate, question.

interrumpir [interrumpír] *t.* to interrupt, break off, block, hold up.

intervención [interβen-θjón] *f.* intervention. 2 mediation.

intervenir [interβenír] *i.* to intervene. 2 to intercede. 3 *t.* SURG. to operate upon.

intimidad [intimiðáð] *f.* intimacy.

íntimo [íntimo] *a.* intimate. 2 private. 3 close.

intranquilo [intraŋkílo] *a.* restless, uneasy.

introducción [introðuy-θjón] *f.* introduction.

introducir [introðuθír] *t.* to introduce. 2 *p.* to get in(to.

inundación [inundaθjón] *f.* inundation, flood.

inundar [inundár] *t.* to inundate, flood.

inútil [inútil] *a.* useless. 2 **-mente** *adv.* uselessly.

invadir [imbaðír] *t.* to invade, overrun.

invasión [imbasjón] *f.* invasion.

inventar [imbentár] *t.* to invent, find out.

invento [imbénto] *m.* invention, discovery.

inversión [imbersjón] *f.* investment.

invertir [imbertír] *f.* to invert. 2 to spend [time]. 3 COM. to invest. ¶ CONJUG. like *hervir.*

investigación [imbestiɣa-θjón] *f.* investigation, research.

investigar [imbestiɣár] *t.* to investigate, do research on.

invicto [imbíyto] *a.* unconquered, unbeaten.

invierno [imbjérno] *m.* winter, wintertime.

invisible [imbisíβle] *a.* invisible.

invitación [imbitaθjón] *f.* invitation.

invitado [imbitáðo] *m.-f.* guest.

invitar [imbitár] *t.* to invite.

invocar [imbokár] *t.* to invoke, call on.

inyección [injeyθjón] *f.* injection.

ir [ir] *i.* to go: ~ *a caballo,* to ride on horseback; ~ *pie,* to go on foot; *¡vamos!,* come on!, let's go! 2 *p.* to go away. ‖ CONJUG. INDIC. Pres.: *voy, vas, va; vamos, vais, van.* | Imperf.: *iba, ibas,* etc. | Pret.: *fui, fuiste,* etc. | Fut.: *iré, irás,* etc. ‖ COND.: *iría, irías,* etc. ‖ SUBJ. Pres.: *vaya, vayas,* etc. | Imperf.: *fuera, fueras,*

etc., or *fuese, fueses,* etc. | Fut.: *fuere, fueres,* etc. ‖ IMPER.: *ve, vaya; vayamos, id, vayan.* ‖ PAST. P.: *ido.* ‖ GER.: *yendo.*

ira [ira] *f.* anger, wrath.

iracundo [irakúndo] *a.* irate, irascible.

irritar [irritár] *t.* to irritate. 2 *p.* to become irritated.

isla [ízla] *f.* island; isle.

italiano [italjáno] *a.-n.* Italian.

itinerario [itinerárjo] *m.* itinerary, route.

izquierdo [iθkjérðo] *a.* left-handed; crooked. 2 *f.* left hand: *a la ~,* to the left. 3 POL. the Left [wing].

J

jabón [xaβón] m. soap.

jaguar [xaɣwár] m. ZOOL. jaguar.

jalea [xaléa] f. jelly.

jamás [xamás] adv. never, (not) ever.

jamón [xamón] m. ham.

japonés [xaponés] a.-n. japanese.

jaqueca [xakéka] f. headache.

jardín [xarðín] m. garden, flower garden.

jardinero [xarðinéro] m. gardener.

jarro [xárro] m. jug, pitcher.

jaula [xáula] f. cage.

jefe [xéfe] m. chief, head, leader.

jerez [xeréθ] m. sherry.

jinete [xinéte] m. horseman, rider.

jornada [xornáða] f. f. day's journey. 2 working day.

jorobado [xoroβáðo] m.-f. hunch-back(ed.

joven [xóβen] a. young. 2 m.-f. youth, young man or woman.

joya [xója] f. jewel; gem.

joyería [xojería] f. jewellery, jeweller's [shop].

judío [xuðío] a. Jewish. 2 m. Jew, Hebrew.

juego [xwéɣo] m. play. 2 game. 3 sport. 4 gambling. 5 set, service: ~ de té, tea set. 6 ~ de palabras, pun; hacer ~, to match; ~ limpio, fair play.

jueves [xwéβes] m. Thursday.

juez [xweθ] *m.* judge, justice; magistrate.

jugada [xuɣáða] *f.* move. 2 mean trick.

jugador [xuɣaðór] *m.-f.* player. 2 gambler.

jugar [xuɣár] *t.-i.* to play. 2 to gamble. ‖ Conjug. Indic. Pres.: *juego, juegas, juega; jugamos, jugáis, juegan.* ‖ Subj. Pres.: *juegue, juegues, juegue;* juguemos, juguéis, *jueguen.* ‖ Imper.: *juega, juegue; juguemos, jugad, jueguen.*

jugo [xúɣo] *m.* juice.

jugoso [xuɣóso] *a.* juicy.

juguete [xuɣéte] *m.* toy.

juicio [xwíθjo] *m.* judgement, wisdom. 2 LAW trial.

julio [xúljo] *m.* July.

junio [xúnjo] *m.* June.

junta [xúnta] *f.* meeting.

juntar [xuntár] *t.* to assemble. 2 to gather,

lay up, store. 3 to join, unite; to connect.

junto [xúnto] *a.* together. 2 *adv.* near, close: ~ *a,* close to.

juramento [xuraménto] *m.* oath: ~ *falso,* perjury. 2 curse.

jurar [xurár] *t.-i.* to swear: ~ *en falso,* to commit perjury.

justicia [xustíθja] *f.* justice. 2 fairness, right.

justificar [xustifikár] *t.* to justify. 2 to vouch. 3 *p.* to justify one's conduct.

1) **justo** [xústo] *adv.* justly, exactly. 2 closely.

2) **justo** [xústo] *a.* just. 2 righteous. 3 exact. 4 tight.

juventud [xuβentúð] *f.* youth. 2 young people.

juzgar [xuðɣár] *i.* to judge. 2 to try. 3 to think.

K

kilo [kílo], **kilogramo** [kiloɣrámo] *m.* kilogram, kilogramme, kilo.

kilómetro [kilómetro] *m.* kilometre, kilometer.

kiosko [kjósko] *m.* kiosk.

L

la [la] *def. art. fem. sing.* the. 2 *obj. pron.* her; it; you.

labio [láβjo] *m.* lip.

labor [laβór] *f.* labour, work, task. 2 needlework.

labrador [laβraðór] *m.-f.* farmer, ploughman.

labrar [laβrár] *t.* to work. 2 to plough, till.

labriego [laβrjéɣo] *m.-f.* farm labourer, peasant.

ladera [laðéra] *f.* slope, hillside.

lado [láðo] *m.* side: *dejar a un ~,* to set aside; *al ~,* near by; *al ~ de,* beside; *por un ~ ... por otro,* on the one hand ... on the other hand.

ladrar [laðrár] *i.* to bark.

ladrillo [laðríʎo] *m.* brick, tile.

ladrón [laðrón] *m.-f.* thief, robber.

lágrima [láɣrima] *f.* tear. 2 drop.

lago [láɣo] *m.* lake.

lamentable [lamentáβle] regrettable, pitiful.

lamentar [lamentár] *t.* to deplore, regret, be sorry for. 2 *p.* to complain.

lamento [laménto] *m.* wail, moan, complaint.

lamer [lamér] *t.* to lick.

lámpara [lámpara] *f.* lamp, light. 2 valve, bulb.

lana [lána] *f.* wool.

langosta [langósta] *f.* locust. 2 lobster.

lanza [lánθa] *f.* lance, spear. 2 shaft.

lanzar [lanθár] t. to throw, cast, fling, hurl. 2 to launch. 3 p. to rush.

lápiz [lápiθ] m. pencil.

largar [laryár] t. to let go. 2 to give [a sigh]. 3 p. to get out, leave.

1) **largo** [láryo] adv. largely. 2 m. long, length. 3 pasar de ~, to pass by.

2) **largo** [láryo] a. long.

larva [lárβa] f. larva; grub, maggot.

las [las] def. art. f. pl. the. 2 obj. pron. f. pl. them; you [formal].

lástima [lástima] f. pity, grief; ¡qué ~!, what a pity!

lastimar [lastimár] t. to hurt, injure; to offend. 2 p. to get hurt.

látigo [látiyo] m. whip.

latir [latír] i. to beat, throb.

latitud [latitúð] f. breadth, width. 2 latitude.

latón [latón] m. brass.

laurel [laurél] m. laurel.

lavabo [laβáβo] m. washstand. 2 washroom. 3 lavatory, toilet.

lavandería [laβandería] f. laundry.

lavar [laβár] t.-i. to wash; to wash up [dishes, etc.]; to clean. 2 to cleanse.

lazo [láθo] m. bow, knot, loop; lasso. 2 tie, bond.

le [le] pers. pron. m. sing.; direct obj. him; you [formal]. 2 indirect obj. to him, to her, to it; to you [formal].

leal [leál] a. loyal, faithful. 2 fair.

lección [leγθjón] f. lesson; class; lecture.

lector [leγtór] m.-f. reader. 2 lecturer.

lectura [leγtúra] f. reading; libro de ~, reader.

leche [létʃe] f. milk.

lechería [letʃería] f. dairy.

lechero [letʃéro] a. milky. 2 m. milkman. 3 f. milkmaid.

lecho [létʃo] m. bed. 2 river-bed. 3 stratum.

lechuga [letʃúya] f. lettuce.

leer [leér] t.-i. to read.

legal [leγál] a. legal, lawful.

legión [lexjón] f. legion.

legislación [lexislaθjón] f. legislation.

legislador [lexislaðór] m. legislator.

legislatura [lexislatúra]

f. legislature. 2 legislative assembly [or body].

legítimo [lexítimo] *a.* legitimate. 2 genuine, real.

legua [léɣwa] *f.* league.

legumbre [leɣúmbre] *f. pl.* vegetables.

lejano [lexáno] *a* distant, remote, far off.

lejos [léxos] *adv.* far, far away, far off.

lengua [léŋgwa] *f.* tongue. 2 language.

lenguaje [leŋgwáxe] *m.* language. 2 tongue, speech.

lentamente [léntaménte] *adv.* slowly.

lento [lénto] *a.* slow.

leña [léɲa] *f.* firewood.

leñador [leɲaðór] *m.* woodcutter, woodman.

león [león] *m.* lion.

leona [leóna] *f.* lioness.

leopardo [leopárðo] *m.* leopard.

les [les] *pers. pron. m.-f.* them, to them; you, to you [formal].

lesionar [lesjonár] *t.* to hurt, wound, injure. 2 to damage.

letra [létra] *f.* letter. 2 printing type. 3 handwriting. 4 ~ mayúscula,

capital letter; ~ minúscula, small letter. 5 COM. bill of exchange, draft. 6 *pl.* learning.

letrero [letréro] *m.* label. 2 sign, placard, poster, notice.

levantar [leβantár] *t.* to raise, lift, hoist. 2 to build. 3 to pick up. 4 to stir. 5 ~ la mesa, to clear the table. 6 ~ acta to draw up a statement. 7 ~ la sesión, to close the meeting. 8 *p.* to rise, get up; to rebel.

leve [léβe] *a.* light. 2 slight, trifling.

ley [leí] *f.* law; rule; act, statute.

leyenda [lexénda] *f.* legend, story. 2 inscription.

libertad [liβertáð] *f.* liberty, freedom.

libertar [liβertár] *t.* to set free, liberate.

libra [líβra] *f.* pound [weight; coin]: ~ esterlina, pound sterling.

librar [liβrár] *t.* to free, deliver, save [from danger]. 2 to pass [sentence]. 3 to draw [a bill, etc.]. 4 to give [battle]. 5 *p. librarse de,* to get rid of.

libre [líβre] *a.* free: ~

albedrío, free will. 2 vacant. 3 at leisure.

librería [liβrería] f. library; bookcase. 2 bookshop.

libreta [liβréta] f. notebook.

libro [líβro] m. book.

licencia [liθénθja] f. licence, permission. 2 MIL. leave.

licenciado [liθenθjáðo] m. EDUC. licenciate, bachellor. 2 lawyer. 3 discharged soldier.

licor [likór] m. liquor; spirits.

líder [líðer] m. leader.

liebre [ljéβre] f. hare.

lienzo [ljénθo] m. linen cloth. 2 canvas.

liga [líɣa] f. garter. 2 mixture. 3 league.

ligar [liɣár] t. to tie, bind. 2 to join, unite.

ligero [lixéro] a. light. 2 flippant. 3 adv. fast.

lila [líla] f. lilac.

lima [líma] f. file. 2 finish. 3 sweet lime.

limitar [limitár] t. to limit. 2 to cut down. 3 i. to border on. 4 p. to confine oneself to.

límite [límite] m. limit. 2 border.

limón [limón] m. lemon.

limosna [limózna] f. alms, charity.

limpiar [limpjár] t. to clean, cleanse. 2 to wipe. 3 to clear.

limpieza [limpjéθa] f. cleanliness. clean(ing.

limpio [límpjo] a. clean. 2 neat, tidy. 3 honest. 4 clear, net. 5 fair [play].

linaje [lináxe] m. lineage, race: ~ humano. mankind.

línea [línea] f. line.

lino [líno] m. linen; flax.

linterna [lintérna] f. lantern, lamp.: ~ eléctrica, flashlight, torch.

liquidar [likiðár] t.-p. to liquefy. 2 t. to liquidate. 3 to murder.

líquido [líkiðo] a.-n. liquid, fluid. 2 net.

lira [líra] f. lira. 2 lyre.

lírico [líriko] a. lyric(al. 2 m.-f. lyric poet.

lirio [lírjo] m. lily.

liso [líso] a. smooth, flat, even.

lisonjero [lisonxéro] a. flattering; promising.

lista [lísta] f. list, catalogue. 2 roll: pasar ~, to call the roll.

listo [lísto] *a.* ready. 2 quick. 3 finished. 4 clever.

literario [literárjo] *a.* literary.

literato [literáto] *m.-f.* writer, man-of-letters.

literatura [literatúra] *f.* literature.

litoral [litorál] *a.* coastal. 2 *m.* coast, seaboard.

litro [lítro] *m.* litre.

lo [lo] *neut. art.* the. 2 *pers. pron. m. neut.* him; it; you [formal]; *lo que*, what.

lobo [lóβo] *m.* wolf.

local [lokál] *a.* local. 2 *m.* place, premises.

localidad [lokaliðáð] *f.* locality. 2 town. 3 seat.

localizar [lokaliθár] *t.* to localize; to locate, place, site.

loco [lóko] *a.* mad, crazy. 2 *m.-f.* madman, madwoman. 3 fool.

locomotora [lokomotóra] *f.* railway engine.

locura [lokúra] *f.* madness, insanity, folly.

locutor [lokutór] *m.* announcer; tv. newscaster, newsreader; presenter.

lodo [lóðo] *m.* mud, mire.

lógico [lóxiko] *a.* logical. 2 *f.* logic.

lograr [loɣrár] *t.* to get, achieve, attain, obtain. 2 to succeed [in + *ger.*], manage to.

logro [lóɣro] *m.* success, achievement. 2 gain, profit.

lomo [lómo] *m.* back. 2 loin. 3 sirloin.

longitud [lonxitúð] *f.* length, longitude.

loro [lóro] *m.* parrot.

los [los] *def. art. m. pl.* the. 2 ~ *que*, those, or they who or which. 3 *obj. pron. m. pl.* them; you [formal].

losa [lósa] *f.* flagstone, slab. 2 gravestone.

lotería [lotería] *f.* lottery; raffle.

loza [lóθa] *f.* china, fine earthenware, crockery.

lozano [loθáno] *a.* luxuriant. 2 blooming, vigorous.

lucero [luθéro] *m.* morning star, bright star.

lucir [luθír] *i.* to shine, glow. 2 *t.* to display. 3 *p.* to show off. 4 to shine, be successful. ¶ Conjug.: Indic. Pres.: *luzco, luces, luce,* etc. ‖ Subj. Pres.: *luzca, luzcas,* etc. ‖ Imper.:

luce, *luzca;* *luzcamos,*
lucid, *luzcan.*

lucha [lútʃa] *f.* fight.
2 strife, struggle. 3
wrestling.

luchar [lutʃár] *i.* to
fight. 2 to strive, struggle. 3 to wrestle.

luego [lwéyo] *adv.* afterwards, next. 2 im-
mediately. 3 later. 4
desde ~, of course. 5
hasta ~, so long. 6
conj. therefore, then.

lugar [luɣár] *m.* place:
en primer ~, firstly. 2
spot. 3 employment. 4
space. 5 *en* ~ *de,* instead of. 6 *dar* ~ *a,* to

give rise to. 7 *tener* ~,
to take place, happen.

lujo [lúxo] *m.* luxury.

lujoso [luxóso] *a.* luxur-
ious, costly.

luminoso [luminóso] *a.*
bright, shining.

luna [lúna] *f.* moon: ~
de miel, honeymoon;
estar en la ~, fig. to
be absent-minded. 2
mirror.

lunes [lúnes] *m.* Monday.

luz [luθ] *f.* light: ~ *del
dia,* daylight; *dar a* ~,
to give birth to; to
publish.

LL

llaga [ʎáɣa] *f.* ulcer, sore; wound.

llamar [ʎamár] *t.* to call, summon; to name: ~ *por teléfono*, to telephone, call up. 2 *i.* to knock; to ring the bell. 3 *p.* to be called: *me llamo Juan*, my name is John.

llano [ʎáno] *a.* flat, level, smooth. 2 frank. 3 simple [style]. 4 *m.* plain.

llanto [ʎánto] *m.* crying, weeping, tears.

llanura [ʎanúra] *f.* flatness. 2 plain; prairie.

llave [ʎáβe] *f.* key. 2 cock, faucet. 3 wrench. 4 MUS. clef.

llegada [ʎeɣáða] *f.* arrival, coming.

llegar [ʎeɣár] *i.* to arrive [at; in]. 2 to get at, reach. 2 to come to [an agreement]. 3 to amount to. 4 to get to [know]. 5 *p.* to go to.

llenar [ʎenár] *t.* to fill [up]. 2 to fulfil. 3 *p.* to get crowded.

lleno [ʎéno] *a.* full [of]; filled [with]; crowded [with]. 2 *m.* THEAT. full house.

llevar [ʎeβár] *t.* to carry, convey, take. 2 to wear, have on [a hat]. 3 to lead, guide. 4 to keep [books]. 5 *p.* to take off. 6 to win [a prize]. 7 ~ *bien*, to get on well with.

llorar [ʎorár] *i.* to weep, cry.

llover [ʎoβér] *t.* to rain, shower: ~ *a cántaros,* to rain cats and dogs. ¶ CONJUG. like *mover.*

llovizna [ʎoβiðna] *f.* drizzle.

lluvia [ʎúβja] *f.* rain: ~ *menuda,* drizzle.

M

maceta [maθéta] *f.* flower-pot.

machacar [matʃakár] *t.* to pound, crush, mash.

machete [matʃéte] *m.* cutlass, cane knife.

macho [mátʃo] *a.* male. 2 *m.* male. 3 he-mule: ~ cabrío, he-goat. 4 sledge-hammer.

madera [maðéra] *f.* wood.

madrastra [maðrástra] *f.* stepmother.

madre [máðre] *f.* mother: ~ patria, mother country; ~ política, mother-in-law.

madrina [maðrína] *f.* godmother. 2 patroness.

madrugada [maðruɣáða] *f.* dawn; early morning.

madrugar [maðruɣár] *i.* to get up early.

madurar [maðurár] *t.* to mature, ripen. 2 to think over.

maduro [maðúro] *a.* mature, ripe. 2 middle-aged.

maestro [maéstro] *a.* master, main, principal; obra maestra, masterpiece. 2 *m.* master, teacher. 3 *f.* (school)-mistress.

mágico [máxiko] *a.* magic(al.

magnético [maɣnétiko] *a.* magnetic.

magnífico [maɣnífiko] *a.* magnificent, splendid.

mago [máɣo] *m.-f.* magician, wizard. 2 *m.* pl. los Reyes Magos, the Magi, the Three Wise Men.

maíz [maíθ] *m.* maize, Indian corn.

majadero [maxaðéro] *a.* silly, stupid. 2 *m.-f.* dolt, bore.

majestad [maxestáð] *f.* majesty, stateliness.

majestuoso [maxestwóso] *a.* majestic, stately.

1) **mal** [mal] *a.* apocopation of MALO. 2 *adv.* badly, wrongly: ~ que le pese, in spite of him.

2) **mal** [mal] *m.* evil, ill, harm, wrong: tomar a ~, to take ill. 2 illness, disease.

malcriado [malkriáðo] *a.* a. ill-bred, coarse.

maldad [maldáð] *f.* wickedness, badness.

maldecir [maldeθír] *t.-i.* to curse, damn. 2 ~ de, to speak ill of. ¶ CONJUG. like decir.

maldición [maldiθjón] *f.* curse. 2 curse it!, damn!

maldito [maldíto] *a.* accursed, damned. 2 wicked.

malestar [malestár] *m.* discomfort, uneasiness.

maleta [maléta] *f.* valise, suit-case: hacer la ~, to pack up.

maleza [maléθa] *f.* underbrush, thicket.

malgastar [malɣastár] to waste, squander.

malo [málo] *a.* bad, evil, wicked, vicious. 2 ill, harmful. 3 naughty, mischievous. 4 ill, sick: estar malo, to be ill. 5 lo malo es que ..., the trouble is that ... 6 interj. ¡malo!, bad!

malta [málta] *f.* malt.

maltratar [maltratár] *t.* to abuse, illtreat.

malvado [malβáðo] *a.* wicked. 2 *m.-f.* villain.

malla [máʎa] *f.* mesh; network. 2 mail.

mamá [mamá] *f.* mummy [mother].

mamar [mamár] *t.* to suck.

mamífero [mamífero] *m.* mammal.

maná [maná] *m.* manna.

manantial [manantjál] *m.* source, spring.

mancha [mántʃa] *f.* stain, spot, blot.

manchar [mantʃár] *t.* to stain, soil; to defile.

mandamiento [mandamjénto] *m.* order, command. 2 LAW writ. 3 commandment.

mandar [mandár] *t.* to command, order. 2 to send. 3 *i* to govern.

mandato [mandáto] *m.* command, order.

mandíbula [mandíβula] *f.* jaw, jaw-bone.

manejar [manexár] *t.* to manage, handle, wield.

manejo [manéxo] *m.* handling. 2 management. 3 intrigue.

manera [manéra] *f.* manner, mode, fashion: *de ~ que*, so that; *de ninguna ~*, by no means; *de todas maneras*, anyhow. 2 way, means. 3 *pl.* manners, behaviour.

manga [máŋga] *f.* sleeve. 2 hose-pipe.

mango [máŋgo] *m.* handle. 2 BOT. mango.

manguera [maŋgéra] *f.* *f.* hose, hosepipe.

manía [manía] *f.* frenzy. 2 craze, whim. 3 deslike.

manifestación [manifestaθjón] *f.* manifestation. 2 statement. 3 POL. public demonstration.

manifestar [manifestár] *t.* to manifest, show, reveal. 2 to state, declare. ¶ CONJUG. like *acertar*.

manjar [maŋxár] *m.* food.

mano [máno] *f.* hand: *~ de obra*, labourer; *echar una ~*, to lend a

hand; *de segunda ~*, second-hand. 2 hand [of clock, etc.]. 3 round [of game].

mansión [mansjón] *f.* stay, sojourn. 2 dwelling.

manso [mánso] *a.* tame. 2 meek, mild. 3 quiet [water].

manta [mánta] *f.* blanket, travelling rug.

manteca [mantéka] *f.* fat; butter; lard.

mantecado [mantekáðo] *m.* butter bun. 2 ice--cream.

mantel [mantél] *m.* table-cloth.

mantener [mantenér] *t.* to maintain, support, keep. 2 to sustain, hold [up]. 3 *p.* to keep, continue.

mantequilla [mantekíʎa] *f.* butter.

manto [mánto] *m.* mantle, cloak.

manuscrito [manuskríto] *m.* manuscript.

manzana [manθána] *f.* apple. 2 block of houses.

maña [mája] *f.* skill, cunning, knack.

mañana [majána] *f.* morning, forenoon: *de ~*, early in the morning.

2 morrow. 3 *adv.* to-morrow.

mapa [mápa] *m.* map, chart.

maquillaje [makiʎáxe] *m.* make-up.

máquina [mákina] *f.* machine, engine: ~ *de afeitar*, safety-razor; ~ *de escribir*, typewriter; ~ *de vapor*, steam-engine.

maquinaria [makinárja] *f.* machinery.

mar [mar] *m.* or *f.* sea.

maravilla [maraβíʎa] *f.* wonder, marvel.

maravilloso [maraβiʎóso] *a.* wonderful, marvellous.

marca [márka] *f.* mark, brand. 2 SPORT record. 3 *de* ~, first-class quality.

marcar [markár] *t.* to mark, brand; to stencil. 2 SPORT to score. 3 TELEPH. to dial.

marco [márko] *m.* frame, case. 2 mark [German coin].

marcha [mártʃa] *f.* march. 2 course. 3 running, working. 4 departure. 5 pace. 6 *cambio de marchas*, gear-shift.

marchar [mártʃár] *i.* to march, walk. 2 to go, proceed. 3 to work, run. 4 *i.-p.* to leave.

marchitar [martʃitár] *t.-p.* to wither, fade.

marea [maréa] *f.* tide [of sea]: ~ *alta, baja*, high, low tide.

marear [mareár] *t.* to sail. 2 to annoy. 3 *p.* to become nauseated, sick. 4 to get dizzy.

mareo [maréo] *m.* sickness, seasickness. 2 dizziness. 3 annoyance.

marfil [marfil] *m.* ivory.

margarita [maryaríta] *f.* daisy. 2 pearl.

margen [márxen] *m.-f.* margin. 2 border. 3 bank.

marido [maríðo] *m.* husband.

marina [marína] *f.* seacoast. 2 PAINT. sea-scape. 3 ships: ~ *de guerra*, navy; ~ *mercante*, merchant navy.

marinero [marinéro] *m.* mariner, sailor.

marino [maríno] *a.* marine: *azul* ~, navy blue. 2 *m.* mariner, sailor.

mariposa [maripósa] *f.* butterfly.

marítimo [marítimo] *a.* maritime.

mármol [mármol] *m.* marble.

marrón [marrón] *a.* brown, chestnut.

martes [mártes] *m.* Tuesday.

martillo [martíλo] *m.* hammer.

mártir [mártir] *m.-f.* martyr.

martirio [martírjo] *m.* martyrdom. 2 torture.

marzo [márθo] *m.* March.

mas [mas] *conj.* but.

más [mas] *adv.* more. 2 ~ *grande*, bigger. 3 [with definite article] the most, or -est. 4 ~ *bien*, rather; ~ *que*, more than; *por* ~ *que*, however much; *no quiero nada* ~, I don't want anything else. 5 *m.* MATH. plus.

masa [mása] *f.* dough. 2 MAS. mortar. 3 PHYS. mass. 4 ELEC. ground. 5 volume. 6 crowd of pleople; the masses.

mascar [maskár] *t.* to chew. 2 to mumble [words].

máscara [máskara] *f.* mask, disguise; masked person.

masculino [maskulíno] *a.* masculine.

masticar [mastikár] *t.* to chew, masticate.

mata [máta] *f.* bush. 2 sprig. 3 head of hair.

matar [matár] *t.* to kill, slay, murder. 2 to butcher. 3 to cancel [stamps]. 4 *p.* to commit suicide. 5 to kill one another.

materia [matèrja] *f.* matter. 2 substance, stuff: *primera* ~, raw material. 3 subject.

material [materjál] *a.-n.* material.

matinal [matinál] *a.* early morning.

matiz [matié] *m.* hue; shade; nuance; touch.

matrícula [matríkula] *f.* list, roll; registration.

matrimonio [matrimónjo] *m.* marriage. 2 married couple.

maullar [mauλár] *i.* to mew, miaow.

máximo [máysimo] *a.* maximum, greatest, top.

mayo [májo] *m.* May.

mayor [majór] *a.* bigger, older. 2 the biggest; the oldest. 3 of age. 4 chief, main. 5 *m.* head. 6 *m. pl.* elders, superiors. 7 ancestors.

mayoría [majoría] *m.* majority. 2 full age

mayúsculo [majúsku!o] *a.* large. 3 *f.* capital letter.

mazorca [maθórka] *f.* ear of corn.

me [me] *pron.* me.

mecánica [mekánika] *f.* mechanics; mechanism, works.

mecánico [mekániko] *a.* mechanical. 2 *m.* mechanic, engineer.

mecanismo [mekanízmo] *m.* mechanism.

mecer [meθér] *t.-p.* rock, swing.

mecha [métʃa] *f.* wick.

medalla [meðáʎa] *f.* medal.

media [méðja] *f.* stocking. 2 MATH. mean.

mediado [meðjáðo] adv. a mediados de, about the middle of.

mediano [meðjáno] *a.* middling, moderate. 2 mediocre. 3 average.

mediante [meðjánte] *a.* Dios ~, God willing. 2 *adv.* by means of.

medicina [meðiθína] *f.* medicine.

médico [méðiko] *m.* doctor, physician, surgeon.

medida [meðiða] *f.* measure, measurement. 2 proportion: a ~ que,

as. 3 step. 4 moderation.

medio [méðjo] *a.* half. 2 middle, mean, average. 3 medium. 4 mid. 5 *adv.* half, partially. 6 *m.* middle, midst. 7 means: por ~ de, by means of. 8 environment.

mediodía [meðjoðía] *m.* noon, midday; south.

medir [meðír] *t.* to measure. 2 to scan [verse]. ¶ CONJUG. like servir.

meditar [meðitár] *t.-i.* to think over, ponder.

medrar [meðrár] *i.* to grow, thrive, improve.

médula [méðula] *f.* marrow; pith.

mejicano [mexikáno] *a.-n.* Mexican.

mejilla [mexíʎa] *f.* cheek.

mejor [mexór] *comp.* of bueno, better; superl. the best. 2 *adv.* rather.

melancolía [melaŋkolía] *f.* melancholy, low spirits.

melancólico [melaŋkóliko] *a.* melancholy, sad.

melocotón [melokotón] *m.* peach.

melodioso [meloðjóso] *a.* melodious, tuneful.

melón [melón] *m*. BOT. melon.

memoria [memórja] *f*. memory: de ~, by heart. 2 recollection; remembrance: hacer ~, to remind. 3 memoir, record, statement. 4 *pl*. memoirs.

mención [menθjón] *f*. mention.

mencionar [menθjonár] *t*. to mention, cite.

mendigo [mendiɣo] *m.-f*. beggar.

menear [meneár] *t*. to shake, stir. 2 *t.-p*. to wag, move. 3 *p*. to hustle, 4 to be loose.

menester [menestér] *m*. need, want: ser ~, to be necessary.

menor [menór] *a*. smaller, lesser; younger: ~ de edad, under age; minor. 3 *m.-f*. minor. 4 *adv*. al por ~, by [at] retail.

menos [ménos] *adv*. less: al ~, at least; a ~ que, unless; por lo ~, at least; venir a ~, to decline. 2 fewer. 3 minus. 4 to 5 except.

mensaje [mensáxe] *m*. message.

mensajero [mensaxéro] *m.-f*. messenger. 2 carrier [-pigeon].

mensual [menswál] *a*. monthly, a month.

menta [ménta] *f*. peppermint, mint.

mental [mentál] *m*. mental, intellectual. 2 **-mente** *adv*. mentally.

mente [ménte] *f*. mind, intelligence, understanding.

mentir [mentír] *i*. to lie. ¶ CONJUG. like sentir.

mentira [mentíra] *f*. lie, fib, falsehood.

mentiroso [mentiróso] *a*. lying. 2 *m.-f*. liar.

menudo [menúðo] *a*. small, minute, tiny. 2 a ~, often.

mercader [merkaðér] *m*. merchant, dealer, trader.

mercado [merkáðo] *m*. market.

mercancía [merkanθía] *f*. goods, merchandise.

merced [merθéð] *f*. favour. 2 mercy. 3 a ~ de, at the mercy of; vuestra (vuesa, su) Merced, you, sir; ~ a, thanks to.

mercurio [merkúrjo] *m*. quicksilver, mercury.

merecer [mereθér] *t.-i*. to deserve. 2 *t*. to be worth. ¶ CONJUG. like agradecer.

merecimiento [mereθimjénto] *m.* merit, deserts.

merengue [merénge] *i.* meringue.

meridional [meriðjonál] *a.* southern.

merienda [merjénda] *f.* afternoon snack; tea.

mérito [mérito] *m.* merit, worth, value.

mero [méro] *a.* mere, simple. 2 *m.* ICHTH. grouper.

mes [mes] *m.* month.

mesa [mésa] *f.* table: ~ de noche, bed-side table.

meseta [meséta] *f.* table-land, plateau.

metal [metál] *m.* metal.

metálico [metáliko] *a.* metallic. 2 *m.* cash.

meter [metér] *t.* to put [in], place, insert, introduce [in], get [in]. 2 to make [a noise]. 3 *p.* to get involved in. 4 to interfere. 5 ~ con, to quarrel with.

método [métoðo] *m.* method.

metro [métro] *m.* metre. 2 underground, tube.

mezcla [méθkla] *f.* mixture; blend(ing. 2 MAS. mortar.

mezclar [meθklár] *t.-p.* to mix. 2 *p.* to interfere.

mezquino [meθkino] *a.* poor. 2 niggardly. 3 short, mean. 4 wretched.

mi [mi] *poss. a.* my.

mi [mi] *pers. pron.* me, myself.

mico [míko] *m.* monkey.

microbio [mikróβjo] *m.* microbe.

micrófono [mikrófono] *m.* microphone; mouthpiece.

microscopio [mikroskópjo] *m.* microscope.

miedo [mjéðo] *m.* fear, dread: tener ~, to be afraid.

miedoso [mjeðóso] *a.* fearful, fainthearted.

miel [miél] *f.* honey: luna de ~, honey-moon.

miembro [mjémbro] *m.* member, limb. 2 associate.

mientras [mjéntras] *adv.-conj.* while: ~ tanto, meanwhile. 2 ~ que, while.

miércoles [mjérkoles] *m.* Wednesday.

miga [miγa] *f.* bit. 2 crumb. 3 *pl.* fried crumbs. 4 fig. marrow, substance. 5 hacer buenas migas con, to get along well with.

mil [mil] *a.-m.* thousand.

milagro [miláɣro] *m.* miracle, wonder, marvel.

milagroso [milaɣróso] *a.* miraculous.

milicia [milíθja] *f.* art of warfare. 3 militia.

militar [militár] *a.* military. 2 *m.* soldier. 3 *i.* to serve in the army.

milla [miʎa] *f.* mile.

millón [miʎón] *m.* million.

mimar [mimár] *t.* to spoil, pamper, indulge.

mina [mina] *f.* mine. 2 underground passage.

mineral [minerál] *a.-n.* mineral. 2 *m.* ore.

minero [minéro] *m.* miner. 2 *a.* mining.

mínimo [mínimo] *a.* least, smallest. 2 *m.* minimum.

ministerio [ministérjo] *m.* ministry, cabinet. 2 ~ *de Asuntos Exteriores,* Foreing Office; *Department of State; ~ de Gobernación,* Home Office; *Department of the Interior.

ministro [ministro] *m.* minister.

minoría [minoría] *f.* minority.

minutero [minutéro] *a.* minute hand.

minuto [minúto] *m.* minute.

mío [mío] *poss. a.* my, my own, of mine. 2 *poss. pron.* mine.

mirada [miráða] *f.* look, glance; gaze; stare.

mirador [miraðór] *m.* belvedere. 2 oriel window.

mirar [mirár] *t.* to look at, gaze; to watch. 2 to consider; gaze; stare. 4 *¡mira!,* look!, behold!

misa [misa] *f.* mass.

miserable [miseráβle] *a.* miserable, wretched. 2 miserly.

miseria [misérja] *f.* misery, wretchedness. 2 poverty.

mísero [mísero] *a.* miserable, wretched.

misión [misjón] *f.* mission.

mismo [mizmo] *adv.* right: *ahora* ~, right now. 2 *así* ~, likewise. 3 *a.* same. 4 myself, yourself, ourselves, etc.

misterio [mistérjo] *m.* mystery.

misterioso [misterjóso] *a.* mysterious.

mitad [mitáð] *f.* half. 2 middle.

mixto [místo] *a.* mixed. 2 *m.* match. 3 *tren* ~, passenger and goods train.

moda [móða] *f.* fashion, mode, style: *estar de* ~, to be in fashion.

modales [moðáles] *m. pl.* manners.

modelar [moðelár] *t.* to model, mould.

modelo [moðélo] *m.* model, pattern.

moderno [moðérno] *a.* modern, up-to-date.

modestia [moðéstja] *f.* modesty.

modesto [moðésto] *a.* modest, unpretentious.

módico [móðiko] *a.* reasonable, fair, moderate.

modificar [moðifikár] *t.-p.* to modify.

modismo [moðizmo] *m.* idiom.

modo [móðo] *m.* manner, way: ~ *de ser*, nature; *de cualquier* ~, anyway; *de ningún* ~, by no means; *de todos modos*, at any rate. 2 GRAM. mood. 3 *pl.* manners.

mofar [mofár] *i.-p.* to mock, jeer, make fun of.

moho [móo] *m.* mo(u)ld, mildew. 2 rust.

mojado [moxáðo] *a.* wet, damp, moist.

mojar [moxár] *t.* to wet, damp. 2 to dip. 3 *p.* to get wet.

molde [mólde] *m.* mo(u)ld.

moler [molér] *t.* to grind, pound. 2 to beat up. ¶ CONJUG. like *mover*.

molestar [molestár] *t.* to vex, upset, trouble, annoy. 2 *p.* to bother.

molestia [moléstja] *f.* annoyance, nuisance, trouble.

molesto [molésto] *a.* annoying, troublesome.

molino [molíno] *m.* mill.

momento [moménto] *m.* moment, instant: *al* ~, at once.

monarca [monárka] *m.* monarch, sovereign.

monasterio [monastérjo] *m.* monastery.

mondar [mondár] *t.* to trim. 2 to peel.

moneda [monéða] *f.* coin; money; currency.

monería [monería] *f.* grimace. 2 trifle, gewgaw.

monja [mónxa] *f.* nun, sister.

monje [mónxe] *m.* monk.

mono [móno] *a.* pretty,

*cute. 2 *m.* ZOOL. ape.
3 overalls.
monopolio [monopóljo]
m. monopoly.
monótono [monótono]
a. monotonous.
monstruo [mónstrwo] *m.*
monster; freak.
montaña [montáɲa] *f.*
mountain. 2 highlands.
montañoso [montaɲóso]
a. mountainous.
montar [montár] *i.-p.*
to mount, get on; to
stradle. 2 *i.* to ride. 3
~ *en cólera*, to fly into
a rage. 4 *t.* to mount
on a horse. 5 to ride
[a horse, etc.]. 6 to
amount to. 7 to set up
[machinery].
monte [mónte] *m.* mount,
mountain, hill. 2 woods.
3 ~ *de piedad*, public
pawnshop.
montón [montón] *m.*
heap, pile. 2 lot, crowd.
monumento [monuménto]
m. monument, memo-
rial.
morado [moráðo] *a.-n.*
dark purple.
moral [morál] *a.* moral.
2 *f.* morals, morality.
3 [of army] morale.
morar [morár] *i.* to live.
morcilla [morθíʎa] *f.*
blood sausage.

morder [morðér] *t.* to
bite; gnaw. 2 to corode.
¶ CONJUG. like *mover*.
moreno [moréno] *a.*
brown, dark.
moribundo [moriβúndo]
m.-f. moribund, dying
person.
morir [morir] *i.* to die.
¶ CONJUG. like *dormir*.
| P. p.: *muerto*.
moro [móro] *a.* Moorish.
2 Moslem. 3 spotted
[horse]. 4 *m.* Moor.
morral [morrál] *m.* nose-
bag. 2 game-bag. 3
knapsack.
mortal [mortál] *a.-n.*
mortal. 2 **-mente** *adv.*
mortally, deadly.
mortandad [mortandáð]
f. massacre, butchery,
slaughter.
mortificar [mortifikár]
t.-p. to mortify. 2 *t.*
to annoy, vex.
mosca [móska] *f.* fly.
mosquito [moskíto] *m.*
mosquito; gnat.
mostrador [mostraðór]
m. counter.
mostrar [mostrár] *t.* to
show, display. 2 to
point out. 3 to demons-
trate. 4 *p.* to prove to
be. ¶ CONJUG. like *con-
tar*.

motivar [motiβár] *t.* to give rise to.

motivo [motíβo] *m.* motive, reason: con ~ de, owing to.

motor [motór] *m.* motor. 2 engine.

mover [moβér] *t.* to move; to stir, shake; to excite. ‖ Conjug. Indic. Pres.: *muevo, mueves, mueve;* movemos, movéis, *mueven.* ‖ Subj. Pres.: *mueva, muevas, mueva;* movamos, mováis, *muevan.* ‖ Imper.: *mueve, mueva;* movamos, moved, *mueran.*

móvil [móβil] *a.* movable, mobile. 2 *m.* motive.

movimiento [moβimjénto] *m.* movement, motion. 2 agitation.

mozo [móθo] *a.* young. 2 *m.* young man, lad. 3 waiter, porter.

muchacho [mutʃátʃo] *a.* young [person]. 2 *m.* boy, lad. 3 *f.* girl, lass. 4 maidservant.

muchedumbre [mutʃeðúmbre] *f.* multitude, crowd, throng, mass.

mucho [mútʃo] *adv.* much, a great deal, a lot: por ~ que, how-

ever much. 2 long, long-time. 3 *a.-pron.* much, plenty of, a good or great deal of, a lot of. 4 *pl.* many, lots of, a large number of.

mudanza [muðánθa] *f.* change. 2 removal. 3 fickleness.

mudar [muðár] *t.* to change. 2 to remove, move. 3 to mo(u)lt. 4 *p.* to change; to move.

mudo [múðo] *n.* dumb, silent.

mueble [mwéβle] *m.* piece of furniture. 2 *pl.* furniture.

muela [mwéla] *f.* grindstone. 2 molar tooth, grinder.

muelle [mwéʎe] *a.* soft, delicate. 2 *m.* wharf, pier, quay, docks. 3 spring.

muerte [mwérte] *f.* death; murder.

muerto [mwérto] *a.* dead; killed. 2 tired out. 3 faded. 4 *m.-f.* dead person.

muestra [mwéstra] *f.* singboard. 2 sample. 3 pattern. 4 sign.

mujer [muxér] *f.* woman. 2 wife.

mula [múla] *f.* she-mule.

mulo [múlo] *m.* mule.

multa [múlta] *f.* fine.

múltiple [múltiple] *a.* manifold; multiple.

multiplicar [multiplikár] *t.-p.* to multiply.

múltiplo [múltiplo] *a.-m.* multiple.

multitud [multitúð] *f.* multitude, crowd.

mundano [mundáno] *a.* mundane, wordly.

mundial [mundiál] *a.* world-wide.

mundo [múndo] *m.* world; earth, globe: to-do el ~, everybody. 2 trunk.

municipal [muniθipál] *a.* municipal, town. 2 *m.* policeman.

municipalidad [muniθipa-liðáð] *f.,* **municipio** [muniθipjo] *m.* town council.

muñeca [muɲéka] *f.* ANAT. wrist. 2 doll.

muñeco [muɲéko] *m.* puppet. 2 dummy.

muralla [muráʎa] *f.* wall, rampart.

murciélago [murθjélaɣo] *m.* bat.

murmullo [murmúʎo] *m.* murmur, ripple; whisper; rustle.

murmurar [murmurár] *i.* to murmur, whisper. 2 to mutter. 3 to rustle. 4 to ripple. 5 to backbite. 6 to gossip.

muro [múro] *m.* wall.

músculo [múskulo] *m.* muscle.

museo [muséo] *m.* museum.

musgo [múzɣo] *m.* moss.

música [músika] *f.* sic.

músico [músiko] *a.* musical. 2 *m.-f.* musician.

mutuamente [mútwaménte] *adv.* mutually.

mutuo [mútwo] *a.* mutual, reciprocal.

muy [mwi] *adv.* very, very much.

N

nacer [naθér] *i.* to be born. 2 to grow, sprout. 3 to spring, flow. 4 to start. ¶ CONJUG. INDIC. Pres.: *nazco, naces,* etc. ‖ SUBJ. Pres.: *nazca, nazcas,* etc. ‖ IMPER.: *nace, nazca; nazcamos, naced, nazcan.*

nacido [naθíðo] *a.* born.

naciente [naθjénte] *a.* growing. 2 rising [sun].

nacimiento [naθimjénto] *m.* birth. 2 rising [sun]. 3 source. 4 issue. 5 lineage. 6 crib.

nación [naθjón] *f.* nation; people; by birth.

nacional [naθjonál] *a.* national, people.

nada [náða] *f.* naught. 2 *indef. pron.* nothing, not anything.

nadar [naðár] *t.* to swim, take a bath, float.

nadie [náðje] *pron.* nobody, no-one.

naranja [naráŋxa] *f.* orange.

naranjada [naraŋxáða] *f.* orangeade.

nariz [naríθ] *f.* nose; nostril.

narración [narraθjón] *f.* narration, account.

narrar [narrár] *t.* to narrate, tell, recount.

nata [náta] *f.* cream.

natal [natál] *a.* natal, native. 2 *m.* birthday.

nativo [natíβo] *a.* native.

natural [naturál] *a.* natural. 2 *a.-n.* native. 3 *m.* nature.

naturaleza [naturaléθa] *f.* nature. 2 temperament. 3 sort, kind. 5 ~ *muerta*, still life.

naturalmente [naturálménte] *adv.* plainly. 2 of course.

naufragar [naŭfraɣár] *i.* NAUT. to sink; to be shipwrecked.

náufrago [náŭfraɣo] *m.-f.* shipwrecked person.

navaja [naβáxa] *f.* pocketknife: ~ *de afeitar*, razor.

naval [naβál] *a.* naval.

nave [náβe] *f.* ship, vessel. 2 ARCH. ~ *lateral*, aisle.

navegación [naβeɣaθjón] *f.* navigation, sailing.

navegante [naβeɣánte] *m.-f.* navigator.

navegar [naβeɣár] *i.* to navigate, sail, steer.

Navidad [naβiðáð] *f.* Christmas.

navío [naβío] *m.* vessel, ship; ~ *de guerra*, warship.

neblina [neβlína] *f.* mist, haze, thin fog.

necesariamente [neθesárjaménte] *adv.* necessarily.

necesario [neθesárjo] *a.* necessary, needful.

necesidad [neθesiðáð] *f.* necessity; need, want.

necesitar [neθesitár] *t.* to need, want. 2 to have to.

necio [néθjo] *a.-n.* stupid; silly [person].

néctar [néɣtar] *m.* nectar.

negar [neɣár] *t.* to deny. 2 to refuse. ¶ CONJUG. like *acertar*.

negativo [neɣatíβo] *a.-n.* negative.

negociación [neɣoθjaθjón] *f.* business transaction, negotiation.

negociar [neɣoθjár] *i.* to deal, trade. 2 *t.-i.* to negotiate.

negocio [neɣóθjo] *m.* business, affair. 2 trade; concern. 3 profit, gain.

negro [néɣro] *a.* black; dark. 2 *m.* black. 3 Negro. 4 *f.* Negress.

negruzco [neɣrúθko] *a.* blackish.

nene [néne] *m.* baby; dear, darling.

nervio [nérβjo] *m.* nerve. 2 vigour, strength. 3 sinew.

nervioso [nerβjóso] *a.* nervous, excited. 2 vigorous. 3 sinewy.

nevada [neβáða] *f.* snowfall, snowstorm.

nevar [neβár] *impers.* to snow. ¶ Conjug. like *acertar*.

ni [ni] *conj.* ~ ... ~, neither ... nor. 2 ~ *siquiera*, not even.

nido [níðo] *m.* nest. 2 home.

niebla [njéβla] *f.* fog, mist, haze.

nieto [njéto] *m.-f.* grandchild. 2 *m.* grandson 3 *f.* granddaughter.

nieve [njéβe] *f.* snow.

ningun(o [ningún(o] *a.* no, not ~ any. 2 *indef. pron. m.-f.* none, no one, nobody; neither.

niña [níɲa] *f.* female child; little girl. 2 ANAT. pupil, apple of the eye.

niñez [niɲéθ] *f.* childhood, infancy.

niño [níɲo] *m.* male child, little boy.

nivel [niβél] *m.* level: ~ *del mar*, sea level; ~ *de vida*, standard of living; *paso a* ~, level crossing.

no [no] *adv.* no. 2 not; ~ *obstante*, notwithstanding.

noble [nóβle] *a.* noble. 2 *m.-f.* nobleman.

nobleza [noβléθa] *f.* nobility, nobleness.

noción [noθjón] *f.* notion, idea. 2 *pl.* rudiments.

noche [nótʃe] *f.* night; evening: ~ *buena*, Christmas Eve; ~ *vieja*, New Year's Eve; *buenas noches*, good night; *de* or *por la* ~, at night, by night.

nombrar [nombrár] *t.* to name, nominate, appoint.

nombre [nómbre] *m.* name. 2 GRAM. noun. 3 reputation.

norma [nórma] *f.* pattern, standard, norm.

normal [normál] *a.* normal, standard. 2 *f.* training-college.

norte [nórte] *m.* north. 2 North Pole. 3 guide.

norteamericano [norteamerikáno] *a.-n.* North American; American.

nos [nos] *pron.* [object] us; we [subject].

nosotros [nosótros] *pron.* we; us [object]. 2 ourselves.

nota [nóta] *f.* note, footnote. 2 fame. 3 COM. account, bill. 4 EDUC. mark, *grade.

notable [notáβle] *a.* notable, remarkable. 2 no-

ticeable. 3 *m.* EDUC. good
mark. 4 **-mente** *adv.* re-
markably.
notar [notár] *t.* to note,
mark. 2 to notice, ob-
serve, feel, see.
noticia [notíθja] *f.* news,
news item, piece of
news.
notificar [notifikár] *t.*
to inform.
notorio [notórjo] *a.*
evident, obvious.
novedad [noβeδáδ] *f.*
novelty. 2 latest news.
3 *pl.* fancy goods.
novela [noβéla] *f.* novel.
noveno [noβéno] *a.-m.*
ninth.
noviembre [noβjémbre]
m. November.
novillo [noβíʎo] *m.* young
bull. 2 *f.* heifer. 3 *hacer novillos.* to play
truant.
novio [nóβjo] *m.* bride-
groom. 2 fiancé; boy-
friend.
nube [núβe] *f.* cloud.
nudo [núδo] *m.* knot,

noose: ~ *corredizo,* slip
knot. 2 tie. 3 difficulty.
4 *a.* nude, naked.
nuestro [nwéstro] *a.* our.
2 *pron.* ours.
nueva [nwéβa] *f.* news,
tidings. 2 **-mente** *adv.*
again.
nueve [nwéβe] *a.-n.*
nine.
nuevo [nwéβo] *a.* new.
2 fresh. 3 *adv. de* ~,
again, once more.
nuez [nwéθ] *f.* walnut.
2 nut. 3 adam's apple.
número [número] *m.*
ARITH. number. 2 fi-
gure. 3 size.
numeroso [numeróso] *a.*
numerous; large.
nunca [núŋka] *adv.*
never, (not) ever.
nutrición [nutriθjón] *f.*
nutrition.
nutrido [nutríδo] *a.*
nourished. 2 full.
nutrir [nutrír] *t.* to
nourish, feed.
nutritivo [nutritíβo] *a.*
nutritious, nourishing.

Ñ

ñame [ɲáme] *m.* yam.

ñapa [ɲápa] *f.* (Am.)
additional amount.

O

o [o] *conj.* or; either ... or ...

obedecer [oβeðeθér] *t.-i.* to obey. 2 to respond, yield. ¶ Conjug. like *agradecer.*

obediencia [oβeðjénθja] *f.* obedience.

obediente [oβeðjénte] *a.* obedient.

obeso [oβéso] *a.* fat.

obispo [oβíspo] *m.* bishop.

objeción [oβxeθjón] *f.* objection.

objetivo [oβxetiβo] *a.-m.* objective, aim; target.

objeto [oβxéto] *m.* object. 2 thing. 3 subject. 4 purpose.

obligación [oβliɣaθión] obligation. 2 duty. 3 com. bond.

obligar [oβliɣár] *t.* to compel, force, constrain. 2 *p.* to bind oneself.

oblongo [oβlóngo] *a.* oblong.

obra [óβra] *f.* work. 2 deed: ~ *maestra*, masterpiece. 3 THEAT. play. 4 building under construction.

obrar [oβrár] *t.* to work. 2 to build. 3 *i.* to behave.

obrero [oβréro] *a.* working [class]. 2 *m.-f.* worker, labourer; workman.

obscuro [oskúro] *a.* obscure. 2 dark. 3 uncertain.

obsequiar [oβsekjár] *t.* to entertain; ~ *con*, to present with.

obsequio [oβsékjo] *m.* attention, present, gift.

observación [oβserβaθjón] *f.* observation. 2 remark.

observar [oβserβár] *t.* to observe. 2 to notice. 3 to watch,. 4 to remark.

obstáculo [oβstákulo] *m.* obstacle, hindrance.

obstante (no) [oβstánte] *conj.* notwithstanding; nevertheless.

obtener [oβtenér] *t.* to attain, obtain, get.

ocasión [okasjón] *f.* occasion, opportunity, chance. 2 motive.

ocasionar [okasjonár] *t.* to cause, bring about, arouse.

occidental [oyθiðentál] *a.* western. 2 *m.-f.* westerner.

occidente [oyθiðénte] *m.* west.

océano [oθéano] *m.* ocean.

ocioso [oθjóso] *a.* idle; lazy, at leisure.

octavo [oytáβo] *a.-m.* eighth.

octubre [oytúβre] *m.* October.

ocultar [okultár] *t.* to conceal, hide.

oculto [okúlto] *a.* hidden, concealed. 2 secret.

ocupar [okupár] *t.* to occupy. 2 to employ. 3 to fill [a space]. 4 *p.* ~ *en,* to be busy with.

ocurrencia [okurrénθja] *f.* event. 2 witty remark. 3 bright idea.

ocurrir [okurrír] *i.* to happen. 2 *p.* to occur to one.

odiar [oðjár] *t.* to hate.

odio [óðjo] *m.* hatred, ill will, dislike.

odioso [oðjóso] *a.* hateful, nasty, unpleasant.

ofender [ofendér] *t.* to offend, insult. 2 *p.* to take offence.

oferta [oférta] *f.* offer. 2 COM. *la* ~ *y la demanda,* supply and demand.

oficial [ofiθjál] *a.* official. 2 *m.* [skilled] workman. 3 MIL. officer. 4 [government] official. 5 **-mente** *adv.* officially.

oficina [ofiθina] *f.* office.

oficio [ofiθjo] *m.* profession, job: *de* ~, by trade. 2 office [duty, etc.]. 3 official communication. 4 ECCL. service; mass.

oficioso [ofiθjóso] *a.* officious. 2 unofficial. 3 diligent.

ofrecer [ofreθér] t. to offer, present. 2 p. to volunteer. ¶ CONJUG. like *agradecer*.

ofrenda [ofrénda] f. offering.

oido [oído] m. hearing [sense]; ear [organ].

oir [oír] t. to hear; to listen; to understand. ¶ CONJUG. INDIC. Pres.: *oigo, oyes, oye*; oímos, ois, *oyen*. | Pret.: oí, oiste, *oyó*; oímos, oisteis, *oyeron*. ‖ SUBJ. Pres.: *oiga, oigas*, etc. | Imperf.: *oyera, oyeras*, etc., or *oyese, oyeses*, etc. | Fut.: *oyere, oyeres*, etc. ‖ IMPER.: *oye, oiga; oigamos*, oid, *oigan*. ‖ PAST. P.: oído. ‖ GER.: *oyendo*.

¡ojalá! [oxalá] interj. would God! God grant!, I wish!

ojo [óxo] m. eye: *en un abrir y cerrar de ojos*, in the twinkling of an eye; *¡ojo!*, beware! 2 hole. 3 span [of a bridge]. 4 well [of stairs]. 5 keyhole.

ola [óla] f. wave.

oler [olér] t.-i. to smell.

olfatear [olfateár] t. to smell, scent, sniff. 2 to pry into.

olfato [olfáto] m. smell.

olímpico [olímpiko] a. Olympic [games]; Olympian.

olivo [olíβo] m. olive-tree.

olor [olór] m. odour, smell: *mal ~*, stink.

olvidar [olβiðár] t.-p. to forget, leave behind.

olvido [olβíðo] m. fogetfulness; omission, oversight; oblivion.

olla [óλa] f. pot, boiler.

omnipotente [omnipoténte] a. allmighty, all-powerful, omnipotent.

once [ónθe] a.-m. eleven.

onda [ónda] f. wave, ripple; scallop.

onza [ónθa] f. ounce.

opaco [opáko] a. opaque.

ópera [ópera] f. opera.

operación [operaθjón] f. operation, transaction.

operar [operár] t. SURG. to operate upon. 2 i. to take effect, work. 3 to handle. 4 p. to occur.

opinar [opinár] i. to hold an opinion; to think, consider.

opinión [opinjón] f. opinion, view, mind.

oponer [oponér] t. to

oppose; to resist, face. ¶ CONJUG. like *poner*.

oportunidad [oportuniðáð] *f.* opportunity; chance.

oportuno [oportúno] *a.* opportune, suitable.

oposición [oposiθjón] *f.* opposition. 2 *pl.* competitive examination.

oprimir [oprimír] *t.* to press down. 2 to crush. 3 to oppress.

opuesto [opwésto] *a.* opposed. 2 opposite. 3 adverse.

opulento [opulénto] *a.* wealthy; opulent, rich.

oración [oraθjón] *f.* speech. 2 prayer. 3 GRAM. sentence.

orador [oraðór] *m.-f.* speaker, orator.

orar [orár] *i.* to pray.

orden [órðen] *m.* order [arrangement; method]. 2 command.

ordenar [orðenár] *t.* to order, arrange. 2 to comand. 3 *p.* ECCL. to take orders.

ordeñar [orðeñár] *t.* to milk.

ordinario [orðinárjo] *a.* ordinary, usual. 2 common, coarse, vulgar.

oreja [oréxa] *f.* ear.

orgánico [orɣániko] *a.* organic.

organizar [orɣaniθár] *t.* to organize. 2 to set up, start.

órgano [órɣano] *m.* organ. 2 means, medium.

orgullo [orɣúʎo] *m.* pride, haughtiness.

orgulloso [orɣuʎóso] *a.* proud, haughty.

oriental [orjentál] *a.* eastern; oriental.

orientar [orjentár] *t.* to orientate; to direct. 2 *p.* to find one's bearings.

oriente [orjénte] *m.* east.

origen [orixen] *c.* origin. 2 source. 3 native country.

original [orixinál] *a.* original. 2 queer. 3 *m.* original. 4 eccentric. 5 **-mente** *adv.* originally; eccentrically.

originar [orixinár] *t.* to give rise to. 2 *p.* to arise.

orilla [oríʎa] *f.* border, edge, brink. 2 bank; shore.

oro [óro] *m.* gold.

orquesta [orkésta] *f.* orchestra.

oruga [orúɣa] *f.* caterpillar.

os [os] *pron.* you.

osar [osár] *i.* to dare, venture.

oscurecer, oscuridad, etc. [oskur-] = OBSCURECER, OBSCURIDAD.

oso [óso] *m.* bear.

ostentar [ostentár] *t.* to display, show. *2* to show off.

otoño [otóɲo] *m.* autumn, fall.

otorgar [otoɾɣár] *t.* to grant, give. *2* to award [a prize].

otro [ótro] *a.-pron.* another, other.

oveja [oβéxa] *f.* ewe, sheep.

oxígeno [oɣsíxeno] *m.* oxygen.

oyente [oiénte] *m.-f.* hearer. *2* listener.

P

pacer [paθér] *i.-t.* to graze, pasture.

paciente [paθjénte] *a.-n.* patient.

pacífico [paθifiko] *a.* pacific. 2 calm, peaceful. 3 *a.-n.* Pacific [Ocean].

pacto [páɣto] *m.* agreement, covenant, pact.

padecer [paðeθér] *t.-i.* to suffer [from]. ¶ CONJUG. like *agradecer*.

padrastro [paðrástro] *m.* stepfather.

padre [páðre] *m.* father: ~ *político*, father-in--law. 2 *pl.* parents; ancestors.

paga [páɣa] *f.* payment. 2 pay, salary; fee.

pagar [paɣár] *t.* to pay. 2 to pay for.

página [páxina] *f.* page.

pago [páɣo] *m.* payment.

país [país] *m.* country, nattion, land, region.

paisaje [paĭsáxe] *m.* landscape.

paja [páxa] *f.* straw.

pájaro [páxaro] *m.* bird: ~ *carpintero*, woodpecker.

paje [páxe] *m.* page.

pala [pála] *f.* shovel. 2 blade. 3 [baker's] peel.

palabra [paláβra] *f.* word [term; speech, remark].

palacio [paláθjo] *m.* palace.

paladar [palaðár] *s.* palate. 2 taste.

palanca [paláŋka] *m.-f.* lever, crowbar.

palangana [palaŋgána] *f.* washbasin.

palco [pálko] *m.* box.

paleta [paléta] *f.* palette. 2 fire shovel. 3 trowel.

palidez [paliðéθ] *f.* paleness, pallor, sickliness.

pálido [páliðo] *a.* pale.

palillo [palíʎo] *m.* toothpick. 2 drumstick. 2 *pl.* castanets.

paliza [palíθa] *f.* beating, thrashing, dressingdown.

palma [pálma] *f.* palm, palm-tree. 2 palm [of the hand]. 3 *pl.* clapping of hands.

palmada [palmáða] *f.* slap, pat: *dar palmadas,* to clap.

palmera [palméra] *f.* palm-tree.

palo [pálo] *m.* stick. 2 NAUT. mast. 3 suit [at cards]. 4 handle.

paloma [palóma] *f.* dove, pigeon.

palomar [palomár] *m.* dove-cot pigeon loft.

palpitante [palpitánte] *a.* palpitating, throbbing, burning.

palpitar [palpitár] *i.* to beat, throb, palpitate.

pan [pan] *m.* bread; loaf.

pana [pána] *f.* velveteen, corduroy. 2 AUTO. break-down.

panadería [panaðería] *f.* bakery, baker's [shop].

panadero [panaðéro]· *m.* baker.

panal [panál] *m.* honeycomb.

panel [panél] *m.* panel.

pánico [pániko] *a.-m.* panic.

panorama [panoráma] *m.* panorama, vista, view.

pantalón [pantalón] *m.* trousers, pants; slacks.

pantalla [pantáʎa] *f.* lamp-shade. 2 CINEM. screen.

pantano [pantáno] *m.* swamp, marsh.

pantera [pantéra] *f.* panther.

pañal [paɲál] *m.* swaddling-cloth, baby cloth.

pañuelo [paɲwélo] *m.* handkerchief.

papa [pápa] *m.* Pope. 2 potato.

papá [papá] *m.* papa, dad, daddy.

papel [papél] *m.* paper: ~ *secante,* blotting-paper. 2 THEAT. part, rôle.

papeleta [papeléta] *f.* card, ticket: ~ *de votación,* ballot paper.

paquete [pakéte] *m.* packet, parcel.

par [par] *a.* like, equal. 2 even [number]. 3 *m.* pair, couple.

para [pára] *prep.* for, to, in order to: ~ *que*, so that; ¿*para qué?*, what for? 2 towards. 3 by, on.

parada [paráða] *f.* stop, halt. 2 parade.

parador [paraðór] *m.* tourist hotel; inn.

paraguas [paráɣwas] *m.* umbrella.

paraíso [paraíso] *m.* paradise, heaven.

parálisis [parálisis] *f.* paralysis; palsy.

paralítico [paralítiko] *a.-n.* MED. paralytic, palsied.

paralizar [paraliθár] *t.* to paralyse; to stop.

parar [parár] *t.* to stop. 2 ~ *mientes en*, to consider. 3 *i.-p.* to stop. 4 to put up, lodge.

parásito [parásito] *a.* parasitic. 2 *m.* BIOL. parasite. 3 hanger-on. 4 *pl.* RADIO. strays.

parcela [parθéla] *f.* lot, plot [of land].

pardo [párðo] *a.* brown. 2 dark.

1) **parecer** [pareθér] *m.* opinion, mind. 2 looks.

2) **parecer** [pareθér] *i.* to appear, show up. 2 im- *pers.* to seem, look like: *según parece*, as it seems. 3 *p.* to re- semble. ¶ CONJUG. like *agradecer*.

parecido [pareθíðo] *a.* resembling, similar [to|, like. 2 *bien* ~, good- looking. 3 *m.* resem- blance.

pared [paréð] *f.* wall.

pareja [paréxa] *f.* pair, couple. 2 partner.

pariente [parjénte] *m.* relation, relative.

parir [parír] *t.* to give birth to, bring forth, bear.

paro [páro] *m.* stop. 2 strike: ~ *forzoso*, un- employment.

parque [párke] *m.* park.

párrafo [párrafo] *m.* paragraph.

parte [párte] *f.* part, portion, lot, section: *en* ~, partly. 2 share, interest. 3 side: *estar de* ~ *de*, to support. 4 place, region: *por to- das partes*, everywhere. 5 *de* ~ *de*, on behalf of. 6 *por una* ~, ... *por otra* on the one hand,

... on the other hand.
7 official communication. *8 dar ~*, to report.

participante [partiθipánte] *m.-f.* participant, sharer.

participar [partiθipár] *t.* to notify, inform. *2 i.* to share.

particular [partikulár] *a.* particular, peculiar, private. *2* noteworth. *3 m.* private. *4* **-mente** *adv.* particularly; especially.

partida [partíða] *f.* leave. *2* record [in a register]. *3* [birth] certificate. *4* BOOKKEEP. entry, item. *5* COM. shipment. *6* game; match; set. *7* gang.

partido [partíðo] *p. p.* of PARTIR. *2 m.* party. *3* profit. *4* popularity. *5* SPORT team; game, match. *6* territorial district. *7* match [in marriage].

partir [partír] *t.-p.* to divide, split. *2 i.* to depart, leave, start.

parto [párto] *m.* childbirth, delivery.

pasado [pasáðo] *a.* past. *2* last [week, etc.]. *3* spoiled; tainted. *4* ~ *de moda*, out of date. *5*

~ *mañana*, the day after tomorrow. *6 m.* the past.

pasaje [pasáxe] *m.* passage, way. *2* passengers. *3* fare. *4* lane, alley.

pasar [pasár] *t.* to pass. *2* to go [over, in, by, to]. *3* to walk past. *4* to suffer. *5* to overlook. *6* to spend [time] *7 pasarlo bien*, to have a good time. *8 i.* to pass, get through. *9* to come in. *10* ~ *de*, to go beyond. *11 ir pasando*, to get along. *12 impers.* to happen: *¿que pasa?*, what is the matter? *13 p.* to get spoiled. *14* to exceed. *15* ~ *sin*, to do without.

pascua [páskwa] *f.* Easter: ~ *de Resurrección* Easter Sunday.

pasear [paseár] *i.-p.* to walk; to take a walk.

paseo [paséo] *m.* walk, ride: *dar un* ~, to go for a walk. *2* promenade.

pasillo [pasíλo] *m.* corridor, passage; lobby.

pasión [pasjón] *f.* passion.
amazed.

paso [páso] *m.* step, pace: ~ *a* ~, step by

step; *de* ~, by the way;
~ *a nivel*, level crossing; *marcar el* ~, to
mark time. 2 passage.

pasta [pásta] *f.* paste. 2
dough.

pastar [pastár] *t.-i.* to
graze, pasture.

pastel [pastél] *m.* pie,
tart. 2 cake.

pastilla [pastíʎa] *f.* tablet, lozenge; cake [of
soap].

pastor [pastór] *m.* shepherd. 2 ECCL. minister.

pata [páta] *f.* foot and
leg; leg [of table, etc.]:
a cuaro patas, on all
fours; *a* ~, on foot;
meter la ~, to make a
blunder; *tener mala* ~,
to have bad luck.

patada [patáða] *f.* kick.

patata [patáta] *f.* potato: *patatas fritas*, chips.

patente [paténte] *a.* evident. 2 *f.* patent.

patilla [patíʎa] *f.* side-
-whiskers.

patio [pátjo] *m.* court,
yard, courtyard. 2 THEAT.
pit.

pato [páto] *m.* duck. 2
drake.

patria [pátrja] *f.* native
country: ~ *chica*, home
town.

patriota [patrjóta] *m.-f.*
patriot.

patriótico [patrjótiko] *a.*
patriotic.

patriotismo [patrjotízmo]
m. patriotism.

patrón [patrón] *m.* patron. 2 landlord. 3 employer. *4* pattern. *5*
standard.

pausa [páusa] *f.* pause.
2 rest; break.

pavo [páβo] *m.* turkey.
2 ~ *real*, peacock.

pavor [paβór] *m.* fear,
fright, dread, terror.

paz [paθ] *f.* peace, peacetime; quiet.

peca [péka] *f.* freckle,
spot.

pecado [pekáðo] *m.* sin.

pecador [pekaðór] *a.*
sinful. 2 *m.-f.* sinner.

pecar [pekár] *i.* to sin.

peculiar [pekuljár] *a.*
peculiar, characteristic.

pecho [pétʃo] *m.* chest,
breast, bosom; heart:
tomar a ~, to take to
heart.

pedazo [peðáθo] *m.* piece,
bit, portion.

pedir [peðír] *t.* to ask
[for], beg, request, demand. 2 COM. to order.
3 ~ *prestado*, to borrow. ¶ CONJUG. like
servir.

pedrada [peðráða] *f.* blow with a stone.

pegar [peɣár] *t.-i.* to glue, stick. 2 to fasten. 3 to post [bills]. 4 to set [fire]. 4 to hit, slap. 6 *p.* to stick. 7 to come to blows.

peinar [peinár] *t.* to comb. 2 *p.* to comb one's hair, do one's hair.

peine [péine] *m.* comb.

pelado [peláðo] *a.* bald, bare. 2 barren. 3 penniless [person].

pelar [pelár] *t.* to cut or shave the hair of. 2 to pluck. 3 to peel. 4 *p.* to get one's hair cut.

pelea [peléa] *f.* fight. 2 quarrel, row, scuffle.

pelear [peleár] *i.-p.* to fight. 2 to quarrel; to come to blows. 3 *i.* to battle.

película [pelíkula] *f.* film, movie.

peligro [pelíɣro] *m.* danger, peril, risk, hazard.

peligroso [peliɣróso] *a.* dangerous, risky.

pelo [pélo] *m.* hair. 2 fur. 3 down [of birds]. 4 *tomar el* ~, to pull the leg.

pelota [pelóta] *f.* ball; pelota; *en pelotas*, naked.

peludo [pelúðo] *a.* hairy.

peluquería [pelukería] *f.* hairdresser's [shop]; barber's [shop].

pellejo [peʎéxo] *m.* skin, hide. 2 wineskin.

pena [péna] *f.* penalty, punishment, pain. 2 sorrow. 3 *dar* ~, to arouse pity. 4 *valer la* ~, to be worth while.

penal [penál] *a.* penal. 2 *m.* penitentiary.

pendiente [pendjénte] *a.* pending, hanging. 2 depending on. 3 *f.* slope. 4 *m.* ear-ring.

penetrar [penetrár] *t.-i.* to break into. 2 *i.* to be piercing. 3 to comprehend.

península [península] *f.* peninsula.

penitencia [peniténθja] *f.* penance. 2 penitence.

penoso [penóso] *a.* painful, distressing. 2 hard.

pensador [pensaðór] *m.* thinker.

pensamiento [pensamjénto] *m.* thought. 2 idea. 3 BOT. pansy.

pensar [pensár] *t.* to think [of, out, over, about]; to consider; to intend. ¶ CONJUG. like *acertar*.

pensativo [pensatíβo] a. pensive, thoughtful.

pensión [pensjón] f. pension. 2 guest-house.

peña [péŋa] f. rock.

peón [peón] m. day-labourer: ~ de albañil, hodman; ~ caminero, road-mender. 2 (Am.) farm hand. 3 pawn [in chess].

peor [peór] a.-adv. worse. 2 the worst.

pepita [pepita] f. pip. 2 MIN. nugget.

pequeño [pekéŋo] a. little, small. 2 low; short. 3 m.-f. child, kid.

pera [péra] f. pear.

percibir [perθiβír] t. to perceive. 2 to collect.

percha [pértʃa] f. perch. 2 clothes-rack, hanger.

perder [perðér] t. to lose: ~ de vista, to lose sight of. 2 to ruin, spoil. 3 p. to get lost. 4 to be spoiled. ¶ CONJUG. like entender.

pérdida [pérðiða] f. loss: pérdidas y ganancias, COM. profit and loss. 2 waste [of time].

perdido [perðíðo] a. lost. 2 mislaid. 3 wasted.

perdón [perðón] m. pardon, forgiveness.

perdonar [perðonár] t. to pardon, forgive. 2 to excuse.

perecer [pereθér] i. to come to an end, perish, die. ¶ CONJUG. like agradecer.

peregrino [pereɣríno] a. strange, rare. 2 wandering. 3 m.-f. pilgrim.

pereza [peréθa] f. laziness, idleness.

perezoso [pereθóso] a. lazy, idle.

perfección [perfeɣθjón] perfection, completion.

perfeccionar [perfeɣθjonár] t. to perfect; to improve; to complete.

perfectamente [perféytaménte] adv. perfectly.

perfecto [perféyto] a. perfect, complete.

perfilar [perfilár] t. to profile. 2 to outline.

perfumar [perfumár] t. to perfume, scent.

perfume [perfúme] m. perfume; scent. 2 fragance.

periódico [perjóðiko] a. periodic(al. 2 m. journal, newspaper.

periodista [perjoðísta] m.-f. journalist.

periodo [períoðo] m. period.

perjudicar [perxuðikár] *t.* to hurt, damage, injure.

perjudicial [perxuðiθjál] *a.* harmful, damaging.

perjuicio [perxwiθjo] *m.* harm, injury, prejudice.

perla [pérla] *f.* pearl.

permanecer [permaneθér] *i.* to remain, stay. 2 to last. ¶ CONJUG. like *agradecer*.

permanente [permanénte] *a.* permanent, lasting. 2 *f.* permanent wave. 3 **-mente** *adv.* permanently.

permiso [permiso] *m.* leave, permit; permission: ~ *de conducir*, driving licence; *con su* ~, by your leave.

permitir [permitir] *t.* to permit, allow, let.

pernil [pernil] *m.* ham.

pero [péro] *conj.* but; yet; except.

perpetuo [perpétwo] *a.* everlasting, perpetual.

perro [pérro] *m.* dog.

persecución [persekuθjón] *f.* persuit, hunt, chase.

perseguir [perseɣir] *t.* to pursue, persecute, chase. ¶ CONJUG. like *servir*.

persiana [persjána] *f.* Venetian blind.

persona [persóna] *f.* person. 2 *pl.* people.

personaje [personáxe] *m.* personage. 2 THEAT. character.

personal [personál] *a.* personal. 2 *m.* staff, personnel. 3 **-mente** *adv.* personally.

perspectiva [perspeɣtiβa] *f.* perspective. 2 prospect, outlook.

persuadir [perswaðir] *t.* to persuade. 2 *p.* to be convinced.

pertenecer [perteneθér] *i.* to belong; to concern, ¶ CONJUG. like *agradecer*.

perteneciente [perteneθiénte] *a.* belonging to.

perturbado [perturβáðo] *a.* disturbed. 2 insane.

perturbar [perturβár] *t.* to disturb, upset. 2 to confuse.

perverso [perβérso] *a.* perverse, wicked, depraved.

pervertir [perβertir] *t.* to pervert, deprave. ¶ CONJUG. like *hervir*.

pesa [pésa] *f.* weight.

pesadilla [pesaðíλa] *f.* nightmare.

pesado [pesáðo] *a.* heavy, weighty. 2 tiresome, boring. 3 deep [sleep].

pésame [pésame] *m.* condolence, expression of sympathy.

1) **pesar** [pesár] *m.* sorrow. 2 regret, grief. 3 *a ~ de*, in spite of.

2) **pesar** [pesár] *t.* to weigh. 2 to consider. 3 *i.* to have weight. 4 to be sorry, regret.

pesca [péska] *f.* fishing. 2 angling. 3 catch of fish.

pescado [peskáðo] *m.* fish. 2 salted codfish.

pescador [peskaðór] *m.* fisher, fisherman: *~ de caña*, angler.

pescar [peskár] *t.* to fish. 2 to angle.

pesebre [peséβre] *m.* crib, manger.

peseta [peséta] *f.* peseta.

peso [péso] *m.* weight: *~ bruto*, gross weight; *~ neto*, net weight. 2 load, burden. 3 peso [monetary unit].

pestaña [pestáɲa] *f.* eyelash.

peste [péste] *f.* pest, plague.

pétalo [pétalo] *m.* petal.

petición [petiθjón] *f.* petition, request.

petróleo [petróleo] *m.* petroleum, oil.

pez [peθ] *m.* fish. 2 *f.* pitch, tar.

pezuña [peθúɲa] *f.* hoof.

piadoso [pjaðóso] *a.* pious, devout.

piar [piár] *i.* to peep, chirp, cheep.

picar [pikár] *t.* to prick, pierce. 2 BULLF. to goat. 3 [of insects] to bite, 4 to spur [a horse]. 5 to mince. 6 *t.-i.* to itch. 7 AER. to dive. 8 *p.* [of teeth] to begin to decay. 9 [of the sea] to get choppy. 10 to take offense.

pícaro [píkaro] *a.* knavish, roguish. 2 sly. 3 *m.-f.* knave, rogue. 4 sly person. 5 *m.* LIT. pícaro.

pico [píko] *m.* beak. 2 mouth; eloquence. 3 peak [of a mountain]. 4 pick [tool], pickaxe: *tres pesetas y ~*, three pesetas odd.

picotazo [pikotáθo] *m.* peck [of a bird]. 2 sting [of insects].

pie [pjé] *m.* foot: *a pie*, on foot; *en ~*, standing; *al ~ de la letra*, literally. 2 bottom. 3 base, stand. 4 trunk, stalk.

piedad [pjeðáð] *f.* piety.

piedra [pjéðra] *f.* stone.

piel [pjél] *f.* skin. 2 hide, pelt. 3 leather. 4 fur. 5 m. ~ *roja*, red-skin.

pierna [pjérna] *f.* leg.

pieza [pjéθa] *f.* piece. 2 game.

pila [píla] *f.* trough. 2 baptismal font. 3 heap.

píldora [píldora] *f.* pill.

piloto [pilóto] *m.* pilot. plunder, catch, grasp.

pillo [píʎo] *m.-f.* rogue, rascal. 2 urchin.

pimienta [pimjénta] *f.* pepper [spice].

pimiento [pimjénto] *m.* [green, red] pepper.

pincel [pinθél] *m.* brush.

pinchar [pintʃár] *t.* to prick, puncture.

pino [píno] *m.* pine, pine-tree.

pintar [pintár] *t.* to paint. 2 to describe. 3 *p.* to make up one's face.

pintor [pintór] *m.* painter; house painter.

pintoresco [pintorésko] *a.* picturesque.

pintura [pintúra] *f.* painting.

piña [píɲa] *f.* pine cone. 2 ~ *de América*, pine-apple.

pipa [pípa] *f.* pipe. 2 cask. 3 pip, seed.

pirata [piráta] *m.* pirate.

pisar [pisár] *t.* to tread on, step on. 2 to trample under foot.

piscina [pisθína] *f.* swimming-pool.

piso [píso] *m.* floor; storey: ~ *bajo*, ground floor. 2 flat, apartment.

pista [písta] *f.* trail, trace, scent. 2 clue. 3 SPORT race-track. 4 ring. 5 AER. runway, landing-field.

pistola [pistóla] *f.* pistol.

pitar [pitár] *i.* to blow a whistle; to whistle at; to hiss.

pito [píto] *m.* whistle.

pizarra [piθárra] *f.* slate. 2 blackboard.

placa [pláka] *f.* plaque. 2 PHOT. plate.

placentero [plaθentéro] *a.* joyful, pleasant, agreeable.

1) **placer** [plaθér] *m.* pleasure. 2 will.

2) **placer** [plaθér] *t.* to please. ¶ CONJUG. INDIC. Pres.: *plazco*, *places*, *place*, etc. | Pret.:

plació or *plugo;* placieron or *pluguieron.* ‖ SUBJ. Pres.: *plazca, plazcas,* etc. | Imperf.: placiera or *pluguiera.* | Fut.: placiere or *pluguiere,* etc. ‖ IMPER.: place, *plazca; plazcamos,* placed, *plazcan.*

plaga [pláɣa] *f.* plague, pest, scourge.

plan [plan] *m.* plan, project, scheme.

plancha [plántʃa] *f.* plate, sheet. 2 iron [for clothes].

planchar [plantʃár] *t.* to iron, press.

planear [planeár] *t.* to plan, outline. 2 *i.* AER. to glide.

planeta [planéta] *m.* planet.

plano [pláno] *a.* plane. 2 flat, even. 3 *m.* plane. 4 plan [map].

planta [plánta] *f.* plant. 2 sole of the foot. 3 ~ *baja,* ground floor.

plantar [plantár] *t.* to plant. 2 to set up, place 3 to jilt. 4 *p.* to stand firm.

plantel [plantél] *m.* nursery; nursery school.

plata [pláta] *f.* silver. 2 money.

plataforma [platafórma] *f.* platform.

plátano [plátano] *m.* banana.

plateado [plateáðo] *a.* silver-plated. 2 silvery.

plato [pláto] *m.* plate, dish. 2 course [at meals].

playa [plája] *f.* beach, seaside, shore.

plaza [pláθa] *f.* public square. 2 market-place. 3 fortress. 4 seat. 5 job. 6 town, city. 7 ~ *de toros,* bullring.

plazo [pláθo] *m.* term: time-limit: *a plazos,* by instalments.

pleito [pléito] *m.* litigation, law-suit. 2 debate.

pleno [pléno] *a.* full, complete. *ciones,* specifications.

pliegue [pljéɣe] *m.* fold, crease.

plomo [plómo] *m.* lead. 2 sinker.

pluma [plúma] *f.* feather. 2 [writing] pen, nib.

población [poβlaθjón] *f.* population. 2 city, town.

poblado [poβláðo] *a.* populated. 2 thick. 3 *m.* town.

pobre [póβre] *a.* poor. 2 *m.-f.* beggar.

pobreza [poβréθa] *f.* poverty; need; lack.

1) **poco** [póko] *adv.* little, not much: *dentro de ~,* presently; *~ más o menos,* more or less.

2) **poco** [póko] *a.* little, scanty. 2 *pl.* few.

podar [poðár] *t.* to prune, lop off, trim [off].

1) **poder** [poðér] *m.* power; authority. 2 force, strength, might.

2) **poder** [poðér] *t.-i.* to be able [to], can, may. 2 *i.* to have power or influence. 3 *impers.* to be possible, may. ‖ CONJUG. INDIC. Pres.: *puedo, puedes, puede, podemos, podéis, pueden.* | Pret.: *pude, pudiste,* etc. | Fut.: *podré, podrás,* etc. ‖ COND.: *podría, podrías,* etc. ‖ SUBJ. Pres.: Pres.: *pueda, puedas, pueda, podamos, podáis, puedan.* | Imperf.: *pudiera, pudieras,* etc., or *pudiese, pudieses,* etc. | Fut.: *pudiere, pudieres,* etc. ‖ IMPER.: *puede, pueda, podamos, poded, puedan.* ‖ GER.: *pudiendo.*

poderoso [poðeróso] *a.* powerful, mighty. 2 wealthy.

poema [poéma] *m.* poem.

poesía [poesía] *f.* poetry. 2 poem.

poeta [poéta] *m.* poet.

policía [poliθía] *m.* policeman, detective. 2 police force: *~ secreta,* secret police.

policíaco [poliθíako] *a.* [pertaining to the] police. 2 *novela policíaca,* detective story.

polilla [políʎa] *f.* moth.

política [polítika] *f.* politics.

político [polítiko] *a.* politic(al. 2 tactful. 3 *-in-law: padre ~,* father-in-law. *4 m.* politician.

polo [pólo] *m.* pole. 2 SPORTS polo.

polvo [pólβo] *m.* dust. 2 powder.

pólvora [pólβora] *f.* gunpowder.

pollo [póʎo] *m.* chicken. 2 young man.

pompa [pómpa] *f.* pomp; show: *pompas fúnebres,* funeral. 2 pageant. 3 bubble. *4* pump.

poner [ponér] *t.* to place, put, set: *~ en libertad,* to set free; *~ en práctica,* to carry out. 2

to lay [eggs]. 3 to render [furious]. 4 ~ de manifiesto, to make evident; ~ de relieve, to emphasize; ~ reparos, to make objections. 5 p. to put on [one's hat]. 6 [of the sun] to set. 7 to become. 8 ~ a, to begin to. 9 ~ al corriente, to get informed. 10 ~ de acuerdo, to agree. 11 ponerse en pie, to stand up. ‖ Conjug. Indic. Pres.: pongo, pones, pone, etc. | Pret.: puse, pusiste, puso, etc. | Fut.: pondré, pondrás, etc. ‖ Cond.: pondría, pondrías, etc. ‖ Subj. Pres.: ponga, pongas, etc. | Imperf.: pusiera, pusieras, or pusiese, pusieses, etc. | Fut.: pusiere, pusieres, etc. ‖ Imper.: pon, ponga; pongamos, poned, pongan. ‖ Past. p.: puesto.

popular [populár] a. popular; colloquial.

popularidad [populariðáð] f. popularity.

por [por] prep. by, for, as, along, around, across, through, from, out of, at, in, on, to, etc.:

~ la noche, in the night, by night. 2 ~ ciento, per cent; ~ tanto, therefore; ~ más que, ~ mucho que, however much; ¿~ qué?, why?; ~ supuesto, of course.

porcelana [porθelána] f. china, porcelain.

porción [porθjón] f. part, share, lot, portion.

pordiosero [porðjoséro] n. beggar.

poro [póro] m. pore.

porque [pórke] conj. for, because, since.

¿por qué? [porké] conj. why?

porqué [porké] m. cause, reason; why.

porquería [porkería] f. dirt, filth. 2 filthy act or word.

porta(a)viones [portaβjónes] m. aircraft carrier.

portal [portál] m. doorway, vestibule. 2 porch, portico, entrance.

portarse [portárse] p. behave, act.

porte [pórte] m. portage, carriage; freight: ~ pagado, portage prepaid. 2 behaviour; appearance [of a person].

portero [portéro] m.

doorkeeper, porter. 2 SPORT goalkeeper.

porvenir [porβenír] *m.* future.

posada [posáða] *f.* lodg-ing-house, inn.

posar [posár] *i.* to lodge. 2 to rest. 3 F. ATRS to sit, pose. 4 *i.-p.* [of birds, etc.] to alight, perch. 5 *t.* to lay down. 6 *p.* to settle.

poseer [poseér] *t.* to possess, own, hold, have. 2 to master. ¶ CONJUG. INDIC. Pret.: poseí, poseíste, poseyó; poseímos, poseísteis, poseyeron. ‖ SUBJ. Imperf.: poseyera, poseyeras, etc., or pose-yese, poseyeses, etc. ‖ PAST. P.: poseído or po-seso. ‖ GER.: poseyendo.

posesión [posesjón] *f.* possession, holding.

posibilidad [posiβiliðáð] *f.* possibility, chance. 2 *pl.* means.

posible [posíβle] *a.* possible: nacer todo lo ~, to do one's best.

positivo [positíβo] *a.* positive, practical.

posponer [posponér] *t.* to postpone, delay, put off.

postal [postál] *a.* postal. 2 *f.* postcard.

poste [póste] *m.* pillar; post, pole: ~ indicador, finger-post.

postrar [postrár] *t.* to prostrate, cast down. 2 *p.* to kneel down.

postre [póstre] *a.* POS-TRERO. 2 *m.* dessert. 3 adv. a la ~, at last.

postrero [postréro] *a.* last. 2 *m.-f.* last one.

pote [póte] *m.* pot; jug; jar.

potencia [poténθja] *f.* power; faculty, ability; strength. 2 powerful nation.

potente [poténte] *a.* potent, powerful, mighty. 2 strong.

potestad [potestáð] *f.* power, faculty. 2 authority.

potro [pótro] *m.-f.* colt, foal. 2 *m.* horse [for torture]. 3 *f.* filly.

pozo [póθo] *m.* well, pit. 2 shaft.

práctica [práytika] *f.* practice: poner en ~, to put into practice. 2 skill. 3 *pl.* training.

práctico [práytiko] *a.* practical. 2 skilful. 3 *m.* NAUT. pilot.

pradera [praðéra] *f.* prairie, meadow.

prado [prádo] *f.* field, meadow, lawn.

precaución [prekauθjón] *f.* precaution.

precedente [preθeδénte] *a.* preceding. 2 *m.* precedent.

preceder [preθeδér] *t.-i.* to precede, go ahead of.

precepto [preθéβto] *m.* rule; order: *dia de ~*, holiday.

precio [préθjo] *m.* price, cost, value. 2 worth.

precioso [preθjóso] *a.* precious, valuable, costly. 2 beautiful.

precipitar [preθipitár] *t.* to throw headlong, hurl, hurry. 2 *p.* to be hasty or rash..

precisamente [preθisaménte] *adv.* precisely, exactly. 2 just.

preciso [preθiso] *a.* precise, accurate; just. 2 necessary.

predecir [preδeθír] *t.* to foretell, forecast.

predicador [preδikaδór] *m.-f.* preacher.

predicar [preδikár] *t.-i.* to preach.

predilecto [preδiléɣto] *a.* favourite.

predominar [preδominár] to prevail. 2 to overlook.

preferencia [preferénθja] *f.* choice, preference.

preferible [preferíβle] *a.* preferable.

preferir [preferír] *t.* to prefer, choose: *yo preferiría ir*, I'd rather go.

pregunta [preɣúnta] *f.* question, inquiry: *hacer una ~*, to ask a question.

preguntar [preɣuntár] *t.-i.* to ask, inquire. 2 *p.* to wonder.

prejuicio [prexwíθjo] *m.* prejudice, bias.

premiar [premjár] *t.* to reward.

premio [prémjo] *m.* reward. 2 prize, award.

prenda [prénda] *f.* pledge, security, pawn; token, proof. 2 garment.

prender [prendér] *t.* to seize, catch. 2 to attach, pin. 3 to arrest. 4 to set [fire]. 5 *i.* to take root. 6 to catch.

prensa [prénsa] *f.* press; printing press. 2 journalism, daily press.

preocupación [preokupaθjón] *f.* preoccupation. 2 care, concern, worry.

preocupar [preokupár] *t.* to preoccupy. 2 to concern, worry, bother. 3 *p.* worry about.

preparación [prepara-θjón] *f.* preparation.

preparar [preparár] *t.* to prepare. 2 *p.* to get ready.

preparativo [preparatíβo] *a.* preparatory. 2 *m. pl.* arrangements.

presa [présa] *f.* catch, grip, hold. 2 capture. 3 prize, booty. 4 prey. 5 claw. 6 dam.

presencia [presénθja] *f.* presence.

presenciar [presenθjár] *t.* to be present at, witness.

presentar [presentár] *t.* to present. 2 to display, show. 3 to introduce. 4 *p.* to appear.

presente [presénte] *a.* present; hacer ~, to remind of; tener ~, to bear in mind. 2 current [month, etc.]. 3 *a.-m.* GRAM. present. 4 *m.* present, gift.

preservar [preserβár] *t.* to preserve, guard, keep safe.

presidencia [presiðénθja] *f.* presidency. 2 chairmanship.

presidente [presiðénte] *m.* president. 2 chairman.

presidir [presiðír] *t.-i.* to preside over or at, take the chair at, rule.

presión [presjón] *f.* pressure; press, squeeze.

preso [préso] *a.* imprisoned. 2 *m.-f.* prisoner.

préstamo [préstamo] *m.* loan, lending, borrowing.

prestar [prestár] *t.* to lend, loan. 2 to give. 3 to do, render [service, etc.]. 4 to pay [attention]. 5 to take [oath]. 6 *p.* to lend oneself. 7 se presta a, it gives rise to.

prestigio [prestíxjo] *m.* prestige; good name.

presto [présto] *adv.* quickly. 2 soon. 3 *a.* prompt, quick. 2 ready.

presumir [presumír] *t.* to presume, conjecture. 2 *i.* to boast.

presupuesto [presupwésto] *a.* presupposed. 2 *m.* budget. 3 estimate.

pretender [pretendér] *t.* to pretend to, claim. 3 to try to.

pretensión [pretensjón] *f.* claim. 2 aim, object.

pretexto [pretésto] *m.* pretext, excuse, plea.

prevalecer [preβaleθér] *i.* to prevail.

prevención [preβenθjón] *f.* supply. 2 foresight. 3 dislike. 4 warning. 5 police station.

prevenir [preβenír] *t.* prepare. 2 to forestall. 3 to warn. 4 to prevent. 5 *p.* to get ready.

previo [préβjo] *a.* previous.

prieto [prjéto] *a.* tight. 2 mean. 3 dark.

primario [primárjo] *a.* primary.

primavera [primaβéra] *f.* spring, springtime.

primero [priméro] *adv.* first. 2 *a.* first. 3 early.

primitivo [primitíβo] *a.* primitive, original, early.

primo [prímo] *a.* first. 2 raw [material]. 3 *m.-f.* cousin. 4 simpleton.

primogénito [primoxénito] *a.-n.* first-born, eldest [son].

primoroso [primoróso] *a.* exquisite. 2 skilful, fine.

principal [prinθipál] *a.* principal. 2 *m.* head [of a firm, etc.]. 3 first floor. 4 **-mente** *adv.* principally, mainly.

principio [prinθípjo] *m.* beginning. 2 principle. 3 *pl.* principles.

prisa [prísa] *f.* haste, hurry: *tener* ~, to be in a hurry.

prisión [prisjón] *f.* prison, jail; imprisonment.

prisionero [prisjonéro] *m.-f.* prisoner.

privación [priβaθjón] *f.* want, deprivation, loss.

privar [priβár] *t.* to forbid. 2 to prevail.

privilegio [priβiléxjo] *m.* privilege, grant, exemption.

pro [pro] *m.-f.* profit: *el* ~ *y el contra*, the pros and cons.

probabilidad [proβaβiliðáθ] *f.* probability, likelihood.

probable [proβáβle] *a.* probable, likely. 2 **-mente** *adv.* probably.

probar [proβár] *t.* to prove. 2 to test, try out. 3 to taste. 4 to try on [clothes]. 5 *i.* ~ *a*, to endeavour to.

problema [proβléma] *m.* problem.

proceder [proθeðér] *i.* to proceed. 2 to come from. 3 to behave. 4 to take action [against]. 5 to be proper.

procedimiento [proθeðimjénto] *m.* procedure; method, way.

procesión [proθesjón] *f.*
procession.

proceso [proθéso] *m.*
process. 2 lapse of time.
3 LAW proceedings. 4
law-suit.

proclamar [proklamár] *t.*
to proclaim.

procurador [prokuraðór]
m. attorney. 2 solicitor.

procurar [prokurár] *t.*
to try to. 2 to get. 3 to
manage.

prodigar [proðiɣár] *t.* to
lavish, squander.

prodigio [proðixjo] *m.*
prodigy, miracle.

prodigioso [proðixjóso]
a. marvellous, prodi-
gious. 2 exquisite.

pródigo [próðiɣo] *a.-n.*
prodigal. 2 *a.* lavish,
wasteful, extravagant.

producción [proðuɣθjón]
f. production. 2 pro-
duct, output, yield.

producir [proðuθír] *t.* to
produce, yield, bring
forth. 2 to cause. 3
p. to happen.

producto [proðúɣto] *m.*
product, produce.

productor [proðuɣtór] *a.*
productive. 2 *m.-f.* producer.

profecía [profeθía] *f.*
prophecy.

profesar [profesár] *t.-i.*
to profess. 2 *t.* to show,
manifest.

profesión [profesjón] *f.*
profession. 2 avowal,
declaration.

profesor [profesór] *m.-f.*
professor, teacher.

profeta [proféta] *m.*
prophet.

profundamente [profún-
ðaménte] *adv.* deeply.

profundidad [profundi-
ðáð] *f.* depth.

profundo [profúndo] *a.*
profound, deep.

progresar [proɣresár] *i.*
to progress, advance,
develop.

progreso [proɣréso] *m.*
progress, advance.

prohibir [proiβír] *t.* to
prohibit, forbid, stop,
ban.

prójimo [próximo] *m.*
neighbour, fellow man
[or creature].

prolongar [prolongár] *t.*
to lengthen. 2 to pro-
long. 3 *p.* to go on, extend.

promedio [proméðjo] *m.*
middle. 2 average.

promesa [promésa] *f.*
promise.

prometer [prometér] *t.-i.*
to promise. 2 *p.* to be-
come engaged, betrothed.

prometido [prometiðo] a. promised. 2 engaged, betrothed. 3 m. fiancé. 4 f. fiancée.

prominente [prominénte] a. prominent, projecting.

promover [promoβér] t. to promote, start. 2 to cause, stir up, raise.

pronombre [pronómbre] m. pronoun.

pronto [prónto] adv. soon: lo más ~ posible, as soon as possible. 2 quickly: de ~, suddenly. 3 a. ready.

pronunciar [pronunθjár] t. to pronounce, utter. 2 to deliver, make [a speech].

propaganda [propaγánda] f. propaganda. 2 advertising.

propagar [propaγár] t. to propagate, spread. 2 p. to be diffused.

propicio [propíθjo] a. propitious, favourable.

propiedad [propjeðáð] f. ownership, property.

propietario [propjetárjo] m. owner, landlord.

propio [própjo] a. proper, peculiar. 3 suitable. 4 amor ~, pride; nombre ~, proper noun.

proponer [proponér] t. to put forward. 2 p. to to plan, intend.

proporcionar [proporθjonár] t. to adjust. 2 to supply. 3 p. to get.

proposición [proposiθjón] f. proposition; proposal, offer.

propósito [propósito] m. purpose, aim: a ~, by the way; de ~, on purpose; fuera de ~, irrelevant.

prosa [prósa] f. prose.

proseguir [proseγír] t. to continue. 2 i. to go on, carry on.

prosperar [prosperár] i. to prosper, thrive, flourish.

prosperidad [prosperiðáð] f. prosperity. 2 success.

próspero [próspero] a. prosperous. 2 successful.

proteger [protexér] t. to protect, defend, shelter.

protesta [protésta] f. protest.

protestar [protestár] t.-i. to protest, object, remonstrate.

provecho [proβétʃo] m. profit, advantage, benefit.

provechoso [proβetʃóso] a. profitable, advantageous, useful.

proveedor [proβeeðór] *m.* supplier, furnisher, purveyor.

proveer [proveér] *t.* to supply with, provide, furnish.

proverbio [proβérβjo] *m.* proverb, saying.

providencia [proβiðénθja] *f.* providence, foresight.

providencial [proβiðénθjál] *a.* providencial.

provincia [proβinθja] *f.* province.

provisional [proβisjonál] temporary.

provocar [proβokár] *t.* to provoke, defy, challenge.

próximamente [próysima-ménte] *adv.* soon, before long, shortly.

proximidad [proysimiðáð] *f.* nearness.

próximo [próysimo] *a.* near, close to. 2 next: *el mes* ~, next month.

proyección [projeyθjón] *f.* projection. 2 showing.

proyectar [projeytár] *t.* to throw. 2 to show [a film, etc.]. 3 to plan, intend. 4 *p.* to jut out, stand out. 5 [of a shadow] to fall on.

proyecto [projéyto] *m.* project, plan, scheme. 2 ~ *de ley*, bill.

prudente [pruðénte] *a.* wise. 2 cautious.

prueba [prwéβa] *f.* proof; evidence. 2 sign. 3 test, trial. 4 sample. 5 fitting. 6 ordeal, trial. 7 poner *a* ~, to put to test.

psicológico [sikolóxiko] *a.* psychological.

publicación [puβlikaθjón] *f.* publication.

publicar [puβlikár] *t.* to publish. 2 to issue. 3 *p.* to come out.

publicidad [puβliθiðáð] *f.* publicity 2 advertising.

público [púβliko] *a.* public. 2 *m.* public; audience; spectators, crowd.

pueblo [pwéβlo] *m.* town. 2 common people. 3 nation.

puente [pwénte] *m.-f.* bridge. 2 deck.

puerco [pwérko] *a.* dirty, filthy. 2 *m.* hog, pig, swine. 3 ~ *espín*, porcupine. 4 *f.* sow.

puerta [pwérta] *f.* door; gate; entrance.

puerto [pwérto] *m.* port, harbour. 2 refuge. 3 mountain pass.

pues [pwes] *conj.* because, for, since. 2

then: *así* ~, so then; ~ *bien*, well then.

puesta [pwésta] *f.* setting: ~ *de sol*, sunset. 2 stake. 3 egg-laying.

puesto [pwésto] *p. p.* of PONER. 2 placed, put. 3 *m.* place, spot. 4 stall, stand. 5 job. 6 MIL. post, station: ~ *de socorro*, first-aid station. 7 conj. ~ *que*, since, inasmuch as.

púgil [púxil] *m.* boxer, pugilist.

pulga [púlɣa] *f.* flea.

pulmón [pulmón] *m.* lung.

pulpo [púlpo] *m.* octopus.

pulsera [pulséra] *f.* bracelet: *reloj de* ~, wristwatch.

punta [púnta] *f.* point. 2 head. 3 nib. 4 top. 5 horn. 6 tine. 7 *está de* ~ *con*, to be on bad terms with.

puntilla [puntiʎa] *f.* lace edging. 2 BULLF. short dagger. 3 *de puntillas*, on tiptoe.

punto [púnto] *m.* point; dot; stop: ~ *final*, full stop; ~ *y coma*, semicolon; *dos puntos*, colon. 2 SEW. stitch. 3 *géneros de* ~, hosiery. 4 place, spot: ~ *de partida*, starting-point; ~ *de vista*, point of view.

puntuación [puntwaθjón] *f.* punctuation. 2 score. 3 mark(s.

puntual [puntuál] *a.* punctual; exact.

puñado [puɲáðo] *m.* handful.

puñal [puɲál] *m.* dagger.

puño [púɲo] *m.* fist. 2 cuff. 3 hilt. 4 handle.

pupila [pupíla] *f.* pupil.

pupilo [pupílo] *m.* ward. 2 boarder, inmate.

pupitre [pupítre] *m.* desk.

pureza [puréθa] *f.* purity.

purificar [purifikár] *t.* to purify, cleanse.

puro [púro] *a.* pure, sheer; chaste. 2 *m.* cigar.

púrpura [púrpura] *f.* purple.

Q

que [ke] *rel. pron.* that; which; who; whom. *2 conj.* that. *3* than. *4* and. *5 con tal* ~, provided [that]. *6* for, because, since.

qué [ké] *exclam. pron.* how, what [a]. *2 interr. pron.* what?, which? *3 ¿por* ~?, why?

quebrantar [keβrantár] *t.* to break. *2* to pound, crash. *3* to transgress [a law]. *4* to weaken.

quebrar [keβrár] *t.* to break, crush. *2 i.* to go bankrupt. ¶ CONJUG. like *acertar*.

quedar [keðár] *t.-p.* to remain, stay, be left.

queja [kéxa] *f.* complaint.

quejarse [kexárse] *p.* to complain, moan.

quemar [kemár] *t.* to burn, scald, scorch. *2 p.* to burn up, get scorched. *2* plaint. 2 quarrel.

querella [keréʎa] *f.* complaint. *2* quarrel.

querer [kerér] *t.* to love [be in love with]. *2* to want, will, wish, desire. *3* ~ *decir*, to mean. *4 sin* ~, unintentionally. ¶ CONJUG. INDIC. Pres.: *quiero, quieres, quiere; queremos, queréis, quieren.* | Pret.: *quise, quisiste, quiso*, etc. | Fut.: *querré, querrás*, etc. ‖ SUBJ. Pres.: *quiera, quieras, quiera; queramos, queráis, quieran.* | Imperf.: *quisiera, quisieras,* etc., or *quisiese, quisieses,* etc. | Fut.: *quisiere, quisieres,* etc. ‖ IMPER.: *quiere,* *quiera;* queramos, quered, *quieran.*

querido [kerído] *a.* dear, beloved. 2 *m.-f.* lover. 3 *f.* mistress.

queso [késo] *m.* cheese.

quiebra [kjéβra] *f.* break, crack; fissure. 2 failure, bankrupcy.

quien [kjen] *pron.* who, whom.

quienquiera [kjeŋkjéra], *pl.* **quienesquiera** [kjeneskjéra] *pron.* whoever, whomever, whosoever.

quieto [kjéto] *a.* quiet, still, motionless; calm.

quietud [kjetúð] *f.* calmness, stillness, quiet.

química [kímika] *f.* chemistry.

químico [kímiko] *a.* chemical. 2 *m.-f.* chemist.

quince [kínθe] *a.-n.* fifteen.

quinqué [kiŋké] *m.* oil lamp.

quinto [kínto] *a.* fifth. 2 *m.* recruit.

quitar [kitár] *t.* to remove, take [away, off, from, out]. 2 to steal, rob of. 3 to clear [the table]. 4 *p.* to move away. 5 to take off [one's clothes, etc.]. 6 *quitarse de encima,* to get rid of.

quizá(s [kiθá(s)] *adv.* perhaps, maybe.

R

rabia [rráβja] *f.* rabies. 2 rage, fury.

rabioso [rraβjóso] *a.* rabid; mad. 2 furious, angry.

rabo [rráβo] *m.* tail; end: *de cabo a ~*, from beginning to end.

racimo [rraθímo] *m.* bunch, cluster.

racional [rraθjonál] *a.* rational. 2 reasonable.

radiante [rraðjánte] *a.* radiant; beaming.

radical [rraðikál] *a.* radical. 2 *m.* root.

radio [rráðjo] *m.* radius. 2 radium. 3 spoke. 4 scope. 5 radiogram. 6 *f.* boadcasting. 7 radio, wireless set.

raíz [rraíθ] *f.* root.

rama [rráma] *f.* branch, bough.

ramaje [rramáxe] *m.* foliage, branches.

ramillete [rramiλéte] *m.* bouquet, nosegal. 2 centrepiece.

ramo [rrámo] *m.* bough, branch. 2 bunch, cluster.

rana [rrána] *f.* frog.

rancho [rrántʃo] *m.* MIL. mess. 2 (Am.) cattle ranch.

rapidez [rrapiðéθ] *f.* speed, quickness.

rápido [rrápiðo] *a.* fast, quick, swift.

rapto [rráβto] *m.* ravishment. 2 kidnapping. 3 rapture.

raro [rráro] *a.* rare. 2 scarce: *raras veces*, seldom. 3 odd, queer.

rascar [rraskár] *t.* to scrape, scrath.

rasgar [rrazɣár] *t.* to tear, rend, rip, slash.

rasgo [rrázɣo] *m.* dash, stroke. 2 deed, feat. 3 trait. 4 *pl.* features.

raso [rráso] *a.* flat, level. 2 clear. 3 *m.* satin.

raspar [rraspár] *t.* to scrape, erase.

rastrillo [rrastríʎo] *m.* rake.

rata [rráta] *f.* rat.

rato [rráto] *m.* time, while: al poco ~, shortly after.

ratón [rratón] *m.* mouse.

raudal [rrauðál] *m.* stream, torrent, flood.

raya [rrája] *f.* ray. 2 line. 3 score. 4 stripe. 5 crease 6 parting.

rayar [rrajár] *t.* to draw lines on, line. 2 to scratch. 3 to stripe. 4 to cross out. 5 i. ~ con or en, to border on.

rayo [rrájo] *m.* ray, beam. 2 lightning. 3 rayos X, X-rays.

raza [rráθa] *f.* race, breed: de pura ~, thoroughbred.

razón [rraθón] *f.* reason. 2 right: tener ~, to be right; no tener ~, to be wrong. 3 account. 4 ~ social, trade name, firm.

razonable [rraθonáβle] *a.* reasonable, sensible. 2 fair.

reacción [rreaɣθjón] *f.* reaction; avión a ~, jet.

reaccionar [rreaɣθjonár] *i.* to react, respond to.

real [rreál] *a.* real. 2 royal. 3 magnificent. 4 *m.* real [Spanish coin].

realidad [rrealiðáð] *f.* reality. 2 sincerity 3 en ~, really, in fact.

realizar [rrealiθár] *t.* to accomplish, carry out, do, fulfill.

reanudar [rreanuðár] *t.* to renew, resume.

rebaja [rreβáxa] *f.* reduction. 2 rebate, discount.

rebajar [rreβaxár] *t.* to reduce, rebate, discount 2 to disparage. 3 *p.* to humble oneself.

rebaño [rreβáɲo] *m.* herd, flock, drove.

rebelarse [rreβelárse] *p.* to rebel, revolt, rise.

rebelde [rreβélde] *a.* rebellious. 2 *m.-f.* rebel, insurgent.

rebosar [rreβosár] *i.-p.* to overflow, run over.

receptor [rreθeptór] *m.* receiver, television set.

receta [rreθéta] *f.* MED. prescription. 2 recipe.

recetar [rreθetár] *t.* to prescribe.

recibir [rreθiβír] *t.* to receive. 2 to admit. 3 to meet.

recibo [rreθíβo] *m.* reception, receipt: *acusar* ~ *de*, to acknowledge receipt of.

reciente [rreθjénte] *a.* recent, fresh. 2 **-mente** *adv.* recently, lately, newly.

recio [rreθjo] *a.* strong. 2 thick, stout. 3 hard: *hablar* ~, to speak loudly.

recitar [rreθitár] *t.* to recite.

reclamar [rreklamár] *t.* to claim, demand. 2 to complain.

recobrar [rrekoβrár] *t.* to recover, retrieve. 2 *p.* to get better.

recoger [rrekoxér] *t.* to gather, collect, pick up, retake. 2 to fetch, get. 3 to give shelter to. 4 *p.* to retire, go home.

recomendación [rrekomendaθjón] *f.* recomendation: *carta de* ~, letter of introduction.

recomendar [rrekomendár] *t.* to recommend. ¶ CONJUG. like *acertar*.

recompensa [rrekompén-sa] *f.* reward; compensation.

recompensar [rrekompensár] *t.* to recompense, reward.

reconocer [rrekonoθér] *t.* to inspect, examine. 2 MIL. to reconnoitre. 3 to recognize, admit, acknowledge. 4 *p.* to know oneself. ¶ CONJUG. like *agradecer*.

reconocimiento [rrekonoθimjénto] *m.* inspection. 2 MIL. reconnaissance. 3 survey. 4 acknowledgement. 5 gratitude. 6 MED. check-up.

reconstruir [rrekonstruír] *t.* to rebuild, reconstruct.

récord [rrékor] *m.* record.

recordar [rrekorðár] *t.* to remember, recollect, recall. 2 to remind. ¶ CONJUG. like *contar*.

recorrer [rrekorrér] *t.* to go over, walk. 2 to read over.

recorrido [rrekorríðo] *m.* journey, run, course.

recortar [rrekortár] *t.* to cut away, clip, trim. 2 to cut out.

recrear [rrekreár] *t.* to amuse, entertain. 2 to please, delight. 3 *p.*

to amuse oneself, take delight.

recreo [rrekréo] *m.* amusement; break [at school]| 2 playground, play-field, pitch.

rectángulo [rreytángulo] *m.* rectangle.

recto [rréyto] *a.* straight; right [angle]. 2 just, honest. 3 *f.* straight line.

rector [rreytór] *a.* ruling. 2 *m.* principal, head; vice-chancellor. 3 ECCL. parish priest.

recuerdo [rrekwérðo] *m.* remembrance. 2 souvenir. 3 *pl.* regards.

recuperar [rrekuperár] *t.* to recover, retrieve. 2 *p.* to recover oneself.

recurrir [rrekurrír] *i.* to appeal, resort to.

rechazar [rretʃaθár] *t.* to drive back. 2 to reject.

red [rreð] *f.* net. 2 network. 3 trap.

redacción [rreðayθjón] *f.* wording, redaction. 2 editing. 3 editorial office. 4 editorial staff.

redactar [rreðaytár] *t.* to draw up, compose, write, edit.

redil [rreðíl] *m.* sheepfold.

redimir [rreðimír] *t.* to redeem. 2 to ransom.

redondo [rreðóndo] *a.* round.

reducir [rreðuθír] *t.* to reduce, diminish. 2 to convert [into]. 3 to subdue.

reemplazar [rreemplaθár] *t.* to replace [with, by].

referencia [rreferénθja] *f.* account. 2 reference.

referente [rreferénte] *a.* concerning to.

referir [rreferir] *t.* to relate, tell; to report. 2 *p.* ~ a, to refer to. ¶ CONJUG. like *hervir*.

reflector [rrefleytór] *m.* searchlight. 3 floodlight.

reflejar [rreflexár] *t.* to reflect. 2 to show, reveal.

reflejo [rrefléxo] *a.* reflected. 2 GRAM. reflexive. 3 *m.* PHYSIOL. reflex. 4 reflection.

reflexión [rrefleysjón] *f.* reflexion. 2 meditation.

reflexionar [rrefleysjonár] *t.-i.* to think over, consider.

reforma [rrefórma] *f.* reform. 2 ECCL. Reformation.

reforzar [rreforθár] *t.* to strengthen. ¶ CONJUG. like *contar*.

refrán [rrefrán] *m*. proverb, saying.

refrescante [rrefreskánte] *a*. cooling; refreshing.

refrescar [rrefreskár] *t*. to cool, refresh. 2 *i*. to get cool. 3 *i.-p*. to take the air, have a drink. 4 to cool down.

refresco [rrefrésko] *m*. refreshment. 2 cooling drink. 3 *de* ~, new, fresh [troops, etc.].

refugiar [rrefuxjár] *t*. to shelter. 2 *p*. to take refuge.

refugio [rrefúxjo] *m*. shelter, refuge.

regalar [rreɣalár] *t*. to present, give; to entertain. 2 to flater. 3 *p*. to treat oneself with.

regalo [rreɣálo] *m*. gift, present. 2 comfort.

regañar [rreɣaɲár] *i*. to snarl, rebuke. 2 to quarrel. 3 *t*. to scold.

regar [rreɣár] *t*. to water, irrigate. ¶ CONJUG.. like *acertar*.

régimen [rréximen] *m*. regime, rule, system of government. 2 diet.

regio [rréxjo] *a*. royal.

región [rrexjón] *f*. region; area, district.

regir [rrexír] *t*. to gov-

ern, rule. 2 to manage. 3 *i*. to be in force; to prevail. ¶ CONJUG. like *servir*.

registro [rrexístro] *m*. search, inspection. 2 register. 3 book-mark.

regla [rréɣla] *f*. rule, norm, precept: *por* ~ *general*, as a rule. 2 ruler [for lines].

reglamento [rreɣlaménto] *m*. regulations, by-law.

regocijar [rreɣoθixár] *t.-p*. to rejoice, cheer up.

regocijo [rreɣoθixo] *m*. rejoicing, joy. 2 *pl*. festivities.

regresar [rreɣresár] *i*. to return, come back, go back.

regreso [rreɣréso] *m*. return: *estar de* ~, to be back.

rehabilitación [rreaβilitaθjón] *f*. rehabilitation.

rehusar [rreusár] *t*. to refuse, decline.

reina [rréina] *f*. queen.

reinado [rreináðo] *m*. reign.

reinar [rreinár] *i*. to reign. 2 to rule, prevail.

reino [rréino] *m*. kingdom.

reir [rreír] *i. - p.* to laugh at. ¶ CONJUG. INDIC. Pres.: *río, ríes, ríe;* reimos, reis, *ríen.* | Pret.: reí, reíste, *rió;* reimos, reísteis, *rieron.* ‖ SUBJ. Pres.: *ría, rías,* etc. | Imperf.: *riera, rieras,* etc., or *riese, rieses,* etc. | Fut.: *riere, rieres,* etc. ‖ IMPER.: *ríe, ría; riamos,* reid, *rían.* ¶ GER.: riendo.

relación [rrelaθjón] *f.* relation, account, narrative. 2 reference. 3 list of particulars. 4 *pl.* intercourse. 5 courtship. 6 connections, friends.

relacionar [rrelaθjonár] *t.* to relate, connect. 2 *p.* to be acquainted with or connected with.

relámpago [rrelámpaɣo] *m.* lightning, flash of lightning.

relatar [rrelatár] *t.* to tell, state, report.

relativo [rrelatíβo] *a.-m.* relative.

relato [rreláto] *m.* story, tale, report.

relevar [rreleβár] *t.* to relieve. 2 to release. 3 to remove [from office].

relieve [rreljéβe] *m.* [high, low] relief. 2 *poner de* ~, to emphasize.

religión [rrelixjón] *f.* religion, faith, creed.

religioso [rrelixjóso] *a.* religious. 2 *m.* religious. 3 *f.* nun.

reloj [rreló(x)] *m.* clock; watch; ~ *de pared,* clock; ~ *de pulsera,* wrist watch; ~ *de sol,* sundial; ~ *despertador,* alarm-clock.

reluciente [rreluθjénte] bright, shining; glossy.

relucir [rreluθír] *i.* to shine, glisten, gleam.

remar [rremár] *i.* to row.

remediar [rremeðjár] *t.* to remedy. 2 to help: *no lo puedo* ~, I can't help that.

remedio [rreméðjo] *m.* remedy, cure. 2 help, relief; *sin* ~, hopeless.

remendar [rremendár] *t.* to mend. 2 to patch; to darn. ¶ CONJUG. like *acertar.*

remitir [rremitír] *t.* to remit, send. 2 to forgive.

remo [rrémo] *m.* oar, paddle.

remolacha [rremolátʃa] *f.* beet; beetroot. 2 sugar-beet.

remontar [rremontár] *t.* to rouse, beat [game]. 2 to raise. 3 *p.* to go back to. 4 to soar.

remoto [rremóto] *a.* remote, distant. 2 unlikely.

remover [rremoβér] *i.* to remove. 3 to stir.

renacer [rrenaθér] *i.* to be reborn, revive.

rencor [rrenkór] *m.* ranco(u)r, grudge, spite.

rendija [rrendíxa] *f.* chink, crack, crevice.

rendir [rrendír] *t.* to conquer, subdue. 2 to give up. 3 MIL. to lower [arms, flags]. 4 to pay. 5 to yield, produce. 6 *p.* to surrender. 7 to become tired out. ¶ CONJUG. like *servir*.

renovar [rrenoβár] *t.* to renew; to change. ¶ CONJUG. like *contar*.

renta [rrénta] *f.* rent. 2 interest; profit, income. 3 revenue.

rentar [rrentár] *t.* to yield, produce.

renuncia [rrenúnθja] *f.* renouncement, resignation.

renunciar [rrenunθjár] *t.* to renounce, resign. 2 to refuse.

reñido [rreɲído] *a.* on bad terms, at variance.

reñir [rreɲír] *i.* to quarrel, fight, come to blows. 2 *t.* to scold. ¶ CONJUG. like *reir*.

reorganizar [rreoryaniθár] *t.* to reorganize.

reparación [rreparaθjón] *f.* repair. 2 satisfaction.

reparar [rreparár] *t.* to repair, mend. 2 to notice. 3 to restore [one's strength].

repartir [rrepartír] *t.* to distribute, allot, deliver.

repasar [rrepasár] *t.* to revise, review. 2 to check; to go over [one's lesson, etc.]. 3 to mend [clothes].

repaso [rrepáso] *m.* revision, review, check.

repente [rrepénte] *m.* sudden impulse. 2 *de ~*, suddenly.

repetir [rrepetír] *t.* to repeat. ¶ CONJUG. like *servir*.

replicar [rreplikár] *i.* to answer back, reply, retort.

reponer [rreponér] *t.* to replace, put back 2 THEAT. to revive. 3 to reply. 4 *p.* to recover.

reposar [rreposár] *i.* to rest; to sleep, lie.

reposo [rrepóso] *m.* rest, repose, relax.

reprender [rreprendér] *t.* to reprimand, rebuke, scold.

representante [rrepresentánte] *m.-f.* representative.

representar [rrepresentár] [rrepresentár] *t.* to represent. 2 THEAT. to perform. 3 *p.* to imagine.

representativo [rrepresentatíβo] *a.* representative.

reproducción [rreproðuɣθjón] *f.* reproduction.

reproducir [rreproðuθír] *t.-p.* to reproduce. ¶ CONJUG. like *conducir*.

reptil [rreβtil] *m.* reptile.

república [rrepúβlika] *f.* republic.

republicano [rrepuβlikáno] *a.-n.* republican.

repugnante [rrepuɣnánte] *a.* repugnant, disgusting.

reputación [rreputaθjón] *f.* reputation, renown.

requerir [rrekerír] *t.* to intimate. 2 to require; to request. 3 to need.

4 to court. ¶ CONJUG. like *hervir*.

requisito [rrekisíto] *m.* requisite, requirement.

res [rres] *f.* head of cattle, beast.

resbalar [rrezβalár] *i.-p.* to slip, slide. 2 to skid.

rescate [rreskáte] *m.* ransom, rescue.

reserva [rresérβa] *f.* reserve, reservation. 2 reticence: sin ~, openly.

reservado [rreserβáðo] *a.* reserved. 2 *m.* private room.

reservar [rreserβár] *t.* to reserve, keep [in], book.

resfriado [rresfriáðo] *m.* cold; chill.

residencia [rresiðénθja] *f.* residence.

residente [rresiðénte] *a.-n.* resident.

residir [rresiðír] *i.* to reside, live. 2 fig. to consist.

resignación [rresiɣnaθjón] *f.* resignation.

resistencia [rresisténθja] *f.* resistance. 2 endurance. 3 reluctance.

resistente [rresisténte] *a.* resistant, tough.

resistir [rresistír] *t.* to endure, stand. 2 to resist. 3 i. to stand up to. 4 p. to refuse to.

resolución [rresoluθjón] f. resolution, decision, courage.

resolver [rresolβér] t. to resolve, decide [upon]. 2 to solve. 3 p. to make up one's mind. ¶ CONJUG. like *mover*.

respaldo [rrespáldo] m. back. 2 support; help.

respectar [rrespeɣtár] i. to concern, relate to.

respectivamente [rrespeɣtíβaménte] adv. respectively.

respectivo [rrespeɣtíβo] a. respective.

respecto [rrespéɣto] m. respect, relation: con ~ a or de, ~ a or de, with regard to.

respetable [rrespetáβle] a. respectable, worthy.

respetar [rrespetár] t. to respect, revere.

respeto [rrespéto] m. respect. 2 reverence. 3 pl. respects.

respetuoso [rrespetuóso] a. respectful.

respirar [rrespirár] to breathe [in], inhale.

resplandecer [rresplandeθér] i. to shine, glitter, glow. 2 to stand out.

¶ CONJUG. like *agradecer*.

resplandeciente [rresplandeθjénte] a. bright, shining, glittering, blazing.

responder [rrespondér] t. to answer, reply. 2 to be responsible for. 3 to answer back.

responsabilidad [rresponsaβiliðáð] f. responsibility.

respuesta [rrespwésta] f. answer, reply.

restablecer [rrestaβleθér] t. to re-establish, restore. 2 p. to recover, get better.

restar [rrestár] t. to take away, reduce, subtract. 2 i. to be left.

restaurante [rrestaŭránte] m. restaurant.

restituir [rrestituír] t. to restore, return, pay back. ¶ CONJUG. like *huir*.

resto [rrésto] m. remainder, rest. 2 pl. remains.

resucitar [rresuθitár] t.-i. to revive, resuscitate.

resultado [rresultáðo] m. result, effect, outcome.

resultar [rresultár] i. to result. 2 to turn out to

be. 3 to come out [well, badly, etc.].

resumen [rresúmen] *m.* summary: *en* ~, in short.

resumir [rresumír] *t.* to summarize, sum up.

resurrección [rresurreyθjón] *f.* resurrection, revival.

retener [rretenér] *t.* to retain, keep back.

retirar [rretirár] *t.-p.* to retire, withdraw. 2 *t.* to put back or aside. 3 MIL. to retreat.

retiro [rretíro] *m.* retirement. 2 withdrawal; ECCL. retreat; seclusion.

retozar [rretoθár] *i.* to frisk, frolic, romp. 2 to bubble, gambol.

retozo [rretóθo] *m.* gambol, frolic.

retratar [rretratár] *t.* to portray, depict. 3 *p.* to have one's photograph taken.

retrato [rretráto] *m.* portrait. 2 photograph. 3 description.

retroceder [rretroθeðér] *i.* to turn back, fall or go back.

reunión [rreunjón] *f.* reunion. 2 gathering, meeting, party.

reunir [rreunír] *t.* to unite, gather. 2 to raise [funds]. 3 *p.* to meet, gather.

revelar [rreβelár] *t.* to reveal. 2 PHOT. to develop.

reventar [rreβentár] *i.-p.* to burst, crack, blow up. 2 *i.* to break. 3 *t.* to weary, annoy. ¶ CONJUG. like *acertar.*

reverencia [rreβerénθja] *f.* reverence. 2 bow, curtsy.

reverendo [rreβeréndo] *a.* reverend.

revés [rreβés] *m.* back, wrong-side. 2 slap [with back of hand]. 3 *al* ~, on the contrary; wrong side out.

revestir [rreβestír] *t.* to clothe, cover.

revisar [rreβisár] *t.* to revise, review, check.

revista [rreβísta] *f.* review, inspection. 2 MIL. parade. 3 magazine. 4 THEAT. revue.

revivir [rreβiβír] *i.* to revive, live again.

revolución [rreβoluθjón] *f.* revolution.

revolucionario [rreβoluθjonárjo] *a.-n.* revolutionary.

revólver [rreβólβer] *m.* pistol, revolver.

revolver [rreβolβér] *t.* to stir. 2 to turn round. 3 *p.* to turn upon. ¶ CONJUG. like *mover.*

rey [rreï] *m.* king: *dia de Reyes,* Twelfth Night; *los Reyes Magos,* the Three Wise Men.

rezar [rreθár] *t.-i.* to say. 3 *i.* to pray.

rezo [rréθo] *m.* prayer.

riachuelo [rrjatʃwélo] *m.* rivulet, stream, brook.

ribera [rriβéra] *f.* bank. 2 shore.

rico [rríko] *a.* rich, wealthy. 2 tasty. 3 sweet [baby].

ridiculo [rriðíkulo] *a.* ridiculous, laughable: *poner en ~,* to make a fool of.

riego [rrjéɣo] *m.* irrigation, watering.

riesgo [rrjézɣo] *m.* risk, danger: *correr el ~,* to run the risk.

rifa [rrífa] *f.* raffle.

rifle [rrífle] *m.* rifle.

riguroso [rriɣuróso] *a.* rigorous, severe. 2 strict.

rincón [rriŋkón] *m.* corner.

rio [rrío] *m.* river,

stream; *a ~ revuelto,* in troubled waters.

riqueza [rrikéθa] *f.* riches, wealth. 2 richness.

risa [rrísa] *f.* laugh, laughter, giggle, titter.

risueño [rriswéɲo] *a.* smiling, cheerful. 2 hopeful.

ritmo [rríðmo] *m.* rhythm.

rival [rriβál] *m.-f.* rival, competitor.

rivalidad [rriβaliðáð] *f.* rivalry, competition.

rizar [rriθár] *t.-p.* to curl [hair]. 2 to ripple [water].

rizo [rríθo] *a.* curly. 2 *m.* curl, ringlet. 3 ripple.

robar [rroβár] *t.* to rob, steal, break into.

roble [rróβle] *m.* oaktree.

robo [rróβo] *m.* theft, robbery, housebreaking.

robusto [rroβústo] *a.* strong, tough, robust.

roca [rróka] *f.* rock. 2 cliff.

rociar [rroθjár] *t.* to sprinkle, spray.

rocío [rroθío] *m.* dew.

rodear [rroðeár] *i.* to go round. 2 *t.* to surround.

rodilla [rroðíʎa] *f.* knee.

roer [rroér] *t.* to gnaw.
2 to eat away. 3 to
pick [a bone]. ¶ Con-
jug. Indic. Pres.: roo,
roes, etc. | Pret.: roí,
roíste, royó; roímos,
roísteis, royeron. ‖ Subj.
Pres.: roa, roas, etc. |
Imperf.: royera, roye-
ras, etc., or royese, ro-
yeses, etc. | Fut.:
royere, royeres, etc. ‖
Imper.: roe, roa; roi-
gamos, roed, roigan. ‖
Past. p.: roído. ‖ Ger.:
royendo.

rogar [rroγár] *t.* to ask,
beg, pray, entreat. ¶
Conjug. like *contar*.

rojo [rróxo] *a.* red.

rollo [rróʎo] *m.* roll.

romance [rrománθe] *a.*
Romance [languages]. 2
m. ballad.

romano [rrománo] *a.*
Roman.

romántico [rromántiko]
a.-n. romantic.

romper [rrompér] *t.-p.*
to break, smash. 2 to
wear out. ¶ P. p.: *roto*.

ron [rron] *m.* rum.

ronco [rróŋko] *a.* hoarse,
harsh.

ronda [rrónda] *f.* night
patrol. 2 rounds, beat.
3 round [of drinks].

ropa [rrópa] *f.* clothing,
clothes; dress: ~ *blan-*

ca, linen; ~ *interior,*
underwear; *a quema* ~,
at point-blank.

rosa [rrósa] *f.* rose.

rosado [rrosáðo] *a.* rosy,
pink.

rosal [rrosál] *m.* rose-
bush.

rosario [rrosárjo] *m.* ro-
sary.

rostro [rróstro] *m.* face,
countenance. 2 beak.

rotación [rrotaθjón] *f.*
rotation, turnover.

roto [rróto] *a.* broken.
3 torn.

rozar [rroθár] *t.-i.* to
touch [lightly].

rubí [rruβí] *m.* ruby.

rubio [rrúβjo] *a.* blond(e,
fair, fair-haired.

rudo [rrúðo] *a.* rough,
coarse. 2 hard.

rueda [rrwéða] *f.* wheel.

ruego [rrwéγo] *m.* entreaty, prayer, request.

rugir [rruxír] *i.* to roar,
bellow; to howl [of
wind].

ruido [rrwíðo] *m.* noise,
sound. 2 report. 3 ado.

ruin [rrwin] *a.* mean,
base. 2 miserly.

ruina [rrwína] *f.* ruin.
2 *pl.* ruins, remains.

ruiseñor [rrwiseɲór] *m.*
nightingale.

rumbo [rrúmbo] *m.*

course, direction; *con ~ a*, bound for. 2 ostentation.

rumor [rrumór] *m.* murmur; noise. 2 rumour.

tica, paper-backed.

ruta [rrúta] *f.* way, route. 2 course.

S

sábado [sáβaðo] *m.* Saturday; Sabbath.

sábana [sáβana] *f.* bed sheet.

1) **saber** [saβér] *m.* knowledge, learning.

2) **saber** [saβér] *t.* to know; to know how to [write]; to be able to. 2 ~ *a*, to taste of. ¶ CONJUG. INDIC. Pres.: sé, sabes, sabe, etc. | Imperf.: sabia, sabias, etc. | Pret.: *supe, supiste,* etc. | Fut.: sabré, sabrás, etc. ‖ COND.: *sabria, sabrías,* etc. ‖ SUBJ. Pres.: *sepa, sepas,* etc. | Imperf.: *supiera, supieras,* etc., or *supiese, supieses,* etc. | Fut.: *supiere, supieres,* etc. ‖ IMPER.: sabe, sepa; sepamos, sabed, sepan. ‖ PAST. P.: *sabido.* ‖ GER.: sabiendo.

sabiduría [saβiðuría] *f.* knowledge, learning. 2 wisdom.

sabio [sáβjo] *a.* learned; wise. 2 *m.-f.* learned person, scholar.

sabor [saβór] *m.* taste, flavour, savour.

sabroso [saβróso] *a.* savoury, tasty. 2 delightful.

sacar [sakár] *t.* to draw [out], pull out, take out. 2 to get. 3 to solve. 4 to take [a photo]. 5 to make [a copy]. 6 to buy [a ticket]. 7 ~ *a luz,* to publish, print. 8 ~ *a relucir,* to mention.

sacerdote [saθerðóte] *m.* priest.

saco [sáko] *m.* bag; sack. 2 bagful, sackful. 3 (Am.) coat.

sacramento [sakraménto] *m.* sacrament.

sacrificar [sakrifikár] *t.* to sacrifice. 2 to slaughter.

sacrificio [sakrifíθjo] *m.* sacrifice.

sacudir [sakuðir] *t.* to shake, jerk, jolt. 2 to beat, dust. 3 to deal [a blow]. 4 *p.* to shake off.

sagaz [saɣáθ] *a.* sagacious, shrewd, clever.

sagrado [saɣráðo] *a.* sacred, holy. 2 *m.* refuge.

sal [sal] *f.* salt. 2 wit.

sala [sála] *f.* drawing-room, living-room. 2 room, hall.

salado [saláðo] *a.* salty. 2 witty; graceful.

salario [salárjo] *m.* wages, salary, pay.

salchicha [saltʃitʃa] *f.* pork sausage.

salida [salíða] *f.* start, departure. 2 excursion. 3 rise. 4 exit, outlet; way out.

salir [salir] *i.* to go out, come out. 2 to depart, leave, start, set out. 3 to project, stand out. 4 [of a book] to come

out. 5 [of the sun] to rise. 6 ~ *bien* [*mal*], to turn out well [badly]. 7 ~ *adelante*, to be successful. 8 *p.* to leak; to overflow. ‖ CONJUG. INDIC. Pres.: *salgo*, *sales*, *sale*; *salimos*, etc. ‖ Fut.: *saldré*, *saldrás*, etc. ‖ COND.: *saldría*, *saldrías*, etc. ‖ SUBJ. Pres.: *salga*, *salgas*, etc. ‖ IMPER.: *sal*, *salga*; *salgamos*, *salid*, *salgan.*

salmo [sálmo] *m.* psalm.

salmón [salmón] *m.* salmon.

salpicar [salpikár] *t.* to splash, spatter, sprinkle.

salsa [sálsa] *f.* gravy, sauce.

saltar [saltár] *i.* to spring, jump, hop, skip. 2 ~ *a la vista*, to be self-evident. 3 *t.* to leap.

salto [sálto] *m.* spring, jump, leap, hop, skip; ~ *de agua*, water-fall, falls.

salud [salúð] *f.* health. 2 welfare.

saludable [saluðáβle] *a.* wholesome, healthy.

saludar [saluðár] *t.* to greet, salute, bow to.

saludo [salúðo] *m.* greeting, bow. 2 *pl.* compliments, regards.

salvación [salβaθjón] *f.* salvation. 2 rescue.

salvador [salβaðór] *a.* saving. 2 *m.-f.* saviour; El Salvador [American country].

salvaje [salβáxe] *a.* wild, savage. 2 *m.-f.* savage.

salvar [salβár] *t.* to save, rescue. 2 to overcome. 3 to go over. 4 *p.* to be saved. 5 to escape danger.

salvo [sálβo] *adv.* save, except, but. 2 *a.* saved, safe: *sano y* ~, safe and sound.

sanatorio [sanatórjo] *m.* sanatorium, nursing home.

sangrar [saŋgrár] *t.* to bleed. 2 to drain.

sangriento [saŋgrjénto] *a.* bleeding, bloody. 2 bloodthirsty.

sano [sáno] *a.* healthy, wholesome. 2 sound.

santidad [santiðáð] *f.* sanctity, holiness.

santo [sánto] *a.* holy, blessed, sacred. 2 saintly, godly. 3 *m.-f.* saint. 4 saint's day. 5 ~ *y seña*, password.

sapo [sápo] *m.* toad.

sardina [sarðína] *f.* sardine.

sargento [sarxénto] *m.* sergeant.

sartén [sartén] *f.* frying-pan.

sastre [sástre] *m.* tailor.

satisfacción [satisfaɣθjón] *f.* satisfaction; pleasure.

satisfacer [satisfaθér] *t.* to satisfy; to please. 2 to pay.

satisfactorio [satisfaɣtórjo] *a.* satisfactory.

satisfecho [satisfétʃo] *a.* satisfied, pleased.

savia [sáβja] *f.* sap.

sazonar [saθonár] *t.-p.* to ripen. 2 *t.* to flavour.

se [se] *ref. pron.* himself; herself; itself; yourself, yourselves [formal]; themselves. 2 *obj. pron.* to him, to her, to it, to you [formal], to them. 3 *reciprocal pron.* each other, one another. 4 *passive*: *se dice*, it is said.

secar [sekár] *t.* to dry [up]. 2 *p.* to get dry.

sección [seɣθjón] *f.* section. 2 department.

seco [séko] *a.* dry; bare, arid. 2 withered, dead. 3 lean, thin.

secretaria [sekretaría] *f.* secretary's office.

secretario, ria [sekretárjo, rja] *m.-f.* secretary.

secreto [sekréto] *a.* secret. 2 *m.* secret.

sector [seytór] *m.* sector.

secular [sekulár] *a.* secular. 2 lay.

secundar [sekundár] *t.* to back up, aid, help.

secundario [sekundárjo] *a.* secondary.

sed [seð] *f.* thirst: *tener ~*, to be thirsty. 2 desire.

seda [séða] *f.* silk.

sediento [seðjénto] *a.* thirsty; dry. 2 anxious.

segar [seɣár] *t.* AGR. to havest, reap, mow. ¶ CONJUG. like *acertar*.

seguidamente [seɣiðaménte] *adv.* immediately, at once.

seguir [seɣír] *t.* to follow. 2 to pursue, chase. 3 to go on [doing something]. 4 *p.* to follow as a consequence. ¶ CONJUG. like *servir*.

según [seɣún] *prep.* according to, as. 2 *adv.* *~ y como*, that depends.

segundo [seɣúndo] *a.-m.* second.

seguridad [seɣuriðáð] *f.* security, safety.

seguro [seɣúro] *a.* secure, safe. 2 firm, steady. 3 certain, sure. 4 *m.* COM. insurance. 5 safety-lock. 6 MECH. click, stop.

seis [séis] *a.-m.* six.

selección [seleɣθjón] *f.* selection.

seleccionar [seleɣθjonár] *t.* to select, choose, pick.

selecto [seléyto] *a.* select, choice.

selva [sélβa] *f.* forest; jungle, woods.

sello [séʎo] *m.* seal. 2 stamp.

semana [semána] *f.* week.

semblante [semblánte] *m.* face, countenance, look.

sembrar [sembrár] *t.-i.* to sow. 2 *t.* to scatter. ¶ CONJUG. like *acertar*.

semejante [semexánte] *a.* resembling, similar, like, such. 2 *m.* fellow.

semejanza [semexánθa] *f.* resemblance, likeness.

semestre [seméstre] *m.* semester.

semilla [semíʎa] *f.* seed.

senador [senaðór] *m.* senator.

sencillez [senθiʎéθ] *f.* simplicity. 2 plainness.

sencillo [senθíʎo] *a.* simple. 2 plain, natural.

senda [sénda] *f.*, **sendero** [sendéro] *m.* path, foot-path, track.

sensación [sensaθjón] *f.* sensation, feeling.

sensacional [sensaθjonál] *a.* sensational.

sensible [sensíβle] *a.* perceptible. 2 sensitive. 3 regrettable. 4 **-mente** *adv.* perceptibly.

sentencia [sénténθja] *f.* judgement, sentence; verdict. 2 proverb, maxim.

sentenciar [sentenθjár] *t.* to sentence, pass judgement, condemn.

sentido [sentíðo] *a.* felt. 2 touchy. 3 *m.* feeling, sense: ~ común, common sense. 4 meaning. 5 consciousness: *perder el* ~, to faint. 6 course, direction.

sentimental [sentimentál] *a.* sentimental, emotional.

sentimiento [sentimjénto] *m.* feeling. 2 sorrow, regret.

sentir [sentír] *t.* to feel, perceive; to hear. 2 ~ *frío*, to be cold. 3 to regret, be sorry for. 4 *p.* to feel [well, ill], suffer pain. ¶ CONJUG. like *hervir*.

seña [séɲa] *f.* sign, token. 2 mark. 3 *pl.* address.

señal [seɲál] *f.* sign, mark, token. 2 trace. 3 scar.

señor [seɲór] *m.* mister, Mr.; sir; gentleman. 2 owner, master; the Lord.

señora [seɲóra] *f.* Mrs.; madam; lady. 2 landlady, owner, mistress.

señorita [seɲoríta] *f.* young lady, miss.

separar [separár] *t.-p.* to separate. 2 *t.* to dismiss. 3 to remove.

septiembre [sepˈtjémbre] *m.* September.

séptimo [séptimo] *a.-n.* seventh.

sepulcro [sepúlkro] *m.* sepulchre. 2 grave, tomb.

sepultura [sepultúra] *f.* burial; grave, tomb.

sequía [sekía] *f.* drought, dry season.

1) **ser** [ser] *m.* being; essence.

2) **ser** [ser] *v.* to be; to exist. 2 to belong to. 3 to be made of. 4 to come from, be native of. ¶ CONJUG. INDIC. Pres.: *soy, eres, es; somos, sois, son.* | Imperf.: *era, eras,* etc. | Pret.:

fui, fuiste, etc. ‖ Fut.: *seré serás,* etc. ‖ Cond.: *sería, serías,* etc. ‖ Subj. Pres.: *sea, seas,* etc. | Imperf.: *fuera, fueras,* etc., or *fuese, fueses,* etc. | Fut.: *fuere, fueres,* etc. ‖ Imper.: *sé, sea; seamos, sed, sean.* ‖ Past. p.: *sido.* ‖ Ger.: *siendo.*

sereno [seréno] *a.* serene. 2 clear, cloudless. 3 calm, cool. 4 sober. 5 *m.* night watchman.

serie [sérje] *f.* series: *producción en ~,* mass production.

serio [sérjo] *a.* serious. 2 grave, earnest. 3 reliable. 4 *en ~,* seriously.

sermón [sermón] *m.* sermon.

serpiente [serpjénte] *f.* serpent, snake: *~ de cascabel,* rattle-snake.

serrar [serrár] *t.* to saw. ¶ Conjug. like *acertar.*

serrucho [serrútʃo] *m.* handsaw.

servicio [serβiθjo] *m.* service. 2 duty. 3 servants. 4 favour, good [ill] turn. 5 use. 6 service [set of dishes, etc.].

servilleta [serβiʎéta] *f.* napkin, serviette.

servir [serβir] *i.-t.* to serve, be useful. 2 *~ de,* to act as, be used as; *~ para,* to be good [used] for. 3 to wait upon [a customer]. 4 *p.* to serve or help oneself: *servirse de,* to make use of; *sírvase hacerlo,* please, do it. ¶ Conjug. Indic. Pres.: *sirvo, sirves, sirve; servimos, servís, sirven.* | Pret.: *serví, serviste, sirvió; servimos, servisteis, sirvieron.* ‖ Subj. Pres.: *sirva, sirvas,* etc. | Imperf.: *sirviera, sirvieras,* etc., or *sirviese, sirvieses,* etc. | Fut.: *sirviere, sirvieres,* etc. ‖ Imper.: *sirve, sirva; sirvamos, servid, sirvan.* ‖ Ger.: *sirviendo.*

sesenta [sesénta] *a.-m.* sixty.

sesión [sesjón] *f.* session; meeting. 2 show.

setenta [seténta] *a.-m.* seventy.

severo [seβéro] *a.* severe, rigid, harsh.

sexo [séyso] *m.* sex.

sexto [sésto] *a.-n.* sixth. sexual; sex.

si [si] *conj.* if; whether: *~ bien,* although.

si [si] *adv.* yes; indeed, certainly. 2 *ref. pron.* himself, herself, itself, oneself, themselves; yourself, yourselves [formal]: *entre ~*, each other.

siembra [sjémbra] *f.* sowing [time].

silaba [sílaβa] *f.* syllable.

siempre [sjémpre] *adv.* always, ever: *para ~*, forever, for good; *~ que*, whenever; provided that.

sierra [sjérra] *f.* saw. 2 mountain range.

siervo [sjérβo] *m.-f.* serf; slave.

siesta [sjésta] *f.* afternoon nap, siesta.

siete [sjéte] *a.-m.* seven.

siglo [síγlo] *m.* century.

significación [siγnifika-θjón] *f.*, **significado** [siγnifikáδo] *m.* meaning.

significar [siγnifikár] *t.* to signify; to mean; to make known. 2 to have importance. 3 *p.* to become known [as].

signo [síγno] *m.* sign, mark; symbol.

siguiente [siγjénte] *a.* following, next.

silbar [silβár] *i.* to whistle; to hiss.

silbido [silβíδo] *m.* whistle, whistling; hissing.

silencio [silénθjo] *m.* silence, quiet, hush.

silla [síʎa] *f.* chair; seat; *~ de montar*, saddle.

simbolo [símbolo] *m.* symbol.

simiente [simjénte] *f.* seed.

similar [similár] *a.* similar, like.

simpatia [simpatía] *f.* liking, charm, attractiveness. 2 sympathy.

simpático [simpátiko] *a.* pleasant, nice, charming.

simple [símple] *a.* simple. 2 innocent. 3 silly. 4 *-mente adv.* simply.

sin [sin] *prep.* without: *~ embargo*, nevertheless.

sinceramente [sinθéra-ménte] *adv.* sincerely.

sinceridad [sinθeriδáδ] *f.* sincerity.

sincero [sinθéro] *a.* sincere.

sindicato [sindikáto] *m.* syndicate. 2 trade(s) union, *labor union.

sinfonia [simfonía] *f.* symphony.

singular [siŋgulár] *a.* singular; single. 2 extraordinary. 3 odd.

siniestro [sinjéstro] *a.* left, left-hand. 2 sinister. 3 *m.* disaster. 4 *f.* left hand.

sino [sinó] *conj.* but: *no sólo... ~ (también)*, not only... but (also).

sino [sino] *m.* fate.

sinvergüenza [simberɣwénθa] *a.* brazen, barefaced. 2 *m.-f.* rascal, scoundrel.

siquiera [sikjéra] *conj.* although. 2 *adv.* at least. 3 *ni ~*, not even.

sirvienta [sirβjénta] *f.* maidservant, maid.

sistema [sistéma] *m.* system; method.

sitiar [sitjár] *t.* to besiege, surround.

sitio [sitjo] *m.* place, spot. 2 seat, room. 3 site. 4 MIL. siege.

situación [sitwaθjón] *f.* situation, position.

situar [sitwár] *t.* to place, put, set, locate, situate, site. 2 *p.* to be placed.

so [so] *prep.* under.

soberanía [soβeranía] *f.* sovereignty.

soberano [soβeráno] *a.-n.* sovereign.

soberbia [soβérβja] *f.* arrogance, pride, haughtiness.

soberbio [soβérβjo] *a.* arrogant, proud, haughty.

sobra [sóβra] *f.* excess, surplus: *de ~*, in excess.

sobrar [soβrár] *i.* to be left over, exceed, surpass. 2 to be superfluous.

sobre [sóβre] *prep.* on, upon. 2 over; above: *~ todo*, above all. 3 *m.* envelope.

surprise. 2 *p.* to be startled.

sobrenatural [soβrenaturál] *a.* supernatural.

sobrepasar [soβrepasár] *t.* to exceed. 2 *p.* to go too far.

sobresaliente [soβresaljénte] *a.* outstanding. 2 *m.* distinction, first class [mark].

sobresalir [soβresalir] *i.* to stand out, project, jut out.

sobrevivir [soβreβiβir] *i.* to survive. 2 *~ a*, to outlive.

sobrina [soβrina] *f.* niece.

sobrino [soβrino] *m.* nephew.

social [soθjál] *a.* social, friendly.

socialista [soθjalista] *a.-n.* socialist.

sociedad [soθjeðáð] *f.*
society. 2 company, cor-
poration.

socio [sóθjo] *m.-f.* associate; member. 2 part-
ner.

socorrer [sokorrér] *t.* to
help, aid, succour.

socorro [sokórro] *m.*
help, aid, assistance;
relief.

sofá [sofá] *m.* sofa, set-
tee.

sofocar [sofokár] *t.* to
choke, suffocate, smoth-
er. 2 to stifle. 3 *p.* to
blush.

sol [sol] *m.* sun; sunshine: *hace* ~ it is
sunny.

solamente [sólaménte]
adv. only, solely.

soldado [soldáðo] *m.*
soldier.

soledad [soleðáð] *f.* solit-
itude, loneliness.

solemne [solémne] *a.* solemn, impressive.
malities.

soler [solér] *i.* translate
the present of SOLER by
usually: *suele venir el
lunes*, he usually comes
on Monday. | *Imperf.*:
used to: *solía venir el
lunes*, he used to come
cn Monday. ¶ CONJUG.
like *mover*.

sólido [sóliðo] *a.* firm,
strong, solid.

solitario [solitárjo] *a.*
solitary, lone, lonely. 2
secluded. 3 *m.* solitaire
[diamond; game].

solo [sólo] *a.* alone; by
himself, itself, etc. 2
lone, lonely. 3 only,
sole. 4 *m.* MUS. solo.

sólo [sólo] *adv.* only,
solely.

soltar [soltár] *t.* to unfasten, loosen. 2 to let
out, set free, release.
3 to let go. 4 coll. to
give [a blow]. 5 *p.* to
get loose; get free. ¶
CONJUG. like *contar*.

soltero [soltéro] *a.* single.
2 *m.* bachelor, single
man.

solución [soluθjón] *f.*
solution, outcome, break.

sollozar [soλoθár] *i.* to
sob.

sollozo [soλóθo] *m.* sob.

sombra [sómbra] *f.*
shade; shadow.

sombrero [sombréro] *m.*
hat: ~ *de copa*, top
hat; ~ *hongo*, bowler
[hat].

sombrío [sombrío] *a.* gloomy, dark; sad, dismal.

someter [sometér] *t.* to
submit, subject, subdue.
2 *p.* to submit.

sonámbulo [sonámbulo] *a.-n.* sleep-walker.

sonar [sonár] *t.-i.* to sound, ring. 2 *i.* to strike: ~ *a*, to seem like. 3 *p.* to blow one's nose. ¶ CONJUG. like *contar*.

sonido [soníðo] *m.* sound.

sonoro [sonóro] *a.* sonorous: *banda sonora*, sound track.

sonreír(se [sonrreír(se] *i.-p.* to smile.

sonriente [sonrrjénte] *a.* smiling.

sonrisa [sonrrísa] *f.* smile.

soñador [soɲaðór] *a.* dreaming. 2 *m.- f.* dreamer.

soñar [soɲár] *t.-i.* to dream [of]. ¶ CONJUG. like *contar*.

sopa [sópa] *f.* soup.

soplar [soplár] *i.* to blow.

soplo [sóplo] *m.* blowing. 2 breath, puff of wind.

soportar [soportár] *t.* to bear, endure, tolerate.

sordo [sórðo] *a.* deaf. 2 dull, low. 3 *m.-f.* deaf person.

sorprendente [sorprendénte] *a.* surprising.

sorprender [sorprendér] *t.* to surprise, astonish. 2 *p.* to be surprised.

sorpresa [sorprésa] *f.* surprise.

sortija [sortíxa] *f.* finger ring.

sosegar [soseɣár] *t.* to calm, quiet. 2 *p.* to quiet down. ¶ CONJUG. like *acertar*.

soso [sóso] *a.* tasteless. 2 dull, uninteresting.

sospecha [sospétʃa] *f.* suspicion, mistrust.

sospechar [sospetʃár] *t.* to suspect, mistrust.

sospechoso [sospetʃóso] *a.* suspicious. 2 *m.-f.* suspect.

sostener [sostenér] *t.* to support, hold up. 2 to maintain.

sótano [sótano] *m.* basement; cellar; vault.

soviético [soβjétiko] *a.* soviet.

su [su] *poss. a.* his, her, its, their; 2nd. pers. [formal] your.

suave [swáβe] *a.* soft, smooth. 2 mild.

súbdito [súβðito] *m.-f.* subject; citizen.

subir [suβír] *i.* to go up, come up, rise, climb. 2 *t.* to raise, bring up.

súbito [súβito] *a.* sudden: *de* ~, suddenly.

sublime [suβlíme] *a.* sublime, noble.

submarino [suβmaríno] *a.-m.* submarine.

subsistir [suβsistír] *i.* to subsist. 2 to last. 3 to live on.

substancia [sustánθja] *f.* substance, essence. 2 juice.

substantivo [sustantíβo] *a.* substantive. 2 *m.* GRAM. noun.

substituir [sustituír] *t.* to substitute. replace. ¶ CONJUG. like *huir*.

subterráneo [suβterráneo] *a.* subterranean, underground.

suceder [suθeðér] *i.* ~ *a,* to succeed. 2 to follow. 3 *impers.* to happen.

sucesivo [suθesíβo] *a.* successive, consecutive. 2 *en lo* ~, hereafter.

suceso [suθéso] *m.* event, happening. 2 incident.

sucesor [suθesór] *m.-f.* successor; heir, heiress.

sucio [súθjo] *a.* dirty, filthy, grimy; obscene.

sucursal [sukursál] *a.-f.* branch.

sudar [suðár] *i.* to perspire; to sweat.

sudor [suðór] *m.* perspiration; sweat; toil.

suegra [swéɣra] *f.* mother-in-law.

suegro [swéɣro] *m.* father-in-law.

suela [swéla] *f.* sole.

sueldo [swéldo] *m.* salary, pay.

suelo [swélo] *m.* ground, floor, pavement. 2 soil.

sueño [swéɲo] *m.* sleep. 2 dream.

suerte [swérte] *f.* chance; fortune, fate. 2 luck. 3 sort. 4 *de* ~ *que,* so that; *tener* ~, to be lucky.

suficiente [sufiθjénte] *a.* sufficient, enough. 2 able. 3 **-mente** *adv.* sufficiently.

sufrimiento [sufrimjénto] *m.* suffering. 2 endurance.

sufrir [sufrír] *t.* to suffer, endure. 2 to allow. 3 to undergo [an operation, etc.].

sugerir [suxerír] *t.* to suggest, hint. ¶ CONJUG. like *hervir*.

sugestión [suxestjón] *f.* suggestion, hint.

suicidarse [swiθiðárse] *p.* to commit suicide.

suicidio [swiθiðjo] *m.* suicide.

sujetar [suxetár] *t.* to subject, subdue. 2 to

hold. *3* to fasten. *4* *p.* to subject oneself to.

sujeto [suxéto] *a.* subject; liable. *2* fastened. *3* *m.* GRAM. subject. *4* individual. *5* subject, matter.

suma [súma] *f.* sum, amount: en ~, in short. *2* **-mente** *adv.* extremely.

sumar [sumár] *t.* to add up, amount to. *2* *p.* ~ a, to join [in]

sumergir [sumerxir] *t.-p.* to submerge, sink.

suministrar [suministrár] *t.* to provide with, supply with, give.

suministro [suministro] *m.* supply, furnishing, provision.

sumiso [sumíso] *a.* submissive, obedient.

sumo [súmo] *a.* very great: a lo ~, at most.

superar [superár] *t.* to surpass, exceed. *2* to overcome.

superficie [superfíθje] *f.* surface. *2* area.

superior [superjór] *a.* superior. *2* upper. *3* *m.* director, head.

súplica [súplika] *f.* entreaty, request, prayer.

suplicar [suplikár] *t.* to entreat, pray, beg.

suplir [suplir] *t.* to make up for. *2* to replace.

suponer [suponér] *t.* to suppose, assume.

supremo [suprémo] *a.* supreme.

suprimir [suprimír] *t.* to suppress, cut out.

supuesto [supwésto] *a.* supposed, assumed. *2* dar por ~, to take for granted; por ~, of course. *3* *m.* supposition.

sur [sur] *m.* south.

surco [súrko] *m.* furrow, groove. *2* track [of ship].

surgir [surxír] *i.* to spurt, spring. *2* to appear, arise, come up.

surtir [surtír] *t.* to supply. *2* ~ efecto, to work.

suscribir [suskriβír] *t.* to sign. *2* *p.* to subscribe to.

suspender [suspendér] *t.* to hang up. *2* to stop; to delay. *2* to fail [in an examination].

suspensión [suspensjón] *f.* postponement, delay.

suspirar [suspirár] *i.* to sigh. *2* to long for.

suspiro [suspíro] *m.* sigh.

sustentar [sustentár] *t.*

to sustain, support, feed. *2* to hold up.

sustento [susténto] *m.* sustenance. *2* food. *3* support. *4* livelihood.

sustituir [sustituír] = SUBSTITUIR.

susto [sústo] *m.* fright, scare.

sutil [sutil] *a.* subtle. *2* thin.

suyo [sújo] *poss. a.* his, her, its, one's, their; your [formal]. *2 poss. pron.* his, hers, its, one's, theirs; yours [formal].

T

tabaco [taβáko] *m.* tobaco; cigarettes. cigar.

taberna [taβérna] *f.* tavern; bar, pub.

tabla [táβla] *f.* board. 2 plank. 3 table. 4 *pl.* draw [at chess, etc.]. 5 THEAT. stage.

taburete [taβuréte] *m.* stool.

taco [táko] *m.* stopper, plug. 2 billiard-cue. 3 swear word, curse.

tacto [tákto] *m.* tact, finesse. 2 feel, touch.

tachuela [tatʃwéla] *f.* tack, tintack.

tajo [táxo] *m.* cut. 2 steep cliff. 3 cutting edge.

tal [tal] *a.* such, such a: ~ *vez*, perhaps; *un* ~ *Pérez*, a certain Pérez; ~ *como*, just as;

con ~ *que*, provided that; *¿qué* ~?, how are you?

tala [tála] *f.* felling.

talento [talénto] *m.* talent; ability, gift.

talón [talón] *m.* heel. 2 voucher.

talla [tá ʎa] *f.* carving. 2 size; height, stature.

taller [ta ʎér] *m.* workshop, mill, factory.

tallo [tá ʎo] *m.* stem. 2 shoot, stalk.

tamaño [tamáɲo] *a.* so big, so small. 2 *m.* size.

también [tambjén] *adv.* also, too, as well.

tambor [tambór] *m.* drum. 2 drummer.

tampoco [tampóko] *adv.* neither, not ... either; nor.

tan [tan] *adv.* so, as, such. 2 ~ *sólo*, only.

tanque [táŋke] *f.* water tank. 2 MIL. tank.

tanto [tánto] *a.-pron.-adv.* so much, as much. 2 *pl.* so many, as many. 3 *m.* certain amount. 4 ~ *por ciento*, percentage; ~ *como*, as well as; ~ ... *como*, both ... and; *entre* ~ or *mientras* ~, meanwhile; *por lo* ~, therefore.

tapa [tápa] *f.* lid, cover. 2 snack, delicacy.

tapar [tapár] *t.* to cover. 2 to stop up. 3 to conceal. 4 to wrap up.

tapiz [tapiθ] *m.* tapestry.

tapón [tapón] *m.* stopper, cork.

taquigrafía [takiɣafía] *f.* shorthand, stenography.

taquígrafo [takiɣrafo] *m.* stenographer.

taquilla [takíʎa] *f.* booking-office; box-office.

tardanza [tarðánθa] *f.* delay; slowness.

tardar [tarðár] *i.-p.* to delay; to be late.

tarde [tárðe] *adv.* late. 2 *f.* afternoon; evening.

tarea [taréa] *f.* task, work.

tarifa [tarifa] *f.* tariff. 2 price list, rate, fare.

tarjeta [tarxéta] *f.* card: ~ *postal*, postcard.

taxi [táɣsi] *m.* taxi, taxicab, cab.

taza [táθa] *f.* cup, cupful. 2 bowl; basin.

te [te] *pron.* [to] you, yourself.

té [te] *m.* tea. 2 tea-party.

teatro [teátro] *m.* theatre. 2 stage, scene; play-house.

técnico [téɣniko] *a.* technical. 2 *m.* technician.

techo [tétʃo] *m.* ceiling; roof.

teja [téxa] *f.* tile, slate.

tejado [texáðo] *m.* roof.

tejer [texér] *t.* to weave.

tejido [texiðo] *a.* woven. 2 *m.* fabric, textile.

tela [téla] *f.* cloth, fabric. 2 canvas.

telar [telár] *m.* loom.

teléfono [teléfono] *m.* telephone, phone.

telegráfico [teleɣráfiko] *a.* telegraphic, telegraph.

telégrafo [teléɣrafo] *m.* telegraph.

telegrama [teleɣráma] *m.* telegram, wire.

televisión [teleβisjón] *f.* television.

televisor [teleβisór] *m.* television set.

telón [telón] *m.* curtain.

tema [téma] *m.* theme, subject, topic.

temblar [temblár] *i.* to tremble, quake, shake.

temblor [temblór] *m.* tremble; ~ *de tierra*, earthquake.

temer [temér] *t.-i.* to fear, dread; to be afraid of.

temeroso [temeróso] *a.* fearful, afraid.

temible [temíβle] *a.* dreadful, frigtful.

temor [temór] *m.* dread, fear.

temperamento [temperaménto] *m.* temperament, nature, disposition.

temperatura [temperatúra] *f.* temperature.

tempestad [tempestáð] *f.* storm.

tempestuoso [tempestwóso] *a.* stormy.

templado [templáðo] *a.* temperate. 2 lukewarm.

templo [témplo] *m.* temple, church, chapel.

temporada [temporáða] *f.* period of time. 2 season.

temporal [temporál] *a.* temporary; worldly. 2 *m.* gale, storm. 3 **-mente** *adv.* temporarily.

temprano [tempráno] *a.* early; premature. 2 *adv.* early.

tenaz [tenáθ] *a.* tenacious, dogged, stubborn.

tender [tendér] *t.* to spread [out], stretch out. 2 to hang up [to dry]. 3 to lay [a cable, etc.]; to build [a bridge]. 4 *i.* to have a tendency to. 5 *p.* to stretch oneself out, lie down. ¶ CONJUG. like *entender*.

tenebroso [teneβróso] *a.* dark; gloomy, dismal.

tenedor [teneðór] *m.* fork. 2 holder; ~ *de libros*, book-keeper.

tener [tenér] *t.* to have; possess, own; to hold, keep. 2 ~ *hambre*, to be hungry; ~ *sed*, to be thirsty; ~ *sueño*, to be sleepy; *tengo diez años*, to be ten years old; ~ *calor*, to be hot; ~ *frío*, to be cold; *tiene usted razón*, you are right. 3 aux. *tengo que estudiar*, I have to study; I must study. ¶ CONJUG. INDIC. Pres.: *tengo, tienes, tiene; tenemos, tenéis, tienen.* | Pret.: *tuve, tuviste,* etc. | Fut.: *tendré, tendrás,* etc. ‖ COND.:

tendría, tendrías, etc. |
SUBJ. PRES.: *tenga, tengas*, etc. | Imperf.: *tuviera, tuvieras*, etc., or *tuviese, tuvieses*, etc. | Fut.: *tuviere, tuvieres*, etc. ‖ IMPER.: *ten, tenga; tengamos, tened, tengan.*

teniente [tenjénte] *m.* lieutenant.

tenis [ténis] *m.* tennis.

tenor [tenór] *m.* tenor. stress.

tentación [tentaθjón] *f.* temptation.

tentar [tentár] *t.* to feel, touch. 2 to try. 3 to tempt.

tenue [ténwe] *a.* thin, slender.

teñir [tepír] *t.* to dye, tinge.

teoria [teoría] *f.* theory.

tercer(o [terθér(o] *a.-n.* third. giment.

terciopelo [terθjopélo] *m.* velvet.

terminar [terminár] *t.* to end, close, finish. 2 *i.* to be over.

término [término] *m.* end. 2 boundary. 3 aim. 4 word.

termómetro [termómetro] *m.* thermometer.

ternera [ternéra] *f.* female calf, heifer. 2 veal.

ternero [ternéro] *m.* calf, bull calf.

ternura [ternúra] *f.* tenderness, fondness.

terrado [terráðo] *m.*, **terraza** [terráθa] *f.* terrace. 2 flat roof.

terremoto [terremóto] *m.* earthquake, seism.

terreno [terréno] *a.* worldly. 2 *m.* plot, piece of ground, land.

terrible [terríβle] *a.* terrible, frightful. 2 **-mente** *adv.* terribly.

territorio [territórjo] *m.* territory, region.

terror [terrór] *m.* terror, fright.

tertulia [tertúlja] *f.* gathering, meeting of friends.

tesorero [tesoréro] *m.-f.* treasurer.

tesoro [tesóro] *m.* treasure.

testamento [testaménto] *m.* testament, will.

testificar [testifikár] *t.* to attest, give evidence.

testigo [testiγo] *m.-f.* witness.

testimonio [testimónjo] *m.* testimony, evidence.

texto [tésto] *m.* text.

tez [teθ] *f.* complexion.

ti [ti] *pers. pron.* you.

tía [tía] *f.* aunt.

tibio [tíβjo] *a.* lukewarm. 2 cool, indifferent.

tiburón [tiβurón] *m.* shark.

tiempo [tjémpo] *m.* time; epoch. 2 weather. 3 GRAM. tense.

tienda [tjénda] *f.* shop, *store. 2 tent.

tierno [tjérno] *a.* tender; loving. 2 fresh [bread].

tierra [tjérra] *f.* earth; land; ground. 2 country. 3 soil. 4 dust.

tieso [tjéso] *a.* stiff, rigid. 2 tight, taut.

tigre [tíyre] *m.* tiger; (Am.) jaguar. 2 *f.* tigress.

tijera [tixéra] *f.* scissors, shears; *silla de* ~, folding chair.

timbre [tímbre] *m.* stamp, seal. 2 bell: *tocar el* ~, to ring the bell.

tímido [tímiðo] *a.* timid, shy.

tina [tína] *f.* large jar.

tinaja [tináxa] *f.* large earthen jar.

tiniebla [tinjéβla] *f.* darkness. 2 *pl.* night; hell.

tinta [tínta] *f.* ink.

tintero [tintéro] *m.* inkstand, ink-pot.

tío [tío] *m.* uncle.

típico [típiko] *a.* typical.

tipo [típo] *m.* type. 2 build [of a person]. 3 guy.

tira [tíra] *f.* narrow strip; strap.

tiranía [tiranía] *f.* tyranny.

tirano [tiráno] *a.* tyrannical. 2 *m.-f.* tyrant.

tirar [tirár] *to* throw, cast, fling. 2 to fire [a shot]. 3 to draw, stretch. 4 to knock down, pull down. 5 to waste [money]. 6 *i.* to attract. 7 to last, endure. 8 to shoot at; to aim at. 9 to pull [at; on]. 10 *p.* to rush, throw oneself. 11 to jump. 12 to lie down.

tiro [tíro] *m.* throw. 2 shot. 3 report. 4 team. 5 draft, draught [of a chimney].

1) **titular** [titulár] *a.* titular. 2 *m.-f.* holder. 3 *m. pl.* headlines.

2) **titular** [titulár] *t.* to title, entitle, call.

título [título] *m.* title. 2 heading. 3 diplome. 4 qualification.

tiza [tíθa] *f.* chalk.

toalla [toáʎa] *f.* towel.

tocador [tokaðór] *m.* dressing-table. 2 dressing-room. 3 *jabón de ~*, toilet soap.

tocar [tokár] *t.* to touch, feel [with hands]. 2 to play [the piano]; to ring [a bell]; to beat [a drum]. 3 to blow [the horn]. 4 to win [lottery]. 5 *~ a muerto*, to toll. 6 to move. 7 *i.* to be one's turn. 8 to call [at a port]. 9 *p.* to touch each other 10 to cover one's head.

todavía [toðaβía] *adv.* still, even, yet. 2 nevertheless.

todo [tóðo] *a.* all, every, each, entire, whole. 2 *m.-f.* a whole. 3 *adv.* entirely, all. 4 *first of all*; *con ~*, however; *sobre ~*, above all.

tomar [tomár] *t.* to take. 2 to seize, catch. 3 to have [a meal, a drink, etc.]. 4 *~ el pelo*, to pull one's leg; *~ a mal*, to take it amiss; *~ las de Villadiego*, to take to one's heels.

tomate [tomáte] *m.* tomato.

tonada [tonáða] *f.* tune, song, air.

tonelada [toneláða] *f.* ton.

tono [tóno] *m.* tone; tune. 2 pitch. 3 vigour. 4 accent. 5 *darse ~*, to put on airs; *de buen* or *mal ~*, fashionable, or vulgar.

tontada [tontáða], **tontería** [tontería] *f.* silliness, stupidity. 2 nonsense.

tonto [tónto] *a.* silly, stupid. 2 *m.-f.* dolt.

topo [tópo] *m.* mole.

toque [tóke] *m.* touch. 2 blow. 3 sound; ringing [of a bell]; beat [of a drum]. 4 trial. 5 *piedra de ~*, touchstone; *~ de queda*, curfew.

torcer [torθér] *t.* to twist, wrench, bend, crook. 2 *i.* to turn to [the right, etc.]. 3 *p.* to become twisted, bent. 4 *~ el tobillo*, to sprain one's ankle. ¶ Conjug. like *mover.*

torear [toreár] *i.-t.* to fight bulls.

toreo [toréo] *m.* bullfighting.

torero [toréro] *m.-f.* bullfighter.

tormenta [torménta] *f.* storm, tempest.

tormento [torménto] *m.* torment, pain. 2 torture.

tormentoso [tormentóso] *a.* stormy.

torneo [tornéo] *m.* tournament; competition.

tornillo [torníʎo] *m.* screw. 2 clamp. 3 vice.

torpe [tórpe] *a.* awkward, clumsy. 2 lewd. 3 **-mente** *adv.* awkwardly.

torpedo [torpédo] *m.* torpedo.

torre [tórre] *f.* tower. 2 turret. 3 country-house. 4 CHESS rook, castle.

torrente [torrénte] *m.* torrent, stream.

torta [tórta] *f.* cake, pie. 2 slap.

tortilla [tortíʎa] *f.* omelet. 2 (Am.) pancake.

tortuga [tortúγa] *f.* tortoise; turtle.

tortura [tortúra] *f.* torture, torment; grief.

tos [tos] *f.* cough.

tosco [tósko] *a.* rough, coarse. 2 rude, uncouth.

toser [tosér] *i.* to cough.

tostar [tostár] *t.* to toast; to roast. 2 to tan, sunburn.

total [totál] *a.* total. 2 *m.* total, sum. 3 *adv.* in short.

trabajador [traβaxaδór] *a.* hard-working. 2 *m.-f.* worker.

trabajar [traβaxár] *i.* to work, labour, toil. 2 to till the soil.

trabajo [traβáxo] *m.* work, labour, toil. 2 task, job.

trabuco [traβúko] *m.* blunderbuss.

tractor [traɣtór] *m.* tractor.

tradición [traδiθjón] *f.* tradition.

tradicional [traδiθjonál] *a.* traditional. 2 **-mente** *adv.* traditionally.

traducir [traδuθír] *t.* to translate [into; from].

traer [traér] *t.* to bring. 2 to draw, attract. 3 to bring over. 4 to make, keep. 5 ~ *entre manos*, to be engaged in. ¶ CONJUG. INDIC. Pres.: *traigo*, traes, trae, etc. | Pret.: *traje, trajiste*, etc. | Fut.: traeré, traerás, etc. ‖ COND.: traería, traerías, etc. ‖ SUBJ. Pres.: *traiga, traigas*, etc. | Imperf.: *trajera, trajeras*, etc., or *trajese, trajeses*, etc.

| Fut.: *trajere, trajeres,* etc. || IMPER.: trae, traiga; *traigamos,* traed, traigan. | PAST. P.: traído. || GER.: *trayendo.*

tráfico [tráfiko] *m.* traffic; trade, business.

tragar [trayár] *t.-p.* to swallow [up]; to gulp down: ~ *el anzuelo,* to be taken in.

tragedia [traxéðja] *f.* tragedy.

trágico [tráxiko] *a.* tragic(al. 2 *m.* tragedian.

traición [traiθjón] *f.* treason; treachery; betrayal.

traidor [traiðór] *a.* treacherous. 2 *m.* traitor. 3 *f.* traitress.

traje [tráxe] *m.* suit [for men]; dress [for women]; clothes [in general]; [historical] costume; gown [for women; judges, etc.]; ~ *de baño,* bathing-suit; ~*de etiqueta,* full dress; ~ *de luces,* bullfighter's costume.

tramo [trámo] *m.* stretch. 2 flight of stairs.

trampa [trámpa] *f.* trap; snare. 2 trapdoor. 4 trick.

tramposo [trampóso] *a.* deceitful, tricky. 2 *m.- f.* swindler.

tranquilo [traṇkilo] *a.* calm, quiet, peaceful.

transcurrir [tra(n)skurrir] *i.* to pass, elapse.

transcurso [tra(n)skúrso] *m.* course [of time].

transferir [tra(n)sferir] *t.* to transfer. ¶ CONJUG. like *hervir.*

transformación [tra(n)sformaθjón] *f.* transformation.

transformar [tra(n)sformár] *t.* to transform. 2 *p.* to change.

transitar [transitár] *i.* to pass, go, walk.

tránsito [tránsito] *m.* passage, crossing. 2 traffic.

transmitir [tra(n)zmitir] *t.* to transmit. 2 to broadcast.

transparente [tra(n)sparénte] *a.* transparent. 2 translucent.

transportar [tra(n)sportár] *t.* to transport, carry, convey. 2 *p.* to be enraptured.

transporte [tra(n)spórte] *m.* transportation, transport, carriage.

tranvía [trambía] *m.*

tramway, tram; *street-
car.

trapo [trápo] *m.* rag. 2
pl. clothes, dresses.

tras [tras] *prep.* after,
behind.

trasero [traséro] *a.* back,
hind, rear. 2 *m.* coll.
rump, buttocks.

trasladar [trazlaðár] *t.*
to move, remove. 2 to
adjourn. 3 *p.* to move
from ... to.

trastornar [trastornár] *t.*
to upset, overturn, turn
upside down.

trastorno [trastórno] *m.*
upset. 2 riot. 3 trouble.

tratamiento [tratamjén-
to] *m.* treatment. 2 title.

tratar [tratár] *t.* to
treat [a pers. well]. 2
to deal with [people].
3 to call [someone a
liar]. 4 to address [as
tú]. 5 i. ~ *de* [*with in-
finitive*], to try, at-
tempt. 6 ~ *en*, to deal,
trade in. 7 *p.* to live
[well]. 8 to be on good
terms. 9 *se trata de*, it
is a question of. 10 *¿de
qué se trata?*, what is it
all about?

trato [tráto] *m.* treatment. 2 behaviour. 3

agreement. 4 negotia-
tion. 5 relationship.

través [traβés] *m.* bias.
2 *a* ~ *de*, through,
across; *al* or *de* ~,
slantwise, crosswise.

travesía [traβesía] *f.*
cross-roads. 2 passage,
crossing [the *sea*].

travieso [traβjéso] *a.*
mischievous, naughty.

traza [tráθa] *f.* sketch,
plan. 2 appearance, as-
pect.

trazar [traθár] *t.* to
draw, sketch. 2 to lay
out.

trece [tréθe] *a.-m.* thirteen.

trecho [trétʃo] *m.* distance, stretch.

tregua [tréɣwa] *f.* truce,
respite.

treinta [tréïnta] *a.-m.*
thirty.

tremendo [treméndo] *a.*
imposing. 2 huge, tre-
mendous.

tren [tren] *m.* train.

trenza [trénθa] *f.* braid,
plait, pigtail.

trepar [trepár] *i.-t.* to
climb [up], clamber up,
scale.

tres [tres] *a.-m.* three.

triángulo [triáŋgulo] *m.*
triangle.

tribu [tríβu] *f.* tribe.

tribulación [triβulaθjón] *f.* tribulation, trouble.

tribuna [triβúna] *f.* tribune, platform. 2 grand-stand.

tribunal [triβunál] *m.* court of justice. 2 examining board.

tributo [triβúto] *m.* tribute, tax.

trigo [tríɣo] *m.* wheat.

trinar [trinár] *i.* to trill; to warble, chirp.

trino [tríno] *a.* trine. 2 *m.* trill.

trio [trío] *m.* trio.

tripa [trípa] *f.* gut, bowels; intestine.

triple [triple] *a.-m.* triple, treble, three times.

triste [tríste] *a.* sad. 2 gloomy. 3 sorrowful. 4 **-mente** *adv.* sadly.

tristeza [tristéθa] *f.* sadness, melancholy. 2 sorrow, misery, gloom.

triunfar [trjumfár] *i.* to triumph, win.

triunfo [triúmfo] *m.* triumph, win, victory. 2 trump [at cards].

trofeo [troféo] *m.* trophy; victory.

trompa [trómpa] *f.* horn. 2 trunk [of elephant].

trompeta [trompéta] *f.* trumpet; bugle. 2 *m.* trumpeter.

trompo [trómpo] *m.* spinning-top.

tronco [trónko] *m.* trunk; log; stem. 2 team [of horses]. 3 stock.

tronchar [trontʃár] *t.* to break off, lop off. 2 *p.* ~ *de risa*, to burst with laughing.

trono [tróno] *m.* throne.

tropa [trópa] *f.* troop; army, soldiers.

tropezar [tropeθár] *i.* to trip, stumble. 2 to come across. 3 to come up against [a difficulty].

tropical [tropikál] *a.* tropical, tropic.

trópico [trópiko] *m.* tropic.

trozo [tróθo] *m.* piece, bit, chunk. 2 passage.

truco [trúko] *m.* trick.

trucha [trútʃa] *f.* trout.

trueno [trwéno] *m.* thunder, thunderclap.

trueque [trwéke] *m.* exchange.

tú [tu] *pron.* you; thou

tu [tu], *pl.* **tus** [tus] *poss. a.* your; thy.

tuberculosis [tuβerkulósis] *f.* tuberculosis, consumption.

tuberculoso [tuβerkulóso] *a.* tuberculous. 2 *a.-n.* consumptive.

tubo [túβo] *m.* tube, pipe.

tuerto [twérto] *a.* one-eyed. 2 *m.* wrong, injury.

tulipa [tulípa] *f.* glass lampshade.

tulipán [tulipán] *m.* tulip.

tumba [túmba] *f.* tomb, grave.

túnel [túnel] *m.* tunne!.

túnica [túnika] *f.* tunic.

turba [túrβa] *f.* crowd, mob, throng, swarm.

turbar [turβár] *t.* to disturb, upset, trouble. 2 *p.* to get embarrassed.

turismo [turízmo] *m.* tourism. 2 touring car.

turista [turísta] *m.-f.* tourist, sightseer.

turno [túrno] *m.* turn. 2 shift.

tuyo [tújo] *poss. pron.* yours. 2 *poss. a.* your.

U

u [u] *conj.* [replaces o before a word beginning with o or *ho*] or.

ufano [ufáno] *a.* proud, conceited. 2 cheerful.

últimaménte [últimaménte] *adv.* finally, lastly. 2 recently.

ultimar [ultimár] *t.* to end, finish, complete.

último [último] *a.* last, final; latest. 2 por ~, lastly, at last.

un [un] *indef. art.* a. an. 2 *pl.* some, any.

ungir [unxír] *t.* to anoint, put ointment on.

ungüento [ungwénto] *m.* ointment, unguent.

unidad [uniðáð] *f.* unity. 2 unit.

uniforme [unifórme] *a.- m.* uniform.

unión [unjón] *f.* union. 2 concord.

unir [unír] *t.* to join, unite. 2 to connect.

unisono [unísono] *a.* unison: al ~, altogether, in unison.

universal [uniβersál] *a.* universal, world-wide.

universidad [uniβersiðáð] *f.* university.

universitario [uniβersitárjo] *a.* university [professor, student].

universo [uniβérso] *m.* universe, world.

uno [úno] *a.* one. 2 *pl.* a few, some.

untar [untár] *t.* to anoint, grease, smear.

uña [úɲa] *f.* nail, fingernail, toenail. 2 claw; hoof.

urgente [urxénte] *a.* urgent, pressing 2 **-mente** *adv.* urgently.

urgir [urxír] *i.* to press, be urgent.

usar [usár] *t.* to use. 2 to wear. 3 *t.-i.* to be accustomed to. 4 *p.* to be in use.

uso [úso] *m.* use, employment; wear, wear and tear. 2 usage, fashion.

usted [ustéð] *pers. pron.* you.

utensilio [utensíljo] *m.* implement, tool; utensil.

útil [útil] *a.* useful, profitable. 2 effective. 3 *m. pl.* tools, implements.

utilidad [utiliðáð *f.* utility, usefulness. 2 profit.

utilizar [utiliθár] *t.* to utilize, use, make use of.

uva [úβa] *f.* grape.

V

vaca [báka] *f.* cow. 2 beef [meat].

vacación [bakaθjón] *f. sing-pl.* vacation, holidays.

vacante [bakánte] *a.* vacant, empty. 2 *f.* vacancy, post. 3 vacation.

vacilar [baθilár] *i.* to hesitate, flicker. 2 to waver.

vacío [baθío] *a.* empty, void. 2 *m.* void; PHYS. vacuum. 3 blank.

vacuna [bakúna] *f.* vaccine.

vago [báγo] *a.* roving, errant. 2 vague. 3 *m.* loafer, tramp.

vagón [baγón] *m.* wagon, carriage, coach.

vajilla [baxíʎa] *f.* table service. 2 crockery: ~

de porcelana, chinaware.

valer [balér] *i.* to be worth, cost, amount to. 2 to deserve; to be equal to: *vale la pena verlo*, it is worth while seeing. ¶ CONJUG. INDIC. Pres.: *valgo, vales, vale,* etc. | Fut.: *valdré, valdrás,* etc. ‖ SUBJ. Pres.: *valga, valgas,* etc. ‖ IMPER.: *val* or *vale, valga; valgamos,* valed, *valgan.*

valeroso [baleróso] *a.* courageous, brave.

valiente [baljénte] *a.* valiant, brave. 2 fig. fine. 3 **-mente** *adv.* bravely.

valioso [baljóso] *a.* expensive, valuable, costly.

valor [balór] *m.* value, worth, price. 2 courage. 3 validity. 4 *pl.* bonds.

vals [bals] *m.* waltz.

valle [báʎe] *m.* valley, vale, dale.

vanidad [baniðáð] *f.* vanity, conceit.

vanidoso [baniðóso] *a.* vain, conceited.

vano [báno] *a.* vain, useless. 2 *m.* ARCH. opening. 3 *en* ~, in vain.

vapor [bapór] *m.* vapo(u)r; steam. 2 steamship.

vaquero [bakéro] *m.-f.* cow-herd, cowboy.

vara [bára] *f.* stick, rod. 2 wand [of office].

variedad [barjeðáð] *f.* variety.

vario [bárjo] *a.* various, different. 2 *pl.* some, several.

varón [barón] *m.* male; man.

vasallo [basáʎo] *m.-f.* vassal, liegeman.

vasija [basixa] *f.* vessel, jar; container, recipient.

vaso [báso] *m.* glass, tumbler. 2 vessel.

vasto [básto] *a.* vast, huge, immense.

vecindad [beθindáð] *f.* **vecindario** [beθindárjo]

m. neighbourhood; neighbours, residents.

vecino [beθino] *a.* nearby, neighbouring, next [to]. 2 *m.-f.* neighbour. 3 tenant; inhabitant.

vedar [beðár] *t.* to prohibit, forbid. 2 to impede, prevent.

vegetación [bexetaθjón] *f.* vegetation; growth.

vegetal [bexetál] *m.* plant, vegetable.

vehículo [beikulo] *m.* vehicle; carrier.

veinte [béinte] *a.-m.* twenty.

vejez [bexéθ] *f.* old age.

vela [béla] *f.* wakefulness. 2 candle. 3 sail: *hacerse a la* ~, to set sail.

velar [belár] *i.* to watch. 2 ~ *por*, to look after. 3 *t.* to hide.

velo [bélo] *m.* veil.

velocidad [beloθiðáð] *f.* speed, velocity.

veloz [belóθ] *a.* fast, speedy, quick, swift. downy, hairy, shaggy.

vena [béna] *f.* vein. 2 MIN. seam. 3 poetical inspiration.

vencedor [benθeðór] *m.-f.* conqueror; victor; winner.

vencer [benθér] *t.* to defeat, beat. 2 to conquer, subdue. 3 *i.* to win. 4 COM. to fall due.

vendedor [bendeðór] *m.-f.* seller.

vender [bendér] *t.* to sell: *se vende*, for sale. 2 to betray.

veneno [benéno] *m.* poison, venom.

venerable [beneráβle] *a.* venerable.

venerar [benerár] *t.* to worship, venerate, revere.

venganza [bengánθa] *f.* vengeance, revenge.

vengar [bengár] *t.* to avenge. 2 *p.* to take revenge, retaliate.

venida [beníða] *f.* coming, arrival. 2 return.

venidero [beniðéro] *a.* a. future, coming.

venir [benír] *i.* to come. 2 ~ *a las manos*, to come to blows; ~ *al caso*, to be relevant; ~ *a menos*, to decay, decline; ~ *bien* [*mal*], [not] to fit, suit; ~ *en conocimiento*, to come to know; ~ *abajo*, to collapse, fall down. ¶ CONJUG. INDIC. Pres.: *vengo, vienes, viene; venimos, venís, vienen.*

| Pret.: *vine, viniste,* etc. | Fut.: *vendré, vendrás,* etc. ‖ SUBJ. Pres.: *venga, vengas,* etc. | Imperf.: *viniera, vinieras,* etc., or *viniese, vinieses,* etc. | Fut.: *viniere, vinieres,* etc. ‖ IMPER.: *ven, venga; vengamos, venid, vengan.* ‖ PAST. P.: *venido.* ‖ GER.: *viniendo.*

venta [bénta] *f.* sale: *en* ~, for sale. 2 roadside inn.

ventaja [bentáxa] *f.* advantage. 2 gain, profit.

ventana [bentána] *f.* window.

ventilación [bentilaθjón] *f.* ventilation, draught.

ventilar [bentilár] *t.* to air, ventilate. 2 to discuss.

ventura [bentúra] *f.* happiness. 2 luck. 3 *por* ~, by chance; *a la* ~, at random.

venturoso [benturóso] *a.* happy, lucky.

ver [ber] *t.* to see. 2 to look [at]. 3 *i.* ~ *de*, to try to. 4 *p.* to be obvious. ¶ CONJUG. INDIC. Pres.: veo, ves, ve, etc. | Imperf.: veía, veías, etc. | Pret.: vi, *viste*, etc. | Fut.: veré, verás, etc. ‖ Cond.: vería, verías, etc. ‖ Subj. Pres.: vea, veas, etc. | Imperf.: *viera*, *vieras*, etc., or *viese*, *vieses*, etc. ‖ Fut.: *viere*, *vieres*, etc. ‖ Imper.: ve, vea, etc. ‖ Past. p.: *visto*. ‖ Ger.: *viendo*.

veraneo [beranéo] *m.* summer holiday.

verano [beráno] *m.* summer.

verbo [bérβo] *m.* verb.

verdad [berðáð] *f.* truth: *en* ~, in truth, really.

verdaderamente [berðaðéraménte] *adv.* truly, really; indeed.

verdadero [berðaðéro] *a.* true. 2 real. 3 truthful.

verde [bérðe] *a.* green [colour]; verdant; unripe; obscene: *poner* ~, to abuse; *viejo* ~, gay, merry old man. 2 *m.* grass; foliage.

verdugo [berðúγo] *m.* hangman, executioner.

verdura [berðúra] *f.* greenness. 2 *sing & pl.* vegetables.

vereda [beréða] *f.* path.

vergel [berxél] *m.* flower and fruit garden.

vergüenza [berγwénθa] *f.* shame; bashfulness: *te-*

ner or *sentir* ~, to be ashamed.

take place, happen.

verja [bérxa] *f.* grating, grille; railing(s); iron gate.

versión [bersjón] *f.* translation.

verso [bérso] *m.* verse, poem. 2 line.

verter [bertér] *t.* to pour. 2 to spill. 3 to empty. 4 *i.* to run, flow. 5 *p.* to flow. ¶ Conjug. like *entender*.

vestido [bestíðo] *m.* dress, clothes, costume, suit.

vestidura [bestiðúra] *f.* clothing, apparel. 2 *pl.* Eccl. vestments.

vestir [bestír] *t.* to clothe, dress. 2 to cover. 3 to cloak. 4 *i.* to dress. 5 *p.* to get dressed. ¶ Conjug. like *servir*.

vestuario [bestwárjo] *m.* clothes. 2 wardrobe; dressing-room.

veterano [beteráno] *a.-n.* veteran.

veto [béto] *m.* veto.

vez [beθ] *f.* turn: *a su* ~, in turn. 2 time: *a la* ~, at one time; *alguna* ~, sometimes; [in questions] ever; *a* *veces,* sometimes; *muchas veces,* often; *otra* ~, again; *pocas veces,* seldom; *tal* ~, perhaps; *en* ~ *de,* instead of; *dos veces,* twice

vía [bía] *f.* road, way, street; ~ *aérea,* airway; ~ *pública,* thoroughfare. 2 manner.

viajar [bjaxár] *i.* to travel, journey, tour.

viaje [biáxe] *m.* travel, journey, voyage, trip; tour.

viajero [bjaxéro] *m.-f.* traveller; passenger.

vianda [bjánda] *f.* food.

vicisitud [biθisitùð] *f.* vicissitude. 2 *pl.* ups and downs.

víctima [bíɣtima] *f.* victim.

victoria [biɣtórja] *f.* victory, triumph.

victorioso [biɣtorjóso] *a.* victorious, triumphant.

vid [bið] *f.* vine, grapevine.

vida [bíða] *f.* life. 2 liveliness. 3 living, livelihood.

vidrio [bíðrjo] *m.* glass; glass pane [of a window].

viejo [bjéxo] *a.* old [antique]. 2 *m.* old man.

viento [bjénto] *m.* wind.

vientre [bjéntre] *m.* belly; womb; abdomen.

viernes [bjérnes] *m.* Friday.

vigilancia [bixilánθja] *f.* vigilance, watchfulness.

vigilar [bixilár] *t.-i.* to watch over, look after.

vigor [biɣór] *m.* vigo(u)r; strength: *en* ~, in force.

vigoroso [biɣoróso] *a.* vigorous, strong, tough.

vil [bil] *a.* vile, mean, base.

villa [bíʎa] *f.* villa. 2 small town. 3 town council.

villano [biʎáno] *a.* rustic. 2 mean. 3 *m.-f.* scoundrel; villain.

vinagre [bináɣre] *m.* vinegar.

vino [bino] *m.* wine: ~ *tinto,* red wine.

viña [bíɲa] *f.,* **viñedo** [biɲéðo] *m.* vineyard.

violar [bjolár] *t.* to violate; to infringe; to ravish; to rape.

violencia [bjolénθja] *f.* violence; force.

violento [bjolénto] *a.* violent; furious, wild.

violeta [bjoléta] *f.* violet.

violín [bjolín] *m.* violin.

virar [birár] *t.-i.* to tack. 2 *i.* to turn.

virgen [bírxen] *a.-n.* virgin, maiden.

virtud [birtúð] *f.* virtue.

virtuoso [birtwóso] *a.* virtuous. 2 *m.-f.* virtuoso.

visible [bisíβle] *a.* visible; plain, evident.

visión [bisjón] *f.* vision, sight.

visita [bisíta] *f.* visit, call. 2 visitor.

visitar [bisitár] *t.* to visit, pay a visit, call upon.

víspera [bíspera] *f.* eve. 2 ECCL. vespers.

vista [bísta] *f.* sight, eyesight, eye(s: *en ~ de,* in view of; *hasta la ~,* good-bye. 2 view, scene. 3 aspect. 4 outlook. 5 LAW trial.

vistoso [vistóso] *a.* showy, colourful.

vital [bitál] *a.* vital. 2 important. 3 lively.

vitamina [bitamína] *f.* vitamin.

vitrina [bitrína] *f.* showcase.

viudo, da [bjúðo, ða] *m.* widower. 2 *f.* widow.

vivir [biβír] *t.* to live. 2 *~ de,* to live on.

vivo [bíβo] *a.* live, alive,

living. 2 bright. 3 lively. 4 sharp.

vocablo [bokáβlo] *m.* word, term.

vocabulario [bokaβulárjo] *m.* vocabulary.

vocal [bokál] *a.* vocal. 2 *a.-f.* GRAM. vowel. 3 *m.* member [of a council].

volar [bolár] *i.* to fly. 2 *t.* to blow up. ¶ CONJUG. like *contar.*

volcán [bolkán] *m.* volcano.

volumen [bolúmen] *m.* volume. 2 bulk.

voluntad [boluntáð] *f.* will. 2 purpose. 3 liking.

volver [bolβér] *t.* to turn [up, over, upside down, inside out]. 2 to make: *~ loco,* to drive crazy. 3 *i.* to return, come back. 4 to turn [to right]. 5 *~ a hacer,* to do again. 6 *~ en sí,* to come to. 7 *p.* to go back. 8 to turn around. 9 to become. 10 *~ loco,* to go crazy. ¶ CONJUG. like *mover.* ‖ PAST. P.: *vuelto.*

vos [bos] *pron.* you.

vosotros [bosótros] *pron.* you.

votar [botár] *i.* to vote.

voto [bóto] *m.* vow. 2 vote. 3 oath.

voz [boθ] *f.* voice: *en ~ alta,* aloud; *en ~ baja,* in a low voice. 2 shout. 3 GRAM. voice. 4 rumour.

vuelo [bwélo] *m.* flight.

vuelta [bwélta] *f.* turn: *dar la ~ a,* to go around. 2 bend, curve. 3 reverse. 4 return: *estar de ~,* to be back. 5 change. 6 ARCH. vault.

vuestro [bwéstro] *adj.* your. 2 *pron.* yours.

vulgar [bulɣár] *a.* vulgar, common, ordinary.

Y

y [i] *conj.* and.

ya [ja] *adv.* already. 2 now. 3 at once. 4 *¡~ lo creo!,* yes, of course! 5 *conj. ya ... ya,* now ... now. 6 *~ que,* since, as.

yacer [jaθér] *i.* to lie.

yanki [jáŋki] *a.-m.* Yankee.

yarda [járða] *f.* yard.

yegua [jéɣwa] *f.* mare.

yema [jéma] *f.* bud. 2 yolk [of egg]. 3 tip of the finger.

yerba [jérβa] *f.* grass.

yerno [jérno] *m.* son-in-law.

yeso [jéso] *m.* gypsum. 2 plaster. 3 chalk.

yo [jo] *pron.* I.

yola [jóla] *f.* yawl.

yuca [júka] *f.* yucca.

yugo [júɣo] *m.* yoke.

yunque [júŋke] *m.* anvil.

Z

zafra [θáfra] *f.* olive-oil can; sugar-making season.

zanahoria [θanaórja] *f.* carrot.

zángano [θángano] *m.* drone. 2 loafer.

zanja [θánxa] *f.* ditch, trench, drainage channel.

zapatería [θapatería] *f.* shoemaking. 2 shoe shop.

zapatero [θapatéro] *m.* shoemaker, cobbler.

zapato [θapáto] *m.* shoe. ear-ring. 2 вот. tendril.

zarpar [θarpár] *i.* to set sail, get under way.

zinc [θin] *m.* zinc.

zona [υóna] *f.* zone, belt, district, area.

zoológico [θoolóxiko] *a.* *a.* zoologic(al: *parque* ~, zoo.

zootecnia [θootéɣnja] *f.* zootechny.

zorro [θórro] *a.* cunning [person]. 2 *m.* fox. 3 *f.* vixen.

zozobra [θoθóβra] *f.* worry, anxiety. be anxious.

zueco [θwéko] *m.* clog. buzzer. 2 hummingbird.

zumbar [θumbár] *i.* to hum, buzz.

zumbido [θumbiðo] *m.* buzz(ing, hum(ming.

APPENDICES
APÉNDICES

MONETARY UNITS/
UNIDADES MONETARIAS

Country / País	Name / Nombre	Symbol / Símbolo
THE AMERICAS / LAS AMÉRICAS		
Argentina	austral	₳
Bahamas	dollar / dólar bahameño	B$
Barbados	dollar / dólar de Barbados	$
Belize / Belice	dollar / dólar	$
Bolivia	peso	$B
Brazil / Brasil	cruzado	$; Cz$
Canada / Canadá	dollar / dólar canadiense	$
Chile	peso / peso chileno	$
Colombia	peso	$; P
Costa Rica	colon / colón	₡; ¢
Cuba	peso	$
Dominican Republic / República Dominicana	peso	RD$
Ecuador	sucre	S/
El Salvador	colon / colón	₡; ¢
Guatemala	quetzal	₡; Q
Guyana	dollar / dólar guayanés	G$
Haiti / Haití	gourde	₲; G; Gde

| | Symbol / | Symbol / |
| Country / País | Name / Nombre | Símbolo |

THE AMERICAS / LAS AMÉRICAS

Country / País	Name / Nombre	Símbolo
Honduras	lempira	L
Jamaica / Jamaica jamaicana	dollar / dólar	$
Mexico / México	peso	$
Nicaragua	cordoba / córdoba	C$
Panama / Panamá	balboa	B/
Paraguay	guarani / guaraní	₡; G
Peru / Perú	sol	S/; $
Puerto Rico	dollar / dólar	$
Suriname / Surinam	guilder / gulder de Surinam	g
Trinidad and Tobago / Trinidad y Tabago	dollar / dólar trinitario	TT$
United States / Estados Unidos	dollar / dólar	$
Uruguay	peso	$
Venezuela	bolivar / bolívar	B

WEIGHTS AND MEASURES

U.S. Customary Weights and Measures / Unidades de pesas y medidas estadounidenses

Linear measure / Medida de longitud

1 foot / pie	=	12 inches / pulgadas
1 yard / yarda	=	36 inches / pulgadas
		3 feet / pies
1 rod	=	5½ yards / yardas
1 mile / milla	=	5,280 feet / 5.280 pies
	=	1,760 yards / 1.760 yardas

Liquid measure / Medida líquida

1 pint / pinta	=	4 gills
1 quart / quart líquido	=	2 pints / pintas
1 gallon / galón	=	4 quarts / quarts líquidos

Area measure / Medida de superficie

1 square foot / pie cuadrado	=	144 square inches / pulgadas cuadradas
1 square yard / yarda cuadrada	=	9 square feet / pies cuadrados
1 square rod / rod cuadrado	=	30¼ square yards / yardas cuadradas
1 acre	=	160 square rods / rods cuadrados
1 square mile / milla cuadrada	=	640 acres

Dry measure / Medida árida

1 quart	=	2 pints / pintas áridas
1 peck	=	8 quarts
1 bushel	=	4 pecks

Some useful measures / Unas medidas útiles

Quantity / Cantidad

1 dozen / docena	=	12 units / unidades
1 gross / gruesa	=	12 dozen / docenas

Electricity / Electricidad

charge / carga	=	coulomb / culombio
power / potencia	=	watt / vatio
		kilowatt / kilovatio
resistance / resistencia	=	ohm / ohmio
strength / fuerza	=	ampere / amperio
voltage / voltaje	=	volt / voltio

Metric System

Unit	Abbreviation	Approximate U.S. Equivalent	
LENGTH			
1 millimeter	mm	0.04	inch
1 centimeter	cm	0.39	inch
1 meter	m	39.37	inches
		1.094	yards
1 kilometer	km	3,281.5	feet
		0.62	mile

AREA

1 square centimeter	sq cm (cm²)	0.155	square inch
1 square meter	m²	10.764	square feet
		1.196	square yards
1 hectare	ha	2.471	acres
1 square kilometer	sq km (km²)	247.105	acres
		0.386	square mile

VOLUME

1 cubic centimeter	cu cm (cm³)	0.061	cubic inch
1 stere	s	1.308	cubic yards
1 cubic meter	m³	1.308	cubic yards

CAPACITY (Liquid Measure)

1 deciliter	dl	0.21	pint
1 liter	l	1.057	quarts
1 dekaliter	dal	2.64	gallons

MASS AND WEIGHT

1 gram	g, gm	0.035	ounce
1 dekagram	dag	0.353	ounce
1 hectogram	hg	3.527	ounces
1 kilogram	kg	2.2046	pounds
1 quintal	q	220.46	pounds
1 metric ton	MT, t	1.1	tons

PESAS Y MEDIDAS

Sistema métrico

Unidad	Abreviatura	Equivalente aproximado del sistema estadounidense	
LONGITUD			
1 milímetro	mm	0,04	pulgada
1 centímetro	cm	0,39	pulgada
1 metro	m	39,37	pulgadas
		1,094	yardas
1 kilómetro	Km	3.281,5	pies
		0,62	milla
ÁREA			
1 centímetro cuadrado	cm²	0,155	pulgada cuadrada
1 metro cuadrado	m²	10,764	pies cuadrados
		1,196	yardas cuadradas
1 hectárea	ha	2,471	acres
1 kilómetro cuadrado	Km²	247,105	acres
		0,386	milla cuadrada
VOLUMEN			
1 centímetro cúbico	cm³	0,061	pulgadas cúbicas
1 metro cúbico	m³	1,308	yardas cúbicas
CAPACIDAD (Medida líquida)			
1 decilitro	dl	0,21	pinta
1 litro	l	1,057	quarts
1 decalitro	Dl	2,64	galones

MASA Y PESO

1 gramo	g	0,035	onza
1 decagramo	Dg	0,353	onza
1 hectogramo	Hg	3,527	onzas
1 kilogramo	Kg	2,2046	libras
1 quintal métrico	q	220,46	libras
1 tonelada métrica	t	1,1	toneladas

NUMBERS / NUMERALES

Cardinal Numbers		Números cardinales
zero	0	cero
one	1	uno
two	2	dos
three	3	tres
four	4	cuatro
five	5	cinco
six	6	seis
seven	7	siete
eight	8	ocho
nine	9	nueve
ten	10	diez
eleven	11	once
twelve	12	doce
thirteen	13	trece
fourteen	14	catorce
fifteen	15	quince
sixteen	16	dieciséis
seventeen	17	diecisiete
eighteen	18	dieciocho
nineteen	19	diecinueve
twenty	20	veinte
twenty-one	21	veintiuno
twenty-two	22	veintidós
twenty-three	23	veintitrés

Cardinal Numbers	Números cardinales	
twenty-four	24	veinticuatro
twenty-five	25	veinticinco
twenty-six	26	veintiséis
twenty-seven	27	veintisiete
twenty-eight	28	veintiocho
twenty-nine	29	veintinueve
thirty	30	treinta
forty	40	cuarenta
fifty	50	cincuenta
sixty	60	sesenta
seventy	70	setenta
eighty	80	ochenta
ninety	90	noventa
one hundred	100	cien, ciento
five hundred	500	quinientos
one thousand	1000	mil

Ordinal Numbers		Números ordinales	
1st	first	1.°, 1.ª	primero, -a
2nd	second	2.°, 2.ª	segundo, -a
3rd	third	3.°, 3.ª	tercero, -a
4th	fourth	4.°, 4.ª	cuarto, -a
5th	fifth	5.°, 5.ª	quinto, -a
6th	sixth	6.°, 6.ª	sexto, -a
7th	seventh	7.°, 7.ª	séptimo, -a
8th	eighth	8.°, 8.ª	octavo, -a
9th	ninth	9.°, 9.ª	noveno, -a
10th	tenth	10.°, 10.ª	décimo, -a
11th	eleventh	11.°, 11.ª	undécimo, -a
12th	twelfth	12.°, 12.ª	duodécimo, -a
13th	thirteenth	13.°, 13.ª	decimotercero, -a decimotercio, -a
14th	fourteenth	14.°, 14.ª	decimocuarto, -a
15th	fifteenth	15.°, 15.ª	decimoquinto, -a
16th	sixteenth	16.°, 16.ª	decimosexto, -a
17th	seventeenth	17.°, 17.ª	decimoséptimo, -a
18th	eighteenth	18.°, 18.ª	decimoctavo, -a
19th	nineteenth	19.°, 19.ª	decimonoveno, -a decimonono, -a
20th	twentieth	20.°, 20.ª	vigésimo, -a

21st	twenty-first	21.°, 21.ᵃ	vigésimo (-a) primero (-a)
22nd	twenty-second	22.°, 22.ᵃ	vigésimo (-a) segundo (-a)
30th	thirtieth	30.°, 30.ᵃ	trigésimo, -a
40th	fortieth	40.°, 40.ᵃ	cuadragésimo, -a
50th	fiftieth	50.°, 50.ᵃ	quincuagésimo, -a
60th	sixtieth	60.°, 60.ᵃ	sexagésimo, -a
70th	seventieth	70.°, 70.ᵃ	septuagésimo, -a
80th	eightieth	80.°, 80.ᵃ	octogésimo, -a
90th	ninetieth	90.°, 90.ᵃ	nonagésimo, -a
100th	hundredth	100.°, 100.ᵃ	centésimo, -a

TEMPERATURE / LA TEMPERATURA

Fahrenheit and Celsius / Grados Fahrenheit y grados Celsius

To convert Fahrenheit to Celsius, subtract 32 degrees, multiply by 5, and divide by 9.

Para convertir grados Fahrenheit a grados Celsius (centígrados), réstese 32 grados, multiplíquese por 5 y divídase por 9.

$$104°F - 32 = 72 \times 5 = 360 \div 9 = 40°C$$

To convert Celsius to Fahrenheit, multiply by 9, divide by 5, and add 32 degrees.

Para convertir grados Celsius (centígrados) a grados Fahrenheit, multiplíquese por 9, divídase por 5 y agréguese 32 grados.

$$40°C \times 9 = 360 \div 5 = 72 + 32 = 104°F$$

At sea level, water boils at Al nivel del mar, se hierve el agua a	212°F / 100°C
Water freezes at Se congela el agua en	32°F / 0°C
Average human temperature Temperatura promedia del ser humano	98.6°F / 37°C

Some normal temperatures in the Americas /
Algunas temperaturas normales en las Américas

	Winter / Invierno	Summer / Verano
North of the equator / **al norte del ecuador**		
Churchill, Manitoba	-11°F / -23.9°C	63°F / 17.2°C
Montreal, Quebec	22°F / -5.6°C	79°F / 26.1°C
Anchorage, Alaska	12°F / -11.1°C	58°F / 14.4°C
Chicago, Illinois	24°F / -4.4°C	75°F / 23.9°C
New York, New York	32°F / 0°C	77°F / 25°C
Dallas, Texas	45°F / 7.2°C	86°F / 30°C
Los Angeles, California	57°F / 13.9°C	73°F / 22.8°C
Phoenix, Arizona	51°F / 10.6°C	94°F / 34.4°C
Tegucigalpa, Honduras	50°F / 10°C	90°F / 32°C
South of the equator / **Al sur del ecuador**		
Tierra del Fuego, Argentina	32°F / 0°C	50°F / 10°C
Sao Paulo, Brazil	57.2°F / 14°C	69.8°F / 21°C

Temperature/La Temperatura

Montevideo, Uruguay	55.4°F / 13°C	71.6°F / 22°C
Buenos Aires, Argentina	52.3°F / 11.3°C	73.8°F / 23.2°C
Lima, Peru	59°F / 15°C	77°F / 25°C

CLOTHING SIZES/
TALLAS DE ROPA

Men's Clothes					
U.S.	36	38	40	42	44
Metric	46	48	50	52	54

Men's Shirts				
U.S.	14	15	16	17
Metric	36	38	40	42

Women's Clothes					
U.S.	12	14	16	18	20
Metric	40	42	44	46	48

Shoes									
U.S.	4½	5½	6½	7½	8½	9½	10½	11½	12½
Metric	35½	36½	38	39	41	42	43	44	45

ABBREVIATIONS MOST COMMONLY USED IN SPANISH

A	Aprobado (*in examinations*)
a	área
(a)	alias
AA.	autores
ab.	abad
abr.	abril
A.C., A. de C.	Año de Cristo
admón.	administración
adm.or	administrador
afmo., affmo.	afectísimo
afto.	afecto
ago.	agosto
a la v/	a la vista
a.m.	ante meridiem, antes del mediodía
anac.	anacoreta
ap.	aparte; apóstol
apdo.	apartado

art., art.°   artículo
att.°, atto.   atento

B   beato; Bueno (*in examinations*)
Barna.   Barcelona
B.L.M.,   besa la mano;
  b.l.m.   besa las manos
B.L.P.,   besa los pies
  b.l.p.
bto.   bulto; bruto

c.   capítulo
c/   caja; cargo; contra
C.A.   corriente alterna
c.ª   compañía
c/a.   cuenta abierta
cap.   capítulo
C.C.   corriente continua
cénts.   céntimos
cf.   compárese
C.G.S.   cegesimal

Cía., cía.	compañía
C.M.B.,	cuya mano beso
c.m.b.	
comis.°	comisario
comp.ª	compañía
comps.	compañeros
Const.	Constitución
corrte.	corriente
C.P.B.,	cuyos pies beso
c.p.b.	
cps.	compañeros
cs.	cuartos;
	céntimos
cta.	cuenta
cte.	corriente
c/u	cada uno
C.V.	caballo (*or*
	caballos) de
	vapor
D.	Don
D.ª	Doña
descto.	descuento
d/f.,	días fecha
d/fha.	

dha.,	dicha, dicho,
dho.,	dichas,
dhas.,	dichos
dhos.	
dic.	diciembre
dls.	dólares
dna.,	docena, docenas
dnas.	
d/p	días plazo
Dr., dr.	Doctor
dra., dro.,	derecha,
dras.,	derecho,
dros.	derechas,
	derechos
dupdo.	duplicado
d/v.	días vista
E	este (*east*)
E.M.	Estado Mayor
E.M.G.	Estado Mayor
	General
ENE	estenordeste
ene.	enero
E.P.D.	en paz descanse

E.P.M.	en propia mano
ESE	estesudeste
etc.	etcétera
f.ª, fact.ª	factura
f/	fardo(s)
f.a.b.	franco a bordo
F.C., f.c.	ferrocarril
fcos.	francos
feb., febr.	febrero
F.E.M.,	fuerza
f.e.m.	electromotriz
fha., fho.	fecha, fecho
f.°, fol.	folio
fra.	factura
fund.	fundador
g/	giro
gde.	guarde
gobno.	gobierno
gob.ʳ	gobernador
gral.	general
gte.	gerente

Hno.,	Hermano,
Hnos.	Hermanos
HP., H.P.	caballo (*or* caballos) de vapor
ib., ibid.	ibídem (en el mismo lugar)
íd.	ídem
i. e.	id est (*that is*)
it.	ítem
izq.ª, izq.°	izquierda, izquierdo
J.C.	Jesucristo
jul.	julio
jun.	junio
L/	letra
L.	ley; libro
Ldo., ldo.	licenciado
lín.	línea
liq.	liquidación
liq.°	líquido

M.	Maestro;
	Majestad;
	Merced
m.	minuto,
	minutos;
	mañana
m/	mes; mi, mis;
	mío, míos
mar.	marzo
m/cta.	mi cuenta
merc.	mercaderías
m/f.	mi favor
milés.	milésimas
m/L.	mi letra
m/o.	mi orden
m/p.	mi pagaré
m/r.	mi remesa
Mtro.	Maestro
m.a.	muchos años
M.S.	manuscrito
N	norte; Notable
	(*in examina-*
	tions)

n.	noche
n/	nuestro, nuestra
N. B.	nota bene
n/cta.	nuestra cuenta
NE	nordeste
NNE	nornoreste
NNO	nornoroeste
NO	noroeste
nov.,	noviembre
novbre.	
núm.,	número,
núms.	números
nto.	neto
ntra.,	nuestra, nuestro,
ntro.,	nuestras,
ntras.,	nuestros
ntros.	
O	oeste
o/	orden
oct.	octubre
ONO	oesnoroeste
OSO	oessudoeste
P.	Papa; padre;
	pregunta

P.A., p.a.	por ausencia; por autorización
pág., págs.	página, páginas
paq.	paquete
Part.	Partida
Patr.	Patriarca
pbro.	presbítero
p/cta.	por cuenta
P.D.	posdata
p. ej.	por ejemplo
P.O., p.o.	por orden
PP.	Padres
P.P., p.p.	porte pagado; por poder
p. pd.°, ppdo.	próximo pasado
pral.	principal
pralte.	principalmente
prof.	profesor
pról.	prólogo
prov.ª	provincia
próx.°	próximo

P.S.	Post Scriptum
ps.	pesos
P.S.M.	por su mandato
pta., ptas.	peseta, pesetas
pte.	parte; presente
pza.	pieza
Q.B.S.M.,	que besa su
q.b.s.m.	mano
Q.B.S.P.,	que besa sus pies
q.b.s.p.	
Q.D.G.,	que Dios guarde
q.D.g.	
q.e.g.e.	que en gloria esté
q.e.p.d.	que en paz
	descanse
q.e.s.m.	que estrecha su
	mano
qq.	quintales
q.s.g.h.	que santa gloria
	haya
R.	respuesta;
	Reprobado (*in*
	examinations)

Rbi.	Recibí
R.D.	Real Decreto
R.I.P.	Requiescat in pace (descanse en paz)
Rl., Rls.	real, reales (*royal*)
rl., rls.	real, reales (*coin*)
r.p.m.	revoluciones por minuto
S.	San, Santo; sur; Sobresaliente (*in examinations*)
s/	su, sus; sobre
S.ª	Señora
s/c.	su cuenta
S.C., s.c.	su casa
s/cta.	su cuenta
S.D.	Se despide
SE	sudeste
sep., sept., sepbre.	septiembre

serv.°	servicio
serv.or	servidor
s. e. u. o.	salvo error u omisión
sigte.	siguiente
Sn.	San
SO	sudoeste
S.r, Sr.	Señor
Sra., Sras.	Señora, Señoras
Sres.	Señores
Sría.	Secretaría
sria., srio.	secretaria, secretario
Srta.	Señorita
S.S.a	Su Señoría
SSE	sudsudeste
SSO	sudsudoeste
S.S.S., s.s.s.	su seguro servidor
SS. SS.	seguros servidores
Sta.	Santa; Señorita
Sto.	Santo
suplte.	suplente

tít., tít.°	título
tpo.	tiempo
trib.	tribunal
U., Ud.	usted
Uds.	ustedes
V.	usted;
	Venerable;
	Véase
V	versículo
vencimto.	vencimiento
vers.°	versículo
vg., v.g.,	verbigracia
v. gr.	
Vmd., V.	vuestra merced;
	usted
V.° B.°	Visto bueno
vol.	volumen;
	voluntad
vols.	volúmenes
VV.	ustedes

The Vox Line of Spanish/English Dictionaries

Vox New College
Spanish and English Dictionary

Vox Modern
Spanish and English Dictionary

Vox Compact
Spanish and English Dictionary

Vox Everyday
Spanish and English Dictionary

Vox Traveler's
Spanish and English Dictionary

Vox Super-Mini
Spanish and English Dictionary

Vox Diccionario Escolar
de la Lengua Española

The Best, By Definition
NTC National Textbook Language Dictionaries